D0938623

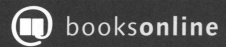 booksonline

Read this book online today:

With SAP PRESS BooksOnline we offer you online access to knowledge from the leading SAP experts. Whether you use it as a beneficial supplement or as an alternative to the printed book, with SAP PRESS BooksOnline you can:

• Access your book anywhere, at any time. All you need is an Internet connection.
• Perform full text searches on your book and on the entire SAP PRESS library.
• Build your own personalized SAP library.

The SAP PRESS customer advantage:

Register this book today at *www.sap-press.com* and obtain exclusive free trial access to its online version. If you like it (and we think you will), you can choose to purchase permanent, unrestricted access to the online edition at a very special price!

Here's how to get started:

1. Visit *www.sap-press.com*.
2. Click on the link for SAP PRESS BooksOnline and login (or create an account).
3. Enter your free trial license key, shown below in the corner of the page.
4. Try out your online book with full, unrestricted access for a limited time!

Your personal free trial **license key** for this online book is:

7rf5-2qij-zdt4-yhxa

Controlling-Profitability Analysis with SAP®

 PRESS

SAP PRESS is a joint initiative of SAP and Galileo Press. The know-how offered by SAP specialists combined with the expertise of the Galileo Press publishing house offers the reader expert books in the field. SAP PRESS features first-hand information and expert advice, and provides useful skills for professional decision-making.

SAP PRESS offers a variety of books on technical and business related topics for the SAP user. For further information, please visit our website: *www.sap-press.com*.

Vanda Reis
Actual Costing with the SAP Material Ledger
2012, 504 pp., hardcover
ISBN 978-1-59229-378-0

John Jordan
100 Things You Should Know About Controlling with SAP
2011, 289 pp., hardcover
ISBN 978-1-59229-341-4

John Jordan
Production Variance Analysis in SAP Controlling (2nd edition)
2011, 292 pp., hardcover
ISBN 978-1-59229-381-0

Rogerio Faleiros and Alison Kreis Ryan
Customizing Controlling in SAP ERP
2012, ~560 pp., hardcover
ISBN 978-1-59229-401-5

Marco Sisfontes-Monge

Controlling-Profitability Analysis
with SAP®

Galileo Press

Bonn • Boston

Galileo Press is named after the Italian physicist, mathematician and philosopher Galileo Galilei (1564—1642). He is known as one of the founders of modern science and an advocate of our contemporary, heliocentric worldview. His words *Eppur si muove* (And yet it moves) have become legendary. The Galileo Press logo depicts Jupiter orbited by the four Galilean moons, which were discovered by Galileo in 1610.

Editor Laura Korslund
Copyeditor Anne Stewart
Cover Design Graham Geary
Photo Credit iStockphoto.com/chill123
Layout Design Vera Brauner
Production Graham Geary
Typesetting SatzPro, Krefeld (Germany)
Printed and bound in the United States of America

ISBN 978-1-59229-386-5

© 2012 by Galileo Press Inc., Boston (MA)
2nd edition 2012

Library of Congress Cataloging-in-Publication Data
Sisfontes-Monge, Marco.
Controlling-profitability analysis with SAP /
Marco Sisfontes-Monge. -- 2nd ed.
p. cm.
Includes bibliographical references.
ISBN 978-1-59229-386-5 -- ISBN 1-59229-386-7
1. Accounting--Computer programs. 2. Profit--Accounting.
3. SAP ERP. I. Title.
HF5636.S57 2012
657'.7--dc23
2011047079

FSC
www.fsc.org
MIX
Paper from
responsible sources
FSC® C014174

All rights reserved. Neither this publication nor any part of it may be copied or reproduced in any form or by any means or translated into another language, without the prior consent of Galileo Press, Rheinwerkallee 4, 53227 Bonn, Germany.

Galileo Press makes no warranties or representations with respect to the content hereof and specifically disclaims any implied warranties of merchantability or fitness for any particular purpose. Galileo Press assumes no responsibility for any errors that may appear in this publication.

"Galileo Press" and the Galileo Press logo are registered trademarks of Galileo Press GmbH, Bonn, Germany, SAP PRESS is an imprint of Galileo Press.

All of the screenshots and graphics reproduced in this book are subject to copyright © SAP AG, Dietmar-Hopp-Allee 16, 69190 Walldorf, Germany.

SAP, the SAP logo, mySAP, mySAP.com, mySAP Business Suite, SAP NetWeaver, SAP R/3, SAP R/2, SAP B2B, SAPtronic, SAPscript, SAP BW, SAP CRM, SAP EarlyWatch, SAP ArchiveLink, SAP GUI, SAP Business Workflow, SAP Business Engineer, SAP Business Navigator, SAP Business Framework, SAP Business Information Warehouse, SAP inter-enterprise solutions, SAP APO, AcceleratedSAP, InterSAP, SAPoffice, SAPfind, SAPfile, SAPtime, SAPmail, SAP-access, SAP-EDI, R/3 Retail, Accelerated HR, Accelerated HiTech, Accelerated Consumer Products, ABAP, ABAP/4, ALE/WEB, Alloy, BAPI, Business Framework, BW Explorer, Duet, Enjoy-SAP, mySAP.com e-business platform, mySAP Enterprise Portals, RIVA, SAPPHIRE, TeamSAP, Webflow and SAP PRESS are registered or unregistered trademarks of SAP AG, Walldorf, Germany.

All other products mentioned in this book are registered or unregistered trademarks of their respective companies.

Contents at a Glance

Dear Reader,

Sometimes I like to think of profit as a type of treasure. It can be tricky to find, with unforeseen obstacles, roadblocks, and even dragons blocking your way! (Okay, maybe not.) However, I think we can all agree that oftentimes there *are* obstacles blocking you from gaining profit, or things that hinder your understanding of the ways a business can create profit. That's where this book comes in—think of it as your treasure map that will enable you to configure your SAP system to find profit for a business.

It's been a pleasure to work with Dr. Marco Sisfontes-Monge on the second edition of this book. I can attest to the fact that he has combed through each chapter to add more information, explain processes and steps more clearly, and provide you with the insight you need to understand what Profitability Analysis tools will work best for your business. He's also provided an overview of recent changes to SAP NetWeaver BI tools, as well as an introduction to how the up and coming SAP HANA will enhance the capabilities of CO-PA. So without hesitation, prepare to dive into CO-PA with SAP and find the information you need to make your business as successful as possible!

We appreciate your business, and welcome your feedback. Your comments and suggestions are the most useful tools to help us improve our books for you, the reader. We encourage you to visit our website at *www.sap-press.com* and share your feedback about this work.

Thank you for purchasing a book from SAP PRESS!

Laura Korslund
Editor, SAP PRESS

Galileo Press
Boston, MA

laura.korslund@galileo-press.com
www.sap-press.com

Contents

9 CO-PA Reporting: Basics ... 363

10 CO-PA Reporting: Configuration ... 391

Acknowledgments

It comes from saying no to 1,000 things to make sure we don't get on the wrong track or try to do too much. We're always thinking about new markets we could enter, but it's only by saying no that you can concentrate on the things that are really important.

—*Steve Jobs, co-founder of Apple Inc.*

I would like to thank all of those individuals that in one way or another influenced this publication. First, I would like to thank my parents, Francisco and Oralia Sisfontes, for their unconditional support in the good and bad times in my life. I would also like to thank John and Carol Reese for being great friends and my family away from home.

I would like to express my special thanks to my great and extremely patient editors, Laura Korslund, Meg Dunkerley, Jawahara Saidullah, and Jutta VanStean, to all of the people involved from Galileo Press, and to SAP AG for their guidance and patience while working on this publication. Also, I would like to thank Lesbia Lemus from the Risk Management Division at Citigroup; Martin Schloegelhofer, Head of Business Development/Banking Division, Hypo Alpe Adria Leasing Holding AG's Austria office; Szu Fen HSing, MS, SAP Consultant, from Abeam Consulting in Taipei, Taiwan; Dr. Naoki Kambe from Kanda University of International Studies in Tokyo, Japan; Hugo Ayala from a Big 4 accounting consulting firm in Chicago, IL; Dr. Elena Davidiak from Stony Brook University, New York; and Adriana Sisfontes, MS, from Dole Corporation in Monterey, California.

Finally, thank you to all of you who have trusted in me to guide you in this learning process. I have tried my best to answer any questions you may have, and hopefully this book will be helpful as you continue with your SAP development.

Dr. Marco Sisfontes-Monge
New York City

Preface

Steve Jobs can be considered one of the greatest visionaries in technology and business in modern history, someone who could make you believe that anything is possible with one idea, that new products or services can be created without *asking* customers what they need but rather *telling* customers what they need, that they ought to have it, and even better, that they need it right now. Steve Jobs proved that innovation and the seeking of perfection are the only ways to guarantee the survival of a company while making shareholders happy with amazing products that people will love.

We therefore pose a question: what makes a company profitable? This sounds more like a philosophical and ethical issue with no correct or incorrect answer rather than a business question. This question puzzles business experts who try to make corporations as lucrative and profitable as possible without negatively affecting shareholders, employees, vendors, suppliers, the environment, and clients.

As professionals in the SAP arena, we know for a fact that the cost of a project going wrong is significant, without mentioning the impact on the reputation of the people involved. It's not a secret that knowledge is power, and in SAP, power means that you have access to good information in a quick and easy way in order to evaluate real situations and translate them into useful working models. Therefore, I hope that the contents of this book will help initiate your learning process with CO-PA and its related systems, and make you a successful decision maker in your implementation.

I encourage you to use the information inside this book to help you achieve the best results for your projects, your clients, and your company. I've tried my best to provide the most complete and accurate information for you, but, as always, not everything can be covered or alternative procedures followed. It's an honor for me to have the support of SAP AG, Galileo Press, my editors, and all of you with this new edition, and I hope I can provide a little more help on this topic.

Thank you,
Dr. Marco Sisfontes-Monge
New York City

Welcome to the world of Profitability Analysis with SAP. This chapter describes the basic objectives and contents of this book, chapter by chapter.

1   Introduction and Overview

We'll start this book with a story. A long time ago, a young engineer was looking for a job right out of school. After studying hard and getting good grades, he had a job offer in hand from a worldwide technology company, to work in the process improvement division (Six Sigma). His future, highly lucrative job was simple—use the latest mathematical and software tools to improve assembly, materials costs, and anything else required to make the best product that money can buy.

The high-tech company was one of the best and biggest technology companies in the world. The human resources manager who interviewed the young engineer assured rapid growth within the company, a close working relationship with the production manager, and that he was the final candidate after many interview rounds. Everything sounded like a dream, and the best part was that a close friend of his was working at the same company and could help him with his training.

Before making a decision, the young engineer also requested a tour of the company to have a look at the systems and processes. He saw the different production lines, packaging, and robotic and manual assemblies scheduled to work 24 hours a day, 7 days a week. One department team had saved over 1.4 million USD improving material usage and flow, making it the most profitable and productive center for the entire corporation, worldwide. Highly impressed with what he saw, and knowing that the name of the company by itself was a boost to his career, the young engineer considered taking the position right away. What more could a young gun want than to join a well-known and profitable company?

However, before accepting the job, the young engineer did one more thing. He went online and checked the company's performance on the New York Stock

Exchange, and what he found was disturbing. The overall corporation inventory turnover was excessively low in comparison with that of the industry, the operating profit was in the red in the last two quarters in comparison to competitors, the yearly demand forecasts were cut in half one week before, and the stock price had gone down more than 30% in less than two months prior to his investigation.

To make things worse, an Asian invention that had been disclosed two weeks before was negatively affecting the demand for the company's main product, and that completely changed the way new technology was provided to the consumer. After reading several news reports about this, the young engineer realized that this invention was threatening almost 40% of the company's product line because it affected the main components of the company's final product. This analysis took a little while, but it was enough to make the young engineer think twice about taking the job and to call the following Monday and kindly decline the offer. He instead decided to join a consulting firm using software that he had never heard of before.

The next month, the young engineer received a call from his friend who had worked at the company, to let him know that he, along with nearly 70% of the workforce of the facility, had been laid off (including the HR manager who had interviewed him). Only one person, the production manager, was left in the department where he was supposed to work. The high-tech equipment was sold as scrap to junk yards or shipped overseas for adaptation to new technology for use in another country. Four additional facilities and research centers around the globe were closed.

After this reality check, the young engineer completely understood that there is more to making a company profitable than massive production, the best technology, and the best qualified individuals. At this point, nobody was interested in the best facility in the world, with the best financial indicators just one month ago, and with the best and most qualified labor force of a technology that was now obsolete. What the young engineer also realized was that profitability, growth, and financial performance were highly interrelated.

Many years have passed since this close encounter with a potentially bitter experience, but from that day forward, and before appearing in front of any client, the engineer always makes sure to completely understand a company's situation—its financials, ethics, shareholder and clients' opinions, and the latest financial news, in order to have a clear picture of the situations he will face. In addition, these analyses can play an important role in deciding whether to ultimately take on a project, regardless of what a company's reputation is and how wonderful of a place it seems to be.

Hopefully, this short story has drawn your attention to some considerations behind profitability analysis and the vision toward the development and implementation of a profitability system. Profitability analysis requires not only financial transactions that measure a company's success, such as revenues or sales, but also strategic decisions that make the products or services of a company attractive in the marketplace to satisfy the changing demands of customers and keep up with the competition.

1.1   The Purpose of This Book

It is a pleasure to once again be able to partner with SAP PRESS to provide enhancements to the first edition of this publication (first released in 2007) and to provide additional content on the demanding world of SAP Finance.

In this edition, we've worked hard to provide more comprehensive coverage on the following topics:

1. Assessment and distribution in order to support the CO-PA planning process.
2. Expanded coverage on the process of transferring data from the Sales and Distribution component, and validation procedures available within SAP ECC to guarantee that the data was transferred without errors.
3. Moving billing documents into CO-PA using specific criteria to guarantee that the correct information is transferred. We also explore the prerequisites required to perform the transfer.
4. Orders and WBS elements settlements to profitability segments.
5. Greater detail is provided on the theory and background of the Order Manager and settlement of WBS elements to profitability segments.
6. We've revised our discussion on how to make direct postings to the Financial Accounting (FI) and Materials Management (MM) components to better understand the relationship between assignment lines and value fields in SAP CO-PA.
7. We've included a completely new chapter that describes the relationship between SAP CO-PA, SAP NetWeaver BW Business Content, and SAP Business-

Objects, including a brief overview of the functionality of SAP BusinessObjects Planning and Consolidation (SAP BPC). Also included in this chapter is a quick overview of SAP HANA and in-memory computing as part of the new enhancements created by SAP to improve system performance and reduce processing time in implementations with large data volumes.

This book will clarify functional and/or technical questions related to implementing CO-PA in your SAP system that could be followed by any beginner, intermediate, or advanced user. This book is not meant to make you a consultant and/or world expert, but to give you a quick start and reference guide of design, structures, functionality, terminology, procedures, and an overall understanding of the role of SAP CO-PA in the SAP ECC environment.

Also, because CO-PA can be considered an integrator within the SAP Controlling (CO) component, a certain minimum level of expertise in other SAP components is required to fully understand CO-PA's potential. SAP Controlling Profitability Analysis (CO-PA) interacts with nearly all the components of SAP ECC. This means that when you need to transfer data from one particular component (say, FI, Sales and Distribution (SD), or MM), a functional and technical knowledge of that specific component is also required so the information from source to target (CO-PA) is configured, transferred, and validated accordingly.

The same logic applies for SAP NetWeaver Business Warehouse (BW) projects when extracting data from SAP ECC into the SAP NetWeaver BW reporting environment because the project requires an understanding of how the data needs to be transferred, the specifics of the component, and the relationships for each SAP ECC field required to be transferred with the extractor and destination fields in the target. For example, when extracting data from the SAP General Ledger, SAP provides a number of pre-defined extractors for SAP NetWeaver BW such as 0FI_GL_10 and 0FI_GL14, and SAP FI consultants are often required to provide the confirmation that the information is correct. The same situation occurs with SAP CO-PA: when performing transfers from MM, SD, FI, and other components, it's necessary to understand the component where the data resides to confirm and validate the required structures to configure in SAP CO-PA to receive the data accordingly.

Note

We recommend taking advantage of other resources when working with other SAP components. For some ideas, take a look at the following resources, available at *www.sap-press.com*:

- *Actual Costing with the SAP Material Ledger*
- *Optimizing Sales and Distribution in SAP ERP—Functionality and Configuration*
- *Financial Reporting with SAP*
- *The SAP General Ledger*
- *SAP BusinessObjects Planning and Consolidation* (2nd Edition)
- *SAP Financials Expert* magazine: *www.financialsexpertonline.com*

This may seem like a lot of information at once for beginners, but with a little extra work, it's possible to master the basic elements required for a successful CO-PA implementation or to just explore the capabilities of the system. In this book, please note that not every element of the component will be explained. Rather, we'll explore the most important functionalities.

The purpose of this book is to explain CO-PA configuration and techniques with a technical, theoretical, but also hands-on approach. CO-PA is a widely used component in the industry that can simplify the data extraction processes and fulfill reporting requirements. It supports the implementation of a revenue, cost, and expense analysis toward the calculation of measures such as net revenue, contribution margins, cost of goods sold, costs of goods manufactured, and operating profit.

Note

The activities performed or explained in this book use the standard SAP IMG help environment. Therefore, if you get lost or want more information, you can quickly complement your learning process using IMG Help information. Additional places to look for help include *http://help.sap.com* and *http://sdn.sap.com*.

1.2 How This Book Is Organized

As we mentioned, this book has been structured following the IMG CO-PA menus. However, depending on the level of implementation of CO-PA within the SAP system in your organization, you might not need to use all of the CO-PA submenus. Also, because costing-based CO-PA is the more complex implementation model, it has been given priority in the discussion and revision of the associated elements; however, most of the functionalities used with this model can be applied with account-based CO-PA as well. For this reason, we can say that if you implement costing-based CO-PA you're getting account-based CO-PA for free. Here's a quick overview of what you'll do and learn while reading this book:

- Gain a basic understanding of CO-PA concepts in **Chapter 2**. This should be useful, especially for beginners who require additional clarification of concepts behind Profitability Analysis with SAP.

- Work with Business Content and get an overview of the functionalities and configuration components of CO-PA in **Chapter 3**.

- Explore the configuration settings to define the basic CO-PA components in **Chapters 4 and 5**.

- Configure a planning application using the CO-PA planning framework in **Chapters 6 and 7**.

- Get an overview of how to transfer actual data from other SAP components such as Financials (FI), Sales and Distribution (SD), Materials Management (MM); projects; WBS elements; and others in **Chapter 8**.

- Create reports within the CO-PA environment using the CO-PA Information System menu in **Chapters 9 and 10**.

- Review briefly the general configuration modifications required to change from a CO-PA costing-based analysis to an account-based analysis in **Chapter 11**.

- Review some useful tips and tricks in **Chapter 12** to improve your reporting and system performance.

- Receive a quick overview in **Chapter 13** of the SAP BusinessObjects suite and integration points with SAP NetWeaver BW, a quick overview of the main SAP BusinessObjects tools along with an extensive explanation on SAP BPC, a tool similar to SAP CO-PA that exists in the SAP NetWeaver Business Intelligence (BI) environment. Finally, SAP HANA and in-memory computing is evaluated as another component part of the new updates for high performance and reporting in SAP CO-PA and SAP ECC.

- Review what you've learned in this book in **Chapter 14**.

Each chapter of the book has been written independently, meaning that you should be able to work with it without the need to move back and forth between chapters. However, there are references between chapters to complement your learning, in case an important concept requires additional clarification that depends on concepts discussed in other chapters. In order to speed up the learning process, SAP-delivered Business Content (CO-PA templates) is used and populated with actual and plan data to get you started with CO-PA tools in no time.

Note that it is not our intention to provide a complete overview of all of the capabilities and configuration steps required to use CO-PA. This component is quite sophisticated, and some of the functions that CO-PA performs are very difficult to replicate with alternative components such as SAP NetWeaver BW, BI, SAP NetWeaver BI Integrated Planning (IP), Business Planning and Simulation (BPS), and others. Only the most significant components are reviewed in this book; however, readers are given pointers to additional documentation, components, transaction codes, and procedures that can support the functionalities reviewed. So, without further delay, welcome to the CO-PA environment!

1.3   Summary

The CO-PA component of your SAP system's CO component is a powerful application with extensive functionality. Although you might not require every single component that we'll review, by reading this book you'll get a broad overview of almost all of the menus available in CO-PA. This will allow you to quickly identify what functionalities you can use and which ones you won't need, which you should make sure to do.

Looking ahead, in Chapter 2 we'll briefly review some general and basic components to consider before initiating your work in CO-PA, as well as the financial and accounting terms to expect during your implementation. It's important to clearly understand the difference, for example, between variable and fixed costs, and what types of documents are available inside the SAP system to accomplish the consolidation.

Chapter 2 will also briefly provide an overview of another key element related to Profitability Analysis in the enterprise: Economic Value Added (EVA). This indicator is often used as the final financial number that many corporate financial officers (CFOs) require that your CO-PA reports deliver.

Before initiating our review of CO-PA, it's important to consider the basic concepts behind the application. Profitability analysis itself is a multidimensional process that allows analysis of different pieces of information. These are based on relevance and importance to the generation of value for the corporation, which in turn is based on concepts such as revenues, profit margins, fixed and variable costs, and EVA.

2 Basics of Profitability Analysis

Key decision makers in any industry have the responsibility to make a business profitable, or at least to make decisions that don't make the company lose money or that reduce the risk of doing so. However, the only way for a manager or decision maker to do so successfully is by having access to a combination of facts and numbers coming from financial data. In this chapter, we'll review and describe basic principles to determine whether a company is making decisions that will help it to be profitable. These are basic principles to consider for your CO-PA applications that will directly affect your implementation.

> **Note**
>
> This chapter provides a brief overview of important elements to consider when working with CO-PA. However, if you lack formal training in the areas of financial and cost accounting, economics, and general business analysis, we recommend that you also consult books on these topics to complement your learning.

2.1 Fundamental Principles

You can perform profitability analysis in three ways:

1. **Historic comparison**
   Evaluation of different time periods to identify the best alternative. For example, you might compare two consecutive time periods, such as month to month; or period to period, such as year to year.

2. **Selecting between different alternatives**

   For example, you might choose between two machines or projects, or include only projects that meet a minimum level of profitability using criteria such as net present value or internal rate of return (IRR).

3. **Differential cost analysis**

   Evaluation of how much money can be obtained from current operations in comparison with an alternative. For example, the analysis with higher net present value or IRR, depending on your decision criteria, might be selected based on its incremental cost or value.

We define profit as the difference between revenues and total costs (that is, revenue − cost = profit). In an SAP system, each of these components is split into multiple accounts and document types, depending on the transaction generated. Furthermore, each of these components requires the creation of cost elements and general ledger (G/L) accounts that control documents inside the system that carry data and information to calculate the relationship between revenues and costs such as:

▶ Billing documents

▶ Purchase orders

▶ Sales orders

▶ Accounts payable

▶ Accounts receivable

▶ Invoices

▶ Allocations

▶ Project order settlements

▶ Internal orders

▶ Credit memos

▶ Production orders

▶ Inventory movements

▶ Overhead

▶ Investments

▶ Rebates

These documents are just a few examples and do not take into consideration any additional company-specified documents required to control debit and credit movements inside the financial system. In addition, some of these documents occur within the SAP Financials (FI) application, and others occur inside the SAP Controlling (CO) application used for external and internal parties, respectively.

Using this information, the SAP system can calculate revenues such as sales — sales discounts, sales rebates, returns, and allowances. Total costs can be classified in multiple ways, depending on a company's operations. Generally, they include expenses such as utilities, office supplies, insurance, shipping, and anything not directly related to a company's operations but that helps support the processes. Costs are more associated with the transactions directly related to maintaining a company's operations, such as labor and materials.

Generally, CO-PA is useful to calculate all of the elements involved in the profit and loss statement (P&L) that quantifies the flows of revenues and costs in the company. However, to generate the balance sheet, additional connections might be required, either using integrators within CO-PA to access information coming from other components, or using SAP NetWeaver Business Warehouse (BW) or SAP NetWeaver business intelligence to complete the generation of the P&L. In the income statement, or P&L, there is an operating section that describes only revenues and expenses, and a non-operating section that describes other revenues and other expenses and losses.

> **Note**
>
> If you're a CPA or a highly accounting-oriented person, the information presented here is likely to be very basic, and is only meant to provide the link between SAP and traditional accounting.

Profitability analysis can be a sophisticated or a simple process within the SAP system, and for this reason is considered to be multidimensional. This topic is discussed in the next section.

2.2 Profitability Analysis as Multidimensional Analysis

Multidimensional analysis is one of the most frequently used terms when working with business intelligence technologies, such as SAP NetWeaver BW and SAP NetWeaver BI. However, this term is also applicable to analytical-oriented and transactional applications delivered with CO-PA without leaving the basic Online

Transaction Processing (OLTP) system. This means that the information is not provided in real time and that there might be some delay in the information reported because some structures require uploading data outside the transactional system and updating the data targets.

CO-PA allows a similar multidimensional analysis without leaving the transactional system. Thus, you can analyze profit contribution for a complete company code, by individual customer or market segment (profitability segment). Using Figure 2.1, you can review how the concept of multidimensional analysis of profitability is defined. At the bottom of Figure 2.1, you see a cube of data or data sets that we're interested in reviewing using specific characteristics, such as region, division, and customer group.

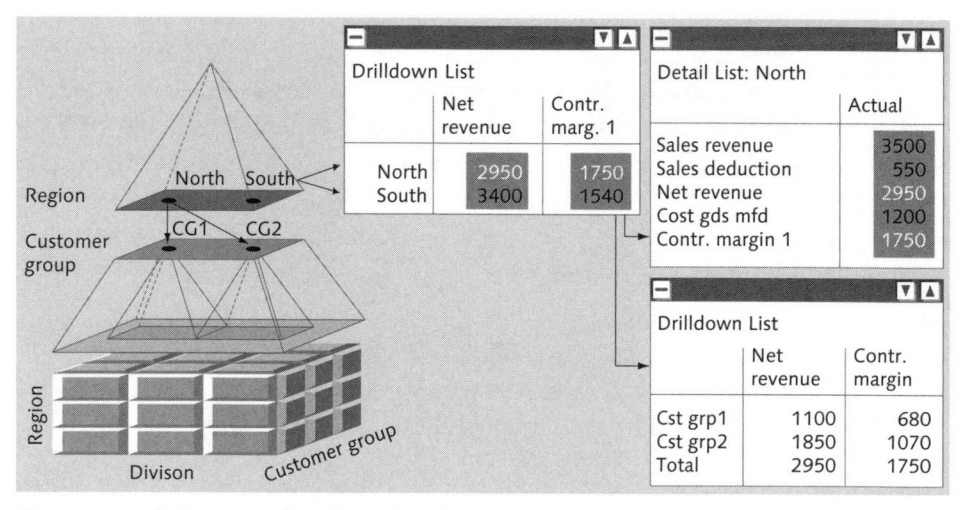

Figure 2.1 Multidimensional Analysis of Profitability

Also, notice that there are small cubes that define small segments that we can use to summarize our data at different hierarchical levels. For example, there is a drilldown displaying NET REVENUE and CONTR. MARGIN (contribution margin) for two customer groups (CST GRP1 and CST GRP2) and also information for the NORTH region with its actual data in a separate environment, shown in DETAIL LIST: NORTH. The small cubes can be used to share information at different levels based on the characteristics available, making it possible to be more selective in how the information can be displayed and modified in the system, depending on the role of the user.

However, CO-PA is a process rather than a data display at different levels. This profitability analysis process is reviewed in the next section, and should be used as a reference when working with your traditional ASAP methodology.

2.3   The Profitability Analysis Process

The process of profitability analysis is intrinsically linked with the concept of Economic Value Added (EVA). EVA-based management links the creation of shareholder wealth over time with a common standard index that measures the differences and growth of the company overall as a single entity. The EVA index is very popular among corporate financial officers (CFOs), corporate executive officers (CEOs), and, of course, many people in human resources (HR) departments. The use of this index, especially in publicly traded companies, provides a general overview of the company's health in its efforts to create value for the shareholders using the minimum rate of return (K) that shareholders and lenders could get by investing their money elsewhere with a similar level of risk.

It is possible to define EVA as:

$$EVA = \textit{Net Operating Profit After Taxes (NOPAT)} - \textit{Capital} \times \textit{Cost of Capital (K)}$$

For our purposes, let's consider profitability analysis as a process that highly depends on how accurate and simplified the information is to calculate the EVA value. With the concept in mind that every single component in an organization is dependent on this EVA index, let's review Figure 2.2.

As shown in Figure 2.2, the goal is to generate the EVA by implementing a *value measuring process* using cost and value drivers. To do so, perform the following steps:

1. **Clearly identify your revenue and cost drivers.**
   Use current reports, management reviews, dashboards, and analytical applications to fully understand your core measurement system.

2. **Identify the sources of your cost drivers and generate profitability segments.**
   Once you know what to measure, spend your time determining how data will flow into your profitability system. Will you have SAP data? Third-party systems? SQL systems from 20 years ago? Make sure you understand your data flow before you even begin with your profitability analysis.

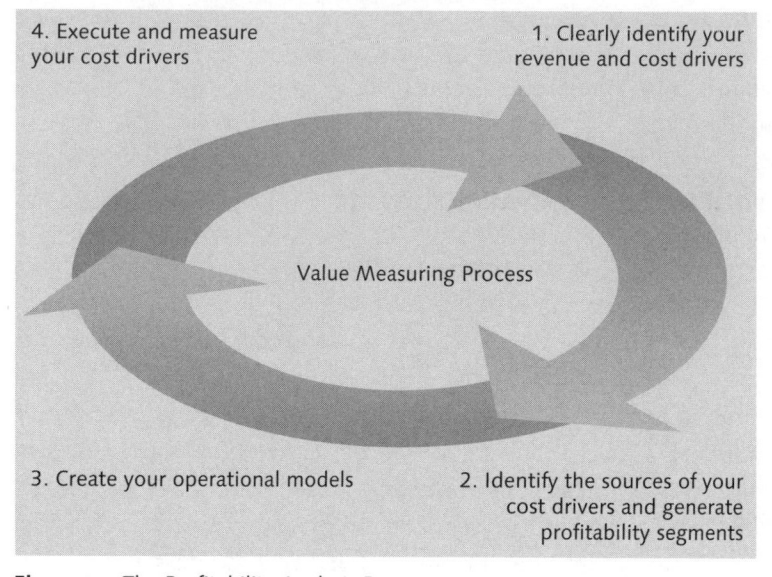

Figure 2.2 The Profitability Analysis Process

3. **Create your operational models.**

   Once you're ready to start building your different CO-PA structures and components, create a model description that includes your data flows, sources, and required outputs, keeping in mind how your users will access your data. Also, consider system performance along the way.

4. **Execute and measure your cost drivers.**

   You can also call these *value drivers* depending on how you handle your value measuring process. Cost drivers are those financial measures identified to describe the performance of your key business areas, such as net revenue, sales per square foot, and revenues per product line. Once you initiate the CO-PA measuring process with reports and planning applications, make sure that your core cost drivers are clearly identified and allocated to the correct levels in your hierarchical organization. You need to design an easy-to-maintain system that allows multiple users to work with it without any problem.

As we mentioned, and as you can see from reading these steps, the profitability analysis process can be a complement to the ASAP methodology, if you desire a more practical approach. However, if you're an EVA consultant, you'll likely prefer using your standard procedures. Either way is fine; the process we outlined in this section is a suggestion, not a requirement.

2.4 Break-Even Analysis

The goal of any manager or company is to at least "break even," which means that the total fixed and variable costs are equal to the total revenues. In other words, the company has the minimum amount of money required to pay all of its liabilities for a particular time period. To know where the break-even point is or how to calculate it, we need to review revenues, fixed and variable costs, and the concept of a break-even analysis in a little more detail.

2.4.1 Revenues, Fixed and Variable Costs

A break-even analysis requires either using a chart or mathematical calculations to estimate the point of equilibrium where costs equal revenues. That point of equilibrium is the minimum level of provided production, sales, or services required for a time period in order to guarantee that you are maintaining value or creating value. It is clear that if you're below that point you are literally "destroying value." Let's review a few terms related to break-even analysis:

- **Revenues**: Describe a relationship, such as *product × price*, that generates the revenue of the company.
- **Fixed costs**: Costs such as direct labor—if you produce 100 parts or 200 parts, you always pay the same. However, in the long term, fixed costs become variable costs.
- **Variable costs**: Costs such as materials, which change depending on the level of production; that is, you don't pay the same if you produce 100 or 200 parts for reasons of volume. However, in the long term, variable costs become fixed.
- **Relationship**: The relationship of the three previously outlined components is thought to be linear, which is not always true but simplifies the calculations.
- **Formula**: Standard formula used to calculate the break-even point is as follows:

$Y = a + bX$

Where:

- Y = revenues or total sales
- a = fixed costs, constant
- b = average cost per unit produced
- X = total production units

For example, a company called ABC has total fixed costs of 4 USD per month and average material cost is 2 USD/unit. The company's previous analysis shows that they must have a minimum of 200 USD per month to cover costs. However, the company wants to know what the minimum number of parts required to break-even is. Let's find out:

$Y = 4 + 2 * X$

This means:

$200\ USD = 4 + 2 * X$

This in turn means:

$(200 - 4) = 2\ X$

Therefore, the company needs to produce X = 98 units in order to achieve 200 USD per month to break even. If they produce more, they will generate a profit.

2.4.2 Sunken Costs

Decision making can only be affected by elements that will affect the future, meaning that any economic resources already committed must be excluded from any new scenario comparison or managerial analysis.

These types of economic effects are called *sunken costs*. For example, if you already invested 1,000 USD as a down payment to build a new facility, and you already committed to a mortgage of 100 USD per month for 30 years, then this money is committed; you've already spent it, so there's no reason to include these costs as part of any new project comparisons.

Therefore, sunken costs are final commitments that are part of the daily life of operations, and there are no increments unless you chose a flexible interest rate, which might require additional analysis. Costs can be classified in different ways, so let's look at different types of cost classifications in the next section.

2.5 Cost Classifications

When working with accounting to measure profitability, you have to identify the cost drivers that truly represent the behavior of your activities, profit centers, cost centers, processes, or systems. For that, it's quite useful to understand the different cost classifications under which your profitability models can be created. We'll review them in detail in the following sections.

2.5.1 Costs Based on Their Function

Costs based on their function are strongly associated with the departments or areas of the organization where they occur, and can be classified as follows:

▶ **Production costs:** These can be further classified as the following:

  ▶ Direct materials: Costs that are directly related to the product, such as sugar in candy.

  ▶ Direct labor: Costs such as the salary of workers on an assembly line.

  ▶ Indirect labor: Costs not directly related to product or services delivered, such as inspections and supervision.

▶ **Distribution or sales costs**: Incurred to move the products from the company's facilities and deliver to the customer. Examples are advertising, shipping costs, and commissions.

▶ **Administrative costs**: Examples are administrative salaries, phone, and general expenses.

Direct vs Indirect.

2.5.2 Costs Based on Activity

Costs based on activity, and that are directly related to the final product or service of a company, can be divided as follows:

▶ **Direct costs**: Identified with an activity, department, or product. For example, the salary of the marketing manager's secretary is a direct cost for the marketing department.

▶ **Indirect costs**: Cannot be identified and associated with a particular activity. For example, the salary of the secretary from marketing is a direct cost for the marketing department, but an indirect cost for the product.

2.5.3 Costs Depending on When They're Charged Against Revenues

Costs that depend on when they're charged against revenues describe the moment when costs are considered reported, depending on their purpose. These costs can be classified as follows:

▶ **Costs of the period**: Identified based on the time interval and not with the products or services. Example: monthly rent for a building, because it's always incurred, regardless of when products or services are provided to customers.

▶ **Costs of the product**: Costs of goods sold (COGS), regardless how goods were sold (via credit or full payment).

2.5.4 Costs Depending on the Authority

Costs that require approval or a certain level of managerial control can be classified as follows:

▶ **Controllable**: One person has the authority to incur the cost. For example, the sales director has the authority to accept (or decline) the expenses of sales representatives.

▶ **Noncontrollable**: These are costs incurred without control; for example, machine depreciation.

2.5.5 Costs Based on Their Importance to Decision Making

When evaluating different options, managers and analysts must focus their attention on costs that are important. For example, when evaluating a multimillion dollar contract, travel expenses might not have a significant impact. Therefore, these types of costs fall into one of the following classifications:

▶ **Relevant costs**: Also known as differential costs. These costs change depending on decisions made, and remove any sunken costs (sunken costs were explained a bit earlier in this chapter) associated with the decision.

▶ **Irrelevant costs**: Not directly related to the activity in question, or too small to make a difference. Therefore, management can decide to remove these costs from the final decision while concentrating only on the relevant costs.

One final point: because working with financial transactions is a delicate task, unless you're an expert on the topic in your region of the world, you should always partner with the accounting and financial departments of your client, company, or organization when working with CO-PA.

2.6   Summary

This chapter provided you with a quick overview of concepts, terminology, and elements that are part of profitability analysis and that you will likely encounter when interacting with other members of your team or organization during your implementation. However, it's not enough to simply understand these terms; it's highly recommended to complement your SAP knowledge with financial and cost accounting information to understand why the different cost elements, general ledger accounts, cost centers, profit centers, internal orders, and other transactions within your transactional system have been set up the way that they have.

Chapter 3 provides a more hands-on overview of the general concepts associated with CO-PA using SAP-delivered templates or Business Content within the SAP ERP ECC 6.0 or R/3 environment. We'll review the general components and structures that create an operating concern, and explore basic reporting capabilities available in CO-PA.

Working with SAP-delivered templates is the best way to get started with your implementation and with basic CO-PA concepts. In this chapter, we'll review the basic functionalities that describe the CO-PA environment.

3   Introducing CO-PA with SAP

Welcome to the SAP Controlling (CO) component for Profitability Analysis or, in technical terms, CO-PA. As its technical name shows, CO-PA is part of the Controlling component of SAP, and is thus related to the internal transactions of a company. In this chapter, we'll review the basic functionalities of CO-PA, including the basic components that define the component and the CO-PA model required to define the approach. We'll also look at how to activate and work with predefined Business Content delivered within the R/3 or SAP ERP Central Component (ECC) 6.0 environment, and how to set up the system to read the information for each structure created (operating concern).

As part of our discussion, we'll provide an overview of the general functionalities of each of the Profitability Analysis menus and functionalities such as master data, planning, flows of actual values, tools, reports and forms, and generation of testing data for our examples. Now, let's have a quick look at CO-PA's capabilities before initiating our detailed discussion in the following chapters.

3.1   General Overview of CO-PA

Controlling Profitability Analysis (CO-PA) is a subcomponent of the SAP Controlling (CO) component that integrates information coming from different platforms in SAP such as Sales and Distribution (SD), Materials Management (MM), Financials (FI), CO, Production (PP), and others. Think of CO-PA as a window to look inside the SAP database using selective extraction and reporting capabilities to either provide static or real-time information.

Regardless of the component on which you have expertise, you likely know that the SAP platform is designed around the financial elements of a company. Thus, it doesn't matter if you work with web technologies, ABAP, MM, SD, or any other component of SAP; the rules defined in the FI component limit the information available in any system. Thus, the FI component becomes the core of the organization in terms of reporting, value and money flow, as well as administration and development. Should you have doubts about this, ask your implementation team what the first component that they implement in your organization is, and the answer would be...yes, financials!

Because high-level enterprise resource planning (ERP) technologies focus first on controlling how money flows in the enterprise and later on how that information will be reported or shared, CO-PA interacts with both of these worlds. In other words, CO-PA allows access to the Online Transaction Processing (OLTP) structures, or the core of SAP database tables, and it also allows the creation of structures that Online Analytical Processing (OLAP) applications later use to generate multidimensional, analytical, and reporting components based on OLTP data such as that delivered in SAP NetWeaver Business Warehouse (BW) 7.0. Let's look at OLTP and OLAP in a bit more detail.

3.1.1 OLTP

OLTP structures are the industry standard for applications that require multiple data entry and retrieval transaction processes, such as creation of purchase orders, invoices, and others. These OLTP databases are also the standard way of storing transactional data that those multiple processes generate, allowing the system to respond faster to database and user requests. However, OLTP databases, like the core database of SAP, have limitations in reporting capabilities because their main purpose is to *generate and store day-to-day data as fast as possible*; general reporting is not their main strength, especially with large data volumes.

3.1.2 OLAP

To resolve these reporting issues, OLAP structures are used separately from OLTP structures, and their main purpose is to *provide a better view of how data is organized* and *identify patterns based on segmentation or limitations in data display*. Some examples of OLAP applications are analytical and reporting operations such as dimensional analysis, slicing and dicing, drill-down, and data mining.

An example of OLAP is SAP NetWeaver BW 7.0 or any other data warehousing application that can extract information from the core of the SAP tables and enhance the reporting capabilities of the data initially stored in OLTP format. Performing advanced reporting processes in the OLTP environment, however, consumes computer resources to a degree that significantly reduces system performance. On the other hand, storing and generating transactional data in OLAP applications causes the same problem. That's why the two structures operate separately; OLTP to store and generate data, and OLAP to read, report, and analyze data.

The concept of system performance in SAP has been enhanced with the release of SAP HANA (High-Performance Analytic Appliance), which is an in-memory computing engine specifically designed to manage data in high volume and granularity. SAP HANA places the data in its main memory, providing a performance boost compared to reading it off of disks. With SAP HANA, customers can analyze data from their SAP systems and other sources near real time, with blazing performance, and according to SAP, with improvements up to 3,600 times.

HANA 1.0 is an analytics appliance has initially been designed for SAP ERP customers, with expansion beyond that group planned for 2012. SAP HANA can be used as the database engine for SAP NetWeaver BW, and consists of certified hardware, an in-memory database (IMDB), an Analytics Engine, and tooling for moving data in and out of SAP HANA. You build the logic and structures yourself, and use a tool (e.g., SAP BusinessObjects) to visualize or analyze data. At the time of this publication (early 2012), SAP HANA is still in its early stages, and the number of customers are very limited. However, SAP has provided guidelines that this technology will permanently replace the previous SAP Business Warehouse Accelerator designed for the same purpose, making SAP HANA the new generation of hardware optimization tools. It's now being considered as a dramatic change to improve performance and processing times in high-data volume environments such as those of utility, oil and gas, pharmaceutical, and financial services. We'll explore a brief overview of SAP HANA in Chapter 13.

3.1.3   Linking OLTP and OLAP

CO-PA is the recommended standard practice to make the link between both worlds (OLTP and OLAP). Using CO-PA, OLTP data can be shared and used in SAP NetWeaver BW. Furthermore, data that exists in SAP NetWeaver BW 7.0 can be stored inside the core tables of SAP and you can use CO-PA as the way to find data inside the SAP database. The beauty of CO-PA lies in the capability of performing somewhat sophisticated planning and reporting processes similar to those available in SAP NetWeaver BW 7.0, but working with OLTP data, which means that your reports can display information available in SAP in real time.

> **Note**
>
> Information displayed in SAP NetWeaver BW 7.0 or higher is not real time; rather, it reflects information with a delay caused by the update and transformation processes.

For this reason, CO-PA allows some level of OLAP reporting while working within an OLTP environment. This is quite useful when the reporting and planning requirements do not demand a high level of sophistication, and the data doesn't need to be transferred to an external platform. However, the drawback of CO-PA is that if the information is not correctly limited when performing the extraction or a search, system performance might be negatively affected. If so, the data will need to be moved to SAP NetWeaver BW 7.0 using special objects to fully deliver more complex requirements.

3.1.4   SAP ERP ECC 6.0—Specific Recommendations

As you've seen, SAP's CO-PA is the window and the door to two worlds: OLTP and OLAP. As such, CO-PA makes it possible to work with transactional data coming directly from SAP tables and in real time while performing reporting, planning, and analytical operations similar to those of SAP NetWeaver BW 7.0 or other components, such as SAP Business Warehouse–Business Planning and Simulation (SAP BW-BPS) or Strategic Enterprise Management–Business Planning and Simulation (SEM-BPS), which basically provide the same functionalities. For this reason, you should use CO-PA as the first choice for SAP ERP ECC 6.0 data analysis and reporting requirements. If your requirements are more complex, then use the more powerful tools available in SAP NetWeaver BW 7.0 using CO-PA as the interface to collect and control the data extraction (from SAP ERP ECC 6.0 to SAP NetWeaver BW 7.0) and retraction (from SAP NetWeaver BW 7.0 to SAP ERP ECC 6.0).

Let's take a detailed look at the CO-PA profitability model and the two types of transactions that can be used: *account-based* and *costing-based*.

3.2 The SAP Profitability Model

From a profitability point of view, SAP ERP ECC 6.0 is a collection of tables and fields that store data, and CO-PA is the interface to access saved (frozen) or real-time data. The main element in CO-PA is called an *operating concern*, which can be understood as an *InfoCube* for those familiar with the SAP data warehouse applications, or simply as a small group of selected data objects that will be extracted from specific SAP tables and that are part of what are called *profitability segments*. Profitability segments can be considered the link between Profitability Analysis and Profit Center Accounting, establishing the connection with the complete SAP ERP ECC 6.0 system into a common analysis, reporting, and display environment.

The SAP system uses two data models: account-based and costing-based. These two data storage or reporting models are the references for any data-sharing applications in the SAP environment, and also limit the type and level of detail of the data reported. These two models control how the information is posted inside the financial components in SAP, and also how CO-PA accesses and reports the information.

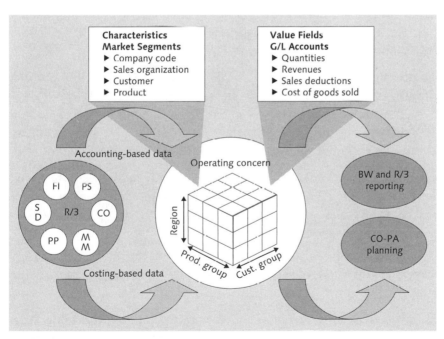

Figure 3.1 SAP Profitability Analysis Model

We can simplify all of these relationships and interactions into a summarized model, as shown in Figure 3.1. This model describes the information flow between the different SAP components and CO-PA. Notice that the SAP R/3 or SAP ERP ECC 6.0 environment is the most important source of data displayed in CO-PA, from components such as FI, CO, SD, PP, MM, and Project Management (PS).

Also, notice that the information transferred into CO-PA can be costing-based, account-based, or both formats reported at the same time. The kind of information that flows from the different SAP components depends on how the transactions are defined in the OLTP system, and thus can be slightly different depending on your reporting and planning requirements, and the account-based or costing-based models that describe how the data is stored or generated.

As you're probably aware, objects inside an SAP system are either called *characteristics* or *value fields*. Characteristics describe the data stored in the system, such as customer ID, billing date, or product ID. These characteristics can be used to limit the data extraction with the definition of profitability segments or market segments. Value fields store data as currency, quantity, or amounts, such as sales, cost of goods sold, and others. For example, if we have the following information in a purchase order: customer ID: AA3223, purchase order number: 11224, and sale = 1,000 USD; then the customer ID and order number are the characteristics, and the sale is the value field.

Once the operating concern is created inside the R/3 or SAP ERP ECC 6.0 platform, the values of the selected tables are transferred, increasing the level of detail by the creation of profitability segments that also limit the information to display outside the operating concern. The SAP system is now ready to initiate two processes, as shown in Figure 3.1:

1. Start reporting the data using the traditional SAP ERP ECC 6.0 reporting environment with the CO-PA reporting capabilities, or initiate the transfer of information from SAP tables to SAP NetWeaver BW 7.0 using the operating concern and the selected characteristics and value fields.

2. Initiate planning of the data using the planning framework available in CO-PA to perform modifications over specific data values associated with a particular object.

This lets you create charts, graphics, and customized reports with information contained in SAP ERP ECC 6.0 using the available reporting environment, or generate a budget or perform transformations over the raw data and store it in a customized value field that only exists in a particular operating concern. With this view in mind of the CO-PA process, you are now ready to explore the different components and elements involved in Profitability Analysis with SAP.

Next, you need to have an idea of what type of information to look for and where to find it, considering that there are more than 17,000 SAP tables available to do the job.

> **Note**
>
> There are several online resources where you can obtain the names of the SAP tables, including *www.erpgenie.com*. For our purposes, we'll limit the discussion to only the tables and fields we're interested in studying.

Table 3.1 provides a general overview of several specific components and documents and information contained in some of the main SAP ERP ECC 6.0 components and their SAP tables. For example, production order, which is part of the PP component, stores production variances that can be assessed in real time and that can be either shared with different users or that can be user specific.

Component	SAP Objects	Data
SD	Billing documents	Quantities, revenues, sales deductions, cost of sales
CO-PC	Cost estimates	Variable and fixed costs of goods manufactured
FI	G/L account posting	Rebates and freights
CO-OM	Cost center Order Process	Sales and administrative costs Marketing costs Variances
PS	Work breakdown structure (WBS) elements Network activity	R&D costs
PP	Production order	Production variances
MM	Material ledger	Quantity flows
CO-PA tables	Additional costs (user defined)	Accrued discounts and rebates

Table 3.1 Some CO-PA Data Sources

Looking at Figure 3.1 and Table 3.1 together, you should have a better understanding of the functionality of CO-PA and its interface with different components. Furthermore, CO-PA not only interacts with other components, but also allows you to create additional information such as user-defined characteristics and value fields that can store customized data.

CO-PA is also important within the CO component as a tool for internal reporting and interaction with other CO components, such as Profit Center Accounting (CO-PCA), Product Cost Controlling (CO-PC), Overhead Cost Controlling (CO-OM), Cost Center Accounting (CO-CCA), Cost Element Accounting (CO-CEL), and others. As shown in Figure 3.2, the goal of SAP financial systems as a whole is to provide the platform to use each major business unit as an income generator instead of a cost carrier with CO-PCA.

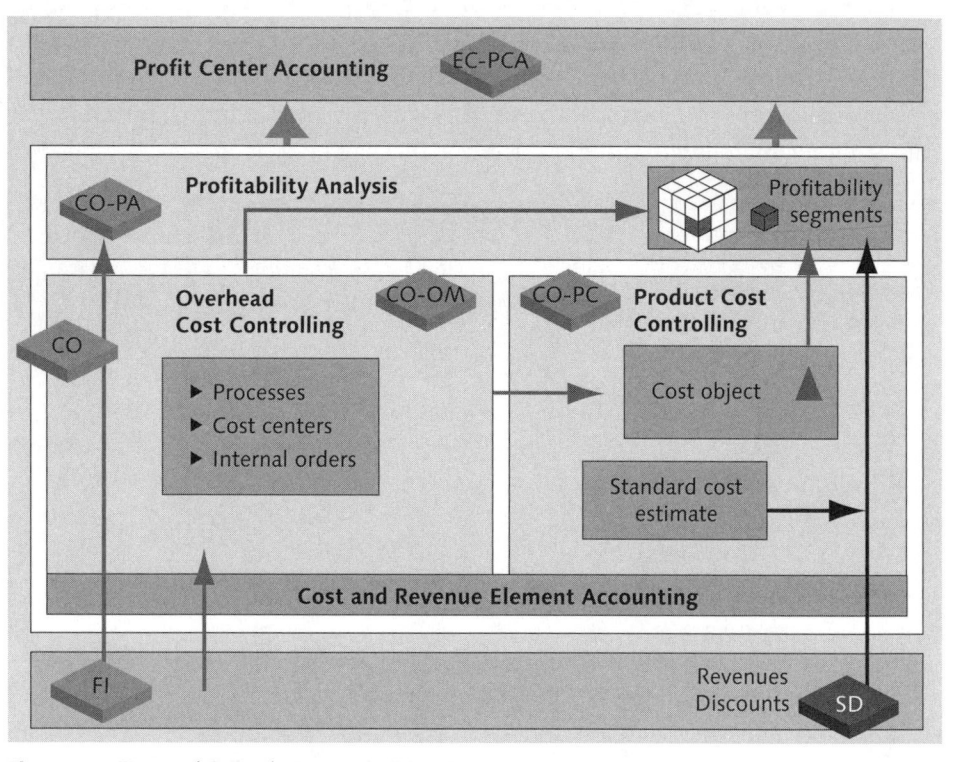

Figure 3.2 Financial Data Flow in an SAP System

The dream of any CEO and shareholder is for each business unit in a corporation to be a profit center rather than a cost center. However, a limited number of profit centers and a large number of cost centers is actually the norm. Cost centers absorb the resources that profit centers generate because their function is limited to support of the strategic process to continue generating income or simply being operational. Also, the role of a profit center can be considered to be more high level in the company's structure, such as that of a division or business unit that carries a considerable number of resources and generates income from a market segment or an important geographical location, such as Germany, the United States as a whole, or New York in particular.

In Figure 3.2, only the most important components are described; however, these components contain subcomponents, so in reality the flow of information is considerably more complex.

You should now have a clear picture of the importance of CO-PA within the R/3 or SAP ERP ECC 6.0 platform, especially to consolidate data for external use, such as in SAP NetWeaver BW, SAP BW-BPS, and SEM.

> **Note**
>
> CO-PA not only allows you to export data, but it also controls the communication structures that import data into SAP ERP ECC 6.0, which is called *retraction*. This is not a very common procedure, but it's useful if you require information that flows from SAP ERP ECC 6.0 into SAP NetWeaver BW 7.0, and vice versa. An example of using data retraction is if you complete your planning outside SAP ERP ECC 6.0 using SAP BW-BPS and then transfer the final budget into the plan data inside SAP ERP ECC 6.0.

In the next section, we'll explore how to access and start working with CO-PA and its components in more detail, and we'll provide you with a general idea of the elements that form part of this component. More detail on each of these elements will be provided in subsequent chapters.

3.3   Components of CO-PA

To work with CO-PA in SAP ERP ECC 6.0, one can choose to work with the traditional menu path ACCOUNTING • CONTROLLING • PROFITABILITY ANALYSIS, as shown in Figure 3.3, or another environment called the IMG. We'll use the IMG because it provides additional help capabilities and a more user-friendly environment to navigate and access the different CO-PA objects and menus, as shown in Figure 3.4.

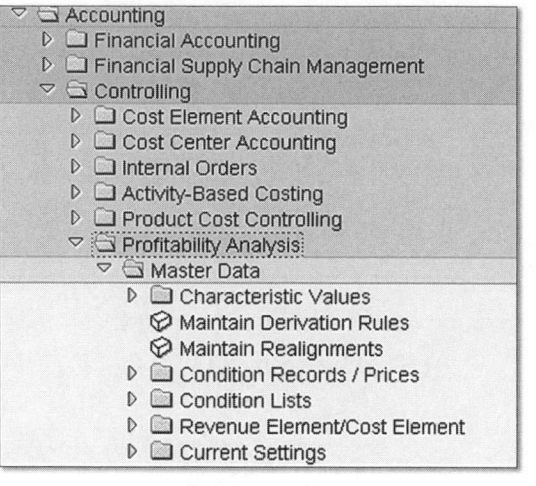

Figure 3.3 Contents of SAP Profitability Analysis Standard Menus

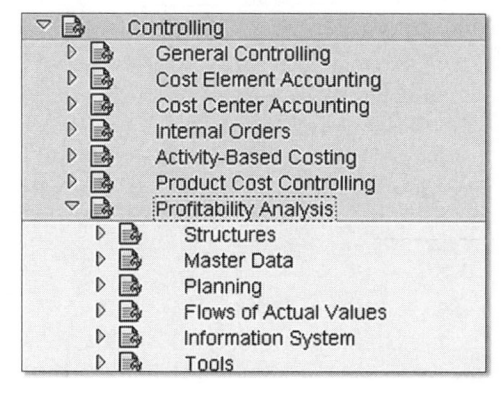

Figure 3.4 Display of the IMG Menu

Tips & Tricks

The menus that display on your screen may be different from those presented in Figure 3.3 and Figure 3.4, depending on your level of authorization and the processes you are allowed to perform. If you have problems accessing the screens presented in this book, contact your system administrator for clarification.

Once you're comfortable working with the application, you can complete your learning by exploring the traditional SAP menus, because the IMG provides access only to the most commonly used functionalities.

3.3.1 Accessing the IMG

To access the IMG, enter Transaction SPRO and follow these steps:

1. Press Enter, and then click on the SAP REFERENCE IMG button.

2. Navigate to CONTROLLING • PROFITABILITY ANALYSIS, shown earlier in Figure 3.4.

3. Notice that CO-PA has a similar component structure as other components in CO, such as CO-CCA.

3.3.2 Profitability Analysis Menu Items

The structure of this book follows the main menu items displayed in the IMG for Profitability Analysis and can be described as follows:

▶ STRUCTURES
These let you define the objects and relationships required to perform CO-PA. Without configuring the structures, you can't work with any CO-PA functionalities.

▶ MASTER DATA
MASTER DATA provides the fundamental data and content of the previously created structures using characteristics and value fields.

▶ PLANNING
PLANNING allows you to perform sales, profit, and revenue planning using selected profitability segments.

▶ FLOWS OF ACTUAL VALUES
You can extract data from the OLTP transactional fields and link it to value fields in CO-PA. This submenu allows you to transfer information coming from components such as FI, SD, or MM.

▶ INFORMATION SYSTEM
Lets you perform drill-down reporting to improve data analysis using individual elements that can be linked to reports.

▶ TOOLS
Tools allow you to access functions applicable to all of CO-PA, including authorizations, summarization levels, Schedule Manager, and others.

In the following subsections, we'll look at the components included in the CO-PA component and analyze SAP-delivered templates to further your understanding of CO-PA.

> **Note**
>
> If you get lost along the way, you can also use the available help information that's part of the IMG to support your learning process.

Structures

As its name implies, *structures* are the basic components of any CO-PA project that control the implementation. As shown in Figure 3.5, the STRUCTURES menu displays different options that control the organization of the following CO-PA information:

- ▶ Characteristics, which describe the data
- ▶ Value fields, which store quantity or amount values
- ▶ Operating concerns, which store characteristics and value fields
- ▶ Profitability segments, which limit the characteristic data displayed inside the operating concern and the data to be transferred as account- or costing-based into the operating concern

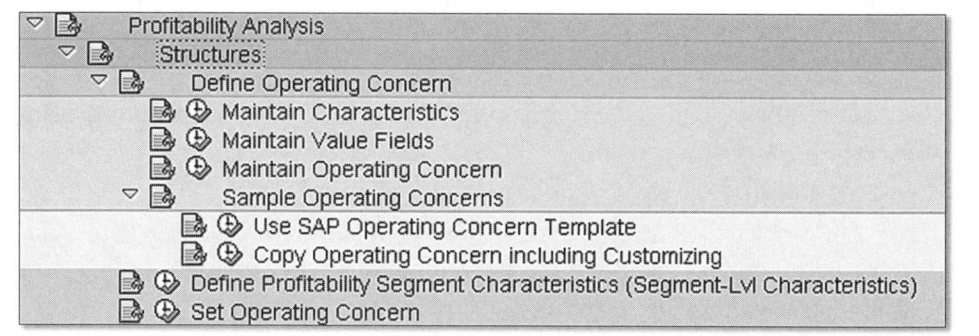

Figure 3.5 Components of the Structures Menu

To access individual elements inside the CO-PA component, click on the EXECUTE icon (identified as a clock with the checkmark), next to the appropriate object. For example, by clicking on this icon for MAINTAIN CHARACTERISTICS (shown in Figure 3.5), you access the screen shown in Figure 3.6, where you can create, change, or display the characteristics available in CO-PA for reporting as part of an operating concern.

Char.	Description	Short text	DTyp	Lgth.	Origin Table	Origin field d
BONUS	Vol. rebate grp	Rebate grp	CHAR	2	MVKE	BONUS
BRSCH	Industry	Industry	CHAR	4	KNA1	BRSCH
BZIRK	Sales district	District	CHAR	6	KNVV	BZIRK
COPA_KOSTL	Cost center	Cost ctr	CHAR	10		
COPA_PRZNR	Business Proc.	BusProcess	CHAR	12		
CRMCSTY	CRM Cost Elmnt	CRM CstElm	CHAR	10		
CRMELEM	Marketing Element	Mrkt.Elem.	NUMC	8		
CRMFIGR	CRM Key Figure	CRM KF	CHAR	16		
EFORM	Form of manufacture	Manuf.form	CHAR	5		
GEBIE	Area	Area	CHAR	4		
KDGRP	Customer group	Cust.group	CHAR	2	KNVV	KDGRP
KMATYP	Aircraft type	Plane type	NUMC	2		
KMBRND	Brand	Brand	NUMC	2		
KMCATG	Business field	Bus. field	NUMC	2		
KMDEST	Destination	Destin.	CHAR	5		
KMFLTN	Flight number	Flight no.	CHAR	6		
KMFLTY	Flight type	FlightType	CHAR	4		
KMHI01	CustomerHier01	CustHier01	CHAR	10	PAPARTNER	HIE01
KMHI02	CustomerHier02	CustHier02	CHAR	10	PAPARTNER	HIE02
KMHI03	CustomerHier03	CustHier03	CHAR	10	PAPARTNER	HIE03
KMIATA	IATA season	IATA seas.	CHAR	5		
KMKDGR	Customer group	Cust.group	CHAR	2	KNVV	KDGRP
KMLAND	Country	Country	CHAR	3	KNA1	LAND1
KMLEGS	Route segment	RouteSegmt	CHAR	7		
KMMAKL	Material Group	Matl Croup	CHAR	9	MARA	MATKL
KMNIEL	Nielsen ID	Nielsen ID	CHAR	2	KNA1	NIELS
KMOPDY	Day of operation	OperatnDay	CHAR	2		
KMODIC	Departure Location	Denart Los	CHAR	5		

Figure 3.6 Maintain Characteristics Overview

The screen displayed in Figure 3.6 shows characteristics that either extracted information contained in the default SAP tables or characteristics that were created by a user for data load. An important part of the STRUCTURES menu is that it allows you to navigate to and identify the complete set of information available in CO-PA to create operating concerns and profitability segments. Also, accessing the screen in Figure 3.6 allows you to access the value field screen. In both cases, the information shown includes a DESCRIPTION, SHORT TEXT, DTYPE (data type), LGTH. (length), ORIGIN TABLE, and ORIGIN FIELD to make sure that you are getting the correct data.

Data structures defined in the STRUCTURES menu of the IMG establish what type of data you can access later on in the MASTER DATA menu. However, they also tell you what information you'll be reporting, planning, or monitoring in CO-PA because you already defined an operating concern and its contents.

The challenge begins in what additional information is necessary to comply with profitability requirements that are not available in the SAP tables because we need to add user-defined values, hierarchies, and automatic rules that control the calculation of additional data based on valuation rules and predefined conditions.

To resolve these issues, you must configure additional rules in the MASTER DATA menu, which we'll look at next. Basically, in the STRUCTURES menu you identify "what" you are interested to find or work with, and in the MASTER DATA menu, you configure additional rules about "how" to work with that data.

3.3.3   Master Data

The MASTER DATA menu, as shown in Figure 3.7, lets you configure the basic settings that determine the structure and contents of Profitability Analysis in your system.

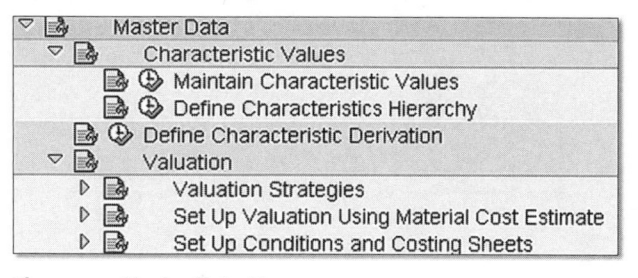

Figure 3.7 Master Data Menu

Using this menu, you access the configuration of the characteristic values, derivation, and valuation to either manually or automatically create values or hierarchies based on predefined criteria to be used in profitability segments.

The elements presented in Figure 3.7 are reviewed in more detail in Chapter 5, where you'll learn how to configure derivation rules and valuation strategies based on predefined criteria. Notice that there is more than just one way to work with valuation, and the way it's configured increases the level of sophistication of your data process.

At this point, we should mention that you do not have to configure each of the options available in the MASTER DATA menu, so always focus on your requirements to identify which components you need to work with besides the definition of your structures. In this book, we'll show you what can be done so you can decide what to apply to your particular project. Note also that sometimes CO-PA is unable to handle the types of transactions required by a massive implementation, and interfaces with SAP NetWeaver BW 7.0 or other external systems to the core of the SAP system are required. As such, the items in the MASTER DATA menu can be considered optional for configuration. You must, however, configure the items in the STRUCTURES menu to be able to work with CO-PA.

In many cases, SAP provides several tools that deliver similar results. For example, the CO-PA planning framework that we'll look at in the next section is similar to other SAP planning applications, such as SAP NetWeaver BI IP, SEM-BPS, and SAP BW-BPS. While the CO-PA planning framework is also not mandatory, you are encouraged to explore its potential as a planning application as much as possible before deciding to increase your application requirements by using one of the other tools mentioned.

3.3.4   Planning

Planning in CO-PA is done with the CO-PA planning framework. As mentioned, this framework is similar to other SAP applications (for example, the SAP BW-BPS application), but they run in different environments. CO-PA allows you to modify and display information from real-time or frozen data inside the R/3 or SAP ERP ECC 6.0 system. In comparison, SAP BW-BPS requires the creation of SAP BW InfoCubes, which are outside the SAP R/3 or SAP ERP ECC 6.0 platform, before any type of reporting and planning is allowed. Furthermore, the use of data in OLAP format is not real time but limited to the creation of data extraction applications.

The capabilities of the CO-PA planning framework are not as powerful as those of SAP NetWeaver BI Integrated Planning or SAP BW-BPS. However, the CO-PA planning framework provides useful functionalities to perform the most common calculations and avoid development or creation of extraction objects that move data outside the SAP ERP ECC 6.0 tables. For this reason, the CO-PA planning framework can provide a great level of sophistication for data planning or manipulation without leaving the SAP ERP ECC 6.0 environment.

The CO-PA planning framework provides different types of planning functions that allow users to revaluate, copy, forecast, and distribute large amounts of data that can later be distributed using the manual planning functions. Another useful feature of the CO-PA planning framework is the transfer of plan data from other applications such as Sales and Operations Planning (SOP), Cost Center Accounting (CO-CCA), or the Logistic Information System (LIS). For those familiar with SAP BW-BPS, this topic is quite easy, but if you are not familiar don't be worried; we'll review these elements extensively in Chapter 7.

Figure 3.8 shows the PLANNING menu and its submenus. For now, just be aware of its existence. In Chapter 7 we'll create a customized application and use the different functions available in this menu to modify the data extracted from the SAP tables, user-defined characteristics, or value fields. Also, an important element of the CO-PA planning framework is its interaction with information created in the MASTER DATA menus, such as valuation strategies, and rules and conditions that can significantly increase the power and complexity of a planning application.

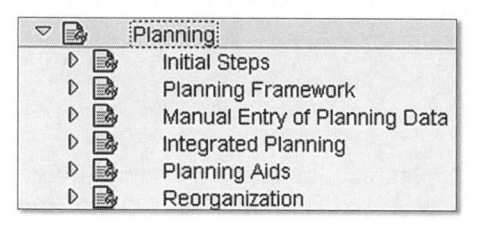

Figure 3.8 The Planning Menu

If you need to interact with different components such as SD or MM, you must configure different interfaces so CO-PA can extract and display the information coming from those applications. The FLOWS OF ACTUAL VALUES menu provides the capability to do so, and these types of requirements allow CO-PA to combine and access data easily and efficiently without the need for major ABAP developments or customizations. Everything comes SAP-delivered or "inside the box" and such interfaces are already configured and ready to use.

3.3.5 Flows of Actual Values

Profitability Analysis with SAP is about combining the sources of revenue and costs into a common communication, reporting, and planning environment. Therefore, we should be able to quantify whether the company is making or losing money at any particular moment because CO-PA allows you to create interfaces to interact with different SAP accounting, financial, and operational components and subcomponents.

To that end, when working with the FLOWS OF ACTUAL VALUES menu, we'll explore the basic settings required to access and consolidate data coming from SD, FI, CO, and other SAP components. For example, to quantify the estimated sales value of an organization for a particular time period, you might require transferring information from incoming sales orders to CO-PA and assigning those to value fields or quantity fields.

Figure 3.9 provides a quick overview of the main menu components of FLOWS OF ACTUAL VALUES, and shows the options to transfer information coming from different components, which include, among others:

▶ TRANSFER OF INCOMING SALES ORDERS

▶ TRANSFER OF BILLING DOCUMENTS

▶ DIRECT POSTING FROM FI/MM

▶ SETTLEMENT OF PRODUCTION VARIANCES

▶ TRANSFER OF OVERHEAD

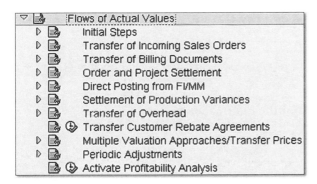

Figure 3.9 Flows of Actual Values Menu

The INFORMATION SYSTEM menu of CO-PA, which we'll look at next, provides great flexibility in the generation of customized reports, forms, and variables (similar to what you can do in SAP NetWeaver BW 7.0). Reporting is one of the most important parts of the SAP system, and the flexibility delivered with CO-PA can satisfy quite complex requirements, thereby reducing the complexity of implementations, especially those that require extensive reports and scenarios.

> **Note**
>
> If you're an advanced user who knows that sometimes these types of extractors are not enough for the type of requirements or functionalities demanded by your projects, you can also perform a generic data extraction into SAP NetWeaver BI or SAP NetWeaver BW. Note that the concept of generic data extraction is not reviewed in this book because its concepts go beyond the scope of our discussion. If necessary, you can consult additional SAP NetWeaver BW documentation for guidance on this subject, such as *http://help.sap.com* or *http://sdn.sap.com*.

3.3.6 Information System

The INFORMATION SYSTEM menu can be considered the most important menu besides the STRUCTURES menu in defining the overall CO-PA environment. In comparison with BEx or similar reporting applications in SAP NetWeaver BI, the INFORMATION SYSTEM menu lets you perform flexible data reporting and analysis using different types of graphics. It also enables the execution of variables behind the scenes within the ABAP environment to automatically update and control the data update to improve reporting performance without coding! As shown in Figure 3.10, you can perform the following in the INFORMATION SYSTEM menu:

- ▶ Create individual components of reports
- ▶ Create reports
- ▶ Store report data
- ▶ Define a report tree
- ▶ Define authorization objects for the information system
- ▶ Reorganize your information system

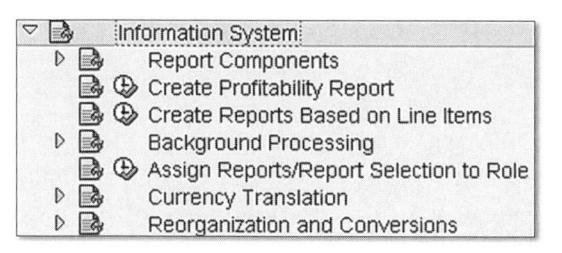

Figure 3.10 Information System Menu

Once an operating concern has been created, activated, and loaded with data, the INFORMATION SYSTEM menu allows you to use system-specific reports or create your own. You can also create sophisticated reports that allow drilldown and filtering using reports or forms. Note that even though CO-PA allows access to see real-time data, this does not mean that you will see the latest data all of the time. If you have a report open, you need to refresh it periodically, or, using variables defined as variants, execute it in the background with an ABAP program and schedule its behavior. All of these options will be reviewed later on in Chapter 9.

Finally, the TOOLS menu delivers additional functionalities, such as summarization levels, SAP enhancements, and access to the authorization management system. These are not required for an implementation, but provide system performance improvements.

3.3.7 Tools

Tools in this case are additional functionalities that are not key elements of CO-PA, but are nice to have. They relate to performance, security, analysis, simulation, and general revision of the objects created in CO-PA. Using the TOOLS menu, you can perform transports, imports, and deletion of transactional data, and post billing documents and sales orders to Profitability Analysis retroactively if you went productive with SD before you implemented CO-PA.

Another important feature available in this menu is AUTHORIZATION MANAGEMENT, which allows setting up authorization levels for CO-PA objects in planning and for basic and baseline items reports. In addition, as with any other SAP application, the definition of roles and profiles is also included in this component.

Figure 3.11 provides a general overview of the contents of this menu, but we'll review this information in detail in Chapter 12. These are important elements that need specific attention, especially when you're ready for implementation. Don't review these elements on your own until we reach that chapter because using them is, for the most part, limited to system administrators or high-level power users.

As is the case with most of the SAP components, predefined content is delivered in SAP ERP ECC or R/3 for CO-PA; namely SAP operating concern templates, which provide you with preconfigured environments you can use as a reference during your implementation. In the next section, we'll explore these templates in detail.

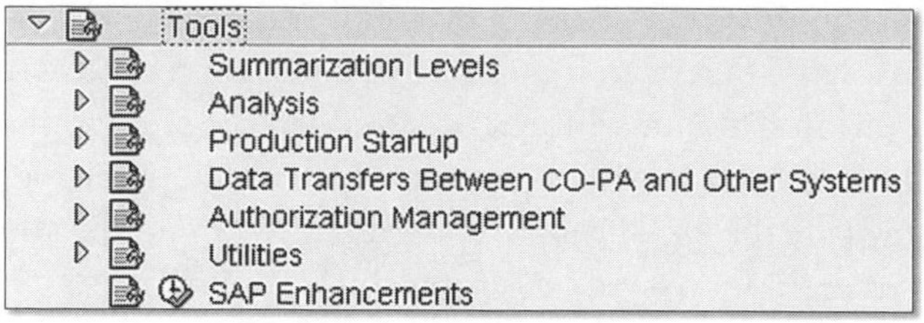

Figure 3.11 Tools Menu

3.4 Working with SAP Operating Concern Templates

SAP-delivered Business Content exists for CO-PA in the form of different templates that can be activated and populated with data to assist your implementation. These templates have predefined operating concerns, which are complete structures that you must generate, activate, and populate with testing data to use them as part of a reference for your implementation. These templates are standard SAP objects that are protected and cannot be modified, so you always have a clean version ready to use as a reference.

> **Note**
>
> You might ask yourself: Why should I use these templates? The answer is simple: they were created to be used as examples for simple and complex implementations providing reports, planning layouts, and other objects that can be used to end up with a successful CO-PA implementation. The only way to learn SAP software, or any other application, is by having a good idea first of what is expected and what kind of general functionalities are available, so you can "play" and learn along the way, without risking or modifying real data or objects.

There are four SAP-delivered templates in the system, as also shown in Figure 3.12:

▶ MODEL BANK E_B1

▶ AIRLINE ROUTE PROFITABILITY S_AL

▶ TEMPLATE CONSUMER GOODS IND S_CP

▶ QUICKSTART TEMPLATE S_GO

To access any of these operating concern templates, follow this path in the IMG: CONTROLLING • PROFITABILITY ANALYSIS • STRUCTURES • DEFINE OPERATING CONCERN • SAMPLE OPERATING CONCERN • USE SAP OPERATING CONCERN TEMPLATE.

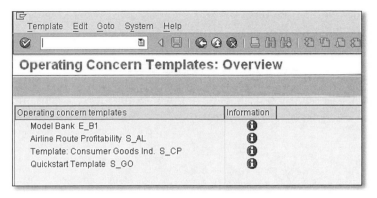

Figure 3.12 SAP-Delivered Operating Concern Templates

Notice in Figure 3.12 that the cells in the INFORMATION column contain an icon with an "i" inside a circle. If you click on this icon, you will access additional help documentation that describes the elements and procedures for each of the objects included in the respective operating concern template. For our purposes, we'll use the operating concern named QUICKSTART S_GO because it's the most basic application of all of the available operating concern templates and thus the easiest to understand.

3.4.1   The Quickstart S_GO Operating Concern Template

This section will describe how to activate and access the different predefined objects included inside the Quickstart S_GO (S_GO is its technical name) operating concern template only, which is similar to the other SAP-delivered operating concern templates. Before we can start working on the information configured in this object, however, we need to generate the objects as well as the data inside this operating concern:

1. Double-click on the operating concern named QUICKSTART TEMPLATE S_GO. You'll receive a message notifying you that the client system (development, production, or testing) will be updated with the test data and the required tables.

2. Click on the checkmark icon. The system will now automatically generate all of the structures and objects required for the Quickstart S_GO template; however, the objects will not contain data. You're only creating the data structures or "buckets" where the data will later be stored or extracted.

Activating and Generating Sample Data

To generate and activate the sample data available with the Quickstart Template S_GO template, follow this procedure:

1. Double-click on QUICKSTART TEMPLATE S_GO again, and you see the information displayed in Figure 3.13, which describes the template and its three submenus: CUSTOMIZING, APPLICATION EXAMPLES, and TOOLS.

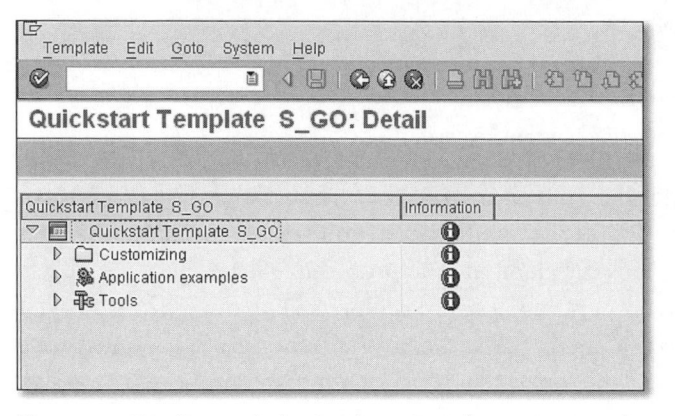

Figure 3.13 Working with the Quickstart Template S_GO Template

2. Next, to generate data for the operating concern Quickstart S_GO, follow this path: APPLICATION EXAMPLES • PREPARE APPLICATION EXAMPLES • CREATE EXAMPLE DATA.

3. Double-click on CREATE EXAMPLE DATA, shown in Figure 3.14.

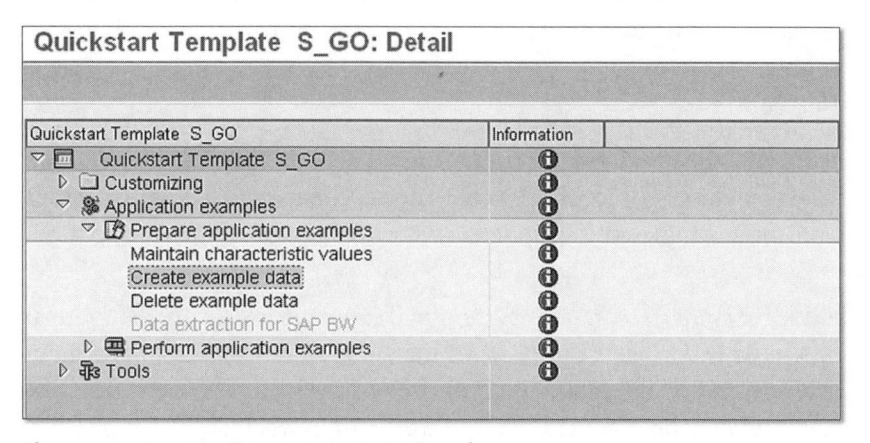

Figure 3.14 Creating Data in Your S_GO Template

4. In the GENERATE EXAMPLE DATA screen shown in Figure 3.15, select the radio button CREATE PLANNING DATA, and enter a fiscal year for which the data is going to be generated, in our case 2009.

5. Click on the green checkmark icon.

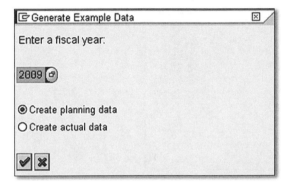

Figure 3.15 Generating Example Data in the Quickstart S_GO Template

6. The message EXAMPLE DATA HAS BEEN CREATED appears on the screen, notifying you that the data was successfully generated. If you want to create actual data, go back and select the CREATE ACTUAL DATA radio button, and then click on the checkmark icon again.

3.4.2 Customizing

Now you're ready to navigate and review the predefined elements inside the CO-PA component using the Quickstart Template S_GO. First, we'll look at each of the functions in the CUSTOMIZING object.

Display Characteristics/Value Fields

The first function in the CUSTOMIZING object is DISPLAY CHARACTERISTICS/VALUE FIELDS:

1. Open the CUSTOMIZING menu and select DISPLAY CHARACTERISTICS/VALUE FIELDS to highlight this menu item, as shown in Figure 3.16.

2. Click on DISPLAY CHARACTERISTICS/VALUE FIELDS again to access the IMG menu that will let us review the structure and configuration of the operating concern, shown in Figure 3.17.

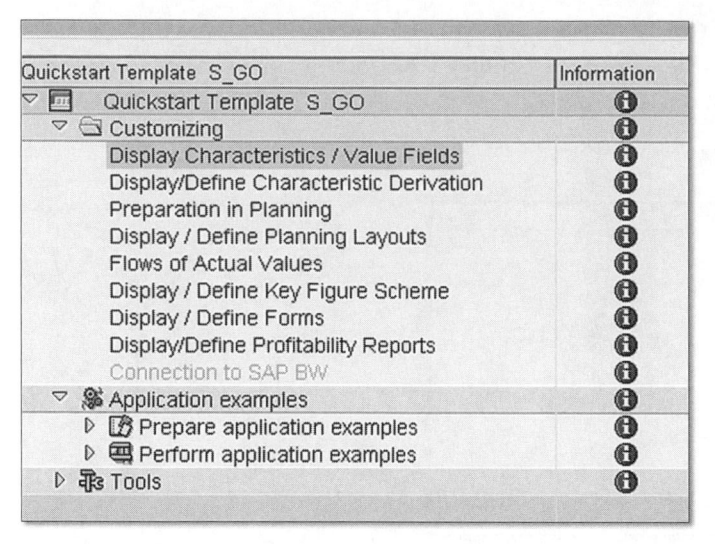

Figure 3.16 Display Characteristics/Value Fields

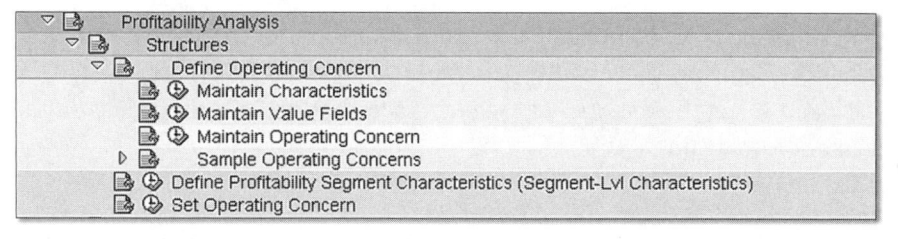

Figure 3.17 Accessing Characteristics/Value Field Information

Note

To access the IMG associated with any item in the menu structure shown in Figure 3.16, you can either select the item to highlight it and then click on it to access the IMG, or you can double-click on the item.

3. Find the item MAINTAIN OPERATING CONCERN and then click on the clock with the checkmark icon to execute the function, shown in Figure 3.17.

4. The screen shown in Figure 3.18 appears, where you can modify the structure of any operating concern. Click on the change/modify icon, (the pencil with glasses), and the message CAUTION! YOU ARE CHANGING/DELETING CROSS-CLIENT SETTINGS appears. The SAP system is letting you know that you are accessing objects used in different components.

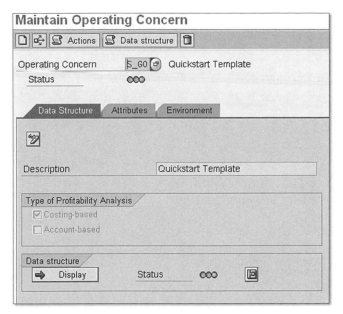

Figure 3.18 Reviewing the Contents of an Operating Concern

5. Click on the green checkmark icon.

Tips & Tricks

When you need to run the activation process, you can click on the change/modify icon, use the combination ⎡Ctrl⎤ + ⎡F3⎤, or click on the cigar icon in the icon bar. Because the Quickstart template is default SAP Business Content, however, you are not actually allowed to modify any part of its configuration; you can only display its contents. However, in an operating concern created from scratch, you can modify any part of the structure and you will need to activate these changes.

6. You can now review the information contained on the CHARS (Characteristics) and VALUE FIELDS tabs of the operating concern, as shown in Figure 3.19 and Figure 3.20. Notice the technical names that identify the characteristics and the origin SAP tables.

7. Once you've finished reviewing this information, click on the BACK icon to return to the original screen of the Quickstart template.

8. After completing your changes, also review the STATUS indicator shown earlier in Figure 3.18, which must be set to green. Otherwise, there might be errors in the latest modifications that you need to review.

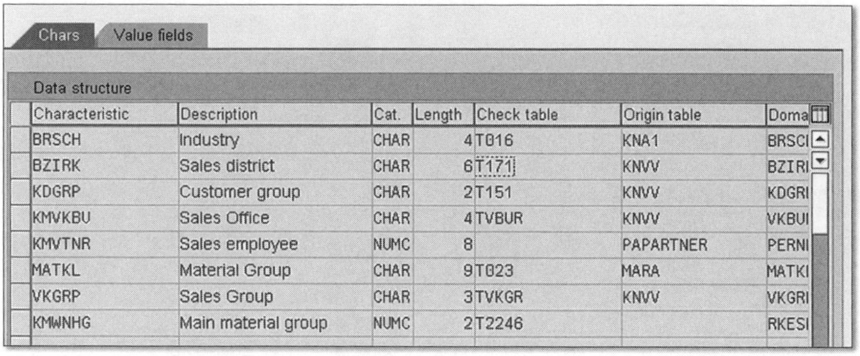
Chars
Value fields
Data structure
Characteristic | Description | Cat. | Length | Check table | Origin table | Doma
BRSCH | Industry | CHAR | 4 | T016 | KNA1 | BRSCI
BZIRK | Sales district | CHAR | 6 | T171 | KNVV | BZIRI
KDGRP | Customer group | CHAR | 2 | T151 | KNVV | KDGRI
KMVKBU | Sales Office | CHAR | 4 | TVBUR | KNVV | VKBUI
KMVTNR | Sales employee | NUMC | 8 | | PAPARTNER | PERNI
MATKL | Material Group | CHAR | 9 | T023 | MARA | MATKI
VKGRP | Sales Group | CHAR | 3 | TVKGR | KNVV | VKGRI
KMWNHG | Main material group | NUMC | 2 | T2246 | | RKESI

Figure 3.19 Characteristics of the Operating Concern Quickstart

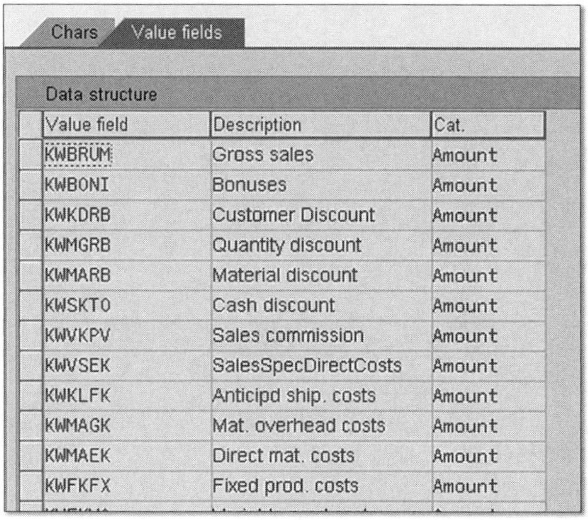
Chars
Value fields
Data structure
Value field | Description | Cat.
KWBRUM | Gross sales | Amount
KWBONI | Bonuses | Amount
KWKDRB | Customer Discount | Amount
KWMGRB | Quantity discount | Amount
KWMARB | Material discount | Amount
KWSKTO | Cash discount | Amount
KWVKPV | Sales commission | Amount
KWVSEK | SalesSpecDirectCosts | Amount
KWKLFK | Anticipd ship. costs | Amount
KWMAGK | Mat. overhead costs | Amount
KWMAEK | Direct mat. costs | Amount
KWFKFX | Fixed prod. costs | Amount

Figure 3.20 Value Fields of the Operating Concern Quickstart

9. Select the ATTRIBUTES tab as shown in Figure 3.21 and notice that the operating concern requires an OPERATING CONCERN CURRENCY for costing-based CO-PA and a FISCAL YEAR VARIANT. Generally, K4 (calendar year with 4 special posting periods) is the most common for SAP reporting.
10. The ENVIRONMENT tab (shown later in Figure 3.33) provides a general review of the status of the operating concern cross-client (programs, screens, and any other objects). Also, this tab provides information if the operating concern has been configured properly. The other status indicator is the client-specific part that identifies whether any objects, such as number range objects, attributes, or control table entries are working properly.

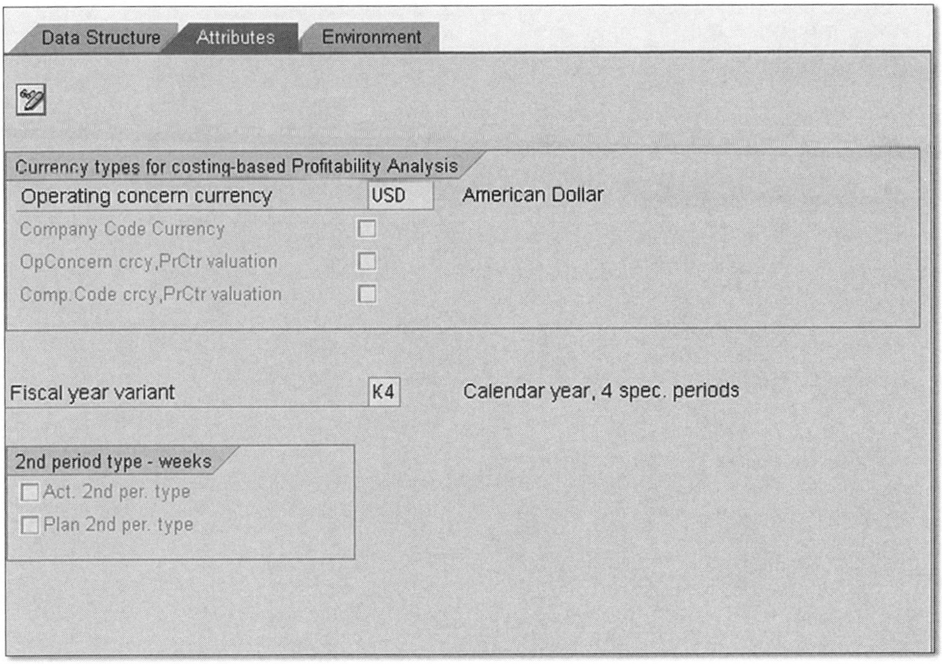

Figure 3.21 Reviewing the Attributes Tabs

Display/Define Characteristic Derivation

We'll now take a quick look at characteristic derivation:

1. Return to the Quickstart main menu, and double-click on DISPLAY/DEFINE CHAR-ACTERISTIC DERIVATION, shown in Figure 3.22. We'll look at derivation in detail in Chapter 5; however, we can say that derivation lets you find values for certain characteristics automatically, based on the known values of other characteristics, where these characteristics are logically dependent on one another.

2. Select PROFITABILITY ANALYSIS, click on the checkmark icon, and then access the IMG menu called DEFINE CHARACTERISTIC DERIVATION, as shown in Figure 3.22.

As shown in Figure 3.23, notice that the main component that controls the DEFINE CHARACTERISTIC DERIVATION menu item is the DERIVATION RULE, which can be considered to be the inference engine that controls the relationships between different characteristics and generates the new data values in the predefined characteristic that exists inside an operation concern.

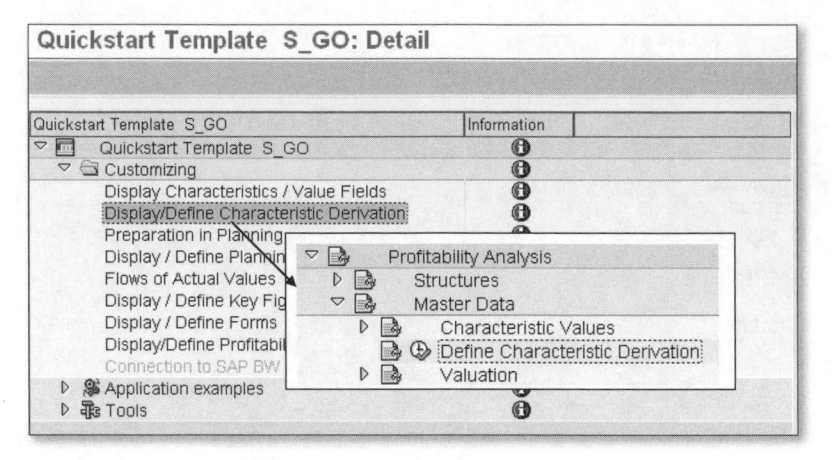

Figure 3.22 Accessing Characteristic Derivation

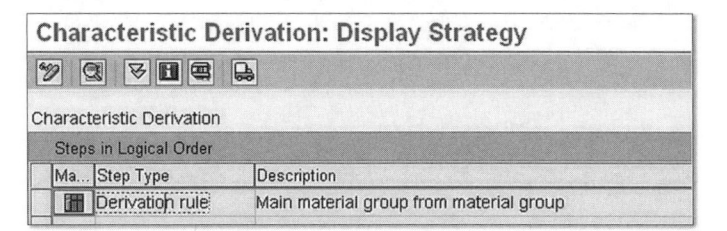

Figure 3.23 Characteristic Derivation

Preparation in Planning

Next, we'll look at preparation in planning:

1. Return to the main menu of the Quickstart template, and follow this path: CUSTOMIZING • PREPARATION IN PLANNING.

2. Select PROFITABILITY ANALYSIS and click on the checkmark. This lets you access the CO-PA PLANNING menu as shown in Figure 3.24. In this menu, you can display the settings made in planning for the operating concern template Quickstart.

   There can be multiple versions of data within the same operating concern, and for this reason the option VERSION MAINTENANCE is available to help you organize the versions across operating concerns, such as plan version 0 which will store a separate set of sample data, and assign it to the Quickstart operating concern template.

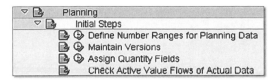

Figure 3.24 Preparation for Planning

Display/Define Planning Layouts

As mentioned earlier, the CO-PA planning framework is an important component in the success of a CO-PA implementation, especially when you start transferring information from other components. We'll explore the CO-PA planning framework features in detail in Chapter 6; for now, we'll simply review the information presented for the Quickstart template using the DISPLAY/DEFINE PLANNING LAYOUTS option:

1. Click on the BACK icon to access the main screen of the Quickstart template.

2. Double-click on DISPLAY/DEFINE PLANNING LAYOUT.

3. Select DEFINE PLANNING LAYOUT, as shown in Figure 3.25, and then click on the EXECUTE icon for DEFINE PLANNING LAYOUT.

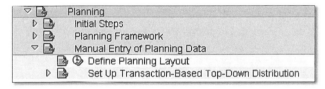

Figure 3.25 Defining Planning Layouts

4. Select CREATE PLANNING LAYOUT, CHANGE PLANNING LAYOUT, or DISPLAY PLANNING LAYOUT, depending on whether you want to create a new planning layout, modify an existing layout object, or display an existing layout object.

The Quickstart template contains several predefined planning layouts, as shown in Figure 3.26. For those familiar with SAP BW-BPS, the concept of *layout* should be more than clear. A *planning layout* is a spreadsheet-like environment that allows you to perform planning operations that can interact with SAP software and Microsoft Excel at the same time. Planning layouts interact directly with the information stored in your operating concern and are created using the SAP ERP ECC 6.0 application called Report Painter, which we'll also review in Chapter 9.

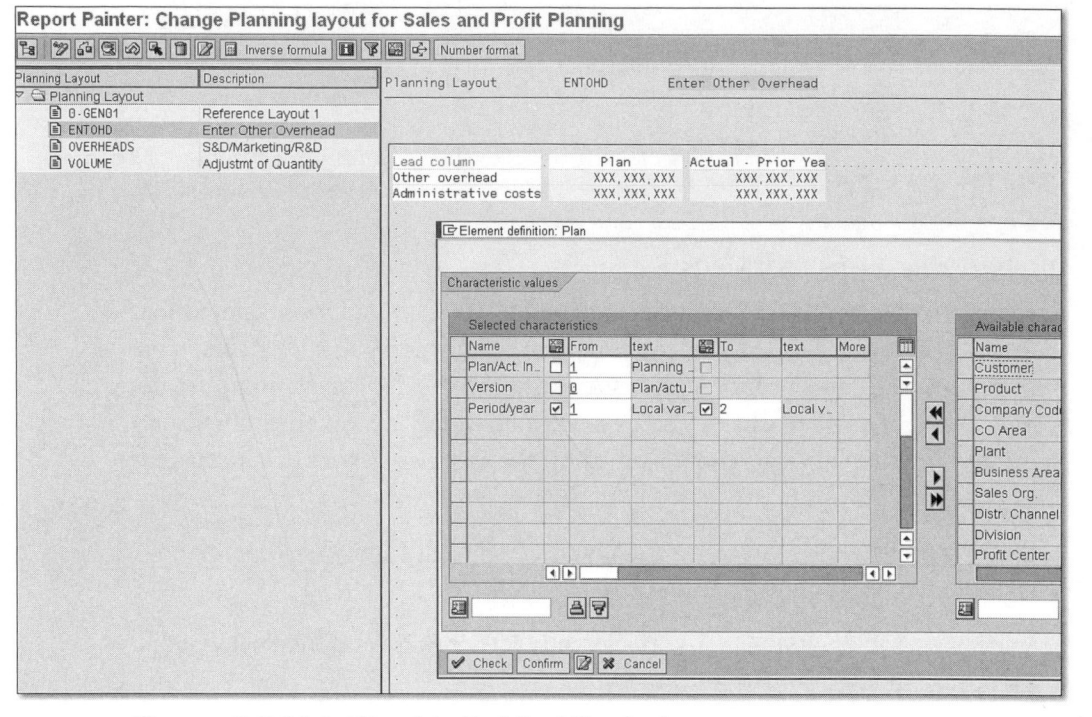

Figure 3.26 Quickstart Template: Predefined Planning Layouts

The functionality of each of the planning layouts shown in Figure 3.26 is as follows:

▶ In planning layout 0-GEN01, the basic layout includes a number of predefined variables that collect and present information based on amount, unit, and distribution key. Use this for a quick reference for a basic layout that you can adapt to other needs, depending on the characteristics of your data.

▶ In planning layout ENTOHD, other overhead costs and administration costs are planned at the highest level under record type D. The numbers from the previous year are displayed for comparison purposes.

▶ Planning layout OVERHEADS is used for entering R&D, marketing, and sales overhead. Planning occurs at the distribution channel and main material group under record type D.

▶ In planning layout VOLUME, you can make adjustments to quantities at the customer group, material group, and distribution channel level under record type F.

> **Note**
>
> An operating concern works quite similar to an SAP BW InfoCube in the sense that it interacts with layouts to extract and modify the information they contain. An operating concern is also the link required to establish data extraction architectures between SAP R/3 or SAP ERP ECC 6.0 and SAP NetWeaver BI, as discussed in Chapter 9. Hopefully, the model presented earlier in Figure 3.1 is clearer now; otherwise, wait until we review each of the components in more detail in later chapters.

Flows of Actual Values

As its name implies, the flows of actual values functionality within the Quickstart template accesses the Flows of Actual Values menu in the IMG. As seen previously in Figure 3.9, this functionality allows interacting and transferring data from different sources, such as billing documents, direct postings, and others. We'll review this in more detail in Chapter 8.

Display/Define Key Figure Scheme

This component is quite important to simplify the calculation of values in CO-PA. This menu of the Quickstart template can be compared to a *calculated key figure* (CKF) or *restricted key figure* (RKF) in SAP BW-BEx because it establishes predefined structures and relationships and stores individual values. For example, we can create a key figure scheme (an object with formulas attached) called Net Sales and place it in a column as part of a report, but in reality it is an object that includes the formula sales-total costs, and its value is what we use in any report. This illustrates that CO-PA is a quick and agile reporting tool and its interaction with Microsoft Excel makes it very desirable for end users.

To work with key figure schemes, follow these steps:

1. Return to the Quickstart main menu and double-click on Display/Define Key Figure Scheme in the Customizing menu.

2. In the IMG, execute the function Define Key Figure Schemes to access the screen shown in Figure 3.27.

Here, the Total var. COGM key figure scheme is shown, and the formula used to calculate its result is presented as:

```
+ 'Direct MaterialCosts' + 'Var. Production costs'
```

DIRECT MATERIALCOSTS and VAR. PRODUCTION COSTS are also key figure schemes with a lower sequence value that extract the information using a specific element based on a VALUE FIELD, FORMULA, and FUNCTION.

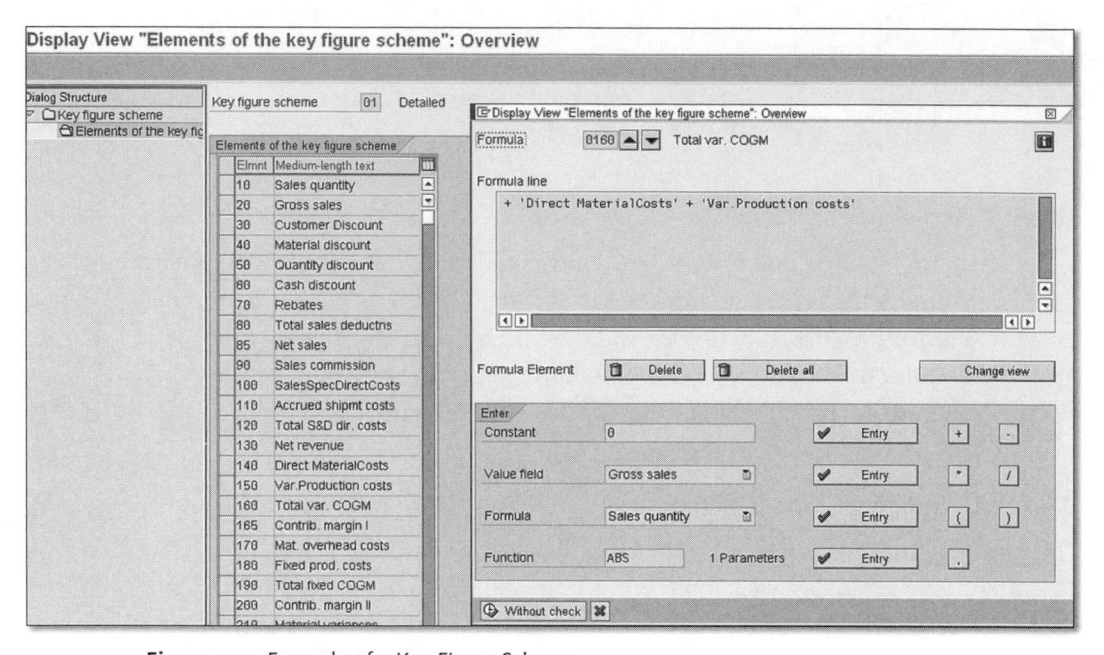

Figure 3.27 Example of a Key Figure Scheme

Note

We'll discuss this topic in more detail in Chapter 10. For now, you just need to understand that you can create your own objects inside CO-PA that allow you to work similarly to how you would work with SAP NetWeaver BW with calculated key figures or with preconfigured formulas, and that they are called key figure schemes.

Display/Define Forms

The DISPLAY/DEFINE FORMS function in the main menu of the Quickstart template allows you to access information of profitability reports that can be based on objects called *forms*. Forms work as templates that define the key figure or value fields to display in rows and columns within a report. You can use forms as a template for complex reports in as many reports as required or to maintain a standard format used by departments or business units with similar information. In addition, the Quickstart template includes seven predefined forms, as shown in Figure 3.28 and described here:

▶ **Sales/Sales Volume (SGOF01)**
Calculates the total value of net sales using the information coming from sales quantity, gross sales, customer discount, material and quantity discount, cash discount, rebates, and total sale deductions.

▶ **Target Achievement (SGOF02)**
Calculates the relative weight or percentage of achievement of the plan versus actual data values inside the operating concern. It provides a formula calculation between actual versus plan to measure achievement of the sales quantity, gross sales, total sales reductions, and net sales.

▶ **Price History (SGOF03)**
Shows the information for twelve periods and a total for the end of the year. The total year value is calculated as the sum of the 12 periods using a predefined formula.

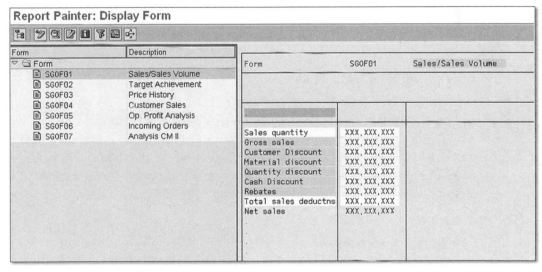

Figure 3.28 Display/Define Forms with the Report Painter

▶ **Customer Sales (SGOF04)**
Displays the total sales for all of the customers, regardless of the time period.

▶ **Operating Profit Analysis (SGOF05)**
Provides a clear view on how the operating profit can be calculated, and additional

features that can be configured as part of a report. For example, you can extract the actual and plan values, and perform comparisons with previous years and make a calculation in the percentages of change for each value type. Also, there are different levels to how the net revenue and the contribution margins are calculated, depending on the desired deductions at each step. However, the values are defined only for predefined value fields without any further definitions.

► **Incoming Orders (SGOF06)**
Extracts information from other SAP components, and how this information can be used and displayed by different users. Most of the value fields have not been preconfigured, and only the calculation of contribution margin per unit (CM II/Unit) and contribution margin per net sales (CM II/Net Sales) have actual formulas assigned to their objects.

► **Analysis CM II (SGOF07)**
Presents a more detailed overview of the calculation of the contribution margin and a comparison with previous years.

You can use these SAP-delivered forms as a template for your own forms, customize them to suit your requirements, or as a reference to create new forms.

Display/Define Profitability Reports

Profitability reports are the ultimate goal of CO-PA because they give managers and users direct access to the information they need that is stored in SAP R/3 or SAP ERP ECC 6.0. In comparison with forms, profitability reports, shown in Figure 3.29, are individual objects that you can customize and modify but that you cannot use as templates to control other reports' behavior. The Quickstart template delivers seven reports using the forms displayed in Figure 3.29 as templates:

► **SGOB01**
Allows you to analyze the short-term sales and volume figures. In particular, you can explore in detail the structure of the discounts granted. Because this information reaches Profitability Analysis from billing documents, you can run an analysis at the customer or product level.

► **SGOB02**
Shows the extent to which planned targets have been attained. Because planning often occurs at a higher level than the customer or product level, you cannot drill down from these characteristics.

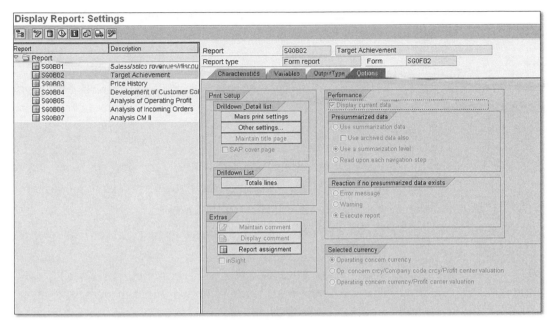

Figure 3.29 Configuration Options for Profitability Report SGOB02

▶ **SGOB03**

Shows the gross and net price history during a given year. Depending on the selection you make, you can display this information for planning or actual data. You can drill down via all of the characteristics in the product hierarchy.

▶ **SGOB04**

Lets you analyze sales volumes in the customer hierarchy. For this, you can either specify a specific period or display an overview of all periods. You can tailor the graphic to meet your requirements.

▶ **SGOB05**

Allows you to compare the actual data—within a given period interval—with the planning data and the data for the previous year (up to the operating profit or loss) for the entire contribution margin scheme. You can drill down from the characteristics if overhead costs occur at that level. The only costs to be represented at the level of the entire company are administration costs.

▶ **SGOB06**

Provides you with a comparison of the incoming sales in a given period interval and the 12 previous periods (that is, the previous year). The information includes everything up to contribution margin II. You can use this report to display early warning information.

► **SGOB07**
Allows you to analyze short-term company success (that is, CM II), without taking periodic overhead into account. Moreover, the report also displays two key figures on the profit-sales ratio.

To access profitability reports in the Quickstart template, follow this procedure:

1. Return to the main menu of the Quickstart template.

2. Double-click on DISPLAY/DEFINE PROFITABILITY in the CUSTOMIZING menu.

3. Select PROFITABILITY ANALYSIS and click on the checkmark icon.

4. Click on the EXECUTE icon for the IMG object named CREATE PROFITABILITY REPORT.

5. Choose an activity: CREATE, CHANGE, or DISPLAY. For our purposes, we'll choose DISPLAY to navigate and review the configurations without changing any important information.

6. Double-click on any object to review its configuration. For example, Figure 3.29 displays the Target Achievement report (SGOB02) and the CHARACTERISTICS, VARIABLES, OUTPUT TYPE, and OPTIONS tabs that control its behavior. For now, access this information and become familiar with it; we'll review it in more detail in Chapter 8.

7. You can execute any profitability report at any time using the same procedure we just used to view the target achievement report.

The final results of executing a profitability report are presented in Figure 3.30 using 1/2009 as the starting period. Notice the different components that are shown such as characteristics used for NAVIGATION, value fields for SALES QUANTITY, GROSS SALES, and others, as well as charts and totals for a particular characteristic for a given time period. The customization options available in the Report Painter allow CO-PA to be a flexible application to design new and improved ways to analyze different sources of data.

CO-PA reporting also requires performance tuning if the amount of data extracted increases with time, so you need to be aware of new techniques or simplifications to avoid performance issues when running your reports.

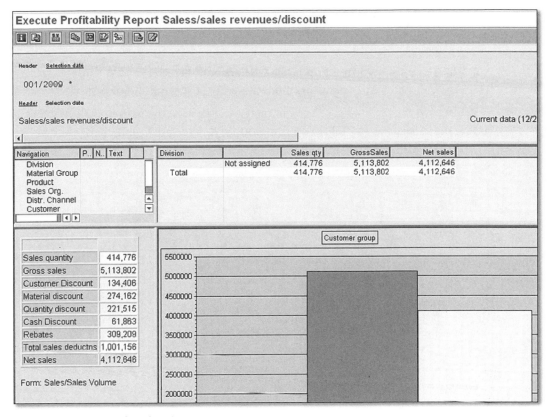

Figure 3.30 Example of Profitability Report SGOB01

3.4.3 Application Examples: Prepare Application Examples

We'll now look at the functions in the APPLICATION EXAMPLES • PREPARE APPLICATION EXAMPLES menu of the Quickstart template, shown earlier in Figure 3.16.

Maintaining Characteristic Values

A market segment is made up of a combination of characteristic values, and the Maintain Characteristic Values function allows you to maintain these values for selected characteristics that can be deleted, changed, or added. Characteristic values are used to generate sample data when activating your Quickstart template. To access this functionality, follow these steps:

1. Follow this path in the Quickstart Template main menu: Application examples • Prepare application examples and double-click on Maintain Characteristic Values.

2. The screen shown in Figure 3.31 appears and displays the available characteristic values for the operating concern S_GO Quickstart Template.

3. Click on the Customer group characteristic and see the values as shown on the right side of Figure 3.31. You can modify, delete, copy, and change the values displayed in your system to match your needs.

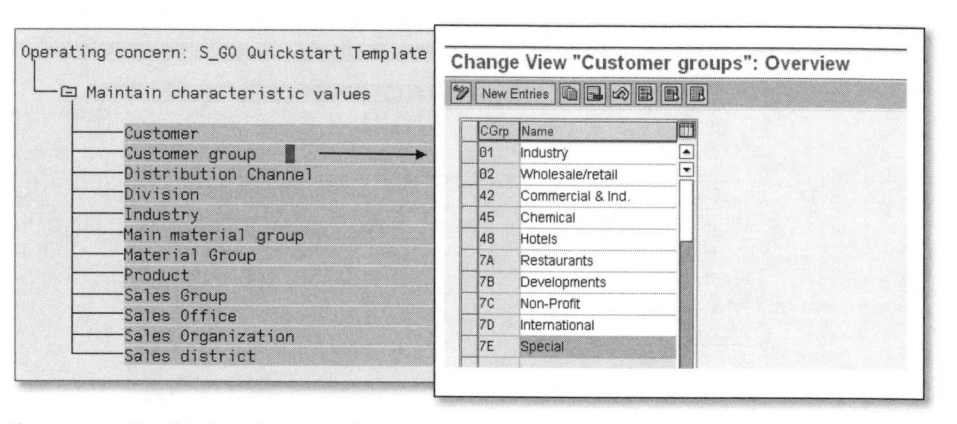

Figure 3.31 Maintaining Characteristic Values

Create/Delete Example Data

We've already covered creating example data earlier in this chapter so we won't look at the Create example data option here. The option Delete example data lets you completely remove the sample data from your system.

3.4.4 Application Examples: Perform Application Examples

We'll now look at the options in the Application examples • Perform application examples menu of the Quickstart template.

Execute Profitability Report

You can access the Execute Profitability Report function by following this path: Perform Application example • Execute Profitability Report. We won't go into further detail here because we've already executed a report and also have a good idea on how to display reports on the screen, based on Figure 3.30. Further detail will be provided in Chapters 9 and 10.

Execute Planning Method

The Execute Planning Method function lets you directly access planning layouts (the objects that allow users to make modifications to data inside the core SAP tables or user-defined values) using the path: APPLICATION EXAMPLES • PERFORM APPLICATION EXAMPLES • EXECUTE PLANNING METHOD. As mentioned before, we'll explain these concepts in more detail in Chapter 6, so for now simply navigate and become familiar with the planning framework environment shown in Figure 3.32.

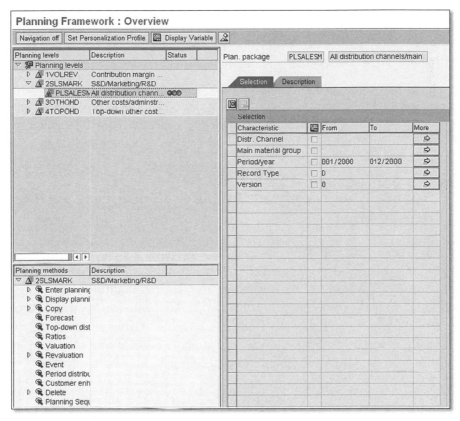

Figure 3.32 The CO-PA Planning Framework

3.4.5   Tools

The last menu of the Quickstart operating concern template is TOOLS. CO-PA provides an extensive number of tools to improve analysis, performance, and other elements. However, the TOOLS menu for Quickstart is limited to the following tools:

▶ **Copy Operating Concern template**
This function lets you copy the selected operating concern template, including the changes you have made to it. You can then make further changes to this copied operating concern and use the relevant customizing settings to integrate it into the other application components. Give the operating concern a name that does not fall within the SAP name range (S_xx).

▶ **Reset Operating Concern template**
This functions lets you reset the operating concern template to its original SAP-delivered state. This process erases any changes you have made to the template and any example data generated. Note that the characteristic values you have maintained are not deleted.

Once all of these components are working and you've finished creating and configuring your CO-PA applications, you must activate each operating concern and set it as current so you can extract your data and generate reports according to your specifications. Let's walk through this process in the following section.

3.5   Manually Activating an Operating Concern and Setting It as Current

For changes made to an operating concern to affect all of the objects included in the operating concern, the operating concern must be activated. You can do this by either answering YES to the message you receive after adding characteristics and value fields to the operating concern when working with the MAINTAIN OPERATING CONCERN function in the STRUCTURES menu (shown earlier in Figure 3.5), or by manually activating the operating concern at a later point in time. To manually activate an operating concern, follow this procedure:

1. Follow this path in the IMG: PROFITABILITY ANALYSIS • STRUCTURES • MAINTAIN OPERATING CONCERN and click on the EXECUTE icon.

2. Select the ENVIRONMENT tab, shown in Figure 3.33.

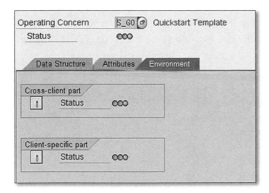

Figure 3.33 Activating Your Operating Concern

3. To activate either of the two available components, CROSS-CLIENT PART (external to CO-PA) or CLIENT-SPECIFIC PART (internal to CO-PA), click on the cigar-like icons in the respective sections. These two components are critical for the data structures and information extracted and shared within the CO-PA application. Your objects are now ready to be accessed by any reports or planning applications.

> **Note**
>
> You should always make sure that the STATUS icons on the ENVIRONMENT tab, as well as those on the DATA STRUCTURE tab are green to be certain that there are no problems or errors left in the system. The SAP system will prompt you if any errors were identified in the data structures of the operating concern that you are trying to activate.

When you're certain that your operating concern only has the group of characteristics and value fields you want, is correctly configured (status green), has been activated (to reflect the latest data structure), and you are clear what you want to do with it, you are ready to make it the current operating concern. Use the SET OPERATING CONCERN function in the IMG STRUCTURES menu.

Only the current operating concern will be affected by any modification, change, report extraction, and update of objects. Furthermore, objects such as planning layouts, forms, and reports that are attached to an operating concern are only available if the correct operating concern has been set up as current. Making sure that the appropriate operating concern is set up as current is extremely important; you don't want to make changes to, or use data from, an incorrect operating concern.

Example

For example, if you have two operating concerns, Europe and USA, and you set Europe as current, the USA information will not be affected by any changes you make in data, reports, layouts, and other information (as long as the two operating concerns' information does not overlap in the data structures). Also, the information contained in the USA operating concern will not be available when working with the Europe operating concern, and vice versa, unless you select the SET OPERATING CONCERN function again, and change this relationship.

To set the Quickstart operating concern as current:

1. Follow the IMG menu path PROFITABILITY ANALYSIS • STRUCTURES • SET OPERATING CONCERN, as shown in Figure 3.34, and click on the EXECUTE icon.

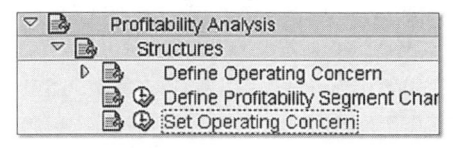

Figure 3.34 The Set Operating Concern Function

2. Review the information presented in the screen shown in Figure 3.35. The STA-TUS icon lets you know if the operating concern is ready to be used. Furthermore, the TYPE OF PROFIT ANALYSIS that this object will perform is identified (either COSTING-BASED or ACCOUNT-BASED), which also affects the way that information is posted and displayed into CO-PA.

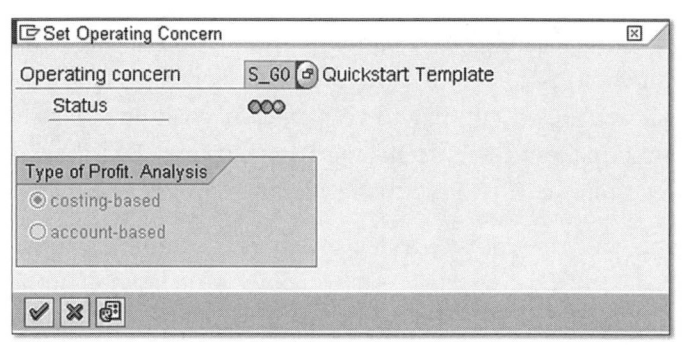

Figure 3.35 Making an Operating Concern Current

3. Click on the checkmark icon to set the current operating concern.

> **Note**
>
> We recommend that you do not perform any additional transactions until you understand the ideas and general concepts presented in the next two chapters. Also, remember that you have several SAP-delivered templates that follow the same format of the Quickstart template that you can activate, and whose structures and configurations you can review to complement your learning.

3.6 Summary

In this chapter we explored the basic functionalities of CO-PA from a general point of view. We showed you what type of information CO-PA can handle in R/3 or SAP ERP ECC 6.0, how you can access this information in a template, and, in general, helped you become familiar with the CO-PA environment.

In Chapter 4, we'll analyze the concept of an operating concern in more detail, as well as CO-PA and its role as main integrator within an SAP system of OLTP and OLAP data. We'll also examine the differences between costing-based and account-based CO-PA.

> **Note**
>
> Should you still be confused about the topics or terms discussed in this chapter or how to navigate inside the SAP IMG, don't worry; we'll continue our discussion in more detail in the chapters that follow and you'll get the hang of things. Also, remember that this book is written for intermediate and advanced users, but beginners of CO-PA can catch up quickly with the help of other team members and by using the material in this book. Remember that the SAP community continuously evolves, so seek the help of a consultant or power user in your firm to get you started.

Costing-based CO-PA is considered the most intensive and common application of Profitability Analysis. However, when you configure costing-based CO-PA, you're also creating an account-based environment at no additional charge.

4 Configuring Costing-Based CO-PA

The most popular type of Profitability Analysis is costing-based CO-PA. It's easy to configure and provides a reasonable level of detail without having to worry about account or cost elements in the system, and it gives meaningful information to decision makers. In this chapter, we'll explore the creation and configuration of a CO-PA costing-based operating concern in detail, as well as the major options required to set it up. In addition, we'll activate all of the account-based CO-PA options along the way so you can review them when we explore account-based CO-PA in more detail in Chapter 11.

4.1 General CO-PA Overview

In general, CO-PA is a component that allows the analysis and combination of different types of documents, such as:

- Invoices from the SD component
- Direct journal entries from FI
- Cost center assessments from CO
- Settlement of production orders from Production Planning (PP)
- Quantity flows from Materials Management (MM)
- Work Breakdown Structure (WBS) elements from Project System (PS), among others

All of this documentation carries information related to customers, billing information, dates, products, variances, cost allocations, and hierarchies, and allows the creation of up to 30 additional user-defined characteristics and up to 120 additional value fields (key figures) to complement the different analyses. Moreover, the creation of CO-PA documents for each line item, sales order, cost assessment, and production order allows creating profitability segments or market segments that identify the data with specific characteristics.

> **Note**
>
> Profitability segments allow CO-PA to perform transactions between controlling objects, such as cost centers or production orders, and the profitability segments. However, once the values have been allocated inside CO-PA, the revenue and cost elements require special processing procedures to be allocated outside this environment.

As you can see in Figure 4.1, the role of CO-PA is to consolidate and access information coming from different areas of the SAP ERP ECC 6.0 system, based on the documents previously discussed. The value flow shown in Figure 4.1 describes the availability of key financial data coming from either Financial Accounting (FI) or Controlling (CO) components, which are the two key elements for any posting inside an SAP system. At the end you can see what management wants to visualize in terms of how each transaction affects financials, while thinking ahead to the balance sheet and the income statement reports.

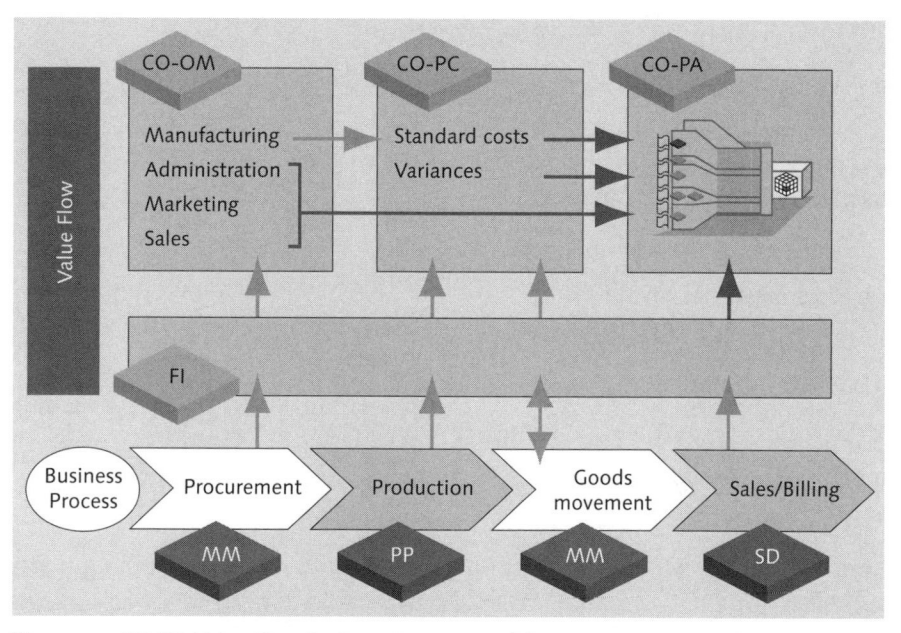

Figure 4.1 CO-PA Value Flow Business Process Model

Note
An operating concern could be understood by SAP NetWeaver BW users as the SAP ERP ECC 6.0 equivalent of an SAP BW InfoCube. Thus, the main function of a SAP CO-PA operating concern is not only storing data, but also creating a door into the SAP ECC tables using a set of pre-defined structures and/or processes that transfer the data from SAP ECC into SAP CO-PA.

4.2 Costing-Based CO-PA versus Account-Based CO-PA

Part of the decisions required to work with CO-PA is how to configure and control how your data flows, which is done using one of two models: costing-based or account-based. Each model allows posting information at different stages of the sales cycle, and the type of information displayed differs slightly. In simple terms, the two basic CO-PA approaches are:

▶ **Costing-based**: Uses value fields and does not use general ledger (G/L) accounts to perform any type of reconciliation with FI or cost-element accounting. Advantages of costing-based CO-PA include:

  ▶ Contribution margin can be calculated, automatically accessing the standard cost estimates of the product valuation approaches.

  ▶ Variance categories can be mapped to value fields.

  ▶ Flexible reporting capabilities are available for analysis of several characteristics.

  ▶ Standard cost estimate is used to show a split by cost component of the bills information extracted from the product costing component.

▶ **Account-based**: Is directly related to G/L account posting and for this reason makes it more exact and requires summarization levels to facilitate data consolidation. The advantage of account-based Profitability Analysis is that it is permanently reconciled with financial accounting. However, the fact that it uses accounts to get values makes it less powerful. No contribution margin planning can be done because it cannot access the standard cost estimate in account-based CO-PA and no variance analysis is readily available.

The main difference between the two CO-PA methods, however, is how and when postings are performed inside the system. Table 4.1 provides a description of these specific differences and how their transactions are posted into the financial and controlling systems, dealing with three major issues:

1. Passing an invoice to accounting updates the revenue, discount, freight, and cost of sales value fields.

2. Settling production order variance updates the variance fields that are related to the cost of goods sold (COGS) cost components.

3. Assessing cost center updates to the cost center variance fields.

Account-Based	Costing-Based
Invoice information and financial postings are performed at the same time when calculating the cost of sales.	Cost of sales captured at the time of invoice but the financial posting is done at the time of delivery, meaning there is a time lag between these two transactions.
The cost of sales is no longer exactly matched with the revenue that is posted at the time of invoicing.	The cost component detail for variances is available for production order settlement and production cost collector hierarchy.
The details of the COGS components are not available.	Cost elements and G/L accounts are not available.
The cost of sales is not captured when invoicing a customer because it was already done when doing the financial entry.	Reconciliation using value fields and high-level characteristics (such as region, business area, and others).
Revenue is posted into CO-PA during billing.	The postings are recorded in a CO-PA document.
Production variances (order settlement and cost collector hierarchy) are not available, but variance is captured via one cost element.	Costing-based CO-PA uses a cost-of-sales approach, where the standard cost of sales is not recognized until a product is sold.
It is more detailed than costing-based because it discloses the different G/L accounts and cost elements.	
The postings are recorded in a standard controlling document.	

Table 4.1 Comparison between Account-Based and Costing-Based CO-PA

> **Note**
>
> If both costing-based and account-based CO-PA are activated, when the settlement to CO-PA takes place, a posting is made to both types of CO-PA. The account-based CO-PA posting is recorded in a standard controlling document and the costing-based CO-PA posting is recorded in a CO-PA document.

If R/3 or SAP ERP ECC 6.0 don't give you the type of information that you want, you can use SAP NetWeaver Business Intelligence (BI). If you want to customize something beyond that, remember the following when using ABAP or another programming language:

▶ Customization affects system performance, and future system upgrades directly affect it.

▶ Modifications to the standard system functionalities centralize power in the hands of a few people who might not be around all of the time.

▶ The lack of documentation generally available during and after a major system customization provides more room for the people who built the system to, under negative circumstances, possibly halt the system.

▶ Customizations mostly add costs rather than value; consultants love to bill you for a new system and the periodic maintenance, but the SAP system has enough tools to avoid major customizations. Limit yourself to what the system provides and you'll find that you are able to access the information that you need without major customizations.

▶ Limit the use of ABAP for the following:

   ▶ Major "your boat is sinking" type of scenarios in SAP and other GUI components.

   ▶ Simple queries using an ABAP query with table joins or direct access.

   ▶ Interacting in the SAP NetWeaver BI 7.0 environment on the web.

   Do not use ABAP for:

   ▶ Major customizations that modify default SAP objects.

   ▶ Creating applications that can be easily delivered with alternative methods, such as FOX code and Formula Editor (available in SAP NetWeaver BI 7.0 and CO-PA Report Painter).

▶ Try to maximize the usage of available standard SAP extractors. SAP Net-Weaver BW generic data extraction can be very handy when exporting information outside SAP ERP ECC 6.0 if the capabilities of CO-PA Report Painter or CO-PA Planning are not enough.

With all these practices and tips in mind, we're now ready to start our discussion of extracting information from R/3 or SAP ERP ECC 6.0 using costing-based CO-PA.

4.3 Creating Characteristics and Value Fields

The following is a general rule in SAP Controlling:

Company codes are assigned to controlling areas, and controlling areas are assigned to operating concerns.

A *controlling area* is the highest level of aggregation that covers the activities of Cost Center Accounting, Product Costing, Profitability Analysis, and Profit Center Accounting. An *operating concern* is the highest node in Profitability Analysis that limits the activities and elements that can be accessed and modified inside SAP ERP ECC 6.0 or R/3 and is limited by characteristics and value fields. Figure 4.2 provides an overview of the major components that are part of the STRUCTURES menu of the IMG (Transaction SPRO) as part of the PROFITABILITY ANALYSIS menu. This is part of the main Profitability Analysis menu that you'll be using to create characteristics and value fields, which provide the backbone of the operating concern.

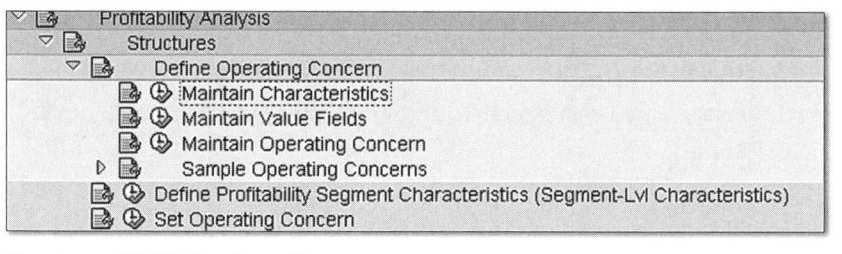

Figure 4.2 CO-PA Structures Menu

The individual configurable items include the following:

▶ MAINTAIN CHARACTERISTICS

Create, modify, or change all available characteristics. Some of the CO-PA characteristics required for reconciliation usually include company code, business area, and cost element. When working with reports, additional characteristics (such as high-level material groups) may also be used or defined as user-defined elements that are part of a derivation rule based on current SAP information to derive new values.

▶ MAINTAIN VALUE FIELDS

Create, modify, or change all available value fields. You can choose to either store or extract data as amount or quantity. For example, the value *Sales* can be stored with a unit of measure such as U.S. dollars or Euros as a quantity, but *Inventory* can simply be stored as "100," regardless of unit value as an amount or vice versa.

▶ MAINTAIN OPERATING CONCERN

Create, modify, or change operating concerns. This is where you establish the link between characteristics and value fields to create your operating concern and control the information displayed in reports or planned in CO-PA.

▶ DEFINE PROFITABILITY SEGMENT CHARACTERISTICS

These elements are additional "partitions" or pieces of your operating concern and are defined via characteristics. You select which characteristics are available for the information system and later on in planning. The remaining characteristics are considered line items and won't be used to generate any type of classification inside the operating concern.

▶ SET OPERATING CONCERN

Determines which operating concern is current in the system, and is affected by any operations, reports, extractions, derivations, and so on. The current operating concern carries the information defined inside the system, such as reports and planning layouts. For example, if operating concern A has report X attached, and operating concern B has report XX attached, only X or XX is available to perform the operations over the respective operating concern and the respective data. For this reason, it's important to know in which operating concern you're working, and that operating concern is current in the system until you exit the system or run this option again to change into another current operating concern.

Let's review and learn how to create the structures that define the basic behavior of the information inside CO-PA and that control the access and display of information—namely characteristics and value fields.

Characteristics

To access the characteristics definition:

1. Follow this IMG path (or use Transaction SPRO): CONTROLLING • PROFITABILITY ANALYSIS • STRUCTURES • DEFINE OPERATING CONCERN • MAINTAIN CHARACTERISTICS.

2. Double-click on the EXECUTE icon (clock with the checkmark), next to MAINTAIN CHARACTERISTICS.

3. You'll see the screen displayed in Figure 4.3. You can now click on CREATE/CHANGE, DISPLAY, or CHANGE, depending on what you want to do.

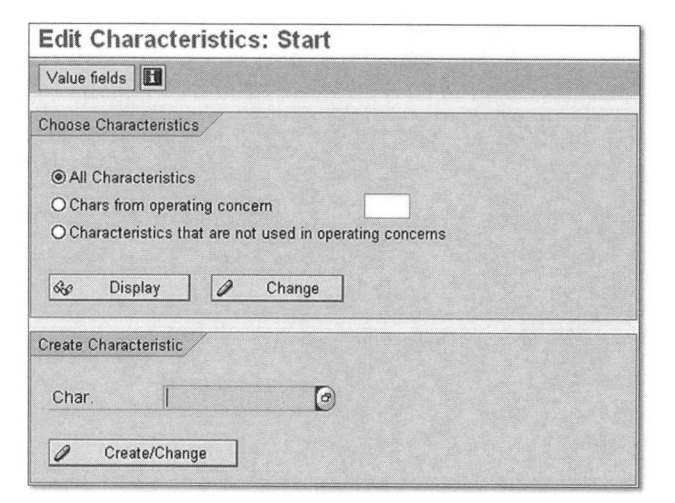

Figure 4.3 Edit Characteristics: Start Screen

4. Click on CREATE/CHANGE. The message CAUTION YOU ARE PROCESSING CROSS-CLIENT DATA STRUCTURES appears.

5. Click on the checkmark icon to accept the message.

6. Review the screen that appears, as shown in Figure 4.4. It displays all of the characteristics available in the system you can allocate to an operating concern. User-defined characteristics are displayed in white and can be modified. SAP standard characteristics extracted from specific SAP tables are grayed out

and can't be modified. For example, BONUS is an SAP default characteristic coming from the origin table MVKE, and EFORM is a user-defined characteristic.

Change Characteristics: Overview

Char.	Description	Short text	DTyp	Lgth.	Origin Table	Origin field d
BONUS	Vol. rebate grp	Rebate grp	CHAR	2	MVKE	BONUS
BRSCH	Industry	Industry	CHAR	4	KNA1	BRSCH
BZIRK	District	District	CHAR	6	KNVV	BZIRK
COPA		Cost ctr	CHAR	10		
COPA		BusProcess	CHAR	12		
CRMCSTY	CRM Cost Elmnt	CRM CstElm	CHAR	10		
CRMELEM	Marketing Element	Mrkt.Elem.	NUMC	8		
CRMFIGR	CRM Key Figure	CRM KF	CHAR	16		
EFORM	Form of manufacture	Manuf.form	CHAR	5		
GEBIE	Area	Area	CHAR	4		
KDGRP	Customer group	Cust.group	CHAR	2	KNVV	KDGRP
KMATYP	Aircraft type	Plane type	NUMC	2		

Create user-defined characteristic

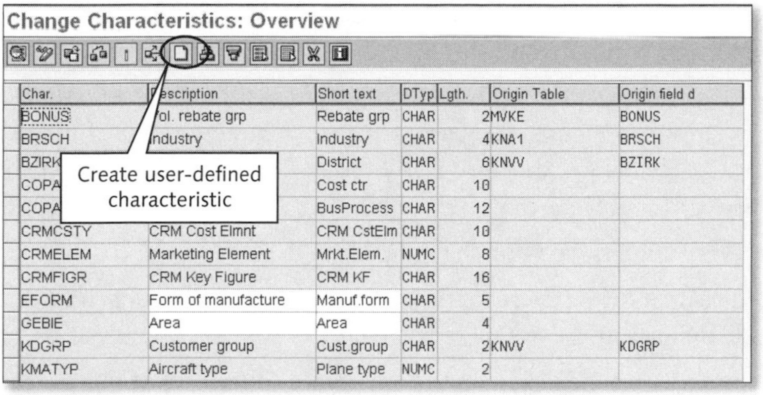

Figure 4.4 Available Characteristics in CO-PA

As discussed in the previous step, SAP default characteristics are clearly identified with their original SAP tables that store the transactional information and data fields. However, you can also create your own characteristics that you will either populate with data or use for different calculations or planning applications later on in the process. To create a user-defined characteristic, follow these steps:

1. Click on the CREATE icon located at the top of the screen shown in Figure 4.4.
2. Select the USER DEFINED radio button, as shown in Figure 4.5.

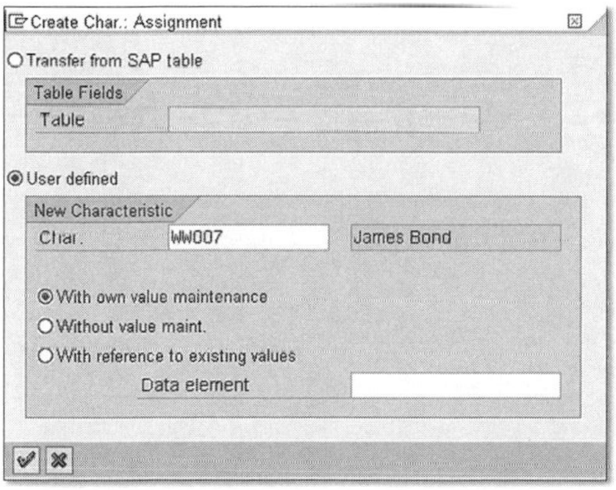

Create Char.: Assignment

- ○ Transfer from SAP table
  - Table Fields
    - Table
- ◉ User defined
  - New Characteristic
    - Char. : WW007   James Bond
  - ◉ With own value maintenance
  - ○ Without value maint.
  - ○ With reference to existing values
    - Data element

Figure 4.5 Creating a User-Defined Characteristic

3. In the NEW CHARACTERISTIC section, configure two input boxes. The first box contains the field name or unique identifier of the characteristic and must begin with "WW," followed by a standard SAP nomenclature to make the system identify these types of characteristics. The second box contains a description. For example, in Figure 4.5, WW007 is a user-defined characteristic. Its name is identifier 007 and the description is JAMES BOND.

4. After configuring the identifier and description, click on the checkmark icon and the screen shown in Figure 4.6 appears. The system now requires the definition of DATA TYPE/LENGTH. Specify "CHAR" to indicate that 007 is alphanumeric and specify "10" for the character length.

5. Click on the SAVE icon to save your changes.

6. Click on the checkmark icon to create the characteristic from scratch, and click on YES, despite the warnings.

7. Click on AUTOMATIC, and then click on the SAVE icon. At the end of this process your screen will look like Figure 4.6. (The system copies the description information from the initial screen shown in Figure 4.5 into the DESCRIPTION and HEADING boxes in the TEXTS section.)

8. To complete the process, click on the ACTIVATION icon, which is located at the top of the screen as shown in Figure 4.6.

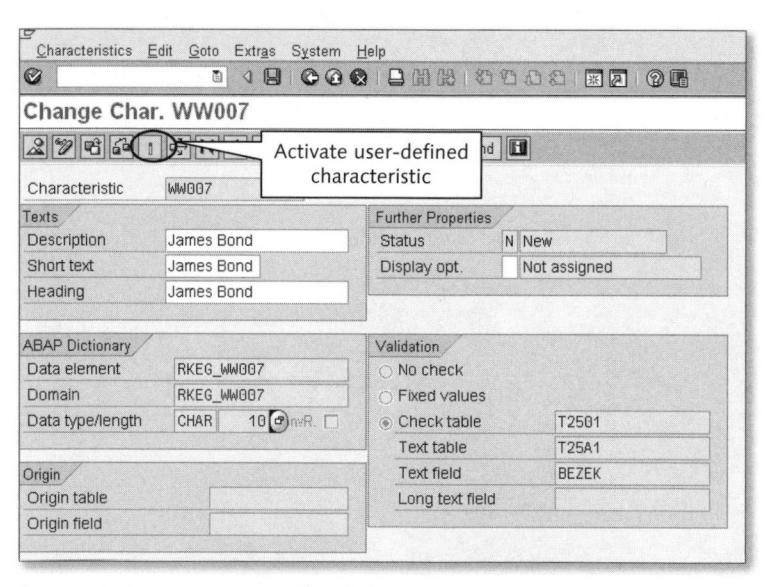

Figure 4.6 Creating a User-Defined Characteristic in CO-PA

This user-defined characteristic is now available for use by different operating concerns.

Note

When creating a user-defined characteristic, a data class can be defined to describe the data format at the user interface. If a table field, structure field, or a data element is used in an ABAP program, the data class is converted to a format used by the ABAP processor. For this reason, when a table is created inside the SAP system, the data class of a table field is converted into a data format of the database system used.

Value Fields

In simple terms, value fields do not store descriptions of data but their results. You can access the information contained in value fields in one of two ways:

▶ Click on the VALUE FIELDS button, shown earlier in Figure 4.3.

▶ Follow the IMG path PROFITABILITY ANALYSIS • STRUCTURES • DEFINE OPERATING CONCERN • MAINTAIN VALUE FIELDS.

As a result, the screen shown in Figure 4.7 appears.

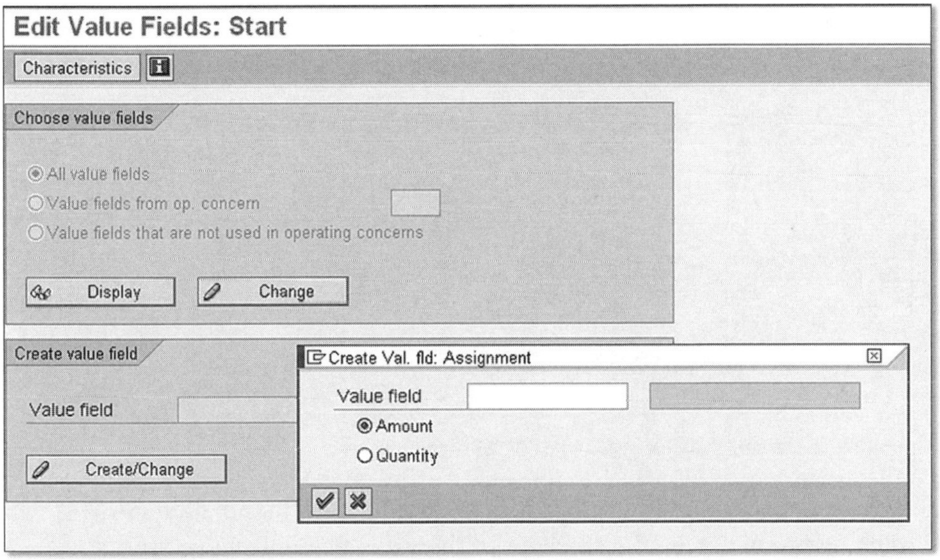

Figure 4.7 Accessing the Edit Value Fields: Start Screen

To create a new value field, follow this procedure:

1. Click on CREATE/CHANGE.

2. Click on the checkmark icon in the dialog box with the message CAUTION YOU ARE PROCESSING CROSS-CLIENT DATA STRUCTURES, and an input box called CREATE VAL. FLD: ASSIGNMENT appears, as shown in Figure 4.7.

3. Select either AMOUNT or QUANTITY, depending on your requirements. We selected AMOUNT for our example.

4. You now need to configure the technical name and a description in the two VALUE FIELD input boxes, as shown in Figure 4.7. The first input box describes the technical name that must start with "VV", followed by xxxx ("VVxxxx"). VV are the initial required letters for the system to identify this field as a value field and xxxx is the name of the value field, which must be either four or five characters long. The second input box is where you enter a description. For our example, we entered "VVTES" in the first box and "test1" in the second box.

5. Click on the checkmark icon to access the change value field screen (CHANGE VAL. FLD VVTES) as shown in Figure 4.8.

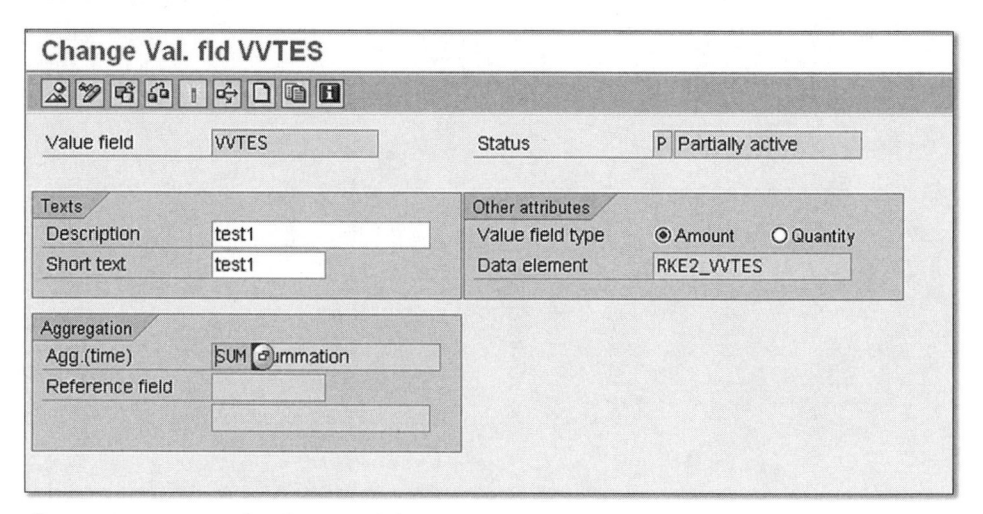

Figure 4.8 Accessing the Change Val. fld VVTES Screen

6. You can now define an aggregation method or leave Summation (SUM) as the default depending on the behavior of the value field during posting.

7. Click on SAVE.

Note

A time-based aggregation rule determines how a key figure is calculated when the reference field is a characteristic with a time dimension with three options:

► Aggregate or Average (AVG) value operation

► Summation (SUM) operation

► Last value (LAS)

The aggregation rule selected depends on the type of value field defined and its real-life behavior. For example, REVENUE is a SUM value field because you want that to be added all of the time. Employees during a time period can be a SUM or an AVG depending on whether our calculations require total employees or average number of employees. Inventory price can be considered a LAS value field because you may only be interested in having the latest value of the price. We recommend that you review the SAP documentation to fully understand this functionality.

Tips & Tricks

The aggregation rules "Last value" and "Average" are only useful for representing statistical and noncumulative values in value fields. Also, the reference period is always the period of a fiscal year. If your data is planned in weeks, the value fields cannot use the aggregation rules AVG or LAS.

---

8. Create additional value fields by clicking on the CHANGE/MODIFY icon.

9. Click on NEW ENTRIES.

10. Type the technical name in the VALUE FIELD column, then provide a DESCRIPTION and SHORT TEXT. For our example, use the information for the value fields VV01, VV012, and VV12, as shown in Figure 4.9.

11. Specify for each value field whether it is an AMOUNT or a QTY. (Amount value fields generally carry information, such as currency, and quantity fields carry data with units of measure, such as kilograms or number of produced units.) Once created, the value fields, as shown in Figure 4.9, are ready for use by any operating concern.

Like with characteristics, grayed out and white boxes are used to differentiate default SAP value fields from user-defined value fields. Notice that for the default SAP value fields, the radio buttons in the AMOUNT and QTY (Quantity) columns are also grayed out, meaning you can't change them.

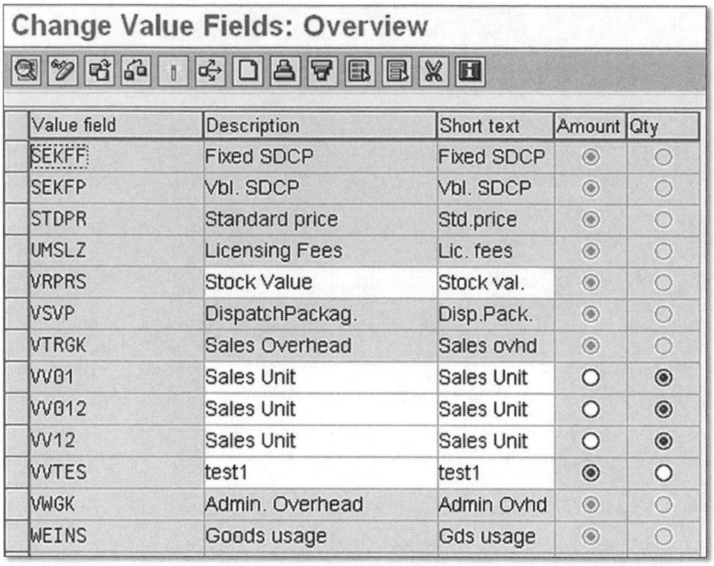

Change Value Fields: Overview

Value field	Description	Short text	Amount	Qty
SEKFF	Fixed SDCP	Fixed SDCP	◉	○
SEKFP	Vbl. SDCP	Vbl. SDCP	◉	○
STDPR	Standard price	Std.price	◉	○
UMSLZ	Licensing Fees	Lic. fees	◉	○
VRPRS	Stock Value	Stock val.	◉	○
VSVP	DispatchPackag.	Disp.Pack.	◉	○
VTRGK	Sales Overhead	Sales ovhd	◉	○
VV01	Sales Unit	Sales Unit	○	◉
VV012	Sales Unit	Sales Unit	○	◉
VV12	Sales Unit	Sales Unit	○	◉
VVTES	test1	test1	◉	○
VWGK	Admin. Overhead	Admin Ovhd	◉	○
WEINS	Goods usage	Gds usage	◉	○

Figure 4.9 Accessing the Change Value Fields: Overview Screen

In the next section we'll explore how to create an operating concern, using value fields and characteristics together to build a common structure that lets you extract or receive information.

> **Note**
>
> An exception exists to the rule that the fields of SAP-defined value fields display in gray: As shown in Figure 4.9, the value field VRPRS is an SAP-defined value field; however, it is possible to change its description and short text. Therefore, the DESCRIPTION and SHORT TEXT fields for this value field display in white.

4.4   Maintaining an Operating Concern

An SAP system requires operating concerns in CO to connect or interact with other structures inside R/3 or SAP ERP ECC 6.0 or external systems, such as SAP NetWeaver BI-IP, SAP SEM-BPS, or SAP BW-BPS.

4.4.1   Accessing and Creating Operating Concerns

To access existing and create new operating concerns, follow these steps:

1. Follow the IMG path CONTROLLING • PROFITABILITY ANALYSIS • STRUCTURES • DEFINE OPERATING CONCERN • MAINTAIN OPERATING CONCERN.

2. Click on the EXECUTE icon to display the screen shown in Figure 4.10.

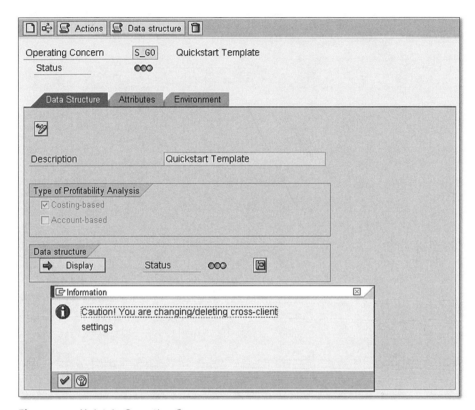

Figure 4.10 Maintain Operating Concern

3. Here you can select any operating concern available in your system. For our example, we selected the S_GO operating concern template. Notice that once you select an operating concern you can check the STATUS of its configuration to give you an idea if the data structures were correctly defined.

4. Review the different options available, especially those on the DATA STRUCTURE and ENVIRONMENT tabs. Also, notice that the operating concern requires defining a type of Profitability Analysis: costing-based, account-based, or both.

5. If necessary, select the DATA STRUCTURE tab shown in Figure 4.10, and click on the change/modify icon (a pencil with glasses), and the message CAUTION! YOU ARE CHANGING/DELETING CROSS-CLIENT SETTINGS will appear.

6. Click on the checkmark icon to acknowledge the message.

7. Notice that the button located at the lower bottom of the screen in the DATA STRUCTURE tab has changed from DISPLAY in Figure 4.10 to ACTIVATE in Figure 4.11.

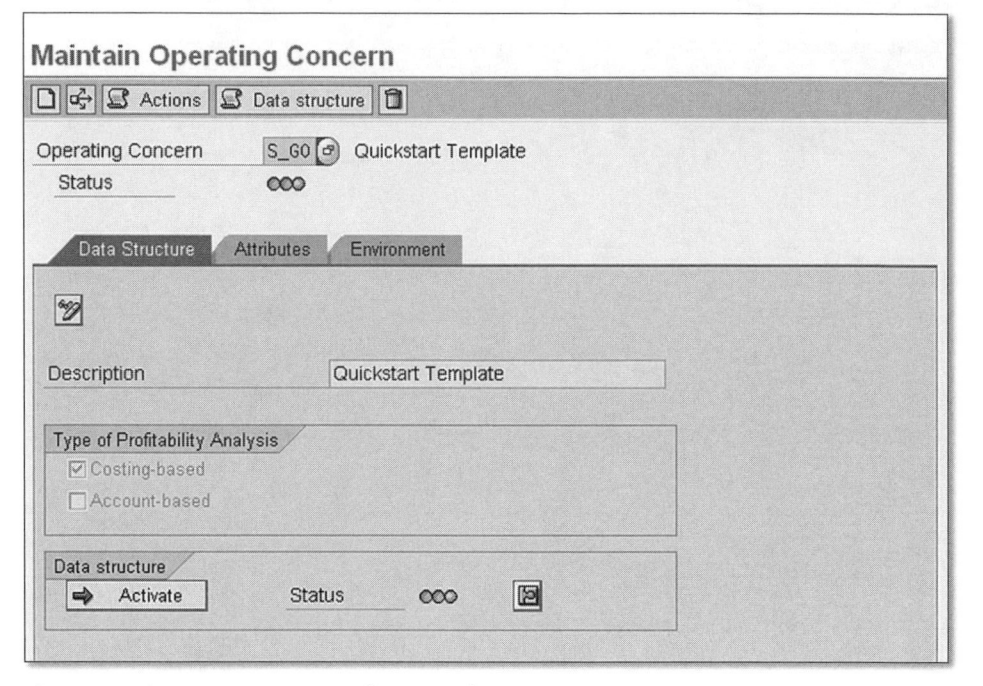

Figure 4.11 Operating Concern in Change Mode

8. Click on ACTIVATE to access the configuration of the operating concern displayed in Figure 4.12.

9. Notice that an operating concern structure contains the CHARS (characteristics) and VALUE FIELDS tabs, as shown in Figure 4.12. You can see here how an operating concern is a collection of predefined objects that you want to have access to from the SAP tables or to store user-defined values. With predefined CO-PA–activated templates, such as S_GO, you're not allowed to make any modifications to the Business Content delivered with R/3. It's only possible to modify the contents of the characteristics and VALUE FIELDS tabs on a brand-new operating concern.

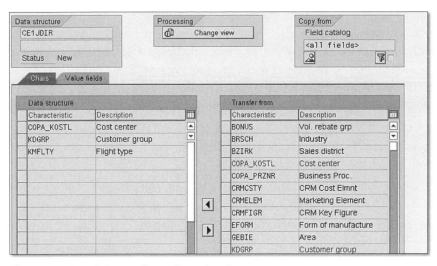

Figure 4.12 Data Structure for an Operating Concern

Now let's create an operating concern from scratch for a company called Jon Dirr Inc., a manufacturer of automotive parts, which is interested in implementing the CO-PA component using both costing-based and account-based CO-PA:

1. Return to the screen shown earlier in Figure 4.11 to start creating an operating concern.

2. Position your cursor in the OPERATING CONCERN input box and type the technical name "JDIR" in the field, as shown in Figure 4.13. In the DESCRIPTION field, type "Jon Dirr Inc."

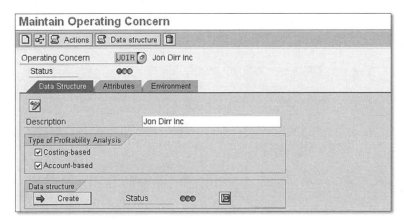

Figure 4.13 Creating a New Operating Concern

3. Select both Costing-based and Account-based checkboxes in the Type of Profitability Analysis section, which allows you to navigate between them later on in the process. We're doing this for our example because Jon Dirr Inc. does not know exactly how it generates revenue and exactly how it is profitable because the results and analysis are based on the final corporate P&L statements each quarter. While each of its plants around the world has its own SAP system, they have not yet been integrated.

4. Click on the standard Create icon (the white page icon). A screen similar to the one shown earlier in Figure 4.12 displays.

5. To include a characteristic or value field in the operating concern, select either the Chars or Value fields tab, then select a line in the Transfer from area and click on the left arrow to move it to the Data structure area.

6. To remove a value field or characteristics from the operating concern, reverse the procedure by selecting a line in the Data structure area and clicking on the right-arrow to move it to the Transfer from area.

7. When you're done, save and activate your structure using the Save and Activate icons. Once completed, a green checkmark will appear at the bottom of your screen to notify you that the update was completed successfully.

At this stage, several tables are created automatically, carrying the name of the operating concern (xxxx reflects the name of the operating concern). For example, if CE1xxxx is created from the SG operating concern, the new table name will carry the information CE1SG. The CO-PA tables generated when you save and activate the operating concern are quite important when performing reporting or extraction operations. Table 4.2 shows the most important tables for costing-based CO-PA and Table 4.3 shows the most important tables for account-based CO-PA.

Table name	Description
CE1xxxx	Actual data, costing-based CO-PA
CE2xxxx	Plan data, costing-based CO-PA
CE3xxxx	Segment level, CO-PA
CE4xxxx	Characteristics table, and also similar to dimension table in SAP NetWeaver BI

Table 4.2 Important Tables for Costing-Based CO-PA

Table name	Description
CE1xxxx_ACCT	Account assignment information, new for release R/3 4.5
K81xxxx	Summarization levels, costing-based CO-PA
TKEBL	Currency of operating concern, costing-based CO-PA
COIX_DATAReport Data	Only converted in costing-based CO-PA
TKEBZ	Exceptions for reports

Table 4.2 Important Tables for Costing-Based CO-PA (Cont.)

Table name	Description
COEJ	Actual/plan line items (by year)
COEP	Actual/plan line items
COSS	Totals records
COSP	Totals records, account-based CO-PA

Table 4.3 Important Tables for Account-Based CO-PA

4.4.2 Creating User-Defined Value Fields and Characteristics Within an Operating Concern

It is also possible to create user-defined value fields and characteristics within an operating concern. To do this:

1. Follow the menu path PROFITABILITY ANALYSIS • STRUCTURES • DEFINE OPERATING CONCERN • MAINTAIN OPERATING CONCERN.

2. Select the CHARS or VALUE FIELDS tab, depending on what type of component you want to create.

3. Select the CREATE icon (showing a white page), as shown in Figure 4.14, ❶.

4. Type the default "VV" or "WW" initial name, depending on whether it is a value field or a characteristic, and type a description ❷.

5. Click on the SAVE icon ❸.

6. Activate your new value field or characteristic by clicking on the ACTIVATE icon ❹.

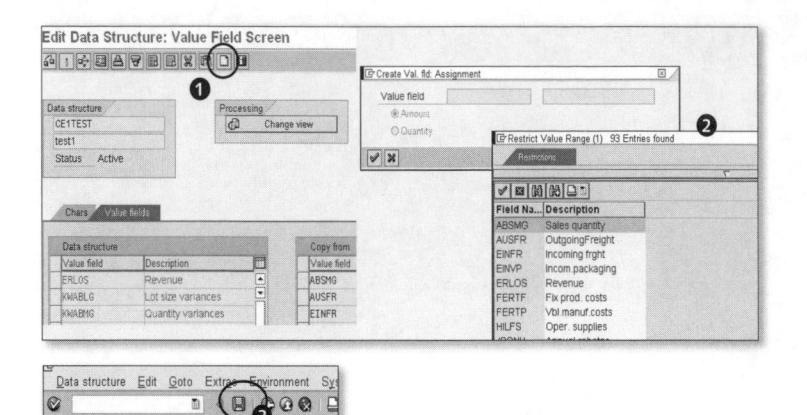

Figure 4.14 Creating User-Defined Value Fields and Characteristics from within an Operating Concern

7. Now the system asks you to generate the operating concern, which means completing the update of the information contained in the operating concern and creating the CO-PA tables. Once you're ready, click on YES, as shown in Figure 4.15, and if everything is correct the STATUS light will be green. Otherwise, go back to your structure and review your characteristics or value fields that caused the problem and correct it.

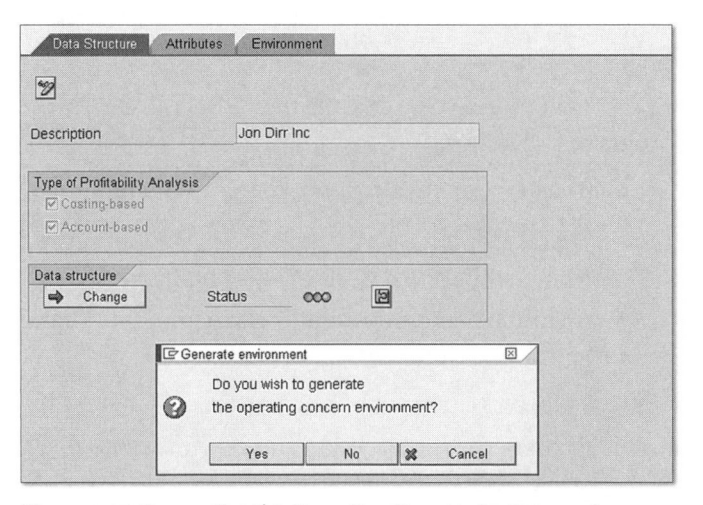

Figure 4.15 Generating the Operating Concern Environment

8. If you clicked on No in the screen shown in Figure 4.15, then, as shown in Figure 4.16, you can go to the operating concern's ENVIRONMENT tab and activate this process manually using the appropriate ACTIVATE buttons. A green light next to the STATUS for the CROSS-CLIENT PART and CLIENT-SPECIFIC PART is displayed if the process was performed successfully.

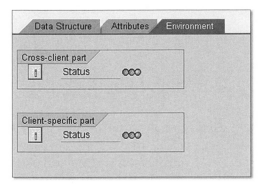

Figure 4.16 Environment Tab of an Operating Concern

4.4.3 Specifying the Operating Concern Currency

Another important factor is the currency of your operating concern. To configure it, follow these steps:

1. Select the ATTRIBUTES tab (shown in detail in Figure 4.20, located later in the chapter in Section 4.6).

2. Select the OPERATING CONCERN CURRENCY; for our example we used USD as the default currency.

3. Specify "K4" as the FISCAL YEAR VARIANT to have a calendar year with four periods of reporting and four special periods.

> **Note**
>
> For further clarification of how attributes, fiscal year variant, and currency affect your reporting and transactions, you should contact your project manager, financial consultant, or someone knowledgeable on your team. Alternatively, review an FI book for information about fiscal year variants and their configuration. You can find several options to suit your specific needs on *www.sap-press.com*.

We now have an operating concern almost ready for use.

However, segments are another important part of the configuration, and using them significantly improves performance, limits the contents of the information inside operating concerns, and depends on the type(s) of accounting selected. Therefore, in the next section we'll explore how to work with profitability segments and also how to include exceptions as part of the configuration. In general, the next section will help illuminate the possibility to perform a multidimensional analysis of R/3 or SAP ERP ECC 6.0 data, which will in turn help you to quickly access the required information.

4.5   Defining Profitability Segments and CO-PA Exceptions

In this section, you'll learn how to specify whether a characteristic in CO-PA is assigned to profitability segments that are later available for use with the INFORMATION SYSTEM and PLANNING menus of CO-PA. Remember that those characteristics that are not involved in the creation of profitability segments remain as line items in CO-PA.

4.5.1   Profitability Segments Overview

Using profitability segments improves the performance of your profitability analysis considerably by excluding characteristics that will otherwise slow down your system. SAP recommends the exclusion of characteristics that occur frequently and that have a different value with each posting (such as "part number" or "bar code"), and are thus not relevant for analysis. Furthermore, you can perform profitability analysis at the customer group level or at the product group level by ceasing to use certain customers or products in that analysis. Most of the time there are simply too many of them, and retrieving all of that information at once as a profitability segment would require a considerable amount of resources.

Caution
Before you execute the first transfer of productive data to CO-PA, you should configure the appropriate setting, specifying which characteristics should be involved in creating profitability segments. The only type of change that you can make subsequently is the deactivation of more characteristics for the determination of a profitability segment. If you later include a characteristic in the determination process, your CO-PA data will be incomplete for all affected characteristics.

4.5.2 Exceptions Overview

Instead of excluding characteristics generally, you have the option of excluding a characteristic under certain conditions and thus define exceptions for how characteristics are used. Because of this option, make-to-order manufacturers with a spare parts business, as an example, can exclude the spare parts business from their analyses, or wholesale manufacturers with a large number of customers can restrict their analysis at the customer level to key customers. The purpose of this function is to reduce the amount of created profitability segments by updating in detail only those values that are relevant for a particular analysis.

4.5.3 Automatically Excluded Characteristics

Elements such as "sales order," "order number," "WBS element," and "cost object" should not be used as characteristics in the formation of profitability segments for the previously discussed reasons (they occur frequently and their values are always different). Thus, when you create a new operating concern, the relevant table is automatically set so that the following characteristics are not used to form the profitability segments:

not used

- ▶ Sales order (KAUFN)
- ▶ Sales order item (KDPOS)
- ▶ Order (RKAUFNR)
- ▶ WBS element (PSPNR)
- ▶ Cost object (KSTRG)

All other characteristics—including "customer" and "product"—are used and therefore are available for profitability reports, planning, and account assignments to profitability segments, for example. No exceptions are defined by default. If you need to make a change to these settings, change the entries accordingly. You should check the index to the object table, especially if you exclude the characteristics "customer" or "product." By defining an index that is most optimally reconciled to how the segment-level characteristics are used, you can improve performance considerably.

4.5.4 Defining Profitability Segment Characteristics

To define profitability segment characteristics follow this procedure:

1. Follow the IMG path CONTROLLING • PROFITABILITY ANALYSIS • STRUCTURES • DEFINE OPERATING CONCERN • DEFINE PROFITABILITY SEGMENT CHARACTERISTICS (SEGMENT-LVL CHARACTERISTICS).

2. Click on the EXECUTE icon that appears next to the DEFINE PROFITABILITY SEGMENT CHARACTERISTICS (SEGMENT-LVL CHARACTERISTICS) option, as shown in Figure 4.17.

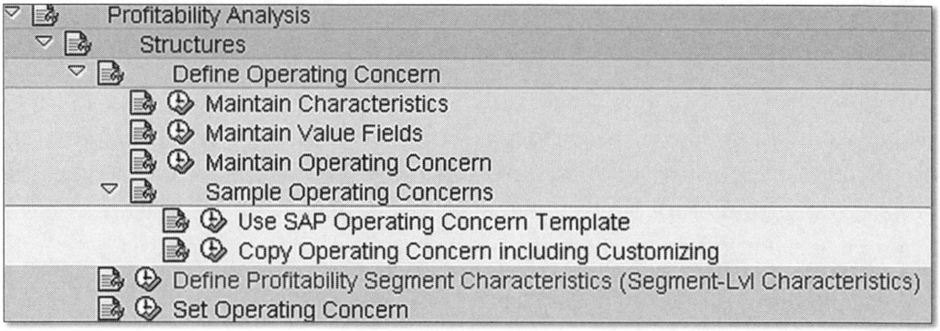

Figure 4.17 Accessing Profitability Segments Window

3. Now the screen displayed in Figure 4.18 shows the characteristics in the OPERATING CONCERN, S_GO in this case, that can be used to configure your profitability segments. You can choose only the COSTING-BASED radio button, COSTING-BASED+ACCOUNT-BASED, or you can exclude the characteristic as a profitability segment and leave it as a CO-PA line item by selecting NOT USED.

4. To modify any contents of the operating concern, click on the change/modify icon (the pencil with glasses), and select the radio button depending on your requirements and future usage of the characteristics. Remember, if you're working in an SAP template, such as the S_GO template shown in Figure 4.18, the SAP system does not allow you to make modifications. However, that's not a problem when using an operating concern created from scratch.

Next, let's look at CO-PA exceptions in more detail.

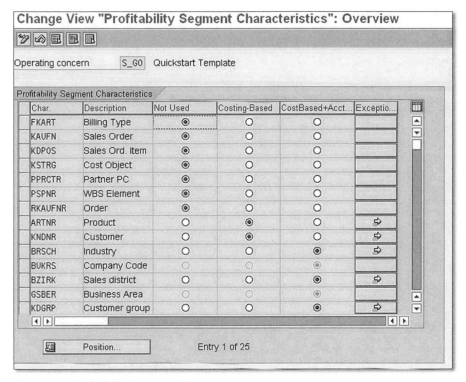

Figure 4.18 Profitability Segment Characteristics

4.5.5 Creating Exceptions

You specify an *exception* for a characteristic you generally do not wish to include in creating profitability segments by defining the conditions when the characteristic should be included among the segment-level characteristics. You do this by specifying the characteristic values. Let's say we're interested in assigning exceptions to a characteristic called *Product*:

1. Click on the yellow arrow for the characteristic PRODUCT, located in the EXCEPTIONS column on the right side of the characteristic, as shown earlier in Figure 4.18. The screen shown in Figure 4.19 appears.

2. There are two areas in this screen that you work with. The uppermost section creates a Boolean logic described as CHARACTERISTIC PRODUCT IS HIDDEN IF:. The one on the right establishes the characteristic values used to limit the data display of the characteristic (PRODUCT in this case).

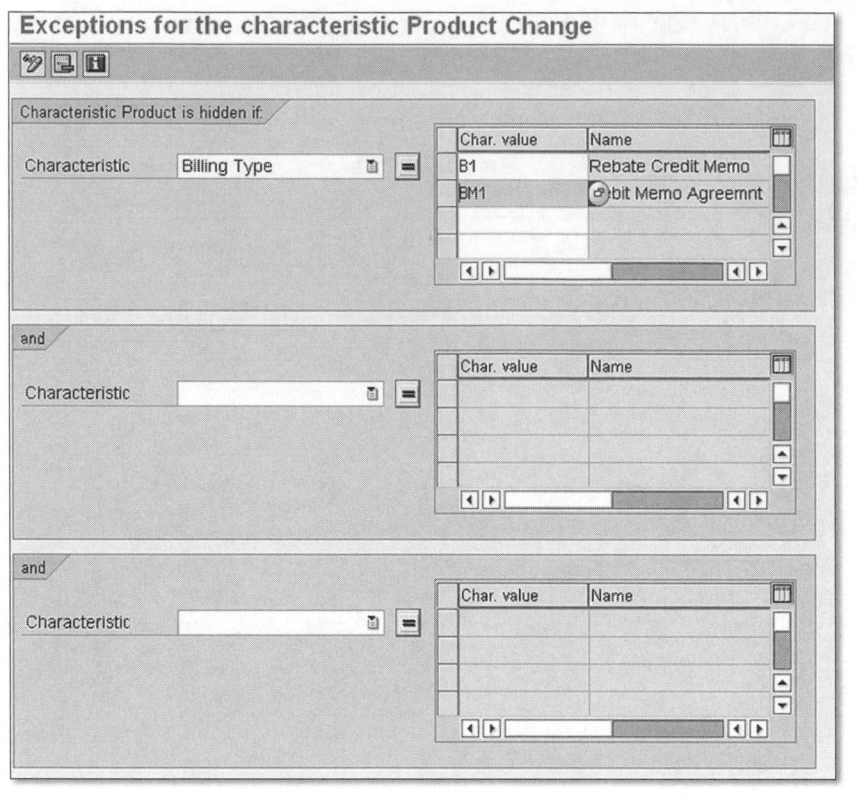

Figure 4.19 Creating Exceptions for a Characteristic

3. Notice that up to three characteristics and their values can be used to hide information that meets certain criteria. For example, as shown in Figure 4.19, the data values for the characteristic PRODUCT are hidden if the characteristic BILLING TYPE is either B1 (REBATE CREDIT MEMO) or BM1 (DEBIT MEMO AGREEMENT).

Characteristics that are hidden due to an exception are still updated in the line item SAP table (CE1xxxx). Furthermore, they remain visible when you display the line items with the current structure. If a line item contains such a characteristic, the system always accesses the line item list to display the line items. This is also the case if you call up the line item display from a profitability report with the current structure. There, the affected characteristic has the value "initial" because the report accesses the segment level (CE4xxxx).

However, the initial value stored in the characteristic is also used to select the line item. Because a value for the characteristic exists in the line item table, the system cannot find the correct line item. You can circumvent this problem by calling up the function GOTO • LINE ITEM at a higher level in the report. That way, the hidden characteristic is not selected.

Let's review some exception examples in detail.

Hiding All Products in the Spare Parts Division

Let's say that an engineering company produces large machinery to order, but also sells custom parts. Detailed analyses at the product level are only necessary for heavy machinery. The operating concern contains two divisions—heavy machinery and engineering analysis—that are determined by appropriately defined derivation steps.

In this case, an exception is defined for the characteristic *Product*. On the exceptions screen, the condition for hiding the data is specified as follows (you can use Figure 4.19 as a reference): when the characteristic "Division" (defined in the left area as shown in Figure 4.18) takes the value "Engineering Analysis" (defined in the right area).

Hiding "Other Customers" by Defining the New Characteristic Key Customer Indicator

A repetitive manufacturer (those that manufacture or assemble large quantities of similar products, such as automotive components) does not want to analyze all of their data at the customer level. Instead, only a selection of key customers should be looked at in detail. However, there is no characteristic in the operating concern that makes any such distinction. Not only is it impossible to define an exception along the lines of "Hide characteristic customer when customer = A and customer = B and ...," but this would not be practical either. Hence, a new characteristic—with which a distinction can be made between key customers and other customers—needs to be created. For example, it's possible for you to define an additional characteristic "key customer indicator" and then, by means of characteristic derivation, set it to X for key customers and leave it empty for all other customers. For data that has already been posted, you have to run a realignment during which these other customers are set to the initial value.

The following exception can then be defined: the characteristic "customer" is hidden when the key customer indicator = initial (for the initial characteristic value, enter "#" [= non assigned] in the entry field). Once this exception has been applied, no further analysis can be run on the other customers at the customer level because the exception cannot be canceled.

4.5.6 Exception Recommendations

Consider the following recommendations when working with exceptions:

▶ You should only define an exception for characteristics representing a detailed level of analysis and that therefore take a large number of characteristic values. The larger portion of these characteristic values should be excluded as a result of the exception.

▶ Complicated conditions should not be defined in an exception because analysis with such a condition counteracts any improvements in performance. It makes better sense to use one or two characteristics as your condition, each having no more than two or three characteristic values. For best results, aim to keep the definition of your exception as basic as possible. To achieve this, you sometimes may need to create an additional characteristic.

▶ Exceptions should not be changed once applied in a productive system. In particular, such exceptions should not be deactivated because this prevents the data from being analyzed correctly. In certain cases, it's possible to maintain extra exceptions. However, you must run a realignment for the affected characteristic beforehand. To do this, select the characteristics and characteristic values in the selection condition that are specified in the exception. In the conversion rule, enter # for the characteristic for which the exception was defined.

▶ Characteristics that have an exception maintained for them cannot be changed by realignments!

▶ To define an exception, you can use almost all characteristics that create profitability segments (technically all of the characteristics from table CE4xxxx, where xxxx = operating concern). This doesn't apply in the case of unit of measure or the characteristic for which the exception has been defined.

▶ If you define an exception with dependent characteristics, then all of the characteristics in those dependencies should be included in that exception.

▶ Note that the definition of the exception applies for all flows of actual data, as well as for the summarized update of data during the transfer of billing documents. The setting doesn't apply in planning; there, the detail level for data entry is specified in the planning level. The detail level for planning should not be greater than that for the flow of actual data in order that useful comparisons between actual and planning data are possible.

Tips & Tricks

When an exception is applied, the number of profitability segments generated is reduced, thereby improving performance in reporting and in the system in general. However, to ensure that system performance is actually enhanced, you should use this function sparingly and only use it in specific cases. Once applied in a productive system, an exception should no longer be changed because changes to it would cause inconsistencies in your data, especially if you remove an exception and thus include the corresponding characteristic in the creation of profitability segments.

Our efforts would not be complete without the configuration of the operating concern attributes that are closely related to the definitions of the data extracted from FI and CO. For this reason, it's highly recommended to review how your company's controlling areas and transaction attributes are related to the attributes used by your operating concern. These elements are discussed in the next section.

4.6   Operating Concern Attributes Tab

The ATTRIBUTES tab of an operating concern as shown in Figure 4.20, contains several options that are important to understand if your implementation increases the complexity of the behavior of your data.

Two main elements of the ATTRIBUTES tab are OPERATING CONCERN CURRENCY and FISCAL YEAR VARIANT, both of which we briefly looked at earlier in Section 4.3, and will look at now in more detail:

▶ OPERATING CONCERN CURRENCY
This setting determines how the operating concern is going to be valuated; it specifies the currency in which values in CO-PA are going to be displayed and planned. In costing-based Profitability Analysis actual data is always updated in

the operating concern currency. You can change the operating concern currency as long as no data has been posted in the operating concern. Once data has been posted, however, a change in the operating concern currency would cause the existing data to be interpreted as if it were posted in the new currency (for example: USD 1,000.00 in the old currency might be reported as 1,000.00 Euros in the new currency).

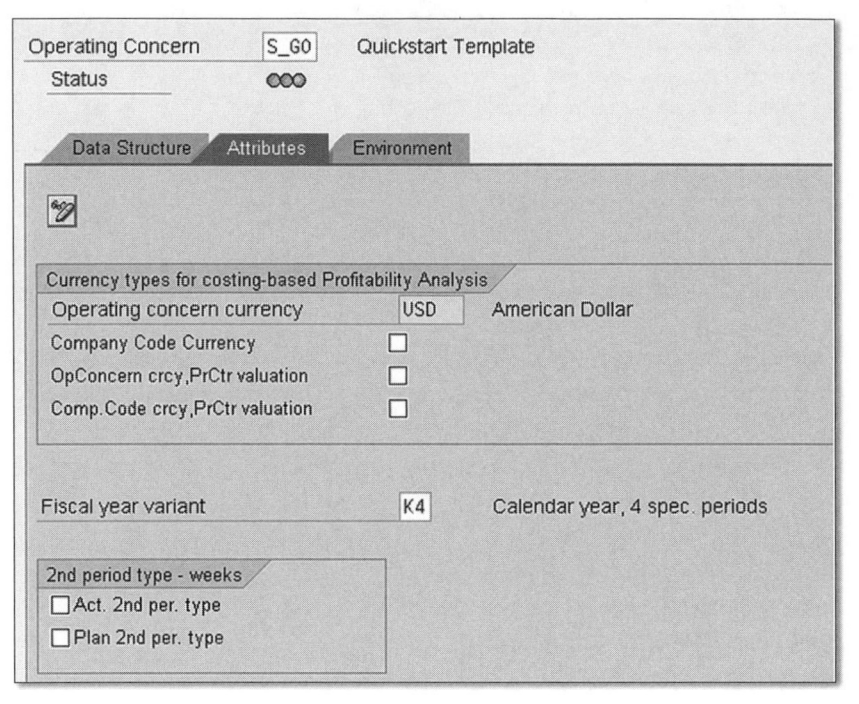

Figure 4.20 Attributes Tab of an Operating Concern

Be aware that actual data can be updated simultaneously in all of the combinations of currency type and valuation, increasing the data volume. In contrast, plan data is updated only with the currency specified in a particular plan version.

▶ FISCAL YEAR VARIANT
This is an important setting that's part of the FI functionality that controls the reporting periods in different SAP software applications. The most common configuration is a period of 12 months for which the company produces financial statements and takes inventory, with four special periods per year allowed for any additional reporting.

A fiscal year may or may not correspond to the calendar year, but depending on the characteristics of the company, it will also require additional special posting periods. A fiscal year can be both internal and legal, so make sure that you review with your FI and CO team members on the current FI practices so you can be sure to configure this setting correctly. (Your options are a fiscal year that follows a calendar year or a fiscal year that does *not* follow the calendar year, which will require FICO configuration.)

Now let's review the rest of the options on the ATTRIBUTES tab in more detail:

► COMPANY CODE CURRENCY

In addition to the operating concern currency, you can also store all data in the currency of the relevant company code using the COMPANY CODE CURRENCY setting. It makes sense to activate this setting if your organization operates internationally and deals with exchange rates that change daily. It allows you to avoid differences due to different exchange rates and lets you reconcile CO-PA data directly with FI.

You can activate the company code currency at any time, but note that this will not make any changes to data that has already been posted. If you deactivate the company code currency, you can no longer use plan versions and reports that use the company code currency.

► PROFIT CENTER VALUATION

In addition to storing data in these two currencies (company code and operating concern currencies) using the legal (= company code) valuation view, you can also store data in both of these currencies valuated from the viewpoint of individual profit centers. This yields the following possible combinations of currency type and valuation view (also called valuation approaches) as shown in Table 4.4.

Currency Type	Valuation View
Operating concern currency	Legal valuation
Company code currency	Legal valuation
Operating concern currency	Profit center valuation
Company code currency	Profit center valuation

Table 4.4 Currency Type and Valuation View Combinations

With this information, you can set up actual data valuation from the profit center viewpoint using the IMG menu path PROFITABILITY ANALYSIS • FLOWS OF ACTUAL VALUES • MULTIPLE VALUATION APPROACHES • TRANSFER PRICES. Whereas actual data is updated simultaneously in all of the selected combinations of currency type and valuation, plan data is always updated in one currency only—the currency specified for that particular plan version.

▶ SECOND PERIOD TYPE—WEEKS
If you set any of the two indicators available in this area, namely ACT. 2ND PER. TYPE or PLAN 2ND PER TYPE, the system stores the actual or plan data in weeks when using costing-based Profitability Analysis. This increases the data volume in CO-PA and could lead to slow response times in the information system.

However, when using these indicators with account-based CO-PA, there's no effect because there is no alternative period type available.

None of these configuration steps and functionalities will take effect until you assign the controlling area to an operating concern. This procedure is discussed in the following section.

4.7 Assigning a Controlling Area to an Operating Concern

As mentioned earlier, it's essential to make sure that there's a clear relationship between controlling areas and operating concerns if you want to build a framework to create business transactions and an integrated financial architecture that allows carrying out cross-company code cost accounting. In other words, you need to make sure that data is transferred from other financial components correctly.

To do so, assign the controlling areas you want to analyze to an operating concern together in Profitability Analysis because the goal is to connect to the rest of the architectures (shown previously in Chapter 3, Figure 3.2) to CO-PA. In order to start this assignment there are several steps and requirements. Let's look at them in detail in the following sections.

4.7.1 Reviewing Controlling Area Components and Verifying the Existence of Operating Concerns

First, let's make sure you're familiar with what a controlling area and its components look like, and also verify that an operating concern has been created in your system.

Note

Before you get started, a controlling area must already exist and be correctly configured. SAP provides several preconfigured controlling areas as part of the SAP pre-delivered master data components that can be reused and integrated as part of your CO-PA templates.

1. Access the controlling areas by following the IMG path CONTROLLING • GENERAL CONTROLLING • ORGANIZATION • MAINTAIN CONTROLLING AREA.
2. Select the appropriate controlling area; for example, the 0001 SAP controlling area, as shown in Figure 4.21.

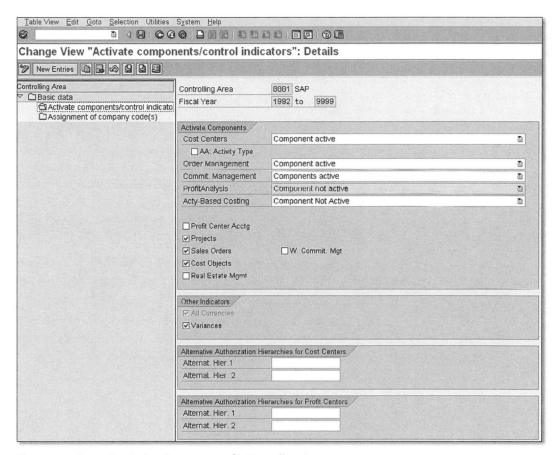

Figure 4.21 Reviewing Active Components of a Controlling Area

In this screen, you can determine which components of a controlling area are active. For example, Figure 4.21 shows that only Profitability Analysis and activity-based costing are not active in the controlling area 0001 SAP, and we want to have CO-PA activated. For now, however, we're just exploring these options; you'll learn how to activate CO-PA in Section 4.8—it requires additional configuration to do so (notice that the option PROFITANALYSIS is currently grayed out). Primarily, knowing that CO-PA hasn't been activated leaves you certain that no postings or any transactions have been affected in the controlling area with any information from CO-PA.

3. Next, use the IMG path CONTROLLING • PROFITABILITY ANALYSIS • STRUCTURES • DEFINE OPERATING CONCERN • MAINTAIN OPERATING CONCERN to access the screen shown in Figure 4.22. Here, you'll verify that an operating concern that contains the elements you need does indeed exist, and thus can be assigned to a CONTROLLING AREA. If there is none, create one as previously explained in Section 4.5.

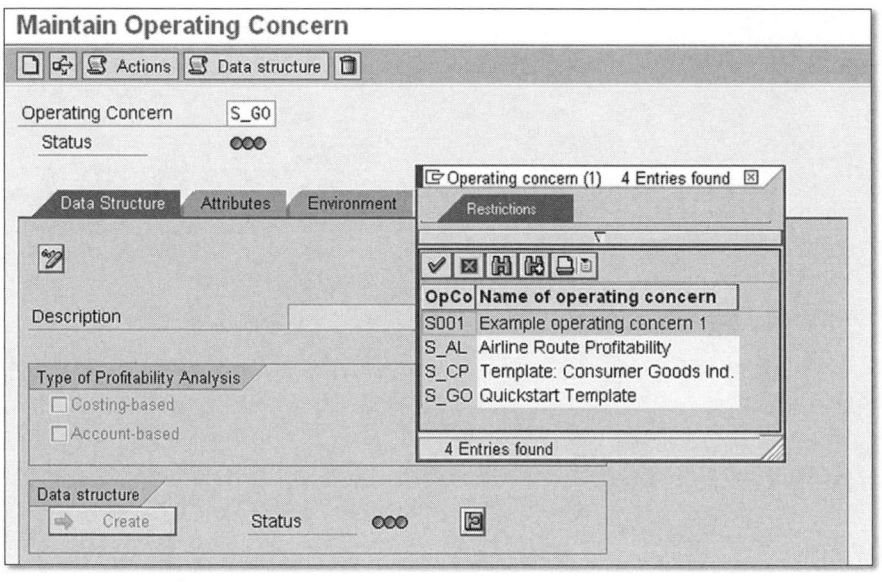

Figure 4.22 Creating or Maintaining an Operating Concern

Be aware that a company code will be affected by different transactions in different business areas, and you must make sure that it has been correctly configured to avoid posting problems later on in the process. Next, we'll look at assigning a company code to a controlling area.

> **Note**
>
> You'll need additional background information in FI regarding the configuration and analysis of company codes. Review this information with your implementation team or project manager.

4.7.2 Assigning a Company Code to a Controlling Area

To assign a company code to a controlling area, follow these steps:

1. Follow the IMG path ENTERPRISE STRUCTURE • ASSIGNMENT • CONTROLLING • ASSIGN COMPANY CODE TO CONTROLLING AREA.

2. Figure 4.23 shows the available controlling areas to which we can assign company codes so that the transactions in that area are limited to those company codes. For our purposes, 0001 SAP is our controlling area, so select the appropriate line on the right side of the screen, and then double-click on ASSIGNMENT OF COMPANY CODES on the left side of the screen.

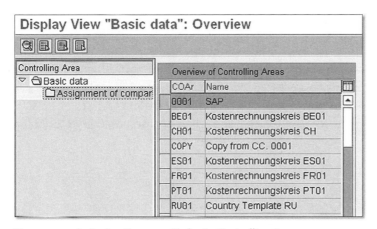

Figure 4.23 Assigning Company Codes to Controlling Areas

3. The ASSIGNED COMPANY CODES are shown on the right side of Figure 4.24. If the required company code is not assigned or the ASSIGNED COMPANY CODES section shows no assignments, click on the change/modify icon, and manually input the company code in the COCD column in the ASSIGNED COMPANY CODES section.

In our example in Figure 4.24, we're assigning company code 0001 SAP to controlling area 0001 SAP. The fact that they have the same name and code is a coincidence. Therefore, review these assignments with your project manager and FI or CO implementation team before proceeding any further. Once this relationship has been created, all transactions associated with the company code will be limited to the controlling area definitions.

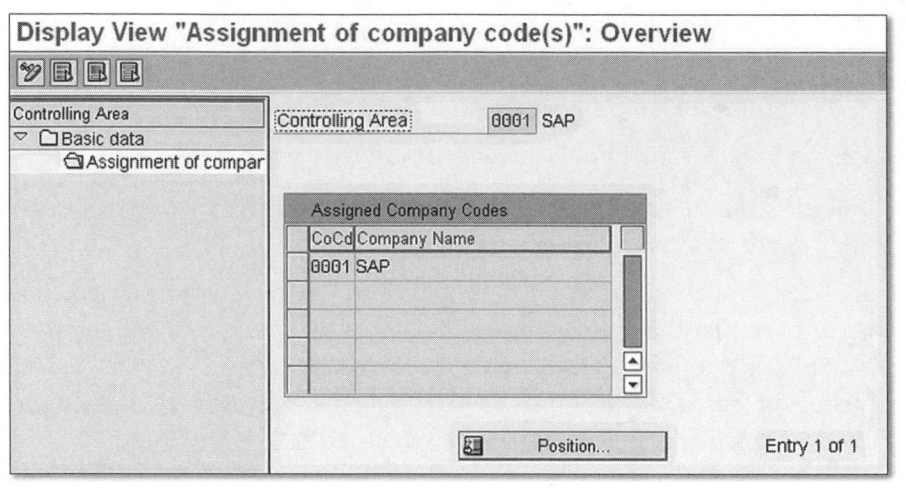

Figure 4.24 Linking Company Codes with Controlling Areas

Company codes, controlling areas, and operating concerns must have identical fiscal year variants, as shown in Figure 4.25, to avoid error messages or serious data inconsistencies during cost center assessments, settlements, or other types of postings. Review this issue with your FI or CO implementation team to make sure that all settings are correctly configured according to the company's ongoing implementation.

The relationships shown in Figure 4.25 between operating concerns, company codes, and controlling areas allow cross-application data transfers using the path ENTERPRISE STRUCTURE • ASSIGNMENT • CONTROLLING • ASSIGN CONTROLLING AREA TO OPERATING CONCERN, shown in Figure 4.26. This screen lets you complete the link by assigning an operating concern to a controlling area. To do this, click on the ASSIGN CONTROLLING AREA TO OPERATING CONCERN option as shown in the CONTROLLING submenu, and simply choose the controlling code and assign it to your operating concern option.

> **Note**
>
> The screen shown in Figure 4.26 is also where you specify the assignments between company codes and controlling areas, as we did a moment ago.

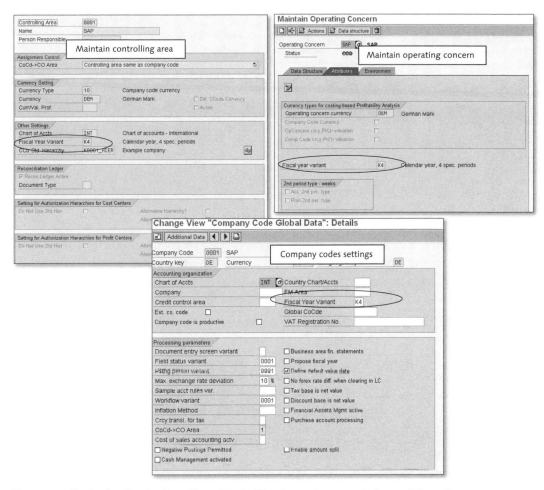

Figure 4.25 Reviewing the Configuration of Controlling Areas, Company Codes, and Operating Concerns

Tips & Tricks

It's important to make sure that Profitability Analysis is activated in your controlling area to make the connection in both directions, meaning postings from FI and other CO components can be accessed using the controlling area as the gate, and postings from CO-PA can be shared with other components. We'll look at how to activate CO-PA in the next section.

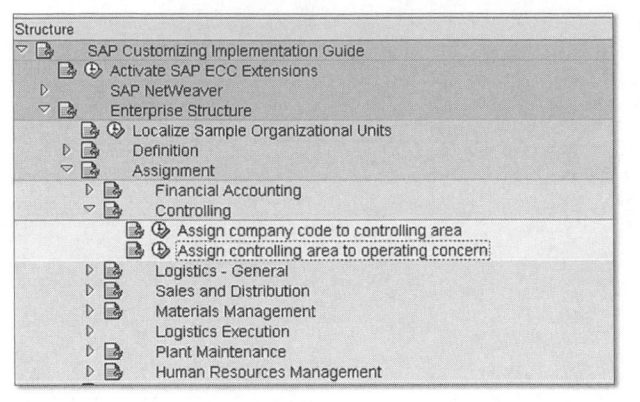

Figure 4.26 Linking Company Codes, Controlling Areas, and Operating Concerns

You must also maintain a correct configuration of elements, such as assignment control indicator, chart of accounts, fiscal year variants, G/L accounts, cost elements, currency settings, and others to make sure that transactions flow between FI and CO. For this reason, make sure that when making these assignments you are working closely with your FI/CO team because further clarifications go beyond the scope of this book.

> **Note**
>
> Because some of the components (such as controlling area, company codes, cost centers, and so on) require knowledge of other components of FI and CO, we won't go into much detail about them. Instead, we'll limit our discussion to how to establish the relationships to link Profitability Analysis with the other controlling structures. The actual configuration, analysis, and requirements to correctly allow transactions between these systems go beyond the scope of the book.

> **Tips & Tricks**
>
> Before going any further with CO-PA, you should have a clear representation of the financial structures that control your different transactions inside your financial accounting and controlling areas. Therefore, you should link CO-PA to controlling areas to review the impact in your operations with your implementation team, and match the settings of your objects on both sides so the different postings behave the way they are supposed to.

Next, you'll learn how to activate the CO-PA component inside the R/3 or SAP ERP ECC 6.0 platform.

4.8 Activating CO-PA in R/3 or SAP ERP ECC 6.0

It isn't enough to create an operating concern and a link between company codes and controlling areas. You must also perform a specific activation procedure to make sure that all of the individual components are ready to accept and share information between CO-PA and other components in FI/CO. First, however, let's review the status of Profitability Analysis in your controlling area; Profitability Analysis may already be activated, in which case you would not need to do anything else.

4.8.1 Checking the Current Profitability Analysis Activation Status

To check the current status of the Profitability Analysis activation, perform the following procedure:

1. Use Transaction OKKP to go to MAINTAIN CONTROLLING AREA SETTINGS and review the information as shown in Figure 4.27.

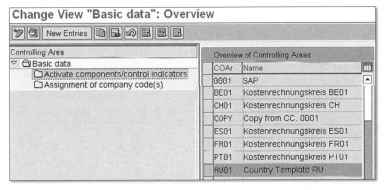

Figure 4.27 Reviewing the Activation Components for Controlling Area RU01

2. Select the Controlling Area RU01 COUNTRY TEMPLATE RU on the right side of the screen, and click on ACTIVATE COMPONENTS/CONTROL INDICATORS on the left-hand side.

3. The status of the CONTROLLING AREA RU01 COUNTRY TEMPLATE RU displays, as shown in Figure 4.28. You can see that the Profitability Analysis (PROFITANALYSIS) and activity-based costing (ACTY-BASED COSTING) components are not activated. Also, Profitability Analysis shows as COMPONENT NOT ACTIVE, and is grayed out, so you cannot use the appropriate option from the dropdown

menu to activate it like you can with the other components. Instead, you need to perform additional configuration steps.

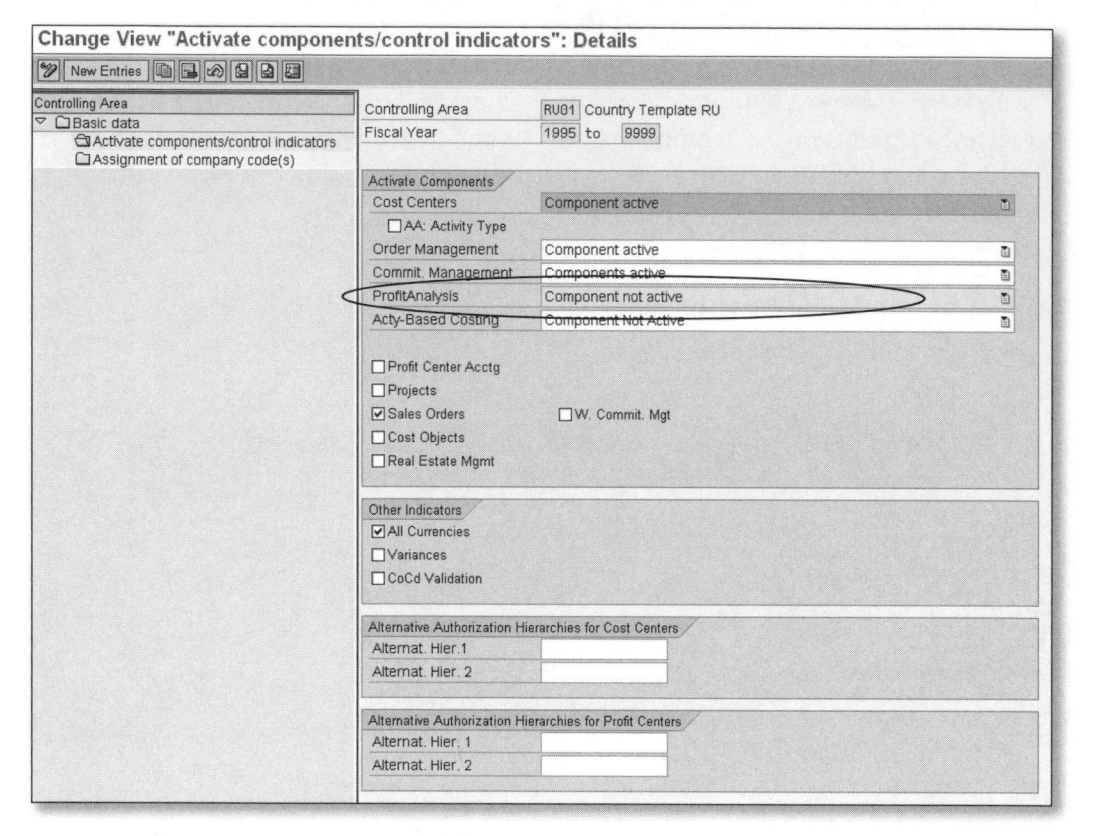

Figure 4.28 Reviewing Activation Status of CO-PA for RU01

4.8.2 Performing the Activation

Once you've finished all of the previous steps, you're ready to activate CO-PA by using the following procedure:

1. Follow the IMG path CONTROLLING • PROFITABILITY ANALYSIS • FLOWS OF ACTUAL VALUES • ACTIVATE PROFITABILITY ANALYSIS, as shown in Figure 4.29.

2. Execute the function ACTIVATE PROFITABILITY ANALYSIS by clicking on the EXECUTE icon, located next to the function.

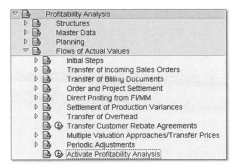

Figure 4.29 Activating Profitability Analysis

Tips & Tricks

If someone else is using the active operating concern when you attempt to activate Profitability Analysis, the SAP system displays a message that the data is locked by a specific user ID, who is probably working in one of the configuration menus we discussed in this chapter. Contact that user to have him exit the objects he is modifying, or wait until his work is finished to perform the activation.

3. Next, the screen shown in Figure 4.30 appears, showing the CO-PA: ACTIVATE FLAG FOR PROFITABILITY ANALYSIS table.

Change View "CO-PA: Active Flag for Profitability Analysis": Overview

COAr	Name	From FY	Op.c..	Active status
0001	SAP	1992		
BE01	Kostenrechnungskreis BE01	1995		
ES01	Kostenrechnungskreis ES01	1995		
FR01	Kostenrechnungskreis FR01	1995		
PT01	Kostenrechnungskreis PT01	1995		
RU01	Country Template RU	1995	TEST	
RF01	Kostenrechnungskreis BE01	1995		
ES01	Kostenrechnungskreis ES01	1995		

Profitability analysis active (2)   4 Entries found

PA	Short text
	Component not active
2	Component active for costing-based Profitability Analysis
3	Component active for account-based Profitability Analysis
4	Component active for both types of Profitability Analysis

Figure 4.30 CO-PA: Activate Flag for Profitability Analysis

Caution

It's important to know that the CO-PA: Activate Flag for Profitability Analysis table is the same table used when performing the function ACTIVATE TRANSFER OF INCOMING SALES ORDERS, as explained later in Chapter 8. Therefore, keep in mind that any changes to this table affect both CO-PA activation and the activation of transfer of incoming sales orders.

4. Verify that the controlling area (COAR) you're looking for is available. In our case, this is RU01. Also, notice in the OP C. column that the operating concern TEST has been assigned.

5. Click on the blank field ACTIVE STATUS for controlling area RU01, and the window shown on the right-hand side of Figure 4.30 is displayed. Let's review the options in this window in more detail to complete the CO-PA activation:

   ▶ **Blank**: Component not active

   ▶ **2**: Component active for costing-based Profitability Analysis

   ▶ **3**: Component active for account-based Profitability Analysis

   ▶ **4**: Component active for both types of Profitability Analysis

   Because there are several options from which to select, the SAP system does not allow you to activate CO-PA using the dropdown list shown earlier; selection of the correct option is a procedure that requires analysis and review to make sure that your components will do what you want them to do. For example, you don't want the system to perform account-based CO-PA when you need to use costing-based CO-PA, or vice versa.

6. Option 4 (activating CO-PA for any type of analysis, costing- or account-based) will make things easiest for you if you want to use an operating concern in costing-based or account-based CO-PA modes, and your data will be changed depending on the option selected. We recommend selecting this option in order to maintain this flexibility as you move forward in your implementation. The ACTIVE STATUS field will now look like that shown in Figure 4.31.

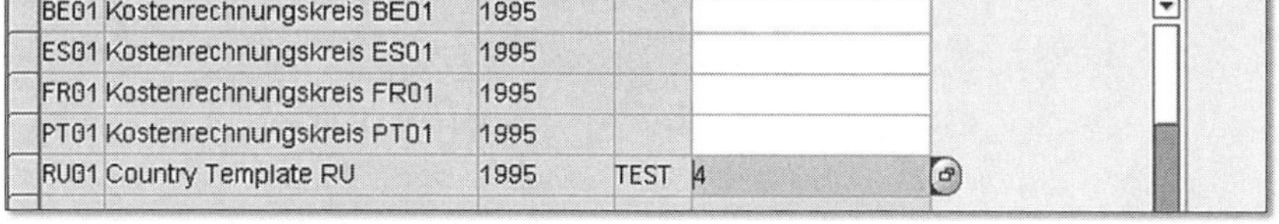

| Table View | Edit | Goto | Selection | Utilities | System | Help |

Change View "CO-PA: Active Flag for Profitability Analysis": Overview

COAr	Name	From FY	Op.c...	Active status
0001	SAP	1992		
BE01	Kostenrechnungskreis BE01	1995		
ES01	Kostenrechnungskreis ES01	1995		
FR01	Kostenrechnungskreis FR01	1995		
PT01	Kostenrechnungskreis PT01	1995		
RU01	Country Template RU	1995	TEST	4

Figure 4.31 Activating Controlling Area RU01 and Operating Concern TEST to Use Both Costing-Based and Account-Based CO-PA

7. Click on the SAVE icon to save your changes. CO-PA has now been activated for all types of Profitability Analysis.

4.8.3   Verifying the Activation

At this point, we also need to confirm the activation, following this procedure:

1. Run Transaction OKKP again.

2. Review the activation options of the RU01 CONTROLLING AREA, as shown in Figure 4.32. The grayed-out menu option has changed from the previous COMPONENT NOT ACTIVE to COMPONENT ACTIVE FOR BOTH TYPES OF PROFITABILITY ANALYSIS.

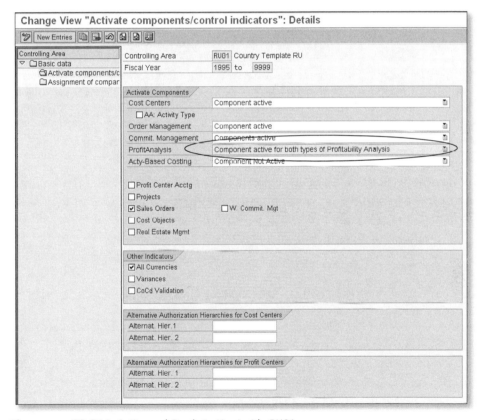

Figure 4.32 CO-PA is Active and Ready to Use Inside RU01

Once the Profitability Analysis component is activated, you can start transferring the actual postings into the predefined profitability segments. We'll outline these elements briefly here; they're reviewed in more detail in Chapter 8:

- Automatic transfers of billing document data from SD
- Direct postings from FI
- Settlement of orders and projects
- Period-based allocations, such as the transfer of overhead
- Invoice receipt postings from MM

Also, you can now make plan data postings, such as the following:

- Period-based allocations, such as the transfer of planned overhead
- Settlement of planning data from orders and projects

Caution
It's very important to understand that when you carry out the activities ACTIVATE PROFITABILITY ANALYSIS and ACTIVATE TRANSFER OF INCOMING SALES ORDERS (the latter will be described in detail in Chapter 8), you are accessing the same table. Consequently, if you delete an entry on one of these screens, you affect the functionality in both components, so be careful!

In the next section, we'll briefly explore a few additional functionalities available in CO-PA as part of the initial configuration settings required to start the CO-PA implementation. You don't have to perform or work with all of them, but it's important to remember that they're available.

4.9   CO-PA: Additional Functionalities

In this section we'll explore additional elements that are useful when working with CO-PA. You'll learn about the more user-oriented functionalities on the STRUCTURES menu, such as importing and copying an operating concern, copying specific objects inside an operating concern, using action and data structure buttons, and performing CO-PA transports.

Note

If you feel confident using these elements, feel free to continue with other parts of this book. Keep this section in mind, however, if you're interested in exploring the additional functionalities available in CO-PA if they are required later on in your implementation.

To access the copy functionality in CO-PA, follow the IMG path CONTROLLING • PROFITABILITY ANALYSIS • STRUCTURES • COPY OPERATING CONCERN INCLUDING CUSTOMIZING.

The screen shown in Figure 4.33 appears. There are three different tabs:

▶ IMPORT OPERATING CONCERN

▶ COPY OPERATING CONCERN

▶ COPY SPECIFIC OBJECTS

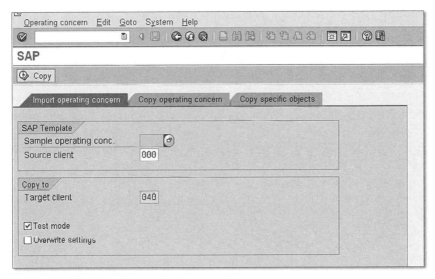

Figure 4.33 The Import Operating Concern Tab

In addition, there is the COPY button at the top of the screen. Let's look at the first tab, the IMPORT OPERATING CONCERN tab, in more detail.

Caution

Copy operations don't make copies of the transaction data stored in any of the operating concerns. That is, they perform changes to the objects of the operating concern, but not the data. Therefore, these operations are not meant for archiving or storage of data. For these functions, use the proper SAP tools; your SAP basis or security teams in your company should be able to assist you with this.

4.9.1 Import Operating Concern

The IMPORT OPERATING CONCERN tab (see Figure 4.33) lets you select one of the sample SAP operating concern templates in source client 000 and copy it to a target client. The SAP template can't exist in the target client, and the source and target clients must have different values.

In addition, the TEST MODE checkbox lets you copy the customizing settings in the test mode (with no changes being made to the database). A log tells you which tables and settings are copied when you select this feature and click on the COPY button.

Furthermore, the OVERWRITE SETTINGS checkbox determines how the system handles table entries that are not directly dependent on the operating concern but are still part of the customizing settings for the operating concern. If this field is not selected (default), these settings are not copied to the target client. Consequently, no existing settings in the target client are overwritten. If this field is selected, the existing settings in the target client are overwritten. This can lead to changes in the settings for other operating concerns that are in use.

Tips & Tricks

Only select the OVERWRITE SETTINGS checkbox if the target client (= current client) has not yet been customized for any operating concerns, or if you want the source and target clients customized identically. Unlike the function import objects, this function copies all of the settings for the operating concern, not just individual objects. The logic for copying settings is different from the logic for transporting in that settings that simply reference the operating concern instead of being dependent on it (such as PA transfer structures) are copied as well. To avoid inadvertently overwriting settings in the target client, you should only use this function when the target client does not contain any customizing settings yet, or when you want customizing in the source and target clients to be identical.

4.9.2 Copy Operating Concern

Next, we'll look at the Copy operating concern tab, as shown in Figure 4.34. With this tab, you can copy an entire operating concern within the same client, which becomes useful when you need multiple concerns within the same system; for instance, if you'd like to have independent operating concerns, one with costing-based settings and another one with account-based settings. In addition, you can always use another operating concern in order to start building a new one from scratch. You can specify whether you want to copy the data structures only, the customizing settings only, or both. These are copied in separate steps.

1. Select the Source operating concern from the current client system, and then create a name for the Copy to section. Later on, this becomes the Target operating concern.

2. Copy the Data structures and Generate the environment (cross-client).

3. Finally, you can copy the Customizing settings in Test Mode in order to evaluate the effect to the database when you perform the updates without worrying of updating the database with incorrect data, since this is basically a simulation. A log tells you which tables and settings are copied.

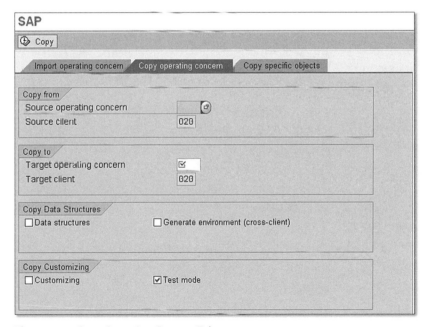

Figure 4.34 Copy Operating Concern Tab

> **Tips & Tricks**
>
> TEST MODE cannot be used to copy data structures of the operating concern because those can be copied when you execute the function, provided that TEST MODE has been activated for Customizing.

Once you've generated the environment (cross-client) and the customizing in test mode as described in Figure 4.34, you can copy the Customizing settings by simply selecting the checkbox with the same name. You can also repeat this step as often as required—each time, the system will overwrite any existing settings. The data structures in the target operating concern must be active, and they must contain at least the same characteristics and value fields as the source operating concern. Next, let's look at the COPY SPECIFIC OBJECTS tab.

4.9.3 Copy Specific Objects

The COPY SPECIFIC OBJECTS tab allows copying specific customizing settings between clients or between operating concerns within one client. This means that you can only copy the objects inside an operating concern to another one as long as it is within the same SAP system (production, QA, or test). For this, simply follow these steps:

1. Collect all of the relevant tables in a transport request using the Transport Objects transaction (SE10) or the manual transport function in the transaction for each setting (the truck icon).

2. Do not release the transport request. When you call up this function, enter the number of the task (not the request) or look for it using the search capabilities shown in Figure 4.35.

3. The SOURCE CLIENT is determined based on the client for which the transport request is defined. If you're copying between clients, you cannot change the operating concern. If you're copying between operating concerns, they must be in the same client.

4. Once you find the desired objects, select the REQUEST/TASK number that contains the objects that you want to copy and then select the SOURCE OPERATING CONCERN as shown in Figure 4.36.

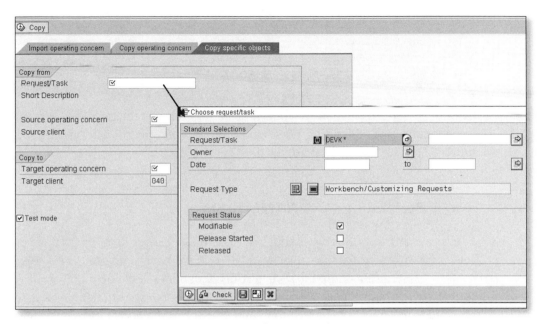

Figure 4.35 Choose Request/Task on the Copy Specific Objects Tab

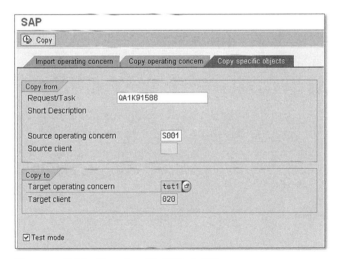

Figure 4.36 The Copy Specific Objects Tab

5. In the COPY TO section, create a name for the TARGET OPERATING CONCERN. This needs to be a four-character description, as shown in Figure 4.36.

6. Click on the COPY button located on the top of the screen to perform the copy.

> **Caution**
>
> The system cannot automatically check whether all of the table entries in the transport request belong to the specified source operating concern. You need to pay special attention to this when you use this function.

Eventually you'll need to move your information from a testing environment into a production system. For this, it's important to review how to perform transports in CO-PA, as we'll do in the next section.

4.10   Performing CO-PA Transports

You move or transport objects (but not data) that exist inside an operating concern to another system for final testing or implementation using a *transport request*. With this function, the system collects all of the dependent objects in the source system and places them in the transport request. After importing the objects to the target system, it automatically activates the necessary objects in the *ABAP Data Dictionary* (the data structures of the operating concern). For that, both the source and target systems must be of the same release and update level.

A Best Practice is to use the following client sequence:

1. From development to testing (QA)

2. From testing to production

This sequence, or object flow, describes a secure way to avoid losing information on any server because it is unique, and reassures the implementation team that objects exist more than once in a client system. Also, because the original always exists in the development environment and can be transported again, objects are secure in case of corruption or failure.

The process of a CO-PA transport is described as follows:

1. Click on the EXECUTE icon next to TRANSPORT in the PRODUCTION STARTUP menu, as shown in Figure 4.37. You can also use the IMG path CONTROLLING • PROFITABILITY ANALYSIS • TOOLS • PRODUCTION STARTUP • TRANSPORT or use Transaction KE3I.

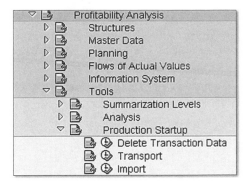

Figure 4.37 Accessing the Transport Functionality

2. The SAP Executive Information System (EIS) transport tool starts and the screen shown in Figure 4.38 appears. You can now collect the objects that are linked to your CO-PA settings (table entries, data elements, domains, tables, and so on) in a transport request.

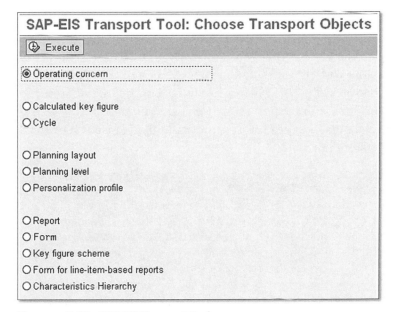

Figure 4.38 The SAP-EIS Transport Tool

3. For our example, we want to transport operating concerns, so select the OPERATING CONCERN radio button and click on EXECUTE.

4. Next, the SAP system needs to find the customizing request that stores the information that you're looking to transport. Remember, we've created structures that interact with other objects. If those objects are already in a customizing or workbench request (if you aren't familiar with these request types, we'll explain what they are in more detail a little later in this section), we need to find them in the system. Click on the icon to the right of the CUSTOMIZING REQUEST box, as shown in Figure 4.39, to see the different options available, or you can create your own customizing request.

Figure 4.39 Accessing the Customizing Requests

5. You can work with the Transport Organizer (Transaction SE10) by clicking on the TRANSPORT ORGANIZER button shown in Figure 4.39 and allowing any user to review any transport objects available in the system. Using the Transport Organizer, you can create a transport request that lets you transport objects to a target system. Note that detailed information about the Transport Organizer is beyond the scope of this book.

Tips & Tricks

Using the transport functionality creates a transport request based on the current settings of the operating concern; thus, no new CO-PA objects should be added and no setting changed while the transaction is running. A transport request can be created and data transferred at different points in time. However, if you change any settings between the time when you create the transport request and when you carry out the transport, the system recognizes some of the changes but does not add any new objects to the transport request. This can lead to inconsistencies in the target system following the transport. For this reason, SAP recommends that you make no further changes in CO-PA between the time you create the request and when you export the settings.

When you create a transport request, the system is not able to check which of the objects to transport already exist in the target system. However, if objects already exist in the target system, they are overwritten. To avoid this, set up one source system with the defined objects and then transfer the settings defined in this source system to other target system(s). Do not create any new CO-PA objects, such as operating concerns, characteristics, or value fields in the target systems if you're going to have transports between a source (development) and different target systems.

There are different types of CO-PA transports:

▶ Automatic transport or manual transport
▶ Transporting client-specific and cross-client settings
▶ Transporting translated settings (settings in different languages)

Next, we'll analyze these to get a better understanding of the CO-PA transport process and the types of transports available in the R/3 or SAP ERP ECC 6.0 systems.

4.10.1 Automatic Transport or Manual Transport

Even though CO-PA automatically collects the objects and stores them in a transport request, not all of the desired settings may be correctly collected and some objects might still be missing. To address this, you can use automatic transport to set up the overall structure of the required objects in the new system when performing the first move of individual objects to a new system.

If changes have happened to previously transported objects or not all of the objects that are found in the new system, you can generate a manual transport, selecting individual components to include in a specific transport request. This is quite useful for large applications. Manual transports are also called *delta transports* because you only move the elements that have changed to the new system and not the complete set of objects.

You should use the Transport Organizer to manage your transported objects. However, coordinate with your SAP basis team, project manager, and security administrators about the company's procedure to perform and release transports to other systems before you generate one or verify that you're allowed to perform this process based on your individual role in the implementation.

4.10.2   Client-Specific and Cross-Client Settings

In CO-PA, customizing consists of cross-client settings (such as tables and data elements) and client-specific settings (such as customizing value flows). Two request categories are usually used in the SAP system, which are also available in the Transport Organizer:

- ▶ **Customizing requests**
  Record the changes to the customizing settings. When you release the requests, the current status of the recorded settings is exported, and can then be imported into the consolidation system and, if necessary, into subsequent delivery systems. When you create customizing requests, the transport target is automatically assigned the standard transport layer by the SAP system.

- ▶ **Workbench requests**
  These types of requests record the changes made to ABAP workbench objects, and can be either local or transportable workbench requests. The package of the object and the transport route settings in the transport management system is what determines if the changes are recorded in a local or transportable workbench request.

The customizing settings in CO-PA are split by default into these two request categories, depending on whether they are cross-client or client-specific settings. You can deactivate this splitting by using the GOTO • SETTINGS path in the SAP-EIS transport tool, as shown in Figure 4.40, and deselecting the option SPLIT INTO WORKBENCH AND CUSTOMIZING REQUESTS.

You use the customizing settings to specifically configure the transport options for CO-PA and how the transported information will behave. There are two options on the ORDER CATEGORY dropdown list, as shown in Figure 4.40: WORKBENCH REQUEST (default) and TRANSPORT OF COPIES. You can also select the request type for cross-client objects in the CO-PA TRANSPORT SETTINGS • ORDER CATEGORY section for cross-client objects.

The WORKBENCH REQUEST (also called consolidation requests) option is set as the default request type. If the system has not been configured for transporting objects, it's possible to transfer the objects using the TRANSPORTS OF COPIES option. During a transport of copies, however, it isn't possible to run checks on the transport system, and for this reason, this setting should only be used in exceptional cases.

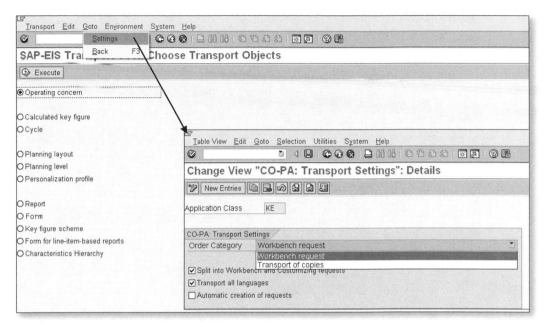

Figure 4.40 Accessing CO-PA Transport Settings

If you select the AUTOMATIC CREATION OF REQUESTS option, the system automatically creates the required transport requests depending on the category of the objects that will be transported: either client-specific or cross-client. Finally, if the sequence in which the transport occurs is important and if the split function is activated, make sure that the workbench request is released first (by following the proper transport release procedures) and then the customizing request. This is because the first request moves the objects, and the second request updates any changes generated over these objects that exist in your transport system.

4.10.3 Transporting Translated Settings

If you work for a multinational company and you have a big implementation, especially one that uses different currencies and languages, the transporting translated settings feature will be important to know. Objects that exist in different languages can be taken into account during the transport process. For this, proceed as follows:

1. In the SAP-EIS transport tool, select EDIT • ADD LANGUAGES, as shown in Figure 4.41. This opens the ADDING FOREIGN LANGUAGES TO A TRANSPORT REQUEST screen.

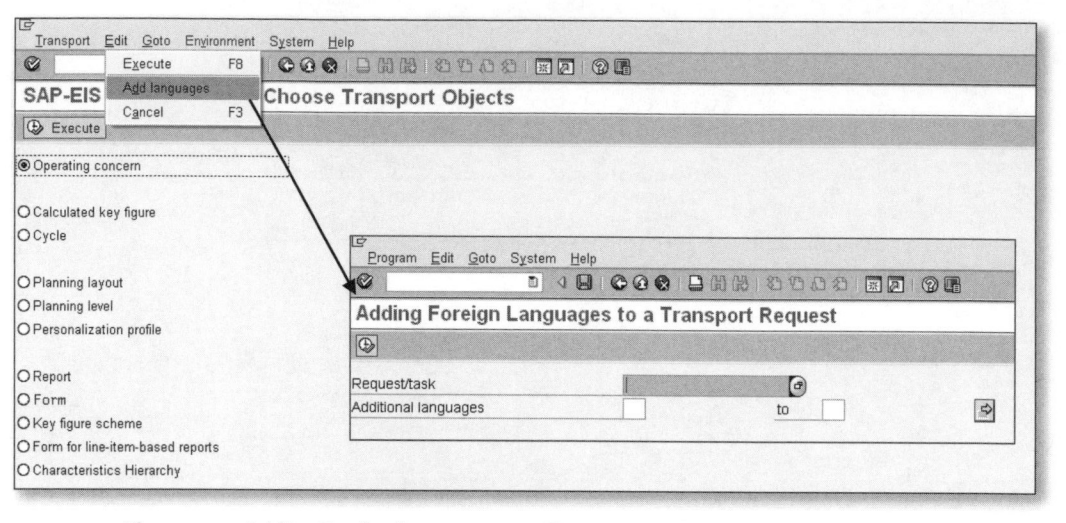

Figure 4.41 Adding Foreign Languages to a Transport Request

2. Select the REQUEST/TASK that will contain the objects in other languages. In the ADDITIONAL LANGUAGES field, enter exactly the names that you require. For example, if you only want to include objects in English (EN) and German (DE) as part of a REQUEST/TASK as shown in Figure 4.42, select the input box, right-click, and select the MULTIPLE SELECTION option as shown.

3. Now the MULTIPLE SELECTION FOR ADDITIONAL LANGUAGES screen appears, as also shown in Figure 4.42, which has several tabs. For our example, we only want English (EN) and German (DE) objects attached, so you should work within the SELECT SINGLE VALUES (1) tab.

   The remaining tabs let you select different options to limit the selection, such as transaction ranges, exclude single values from a selection, or exclude certain ranges from being transported or linked to the request or task, based on their language. Explore these additional tabs on your own; they are self-explanatory. Finally, remember that all language objects are transported by default unless you limit that process using the tools discussed in this section.

4. Once satisfied with your selections, click on the green checkmark icon located in the lower menu bar to accept your changes.

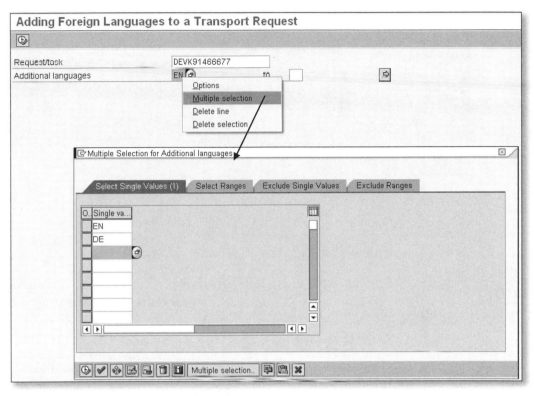

Figure 4.42 Multiple Selections for Additional Languages

4.10.4 Transporting CO-PA Assessment Cycles

In Chapter 7 we'll explore the concept of CO-PA Assessment Cycles and its configuration. However, this is simply just one more object that you need to move to the Production system at the moment; the SAP-EIS transport tool can be used to perform this process. In order to transport a CO-PA Assessment Cycle object (from Development environment into the Production system, for example), follow these steps:

1. Access the SAP-EIS Transport Tool by using Transaction KE3I, and select the CYCLE radio button as shown in Figure 4.43. This allows you to access the available assessment cycles in the system.

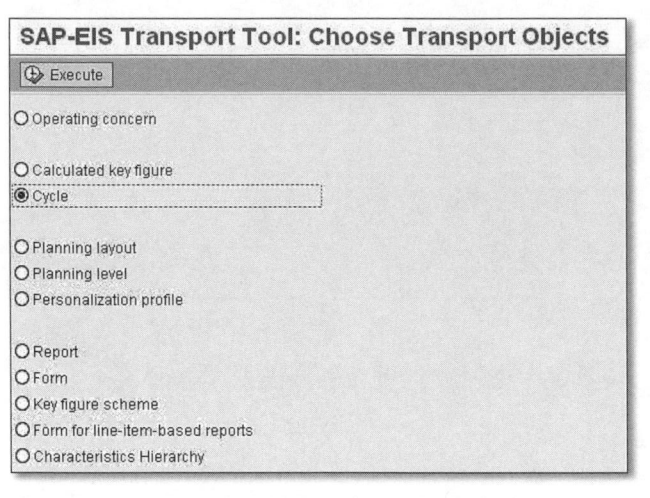

Figure 4.43 Transporting CO-PA Assessment Cycles

2. Click on the EXECUTE button, and the system will prompt you to either assign or create a Workbench and a Customizing request. Click on the checkmark two times if you've already defined it; otherwise, create the Workbench and Customizing request as needed.

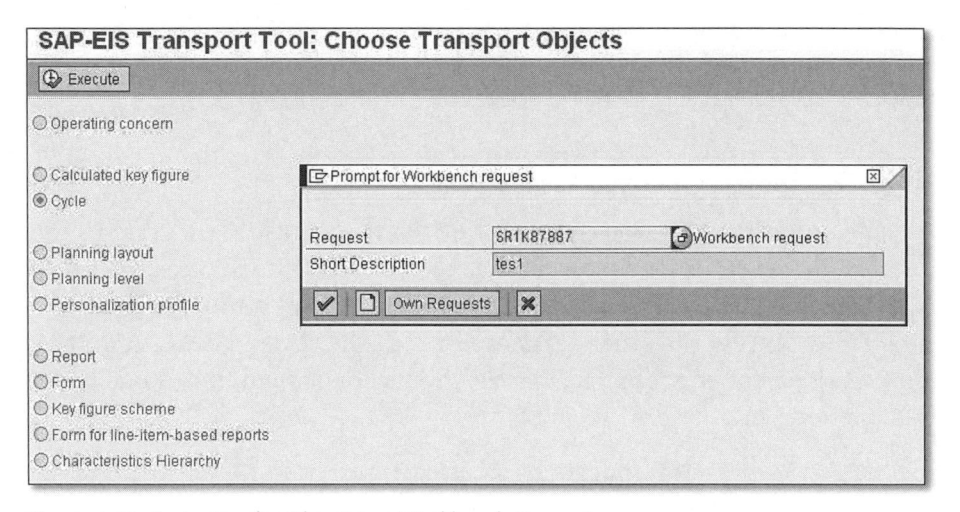

Figure 4.44 Assigning the Object to a Workbench Request

3. After clicking on the EXECUTE button the screen shown in Figure 4.45 appears, and the system identifies that only one assessment cycle is available (in this case, TYB2, which is the example discussed later on in Chapter 7).

SAP-EIS Transport Tool: Choose Transport Objects

| Execute in Background | ⊕ Execute |

Obj. Type	Object	Description	🖩
Cycle	TYB2 20110905 I	This is a Test Cycle	▲ ▼

Figure 4.45 Identifying the CO-PA Assessment Cycle to Transport

4. Select the line where the Cycle TYB2 is located, and click on either the EXECUTE or EXECUTE IN BACKGROUND button. EXECUTE runs the transport tool in the frontend, and the second option runs the tool in the backend, which improves system performance. As shown in Figure 4.46, each of the steps required to attach the Assessment Cycle object are described from selecting the EXECUTE button until the object has successfully been attached as part of a Customizing order. To clearly understand the different transport components in SAP ECC, we recommend that you contact your system administrator or SAP Basis team to further clarify this process.

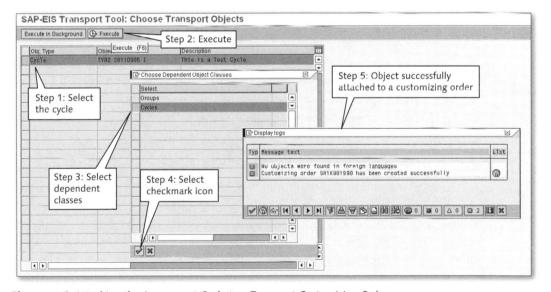

Figure 4.46 Attaching the Assessment Cycle to a Transport Customizing Order

5. In order to confirm that the generation was successful, use Transaction SE10 (see Figure 4.47) to validate that the order has been successfully generated. Otherwise, you'll be able to review any error messages that were generated in the process.

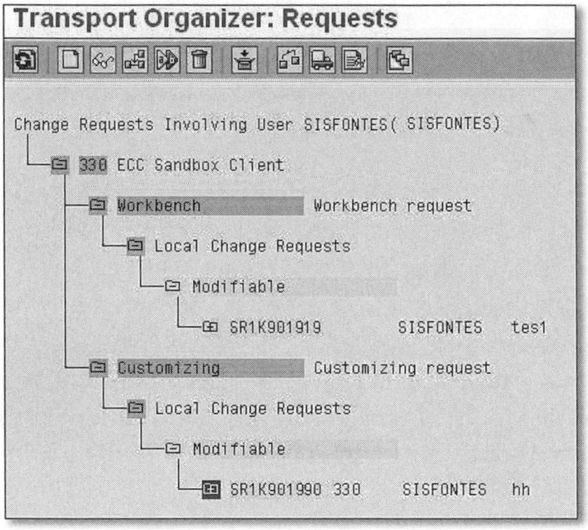

Figure 4.47 Reviewing that the Customizing Request was Generated Successfully

At this point, you've successfully transported the CO-PA Assessment Cycle object, and you have informed your SAP Basis team to move it to the desired system: Testing, Production, or any other server. It's important to understand which server will become the source and the target of the object to be transported in order to avoid overwriting the original object by mistake.

4.10.5 Transporting CO-PA Layouts

When working within the planning environment of SAP CO-PA using Transaction KEPM, we can use layouts to display and/or enter data. Layouts are the main components of the CO-PA Planning component, and it's likely that customized layouts will be used for your implementation, which causes the need to move them between systems and avoid recreating them in Development, Testing, and Production environments.

As shown in Figure 4.48, layouts are basically objects that are created to arrange the data available in the database.

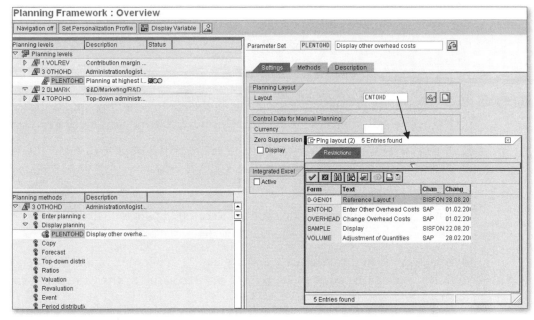

Figure 4.48 Reviewing the Available Layouts in Your CO-PA Planning Framework

As shown in Figure 4.48, there are multiple layouts available that you can use, or you can alternatively review them by clicking on the icon with glasses or create a new one by clicking on the New icon. By clicking on any of these icons, you access the Report Painter environment as shown in Figure 4.49. Notice that each layout object is simply a template where you can arrange the data that's available in the database.

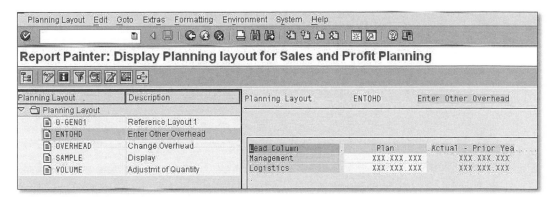

Figure 4.49 Reviewing the Layouts in the Report Painter Environment

For the purpose of this section, we need to know how to move these objects from one server to another, which once again will require us to have a transport object. To move layouts from one system to another, follow these steps as shown in Figure 4.50:

❶ Access the SAP-EIS transport tool using Transaction KE3I, and select the radio button next to PLANNING LAYOUT. Click on the EXECUTE button, and the system will ask you to assign or create a Workbench request and Customizing request.

❷ A new screen appears, requesting you to select the objects to transport. As shown in Figure 4.50, we've selected the LAYOUT 0-GEN01. Click on the EXECUTE button.

❸ A new window appears, asking you to select the Dependent Object Classes. As shown, both FORM and INTEGRATED EXCEL have been selected.

❹ Finally, click on the checkmark to complete the generation of the Workbench order. Make sure you go to Transaction SE10 to verify that the object was created.

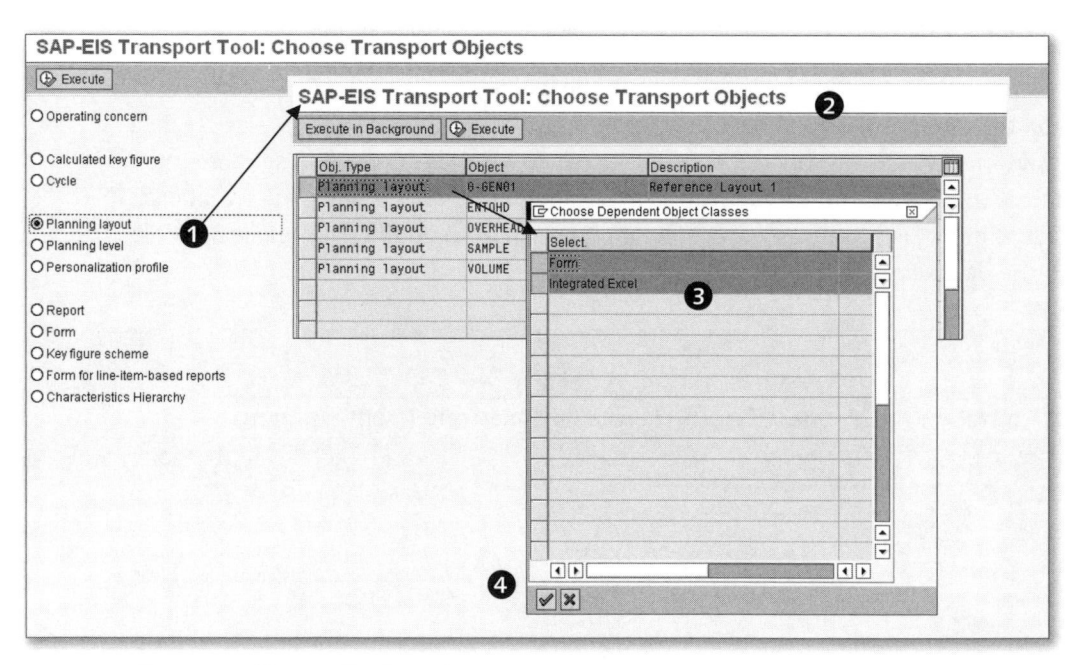

Figure 4.50 Transporting Layouts

4.10.6 Transporting Planning Levels

As part of the SAP CO-PA planning framework, the planning levels are the first objects required to develop your planning applications, and are a subset of the characteristics available in your operating concern. As shown in Figure 4.51, we have four planning levels in our current environment when accessing Transaction KEPM.

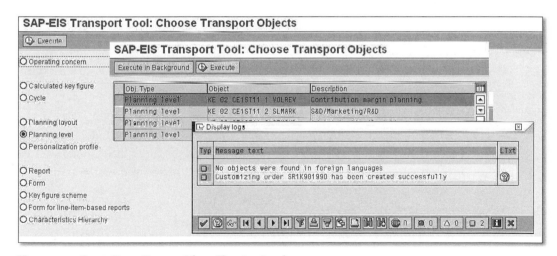

Figure 4.51 Reviewing the Available Planning Levels

Next, we need to access Transaction KE3I, select the planning level (you can only choose one at a time), click on the EXECUTE button, assign the Workbench request and Customizing request, and select the planning level to transport. As shown in Figure 4.52, we've selected the CONTRIBUTION MARGIN PLANNING level, and the Workbench has been generated.

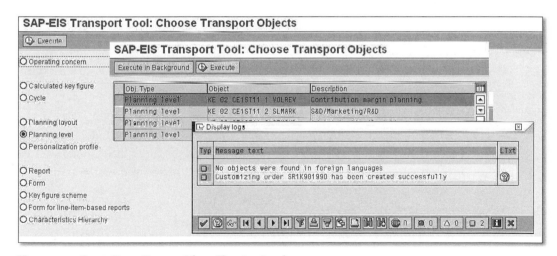

Figure 4.52 Generating a Transport for a Planning Level

It's clear that the object that you need to move from one server to another when working with transports within the SAP system will be associated with a transport request number. Generally you must guarantee that the information stored in the object is the most up to date, and it's recommended that no other user is working and/or modifying that particular object. The SAP Basis team will take care of moving the data from the intermediate location where the objects generated using the Transport Tool are moved, and from that location moved into the destination server.

4.11   Summary

In this chapter, we've extensively reviewed the different options available to allow the system to understand what type of value fields, characteristics, and accounting type you want to use as part of your costing-based CO-PA configuration.

We also explored the differences and similarities between account-based and costing-based CO-PA. However, our discussion on elements such as company code, controlling areas, profit centers, fiscal year variants, and other important elements of the SAP financial system were limited because they require further analysis outside the scope of this book.

One of the most important parts when working with CO-PA is making sure that you've created a correct operating concern, and that the operating concern is assigned to a controlling area. Furthermore, it's very important that CO-PA itself is activated so that the SAP system "knows" that you're working with this application.

The SAP-EIS transport tool was extensively discussed in this chapter, and it's one of the main components that you'll be referring to when your system is going live or into production status. It is highly recommended to follow the standard design of development, testing, and production, while maintaining the original objects in the development system.

The SAP-EIS transport tool doesn't move the data or upload it in a particular system; it only moves the data structures or objects that will be populated with real data once the appropriate processes are executed in SAP ECC to load the specific tables with data applicable to the system where the objects were moved to. If you need to move the data from one system to another, check with your SAP Basis and implementation team to find the recommended practices to perform this task. Remember, once your objects are transported into the Production system, they'll be locked for modification and only available to be executed with limited modification options.

In Chapter 5, we'll explore how to take advantage of the CO-PA structures in more detail, now that they're activated and ready to accept data from other systems. Note that it will be helpful to have some finance or business background to understand the functions and methods discussed in the next chapter.

Master data provides organizational rules that control the behavior of the data values stored in different characteristics inside the operating concern. In addition, master data allows you to perform characteristic valuation and derivation using predefined rules to generate new values that are based on stored data.

5   Master Data in CO-PA

In Profitability Analysis, master data provides you with the basis to build content within the structures you've already created with characteristics and value fields. In other words, master data in CO-PA is the organizational rule for the structures created and stored inside an operating concern that limit the values, postings, and extraction procedures.

Master data defines the general components used in your CO-PA applications and will control how your data is reported, displayed, and analyzed. It's important to understand that master data is not actual data, but rather metadata that regulates and controls the CO-PA structures discussed in Chapters 3 and 4. This is similar to the concept of InfoObjects, which define the structure of InfoCubes in SAP Business Warehouse (BW) or SAP NetWeaver Business Intelligence (BI). In this chapter, we'll closely look at master data, how it relates to CO-PA, and how to configure it.

5.1   Components of Master Data Menus in CO-PA

Figure 5.1 provides a complete overview of the components inside the MASTER DATA menu of CO-PA (Transaction SPRO); we'll now take a closer look at the most important of these components:

Tips & Tricks

It isn't always necessary to configure or add any of the MASTER DATA menu components, especially if your only goal in CO-PA is to use it as a basic data layer to access OLTP data and move it to SAP NetWeaver BI/SAP NetWeaver BW for reporting and additional manipulation.

▶ MAINTAIN CHARACTERISTIC VALUES

Lets you define specific sets of values for a particular characteristic included in an operating concern and also affecting profitability segments.

▶ DEFINE CHARACTERISTICS HIERARCHY

Lets you define hierarchies that control the behavior and display of the characteristic values stored in a particular characteristic.

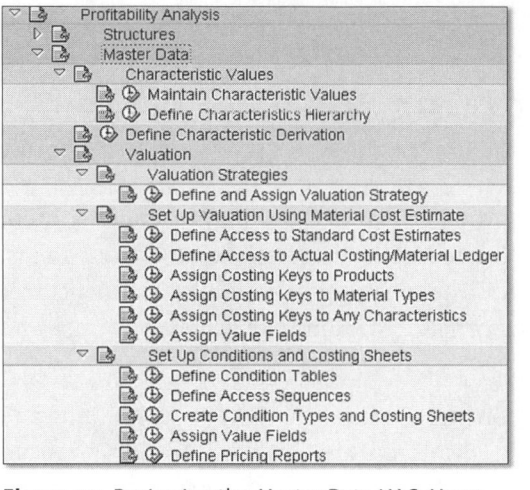

Figure 5.1 Reviewing the Master Data IMG Menu

▶ DEFINE CHARACTERISTIC DERIVATION

Lets you generate values based on predefined rules and relationships to generate additional characteristic values inferred from the previously stored data. For example, if material type A and supplier B are data values that are available in the system, then we can find the characteristic C because it's only provided by supplier B and is made of material A.

▶ VALUATION

Valuation has several sub-items that are of importance and are as follows (note that some items in the following list are summaries of multiple sub items):

  ▶ VALUATION STRATEGIES: Lets you configure automatic procedures based on specific rules and relationships following a sequence of events. For example, automatic calculation of commissions and discounts for specific material types.

  ▶ Keys for accessing material cost estimates, characteristics, and products: Lets you configure automatic procedures to search or locate information using predefined criteria to access specific information based on data attributes. For example, for the calculation of the cost of goods manufactured, you can subdivide your company's material value into fixed and variable cost components. Their classification is identified by their costing key to differentiate between the two when calculating your profit margin.

▶ Assignment of value fields: Lets you specify the value fields (key figures) to consider as part of the component structure to analyze with CO-PA. For example, you could specify the gross sales value field from operating concern A to be a variable amount and its actual data to be extracted using a real-time procedure (point of valuation).

CO-PA uses a combination of characteristic values to automatically create the affected market segment or profitability segment we discussed in Chapter 4 (and that can be considered SAP ERP ECC 6.0 InfoCubes but are completely transactional in nature from an SAP NetWeaver BW/SAP NetWeaver BI perspective).

These specifications for the characteristic values form the basis for the automatic determination of the profitability segment. Now you can specify the valid characteristic values for the new characteristics you've defined using the master data stored in your characteristics by limiting and controlling the types of transactions allowed inside the system.

Of the topics reviewed in this section, valuation and derivation are the most complex and sophisticated topics in master data CO-PA. This is because if they aren't configured correctly, they can negatively affect system performance when working on a massive scale. However, they can also allow the user to generate sophisticated scenarios for calculating multiple pricing or costing procedures for multiple numbers of materials, products, parts, and others, and replicating such processes using SAP NetWeaver BI or SAP NetWeaver BW, SAP NetWeaver BI Integrated Planning (IP), and Business Planning and Simulation (BPS) might not be worth the effort. Let's take a closer look at the topic of maintaining characteristic values.

5.2 Maintaining Characteristic Values

In this section, you'll learn how to maintain the values of the characteristics that you already defined in your operating concern in Chapter 4 within the SAP ERP ECC 6.0 environment.

You can also use a characteristics hierarchy to arrange the characteristic values in a tree-like environment and use it as part of a report or planning application in the CO-PA information system. As shown earlier in Figure 5.1, you'll see the corresponding options of MAINTAIN CHARACTERISTIC VALUES and DEFINE CHARACTERISTICS HIERARCHY in the CHARACTERISTIC VALUES menu.

Now, let's begin maintaining characteristic values (carrying the data) and texts (describing the data):

1. Set an operating concern as current (as described in Chapter 3), making sure you are working with the object you actually want to modify or affect.

> **Note**
>
> Remember from our discussion in Chapter 3 that to modify the contents of any elements in CO-PA that are included as part of an operating concern, the operating concern must be set up as current, using the IMG path PROFITABILITY ANALYSIS • STRUCTURES • DEFINE OPERATING CONCERN • SET OPERATING CONCERN, otherwise nothing will appear or your changes will be stored in the wrong operating concern.

2. Click on the MAINTAIN CHARACTERISTIC VALUES option shown earlier in Figure 5.1.

3. Now the operating concern is set up as current (in this case S_GO QUICKSTART TEMPLATE), and its available characteristics are displayed. This is shown in the box on the left of Figure 5.2.

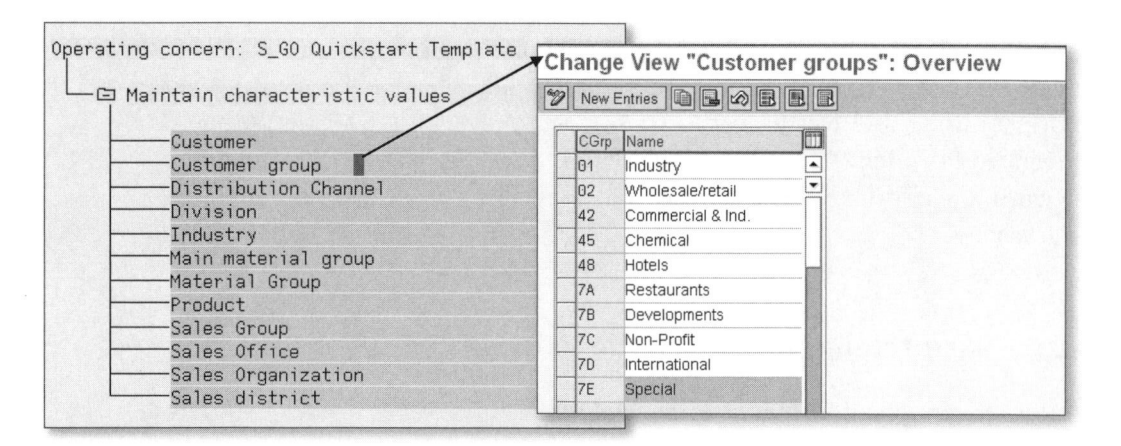

Figure 5.2 Maintaining the Characteristic Values

4. Double-click on the CUSTOMER GROUP characteristic and the screen CHANGE VIEW "CUSTOMER GROUPS": OVERVIEW appears, as shown on the right side of Figure 5.2. Notice that there are two columns: CGRP for the technical name and NAME for the description.

5. Click on the change/modify icon (pencil with glasses).

6. Click on the NEW ENTRIES button and provide the necessary information to create your master data values attached to the CUSTOMER GROUP characteristic.

7. Save your work by clicking on the SAVE icon, and now all cross-client and client objects will be compiled and activated with this change.

At this point, only the values set up in the master data characteristic are allowed for selection or generation inside CO-PA. In addition, you can organize characteristics using hierarchies to improve performance, planning, or reporting, depending on the complexity of the project or if the project requires several levels of organization. Let's look at this option in the next section.

5.2.1 Define Characteristics Hierarchy

Hierarchies are one of the most important components in an SAP system, regardless of the environment. They are structures for characteristics that help to simplify and analyze data using the Information System menu for planning and reporting that will be discussed in Chapters 6, 7, 9, and 10. For example, you can set up a hierarchy structure for products or customers and categorize it by region.

Different characteristics that use the same master data table are grouped in the same characteristics hierarchy. It isn't difficult to define external hierarchies for characteristics that don't have a check table or text table. In addition, only the characteristic values for one characteristic are grouped hierarchically for each hierarchy. Each characteristic value can occur only once in the hierarchy, which means that each value is unique within the entire hierarchy. You can define alternative hierarchies for the same characteristic to simulate different ways of grouping the characteristic values. These alternative hierarchies are stored as hierarchy variants. You can define up to 999 different variants for each characteristic.

To define a characteristic hierarchy, follow these steps:

1. With the appropriate operating concern still set as current, click on the DEFINE CHARACTERISTICS HIERARCHY object as shown in Figure 5.3.

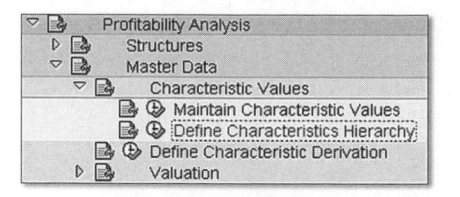

Figure 5.3 Define Characteristics Hierarchy

2. The screen displayed in Figure 5.4 appears, showing the CHAR. (characteristic) TABLE on the left. On the right side is the section CHOOSE HIERARCHY, where you can create a characteristic hierarchy associated with a specific characteristic.

3. To do this, select the characteristic ZONE in the CHAR. TABLE, and enter "TST" in the VARIANT field to start creating a characteristic hierarchy associated with a variant called TST.

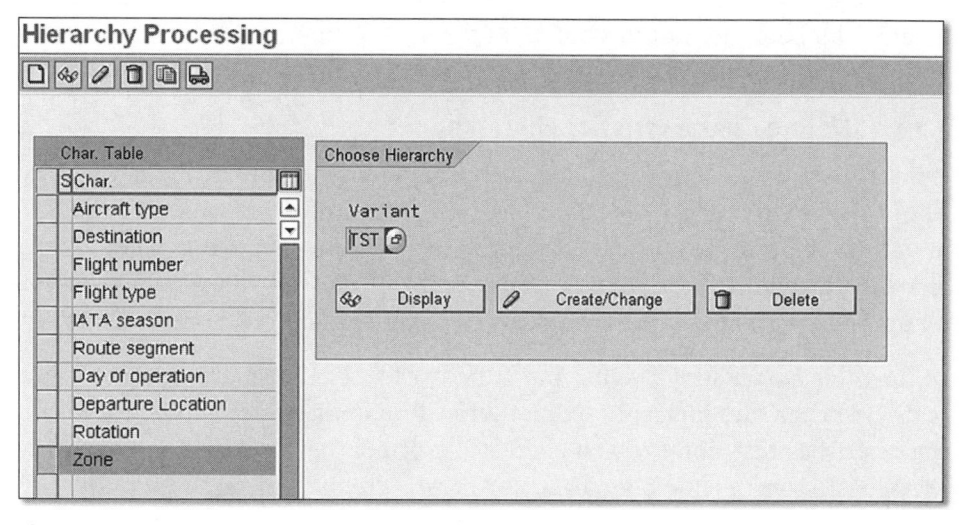

Figure 5.4 Creating a Hierarchy in CO-PA

4. Click on the CREATE/CHANGE button shown in Figure 5.4 to create the variant variable that will store the characteristic hierarchy information. Notice that you can also DISPLAY or DELETE a selected variant.

5. The screen displayed in Figure 5.5 appears. To complete the configuration of your hierarchy variant TST, type "This is a characteristic hierarchy" or any other description that you might require into the SHORT DESCRIPTION box, and click on the HIERARCHY button.

Tips & Tricks

Notice that in the ATTRIBUTES section in Figure 5.5 there is a checkbox called VISIBLE SYSTEM-WIDE. This controls whether the hierarchy variant will be active for all applications where master data hierarchies can be maintained. If not selected, the hierarchy variant is only available in the Enterprise Controlling Executive Information System (EC-EIS). In other words, the attribute is available across the system or limited to a specific environment.

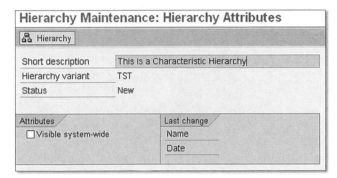

Figure 5.5 Configuring Your TST Hierarchy Variant

6. After completing the previous steps, your screen should now look similar to the HIERARCHY PROCESSING: MAINTAIN HIERARCHY screen shown in Figure 5.6. Here, the different standard nodes and levels that you can define are displayed as a hierarchical tree. There are several buttons at the top of the screen, such as SAME LEVEL (create object at the same level), LOWER LEVEL (create object at lower level), delete icon, cut icon, SAME LEVEL (paste operation at same level), LOWER LEVEL (paste operation at lower level), and EMPTY NODE. All of these buttons and icons can be used to enhance or remove elements of the hierarchy.

You can now fill in the blanks of the different nodes and create your own hierarchy, or use the buttons to add, remove, or modify the current standard hierarchy configuration.

7. Position the cursor on a node and press F4 to display the valid characteristic values to which data can be posted.

Tips & Tricks

Each characteristic value can only be present once in the hierarchy variant. If a characteristic value is already present in the hierarchy, it no longer appears in the list of possible entries.

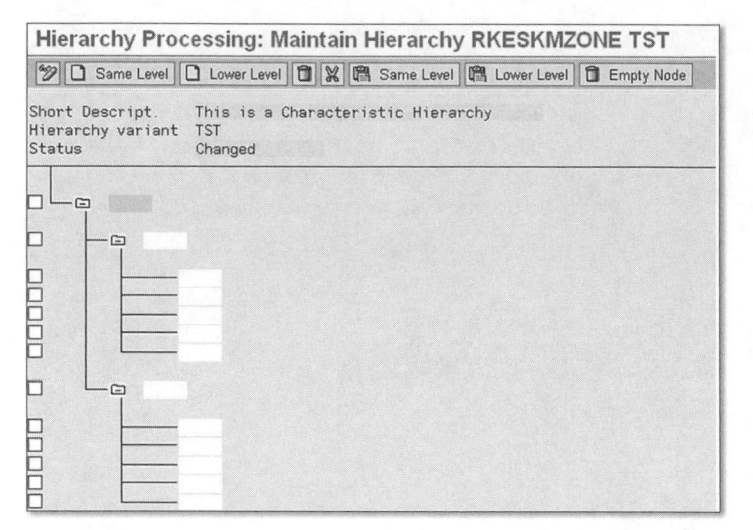

Figure 5.6 Empty Characteristic Hierarchy

8. Choose the desired value or any existing node that cannot receive postings.

Tips & Tricks

If you enter data for a nonchargeable node, this data is transferred to a table. To access this table, choose GOTO • MAINTAIN NONCHARGEABLE NODES.

---

9. Take a look at Figure 5.7, which shows a completed hierarchy for the ZONE characteristic. The first node, called ORIGIN NODE, is considered the root node or dummy node, to which every other component is attached.

10. Save your work. Your hierarchy is now ready for use by the components of the INFORMATION SYSTEM menu and the CO-PA planning framework.

11. To open and close the hierarchy tree, click on the nodes at each of the higher levels to expand or collapse the structure below. Nodes that can be expanded have a plus (+) sign next to their name, and nodes that can be collapsed have a minus (–) sign next to their name.

Tips & Tricks

Now you can use the hierarchy TST in the INFORMATION SYSTEM menu to improve the system's performance and access the information in different levels of data instead of all at once. You can consider each level node a level of aggregation that limits the search to that level, if selected in reporting or planning.

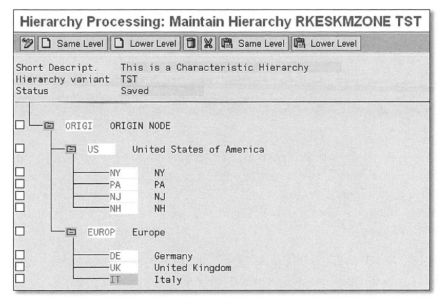

Figure 5.7 TST Characteristic Hierarchy for the Zone Characteristic

Additional functionalities are available when you create hierarchy variants. For example, explore the EDIT option, as shown in Figure 5.8.

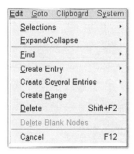

Figure 5.8 Reviewing the Edit Menu

There are several ways to create new nodes in the hierarchy as we describe here:

▶ EDIT • CREATE ENTRY • SAME LEVEL: Inserts a blank node at the same level as the selected node.

▶ EDIT • CREATE ENTRY • ONE LEVEL LOWER: Inserts a new node at the next level down.

▶ EDIT • CREATE SEVERAL ENTRIES • SAME LEVEL: Inserts several blank nodes at the same level.

▶ EDIT • CREATE SEVERAL ENTRIES • ONE LEVEL LOWER: Inserts several blank nodes at the next level down.

▶ EDIT • CREATE RANGE • SAME LEVEL • EDIT • CREATE RANGE • ONE LEVEL LOWER: Lets you enter a range, such as "characteristic value X through characteristic value Z."

You can change, display, copy, transport, delete, and modify the master data of the characteristic values at any time to update or adjust your hierarchy variant. You can also copy a hierarchy variant and change it to generate a brand new one. For example, follow the steps shown in Figure 5.9 to copy a hierarchy variant and described as follows:

1. Select the characteristic, in this case ZONE.

2. Open the HIERARCHY menu as shown in Figure 5.9, and select COPY.

3. The system will display the name of the FIELD NAME to copy, and select the HIERARCHY VARIANT to generate as shown in steps ❸ and ❹.

4. Finally, click on the COPY icon as shown in step ❺, identified with the icon with two pages.

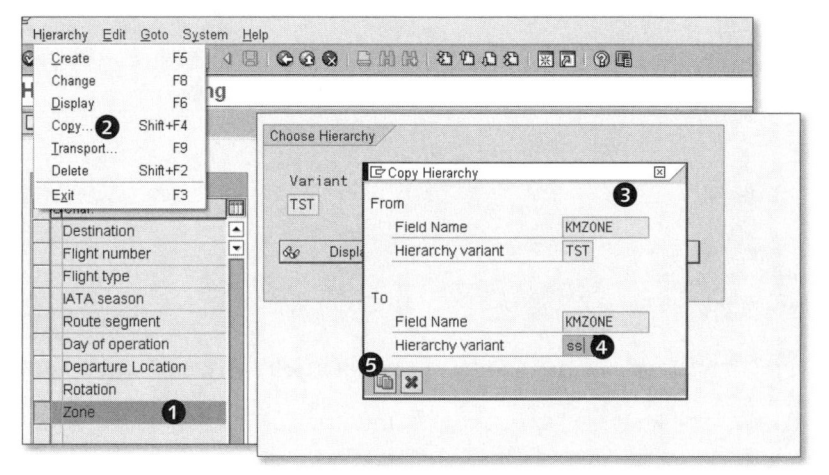

Figure 5.9 Copying a Hierarchy Variant for the Zone Characteristic

There are additional functionalities available in the screen presented in Figure 5.9 that are beyond the scope of this book. Feel free to explore and play with these options as long as you are working in a Sandbox or Development environment and based on the security limitations assigned to your user ID. Remember, hierarchies become quite handy, especially when the number of products, materials, customers, regions, and their relationships becomes so large that it confuses data analysis and affects system performance due to the data volume.

In the following section, we'll review the concept of derivation in more detail and the different types of rules that can be utilized to generate new characteristic values based on the relationships described, with data originally stored in the database.

> **Note**
>
> We won't be able to cover the concepts of derivation and valuation in great detail in this book because of their sophistication. This book will help you understand the basic functionalities and see how they can be integrated into more complex environments to automatically control and calculate the generation of new information and store it as part of your operating concern.

5.2.2 Derivation, Derivation Tables, and Rules Overview

Characteristic derivation is the process of inferring or estimating relationships for CO-PA values to a specific profitability-relevant business transaction. Think of characteristic derivation as a process that's based on specific sets of *rules* that are created using controlled and logically organized sequences of tasks in a *derivation table*. This entire process is called the *derivation strategy*.

A caution right up front: Be careful when generating new values while working with derivation and valuation—their effect might seriously affect your final data, especially when the calculations run in the background. Depending on complexity, potential problems might be very difficult to resolve. Therefore, pay special attention to the alternative usage of valuation and derivation as shown in the planning framework and reviewed in Chapter 7.

With derivation, not all of the desired outputs are generated at once because one task can generate outputs required to execute or generate the following set of activities to come up with the desired result. Let's review a traditional philosophical example: If characteristics material type = "wood," tool type = "ladder," and object = "tree," our characteristic derivation rules might look like this:

▶ **Rule 1**: Ladder is made of wood: the system will understand it if tool type = "ladder" and material type = "wood."

▶ **Rule 2**: Tree is made of wood: the system will be able to say that we have a tree if object = "tree" and material type = "wood."

When these rules are met, our new characteristic value "tree is a ladder" can be populated. In other words, we would say "yes" to the statement "tree is a ladder" only when object = "tree" and tool type = "ladder" are true and if both have material type = "wood." These relationships can be generated combining both rules in a derivation table to generate a third and true statement based on the information that's available.

As shown in Figure 5.10, derivation requires a sequence of events that is logically organized to use the current input data, shown on the left side of the figure, and transform and generate additional data to store in CO-PA and create an enhanced output, shown on the right side of the figure. As also shown in Figure 5.10, we're using three characteristics and their values (Customer, Product, and Sales rep.) to generate data for six different characteristics populated based on the relationships of the characteristic values of the initial three characteristics.

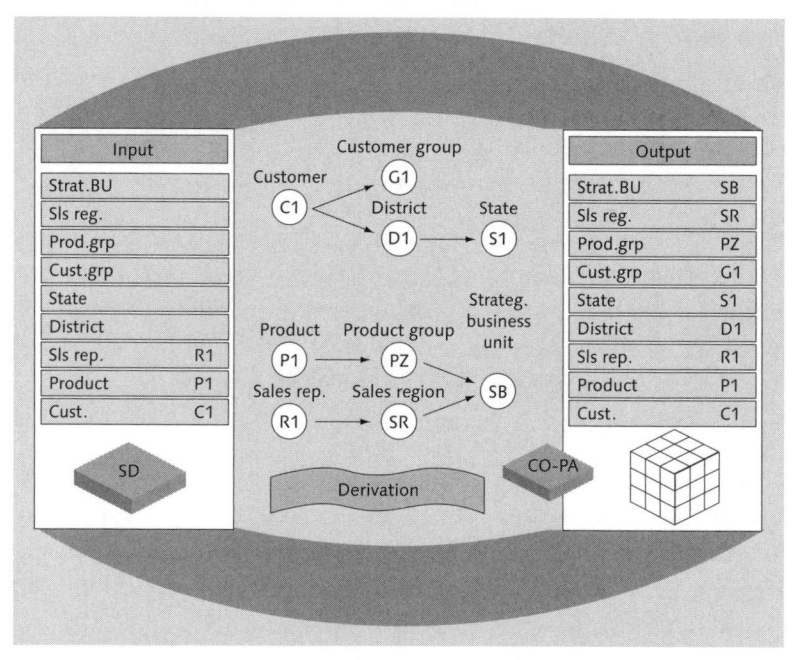

Figure 5.10 The Derivation Concept

The same idea behind these rules is what controls the generation of values using derivation. We can generate a third characteristic that we don't currently have based on the characteristic values of our current data values stored in a characteristic. For example, if product A and region B are in the same transaction line, we can generate values for a characteristic called "industry sector" and generate a characteristic value called "heavy materials." The characteristic value "heavy materials" is not currently available in our database or included in the industry sector characteristic, but we know for a fact that we can infer that the "heavy materials" rule follows this relationship to populate an additional column in the same transaction line in our database.

Derivation Steps

It's important to identify the different types of *derivation steps* that can be created as part of a derivation strategy. Derivation steps are series of steps or tasks that perform specific processes to achieve a specific final outcome. Derivation steps that describe the different functionalities are described as follows:

▶ **Derivation rule:** Performs inference on the values of characteristics that are based on the values of other characteristics.

▶ **Table lookup**: Performs a search inside the data stored in the operating concern that are based on conditions. Doesn't make any modifications to the data; instead, it simply informs whether data has been found that meets certain criteria.

▶ **Move:** Performs an assignment to a target field that is based on a source field or a constant.

▶ **Clear:** Performs a delete operation to a specified field that is based on predefined conditions.

▶ **Enhancement:** Uses ABAP programs to create routines to develop more customized applications using both customized and standard user conditions.

Tips & Tricks

Only characteristics created inside of your operating concern can be manipulated to be used in existing rules or to generate new values. Also, the profitability segment to which the account assignments will need to be made is determined using the quantity of characteristic values drawn from characteristic derivation.

Steps follow a chain or cause-effect reaction, so if there is an incorrect procedure inside a derivation strategy, the final outcome might not be the most desirable one. Therefore, make sure to review that each process is delivering the information that it's supposed to.

Applicable Object Types

It's important to clearly understand the types of objects for which derivation is applicable. You first have manual account assignments, which include the following:

▶ **Settling orders and projects**
In the SAP system, you can settle internal orders (Controlling component), sales orders (Sales and Distribution component), projects (Project System component), production orders and production cost collectors (Production Planning component), and then you can transfer these internal orders to SAP CO-PA profitability segments. To settle data to CO-PA, you also need a settlement profile that contains an allocation structure, which in turn defines how the order or project will be credited. By assigning this profile to the master data of the objects that you need to settle, you'll also map the value fields in the operating concern in CO-PA (refer to Chapter 8 for more details). Figure 5.11 shows a simplified version of the overall process.

▶ **Direct postings from Financials (FI)**
Direct postings from the SAP Financials (FI) component can be transferred to CO-PA profitability segments as described in Chapter 8. As shown in Figure 5.12, the transfer can be performed in real-time, providing that the Controlling area has been activated. Additionally, you can assign revenue, sales deductions, and costs directly from Financial Accounting to profitability segments (such as customers and products) when you use the POST DOCUMENT function.

As shown in Figure 5.12, once the FI document has been posted, the system creates a line item in CO-PA and updates each line that's assigned to the chosen profitability segment. Direct postings from FI would be controlled by a PA Transfer Structure (discussed in Chapter 8) that can be adapted depending on the characteristics of the operating concern: costing-based or account-based CO-PA.

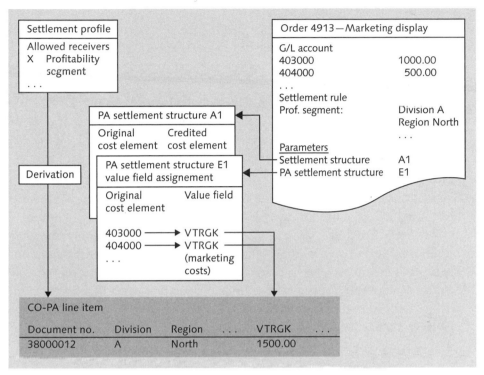

Figure 5.11 Sample Process of Settling Orders/Projects to CO-PA Profitability Segments

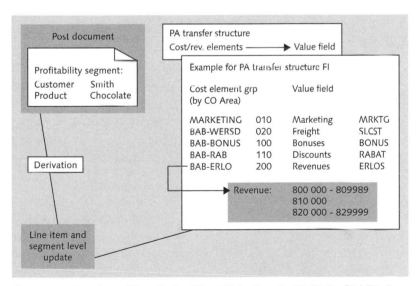

Figure 5.12 Overview of Transferring Direct FI Postings to CO-PA Profitability Segments

▶ **Manually created CO-PA line items**

This is a very particular case of data that exist only in CO-PA. Generally, data would be transferred from multiple components into a CO-PA profitability segment. However, there can be errors in the transferred postings that might require further adjustments, and for these cases, manually created CO-PA line items are useful in that they can also be complemented with the CO-PA planning framework functionalities described in Chapter 6. However, using CO-PA line items sometimes can be more cumbersome and less flexible than the CO-PA planning framework environment.

▶ **Manual entry of planning data**

As mentioned in the previous point, the CO-PA planning framework is the preferred way to add, adjust, or include data as part of the contents of your operating concern. You can create manual entries using CO-PA planning framework by creating a parameter set for the ENTER PLAN DATA method, and configuring the settings in order to perform the required data input depending on the characteristics and value fields available in your operating concern, as well as the settings defined in the planning level. We'll explore how to work with CO-PA planning framework in more detail in Chapter 6.

To create CO-PA line items, follow these steps:

1. For costing-based CO-PA, using Transaction KE21 allows you to create line items postings. If you're working with account-based CO-PA, you need to use Transaction FB01. You can also use Transaction KE21N from the standard menu as the starting point, and the SAP ECC system will inform you of any further adjustments depending on the characteristics of the different SAP objects such as Controlling area and company code.

2. You can choose to post line items in both operating concern and company code currency, only in operating concern currency, or only to company code currency. In addition, select the RECORD TYPE (incoming sales order, direct posting from FI, single transaction costing, billing data, customer agreements, statistical key figures, and order-related projects).

3. The CO-PA operating concern that you are working with must be assigned to a controlling area using Transaction KEKK, and both objects must have the same fiscal year variant. Note that there are relationships that must have already been clearly defined in your FICO design, such as sales prganization assigned to a company code, distribution channels must be created and available, and more. Before configuring the header of the line item, make sure to

check with your SAP FICO and sales and distribution teams for guidance on the current design for your project.

You only have to enter a few characteristic values manually. The remaining characteristic values can be entered via characteristic derivation, which we discuss in the following section. You can automatically transfer data from other applications, including billing documents. This function allows you to post in CO-PA billing documents that have already been posted in Financial Accounting (FI). This is particularly useful if you implement CO-PA after SD and you wish to import the data for the current or previous periods to CO-PA. Before billing documents can be transferred to CO-PA, the Controlling area must be activated and assigned to the operating concern using Transaction KEKK.

You can perform the transfer of the billing documents by following these steps:

1. Access the TRANSFER SD BILLING DOCUMENTS TO CO-PA screen using Transaction KE4S.

2. On the screen that appears, specify the billing documents to be transferred by entering the billing document number, billing date, sales organization, distribution channel, and/or division.

3. Select the TEST RUN option in the CONTROL PARAMETERS menu in order to simulate the program execution, or uncheck that option to perform the transfer. Also, click on the CHECK FOR EXISTING RECORDS OPTION in the UPDATE CONTROL section, and then click on the EXECUTE button.

   When the program is executed, the system checks whether the billing data has been already posted to CO-PA in order to prevent documents from being posted twice in the operating concern. After completing the posting, the program will display a transfer log and an error log to identify the status of the data transferred. Any errors identified during the transfer require you to correct them manually, and then to execute Transaction KE4S one more time. This process will be discussed in more detail in Chapter 8.

Transferring Overhead

Calculation and transferring of overhead costs can be one of the most challenging tasks in SAP ECC and during any migration project. This isn't because the functionality is sophisticated in SAP, but because of the time required to fully define, understand, and identify the kinds of rules that control the overhead allocation processes within SAP ECC, and then determine that the information generated is correct and required in SAP CO-PA.

Figure 5.13 shows the different types of overhead allocations that can occur in the SAP CO component, specifically coming from Cost Center Accounting (cost centers) and activity–based costing (processes), and how this data can be transferred to an SAP CO-PA operating concern.

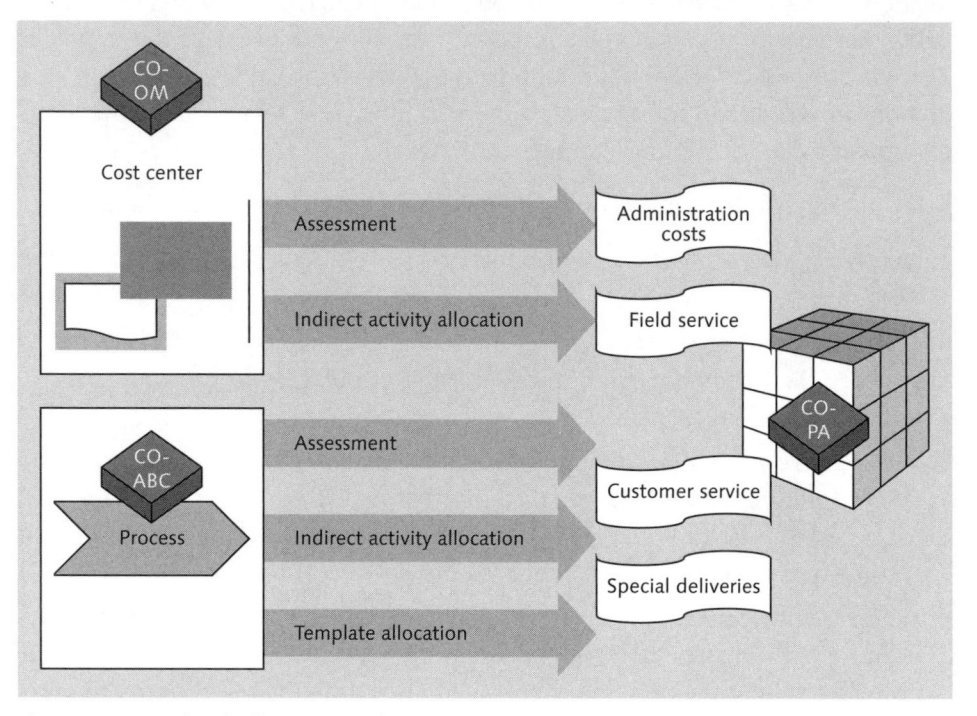

Figure 5.13 Overhead Allocation Methods

There are multiple ways available in SAP ECC to manage overhead, such as:

▶ **Assessment**
This is an allocating method of primary and secondary costs. This choice is available in Cost Center Accounting and activity-based costing using a sender and receiver. Allocation through assessment is useful when the composition of the costs is unimportant for the receiver.

▶ **Indirect activity**
This is a method used for periodic allocation to determine the input of activity

that's indirectly allocated from the sender (cost center or activity type) from the perspective of the receiver. If you are not able to enter the activity consumed by the receiver, or it's too time-consuming, this method can be used to distribute the total activity quantity from the sender to the receivers.

▶ **Template allocation**
This is a method of quantity-based cost allocation that uses templates. With this method, information such as the sender, quantities, and costs don't need to be entered. Instead, they can be determined dynamically when the values are calculated using the template. The senders of template allocation can be business processes, cost centers, or activity types. The receiver objects can be cost objects, profitability segments, business processes, cost centers, or activity types. Chapter 8 also discusses the process of transfer of overhead to CO-PA.

External Data Transfer

When the data that you want to include into your SAP CO-PA operating concern comes from non-SAP systems or legacy systems, SAP CO-PA provides the functionality to be able to accept this data using a direct input procedure. In a costing-based Profitability Analysis, you can import both plan and actual data, as compared to account-based Profitability Analysis where you can only import plan data. You can perform transfers simultaneously without locking the system.

To load data from external systems, follow these steps:

1. Access Transaction SPRO, and access PROFITABILITY ANALYSIS • TOOLS • DATA TRANSFERS BETWEEN CO-PA AND OTHER SYSTEMS • CO-PA EXTERNAL DATA TRANSFER, as shown in Figure 5.14.

2. Now you need to define the structure of the data that you want to import or the structure of the source file that you'll read and upload into CO-PA. This configuration makes it possible to transfer the data in the format provided by the legacy system. SAP CO-PA has a structure called COPA999, which has already been defined as an example for your reference (note that you can copy the structure if you'd like to create a new one). To access this sample structure, simply click on the DEFINE STRUCTURE OF EXTERNAL DATA as shown in Figure 5.14, enter the name COPA999 in the DATABASE TABLE menu option, and click on the DISPLAY button as shown in Figure 5.15. You may require assistance from your ABAP developers to accomplish this task.

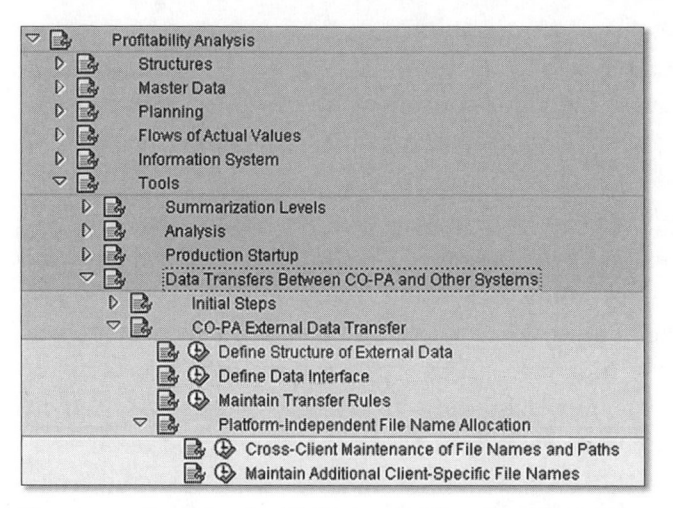

Figure 5.14 Accessing the CO-PA External Data Transfer Menu

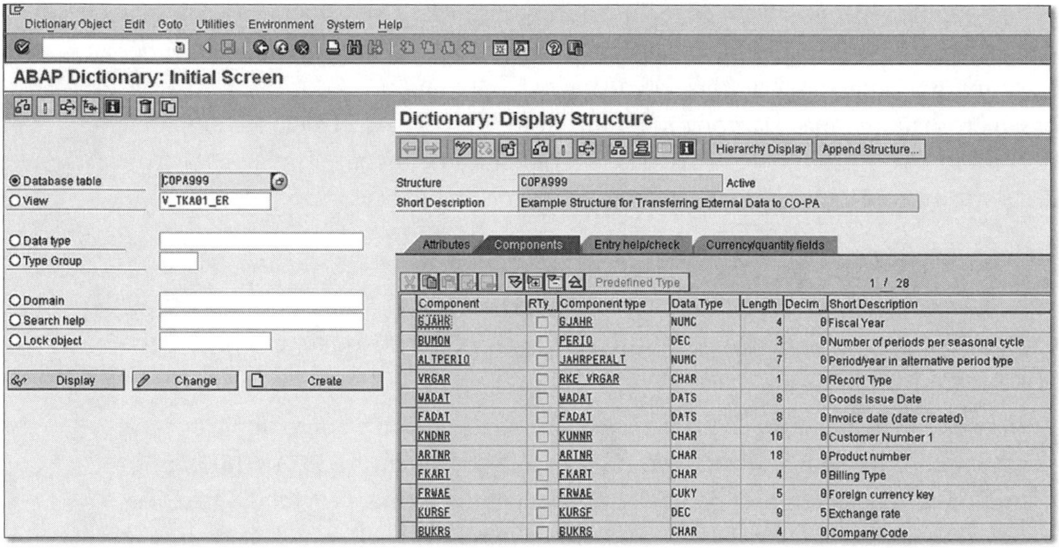

Figure 5.15 Reviewing the Pre-Delivered Structure COPA999

3. Next, you need to define the sender structure or data interface. You access this by clicking on the menu shown in Figure 5.14 with the name DEFINE DATA INTERFACE. In this activity, the data interface the system uses to import external data to CO-PA is created, and will be referred to as the *sender structure*. This structure contains the required mappings of one or more ABAP Dictionary

structures to an operating concern. The ABAP Dictionary structure defines the format of the external data to be imported to the CO-PA operating concern using an account-based or costing-based approach for either plan or actual data.

4. As shown in Figure 5.16, the Data interface can be created using a table, pre-defined structures, Dictionary structures generated for sender structure, and create a new Dictionary structure. Notice that the interface can be created for ACTUAL DATA or PLAN DATA by clicking on the respective radio buttons, and also is specific for an operating concern and applicable to either costing-based or account-based CO-PA.

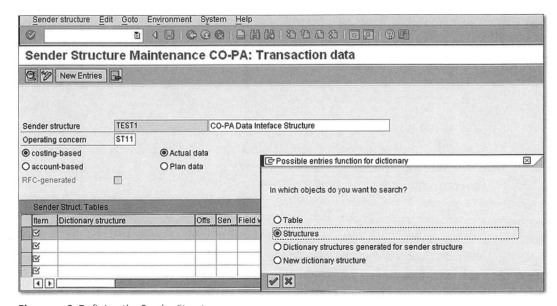

Figure 5.16 Defining the Sender Structure

5. Now you need to define the transfer rules: once the sender structure has been defined, similarly to SAP NetWeaver BW, you need to create rules that connect your sender structure to your CO-PA fields. As shown in Figure 5.17, you can also request CO-PA to propose the rules associated with the transfer structure.

In practical terms, it is recommended to have your SAP ECC team explore a more simple interface using a custom ABAP program that will have all the rules required for you to load the data into your operating concern embedded in the correct field mapping. We've discussed this functionality to make you aware of its existence, but we don't recommend that you initiate its implementation.

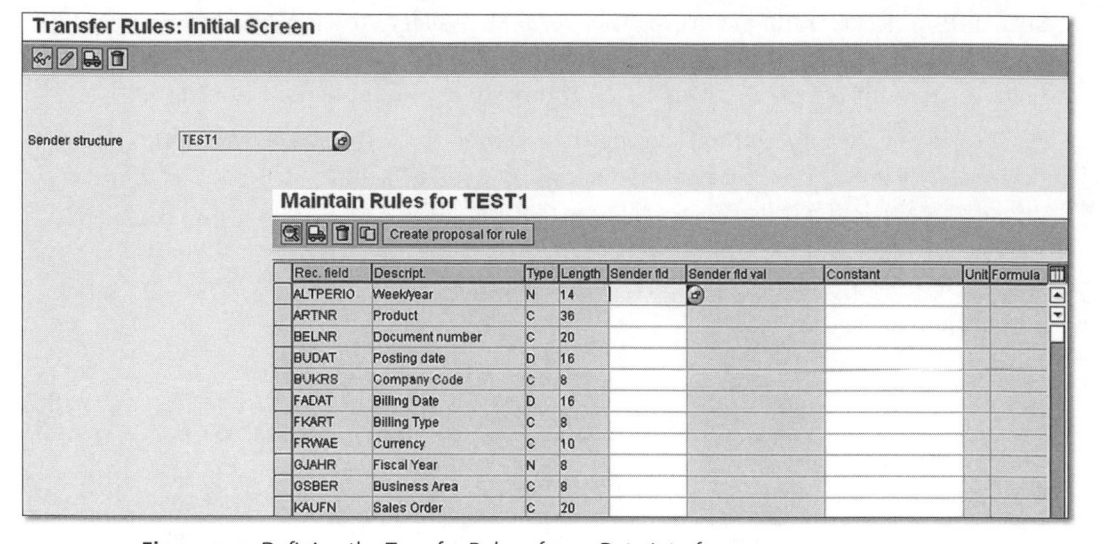

Figure 5.17 Defining the Transfer Rules of your Data Interface

In the next section, we'll explore how to create derivation steps along with the procedure to generate each of them. We'll also look more closely at the concepts of the derivation rules and derivation steps by reviewing the general configuration procedures for each of the step types.

5.2.3 Creating Characteristic Derivations and Derivation Rules

Now that we have a good idea of the logic behind derivation, let's begin with a more detailed discussion on how to create a derivation strategy to generate new values using derivation steps.

Creating Derivation Rules

First, let's create a derivation rule following these steps:

> **Note**
>
> Before you start creating objects in the SAP system, remember to rehearse the steps or processes that you want to create on paper and correctly identify them to improve your development efforts using a Sandbox or Development environment.

1. Follow the IMG path CONTROLLING • PROFITABILITY ANALYSIS • MASTER DATA • DEFINE CHARACTERISTIC DERIVATION, as shown in Figure 5.18.

Figure 5.18 Accessing Define Characteristic Derivation

Tips & Tricks

When an operating concern is generated, the system produces a standard derivation strategy that contains all known dependencies between characteristics. You can display these by choosing VIEW • DISPLAY ALL STEPS. Also, you can change the derivation strategy by adding more steps, changing previous steps, deleting steps, or changing the step sequence.

2. The screen CHARACTERISTIC DERIVATION: CHANGE STRATEGY appears, as shown in Figure 5.19. Click on the change/modify icon (pencil with glasses).

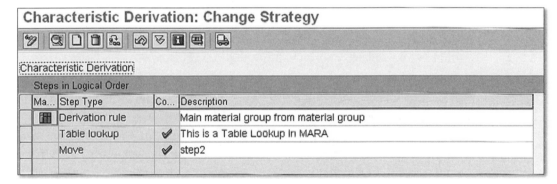

Figure 5.19 Characteristic Derivation: Change Strategy Screen

3. Click on the CREATE icon (white page icon) to start creating a derivation step.

4. In the CREATE STEP box that appears, as shown in Figure 5.20, select DERIVATION RULE and click on the checkmark icon.

> **Note**
>
> As you can see, there are four additional types of derivation steps that can be created: TABLE LOOKUP, MOVE, CLEAR, and ENHANCEMENT. We'll review the remaining functions in more detail in the following sections.

Create Step

- ⦿ Derivation rule
- ○ Table lookup
- ○ Move
- ○ Clear
- ○ Enhancement

Figure 5.20 Types of Derivation Steps Available in CO-PA

5. The CHARACTERISTIC DERIVATION: DISPLAY STRATEGY screen appears after clicking on the checkmark icon in Figure 5.20. For this type of derivation there are some additional options to consider:

   ▸ Under MAINTAIN RULE VALUES, enter which values in the target fields should be placed in which characteristic values of the source fields.

   ▸ Under CHARACTERISTICS, you can make additional entries that, for example, make it possible to enter a validity date for the step.

6. As shown in Figure 5.21, characteristic derivation has three columns: MAINTAIN ENTRIES, STEP TYPE (which identifies the type of derivation being performed in the step, in this case DERIVATION RULE), and finally a DESCRIPTION of the rule, in this case MAIN MATERIAL GROUP FROM MATERIAL GROUP. In other words, we have two MAIN MATERIAL characteristics and we're going to generate values for a characteristic called MATERIAL GROUP as shown in Figure 5.22.

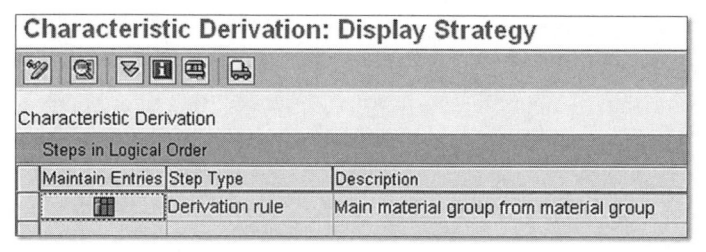

Characteristic Derivation: Display Strategy

Characteristic Derivation

Steps in Logical Order

Maintain Entries	Step Type	Description
▦	Derivation rule	Main material group from material group

Figure 5.21 Configuration of a Derivation Rule

7. Click on the icon in the MAINTAIN ENTRIES column to access the derivation rule filtering options. As shown in Figure 5.22, we have two characteristics—MATERIAL GROUP NAME and MAIN MATERIAL GROUP (derived characteristic). We'll take values from MATERIAL GROUP NAME to generate user-defined values in the MAIN MATERIAL GROUP characteristic.

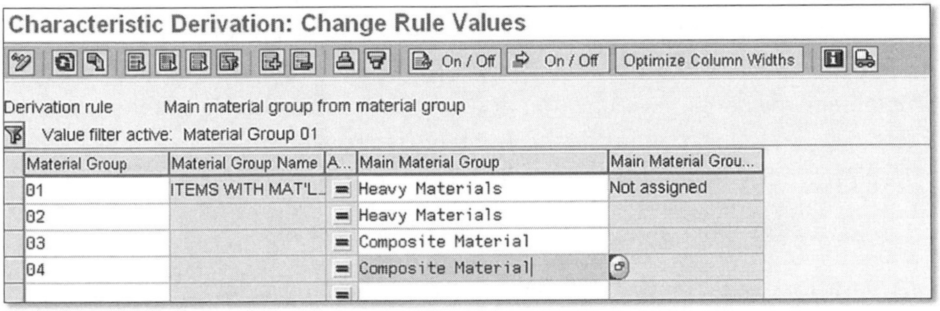

Characteristic Derivation: Change Rule Values

Derivation rule   Main material group from material group

Value filter active: Material Group 01

Material Group	Material Group Name	A...	Main Material Group	Main Material Grou...
01	ITEMS WITH MAT'L...	=	Heavy Materials	Not assigned
02		=	Heavy Materials	
03		=	Composite Material	
04		=	Composite Material	
		=		

Figure 5.22 Definition of the Derivation Rule

For example (as shown in Figure 5.22), we have four entries in the MATERIAL GROUP column (01, 02, 03, and 04). On the right side of the screen we define that for material groups 01 and 02, we'll derive those values as HEAVY MATERIALS (shown in the MAIN MATERIAL GROUP column). The same logic applies to the MATERIAL GROUPS groups 03 and 04 as shown in Figure 5.22 when we define these two values as composite material as part of the derivation rule created. Basically, we're deriving one material with two sets of values and another material based on a different two sets of values.

There are several steps you can complete when creating derivation tables, and each of them is defined in a step sequence that controls the order in which each rule is applied to the operating concern. For example, step 1 can derive characteristic A, step 2 uses characteristic A to derive characteristic B, and so on.

In addition, you can delete, move, and change your steps. For this, simply select the line that defines the step and perform the process as required, either using the menu displayed on top of the screen shown in Figure 5.22 that allows you to add, remove, filter, copy, and other operations, or using the standard SAP software menu bars.

However, not all of the steps require generating additional values to other user-defined characteristics. As seen previously in Figure 5.18, you can also use something called a TABLE LOOKUP. As its name suggests, a lookup doesn't generate additional values, but rather searches inside a database to confirm if certain conditions of values are available.

Let's take a closer look at this process.

Creating Table Lookups

A *table lookup* lets you determine characteristic values by reading them from an SAP table using the target value (the desired value to find inside a table) based on the source fields (location inside the SAP table where you might locate the desired values previously defined in the target value).

To create a table lookup you must perform the following:

1. Access the CHARACTERISTIC DERIVATION screen shown previously in Figure 5.19.

2. Click on the change/modify icon and the create step icon as previously done for the derivation rule procedure.

3. When the CREATE STEP screen displayed in Figure 5.20 appears, select the TABLE LOOKUP option and click on the checkmark icon.

4. The ENTER TABLE NAME dialog box appears, as shown in Figure 5.23. This required table name is delivered by SAP where specific transactions or information is stored.

   As shown in Figure 5.23, we'll be searching in the Materials Management (MM) table called MARA.

> **Note**
>
> Don't worry about not knowing the names of all of the SAP tables; they are too complicated and numerous to remember! You can easily find them online on a variety of websites, such as *http://help.sap.com*, *http://sdn.sap.com*, and *www.erpgenie.com*.

5. Click on the checkmark icon to continue.

6. The screen shown in Figure 5.24 displays. Three tabs are available for the table lookup step:

   ▸ DEFINITION: Lets you define the relationships between the SAP table fields and the fields defined in the operating concern. In other words, establishes the relationship between source to target.

▷ CONDITION: Lets you establish the selection criteria for the data extraction from the SAP tables into the operating concern. Basically, this tab controls the filtering options associated with the previous relationship from source to target controlled by the DEFINITION tab.

▷ ATTRIBUTES: Lets you activate the ISSUE AN ERROR MESSAGE IF NO VALUE FOUND option, to assist during execution if desired.

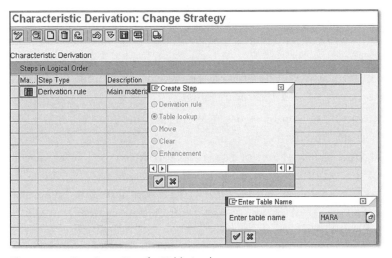

Figure 5.23 Creating a Step for Table Lookup

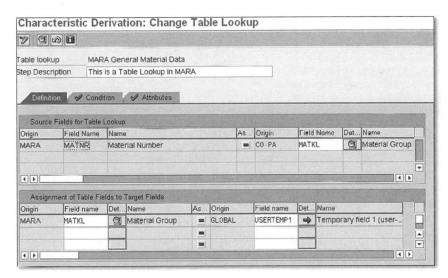

Figure 5.24 Configuring the Definition Tab

7. Now, let's suppose we want to look up the base unit of measure and the material group for a particular product number.

8. Select the Definition tab. Enter MATNR in the Field Name section, which is the material number from the origin table MARA, and it's used as the main field or primary key to perform a search within a table, and match it with the CO-PA fields called MATKL (material group), as shown in Figure 5.24.

9. In the Assignment of Table Fields to Target Fields section, specify where you'll store the information once it's derived by using a condition, which we define next in the Condition tab. Remember, the ultimate destination of the information will be a field in your operating concern, which requires business involvement on how it would be utilized. The reasoning behind these decisions must also be clear to the technical teams.

10. On the Condition tab shown in Figure 5.25, define the CO-PA Origin field Billing Type (FKART) and define the condition greater than (>) and the reference Value B1 with a description of Rebate Credit Memo. In other words, we're defining the condition that needs to be satisfied to execute the table lookup step to find any values that meet the criteria configured in the Assignment of Table Fields to Target Fields section of the screen shown in Figure 5.24. This process is equivalent to the table lookup functionality of MS Excel, but applied to the database level of SAP ECC and integrated with SAP CO-PA.

11. Click on the Save icon.

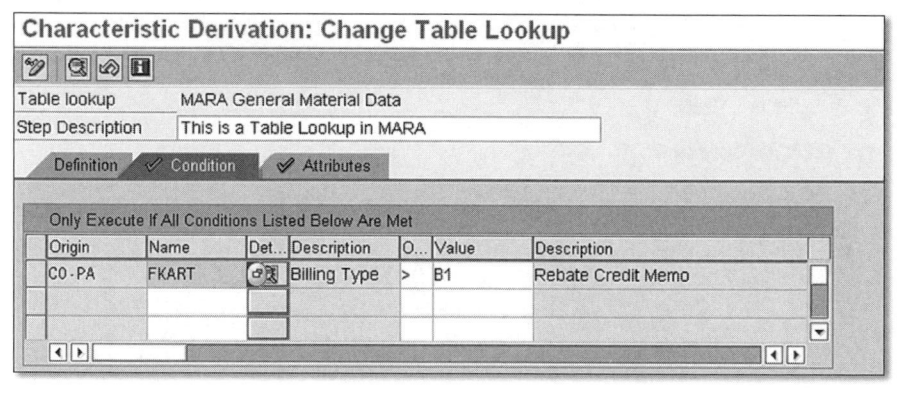

Figure 5.25 Condition Tab

Next, let's execute the table lookup step we configured, as follows:

1. Go back to the main screen CHARACTERISTIC DERIVATION: DISPLAY STRATEGY and click on the new step called THIS IS A TABLE LOOKUP IN MARA, as shown in Figure 5.26.

2. Select the TEST icon (the icon to the left of the transport [truck] icon), also shown in Figure 5.26.

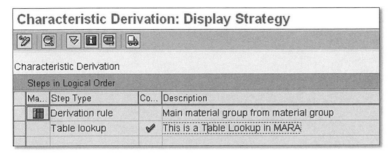

Figure 5.26 Executing the Step Table Lookup

3. The screen shown in Figure 5.27 appears, ready to test the characteristic derivation settings. First, however, you must specify the value you want to find in the SAP tables. For our example, we'll search for the information of product 000011447, so enter this value in the PRODUCT field.

4. Click on the DERIVATION button to start the test. After clicking on the DERIVATION button, two new buttons appear on the same screen: UNDO DERIVATION and ANALYZE DERIVATION. The first button takes you back to the screen shown in Figure 5.25, and undoes any changes. The second button lets you review the conditions defined in the table lookup step and analyze what this rule has performed.

5. Click on ANALYZE DERIVATION to review the CHARACTERISTIC DERIVATION: ANALYZE DERIVATION STEPS screen with the results of the execution of the derivation table lookup step, as shown in Figure 5.28.

6. In steps 12 and 17 the effects of the previous configuration will be reflected, and if you followed the previous steps literally in your environment, you'll be able to see on your screen that the steps that met the criteria defined in the CONDITION tab previously defined in Figure 5.24 are highlighted.

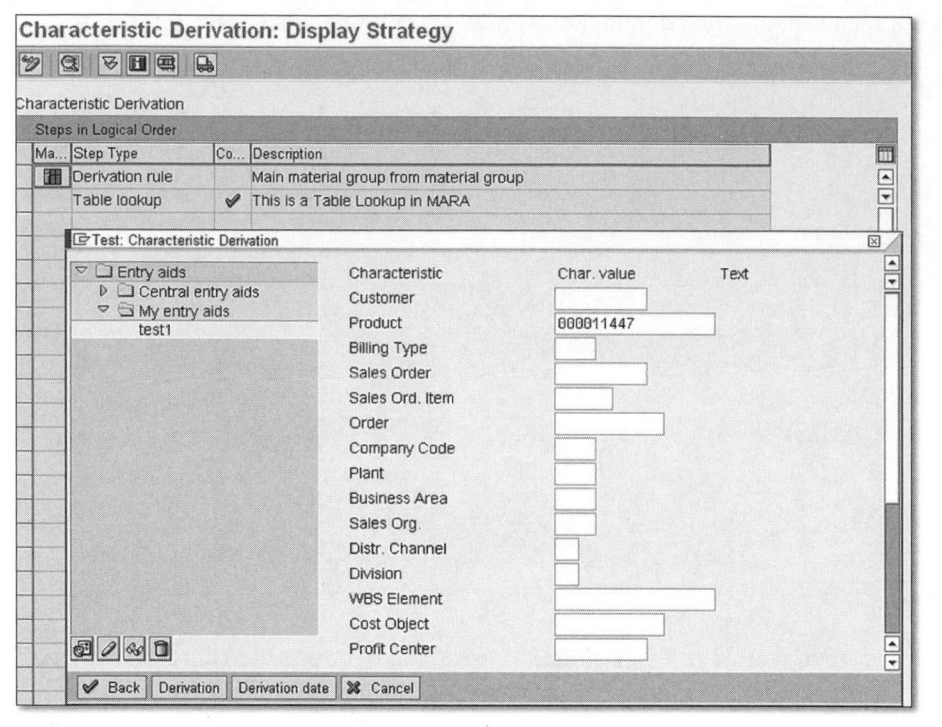

Figure 5.27 Executing Your Table Lookup Step

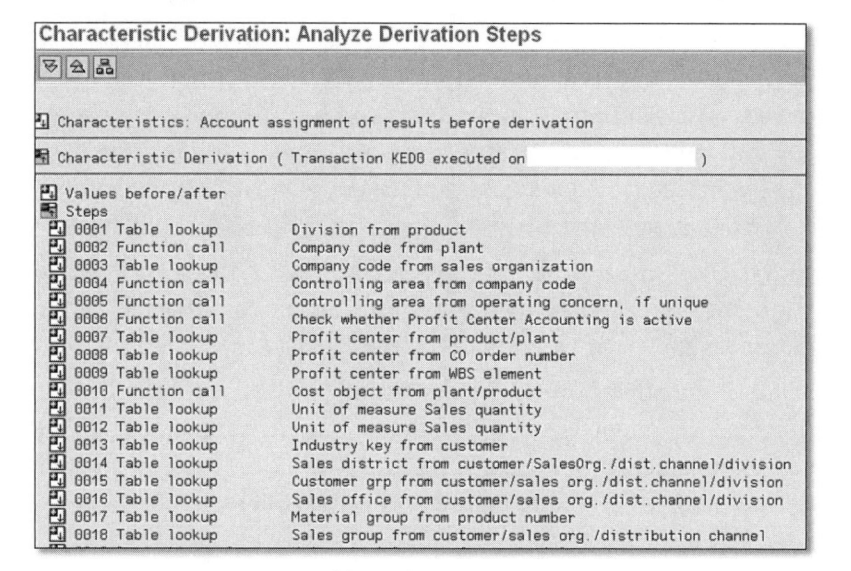

Figure 5.28 Reviewing Your Table Lookup Step Execution

7. You can change the display shown in Figure 5.28 by clicking on the tree icon to get a clearer view to understand the influence of the table lookup derivation step. For example, as shown in Figure 5.29, you can see the VALUE BEFORE and VALUE AFTER, which show that the two items found by our search condition are EA and 01, in line with the CONDITION tab definitions for the table lookup.

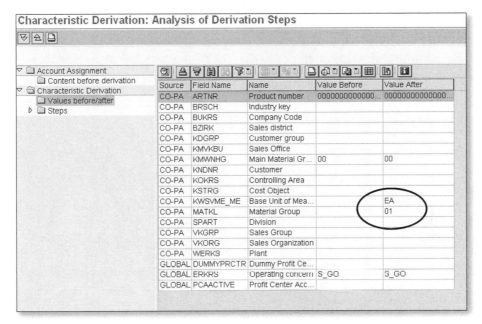

Figure 5.29 Detailed Result for the Valuation Derivation Step Table Lookup

As shown in Figure 5.29, the two values found by using the step table lookup can be adjusted if required once again; simply go back to the the CONDITION tab previously configured in Figure 5.24.

In the next section, we'll explore the move derivation step, and understand how it can be used to adjust and transfer information that is stored in one object into another.

> **Note**
>
> Because these functionalities depend largely on the contents or sequence of events to create a derivation strategy, sometimes a table lookup becomes useful to confirm the values that a previous step generated during the derivation process.

Creating a Move Step

As its name implies, a *move step* lets you transfer the contents of any source field or constant to any target field. The SOURCE FIELD is where the information is coming from and the TARGET FIELD is where the information will be stored. In addition, the CONSTANT value is a default value and can also transfer to a target field, if selected. Figure 5.30 shows the CHARACTERISTIC DERIVATION: CHANGE ASSIGNMENT screen, which is used to perform a move step. Notice that the MOVE STEP screen shown in Figure 5.30 is quite similar to that of Figure 5.24 for characteristic derivation; the main difference is the lack of the ATTRIBUTES tab and that the DEFINITION tab design is more direct to the TARGET FIELD.

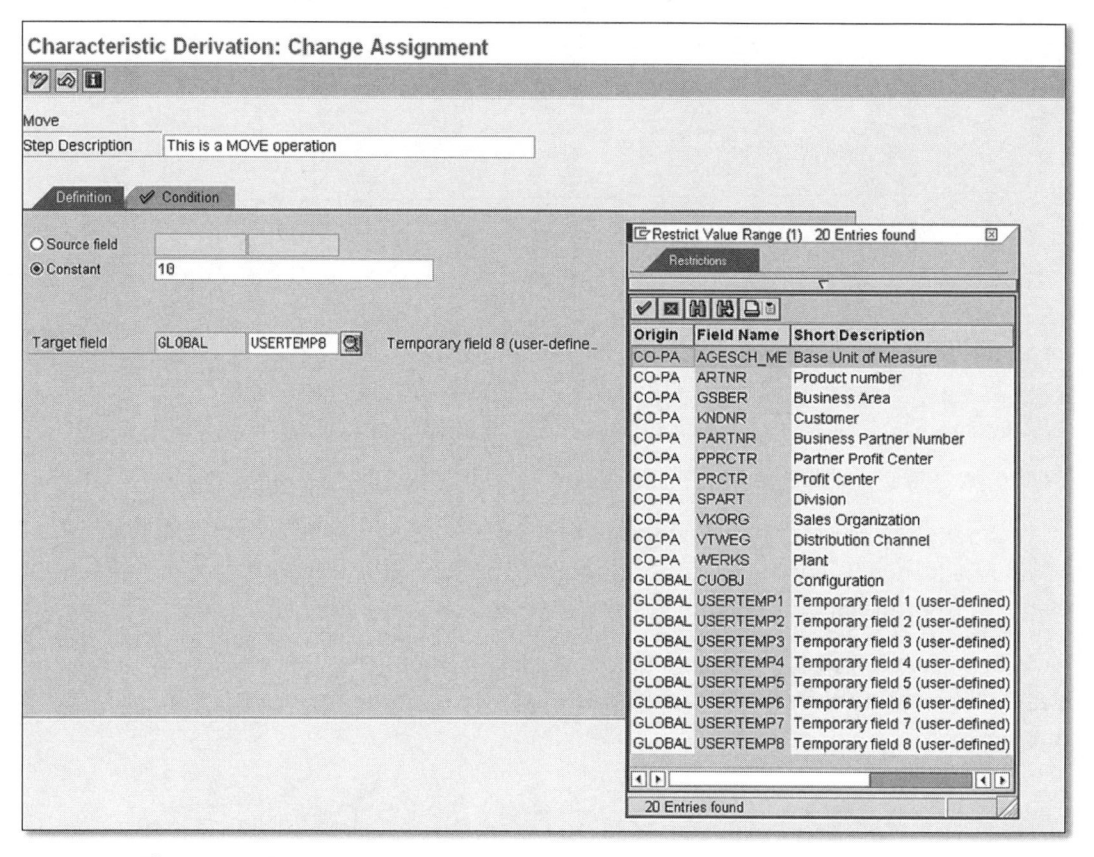

Figure 5.30 Creating a Move Step

The DEFINITION and CONDITION tabs on this screen are used to control the behavior of the step. The DEFINITION tab lets you specify the data origin—either a

SOURCE FIELD or a CONSTANT. On this tab, you also have to specify the TARGET FIELD, as shown in Figure 5.30. For this you must access the objects available in the default operating concern.

Next, as shown in Figure 5.31, the CONDITION tab lets you limit the transfer of data between two or more objects. For example, the assignment of the constant value 10 to USERTEMP8, defined previously as the TARGET FIELD, as shown in Figure 5.30, is determined by the value of the CONTROLLING AREA (KOKRS) to be 0001.

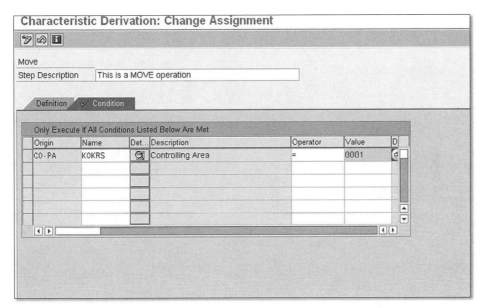

Figure 5.31 The Condition Tab for the Move Step

After configuring the move step, follow the same logic as for any other defined step. That is, select the step, execute it, click on the ANALYZE button, and review your results to see if they are successful. Creating derivation steps in CO-PA and working with the move step functionality follow a similar logic of source to target, and a set of selection criteria is utilized to affect the data in the source and transfer it to the target.

However, sometimes instead of generating, moving, or storing values into new objects, you might want to clear or delete values that currently exist in the database or were previously generated from other steps. This is done using the clear step function that we'll review in the next section.

Creating a Clear Step

The *clear* step lets you delete a characteristic value, or, put differently, reset it to "" (blank) for CHAR fields or "0" for NUMC fields:

1. To start, follow the previously discussed procedure to display the CREATE STEP dialog box, select CLEAR, and click on the checkmark button.

2. Figure 5.32 shows the configuration screen that displays. As with other steps, you need to enter a description, and there is a DEFINITION and a CONDITION tab. However, on the clear step's DEFINITION tab, only one field needs to be defined that identifies the FIELD that has data that you want to clear. In our example, this is USERTEMP8.

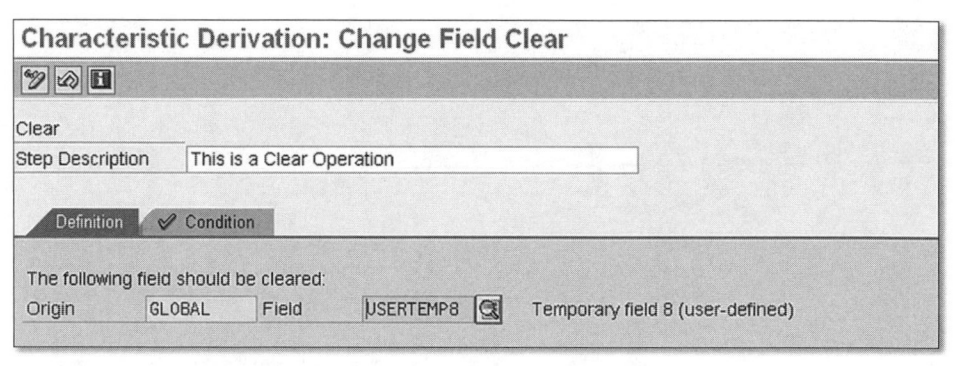

Figure 5.32 Configuring the Change Field Clear Screen

3. Select the CONDITION tab, shown in Figure 5.33, which lets you specify the requirements the step must have to perform the clear or delete operations. Notice that we've defined that we will only delete the condition data from CONTROLLING AREA (KOKRS) with value 0001 in USERTEMP8.

   This procedure can be quite useful, especially if you want to empty the fields of an operating concern before you execute another step that will populate it with data.

> **Caution**
>
> We cannot emphasize enough how careful readers must be when working with this step type. In particular, other objects (such as reports or planning functions) might be value-dependent and final results can be affected by clearing field values.

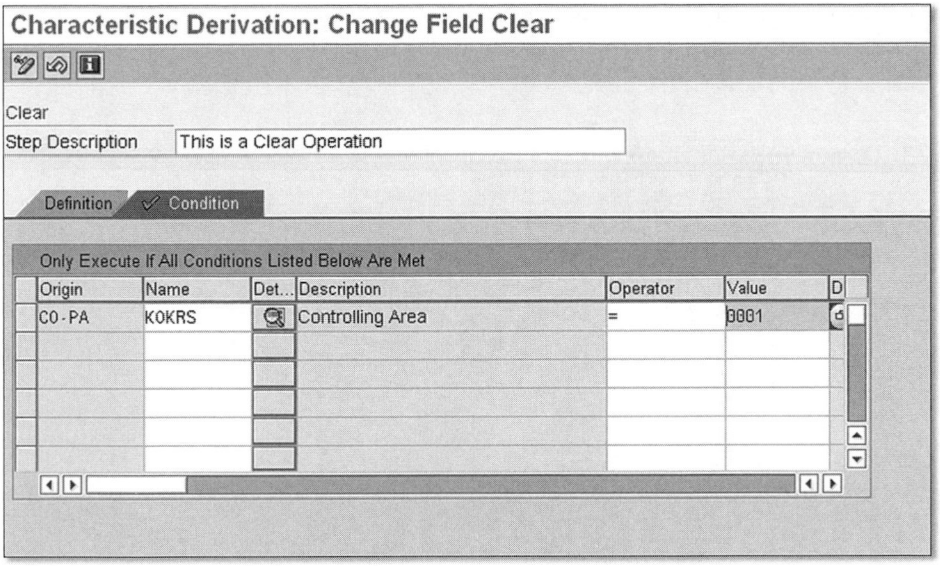

Figure 5.33 Configuring the Condition Tab Screen for the Clear Step

Finally, you can also define your own step using the enhancement functionality. Enhancements are user-defined ABAP programs that interact with SAP tables to generate more sophisticated procedures.

> **Note**
>
> As we've said before, avoid using ABAP as much as you can. ABAP is not a Best Practice because it requires modification of objects that can be highly sensitive and might be affected after an upgrade.

Creating an Enhancement Step

You can use Component 003 of customer enhancement COPA0001 to define your own derivation logic. This enhancement can be inserted anywhere in the derivation strategy, even in more than one place. Note, however, that increasing the complexity of your analysis will also increase the performance requirements of your system. So it's better to use many small steps to complete a sophisticated task rather than generating a few enhancement steps.

As shown in Figure 5.34, an enhancement step using component COPA0001 is being created. Notice that there are multiple Source Fields and multiple Target Fields on the Definition tab.

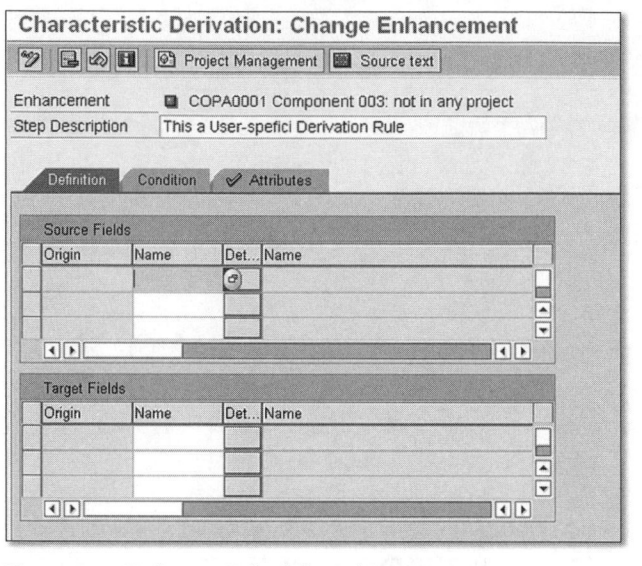

Figure 5.34 Definition Tab of the Enhancement Step

As you can see in Figure 5.35, you can generate multiple conditions on the Condition tab to determine when the Definition tab options should be executed.

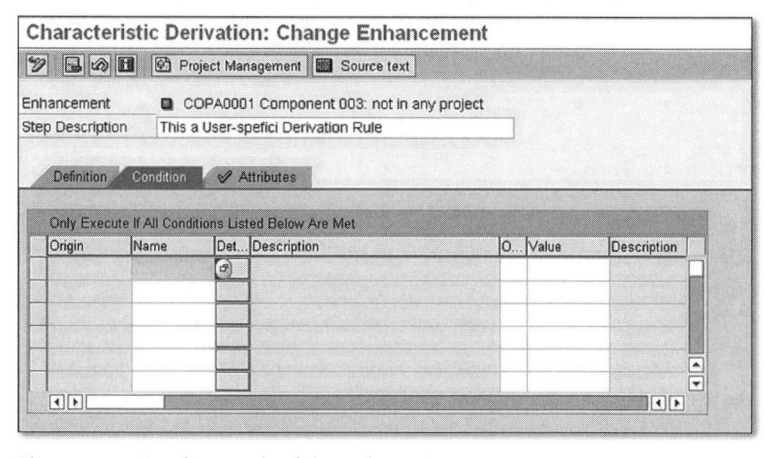

Figure 5.35 Condition Tab of the Enhancement Step

Finally, the ATTRIBUTES tab shown in Figure 5.36 provides an option to issue an error in case of any problem, as is standard for all step types. You can also click on SOURCE TEXT to enter ABAP code via the FUNCTION BUILDER that opens, as shown in Figure 5.37.

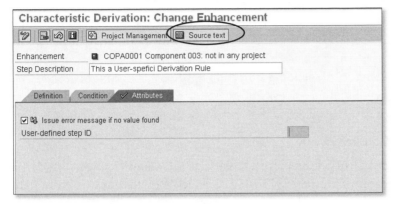

Figure 5.36 Attributes Tab and Source Text Button of the Enhancement Step

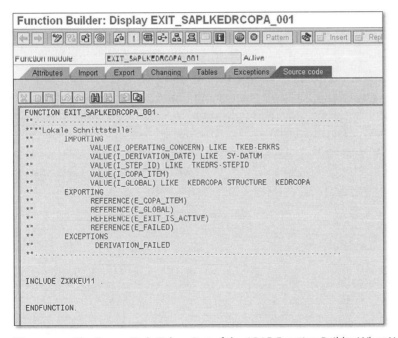

Figure 5.37 The Source Code Tab as Part of the ABAP Function Builder When Using the Enhancement Step

There's one more type of derivation step, called *customer hierarchy*. However, this step is only available if you are using customer hierarchy characteristics in the data structures of an operating concern. For this, you need to create a customer hierarchy step as part of derivation strategy to be able to identify each level of the hierarchy independently.

In the next section, we'll explore the concept of valuation and how this technique works similar to derivation but is more oriented toward automatic calculations inside CO-PA, based on reference data. Valuation applies if you want to generate more complex scenarios depending on product, price, costs, and material structures associated with volume, sales, and revenue.

5.2.4 Valuation in CO-PA

In this section, we'll briefly explore the concept of *valuation*. Valuation is the automatic calculation of values following specific rules for both planning and actual data, but in a costing-based CO-PA environment only. The concept of valuation can be useful for environments with multiple lines of products and materials whose costs and prices are calculated differently depending on the relationship. The alternative to valuation—highly complex relationships in SAP Net-Weaver BW or SAP NetWeaver BI, Business Planning and Simulation (BPS), and ABAP itself—is simply too difficult to manage.

Therefore, for large organizations, it's more advisable to use CO-PA valuation rather than generating a customized application to generate similar processes using ABAP, BPS, Operational Data Source (ODS), Business Explorer (BEx), and other components of the SAP NetWeaver BI application. You can, however, consider the valuation functionality in CO-PA as a component that can later on be used to extract data into SAP NetWeaver BI to generate reports. The transformation processes and relationships, however, are best executed, created, and modified with the valuation menus within the SAP ERP ECC 6.0 environment in a costing-based environment.

> **Note**
>
> Because valuation is such a sophisticated topic, we'll only be able to touch the tip of the iceberg of information available about valuation in this section. You can refer to the book *Actual Costing with the SAP Material Ledger* (SAP PRESS, 2011) as reference.

See material Ledger.

It's quite common to see calculation procedures such as:

▶ The value of marketing commissions is 10% of total sales value or research.

▶ The development budget is 5% of the total net revenue.

These types of relationships can be established by using the Valuation menus in costing-based Profitability Analysis to create values that currently don't exist in the SAP ERP ECC 6.0 platform or require further customization. Note, however, that the usage of valuation can significantly increase processing times, reducing system performance and the speed of different transactions inside SAP ERP ECC 6.0.

The concept of valuation in CO-PA is shown in a simplified manner in Figure 5.38. Using input information from the Sales and Distribution (SD) component, there are three main value fields that we're interested in using as reference for further calculations: QUANTITY, REVENUE, and DISCOUNTS.

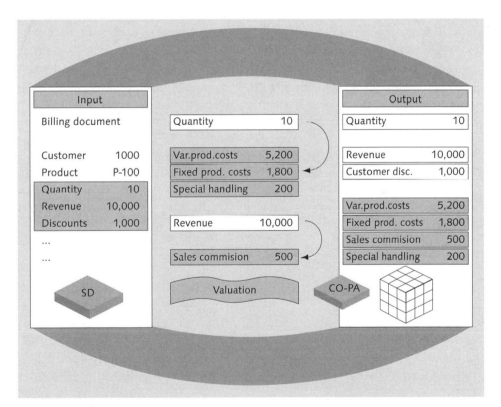

Figure 5.38 Valuation Concept in CO-PA

> **Note**
>
> SAP recommends using different value fields for actual and standard costs calculations in order to provide different levels of detail of information, and to avoid the situation that a calculation stored in a single value field cannot be explained later on because it is stored in a single value field.

With the information in these value fields, we can use valuation to generate costs and expenses associated with the values of each of them. For example, the QUANTITY value generates VAR. PROD. COSTS, FIXED PROD. COSTS, and SPECIAL HANDLING; and the REVENUE value generates the SALES COMMISSION. Once the information has been generated, using different valuation strategies outlined in more detail later in the Valuation Strategies section at the end of this section, the new values can be stored in CO-PA and used for reporting or planning purposes.

As you can see previously in Figure 5.36, when CO-PA storage is performed, it affects the profitability segments of the operating concern. From an accounting point of view, valuation can only be implemented using costing-based CO-PA because of reconciliation purposes for both planning and actual data. In addition, you can valuate or revaluate business transactions before their values are posted, once they have been posted, or after they have been posted when performing periodical updates.

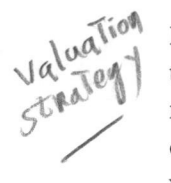

Linked with the concept of valuation is the concept of a *valuation strategy*. A valuation strategy is the final link between the valuation methods and the assignment of those methods to specific quantity or value fields coming from the operating concern. Valuation strategies are useful to combine sophisticated valuation scenarios that use material cost estimates, conditions, and costing sheets.

A valuation strategy has the following elements:

▶ **Point of valuation (PV)**
How and how often the data is updated.

▶ **Record type**
Specifies the type of document that will be updated, such as incoming sales order (A), direct postings from FI (B), order/project settlements (C), and billing data (F), among others. Discussion of these documents goes beyond the scope

of this book; to learn about their characteristics, you should review additional resources, such as *http://sdn.sap.com* and *http://help.sap.com*.

► **Plan version** (if applicable)
Describes different types of scenarios for the data.

You can define a valuation strategy in relation to the PV, the record type, and the plan version (if applicable). You specify which of the valuation methods in the valuation strategy—valuation using material cost estimates, valuation using conditions and costing sheets, or user exit valuation—to use to fill the value fields and in which order these methods are implemented.

Let's continue on to the next section and explore the concept of valuation strategies as a useful way to derive new records or value calculations based on relationships between master data and characteristics stored in your operating concern.

5.3   Working with Valuation Methods

There are multiple ways to generate new sets of data within CO-PA by deriving the relationships between master data and characteristics. CO-PA provides you with the flexibility to either implement pre-delivered functionality or use an ABAP program that will generate the new values. Let's look at four methods in more detail:

► **Valuation using material cost estimate**
You can use material cost estimates from Product Cost Controlling (CO-PC) to determine the cost of goods manufactured in Profitability Analysis. The breakdown of these costs in CO-PC is usually more detailed than that required in CO-PA. Consequently, you can assign more than one cost component to the same value field in CO-PA.

Other than the standard cost estimate, the periodic allocation prices or actual cost estimates from the material ledger can also be used for valuation. This is particularly useful for period revaluation.

► **Valuation using conditions and costing sheets**
This method is useful when you need certain data to evaluate a sale but don't yet know the actual values. This makes it possible to calculate such things as sales commission, discounts, cash discounts, or freight costs. You calculate these values by defining conditions, which are stored and processed in a costing

sheet. Conditions can be scaled and made dependent on certain characteristic values. To valuate actual data, you need to define special conditions in CO-PA. For planning data, you can also access conditions from Sales and Distribution (SD) directly.

▶ **User exit valuation**
If your requirements for valuation go beyond the techniques supported in the standard SAP system, you can program your own valuation routines.

▶ **Valuation with transfer prices**
Valuation using transfer prices is only possible for plan data. For detailed information about transfer prices and multiple valuation approaches in the SAP system, review the information available at *http://help.sap.com* associated with profit center accounting.

From the design of a complex product pricing strategy, to calculation of sophisticated transfer pricing and commissions, cost-of-sales accounting, information on units sold and discount calculation, and others, CO-PA valuation can be a complex process. While it can be achieved using any one of the four methods we described, we'll concentrate on two primary methods: valuation using material cost estimates and valuation using conditions and costing sheets. Detail on the other two methods is beyond the scope of this book—due to their complexity, it probably requires a single book for each of them. User exit valuation is a custom-based method using ABAP custom exit programs, and for this you require the assistance of an ABAP developer. In addition, performing valuation with transfer prices not only depends on the valuation method to analyze external sales, but also on how the cost of goods manufactured is calculated either from a legal or company group standpoint.

The concept of transfer prices is applicable to organizations that want to handle profit centers as independently operating companies, but need to be able to see internal sales between profit centers (exchanges of goods, goods issues, stock transfers, and so on) as well as external sales in order to analyze their profit centers correctly in this environment. Moreover, it may be necessary to valuate both internal and external sales from the viewpoint of the individual profit centers (costs of goods manufactured on the basis of transfer prices) in addition to the legal viewpoint. This process requires a combination of SD, FI, and CO team involvement, and the concept of transfer prices requires a book of its own.

5.3.1 Working with Material Cost Estimates

A material cost estimate is an approximate value for a set of parameters to perform valuation using estimates of the data stored to support the cost of goods manufactured calculations and decision making. For example, in the sales system, a line item is posted with product code 4711 with two units of quantity, and a material cost estimate will link the cost of the product (100 USD) with the number of units billed. In this particular case, we'll be able to generate an automatic calculation of the cost of the material of 100 USD × 2 units = 200 USD.

In this section, we'll discuss the SET UP VALUATION USING MATERIAL COST ESTIMATE menu. Figure 5.39 shows the different submenus available in this menu.

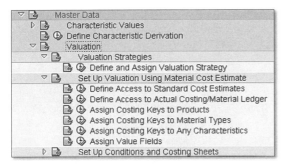

Figure 5.39 Review of the Valuation and Material Cost Estimate Menus

Material cost estimates are quite useful, especially when calculating the cost of goods manufactured or to specifically extract information using a set of parameters that control the behavior and determine the data to be read called *costing keys*. Notice in Figure 5.39 that you can assign costing keys to product, material type, and characteristics, and it is possible, for example, to access "the cost values for only product AB or only the costs for product type HEAVY MATERIAL" to valuate your data. So, with this function, you determine which cost estimates from product cost planning should be used to valuate actual or planning data in CO-PA.

Here, we'll help you understand how to utilize and understand the logic behind the various menu options.

Now, let's explore the steps to create and define material cost estimates:

1. First, define the costing keys. To do so, select the DEFINE ACCESS TO STANDARD COST ESTIMATES object, shown in Figure 5.39. Figure 5.40 shows the CHANGE VIEW "COSTING KEY": OVERVIEW screen that appears.

2. Click on the NEW ENTRIES button.

3. Enter "This is a Costing Key" in the NAME column, and specify a CSTG KEY value of "1," as shown in Figure 5.40.

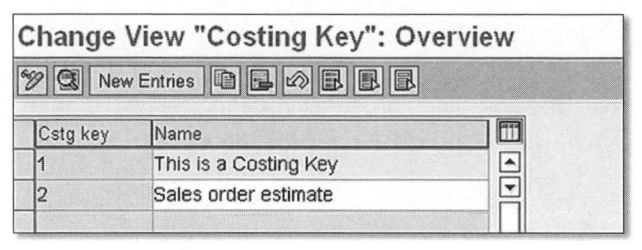

Change View "Costing Key": Overview

Cstg key	Name
1	This is a Costing Key
2	Sales order estimate

Figure 5.40 Creating a New Costing Key

4. Double-click on THIS IS A COSTING KEY to access the screen shown in Figure 5.41.

This screen contains a large number of configuration options for the costing key. The main component is the first area called DETERMINE MATERIAL COST ESTIMATE, which has two options based on CO-PC: TRANSF. STANDARD COST ESTIMATE and TRANSFER SALES ORDER COST ESTIMATE. The first option requires you to define where the system will find the material cost estimate. With the second option, the system uses the cost estimate information stored in the sales order item (already created), thus simplifying the selection.

[handwritten note: He seems to say you use the sales order estimate ↗]

> **Tips & Tricks**
>
> You can only transfer a sales order cost estimate to CO-PA if it was created using material costing. Unit cost estimates cannot be transferred to CO-PA.

5. Review the remaining information presented in Figure 5.39, and then click on the SAVE icon. Remember, you must correctly follow the specifications created in the Product Costing component (CO-PC) to configure how the costing keys are based on the options available in the Product Cost Planning menus.

[handwritten note: material ledger]

When your sales quantities in CO-PA are valuated using periodic allocation prices or actual cost estimates from the material ledger, which typically occurs at the period end during revaluation, another type of costing key needs to be configured using the DEFINE ACCESS TO ACTUAL COSTING/MATERIAL LEDGER option in the IMG path PROFITABILITY ANALYSIS • MASTER DATA • VALUATION • SET UP VALUATION USING MATERIAL COST ESTIMATE, shown earlier in Figure 5.39.

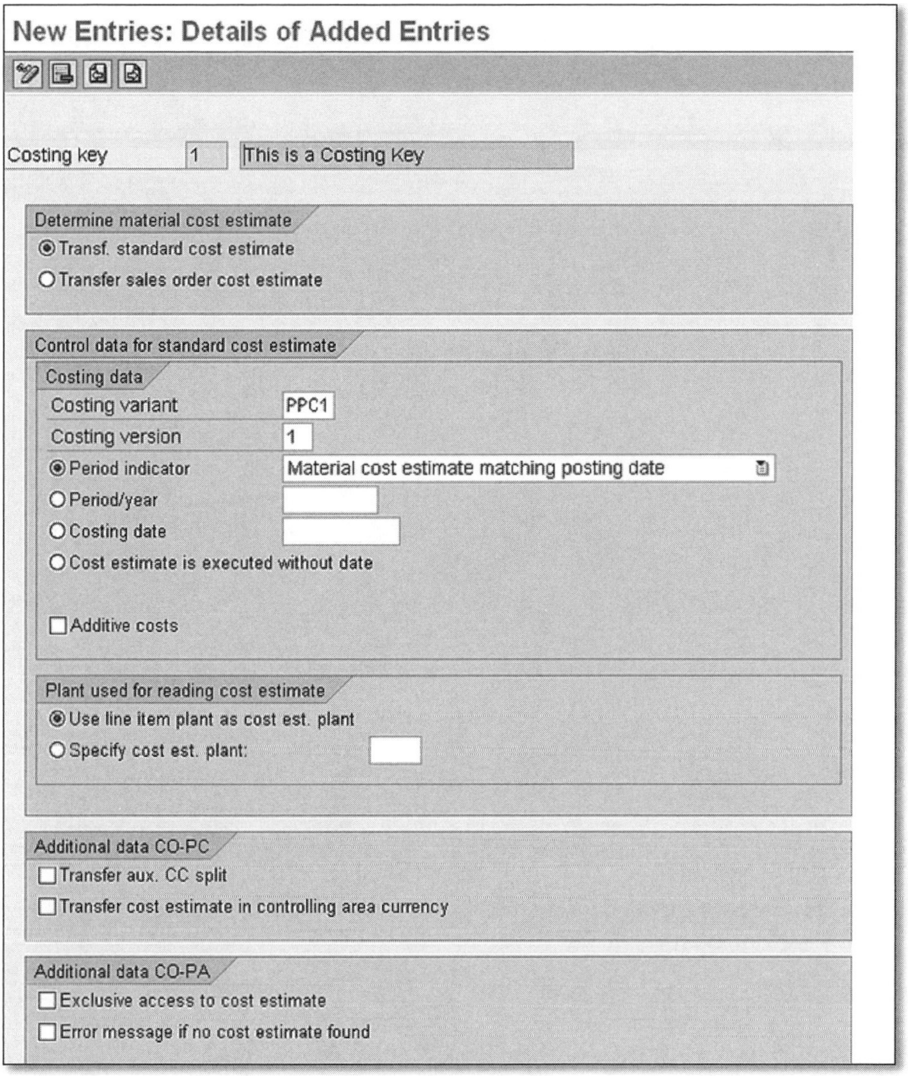

New Entries: Details of Added Entries

Costing key   [1]   This is a Costing Key

Determine material cost estimate
- ⦿ Transf. standard cost estimate
- ○ Transfer sales order cost estimate

Control data for standard cost estimate

Costing data

Costing variant	PPC1
Costing version	1

- ⦿ Period indicator   Material cost estimate matching posting date
- ○ Period/year
- ○ Costing date
- ○ Cost estimate is executed without date

☐ Additive costs

Plant used for reading cost estimate
- ⦿ Use line item plant as cost est. plant
- ○ Specify cost est. plant:

Additional data CO-PC
- ☐ Transfer aux. CC split
- ☐ Transfer cost estimate in controlling area currency

Additional data CO-PA
- ☐ Exclusive access to cost estimate
- ☐ Error message if no cost estimate found

Figure 5.41 Configuring a Costing Key

This takes you to the screen shown in Figure 5.42, where you can specify the system to periodically update the information coming from the CO-PC component. You use the VALU. FLD ALLOCATION FOR PERIODIC MOVING AVERAGE PRICE option to calculate the value assigned to a value field inside the operating concern for a time reference, in this case 001/2009.

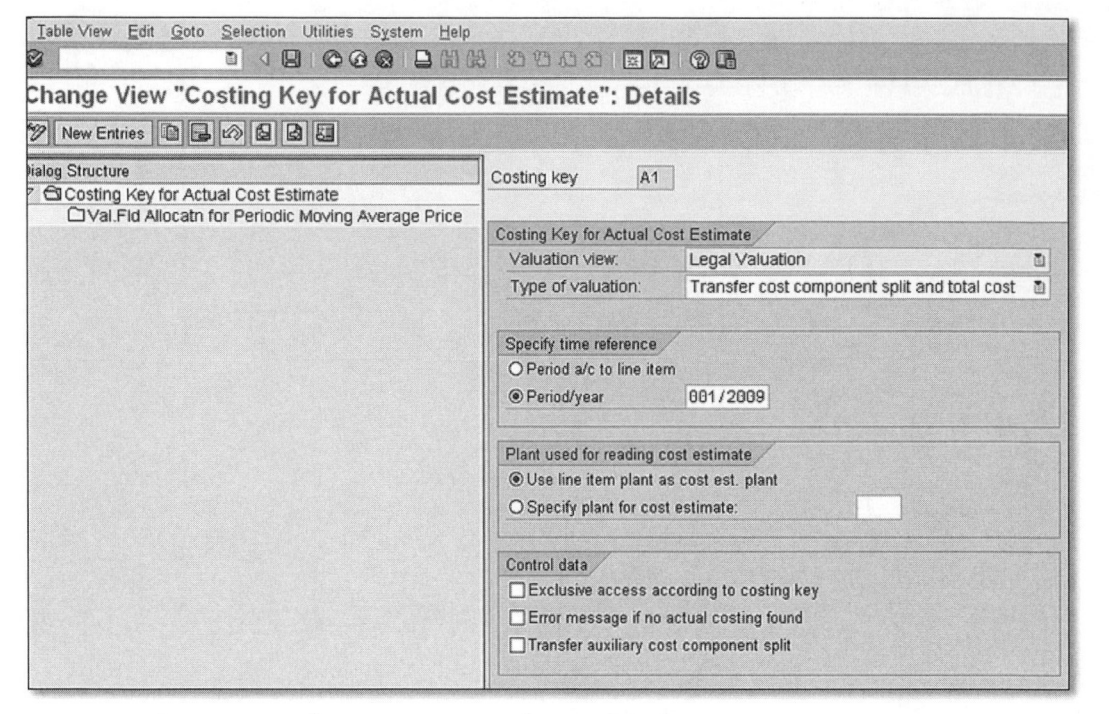

Figure 5.42 Configuring a Costing Key for Actual Cost Estimate

This type of allocation can be transferred depending on the type of valuation:

▸ The complete detail information and totals (transfer cost component split and total cost)

▸ Either total detail or totals, depending on what's available (transfer cost component split or total cost)

▸ Only the total cost

What this does is access the information configured inside CO-PC in the ACTUAL COSTING/MATERIAL LEDGER menus, as shown in Figure 5.43. In other words, we're trying to extract data from CO-PC and use it in CO-PA.

Once you've configured the costing keys information and decided which rules control the data extraction of the different materials from CO-PC, it's time to assign them to our operating concern.

Tips & Tricks

The system applies the costing keys as long as valuation is active, evaluates the information, and transfers the values as configured.

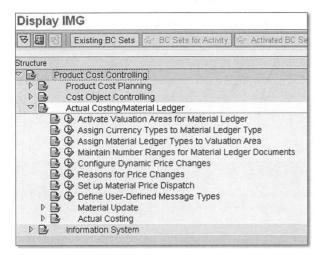

Figure 5.43 Origin of the Data Extracted Using the Costing Keys with the Material Ledger

As shown earlier in Figure 5.37, four types of assignments can be made using the newly configured costing keys:

▶ ASSIGN COSTING KEYS TO PRODUCTS

▶ ASSIGN COSTING KEYS TO MATERIAL TYPES

▶ ASSIGN COSTING KEYS TO ANY CHARACTERISTICS

▶ ASSIGN VALUE FIELDS

You can assign a maximum of three costing keys to control the behavior of products and materials. All of the costing key assignments available in CO-PA valuation require a standard definition of parameters:

▶ **PV:** Controls how the actual data information will be transferred—real time, periodic, manual, or automatic.

▶ **Record Type (RecT):** Defines what kind of information will be transferred—incoming sales order, direct postings from FI, order/project settlements, single trans. costing, billing data, and order-related project.

▸ **Plan Version:** Standard requirement to determine the scenario.

▸ **Assignment:** Material, product, or characteristic.

▸ **Validity:** Determines the validity period during which costing keys apply to a particular object.

[handwritten: See Vish' material son this approach]

The components ASSIGN COSTING KEYS TO ANY CHARACTERISTICS and ASSIGN VALUE FIELDS require additional configuration settings. In cases where the product-dependent or material-dependent call up of material cost estimates in product cost accounting is not flexible enough to meet your requirements, you can determine the costing keys using your own strategy for the "flexible assignment of costing keys" using user-defined tables, table lookups, and customer enhancements.

> **Note**
>
> We won't discuss these flexible assignments in more detail because they're similar to those reviewed in the section on characteristic derivation and derivation steps.

[handwritten: Cost component structure]

Note, however, that for ASSIGN VALUE FIELDS, an additional parameter called a *cost component structure* is required, which comes from CO-PC. In CO-PC, the cost component structure determines how the results of material costing are updated. The cost component structure groups the costs for each material according to cost component (such as material costs, internal activities, external activities, and overhead). If the material is used in the production of another material, the cost component split (which breaks down the costs according to material costs, internal activities, external activities, overhead, and so forth) remains in the system when the costs are rolled up.

As shown in Figure 5.44, it's possible to determine whether some value fields in the operating concern store cost component structures, such as raw materials, overhead, energy, and fixed or variable costs. The F/V column shows whether the cost component is fixed (F) or variable (V).

The concept of material cost estimates is a key strategic and operational challenge by itself, and it requires a high level of organization and is highly company-specific. It's recommended to maintain a clear definition and control of the costing keys because they can dramatically affect the profitability decisions over a product or material, especially if three costing keys control the final output of the cost associated. Also, remember that the functionality of valuation must be activated

[handwritten: → Design considerations. This is not perfunctory config set up.]

in both the CO-PC and CO-PA components so that these processes can be executed successfully.

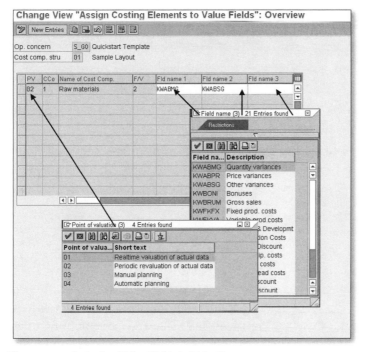

Figure 5.44 Assigning Value Fields in Valuation

Next, let's take a look at working with conditions and costing sheets.

5.3.2 Working with Conditions and Costing Sheets

The conditions technique in CO-PA lets you calculate fictitious values that are needed in CO-PA for analyzing contribution margins but aren't known at the time the original document is posted. In particular, this makes it possible to calculate sales commissions, cash discounts, other discounts, or freight costs for a sales document that is not yet posted or its complete information is not yet available. This function is useful for planning or estimating future cash flows or profitability by customer or other types of analysis.

Conditions are used to calculate values that are based on any number of criteria (such as the quantity sold, the product sold, or the customer who bought the

Amts not known at Time of original posting.

product), and you can define CO-PA-specific costing sheets for valuating data in CO-PA. You do this using the same basic functions as those for defining pricing procedures in SD.

Before we start working with a condition table, follow this high-level sequence of steps as reference:

1. Identify the line items' characteristics and value fields you want to use for valuation.

2. Define a condition table to select the characteristics, the criteria to generate the valuation, and the validity periods for these rules.

3. Create the condition types and costing sheets to control the rules controlling different calculation procedures, such as prices, surcharge or reduction, base condition type, cash discount from customer master, and other condition types.

4. Define the access sequences that control the relationship between the condition table and the value fields that will store the data.

5. Use pricing reports to define the screen layout for analyzing condition records according to different criteria. However, because they are basically ABAP programs, we won't discuss pricing reports here. However, it's possible to access pricing reports in the Customizing menu for Sales and Distributions using Transaction V/LA, and it's recommended to use this functionality unless the predefined reports aren't able to deliver the required needs. In addition, the options used in valuation can be accessed in the planning framework to affect the values of your planning and actual data using a standard layout.

We'll now review the concepts behind performing valuation using costing sheets and conditions in more detail. First, Figure 5.45 shows the different menu items available in the SET UP CONDITIONS AND COSTING SHEETS menu. You'll recognize several of the menu items from the previous list.

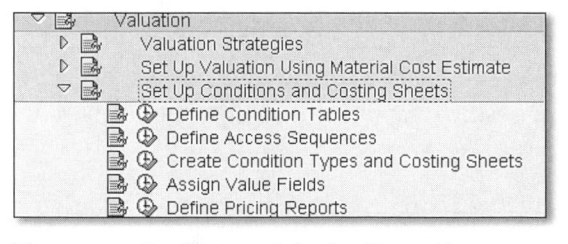

Figure 5.45 Conditions and Costing Sheets Menu

Defining Condition Tables

Condition records in CO-PA are stored in CO-PA-specific *condition tables* whose key consists of specific combinations of characteristic values. Each condition table represents a different combination of characteristics and can be used by any number of conditions. (Different conditions may depend on the same characteristics in the same system, such as customer and product.)

The key of the condition table consists of those characteristics that make up the key of the condition record. You can use all of the characteristics in Profitability Analysis—in all operating concerns—in the keys for condition tables. Thus if you have, for example, two different characteristics that have the same text in different operating concerns, both of these characteristics appear in the field catalog. The fact that they have the same text suggests that a double entry exists.

You should only use characteristics from the same operating concern in a condition table. You can use the FIELD ATTRIBUTES function to display the corresponding data element for a characteristic in the field catalog. By comparing this data element with the data element stored in table CE1xxxx (xxxx = operating concern) for that characteristic, you can see which operating concern the field belongs to.

To create a condition table, proceed as follows:

1. Specify a number between 501 and 999.
2. Enter a name for the condition table and double-click on the characteristics you want to use for the key.
3. Generate the table.

If desired, you can limit the period of validity of the condition table. If you do, all of the condition records in this table are stored with this period of validity. The table must be a *transparent table* (table type "T").

Follow these steps to define a condition table:

1. As was shown in Figure 5.43, click on the DEFINE CONDITION TABLES option. Type the value between 501 and 999 for the table number.
2. Select CONDITION • CREATE from the menu and press ⟨Enter⟩ to access the screen shown in Figure 5.46.

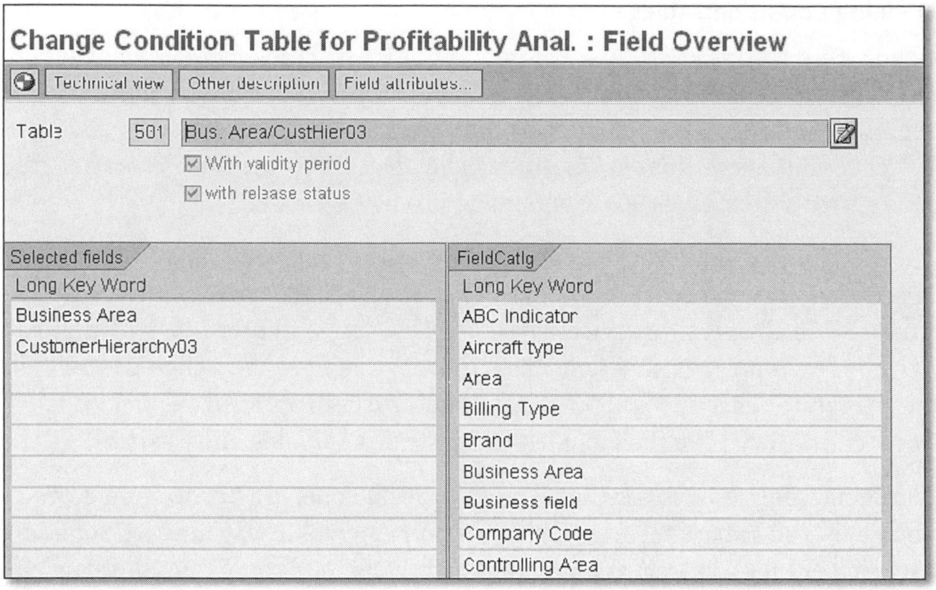

Figure 5.46 Creating a Condition Table

In this screen, you can select the fields on the right and move them to the left using drag and drop. The end result is shown with BUSINESS AREA and CUSTOMERHIERARCHY03.

3. When you're finished, click on the GENERATE icon (the circle split in quarters) or press Shift + F4.

4. The system asks you to confirm whether you want to generate the condition table. Click on the YES button to confirm and configure the required customization request to generate the object or create it as a local object.

5. Finally, the system confirms that Axxx table was generated (where the xxx is the table number), and that the reports and screens are marked for generation and activated.

Next, we'll look at access sequences, which are components required to execute condition tables.

Tips & Tricks

Condition tables can only be accessed by the SD application type "V."

Defining Access Sequences

In this step, you define *access sequences* for your condition types in CO-PA. You must assign an access sequence to each condition type for which you create condition records. The access sequence determines the condition tables in which the system should search for valid condition records for the condition type. Thus the access sequence is a sort of directory that tells the system where condition records for that condition type are stored.

To create an access sequence, do the following:

1. Access the path PROFITABILITY ANALYSIS • MASTER DATA • VALUATION • SET UP CONDITIONS AND COSTING SHEETS • DEFINE ACCESS SEQUENCES, and click on the EXECUTE icon.

2. The screen shown in Figure 5.47 appears. Click on the change/modify icon, and enter the name "Z112" and a short description of "This is an Access Sequence" for the sequence.

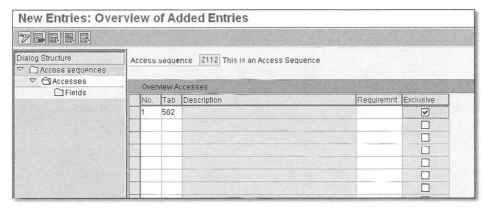

Figure 5.47 Defining an Access Sequence

3. In the TAB column, specify which condition tables to use to access condition records, and in the No. column, specify the order in which these condition tables should be read. For example, in Figure 5.47, condition table 502 will be the first condition table to be read in ACCESS SEQUENCE Z112, as indicated by the entry 1 in the No. column.

4. On the left-hand side of the screen, select ACCESSES, and specify the field contents (characteristics) with which they are read.

5. Click on the SAVE icon to save your access sequence.

In our example, the access sequence Z112 looks for condition records that exist for a certain combination specified in the condition table. If no records are found, the system then looks for a data record for the next condition table, if any, defined in the sequence of events shown in Figure 5.47.

In the following section, let's look at how to define condition types.

Defining Condition Types

If you access the IMG path VALUATION • SET UP CONDITION AND COSTING SHEETS • CREATE CONDITION TYPES AND COSTING SHEETS, you'll see the information shown in Figure 5.48. There are two areas on the left side:

▶ CONDITION TYPES
Defined in the upper left area, used to generate the calculations of values for prices, surcharges, cash discounts, and others based on different criteria.

▶ COSTING SHEETS
Defined in the lower left area, are part of the pricing procedures that are used to generate values based on different levels to generate totals.

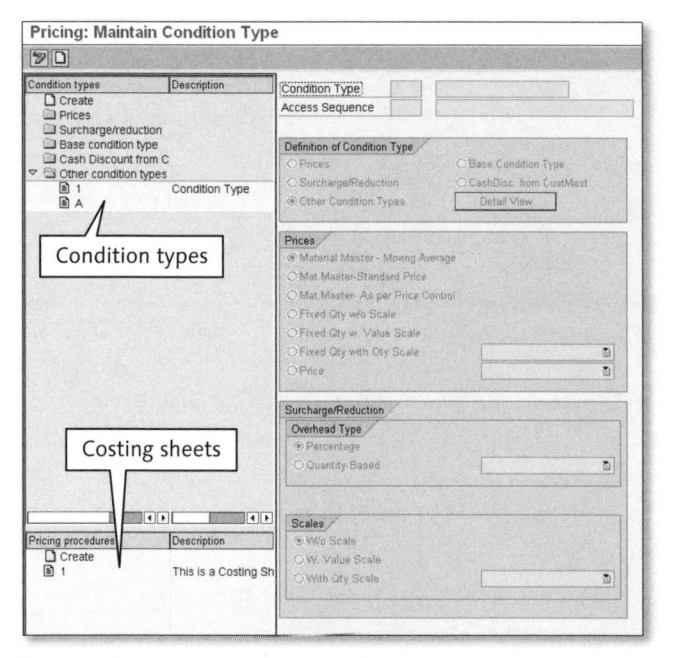

Figure 5.48 Maintaining Condition Types

When working with condition types, you must specify the access sequences in the upper left area that need to be used for the system to find the required characteristics that limit the data extraction to generate the new values. For example, you can generate a condition type that controls the price calculation based on the information coming from MM using moving average based on customer group and material type from the access sequence.

Furthermore, when creating a condition type, you can define the OVERHEAD TYPE as a PERCENTAGE or a QUANTITY-BASED field assigned to specific value fields that will be filled out.

Defining Costing Sheets

To access costing sheets, follow this path: PROFITABILITY ANALYSIS • MASTER DATA • VALUATION • SET UP CONDITIONS AND COSTING SHEETS • CREATE CONDITION TYPES AND COSTING SHEETS. As mentioned previously, to generate costing sheets you must use the lower left area shown in Figure 5.48:

1. Click on the CREATE icon to start the process of generating a pricing procedure associated with the costing sheet.
2. As shown in Figure 5.49, enter "1" as the name for the pricing procedure, and "This is a Costing Sheet" as its description.

   The pricing procedure requires that you specify information in six columns:

   ▶ STEP: Determines the number the step is processed in the condition sequence.

   ▶ CENTR: Condition counter that accesses the step in the pricing procedure.

   ▶ CTYP: The condition type is used for different functions. In pricing, for example, the condition type lets you differentiate between different kinds of discount; in output determination, between different output types, such as order confirmation or delivery note; in batch determination, between different strategy types.

   ▶ FROM: Value of which is the basis for percentage surcharges.

   ▶ TO: Condition step up to which the condition values of the previous steps are totaled. Percentage surcharges are calculated on the basis of the total.

   ▶ DESCRIPTION: Lets you provide a description for the process executed in the step.
3. Save your work by clicking on the SAVE icon.

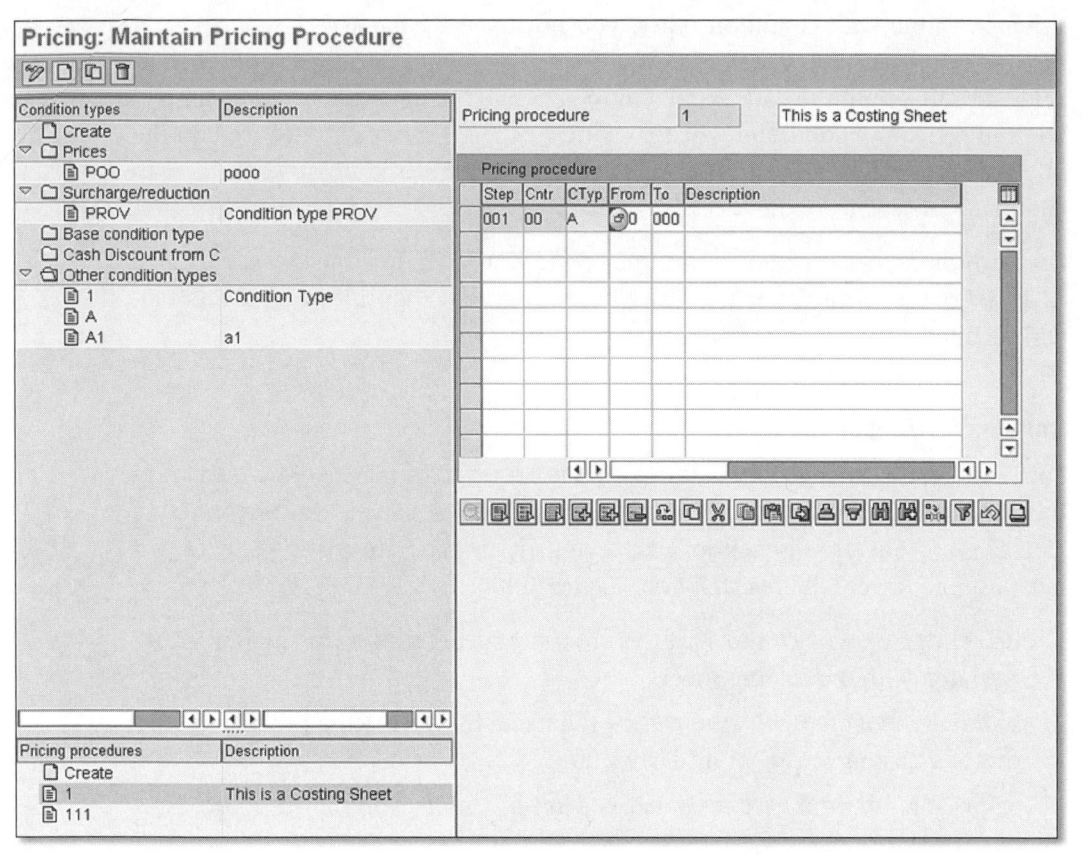

Figure 5.49 Maintain Pricing Procedure Screen

The anticipated costs generated with a costing sheet can be used later in the creation of a valuation strategy (to be discussed later in this chapter). In summary, a costing sheet establishes the link between the different condition types and allows and generates different types of data in a predefined sequence of events. For example, first we can calculate surcharge reductions and cash discounts, then generate the new price considering the previous two components for the selected line items.

The next step is to determine which value fields are affected by the different access sequences, condition types, and costing sheets.

5.3.3 Assigning Condition Types to CO-PA Value Fields

You are now done configuring rules and criteria and ready to assign all of the procedures or conditions developed in the previous sections to the value fields that they are supposed to modify.

> **Note**
>
> Remember, CO-PA value fields are directly associated with the operating concern that contains them. Thus, make sure that you have the correct operation concern set up as current in your system to avoid affecting the incorrect data sets with conditions, access sequences, and other elements.
>
> Also, remember that all of these configuration settings make the calculation automatic, and unless you are aware that a value field is affected by a predefined number of conditions, values, and calculations, it isn't that easy to see or realize. Recall that we're trying to valuate using conditions and costing sheets, meaning that all of the information is not yet posted or not available in the SAP ERP ECC 6.0 system to make the decisions. We're trying to provide a good estimate to make decisions accordingly.

In this IMG activity, you assign the CO-PA condition types you've defined to the corresponding value fields. This determines which condition types are used to value those value fields. For example, you can assign condition type DISC (discounts) to a value field VVPRD (price reduction). The field names are filled automatically. However, if two condition types are applied to the same value field, the values of the two conditions are generated and the displayed value is the sum of the two executed procedures. This is true even if the conditions come from different costing sheets in the valuation strategy.

To assign value fields, start out by using the IMG path PROFITABILITY ANALYSIS • MASTER DATA • VALUATION • SET UP CONDITIONS AND COSTING SHEETS • ASSIGN VALUE FIELDS to access the screen presented in Figure 5.50.

Notice that the assignment requires using a default operating concern, in this case TEST. You also need to assign a costing type and then select a value field (in the VALUE FLD column), as shown in Figure 5.50.

Notice that there is a name on the top of the window called APPLICATION: KE in the CONDITION TYPE window; this notation identifies all applications or components of Profitability Analysis within SAP ERP ECC 6.0. In valuation steps that use a costing sheet (conditions), the application ID determines which application the costing sheet being used comes from. The ID for costing sheets created in Profitability Analysis (actual and plan) is "KE;" the ID "V" is for costing sheets created in the SD. You can only use these costing sheets in planning in CO-PA, but if you want to use product costing or a user exit in a valuation step, do not enter a costing sheet for that step.

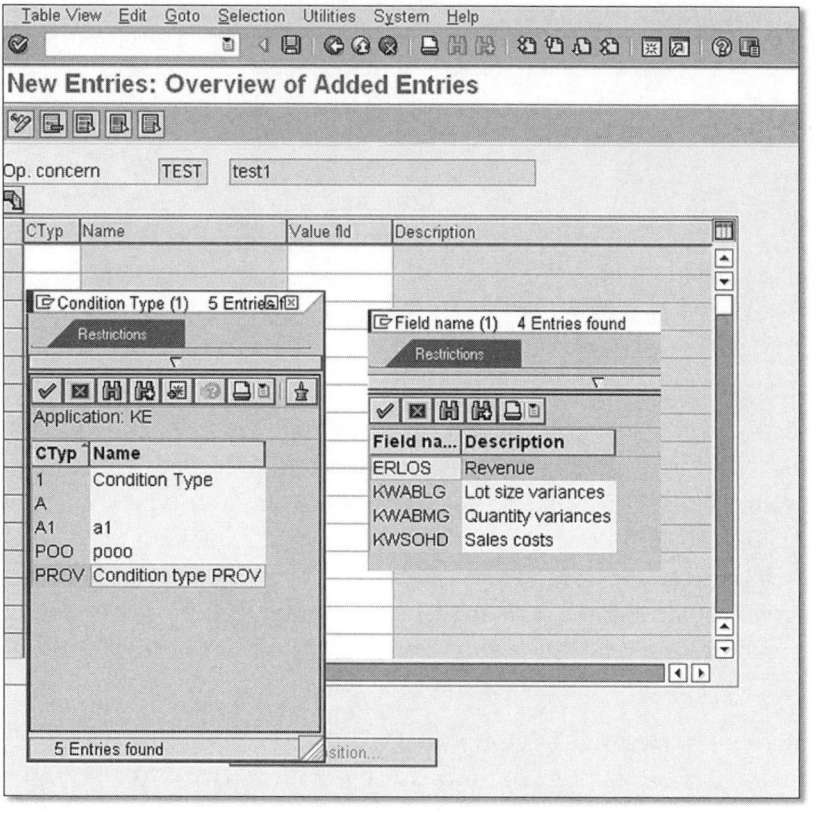

Figure 5.50 Overview of Added Entries Screen

By linking condition types and value fields, you complete the automatic calculation of the values that you want to estimate inside the SAP ERP ECC 6.0 platform. Also, remember that because the value fields are directly related to the contents of the operating concern, only those objects created or assigned to the operating concern are visible. For example, in the TEST operating concern, only the REVENUE, LOT SIZE VARIANCES, QUANTITY VARIANCES, and SALES COSTS are available for assignment, as shown in Figure 5.48.

Now you can assign the elements of cost component structure from CO-PC to the value fields inside your operating concern. Note that for each point of valuation, it's necessary to maintain value field assignments in CO-PA. With this, it's possible to divide the cost components into fixed and variable parts using as many as required (n:1), and then add them together in the value field.

When valuating multiple cost estimates simultaneously, the values of the cost components within the same cost estimate are aggregated and then entered in one CO-PA value field. The value fields with previous cost estimates are not changed by a later cost estimate. Therefore, a value has to be assigned in Customizing so that the values of different cost estimates are entered in different sets of value fields.

You can assign up to six different value fields from your operating concern to a cost component in the cost component structure. These value fields are identified as fields one through six. Finally, different value field assignments are important, especially when you are interested in applying multiple valuation using different cost estimates.

> **Tips & Tricks**
>
> Only six cost estimates can be transferred simultaneously from CO-PC to Profitability Analysis.

5.4 Valuation Strategies

We've now reviewed both the SET UP VALUATION USING MATERIAL COST ESTIMATE and SET UP CONDITIONS AND COSTING SHEETS options of the VALUATION menu in CO-PA. The question that arises, however, is what happens if you want to valuate your materials by combining information from both options for more sophisticated scenarios? For example, the process for calculating your contribution margin can use a number of elements such as conditions and costing sheets for cash discounts, valuation using material cost estimates for calculating material direct costs (and with a valuation strategy in relation to the point of valuation), the record type (such as F for billing documents, C for order settlements, and D for cost center allocations), and plan versions if applicable. Valuation in general can be used to calculate the following:

▶ Sales deductions that don't appear in the invoice, such as cash discounts, rebates, and commissions

▶ Costs of sales (sold products × standard costs of goods manufactured)

▶ Calculated direct costs, referred to as the special direct costs for sales (such as transportation costs, packaging, or insurance)

The answer lies in *valuation strategies.* Valuation strategies allow not only access to CO-PA application components KE, but also to SD elements using the V application that enable access to condition sheets defined in each environment. Note that this isn't allowed for valuation of actual data because there the SD conditions are transferred directly from the billing document or sales order as defined in the value field assignments of the SD interface. If you use an SD pricing procedure for valuation in planning, the system transfers the values of the conditions to the value fields as assigned in the SD interface.

Under certain circumstances, it may not be possible to use all conditions from SD to valuate data in CO-PA. For example, the access sequences used in the SD pricing procedures may contain condition tables with fields that aren't defined as CO-PA characteristics. Consequently, before using an SD pricing procedure, be sure to check whether the fields required by the access sequence are defined as characteristics in your operating concern. Otherwise, the system won't find the condition records, even if they have been maintained in SD.

A valuation strategy requires specifying either a costing sheet (or the appropriate application class), a material cost estimate, a user exit, or a transfer price variant together with the corresponding CO-PA value field.

To work with valuation strategies, follow these steps:

1. Access valuation strategies by following this path: PROFITABILITY ANALYSIS • MASTER DATA • VALUATION • VALUATION STRATEGIES • DEFINE AND ASSIGN VALUATION STRATEGY.

2. Click on the object's EXECUTE icon to see the screen displayed in Figure 5.51. You'll notice that there are several elements that are similar to those we've previously reviewed, such as SEQUENCE, APPL, COSTG SHEET, MAT. CSTG, and QTY FIELD. In the screen shown in Figure 5.51, you can access the costing sheets, quantity fields, and value fields in CO-PA (KE) or SD (V). In addition, a checkmark in the MAT. CSTG column informs you that you can perform valuation using a material cost estimate by defining a quantity field.

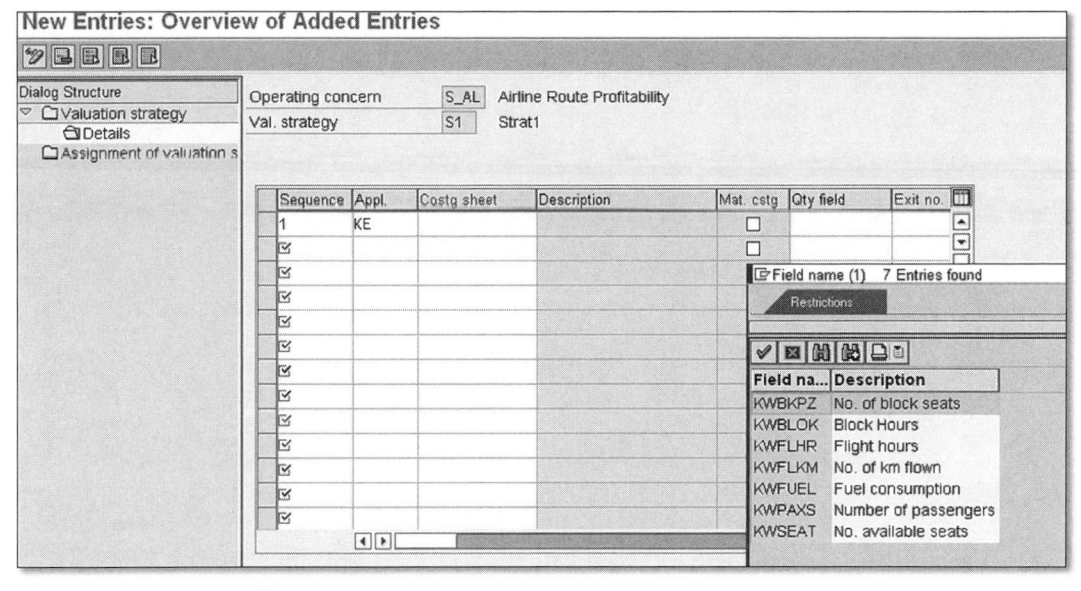

Figure 5.51 Creating a Valuation Strategy

3. Once you've finished configuring the information shown in Figure 5.51, select the next node called ASSIGNMENT OF VALUATION STRATEGY as shown in Figure 5.52.

   ASSIGNMENT OF VALUATION STRATEGY is where you decide the type of PV (method of update). All application functions that transfer data to CO-PA are assigned to one of these PVs. For external data transfers, PVs 01 and 03 are used for actual and plan data, respectively.

> **Tips & Tricks**
>
> In CO-PA there are four PVs: 01 real-time valuation of actual data, 02 periodic valuation of actual data, 03 manual planning, and 04 automatic planning.

4. Notice that there are four basic columns in Figure 5.52: PV for point of valuation, REC. for record type or document type, PLAN VER. for plan version to use in planning, and VAL. STRAT. to represent the valuation strategy to assign for the process. If a valuation strategy calls for valuation using material costing, the system uses the point of valuation to control which cost estimate is read and how the cost components are assigned to value fields in CO-PA.

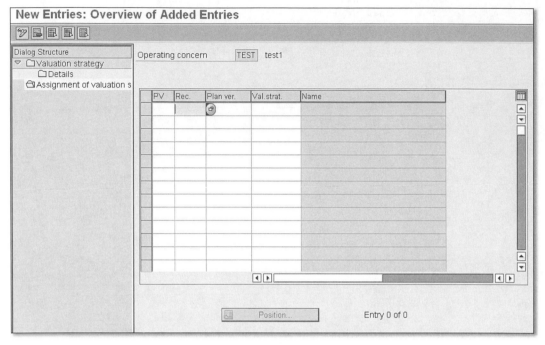

Figure 5.52 Assignment of Valuation Strategy

Tips & Tricks

The plan version enables you to keep two or more sets of data for the same object. You can maintain and evaluate several plan versions at the same time. For example, you can specify the type of assumption for the forecast (optimistic, pessimistic), when the plan was created (original plan, updated forecast), or how binding the plan is.

---

5. Determine the record type in the REC. column, shown in Figure 5.52. There are basically five kinds of record types or document types that CO-PA can affect:

▸ A: Incoming sales orders

▸ B: Direct posting from FI

▸ C: Order/project settlement

▸ E: Single transaction costing

▸ F: Billing data

6. In the PLAN VER. column, select a planning version to use.

7. Finally, select the VAL. STRAT. column to assign the valuation strategy that will affect the chosen record types and the previously selected quantity and value fields.

In addition, you can also create your own customizable CO-PA exits with ABAP programs using either the SAP standard enhancement (Transaction CMOD) or a special program. Moreover, there is an option called VARIANT FOR TP (Transfer Prices) in the screen shown in Figure 5.53, which you access by scrolling to the right in the screen shown in Figure 5.51. Both of these topics are outside the scope of this book, however, so you should review the online SAP information.

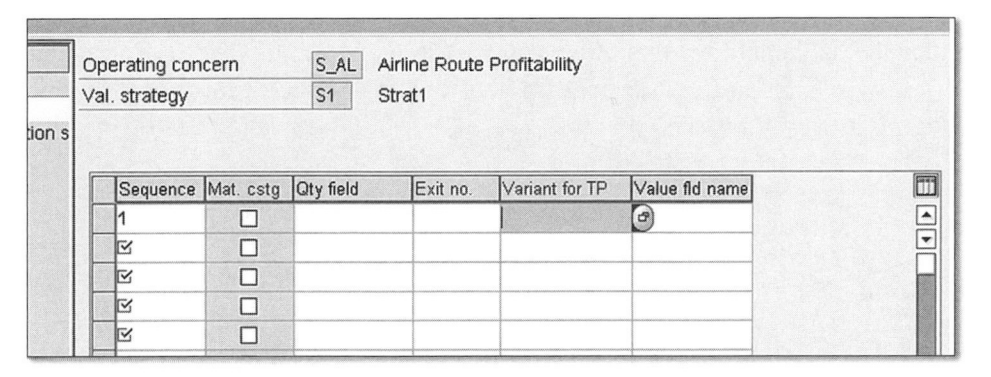

Figure 5.53 Reviewing the Variant for TP Column

> **Note**
>
> Valuation is the generation of different layers of information that are controlled by rules and restrictions. These predefined procedures are ABAP programs that give users flexibility without the need of coding.

To help us summarize the concept of valuation, the logic behind it is simplified in Figure 5.54 in a flow chart that describes each of the steps discussed in this section:

1. First, the ORIGINAL LINE ITEMS (RAW SAP DATA FROM SAP ERP ECC 6.0) are identified and it is determined how valuation would be applied.

2. Then, CONDITION TABLES are created to predefine the criteria to use to perform the valuation.

3. CONDITION TABLES are later on organized in a logic using access sequences that require CONDITION TYPES to define the table of valuation to perform.

4. COSTING SHEETS take the information from ACCESS SEQUENCES and CONDITION TYPES to control how the conditions are executed.

5. Both COSTING SHEETS and CONDITION TYPES can be assigned to control the information contained inside the predefined VALUE FIELDS or VALUATION STRATEGIES.

6. VALUATION STRATEGIES allow you to be more specific about the type of records (billing, sales order, posting from FI, etc.) that are affected by the different conditions specified.

7. VALUE FIELDS are the ultimate goal of assignment of valuation because they identify the fields that are affected by the different rules or conditions that affect the data and value estimation displayed on the user's screen.

8. Finally, all definitions that affect and are assigned to value fields are automatically executed in the user environment and their effects can be seen in line items as NEW GENERATED VALUES.

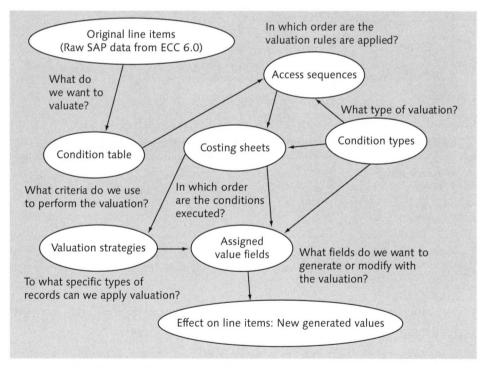

Figure 5.54 Flow Chart for the Concept of Valuation

A final note: valuation and derivation are quite powerful if used correctly; however, avoid using either of these methods if your project does not demand complex selection criteria and multiple relationships of variables. Also, for simpler requirements, some of the capabilities discussed in the MASTER DATA menu for CO-PA can be performed using the CO-PA planning framework, as we'll discuss next in Chapter 6. For complex implementations that require many relationships, valuation can, however, come in handy (as we said earlier, instead of creating and configuring different large number of objects in the SAP NetWeaver BW/SAP NetWeaver BI environment).

> **Note**
>
> As a Best Practice, we suggest avoiding the use of automatically calculated procedures that run in the background, such as costing keys, valuation, and derivation because it's difficult to identify original values from those that are generated. For this reason, we feel it is best to work with the CO-PA planning framework, which lets you control each component affecting your data. You can also review what went wrong in case you detect any errors that can be easily corrected using the same objects. We'll discuss this in more detail in the next chapter.

5.5   Summary

Master data can be used to improve the data manipulation inside CO-PA with automatic calculation procedures. In this chapter, we briefly reviewed how to create hierarchies for use in reporting and planning applications. We covered the creation of derivation rules to generate additional information that can be inferred based on the current data, and we reviewed the concepts of valuation and valuation strategies to generate automatic calculations for estimating the cost of goods sold. Note that the goal of this chapter was to provide you with an overview of the functionalities available in the MASTER DATA menu, but realize that this doesn't mean you need to use them all.

In Chapter 6, we'll explore the CO-PA planning framework, an application similar to SAP NetWeaver BI Integrated Planning (IP) and BPS.

The CO-PA planning framework is the environment that lets you create planning applications without leaving the R/3 or SAP ERP ECC 6.0 environment. CO-PA planning provides powerful functionalities similar to those provided by the Integrated Planning (IP) or the Business Planning and Simulation (BPS) tools in SAP NetWeaver Business Intelligence (BI)/ SAP NetWeaver Business Warehouse (BW).

6 Introduction to CO-PA Planning

In this chapter we'll review the CO-PA planning framework, which is the interface created with the OLTP environment for R/3 or SAP ERP ECC 6.0 to create planning applications. Like other SAP system components, the CO-PA planning framework uses a top-bottom approach to clearly define the data sets used as part of the planning application. We'll start our discussion by giving you an overview of the CO-PA planning framework.

> **Note**
>
> You might not need to implement or use any of the components described in this chapter due to the flexibilities that CO-PA provides to connect to other applications, such as SAP NetWeaver BI or SAP NetWeaver BW. Thus, you might only need to transfer a piece of Sales and Distribution (SD) information into CO-PA and then move that information into SAP NetWeaver BI to complete the planning by including Materials Management (MM) information.
>
> Whatever model your team has decided on to approach your planning needs, make sure that this model is written down on a piece of paper somewhere, your managers know about it, and that the financial reporting of your firm is protected.

6.1 Overview

Profitability planning is likely a part of any yearly activities for every corporation in the world. Depending on its size, a company must estimate, forecast, or develop scenarios for different areas. Profit and sales planning in CO-PA can also be extended to consider elements such as Materials Requirements Planning (MRP), capacity planning, and any other elements that you can extract information from in the OLTP system, and transfer it into CO-PA and other systems. However, oftentimes planning efforts toward quantification or estimation of possible expenses and revenues using data in the SAP system don't become clear until you're actually developing scenarios and sharing them with other people.

When working on a project, it's always good to concentrate on "discovering" the system the client requires first and then focusing on the details when the actual application needs to be created. In other words, you should simplify the requirements for decision makers, regardless of the complexity of the operations to perform.

> **Note**
>
> CO-PA planning might require you to combine information coming from different data sources from inside and outside SAP systems. Sometimes the best approach is to create an environment that even a young student with basic computer skills could use without major difficulty. However, engineers and scientists are often reluctant to simplify their knowledge into common explanations for laymen, so when collecting requirements, you need not only patience, but also to make sure you ask the right questions to collect the correct information.

Planning in Profitability Analysis allows you to plan sales, revenue, and profitability data for any selected profitability segments. You can display the entire planning process of your company in different ways, depending on your business demands, without leaving the SAP ERP ECC 6.0 environment. Some of the applications that can be developed within the CO-PA planning framework can be quite sophisticated and allow you to address the most common requirements without needing to use more complex applications, such as SAP NetWeaver BI Integrated Planning, SAP BW-BPS, SEM-BPS, or others.

You may recall from earlier discussions that CO-PA works and interacts with the OLTP environment (transactional) and the changes performed can be viewed by other users using the regular SAP screens. For example, you can perform adjustments to the purchase order information, run the required processes in the CO-PA planning framework, and the modifications will display on users' screens without them even noticing the processes performed to modify the data.

CO-PA is designed to use revenues and cost data to perform profit and sales planning to produce views that can be assigned to a particular user profile for different roles, such as sales manager, regional manager, sales employee, financial assistants, and others. Distinctions are also often made between the different approaches used, such as central top-down planning and local bottom-up planning

The planning tool in Profitability Analysis offers all of those involved in the planning process a uniform, graphical planning interface that is straightforward. This interface is oriented toward "power users," such as central planning coordinators who model and monitor the planning process, and occasional users (such as sales employees), who only occasionally confirm planning values to make future orders to suppliers, for example.

Because the contents and the level of detail of individual plans vary depending on a person's role and area of responsibility, the CO-PA planning framework allows you to structure planning selectively according to specific planning levels and planning contents. It also allows you to assign the planning structure to individual users. The CO-PA planning structure is represented in a tree hierarchy. From the planning framework, you can execute almost all of the planning functions, from modeling the planning process and monitoring the planning tasks through to manual entry of planning data.

For sales and profit planning, many enterprises have implemented an iterative process consisting of a number of individual planning steps, in which existing planning data is copied, projected into the future, revaluated, adjusted manually, and distributed top-down until they obtain a sales and profit plan that fulfills the enterprise's requirements. For example, automatic methods allow you to produce data automatically for an entire planning application or input data manually into the system. As alternatives to using the standard SAP interface, you can enter planning data locally using Microsoft Excel before loading it centrally into the SAP ERP ECC 6.0 system, or you can enter planning data into the system directly from a corresponding web page.

Another special feature with sales and profit planning is that it isn't a "stand-alone component"; that is, it cannot only send planning data to other applications, but it can also receive planning data from those applications. Accordingly, you have the option, on one hand, of transferring to CO-PA data from Sales and Operations Planning (SOP), from the Logistics Information System (LIS), from internal order planning, and from project planning; and on the other hand, to transfer planning data to profit center accounting or financial accounting.

Planning is not limited to any specific time frame. This means that you can plan more than one fiscal year at once. In addition, you can plan your data by posting periods or calendar weeks. It's also possible to create and store planning data in different plan versions. This allows you to run planning data versions in parallel (such as an optimistic one and a pessimistic one) for the same object.

The CO-PA planning framework allows you to perform modifications of data behind the scenes for actual and plan data, depending on the origin of the data. It's your job as a key decision maker to determine the best business model to follow to deliver the planning applications to your client and make them simple enough that any person feels comfortable to use them and understand them.

6.2   The Framework of Corporate Planning: Sales and Profit Planning in CO-PA

The ultimate goal of CO-PA is to reflect revenue and costing information from the different components of an SAP system and make this information visible to the decision makers. The most important issue here is to have a goal in mind about what you want to achieve, how to achieve it, and what the SAP system has to offer to help you achieve it.

For implementing the CO-PA planning framework, you can either create your own implementation model or follow the ASAP models used in many other implementation projects, but no matter what, it is very important that you have a model in mind. As shown in Figure 6.1, with the CO-PA planning framework, there are always two approaches running parallel to each other. One is strategic planning, and the other the simplified business model that must guide you to clarify the strategy and monitor the implementation.

You start building a simplified business model by collecting the operative knowledge of your business processes that are stored inside your SAP system. In other words, you need to find out if your system or processes are performing as expected, along with indicators that reflect your strategy is doing things right! To prove this, collect the different elements of your system and specifically select those that deliver the type of information that you need. For example, as shown in Figure 6.1, we'll be collecting the operative knowledge of the firm by using quantity, list prices, rebates, and standard costs to generate our business model.

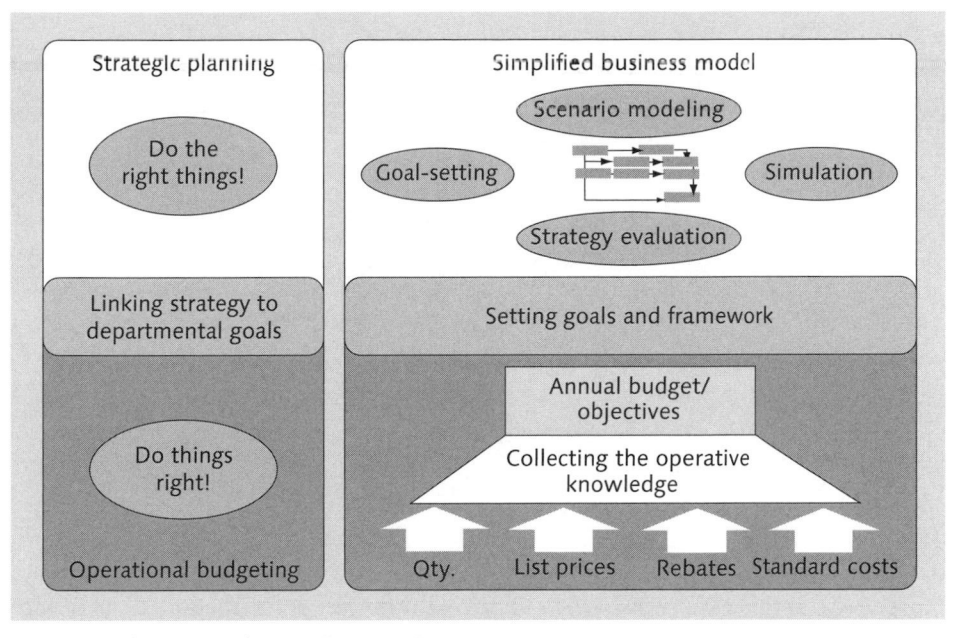

Figure 6.1 The CO-PA Planning Framework

However, before you conceive your business model, you must link the departmental goals to generate an operational budgeting process, for example. From a strategic point of view, you're not quite clear yet on what you need to do, but your business model frame of mind tells you that now you need to set up goals and objectives to direct your measures to a common purpose. Finally, the strategic planning process tells you that linking the strategy and goals will allow you to create planning scenarios directly related to the overall goals of the company.

Using a simplified business model, you can deliver what the strategic planning requires because you can combine multiple elements into one model: goal-setting, strategy evaluation, simulation, and scenario modeling. The idea behind this process is to continuously think of ways to slice and dice your final goal because you don't need to achieve your strategy with one single planning model, but with multiple small models that interact and perform planning processes independently, with one overall goal in mind.

Each of the submodels can be handled with a group or set of indicators that achieve a common purpose and each model can be handled by specific groups of individuals that have access to specific levels of planning, depending on their role in the company. For example, Figure 6.2 provides a general perspective of the concept of planning levels and aggregation, all the way down to a specific set of information that is exactly what our planning applications must deliver to be useful at different levels of our implementation.

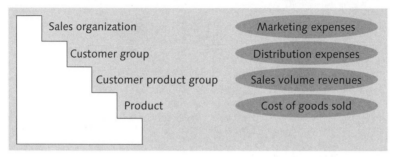

Figure 6.2 Planning at Different Levels of Aggregation

Planning at different levels of aggregation means that we can "cascade," for example, the marketing expenses of the overall organization performed by a sales manager, but each of the division managers is limited to plan the expenses based on a specific customer group. If we continue going down in the organization as shown in Figure 6.2, we can plan sales volumes and revenues by customer and product groups that individual sales managers for each division can assign, and at the end generate demand estimates to calculate the cost of goods sold (COGS) by product.

> **Note**
>
> Solving complex problems using the CO-PA planning framework does not mean creating complex planning applications. The SAP system must be (and can be) adapted and adjusted to your business model to deliver your requirements. Unfortunately, not all project managers or developers think this way, and they turn simple problems into fairly complicated planning applications because "different SAP technologies need to be conquered."

The CO-PA Planning component itself can satisfy most of the planning requirements in most organizations. At the same time, SAP increasingly allows the export of information by creating a data source and performing planning with

SAP NetWeaver BI Integrated Planning, SAP BW-BPS, SAP HANA, SAP BPC, SAP BusinessObjects, or similar applications outside the traditional SAP ERP ECC 6.0 environment. However, CO-PA also allows interacting in a Microsoft Excel environment, and provides a secure platform to run your simplified planning applications without any need of sophisticated data extraction processes.

A key decision needs to be made for under what circumstances should a business stop using CO-PA and instead use the SAP NetWeaver BW environment with tools such as SAP BPC? Is there a boundary that defines when to stop using one and consider using the other? We'll try to answer these questions in the next section. Ultimately, however, the decisions depend on the required level of complexity of your application and the number of processes that you're interested in performing.

6.3   Planning with CO-PA or SAP NetWeaver BI

When you need to decide which planning environment to use, several elements are required to finalize such a decision. The most important is the level of sophistication of your planning requirements. Table 6.1 provides a relatively simple analysis to help you decide whether CO-PA or the SAP NetWeaver BI platform is the best application to use.

Requirement	Level of Complexity	Suggested Application	Reason
Need to plan with high volumes of data external to SAP.	High	BI	CO-PA cannot deliver information external to SAP ERP ECC 6.0.
Work with simple operations with data inside the OLTP system.	Medium-Low	CO-PA	Avoid exporting data to perform simple operations available in CO-PA.
Massive data volume with complex multiple planning levels, data transformation, and web interaction.	High	BI or CO-PA	The SAP NetWeaver BI platform allows you to generate sophisticated reporting and planning operations, and interaction with the enterprise portal. However, CO-PA also allows an interaction with the web environment (but it's not as flexible).

Table 6.1 Comparing CO-PA to SAP NetWeaver BI

Requirement	Level of Complexity	Suggested Application	Reason
Massive reporting of line-item data that is not included at the segment level.	High	BI or other	CO-PA is not designed to manage this level of detail, and might increase reporting times.
Simple reporting requirements without sophisticated drilldown with data inside the OLTP system.	Medium-Low	CO-PA	CO-PA reporting allows delivering the most common requirements with enough flexibility for low-level planning.
Reporting requirement might increase the number of segment levels, table size, or affect system performance.	High	BI	SAP NetWeaver BI handles high-level data requirements better, especially those that require high-level reporting.
Planning requirements demand simple operations over a low volume of data and characteristics, without the need to share the information on the web.	Medium-Low	CO-PA	CO-PA planning functions have similar options as those available in SEM-BPS, SAP BW-BPS, and Integrated Planning when planning within the OLTP environment. Summarization levels in CO-PA are good enough to improve system performance.
Planning requirements demand a high level of complexity using data from SAP and non-SAP applications. Summarization levels, Report-Report Interface (RRI), and Report Splitting (RS), discussed in Chapter 12, are not enough to control system performance, and population of segment levels will affect performance.	High	BI	BI is the best platform to integrate, plan, and report data coming from outside an SAP system, but requires multiple object definitions and processes. Complex systems require a detailed level of analysis and performance optimization, and extensive control of the transports moved within and between systems.
Automatic calculations required inside the OLTP system.	High	CO-PA	CO-PA allows using valuation strategies to automatically perform calculations inside the OLTP system. Automatic valuation calculations have priority over automatic planning functions in the CO-PA planning framework.

Table 6.1 Comparing CO-PA to SAP NetWeaver BI (Cont.)

One of the most important factors that limit CO-PA applications in complex implementations is the reporting of characteristics defined at the segment level with line item data. Drilldown functions in CO-PA are very limited when detailed information is available at the line item level and can only be accessed using Transaction KE23 or the ABAP query tool. However, neither of these tools provides flexible reporting functionalities that are easily accessible to managers or end users. This is when SAP NetWeaver BI becomes the best choice. However, CO-PA can be the first choice inside the SAP ERP ECC 6.0 environment for reporting and planning applications that don't demand an extensive level of drilldown functionalities, and satisfies simple slicing-and-dicing of characteristics defined at the segment level that don't require constant modifications to access additional drilldown reporting applications. Generally speaking, if the level of manipulation is high and the number of processes and transformations is high, move to the SAP NetWeaver BI platform immediately.

You can also split your project into pieces, leaving the simple calculations and reporting inside the OLTP environment working with CO-PA, and running the heavy reporting and planning applications in the SAP NetWeaver BI environment using delta updates to transfer the data into SAP NetWeaver BI to extend and finish the transformation. Whichever way you go, your implementation team should be able to make reports and planning applications available to your users depending on their role, and regardless of where they are located.

> **Note**
>
> Splitting projects into pieces works well, especially because not all of the users will require the same level of access and information because their role limits their information need and access. Your implementation team can control which reports are available to end users and can make reports available to a group of users with similar requirements. End users won't even notice if the information comes from SAP NetWeaver BI or the OLTP system.

The level of manipulation required to arrive at a result in CO-PA can be less complex than in SAP NetWeaver BI because it's simpler to access characteristics that describe a customer or a product in CO-PA compared to having to create complex extraction procedures in SAP NetWeaver BI. Also, complex data manipulation requirements can be eliminated or reduced by using CO-PA assessment cycles that allocate, for example, expenses to profitability analysis characteristics and at the same time allow tracing the method of cost allocation.

In the next section, we'll explore the CO-PA planning framework and its capabilities to deliver customized planning applications within the OLTP environment in more detail.

6.4   A First Look at the CO-PA Planning Framework

Applications created with the CO-PA planning framework are quite similar to those delivered in SEM-BPS, SAP NetWeaver BI Integrated Planning, or SAP-BW-BPS. Figure 6.3 provides a general view of the capabilities of the CO-PA planning framework, including manual planning, planning aids, integrated planning, automatic planning functions, and sales and promotions budgets.

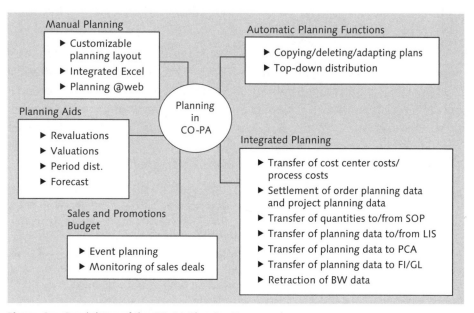

Figure 6.3 Capabilities of the CO-PA Planning Framework

There are no real limits to the types of planning possible within CO-PA; as mentioned before, the goal is to quantify revenues and costs of the firm to have an overall view of the operations, whether it is every single component of the balance sheet, or the profit and loss (P&L) statements. For example, you can decide to include a planning scenario that controls only how overhead expenses or material management expenses are calculated, and another planning scenario that reflects and plans different strategies that only affect operating profit.

Caution

Whatever your final goal for your planning applications is, remember that you'll be interacting within the OLTP system, and thus with real data stored in the SAP ERP ECC 6.0 environment. Therefore, before executing a massive function or modification, be careful to clearly identify the table fields or information that will be modified, and perform multiple tests to make sure that your operations are working as expected.

As shown in Figure 6.3, there are functions that allow you to perform forecasts, revaluations, or valuation-based valuation strategies. However, you don't need to execute or configure all of them at the same time, or use them as part of your planning application. Simply select what is applicable and see every operation as an independent process. For example, you might only be interested in increasing all of your purchase orders by 10%, to be adjusted by inflation using the revaluation function, and then create a forecast using a moving average of the last three periods to have an estimate for a specific company code and controlling areas.

When performing planning, you must also be aware of the type of data that you're working with: plan or actual. For this, you must clearly identify and limit your information when working within the CO-PA planning framework environment using the different planning elements as shown in Figure 6.4. These elements are quite similar to those in SEM-BPS and SAP BW-BPS, and can be described as follows:

▶ **Planning level**
A *planning level* determines a data set of information that aggregates or collects specific types of information. For example, you can have one planning level for marketing expenses, another one for operating costs, and another one for balance sheet planning.

▶ **Planning package**
A *planning package* works as a filter of data (in the SAP NetWeaver BI Integrated Planning application, packages are called filters). Planning packages make the level of planning more specific, such as for a particular fiscal year, business unit, or product line, as long as you've defined the selection criteria to limit the information display and planning operations.

▶ **Planning method**
A *planning method* can be defined as an operation that allows modification of values or display of the data contained inside the OLTP system. For example, the revaluation or valuation functions are planning methods.

▸ **Parameter set**
A *parameter set* allows you to generate the final specific objects required to perform planning. For example, if you would like to make manual data entries, there's a method that allows you to do just that, and the parameter set defines the layout or environment that will control the data entry. As you can see, a parameter set is not only an object, but it is also the final element that modifies the information or displays of the data extracted based on the planning level. A parameter set object is controlled by a planning package, which is also required to execute in order for the parameter set to work.

▸ **Definition screen**
This screen displays the required additional definitions to complete the configuration of the parameter set and also displays the final results of your configured methods, either as a spreadsheet or displaying the results of the execution of the method. We'll review these functions in more detail later in this chapter.

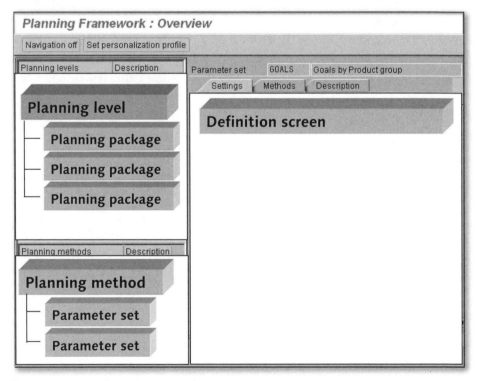

Figure 6.4 CO-PA Planning Framework Components

Figure 6.5 provides an initial overview of the CO-PA planning environment using the IMG menus, with the different components described in Figure 6.4. Also, as shown in Figure 6.5, notice that there is a graphic indicator that describes the status of the planning package that can be manually controlled; that the different automatic planning functions delivered in CO-PA, which can also be limited by user or application, are all included; and that the definition screen that provides the final display of the operations performed by a specific parameter set is shown.

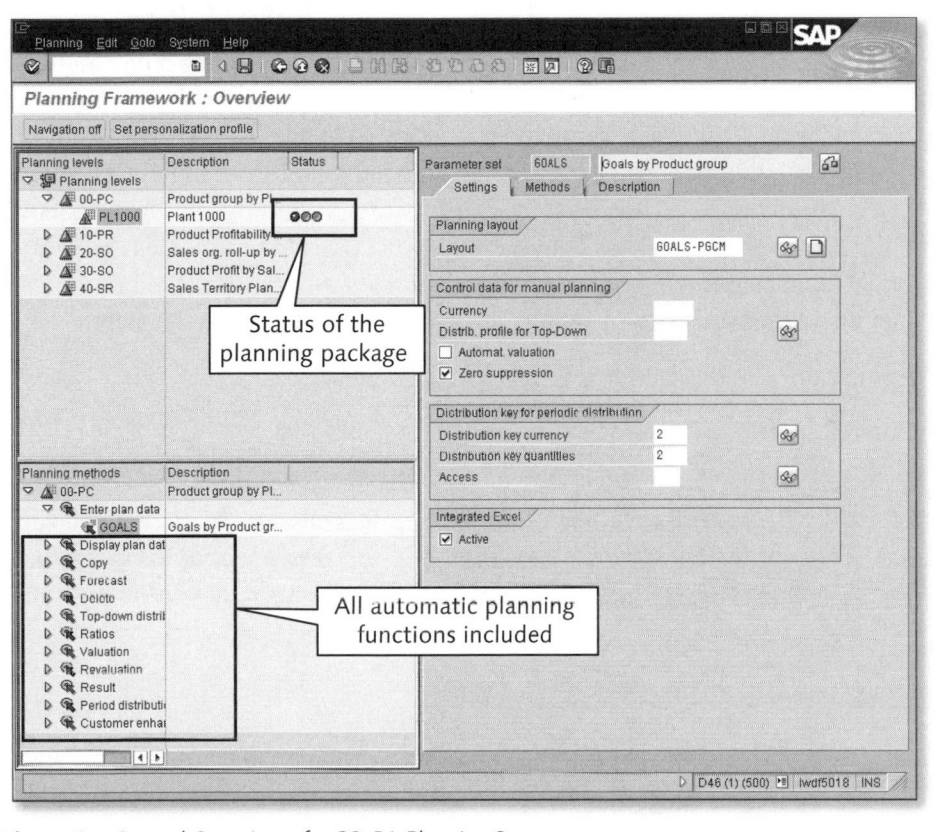

Figure 6.5 General Overview of a CO-PA Planning Screen

Remember, you'll make modifications to the data extracted using the operating concern set up as current, and thus the planning levels, packages, and parameter sets created for that particular operating concern. In other words, you aren't changing any data that you haven't chosen to modify or change. This process might be rather tedious, but guarantees that the user will plan with specific data within an operating concern, and at the same time guarantees that data won't be changed by accident, and that there is security to control the modifications at any specific time.

Based on Figure 6.4 and Figure 6.5, we can visualize how we can plan at different levels of aggregation within CO-PA. For example, we can plan at the product group, material, or the customer level, but in fact it is possible to plan any profitability segment in CO-PA as long as it has been defined correctly within the operating concern and made available following account- or costing-based planning.

An important factor in CO-PA is that the data remains consistent across all levels throughout the planning process, which means that subtotals roll up to totals, or values from different levels are reconciled even if changes are being made at different levels by other users. For example, planned quantities can first be entered at the customer and product level for three customers and five products. Following the previous rule, the totals by product will coincide with the customer and product information, and any changes to the data will be displayed at the customer and product level with an unassigned customer, if that is the case.

To access the CO-PA PLANNING menu, follow these steps:

1. Access the IMG using Transaction SPRO.

2. Navigate to the PROFITABILITY ANALYSIS menu shown in Figure 6.6.

3. Click on the PLANNING submenu to expand it. Notice that there are several components inside this menu such as INITIAL STEPS, PLANNING FRAMEWORK, MANUAL ENTRY OF PLANNING DATA, INTEGRATED PLANNING, PLANNING AIDS, and REORGANIZATION.

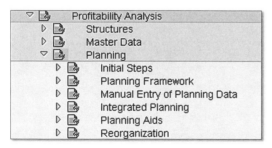

Figure 6.6 Accessing the CO-PA Planning Framework

We've reviewed the capabilities of the SAP CO-PA planning framework, and also the planning functionalities that can interact with LIS, SOP, BW, PCA, and other components within SAP ECC. You should know understand that SAP CO-PA has a dedicated menu, or a specific set of transaction codes designed exclusively for planning.

In the next section, we'll discuss how to implement planning functionality that's applicable to a particular range of accounts using number ranges. Number ranges define how the data will be organized based on a specific set of numbers that control how the different accounts are accessed and what information is displayed in your planning applications.

6.5 Number Ranges for Planning Data

You need to define a number range for updating plan line items (for instance, in each of your operating concerns) using the path CONTROLLING • PROFITABILITY ANALYSIS • PLANNING • INITIAL STEPS • DEFINE NUMBER RANGES FOR PLANNING DATA. When working with profit planning, the SAP system automatically assigns a number that lies within your selected interval, as shown in Figure 6.7.

> **Note**
>
> To define number ranges, you must have authorization from your system administrator to maintain number ranges. In addition, your operating concern must have been completely defined with characteristics and value fields.

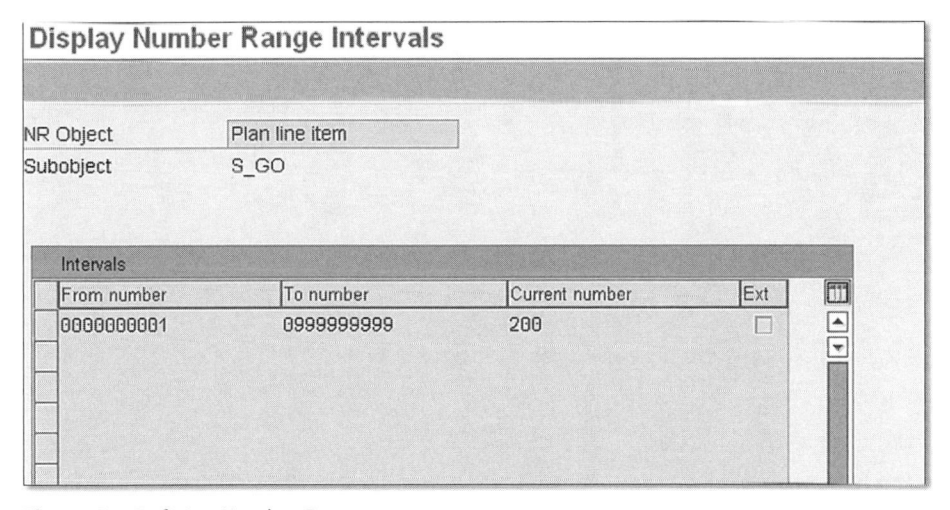

Figure 6.7 Defining Number Ranges

> **Caution**
>
> You shouldn't transport your predefined number ranges into your production system. Instead, define them manually to avoid any confusion or unexpected changes along the way.

When working with CO-PA planning, you must specify versions to separate data for different purposes. For example, one version can control the data stored inside the operating concern for SD and another version may control the data that controls the plan data of MM. This definition is achieved using the MAINTAIN VERSIONS function, discussed in the next section.

6.6 Maintaining Versions

You need to define the Controlling (CO) versions you want to use for your operating concern. These versions are valid for all of CO and for all operating concerns. In Profitability Analysis, you can only use versions for plan data. Consequently, the fields ACTUAL and EXCLUSIVE USE shown in Figure 6.9 (you have to scroll to the right to see EXCLUSIVE USE), are not relevant for CO-PA.

Each version has attributes that are only valid for one operating concern, and this information can be accessed following the path shown in Figure 6.8: CONTROLLING • PROFITABILITY ANALYSIS • PLANNING • INITIAL STEPS • MAINTAIN VERSIONS.

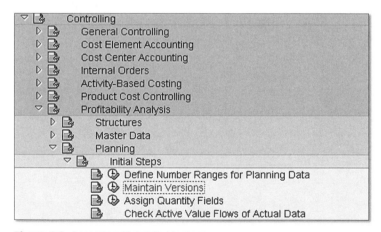

Figure 6.8 Accessing Maintain Versions

As shown in Figure 6.9, different checkboxes are displayed, such as PLAN, ACTUAL, WIP/RA, VARIANCE, and other elements that are attributes to the version that we're interested in creating.

Tips & Tricks

When talking about Work-in-Process/Results Analysis Version (WIP/RA) in Figure 6.9, there are several issues to consider, especially when working with the SAP Production Planning (PP) component. RA is associated with the RA secondary cost element category 31, and these elements are associated with production orders and their movements from work-in-process items to finished goods. You should review related configuration issues with your production team. Refer to Chapter 11 for further discussion on WIP/RA.

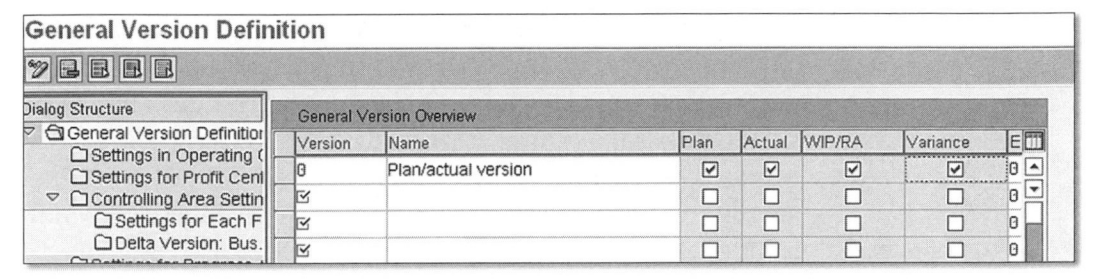

Figure 6.9 Version Attributes

The checkboxes and hierarchy displayed on the left-hand side of the screen shown in Figure 6.9 determine if the version is locked so no changes can be made, the type of currency that should be used to store the data in the version, the company code currency or profit center valuation, the currency type for each version, the exchange rate used to translate foreign currencies to the local currency, and for what date the system should derive characteristics.

If you plan in weeks, you also need to specify which rule is used to distribute the weekly plan values to plan periods. This rule determines how the weekly values are distributed to periods when a week cannot be assigned to one period. Here, as shown in Figure 6.9, we specified that the version handles Plan, Actual, Variance, and we typed "0" and "Plan/actual version" in the VERSION and NAME columns, respectively.

6.7   Planning with the CO-PA Planning Framework

We're now ready to start planning. To access the actual CO-PA planning framework, follow the path in the IMG: CONTROLLING • PROFITABILITY ANALYSIS • PLANNING • PLANNING FRAMEWORK, as shown in Figure 6.10.

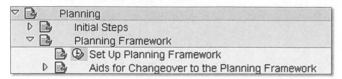

Figure 6.10 Accessing the CO-PA Planning Framework

As shown in Figure 6.11, several components are required to create a planning application using the CO-PA planning framework, including planning levels, planning packages (commonly referred to simply as "packages"), planning methods, and parameter sets. Their main purpose is not only to access the information from the SAP tables, but also to control exactly what elements are extracted, the level of detail required, transformation processes to be used, and values required by users. We already looked at the most important elements within this environment earlier in this chapter and they are discussed in more detail in the following subsections.

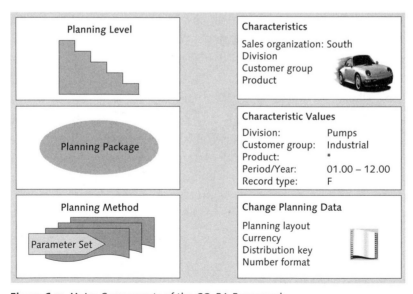

Figure 6.11 Major Components of the CO-PA Framework

Selected fields

6.7.1 Planning Levels

You cannot plan or control every single value of all SAP tables or user-defined fields in your implementation at the same time. However, using planning levels, you can select only the required characteristics and value fields that represent the information for each of the planning areas to include in your planning application, defined inside your operating concern. This lets you plan marketing, operations, and sales expenses and assign all of this information to a common planning application that is simple enough for anyone to use.

To create a planning level, follow these steps:

1. In the screen shown earlier in Figure 6.10, select SET UP PLANNING FRAMEWORK to access the traditional CO-PA PLANNING FRAMEWORK: OVERVIEW screen, shown in Figure 6.12.

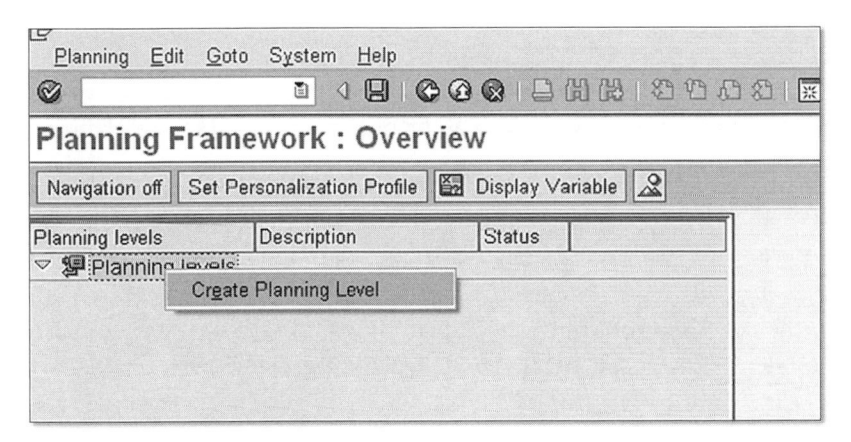

Figure 6.12 Create a Planning Level

2. Review the different elements displayed in Figure 6.12, and notice that there are three columns: PLANNING LEVELS, DESCRIPTION, and STATUS. Because none of these elements have been defined yet, no objects are available.

3. Right-click on the PLANNING LEVELS object and select CREATE PLANNING LEVEL, as shown in Figure 6.12.

4. Another screen appears, shown in Figure 6.13, where you can define the technical name and a description of your planning level. Enter "Level" as the technical name, and "This is a Planning Level" as the description.

5. Click on the checkmark icon to create the planning level.

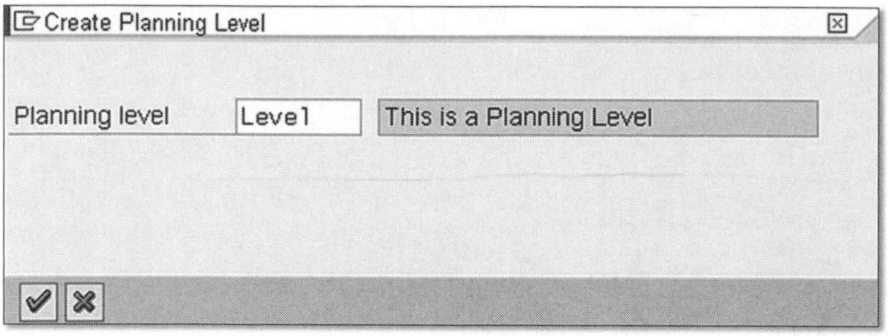

Figure 6.13 Creating a Planning Level

The objects contained in your operating concern are now available for you to plan them. However, you still need to define what type of operations you're interested in performing over those components. To do so, you need to define another component—the planning package—discussed in the next section.

6.7.2 Planning Package

To define a planning package or access any of the objects included in the planning level, follow these steps:

1. Right-click on the planning level we just created and the menu displayed in the upper left portion of the screen shown in Figure 6.14 appears. Notice that in addition to being able to use this menu to create your planning package (to continue with the definition of your CO-PA planning application), there are also different options related specifically to the planning level, such as DISPLAY PLANNING LEVEL, CHANGE PLANNING LEVEL, COPY PLANNING LEVEL, DELETE PLANNING LEVEL, and TRANSPORT PLANNING LEVEL.

2. Select CREATE PLANNING PACKAGE, as shown in Figure 6.14, and the screen shown in Figure 6.15 appears. Enter "Package" as the technical name and "This is a Planning Package" as the description of the object.

3. Click on the checkmark icon to create the planning package.

4. Briefly review the different planning methods at the bottom of the screen shown in Figure 6.14, which are part of your planning package. Planning methods are predefined processes in CO-PA that can be configured to perform modifications over your data, and they are limited by the settings configured on the plan package's SELECTION tab, shown on the right-side of Figure 6.14.

234

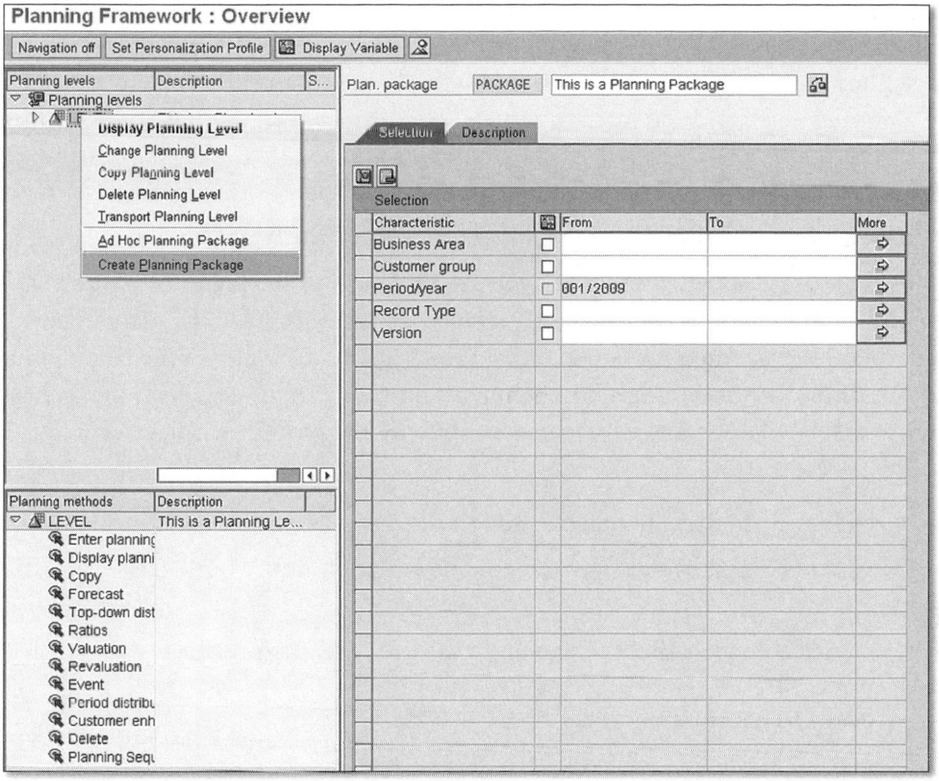

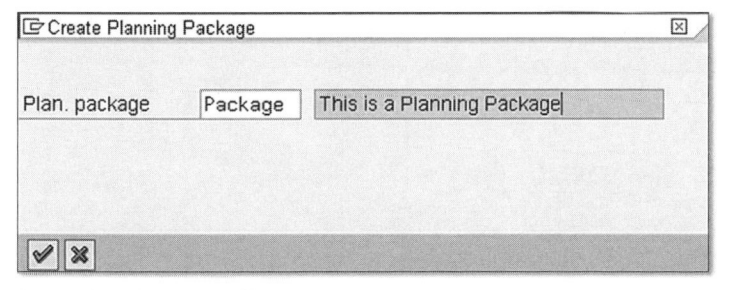

Figure 6.14 Creating a Planning Package as Part of a Planning Level

Notice that the planning methods are attached to your planning level as well, and also notice that the planning package is limiting the display for the elements extracted from the operating concern to starting on 001/2009. We'll look at planning methods in more detail in the next section.

Figure 6.15 Creating a Planning Package

At this point we've configured two key planning elements: planning levels and planning packages. If you want to create additional objects, for example, to manage information for marketing, operations, and sales, then each of them would be a planning level, and the information extracted by each of them is controlled by the selection criteria defined in the planning package. This makes it possible to have *marketing* as a planning level, and marketing expenses for region A and marketing expenses for region B in two separate planning packages.

Finally, if you review Figure 6.16, you see that each of the columns in the PLANNING FRAMEWORK : OVERVIEW screen now contains objects for the planning level and planning package we created. The STATUS column identifies the completion status of the information, using a graphical indicator. Double-click on this indicator to display the SET STATUS screen, also shown in Figure 6.16. You can configure three indicators:

▸ OPEN: Specifies that the object is still in the design stage

▸ IN PROCESSING: Specifies that some work has been done, but changes are still required

▸ COMPLETED: Signals that the planning package is ready for use

Figure 6.16 Changing the Status of Your Planning Package

You don't have to use the STATUS object all of the time, but it helps with organization, especially when you're working with multiple implementation teams or complex planning applications that might require many packages that are stored inside the same planning level.

Now, let's understand how to work with planning methods in case you need to perform specific transformations or modifications to your data. Using planning methods can help you avoid modifications of data outside the SAP OLTP environment, and reduce customization efforts.

planning methods

6.7.3 Working with Planning Methods, Parameter Sets, and Planning Layouts

As was previously mentioned, when working with a planning package you can also see the planning methods that are attached to your planning level.

> **Note**
>
> Remember that even though you can configure planning methods to modify specific data values, they won't work if the correct selection options have not been specified as part of the planning level and planning package. Most likely, the SAP system will let you know of any errors or configuration problems along the way. However, the system won't tell you whether the methods selected and successfully executed are the correct ones; that's up to you to figure out.

use SAP delivered methods

We'll work with the two simplest of the planning methods: ENTER PLANNING DATA and DISPLAY PLANNING DATA, shown in Figure 6.17. As their names imply, the first allows you to enter and modify planning data, and the second is designed to display the extracted information using the planning package as a filter.

To execute any of the planning methods, a planning package must be selected. This object controls what information we want to see when executing these planning methods. The process for working with any of the planning methods available in the CO-PA planning framework is essentially the same, as follows:

1. Select a planning package (in our example, PACKAGE, as shown in Figure 6.17).

2. Select a planning method (in our example, ENTER PLANNING DATA).

3. Right-click on the planning method and choose CREATE A PARAMETER SET.

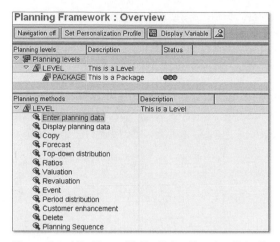

Figure 6.17 Working with the Enter Planning Data Planning Method

4. Configure the options of the parameter set that appear on the right side of the screen to suit your specific business needs, as shown in Figure 6.18.

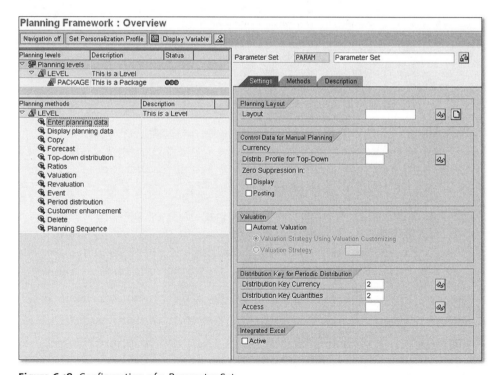

Figure 6.18 Configuration of a Parameter Set

As you can see in Figure 6.18, we've configured a parameter set (required for all of the CO-PA planning methods) called PARAM and there are three tabs: SETTINGS, METHODS, and DESCRIPTION. For the ENTER PLANNING DATA planning method, perform the following steps:

1. Review the different parameter set options shown in Figure 6.18.

2. In the section called PLANNING LAYOUT, select the CREATE icon to define a planning layout. You need to have at least one planning layout to see any data extracted from the SAP tables, and using the information from your operating concern, planning levels, and planning packages on your screen. This is quite similar to the processes in SEM-BPS, SAP NetWeaver BI Integrated Planning, and SAP BW-BPS.

3. Specify a name ("Layout") and description ("LAYOUT") for the planning layout, as shown in Figure 6.19.

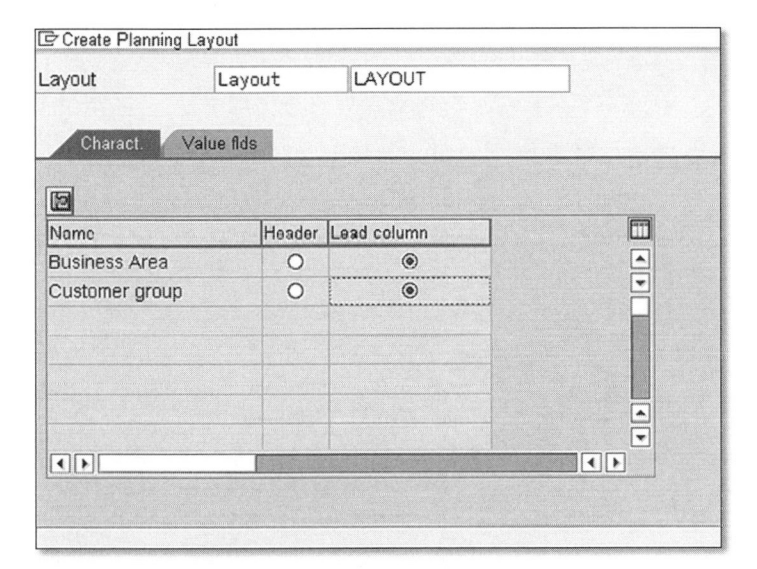

Figure 6.19 Configuring the Characteristics to Include in a Planning Layout

4. Define how you want the characteristics and value fields arranged, using the CHARACT. and VALUE FLDS tabs respectively. As shown in Figure 6.19, we'll use BUSINESS AREA and CUSTOMER GROUP characteristics as lead columns for our planning layout, and, as shown in Figure 6.20, we'll include the value fields ANNUAL REBATES, LOT SIZE VARIANCES, OTHER VARIANCES, and REVENUE in our planning layout.

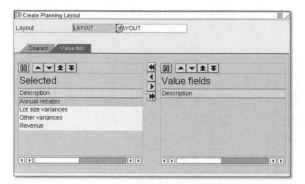

Figure 6.20 Configuring the Value Fields to Include in a Planning Layout

---

Tips & Tricks

We're specifying that the characteristics CUSTOMER GROUP and BUSINESS AREA will be leading columns rather than headers. Generally, headers are reserved for information such as period, fiscal year, fiscal year variant, and other time-related elements or characteristics that require different levels of hierarchies.

---

5. Click on the SAVE icon to create your planning layout.

6. As shown in Figure 6.21, you are returned to the configuration screen for the parameter set PARAM, but now the LAYOUT object has been assigned to the parameter set (which is linked to the ENTER PLANNING DATA planning method).

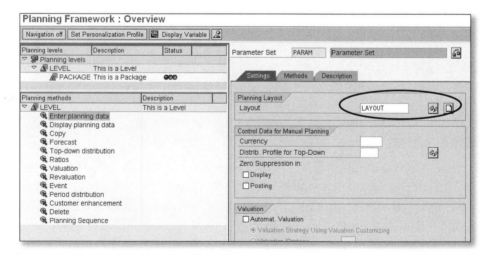

Figure 6.21 Planning Layout Assigned to a Parameter Set

> **Note**
>
> There are several additional options available in the screen shown in Figure 6.21, but they are beyond the scope of this book. You can explore them if you decide to increase the sophistication of your parameter set configuration.

Let's now see how our data looks using the planning layout object we created:

1. Click on the glasses icon shown in Figure 6.21 to open the screen shown in Figure 6.22. As you can see, REPORT PAINTER is the environment used by CO-PA to present a general graphical display of your information.

2. Review the information shown in Figure 6.22. As we configured earlier, the business area (BUSI) and customer group (CU) characteristics are the lead columns for our planning layout, and the value fields ANNUAL REBATES, LOT SIZE VARIANCES, OTHER VARIANCES, and REVENUE are shown.

3. Click on the BACK icon located at the top of the screen, as shown in Figure 6.22, to return to the PLANNING FRAMEWORK : OVERVIEW screen.

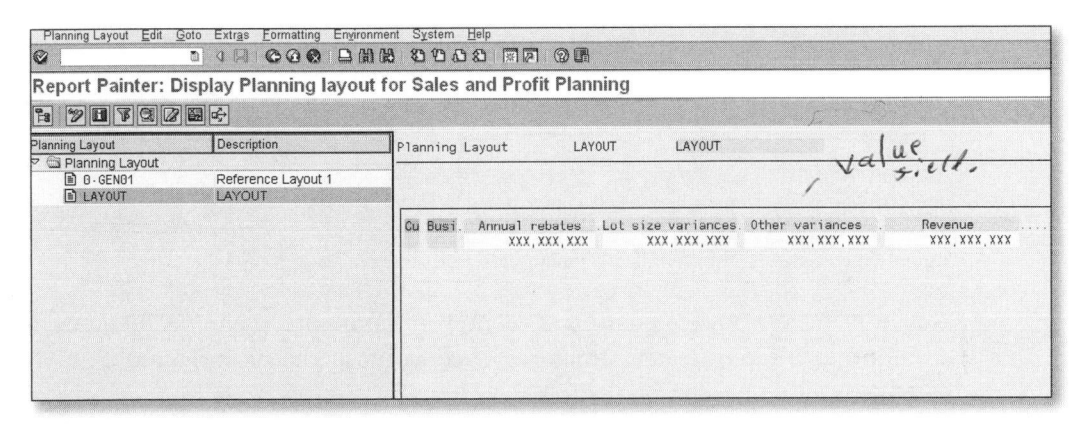

Figure 6.22 Displaying the Structure of Your LAYOUT Planning Layout

You now have a general idea of how your layout looks and feels. However, we need to make sure that the configuration follows your planning requirements for a particular currency. To do so, let's assign U.S. dollars as the standard planning currency for our parameter set.

1. To do this, return to the parameter set's SETTINGS tab, and type "USD" in the CURRENCY field in the CONTROL DATA FOR MANUAL PLANNING area.

2. You can also limit the planning methods associated with our data. To do so, select the METHODS tab, as shown in Figure 6.23, and select the methods that you want to include as PERMITTED METHODS as part of your planning application.

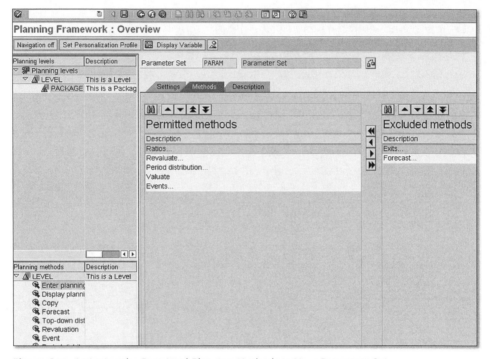

Figure 6.23 Assigning the Permitted Planning Methods to Your Parameter Set

You now have a pretty good idea of how to configure planning methods to develop more sophisticated structures, such as those shown in Figure 6.24. To access this environment, do the following:

1. Save your parameter set by clicking on the SAVE icon.

2. Double-click on the PACKAGE object.

3. Drill down to find the PARAM parameter set we just configured, right-click on it, and select EXECUTE PLANNING METHOD to display your LAYOUT planning layout object on the right side of the screen, with all of the desired information, including the characteristics and value fields previously defined, and default header information at the top that describes the type of data that we're modifying.

4. You can now manually enter the information you require. As shown in Figure 6.24, we've entered the values 100; 1,000; 2,000; and 150 for the key figures CASH DISCOUNT, GROSS SALES, MARKETING DIVISION, and QUANTITY DISCOUNT, respectively. Notice that we chose to provide different value fields in our layout to show that we can add or modify the contents of our layouts to different requirements.

5. Notice that our data is limited in the planning level information to the time frame between 1/2009 and 10/2009, reflecting that the limitations established by the planning level and planning package are key to displaying the information contained in the parameter set of the planning method and showing it in the layout.

6. Click on the SAVE icon.

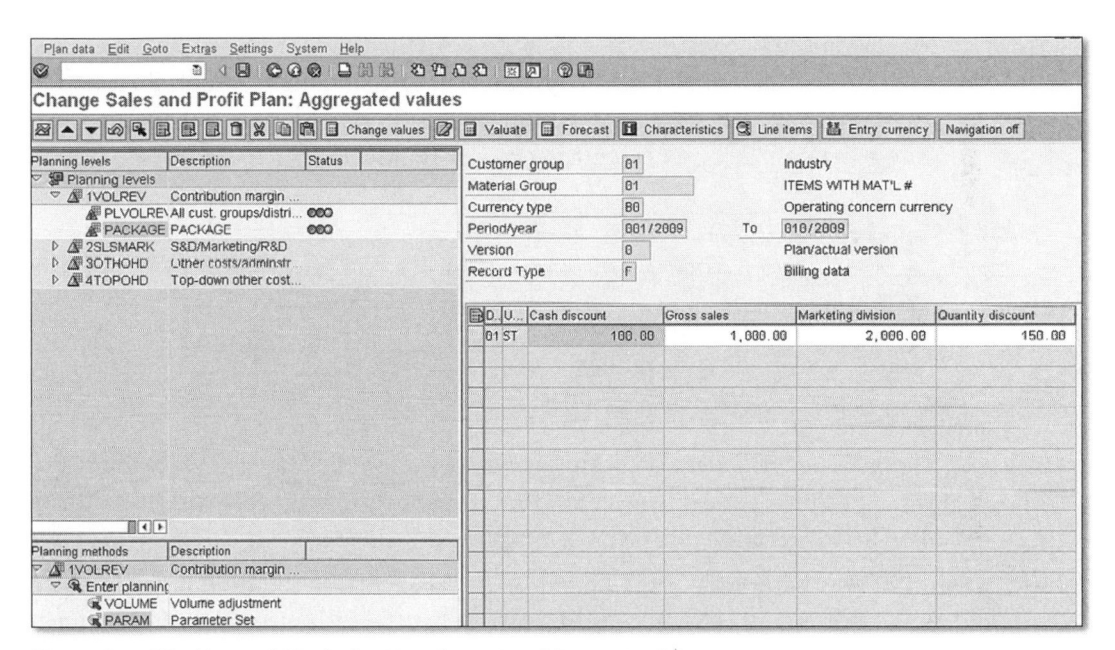

Figure 6.24 Working and Displaying Your Layout and Parameter Set

Once you've executed your parameter set, you can return to the CO-PA configuration screen by clicking on the BACK icon located at the top of the screen.

Note

When you perform any modification or addition to the data in the planning layout, the SAP system asks if you want to post (store) your data, and you either accept or decline. Note that there is a different document number generated each time that you save and change your data, and you're provided the number in the message "Plan data was posted with document number 0000000**XXX**."

Notice that the screen shown in Figure 6.24 contains additional buttons, such as VALUATE, FORECAST, CHANGE VALUES, LINE ITEMS, ENTRY CURRENCY, and NAVIGATION OFF. These buttons are more or less self-explanatory, and you can explore their usage on your own. However, be careful because some of them change or generate new values based on the information displayed on the screen.

Let's look at one example of this, the CHANGE VALUES button:

1. Position the cursor in a field like CASH DISCOUNT, and then click on the CHANGE VALUES button. The screen shown in Figure 6.25 appears, where you can revaluate a field either by a percentage or a constant.

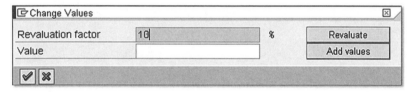

Figure 6.25 Working with the Change Values Screen

2. These values can either be positive or negative, so let's say you want to revaluate the values of cash discount for 10%. Type "10" into the REVALUATION FACTOR field and click on the REVALUATE button.

3. Compare the results in the planning layout shown in Figure 6.26 with those shown previously in Figure 6.24. Notice that the cash discount value changed from 100.00 USD to 110.00 USD because of the 10% revaluation.

4. If a simple method of revaluating data values is what you were looking for, save your changes and click on the BACK icon to return to the design environment of the CO-PA planning framework.

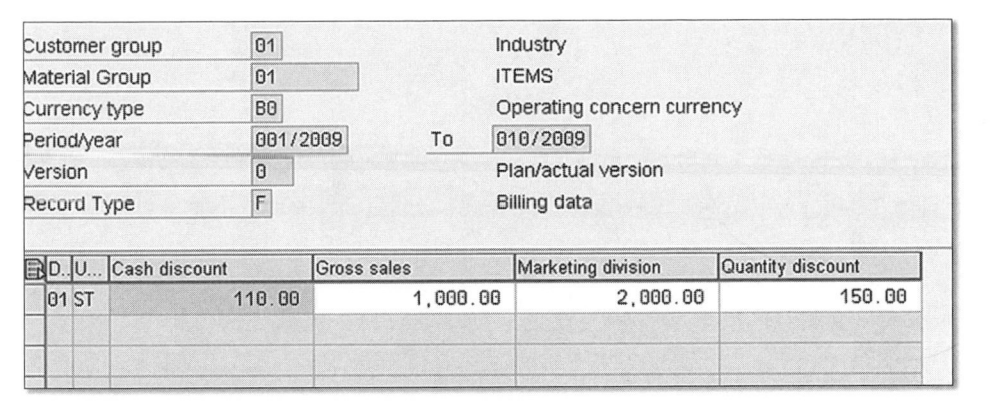

	D..	U...	Cash discount	Gross sales	Marketing division	Quantity discount
	01	ST	110.00	1,000.00	2,000.00	150.00

Figure 6.26 Results of the Change Values Button

Note

Using the predefined CHANGE VALUES button might eliminate the need for you to develop or configure a new planning method. Alternatively, you might expand the revaluation planning method to perform a similar procedure, but one that changes more than just a single value at a time.

Now that we've reviewed this functionality, let's explore how to complement our CO-PA planning framework with variables.

— associated w/ characteristics

6.7.4 Planning Variables

The SAP system lets you create variables to simplify the way information is handled inside your CO-PA planning applications. For example, you can create a variable that has a range stored in it and assign it to a characteristic so you don't need to worry about typing the same information all of the time. Instead, you can call the variable during execution time and the layout will display the required information.

This type of scenario is exactly what we're going to create using the CO-PA planning framework DEFINE VARIABLE function:

1. Make sure that you're working in the design environment of the CO-PA planning framework shown in Figure 6.27.

2. Click on EDIT • VARIABLE • DEFINE VARIABLE, as shown in Figure 6.27, to access the screen shown in Figure 6.28.

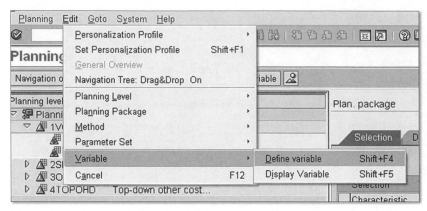

Figure 6.27 Defining a Variable in CO-PA

Note

Before proceeding, know that a CO-PA planning variable is always associated with a specific characteristic.

---

3. As shown in Figure 6.28, create a variable called CUST_GRP and assign it to the characteristic CUSTOMER GROUP as shown in Figure 6.29. You can click on the checkmark icon to identify that it's a variable.

Figure 6.28 Configuring a CO-PA Variable

As shown in Figure 6.28, we have assigned the value wholesale (02) to the VALUE FROM column. This value will be read by the system once it's assigned to the CUSTOMER GROUP characteristic as a variable, and when the planning package is executed, the variable will be read with the value 02. Now your variable CUST_GRP can be used in multiple planning layouts. You only need to maintain the values stored in a variable once, and it will automatically be reflect in any layouts or planning packages are using the same variable.

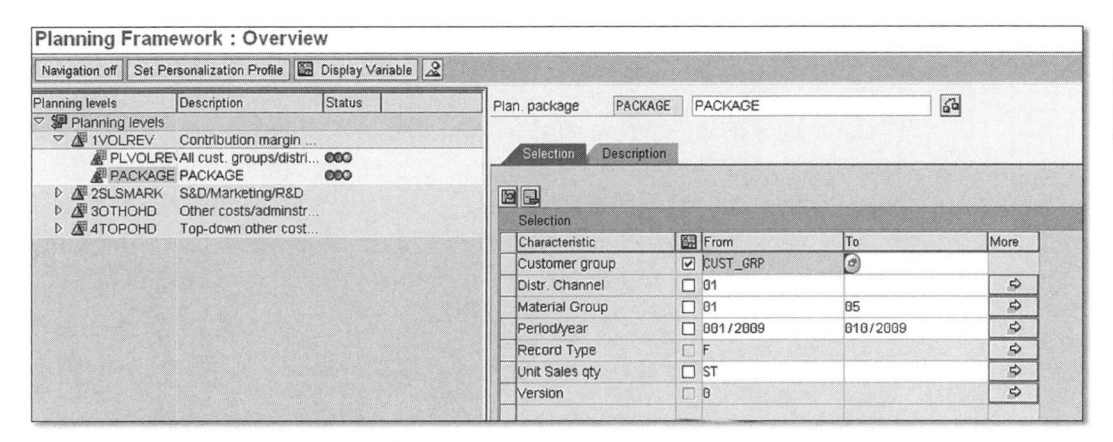

Figure 6.29 Assigning a CO-PA Variable to a Planning Package

4. When you're finished, click on the SAVE icon.

5. Now go to the SELECTION tab in the planning package, as shown in Figure 6.29, and click on the checkbox below the variable icon to access the menu that displays the available characteristic variables. As shown in Figure 6.29, we've selected the checkbox next to CUSTOMER GROUP to access the variable information and assigned the CO-PA variable CUST_GRP to the planning package PACKAGE so when executing your planning layout, the wholesale value will be extracted automatically.

6. Execute the parameter set that's assigned to the planning method ENTER PLANNING DATA, as described earlier. Now the variable CUST_GRP controls the behavior of the characteristic CUSTOMER GROUP, as shown in Figure 6.30, displaying the default value WHOLESALE (02).

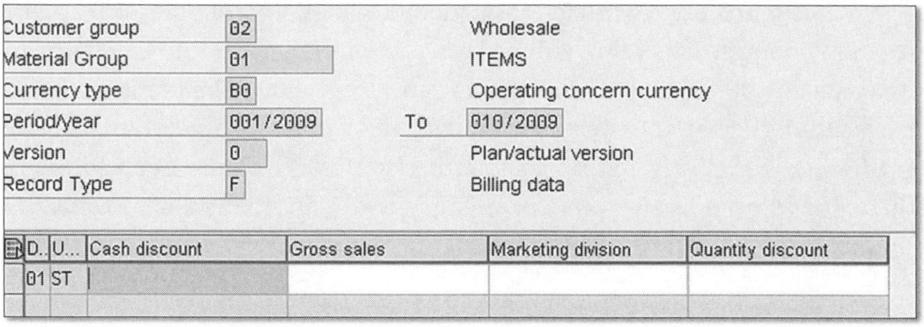

	D.	U...	Cash discount	Gross sales	Marketing division	Quantity discount

Customer group 　02　　　　　　Wholesale
Material Group 　01　　　　　　ITEMS
Currency type 　B0　　　　　　Operating concern currency
Period/year 　001/2009　To　010/2009
Version 　0　　　　　　　Plan/actual version
Record Type 　F　　　　　　Billing data

	D.	U...	Cash discount	Gross sales	Marketing division	Quantity discount
	01	ST				

Figure 6.30 Using the Variable CUST_GRP as Part of Your Layout

CO-PA planning variables are useful in complex implementations that require using the same layout, but the information is required by different users in different departments. In our scenario, the PACKAGE object can control the information for the wholesale division, and another planning package using the same layout might require a second variable to display, for example, only the hospitals division, and both users require the same characteristics and key value fields.

> **Note**
>
> We recommend that you explore the different types of variables that SAP software has to offer in more detail using the CO-PA planning framework. You can either use the available *http://help.sap.com* documentation, or interact with the *http://sdn.sap.com* community.

So far we've used the planning method ENTER PLANNING DATA. The alternative would be to use the planning method DISPLAY PLANNING DATA. This method provides the same type of capabilities, but users can only review the information, not modify it. This can be useful for managers or end users with few SAP system skills who require little or no interaction with the data input processes.

One question that remains is how you can create or design more customized layouts. Together, planning layouts and the Report Painter provide flexibility and customized designs to improve the data display and data manipulation requirements of end users. The next section explores the elements related to configuring CO-PA planning layouts from scratch in more detail as a way to provide a more extensive overview of the reporting capabilities of the CO-PA planning application.

6.8   The Report Painter and CO-PA Planning Layouts

To get started creating more sophisticated environments using Report Painter without creating planning areas, planning methods, and so on, follow this procedure:

1. Follow the path PLANNING • MANUAL ENTRY OF PLANNING DATA • DEFINE PLANNING LAYOUT as shown in Figure 6.31.

2. Select the CREATE PLANNING LAYOUT option, and double-click on it or click on the CHOOSE button. Here, you will manually create a planning layout that you can also modify, display, and later on assign to planning applications.

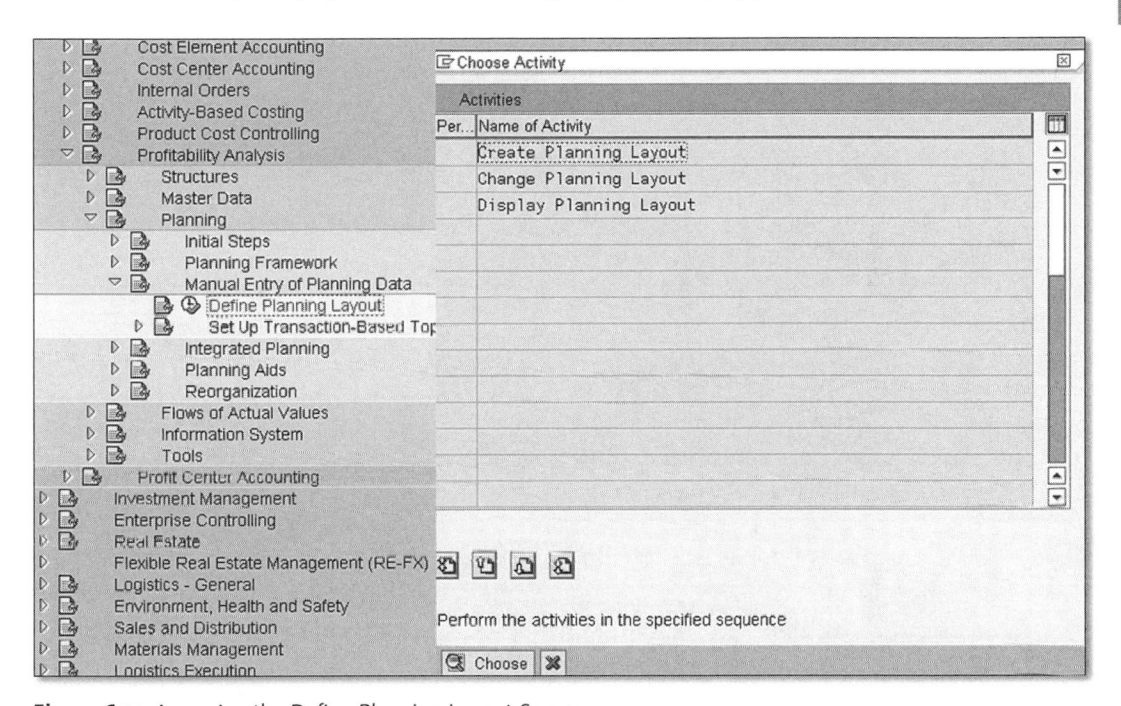

Figure 6.31 Accessing the Define Planning Layout Screen

3. Once completed, as shown in Figure 6.32, click on the CREATE button.

4. Figure 6.33 presents the initial Report Painter screen to perform sales and profit planning. As you can see, a planning layout is defined as a matrix using rows and columns. You can also use a predefined number format to display your key figure's values and perform calculations with a variable assigned to a column as part of a layout.

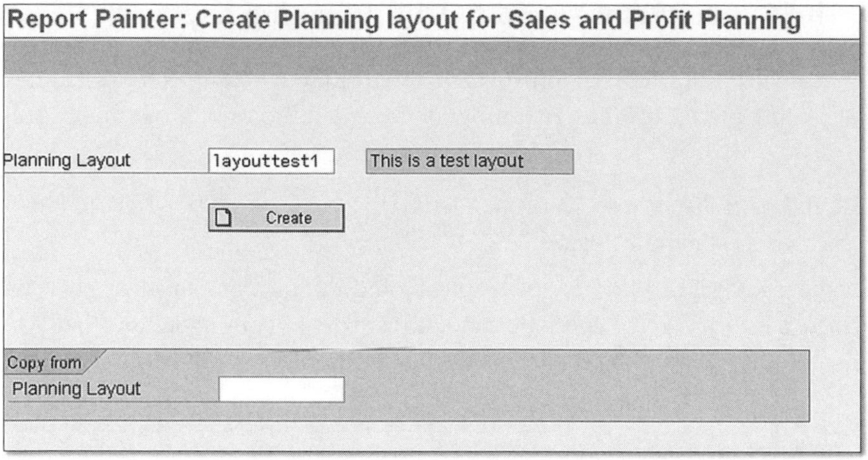

Report Painter: Create Planning layout for Sales and Profit Planning

Planning Layout   layouttest1   This is a test layout

☐   Create

Copy from
Planning Layout   [   ]

Figure 6.32 Configuring a CO-PA Layout

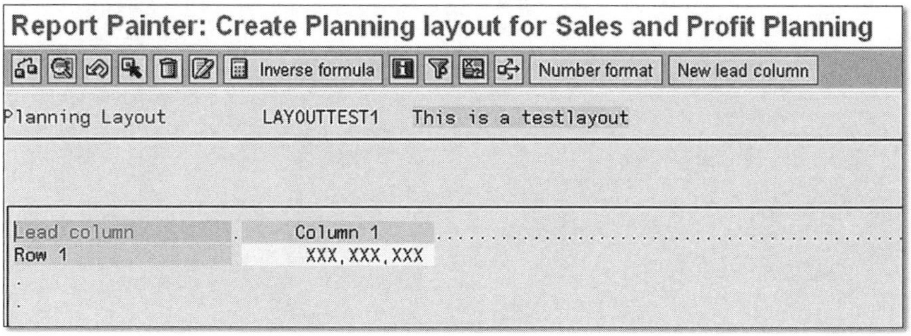

Report Painter: Create Planning layout for Sales and Profit Planning

[toolbar icons] Inverse formula [icons] Number format | New lead column

Planning Layout   LAYOUTTEST1   This is a testlayout

Lead column   .   Column 1 ....
Row 1   XXX,XXX,XXX
.
.

Figure 6.33 Basic Planning Layout in the Report Painter

Although this book is not oriented toward a complete explanation of the Report Painter in the SAP ERP ECC 6.0 environment, we'll provide you with some useful hints. So, let's add information to the rows based on predefined characteristics:

1. Select and then double-click on Row 1 to access the SELECT ELEMENT TYPE screen, as shown in Figure 6.34. You can now either add a characteristic or a value field with characteristics to Row 1. For our example, select CHARACTERISTICS and click on the checkmark icon.

2. Select any of the options available, such as INDUSTRY, CUSTOMER GROUP, or others. For our example, we selected INDUSTRY.

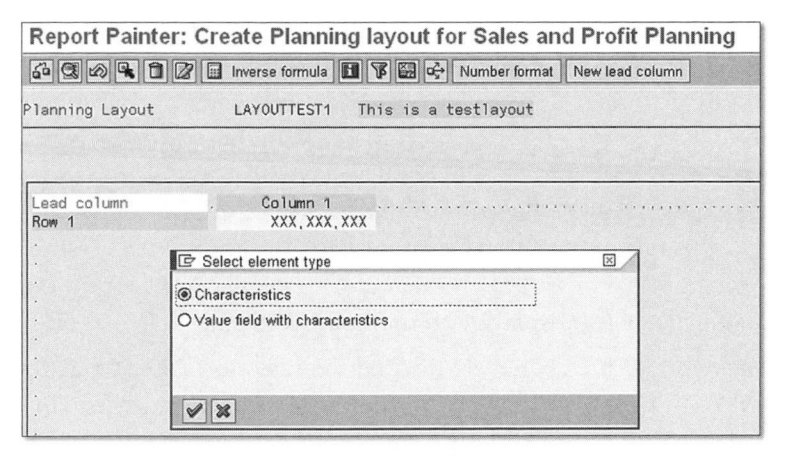

Figure 6.34 Adding a Characteristic to Row 1

3. Now, double-click on COLUMN 1 to perform the assignment and configuration of a value field, following a similar procedure as the one used to assign the characteristic. We're going to create a value field called GROSS SALES and assign it to COLUMN 1 in our layout, as shown in Figure 6.35.

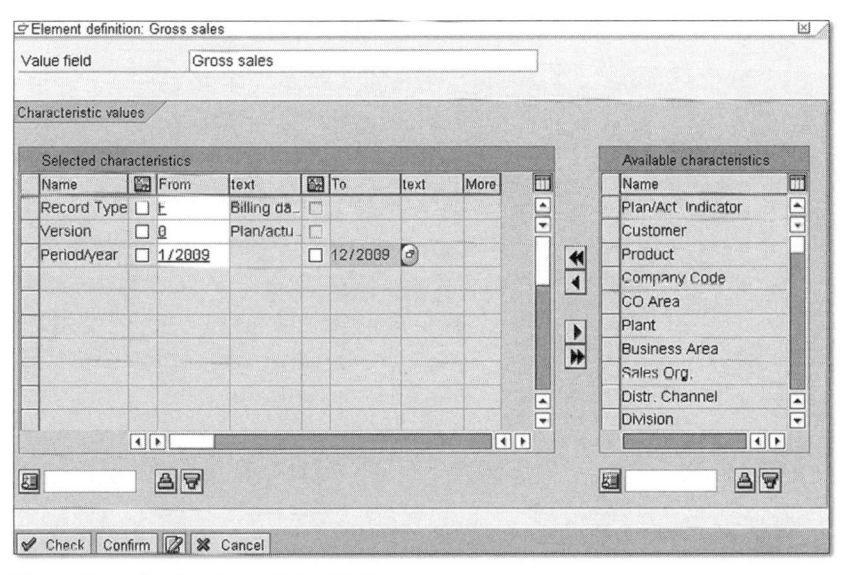

Figure 6.35 Configuring a Value Field

4. For those familiar with the concepts of SAP NetWeaver BI or SAP NetWeaver BW, a value field is the same as a restricted key figure. In other words, we're telling

the SAP system to extract data for a particular key figure that might not exist inside the SAP tables, but we can create a customized name with specific selection criteria to restrict the values extracted. That way, not everything is extracted at once, which improves system performance. In the case of the information shown in Figure 6.35, we're defining the value field gross sales to those values that have Record Type = F, Version = 0, and Period/year between 1/2009 and 12/2009. You can include additional characteristics to improve the restriction of the information that describes a value field. To do so, choose from the Available characteristics list displayed on the right-hand side of the screen.

5. Once you're satisfied with the characteristics and the selection criteria restrictions that describe your value field, click on the Check button to review any inconsistencies and make any corrections.

6. Finally, click on the Confirm button to complete the assignment of the gross sales value field to Column 1.

7. Now, as shown in Figure 6.36, the final results of the assignments to the initial row 1 and column 1 display. You'll see that the characteristic Industry and the value field Gross sales are the only elements displayed in the planning layout LAYOUTTEST1.

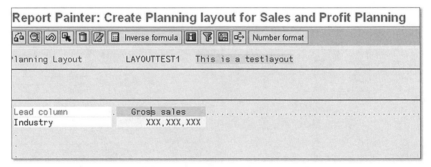

Figure 6.36 Final Results of the Characteristic and Value Field Assignments

> **Note**
>
> It isn't enough that you create a layout with the definition and restriction of values. Any planning layout configured following the procedures shown has to be created thinking of the type of information that is or will be available in the planning levels, planning packages, and parameter sets where it's assigned.

8. Once satisfied, click on the Save icon.

9. Return to the screen shown in Figure 6.31, and select the DISPLAY PLANNING LAYOUT option. The planning layout LAYOUTTEST1 appears on the screen, as shown in Figure 6.37, and you can review its configuration.

Using the DISPLAY PLANNING LAYOUT functionality you can access, review, delete, and transport any of the layouts available. In our case, this includes LAYOUTTEST1, which we just created, as well as LAYOUT, which we created earlier. You'll also see other default SAP layouts.

Explore the rest of the available functionalities in this part of Report Painter for sales and profit planning. There are formatting functionalities to add more rows and columns, limit the number range displayed, add attributes and formulas, and other elements that are important to explore.

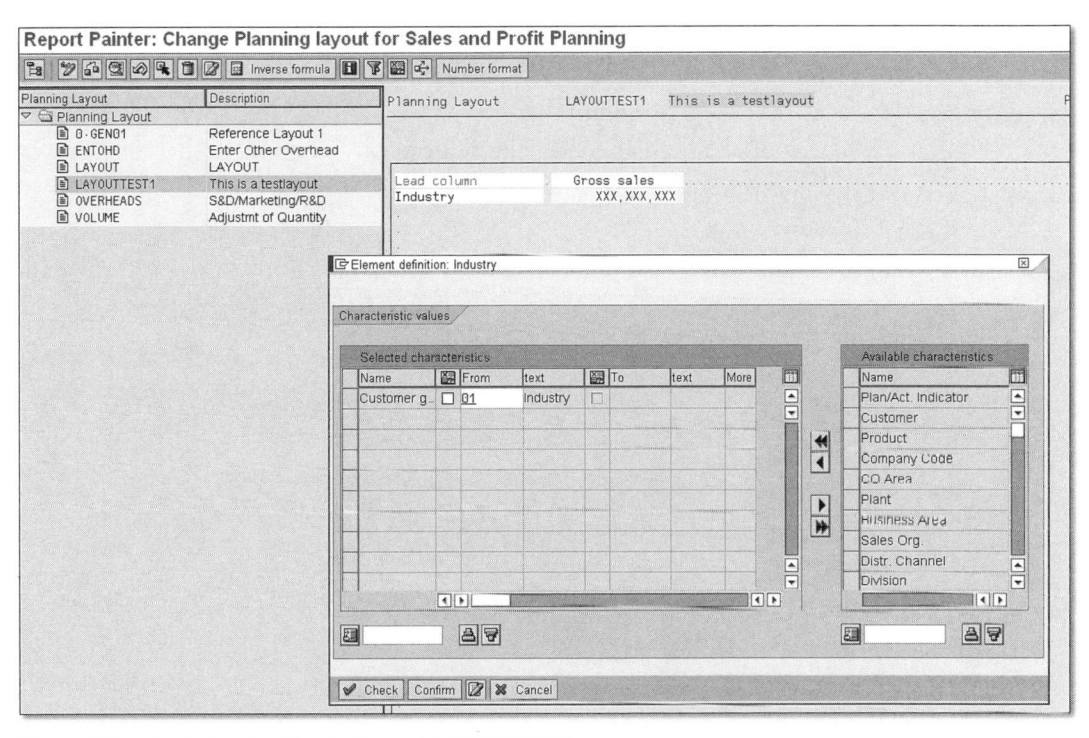

Figure 6.37 Displaying the Newly Created LAYOUTTEST1

In the next section, we'll explore how to control and assign the objects configured in the CO-PA planning framework to users in more detail, as well as roles and functions using planning profiles.

6.9   Planning Profiles

Users plan, use, and monitor information differently depending on their role in the organization. For this reason, a CEO won't require or maintain the same volume of data as a shop floor employee who needs to keep track of production orders. With this example in mind, think of planning profiles as ways to divide the areas of responsibility in your SAP implementation based on the roles of users. Generally, there are three types of users in any SAP implementation, as shown in Figure 6.38, and described in the following list:

▸ **Power users**
Generally, top-level managers, network and system administrators, project managers, team leaders, or developers that control or limit the information displayed or used by super users or end users.

▸ **Super users**
Users that may have a medium- to low-level usage of the application. Super users have authorization and usage limitations placed on them that only power users are allowed to change.

▸ **End users**
Generally, the final customers of any SAP system. End users perform data input operations and execute functions created by power and super users.

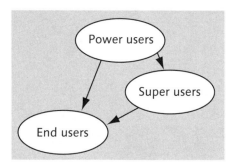

Figure 6.38 Roles and Relationships of an SAP Implementation

In Figure 6.38, the arrows represent the level of influence and relationships between the different types of users. For example, power users can modify information available for themselves, end users, and super users, while super users can modify information for themselves and end users, but are limited by the objects that power users have set up. Finally, end users cannot perform any modifications over the objects assigned to them and they just use the objects available and associated with their user IDs inside the SAP system.

The concept of planning profiles goes along with these classifications because there can be planning applications or views intended only for each of these types of users, depending on their authorizations and roles. For example, if you want certain users to work with specific levels, methods, etc., you can use a planning profile to limit their work and display capabilities:

1. Make sure that you're working in the design environment of the CO-PA planning framework shown earlier in Figure 6.18.

2. As shown in Figure 6.39, select EDIT • PERSONALIZATION PROFILE • CREATE PERSONALIZATION PROFILE.

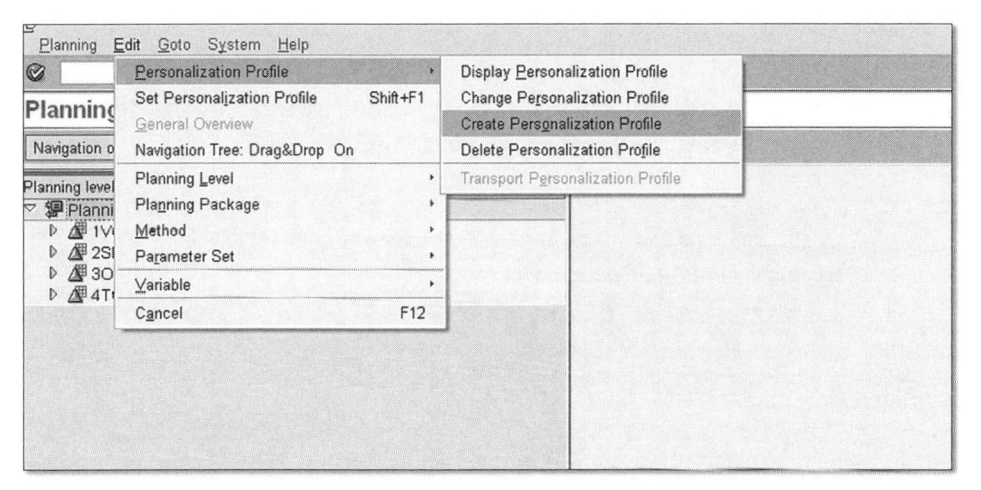

Figure 6.39 Creating a Personalization Profile

3. The screen shown in Figure 6.40 appears. The SAP system requires the initial configuration of the technical name, "USER25," and the description associated with this name, "End-User Profile." The USER25 planning profile is used to assign all of the different end users of the planning application and to limit their modification capabilities.

4. Once you're satisfied with the configuration settings in the CREATE PERSONALIZATION PROFILE screen shown in Figure 6.40, click on the CREATE icon (the white page icon) to generate your planning profile.

Figure 6.40 Configuring a Personalization Profile

5. As shown in Figure 6.41, the USER25 END-USER PROFILE has been created. Notice that on the right side there are two tabs: USER LIST and AUTHORIZATIONS. Also, notice on the left-hand side the planning levels available in your operating concern. You can use the checkboxes to select only those objects contained in the planning levels that you want to include as part of your profile, as shown in Figure 6.41.

On the right-hand side notice that the USER25 planning profile has been assigned to the User IDs MS2006, MWBWTST, and MXJWW2, which must be created inside the SAP system by a system administrator.

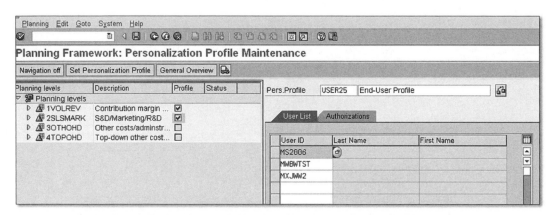

Figure 6.41 Assigning Users and Objects to Your Personalization Profile

> **Note**
>
> The person who creates the planning profile and assigns users will become the administrator of the profile.

6. Select the AUTHORIZATIONS tab, as shown in Figure 6.42.

7. To allow access or execution rights to any of the objects, select the checkbox next to the name of the appropriate function. For example, if you want to allow a user to create a planning level, select the checkbox next to CREATE PLANNING LEVEL and the object ROOT NODE, OBJECT TREE will be displayed.

8. Save the profile. You can always can go back to modify the assignments of the profile, as shown earlier in Figure 6.41. Also, you can change, display, and delete the profile as any other object in an SAP system.

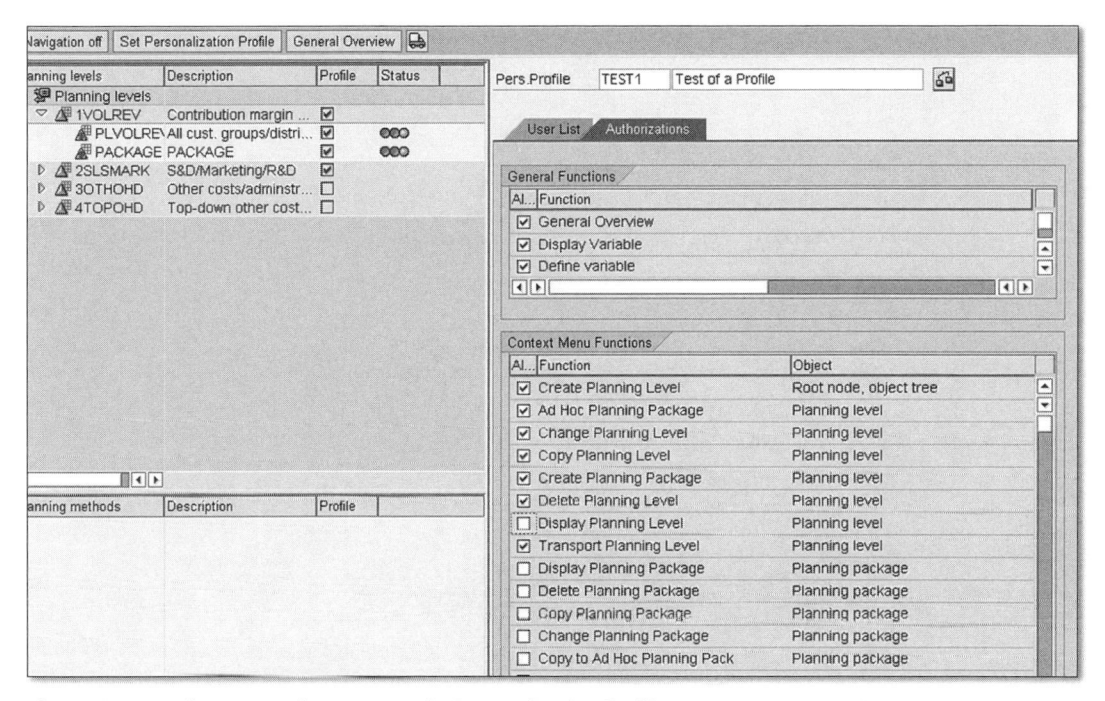

Figure 6.42 Configuring Authorizations of a Personalization Profile

Once users have been assigned to the personalization profile, when they log into the SAP system, the only processes and objects that will display are those configured by the planning administrator.

However, first you need to set a personalization profile, and to do that you need to load it in your system:

1. Click on the SET PERSONALIZATION PROFILE button located at the top of the screen shown in Figure 6.41 and Figure 6.42, or use Shift + F1.

2. Now the screen shown in Figure 6.43 appears, asking you to select the name of your personalized planning profile (PersProfil). In this case we have a profile called TEST1 and we want to review the status and functionalities (which we can do because we're the administrators of this profile).

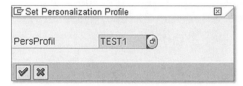

Figure 6.43 Set a Personalization Profile

3. Click on the checkmark icon.

4. Review the information in the screen that displays, shown in Figure 6.44, and notice that only the two planning levels previously selected in Figure 6.42 are displayed.

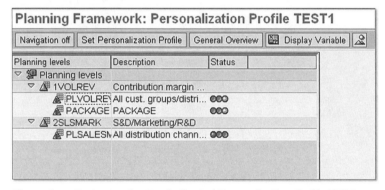

Figure 6.44 Reviewing the Newly Created Personalization Profile TEST1

Now let's review the authorization settings previously configured (shown in Figure 6.42), and how they work from a user's and administrator's point of view:

1. Review Figure 6.45, where we're trying to modify the contents of a predefined planning package, and see that all of the options have been grayed out. In other words, the user is not allowed to modify the package; all they can do is execute it and access any planning layouts associated with this package.

2. Now, in comparison, review the information presented in Figure 6.46, which shows the screen from an administrator's point of view, where all of the functions are available.

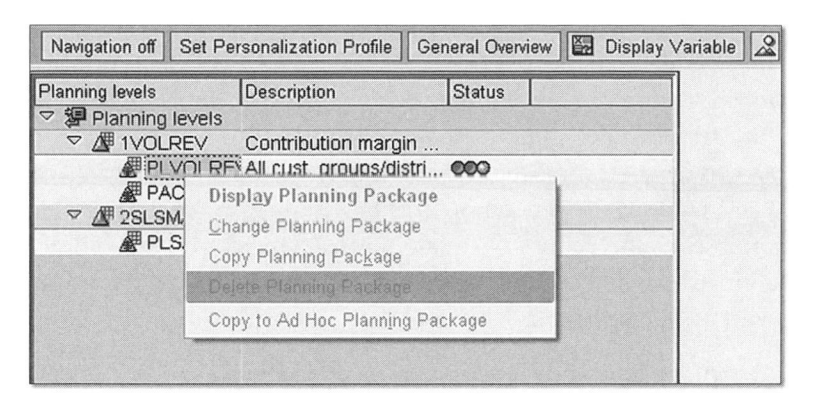

Figure 6.45 Authorization Options Control End-User Options in the Profile TEST1

> **Note**
>
> If you find options that are unavailable or you can't perform a function, always make sure that you know that you're working in the correct environment before thinking that there is a bug in the system or something to that effect.

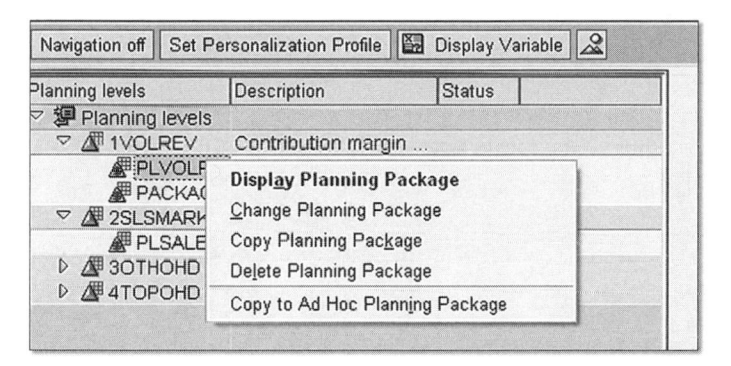

Figure 6.46 General View Without Planning Profiles

You've now learned how to generate and work with a planning profile, which is a useful tool when working with multiple users with different levels of expertise, data input, and requirements. We were also able to perform modifications in the behavior of specific objects inside the CO-PA planning framework, which means that our profile is working and doing what it is supposed to do. We recommend that you experiment more with this application, assigning users to profiles and testing their environments with their IDs to make sure you understand the concepts behind all of this.

6.10 Summary

In this chapter, we've provided a general overview of the components that define the CO-PA planning framework. Think of the CO-PA planning framework as a simple environment to develop sophisticated applications without leaving R/3 or SAP ERP ECC 6.0 and without the generation of cubes, extractors, or using information that is not as current. The CO-PA planning framework provides direct access to the data in its original format and allows performing transformations and sharing data with different users.

In Chapter 7, we'll explore additional functionalities available in the CO-PA planning framework and we'll review the configuration options required to create a planning application in more detail. In addition, we'll explore components such as ratios, key figure schemes, planning functions, and additional planning methods.

This chapter explores more practical components of the CO-PA planning framework such as forecasting, planning profiles, valuation and ratio planning, ratio schemes, and others that enhance the ability to modify data within the OLTP environment. These planning components complete the configuration steps required to generate a CO-PA planning application.

7 CO-PA Planning: Configuration

In Chapter 6, we reviewed the general concepts behind the CO-PA planning framework and briefly discussed some of its components. In this section, we'll move forward to the configuration steps that really define a planning application, and explore how to configure basic planning methods. In addition, we'll review elements such as *key figure schemes* that can be used to improve performance, *ratios*, a sophisticated tool to create formulas and add them to a report, and *planning sequences*, which let you automate running multiple planning methods consecutively. In this updated edition, we've expanded the content to include CO-PA assessment cycles in order to transfer data to your SAP CO-PA profitability segments, explain how to perform top-down distribution, and have provided additional detail on how to work with the SAP CO-PA planning framework environment. Let's get started.

7.1 Basic Planning Methods in the CO-PA Planning Framework

Most of the CO-PA planning methods shown in Figure 7.1 are predefined ABAP programs that run behind the scenes and that require certain parameters to perform the desired processes. In this section, we'll explore the most important of these planning methods, including Display planning data, Copy, Forecast, Valuation, Revaluation, Ratios, and Delete.

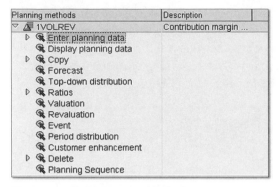

Figure 7.1 CO-PA Planning Methods

In Chapter 6, you already learned how to work with the basic planning method—ENTER PLANNING DATA—if you want to configure a layout and input data manually. However, this isn't always desirable because business applications require data transformation to deliver real planning applications, and these processes will post the data directly into the SAP database in real time. Planning applications and data volume can also affect system performance if they aren't carefully configured.

As a Best Practice, use CO-PA planning methods to extract and modify data within the OLTP system, and limit the usage of custom ABAP programs to highly sophisticated requirements that cannot be delivered with standard SAP functions. You don't want to affect sensitive data because of a mistake in the definition of your ABAP coding.

Now, let's get started with our discussion of the most important planning methods available in CO-PA.

7.1.1 Enter Planning Data

We already explored this functionality in Chapter 6, so we won't discuss it in this section.

7.1.2 Display Planning Data

DISPLAY PLANNING DATA provides similar functionality as ENTER PLANNING DATA, which we also explored in Chapter 6, with the only difference being that you can't change the data displayed and it's for read-only purposes. Similarly to the

ENTER PLANNING DATA method you assign a planning layout, such as the planning layout LAYOUT shown in Figure 7.2, to extract information for display purposes only. Manual input of information is not possible. Depending on the role of your users, you may allow them to use the ENTER PLANNING DATA or DISPLAY PLANNING DATA planning method.

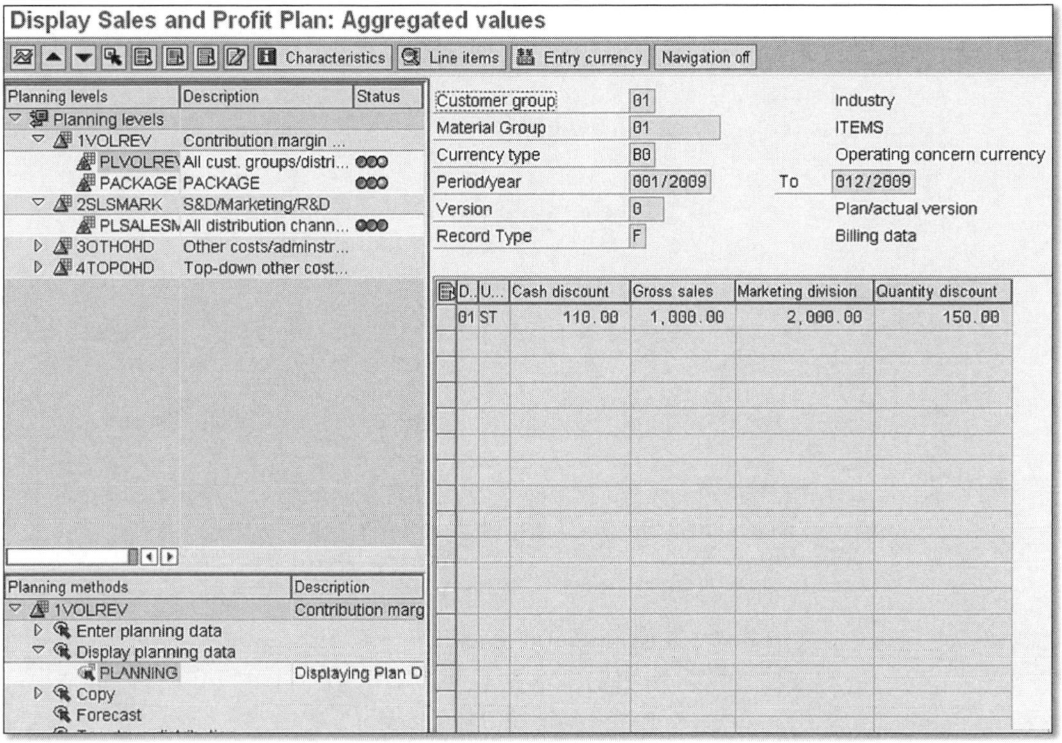

Figure 7.2 Using the Display Planning Data Planning Method

7.1.3 Copy

The COPY planning method is one of the most important functions because it simplifies any operations that perform similar processes based on predefined selection criteria. As an example, the COPY method becomes useful when working with budget, plan, and forecast data, and you would like to reuse actual data from previous years as the starting point. Using the COPY method, you can select the time period to be the source, and copy it to the target time period (so, you could copy actual data from 2009 to budget data for the 2017 time period).

Copy from previous years

Tips & Tricks

In any client or project interview, you'll likely be asked about your knowledge of the Copy function. Knowing this function in either CO-PA, SEM-BPS, BI-BPS, or any other component that performs similarly is sure to be a big plus for you in the interview process.

Three different copy operations exist:

▶ COPY VALUES
Replaces the previous value with a new value.

▶ ADD
Adds the new value to the existing value. Be careful with this operation; you might ending up having double of everything.

▶ SUBTRACT VALUES
You can remove values that already exist in the target based on predefined selection criteria.

Figure 7.3 shows an example of a copy function in CO-PA. On the SETTINGS tab, in the COPY area, you can select the type of copy operation to apply to your data. In addition, you need to specify a REFERENCE DATA time period, which will define the time period to use to select the data to be copied by the system.

To access the COPY planning method, follow these instructions:

1. Click on the COPY planning method, shown in Figure 7.3.

2. Right-click to create the associated parameter group called CPVACT. The screen displayed on the right-hand side of the screen in Figure 7.3 appears.

3. In the PROCESSING area, select TEST RUN from the dropdown box to copy information that we have now as actual data and generate an exact copy of those values in order to generate our plan data, and make modifications later on.

4. Save your new parameter set as CPYACT.

Now, you need to execute the planning method by following this procedure:

1. Select and right-click on CPYACT, then select EXECUTE METHOD, as shown in Figure 7.4. Because we're running the test run environment, the system will let us know if any problems are encountered during execution of the planning method. After this execution is completed you will have successfully copied the data based on the definitions described in Figure 7.3.

Basic Planning Methods in the CO-PA Planning Framework | **7.1**

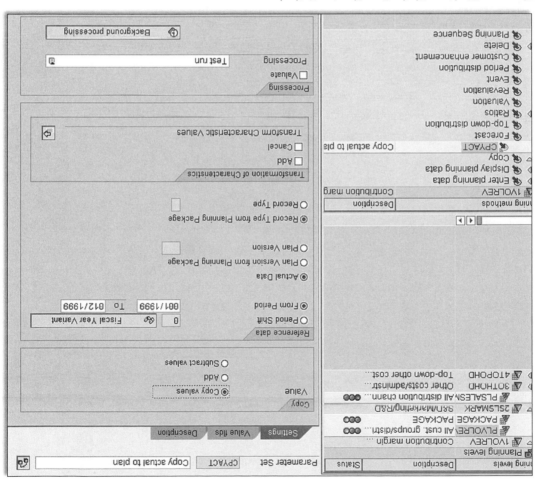

Figure 7.3 Working with the Copy Planning Method

Tips & Tricks

It's important to make sure the procedures and processes you want to execute are doing exactly what they're intended to do. That is, it isn't enough that the system tells you that the execution was performed successfully; you need to verify that the processes are the correct processes for your data transformation requirements. Review this on your own with several tests to make sure your functions are doing what they are supposed to do. Don't transport or assume that your objects are working successfully until you've manually verified the calculations and their effects on the test data, even if you success-fully executed the planning method.

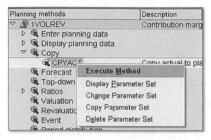

Figure 7.4 Executing the Copy Parameter Set

2. The screen shown in Figure 7.5 displays, showing the results of the test run. You can tell from the text that the parameter set executed successfully.

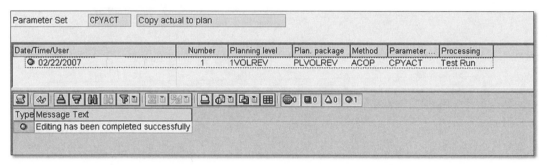

Figure 7.5 Screen Output of the Status of the CPYACT Copy Parameter Set

3. Right-click on the CPYACT planning method and select CHANGE PARAMETER SET.

4. In the PROCESSING area, select UPDATE RUN from the dropdown list. Once executed, this will complete the posting and update the SAP tables in the OLTP system.

5. Right-click on CPYACT and select EXECUTE METHOD again.

Tips & Tricks

Before you execute the function, take a screenshot or write down the values so you can evaluate the final result of the processes.

Figure 7.6 presents the current (before) status of the data included in the planning layout and the different characteristic and value fields selected to which you want to perform the change. The COPY planning method, as shown in Figure 7.3, copied all of the data between 01/2009 and 12/2009.

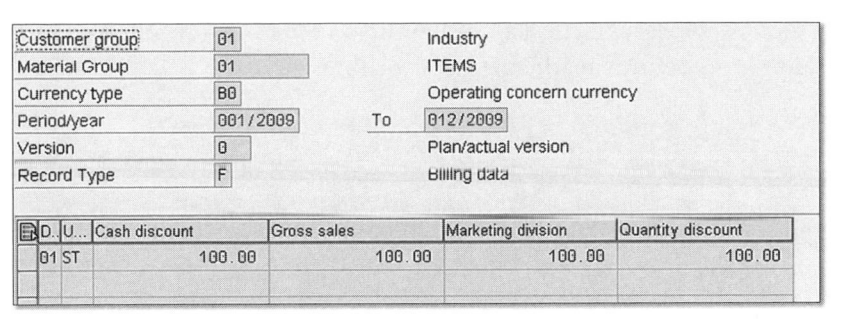

Figure 7.6 Data Status Before Executing the Copy Operation

Figure 7.7 shows the status after executing the COPY planning method, indicating that changes were made to the original data in the CASH DISCOUNT, GROSS SALES, and QUANTITY DISCOUNT columns displayed in Figure 7.6.

Customer group	01		Industry
Material Group	01		ITEMS
Currency type	B0		Operating concern currency
Period/year	001/2009	To 012/2009	
Version	0		Plan/actual version
Record Type	F		Billing data

	D..	U...	Cash discount	Gross sales	Marketing division	Quantity discount
	01	ST	34,852.93	2,901,019.40	100.00	121,754.46

Figure 7.7 Data Values After Executing the Copy Operation

Take your time to analyze and understand the COPY planning method. It's very difficult to avoid using this planning method while developing your planning applications with the CO-PA planning framework. For that reason, the COPY planning method is considered one of the most important planning methods in the SAP system.

> **Tips & Tricks**
>
> You can reset the system to the status before a planning method was executed by using the following path: EDIT • UNDO PLANNING FUNCTION.

7.1.4   Forecast

If you're interested in working with planning applications, you'll want to generate scenarios that describe the future performance of selected values. The FORECAST

Forecast

planning method provides a practical and scientific way to estimate your data into the future, using a predefined mathematical algorithm.

> **Note**
>
> Because this book is designed to present the functionalities of the CO-PA planning framework rather than provide a complete view of financial, mathematical, and other types of analysis, we'll limit our discussion of the forecast planning method to a brief overview.

When working with forecasts in general, there are three types of models:

▶ **Constant**

Used for time-series data in which values don't change much over time. For example, for a supermarket, the sales of frozen pizza is a constant value during the fiscal year, thus if the retailer knows that they will sell around 10 pizzas per day, all of the deliveries from the supplier must be planned using a constant model. In other words, the retailer in this scenario would want 10 packs of pizza available to the public at all times.

▶ **Seasonal**

Also called *cycles*, their behavior might depend on external factors, such as demand or period of the year. For example, for no other day of the year is turkey sold more than for Thanksgiving Day in the United States. For retailers, seasonal products like this might even have their own category for inventory management purposes. In the case of a supermarket or retailer that sells turkeys, for example, a seasonal model will describe the expected sales of turkey for a particular year, and might also affect its classification during that time period. This means that during the rest of the year, turkey can be classified as a nonbasic product (it's ok if it's not in stock because sales are slow; and it could be controlled with a constant model, for example), but during Thanksgiving season, turkey is classified as basic-seasonal. In other words, the retailer must have turkey in stock during this time if he wants to also sell cranberry sauce, spices, stuffing, gravy, and other things that people buy to go along with the turkey. They also need to control the product availability of the complimentary products, using turkey as a product that generates dependable demands.

▶ **Trend**

Trend is a rather complex model because it's a combination of the constant and seasonal models. It uses alpha, beta, and gamma factors as ways to smooth the models' behavior. This model is the most common and you don't have to use all of the parameters.

In addition, the FORECAST planning method requires a parameter set object and a forecast profile that has an alphanumeric name that uniquely identifies it. This forecast profile is a group of parameters with which you can project future values in a time series. You can use the same forecast profile again and again, saving you time, to manage the behavior of one or more key figures based on a forecast strategy.

Generally, you should create a separate planning package to store the forecast data because this planning method requires reference data from before the periods chosen inside the planning package. Once executed, the FORECAST planning method reads the information available at the segment level of the operating concern to perform the forecast of a value field.

Tips & Tricks

A forecast strategy is the same as a forecast model or mathematical algorithm that controls the behavior of the data values generated. There are at least 20 mathematical algorithms designed to create a forecast time series that can be as simple as a first-order equation and moving average, or as complex as the seasonal and Winters methods. The Winters methods (part of the Winters-Whitney methods) are considered to be some of the most mathematically accurate forecasting algorithms for time series and seasonal data.

Not all of the models require the smoothing factors available in the FORECAST planning method, but they are available depending on the mathematical needs and complexity of your time series extracted from the OLTP system.

To successfully apply and develop your FORECAST planning method, you need to perform additional configuration:

1. Go to the CO-PA planning framework, as shown in Figure 7.8, and review the information stored in your planning package for the dates, in this case between 1/2009 and 12/2009, because this information will be used as a reference to forecast the values for 2010.

additional config needed for Forecasting

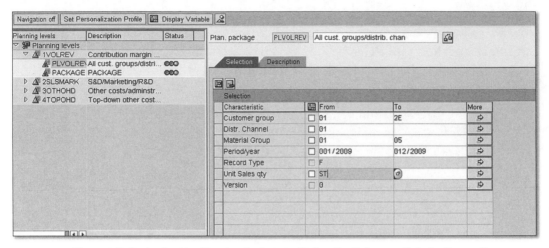

Figure 7.8 Reviewing the Planning Package to Define the Reference Data for Forecasting

2. Next, we need to work with the MAINTAIN FORECAST PROFILES function, following the path PROFITABILITY ANALYSIS • PLANNING AIDS • FORECAST PROFILE • MAINTAIN FORECAST PROFILES, as shown in Figure 7.9.

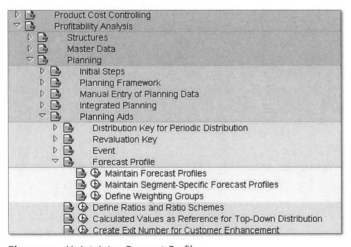

Figure 7.9 Maintaining Forecast Profiles

3. Now you can configure the forecast profile, which is similar to a planning profile but creates a planning strategy associated with an algorithm that generates the planned values. As shown in Figure 7.10, different parameters are required, depending on the forecast strategy. For example, we'll select the

MOVING AVERAGE forecast strategy, which only requires the parameter HIST. PERIODS (number of periods). Define three periods, then complete the information as shown in Figure 7.10.

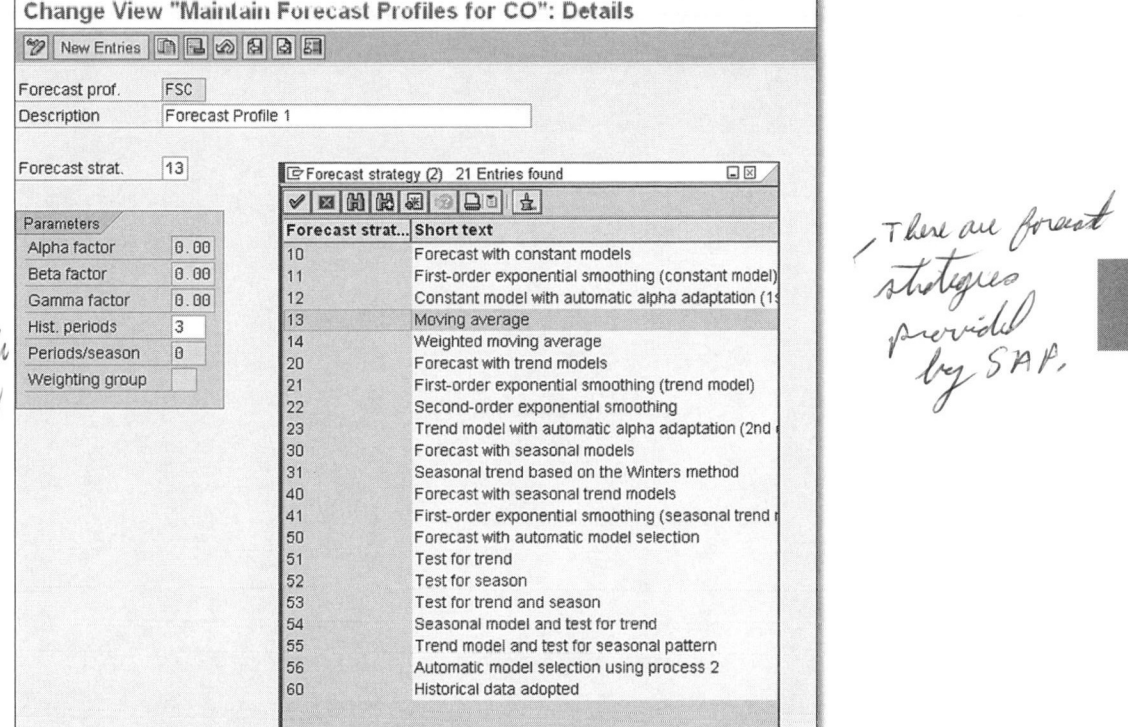

Figure 7.10 Creating a Forecast Strategy and a Forecast Algorithm as Part of a Forecast Profile

> **Note**
>
> When you configure your FORECAST planning method, the HIST. PERIODS (historical periods), PERIODS/SEASON, and WEIGHTING GROUP determine the number of periods that the forecast strategy uses to generate the data. For example, for generally stable data values, using the last three periods of the year is enough, but for very complex behavior, the last 12 periods might help with estimating the next six periods.

4. As shown in Figure 7.10, there's an SAP-defined forecast strategy called FSC that uses a MOVING AVERAGE forecast model and that uses the parameter 3 for the HIST. PERIODS or number of periods used to calculate the moving average.

Now you can use the FSC profile as part of the forecast planning method as shown in Figure 7.11, under PLANNING METHODS. Also, notice that we're using the actual data from 01/2009 until 12/2009 as reference data to generate the new forecasted data using the moving average algorithm.

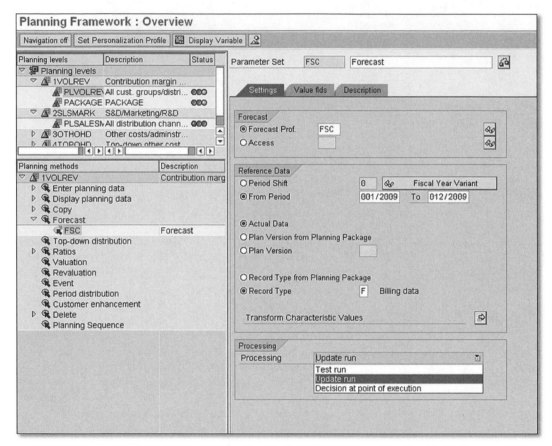

Figure 7.11 Assigning the FSC Planning Profile to Your Forecast Planning Method

The key elements, as we'll configure them on the SETTINGS tab, shown in Figure 7.11, include:

▶ FORECAST PROF. (Forecast Profile)
This has been set to FSC to access the moving average of the previously defined strategy.

▶ REFERENCE DATA
This is the data the SAP system will use to perform the forecast:

- FROM PERIOD
  The time period to use as reference to generate the new data for the time periods limited in the planning package, or 1/2010 to 12/2010.

- ACTUAL DATA
  This specifies that we'll perform a forecast of actual data only.

- RECORD TYPE
  This lets you select the data type. F means that only billing data will be included in the forecasted periods. Other types of documents are reviewed later on in Chapter 8 when transferring data into CO-PA from other SAP components.

▶ PROCESSING
Use TEST RUN twice to make sure you aren't generating values with errors. Once completed, select UPDATE RUN. The option DECISION AT POINT OF EXE-CUTION is only used if you think you'll be working online and you'll decide later whether to execute this function.

Tips & Tricks

You don't use the FORECAST planning method to estimate characteristics values, but to estimate key figures. Characteristics are maintained based on the definitions of the planning levels and planning packages in the CO-PA planning framework.

5. Now, select the VALUE FLDS tab as shown in Figure 7.12, and select the value fields forecasted using the moving average method.

   Notice that on the right side is the list of the different value fields that are available. Select the ones you're interested in and click on the left arrow to add them to the SELECTED region on the left. As shown in Figure 7.12, the CASH DIS-COUNT value field is the only selected key figure to be forecast using the moving average, and the configurations created on the SETTINGS tab, such as RECORD TYPE F, ACTUAL DATA, and FORECAST PROFILE FSC, are displayed in Figure 7.11.

6. Select and right-click on FSC FORECAST on the left.

7. Click on EXECUTE METHOD, as shown in Figure 7.13.

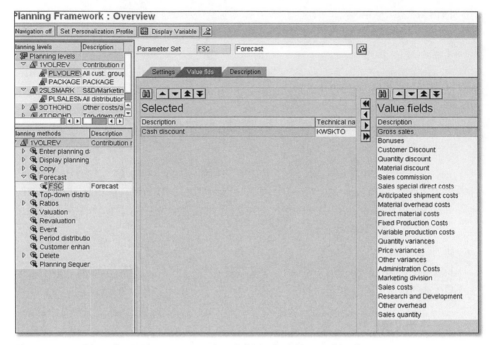

Figure 7.12 Adding the Cash Discount Value Field in the Value Field Tab

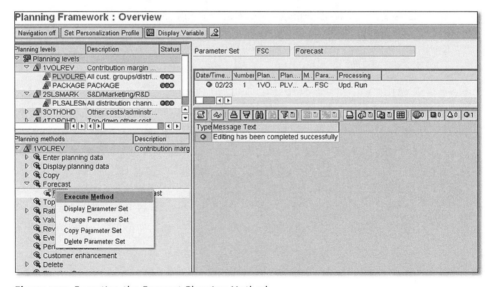

Figure 7.13 Executing the Forecast Planning Method

The SAP system now generates a general check of the information presented and provides the information shown in Figure 7.13, informing you if any errors were detected during the execution of the planning method. Based on the same figure, we can conclude that our FORECAST planning method has been correctly configured and executed. However, we still need to see if the data was generated as expected because regardless of whether the execution was successful, the configuration might still be incorrect.

Remember, we wanted to generate data between 1/2010 and 12/2010 using 2009 data for the same time range as reference and only for the CASH DISCOUNT value field. With this information in mind, and knowing that the planning method ran successfully, let's see if any data was available for the selection criteria.

~ use last years data as a base

As shown in Figure 7.14, using the CO-PA planning framework and the DISPLAY PLANNING DATA planning method, we see that for the time period 1/2010 to 12/2010 the CASH DISCOUNT 34,852.92 was generated, based on the information previously contained in the 1/2009-12/2009 data range. This means that our FORECAST planning method was successfully executed because previously there was no such data in the system (notice that the other value fields contain no data values).

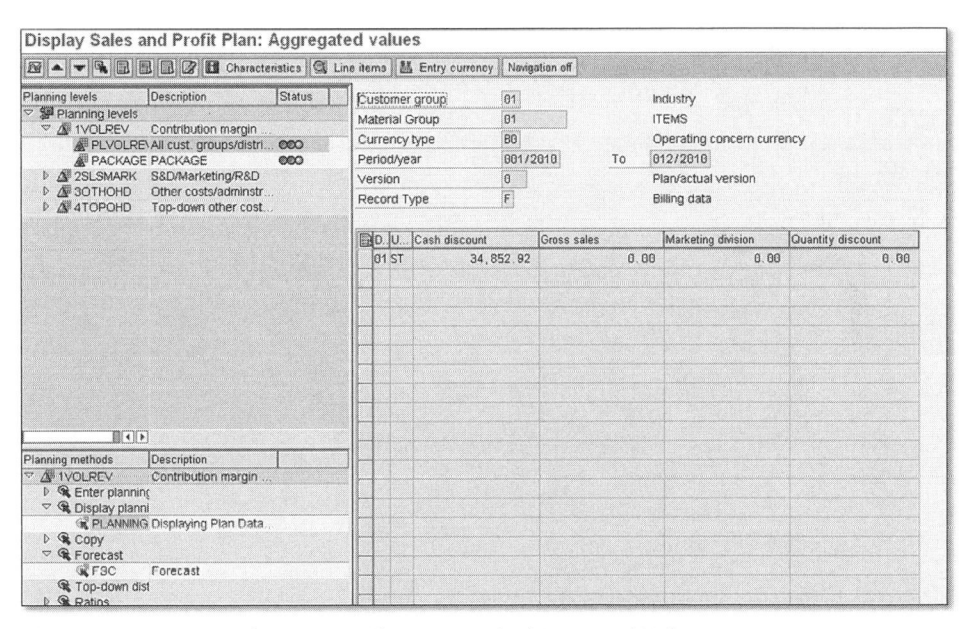

Figure 7.14 Reviewing the Forecast Planning Method Generated Values

7.1.5 Valuation

The VALUATION planning method uses the information defined previously in master data using the path VALUATION STRATEGIES IN PROFITABILITY ANALYSIS • MASTER DATA • VALUATION • VALUATION STRATEGIES • DEFINE AND ASSIGN VALUATION STRATEGIES. This information is now available in the VALUATION planning method as part of the planning framework, and you simply assign it. The steps configured in your valuation strategy will be applied to the data in the planning framework. Refer back to Chapter 5 for the concepts behind this planning function.

[handwritten margin note: This would involve changing the valuation]

7.1.6 Revaluation

In this section, you'll learn about the REVALUATION planning method, which you can use to change values during planning by specified percentages. In comparison with the VALUATION planning method, revaluation requires a planning aid called *revaluation keys*. As is the case with other planning methods in CO-PA planning framework, there are additional objects required to complete the definition and control the behavior of the data selection and generation in the REVALUATION planning method. That is, revaluation requires you to work with either MAINTAIN REVALUATION KEYS, or with MAINTAIN SEGMENT-SPECIFIC REVALUATION KEYS if you want to affect particular characteristics and value fields contained inside your operating concern and defined as a segment.

[handwritten margin note: needs a revaluation key configured]

Follow this procedure to create revaluation keys and use them in your planning applications:

1. Follow the path REVALUATION KEYS OBJECT PROFITABILITY ANALYSIS • PLANNING • REVALUATION KEY • MAINTAIN REVALUATION KEYS, as shown in Figure 7.15, and click on the EXECUTE icon next to MAINTAIN REVALUATION KEYS.

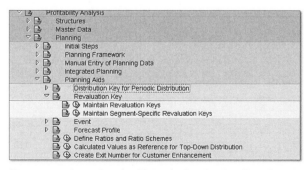

Figure 7.15 Accessing the Maintain Revaluation Keys Function

2. The screen shown in Figure 7.16 is displayed. Notice there are two nodes: REVALUATION KEYS, which defines the name of the object that will carry the value fields and the percentages, and ASSIGN FACTORS, where we create the assignment of value fields and percentages.

3. Select the change/modify icon (the pencil with glasses), and click on NEW ENTRIES. Give the revaluation key a technical name of "RV" (in the REV column) and a name of "This is a Revaluation Key" as shown in Figure 7.16.

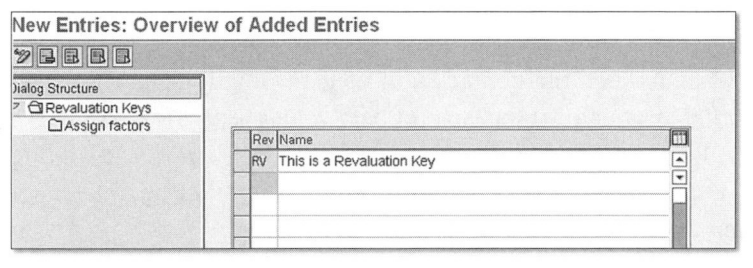

Figure 7.16 Configuring a Revaluation Key

4. Now, select the ASSIGN FACTORS node on the left-hand side of Figure 7.17 to define which key figures will be included as part of revaluation key RV, as shown in the same figure.

5. Assign the value fields that you want to increase or decrease by a specific percentage by finding them using their technical names in the FIELD NAME column, shown in Figure 7.17, and typing the percentage increase in the PERCENTAGE column.

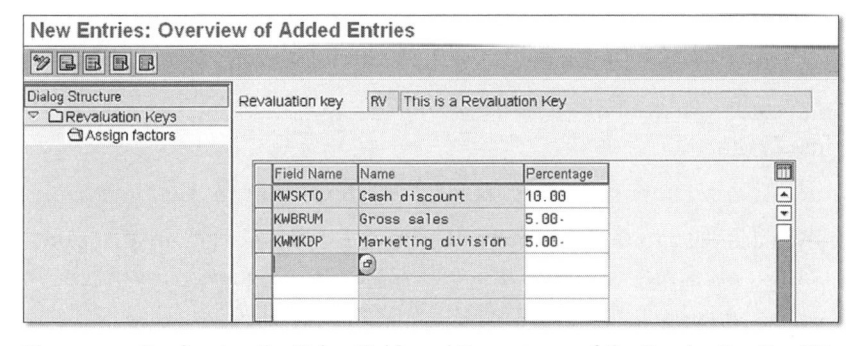

Figure 7.17 Configuring the Value Fields and Percentages of the Revaluation Key RV

As shown in Figure 7.17, we want to work with the following value fields:

▶ KWSKTO (Cash discount) increased by 10%

▶ KWBRUM (Gross sales) reduced by 5%

▶ KWMKDP (Marketing division) reduced by 5%

Notice that the notation for the SAP system to create a reduction is 5.00-, with the minus sign at the end, as also shown in Figure 7.17. To make a percentage increase, just the number is entered (without a sign).

6. Once you're satisfied with your changes, save them.

At this point, you've completed the definition of your revaluation key RV. Now, let's suppose that we want to adjust the current data values with the percentages previously defined. For this, we need to work with the REVALUATION planning method in the CO-PA planning framework and configure another parameter set to access the information contained in the RV revaluation key.

First, let's review the current status of your data for the period from 01/2009 to 12/2009 in your SAP system, as shown in Figure 7.18. This is what the data looks like before executing the REVALUATION planning method.

D..	U...	Cash discount	Gross sales	Marketing division	Quantity discount
01	ST	34,852.93	2,901,019.40	100.00	121,754.46

Figure 7.18 Data Before the Revaluation is Executed

Next, we'll review the SETTINGS tab of the REVALUATION planning method and its parameter set. As shown in Figure 7.19, perform the following:

1. In the REVALUATION section on the SETTINGS tab, assign the REVALUATION KEY RV that we just created.

2. In the PROCESSING section, select TEST RUN to avoid postings for the time being.

3. Select the VALUE FLDS tab to select the value fields GROSS SALES, CASH DISCOUNT, and MARKETING DIVISION, as shown in Figure 7.20. Use the left arrow to move selected value fields from the VALUE FIELDS area to the SELECTED area.

4. Save your work, and go back to the CO-PA planning framework and identify the parameter set that you defined, in this case REVAL, and execute the REVALUATION planning method as shown in Figure 7.21.

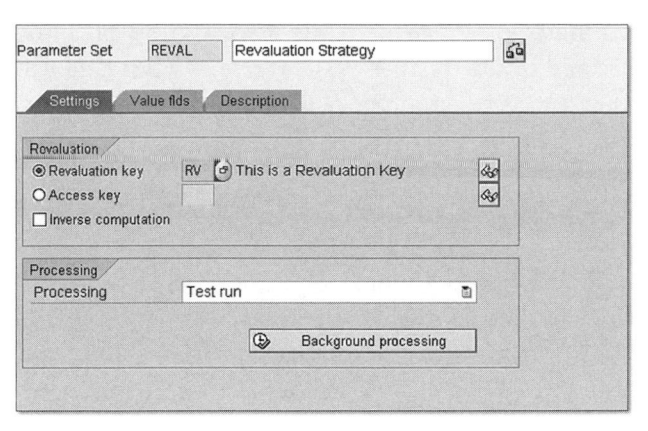

Figure 7.19 Configuring the Revaluation Key Parameter Set

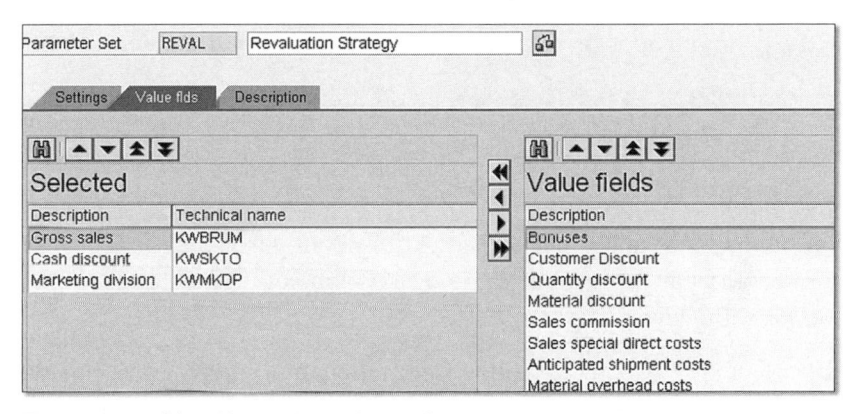

Figure 7.20 Adding Your Value Fields to the REVAL Parameter Set

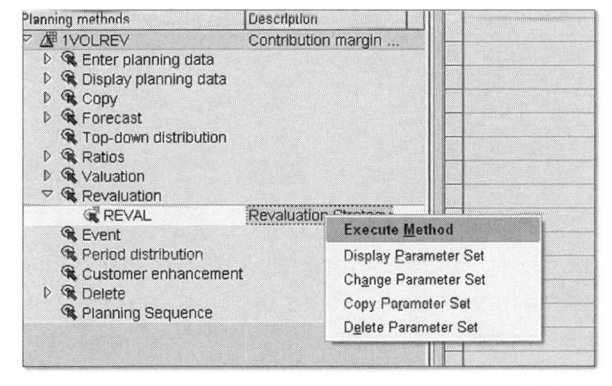

Figure 7.21 Executing the Revaluation Planning Method

To make sure that what you thought you created (the REVALUATION planning method) is actually being executed inside the SAP system, review your data values using a parameter set in the DISPLAY PLANNING DATA planning method with the same layout, as shown in Figure 7.22 and as described previously in Chapter 6.

D.	U...	Cash discount	Gross sales	Marketing division	Quantity discount
01	ST	38,338.24	2,755,968.47	95.00	121,754.46

Figure 7.22 New Values After Executing the Revaluation Planning Method Using the Revaluation Key RV

Compare your original and modified data values shown in Figure 7.18 and Figure 7.22, respectively, to see how effective your design and configuration are:

▶ CASH DISCOUNT: 38,338.24 is 10% more than 34,852.93.

▶ GROSS SALES: 2,755,968.47 is 5% less than 2,901,019.4.

▶ MARKETING DIVISION: 95 is 5% less than 100.

Now you can be confident that you have successfully configured the REVALUATION planning method and you can use the same revaluation key with other planning packages and planning levels.

The flexibility of an SAP system often allows more than one correct way of delivering the same result. Therefore, you can generate the same data values you generated with revaluation keys with an alternative planning method called RATIOS. The RATIOS planning method is typically used when your planning efforts require more sophisticated calculations that demand working with the division and the multiplication operations.

7.1.7   Ratios

The RATIOS planning method lets you valuate a plan version using average prices from a reference version or reference actual data. This means that you can store your price plan and quantity plan separately and then use these prices to valuate the quantity plan. Ratios can be used both in manual planning and in automatic planning.

Ratios are another example of CO-PA planning methods that require additional definitions external to the CO-PA planning framework. Ratios are quite popular among managers because they are the calculation of indexes that divide a numerator by a denominator and are sometimes followed by multiplication.

For example, for just-in-case situations, if we define the equation A/B, A is the numerator, and B is the denominator. A ratio is a division, and sometimes we may find relationships, such as A/B*C. A ratio is the quotient of two value fields, such as sales revenue divided by quantity. In this section you'll define ratios to be used as part of your planning applications with the RATIO planning method.

Ratios can be used in different ways (using an example of a formula with three fields):

▸ If you change one of the fields and only one of the other two fields can be entered manually, the system assumes that it should calculate the field that cannot be entered manually, regardless of which calculation type was chosen.

▸ When you change two of the fields, the system calculates the third field.

▸ If you change all three fields, the system calculates sales as quantity * price and overwrites the manually entered value.

You must assign at least one access-level characteristic to each ratio in a ratio group. Access-level characteristics determine which combination of characteristics the system should use to access the valuation for each ratio. This makes it possible, for example, to calculate the average price for a product group. The calculation types for the ratios aren't involved in this function.

You need to define the ratios separately and place these in a ratio scheme before you can use them to valuate your plan data. The ratio scheme determines which ratios are selected in which order.

With an access-level characteristic, you can specify the planning level (the combination of characteristics) at which the ratio should be used for valuation. This makes it possible, for example, to plan individual products and valuate these using the average price at the product group level. Ratios, ratio schemes, and access-level characteristics are defined in Customizing.

Depending on the industry, the calculation of ratios will vary depending on the performance indicators required to be reported to management. For example, if you're in the automotive industry, you're interested in knowing about cost reduction efforts, inventory flow, and production indicators, such as cycle time and downtimes of machinery, and all of them can be defined as ratios. In the retail industry, it's more important to know inventory turnover, delivery times, profitability by product line, and sales per square foot. If you're in the financial sector, you probably want to know the profitability by client segment, number of transactions per day by product line, and number of new mortgage loans approved because all of them are core indicators that reflect the health of the business.

Regardless of where your CO-PA implementation is taking place, you must clearly define and understand your ratios before creating them, making sure that they measure exactly the relationships that you want to monitor.

> **Note**
>
> The useful and simple calculations that the RATIO planning method performs are a must in any SAP implementation, and therefore you must remember them.

Let's start working with ratios, creating quantity discounts:

1. Follow the path PLANNING • PLANNING AIDS • DEFINE RATIOS AND RATIO SCHEMES to start configuring ratios and ratio schemes, as shown in Figure 7.23. A ratio is one object, and a ratio scheme is a collection of objects with specific relationships. Ratio schemes reuse the information in the ratio objects they contain.

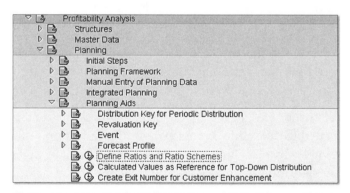

Figure 7.23 Accessing the Define Ratios and Ratio Schemes Object

Part of the ratio definition is the calculation type, which is only relevant in manual planning, but not for ratio schemes. Calculations, such as price = revenue/quantity, revenue = quantity × price, or quantity = revenue/price depend greatly on a number of factors, such as which fields are changed or which fields can or cannot be manually entered.

2. Click on the change/modify icon.

3. Click on the New Entries button to create the ratio with the configuration information shown in Figure 7.24. The ratio is called Rat1, and has two components: Numerator KWSKT0 and Denominator KWMGRB. In addition, the Rat1 ratio uses Calc. type 1 (calculation type 1), which requires recalculating the ratio. Now you can assign the Rat1 ratio to a group of specific ratios called a ratio scheme.

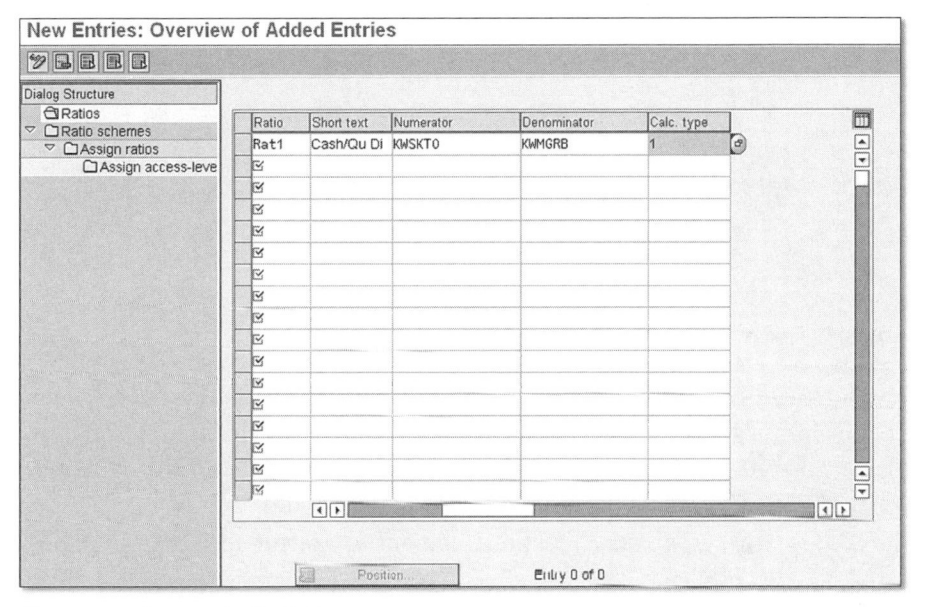

Figure 7.24 Creating Ratio Rat1

4. Click on the Save icon to store your newly created Rat1 ratio.

5. Click on Ratio Schemes, as shown in Figure 7.25.

6. Click on the change/modify icon, and then click on the New Entries button.

7. Using the information shown in Figure 7.25, create a ratio scheme called "TEST" with a description of "This is a test for a Ratio Scheme."

8. Click on the Save icon.

9. Select the line of the newly created TEST ratio scheme to assign ratios inside of this object.

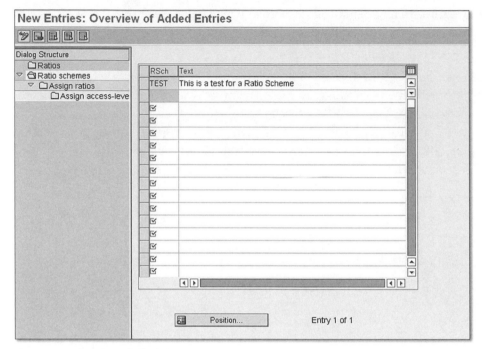

Figure 7.25 Creating a Ratio Scheme

As shown in Figure 7.26, you're assigning two ratios to the ratio scheme TEST. One of them is RAT1 CASH DISC/QUANT DISC (cash discount/quantity discount) and the other is FPROD PROD. FIXED COSTS/PC. Thus, the TEST ratio scheme is an umbrella object that carries the information of several ratios, so the SAP system can access a common element to execute different functions.

10. Save your changes.

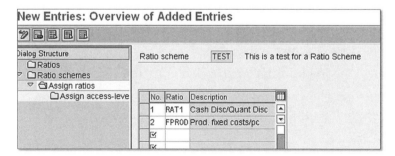

Figure 7.26 Assigning Ratios to a Ratio Scheme

Next, we need to define the level of detail at which the reference data is selected during the calculation of ratios, using access-level characteristics. Access-level characteristics can be simple or sophisticated, depending on your final goal of using ratios in your implementation. Let's review the first example, and create the following ratio relationship:

Price = revenue/quantity

We'll use the reference data shown in Table 7.1 with the intention of generating data to populate Table 7.2.

Product	Customer	Quantity	Revenue
P1	C1	10	100
P1	C2	20	260

Table 7.1 Reference Data for the Price = Revenue/Quantity Ratio

Product	Customer	Quantity	Revenue
P1	C1	11	???
P1	C2	22	???

Table 7.2 Goal of the Price = Revenue/Quantity Generation Ratio

► **Strategy 1**
Using access-level characteristics, you can estimate the values of revenue in different ways. In strategy 1, you use two characteristic relationships—product and customer—to estimate the values of revenue, as shown in Table 7.3. This leads us to ratio calculation strategy 1: revenue is calculated based on the price for each individual customer from Table 7.1 as reference, and then multiplied by the quantity in Table 7.2.

Product	Customer	Quantity	Revenue
P1	C1	11	110
P1	C2	22	286

Table 7.3 Results of the Revenue Ratio with Ratio Calculation Strategy 1

The calculation logic using product and customer as access-level characteristics for the ratio revenue values displayed in Table 7.3 is as follows:

$110 = 11 \times 100 / 10$
$286 = 22 \times 260 / 20$

▶ **Strategy 2**
Alternatively, you can calculate revenue by using the product characteristic as the only access-level characteristic assigned to the ratio revenue, leading us to ratio calculation strategy 2: quantities are valuated using an average price for all customers because only the characteristic product is used to estimate the values of revenue. The results of this change in logic are presented in Table 7.4.

Product	Customer	Quantity	Revenue
P1	C1	11	132
P1	C2	22	264

Table 7.4 Results of the Revenue Ratio with Ratio Calculation Strategy 2

The ratio calculation procedure using strategy 2 is as follows:

$132 = 11 \times (100 + 260) / (10 + 20)$
$264 = 22 \times (100 + 260) / (10 + 20)$

The difference in the results, shown in Table 7.3 and Table 7.4, by simply changing the number of characteristics assigned in the access-level characteristic, is significant. In general, the number of characteristics assigned greatly depends on the logic behind your ratio calculation. Based on this information, you can see that the calculation of ratio schemes can be a sophisticated issue, depending on the number of characteristics involved.

For our purpose, define access-level characteristics as follows:

1. Define CUSTOMER GROUP and MATERIAL GROUP as the access-level characteristics for our TEST ratio scheme, as shown in Figure 7.27.

2. Assign the TEST ratio scheme to the RATIO planning method as shown in Figure 7.28.

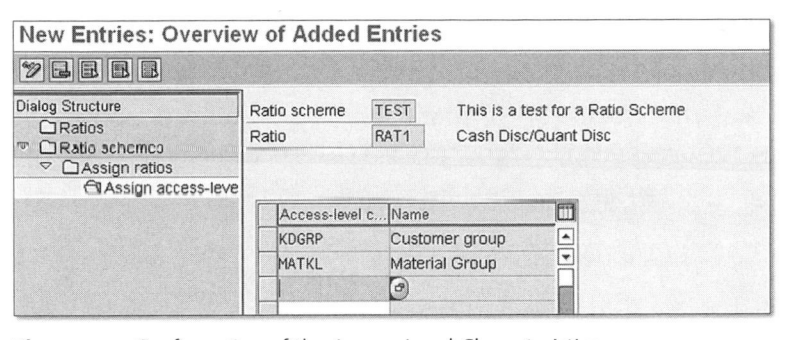

Figure 7.27 Configuration of the Access-Level Characteristics

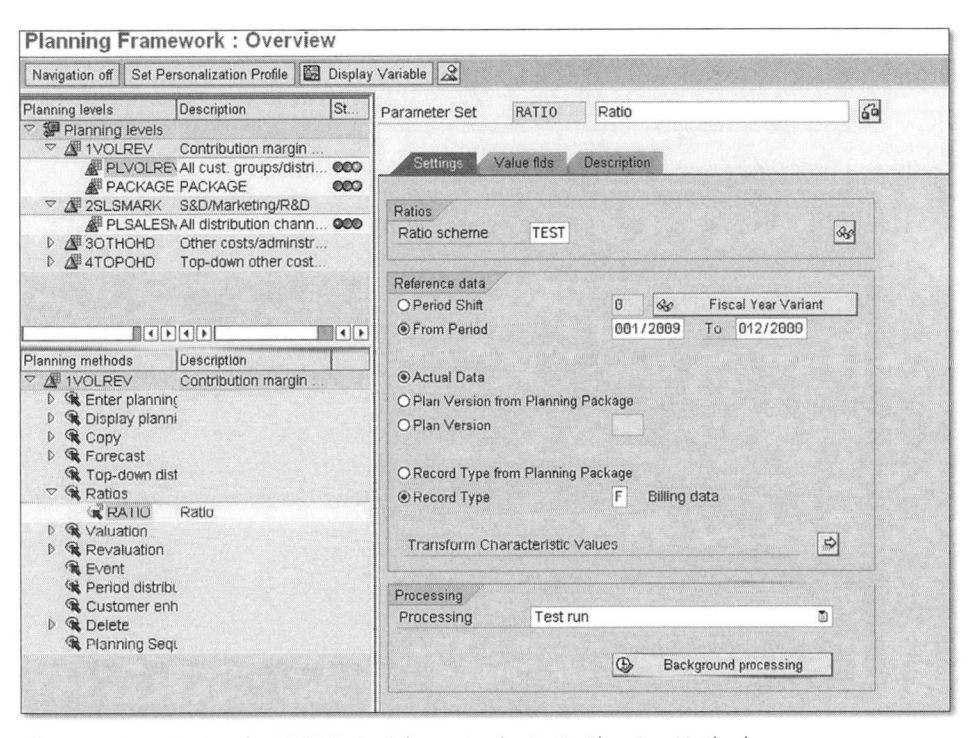

Figure 7.28 Assigning the TEST Ratio Scheme to the Ratio Planning Method

Creating Your Own Ratio Calculation Formulas

Although ratios are an easy function to master, you can also create your own calculation formulas using the Report Painter and adding them to your layout as an additional column, limiting characteristics in that way.

To create your own personalized formulas and calculations, follow this procedure:

1. Follow the path PLANNING • MANUAL ENTRY OF PLANNING DATA • DEFINE PLAN-NING LAYOUT and choose CHANGE PLANNING LAYOUT. Figure 7.29 shows the information from our previously created LAYOUT planning layout in the REPORT PAINTER environment.

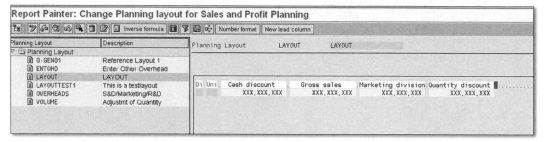

Figure 7.29 Creating a Ratio in a Planning Layout

2. Start creating an additional column as part of the layout by clicking on the end of the column called QUANTITY DISCOUNT, and selecting the element type FOR-MULA, as shown in Figure 7.30.

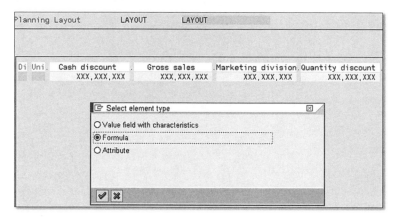

Figure 7.30 Creating a Ratio as a Formula Object

3. Click on the checkmark icon to enter the Report Painter formula editor, shown in Figure 7.31. The formula editor contains different components:

   ▶ FORMULA TABLE
   Describes the relationships or formula calculations of the value fields available.

▶ FORMULA COMPONENTS

Displays the components available to include as part of the Formula table using an ID identifier. For example, X001 identifies the CASH DISCOUNT value field. There are also other components that help to design a formula such as multiplication (*), division (/), parenthesis, individual numbers, and others.

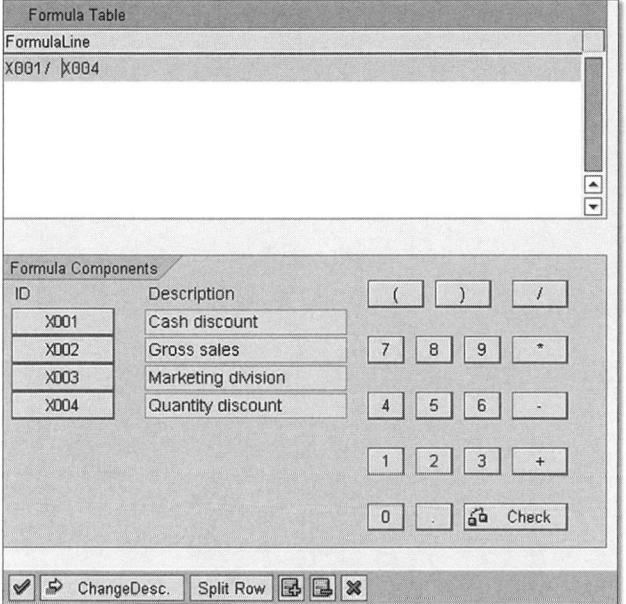

Figure 7.31 Using the Report Painter Formula Editor

4. Click on X001, then click on the division (/) operator, and then click on X004 to configure the formula (or ratio) CASH DISCOUNT/QUANTITY DISCOUNT, as shown under FORMULALINE in Figure 7.31.

5. Click on the checkmark icon.

6. Configure the name and identifiers of the new object by providing SHORT, MEDIUM, and LONG texts, as shown in Figure 7.32.

7. Click on the checkmark icon.

As shown in Figure 7.33, you now have an ALTERNATIVE RATIO calculation as part of your LAYOUT planning layout.

Figure 7.32 Configuring the Names for the New Formula Object

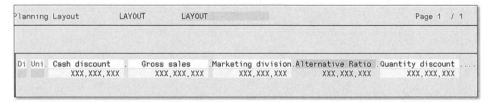

Figure 7.33 Reviewing Your Formula Object in Your Planning Layout

> **Note**
>
> More complicated ratios are better delivered using the RATIO planning method in combination with segment-level characteristics.

If you now run the planning layout LAYOUT, the ALTERNATIVE RATIO ratio displays a value of 0.29, as shown in Figure 7.34, after performing the same procedure used by the RATIO planning method. As you can see, there is more than one way to deliver and achieve the same information.

D.	U...	Cash discount	Gross sales	Marketing division	Alternative Ratio	Quantity discount
01	ST	34,803.90	2,755,968.47	95.00	0.29	121,754.46

Figure 7.34 Reviewing the Alternative Ratio Information After Executing the LAYOUT Planning Layout

In summary, review Figure 7.35 for a final look at the ratio concept. On the right side of the figure, you see that you require a reference version of data that you'll use to calculate the ratio $R1=Q1*R2/Q2$. This relationship is maintained in the generation of the current plan version, shown on the left side of Figure 7.35.

Notice that we're using two access-level characteristics, product and customer, to make the calculation.

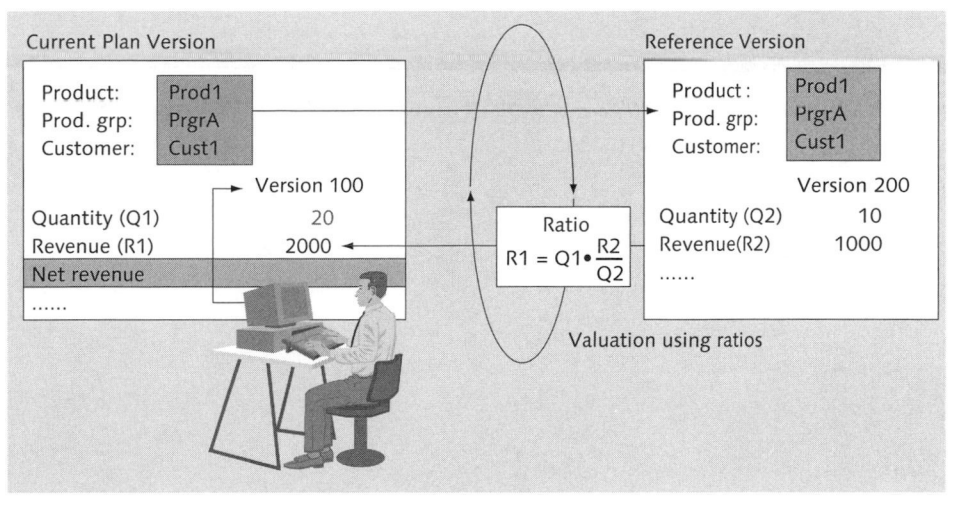

Figure 7.35 Valuation Using Ratios from a Reference Version

7.1.8 Delete

Another very important planning method is the DELETE planning method. Sometimes you need to remove data generated by error or data that's no longer needed. For example, using the FORECAST planning method for the CASH DISCOUNT value field, we generated data for the period between 1/2010 and 12/2010. We now want to get rid of this information, which you can do by following this procedure:

> **Note**
>
> By now you should know how to navigate the CO-PA planning framework to access the screen shown in Figure 7.36. If not, go back to previous activities to review this information.

1. Select a planning package, such as PLVOLREV, in the CO-PA planning framework, as shown in Figure 7.36.

2. Select the DELETE planning method, and create a PARAMETER SET called DELEFSCT, using the information shown in Figure 7.36.

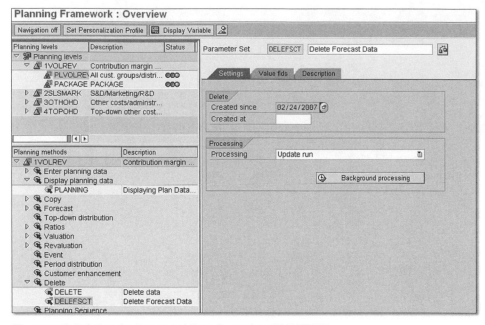

Figure 7.36 Deleting the Forecasted Data Created on 02/24/2007

3. Specify the date when the data to be deleted was generated. In our case, we want to delete the data generated on 02/24/2007.

4. In the PROCESSING section, select UPDATE RUN.

5. Select the VALUE FLDS tab and select the CASH DISCOUNT value field in order to delete *only* the data for that particular object.

6. Save your work, and execute the planning method.

7. You should receive confirmation that the run was successfully completed. Otherwise, you can review any issues on the right side of the screen.

8. Go back to the display planning area layout for the 01/2010 to 12/2010 data range established in the planning package to verify that the data for CASH DISCOUNT for the forecast time periods has been erased from the SAP database, as shown in Figure 7.37.

> **Note**
>
> Exercise extreme caution when using the DELETE planning method to avoid deleting data that is still required in the SAP system.

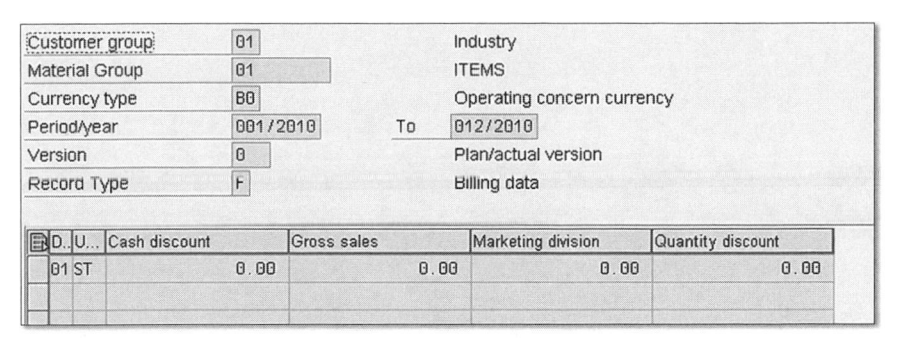

	D..	U...	Cash discount	Gross sales	Marketing division	Quantity discount
	01	ST	0.00	0.00	0.00	0.00

Figure 7.37 Confirming the Deletion of Your 2010 Data

In the next section, we'll briefly explore planning sequences, which are a more controlled and automatic way of managing complex operations by subdividing these operations into small pieces.

7.2 Planning Sequences

A *planning sequence* is a user-defined sequence or process that runs multiple planning methods sequentially to perform changes to the data that's limited by a planning package. This helps avoid errors that might occur if you're executing planning methods manually. Figure 7.38 shows a parameter set that's been configured to sequentially execute different preconfigured planning methods. This means that a complex process has been broken down into multiple small planning methods that change data one after the other, which in turn avoids generating complex architectures that are difficult to modify and update.

For example, based on the information we have previously developed, you may want to use a planning sequence to execute multiple operations, using the following specific logic:

1. Copy actual data from a referenced plan data.

2. Perform a forecast of the actual data.

3. Revaluate the actual data by specific percentages to reflect adjustments for inflation.

4. Delete the data of previously forecasted years.

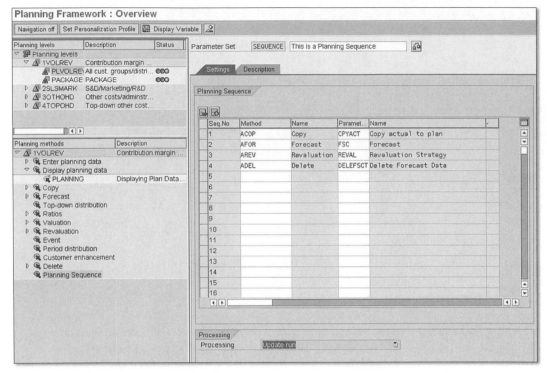

Figure 7.38 Creating a Planning Sequence

For the planning sequence to work properly, you must select a planning method to execute at each part of the sequence, and then associate the parameter set linked to that planning method. For example, in SEQ. No 1, shown in Figure 7.38, the planning method ACOP (COPY) is the first to run, using the parameter set CPY-ACT (COPY ACTUAL TO PLAN) contained in the planning method. The same logic applies to the rest of the objects included in the planning sequence.

In this respect, the goal of the CO-PA planning framework is to visualize complex operations as a planning sequence to simplify a controlled data transformation process.

> **Note**
>
> The CO-PA planning framework has a submenu called INTEGRATED PLANNING that was not discussed in this section. This submenu allows interaction with other components of the SAP system, such as Materials Management (MM), Financials (FI), and SAP NetWeaver Business Warehouse (BW).

7.3   Configuring CO-PA Assessments Cycles

When working in a sophisticated planning environment, you might be required to compare actual versus plan scenarios for your different profitability segments that are configured inside SAP CO-PA. For these cases, you need to transfer the values for the actual and/or plan versions of your data that reside in your cost centers to your SAP CO-PA operating concern.

In these situations, to assess the actual or planned costs stored in your cost centers, you should use an assessment cycle to transfer these costs to SAP CO-PA. Each data set (actual or plan) requires a separate assessment cycle to transfer costs to your profitibility segments and operating concerns. This process is quite useful when performing analysis associated with the contribution margin to visualize your data by sales organization, material, product hierarchy, and others.

Even though allocations, distributions, indirect activity allocation, and reposting are created in other modules such as Cost Center Accounting, the results must be transferred to CO-PA using a specific kind of assessment cycle.

In Cost Center Accounting, allocations can be performed using different methods, and the most common ones are assessments, distributions, and periodic reposting. Assessments allocate primary and secondary costs, whereas the last two only allow you to post primary costs. To perform the data transfer from cost centers to the CO-PA operating concern, you must follow the overall process described as follows:

1. Actual or planned costs must be posted to the cost centers, which must be debited with the costs of salaries and wages. To perform this process, use Transaction FB50 as shown in Figure 7.39.

2. Your next step is to transfer the cost center costs to CO-PA. To do this, use Transaction KEU5 to perform the clearing of the cost centers as shown in Figure 7.40. All costs that had previously been assigned to the cost centers have now been transferred to CO-PA. The balance of all cost centers affected by the assessment is zero after you execute this transaction, and the offsetting entries will appear in any cost center report.

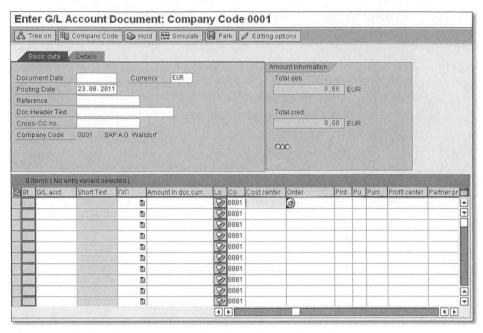

Figure 7.39 Posting Costs to the Cost Centers with Transaction FB50

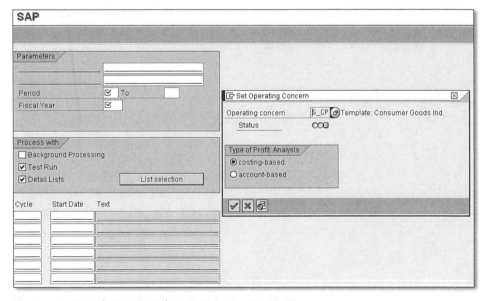

Figure 7.40 Transferring Costs from Cost Centers to CO-PA

As shown in Figure 7.40 when working with Transaction KEU5, we have identified different key parameters:

- OPERATING CONCERN
- TYPE OF PROFITABILITY ANALYSIS
- PERIOD
- BACKGROUND PROCESSING
- TEST RUN
- CYCLE

At this point of the book, you should be familiar with each of these components except CYCLE. CYCLE is a parameter used when performing periodic reposting, assessment, distributions, indirect activity allocation, and other allocation procedures. In a cycle, you need to define a sender-receiver relationship and the corresponding distribution rules associated with it.

These rules defined in a cycle code are processed iteratively; however, if you want to process hierarchies separately, you must define a cycle for each level of the hierarchy by creating a separate assessment as shown in Figure 7.40. You can define several groups within one cycle, and each cycle is independent from each other, making it possible to run cycles in succession, and this is the reason why there are separate lines in Figure 7.40.

After the assessment cycle is executed, the contents of the cost centers affected by the cycle are cleared and the offsetting entries recorded, and these costs are transferred to CO-PA operating concern. At this point, the balance of all cost centers affected by the cycle would be zero.

Finally, you should review the transferred values using Transaction KEPM to confirm that the configured assessment cycle performed the allocation rules correctly, and this information is correctly reflected in the CO-PA planning environment.

In the next section, we'll explore the process of performing the data transfer from Cost Center Accounting to an SAP CO-PA operating concern in more detail, and briefly discuss the general rules that control the cost transfer. Without more delays, let's begin!

7.3.1 Configuring Allocations and Assessment Cycles

When you move costs from one costing object to another using a predefined set of rules, this procedure is defined as an *allocation*. There are three basic types of allocations in SAP ECC: assessments, distributions, and periodic reposting. For assessments and distributions, the sender always requires a cost center, but the receiver of the allocation can be any CO cost object (order, cost object, or cost center). In comparison, periodic repostings allow for any CO object to be a sender or receiver.

Depending on the level of detail required by the analysts, the allocation types can merely provide information relevant to the dollar that is transferred or to the cost elements that are affected by the allocation. Assessments only provide information that's associated to the dollars transferred, and disregard any other objects that were affected during the cycle. Periodic reposting and distributions provide a greater level of detail during the allocation process and should be utilized if more detailed information is required after the allocation procedure is performed.

For the CO-PA assessment process, CYCLE is also an object that behaves similarly to the Cost Center Assessment and Distribution, with the difference that it performs a transfer across components, mapping value fields from the operating concern to the cost centers or cost elements. There can be multiple cycle objects used to transfer data using allocation segments or rules that control the data movement from sender to receiver objects. These cycles are reusable and can be executed every month and updated as the allocation procedure changes over time.

To work with the complete allocation process from start to finish, follow these steps:

1. Define the kind of data your allocation will affect: actual, plan, and other.
2. Using Transaction KCAU, access the screen shown in Figure 7.41, and notice that the ALLOCATION TYPE is ASSESSMENT by default, but there are multiple other types of assessment types available.
3. Select the COST CENTER option to configure the input fields that are available when configuring the allocation rules applicable to cost centers as shown in Figure 7.42. To do this, just access the different indicator fields to make the field mandatory, optional, or blocked.

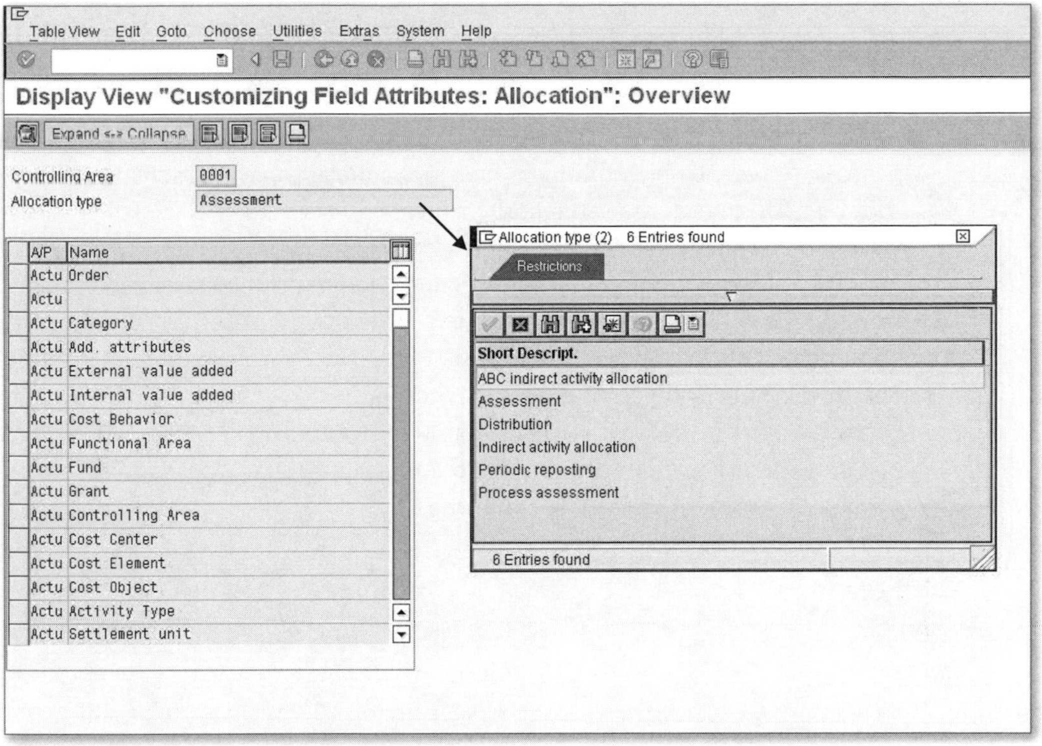

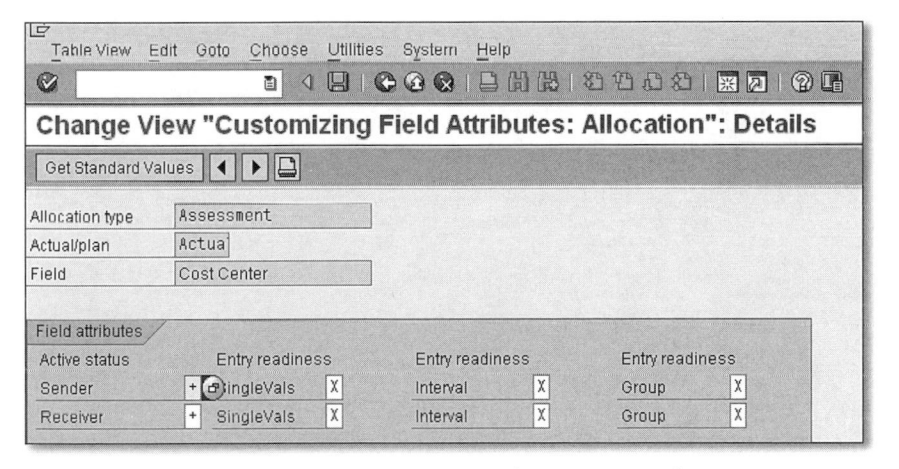

Figure 7.41 Defining the Assessment Receiver Types

Figure 7.42 Configuring the Display Field Options for Cost Center Allocation

> **Note**
>
> If an allocation rule previously had entries, when you access Figure 7.41 and modify the fields available to configure, the previous entries will still be available and valid.

4. Once we have the field options set that we require, we need to create an *assessment element* in order to settle both primary and secondary cost elements used to link the sender and receiver. To create the assessment element, use Transaction KA06, create the numbering for which you want the elements to be processed, select the MASTER menu located on the top of the screen, and you'll access the CREATE COST ELEMENT: BASIC SCREEN shown in Figure 7.43. Notice that in the BASIC DATA section we have chosen the COST ELEMENT TYPE 42, which is the category of the cost element to process (in this case, ASSESSMENT). We recommend using a number specific to this category so it is easier to identify in your database from the different postings.

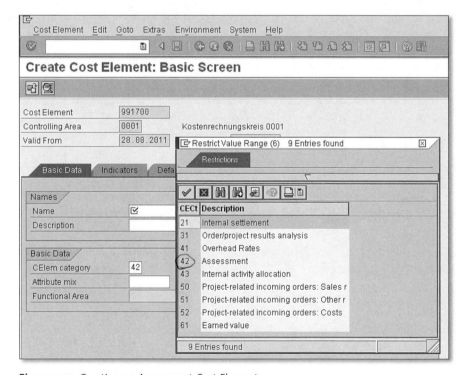

Figure 7.43 Creating an Assessment Cost Element

5. At this point, we're ready to start creating the allocation rules using an assessment cycle object. Working with Transaction KSU1 as shown in Figure 7.44, you can create an assessment cycle called TYB1 with a start date of 05.09.2011. Press the ⌈Enter⌋ key and the ACTUAL ASSESSMENT CYCLE HEADER appears. We generally recommend entering the start date of the cycle as the first date of a fiscal year period in order to register the postings within a particular period.

KSU1

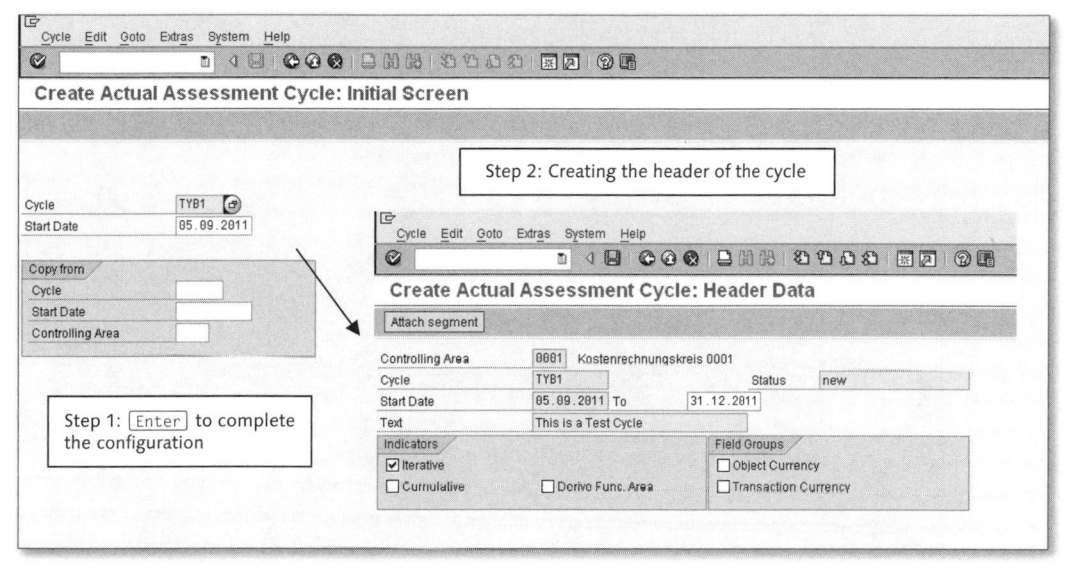

Figure 7.44 Creating an Assessment Cycle

As shown in Figure 7.44, the cycle header stores the general information associated with the ATTACH SEGMENT or RULES that will be executed as part of the cycle, identifying the CONTROLLING AREA, CYCLE, START DATE, and others such as:

▶ ITERATIVE: Using this option, any rules created as part of the cycle are executed in a sequence.

▶ CUMULATIVE: Select this indicator to perform allocation using tracing factors accumulated from period 1 and onwards. In the current period, the allocation amounts determined are posted as less than the amounts allocated in the previous periods.

▶ DERIVE FUNCTIONAL AREA: Use this option if you want the system to take into consideration the functional area during the cycle execution.

▶ OBJECT CURRENCY: Requires that the object currency be considered during the calculation. The system will post the results for the controlling area and the object currency separately.

▶ TRANSACTION CURRENCY: Activate this option if you want the postings to occur in the sender's currency and not the controlling area currency when updating the receiver of the allocation.

6. Once you've completed the configuration of the header for the cycle, click on the ATTACH SEGMENT button and Figure 7.45 appears in order to configure each rule or segment to be executed when running Cycle TYB1.

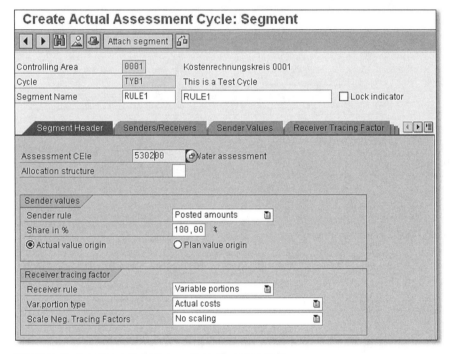

Figure 7.45 Creating a Cycle Segment or Allocation Rule

Notice in Figure 7.45 that there are multiple tabs such as SEGMENT HEADER, SENDERS/RECEIVERS/SENDER VALUES, RECEIVER TRACING FACTOR, and others. As shown in Figure 7.45, when working with the SEGMENT HEAD tab, there are important options; notice that an assessment element is required, which stores the transaction posting, and you can also define the logic behind the transfer from sender to receiver. The rules shown in Figure 7.45 are described as follows:

- SENDER RULES: These options control how the values stored in the sender:
  - POSTED AMOUNTS: Select this option if you want all transactions to be transferred to the receiver object.
  - FIXED AMOUNTS: Choose this option if you want to predefine the exact amounts you want to transfer to the receiver object.
  - FIXED RATES: Use this option to transfer fixed activity prices to transfer the costs to the receiver object.
- SHARE IN %: Percentage of the total sender's value to be moved to the receiver object. If you enter a percentage below 100%, you are defining that not all the values from the sender will be distributed into the receiver. Values greater than 100% aren't allowed.
- ACTUAL/PLAN VALUE ORIGIN: Select the versions of data to transfer, or to which data you want the rules to be applicable.
- RECEIVER RULE (TRACING FACTOR): Use this option to determine how the amount from the sender should be distributed into the receiver:

  Tracing factor

  - VARIABLE PORTION: The system determines the amount to allocate automatically based on tracing factor values defined in the RECEIVER TRACING FACTOR tab.
  - FIXED AMOUNTS: Works with the TRACING FACTOR tab, and configures the system to specifically input the amounts that the system will receive for each of the receiver cost objects.
  - FIXED PERCENTAGES: Distributes the amount from the sender using percentages that are also configured in the RECEIVER/TRACING FACTOR tab. The total sum of the percentages must add up to 100%.
  - FIXED PORTIONS: Similar to fixed percentages; however, it allows the sum to be higher than 100% because this value is a ratio, not a percentage.

Once you've completed the rule configuration associated with the assessment cycle, click on the SAVE icon located on the top of your screen. With this step, you have successfully completed an assessment cycle to transfer data between different cost objects as part of an allocation.

The next step you need to complete is to transfer all the postings available in your cost centers to your SAP CO-PA environment using a CO-PA assessment cycle, which we'll discuss in the next section.

7.3.2 Creating a CO-PA Assessment Cycle

Before the cost stored in your cost centers can be transferred to CO-PA, you need to perform a few different steps as follows:

1. Assign the operating concern to a controlling area using Transaction KEKK (see Figure 7.46). As shown in this figure, we're assigning Operating Concern ST11 to the predelivered Controlling Area 0001 for example purposes. Once completed, click on the SAVE button.

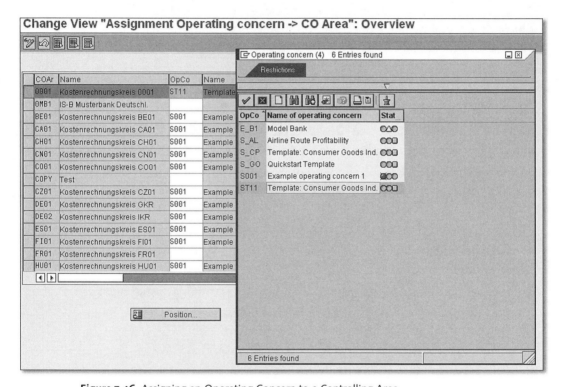

Figure 7.46 Assigning an Operating Concern to a Controlling Area

KEU1

2. Once this assignment has been performed, you can now create the CO-PA assessment cycle using Transaction KEU1 as shown in Figure 7.47. If you need to change your configuration, you can access Transaction KEU2.

3. As shown in Figure 7.47, ❶ assign the cycle name (in this case TYB2) and the START DATE, similar to the cost center assessment. ❷ press Enter in order to start configuring the header of the CO-PA assessment cycle as shown in the second screen in Figure 7.47.

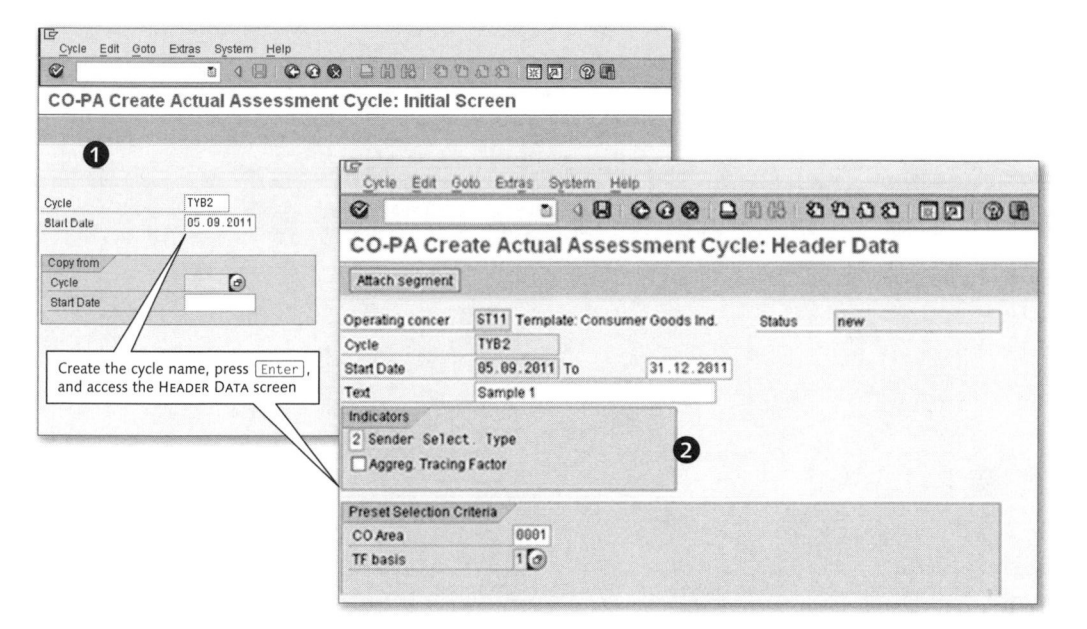

Figure 7.47 Creating a CO-PA Assessment Cycle with Transaction KEU1

4. As part of the configuration of the header for the CO-PA assessment, additional components are required to reflect the options of an operating concern that will receive the costs. As shown in Figure 7.48, you'll need to configure the following elements as is required for your specific needs:

▶ SENDER SELECT. TYPE: Use this indicator to transfer actual costs from cost centers or business processes to your CO-PA operating concern. Choosing option 1 (Unsplit Costs), the overall costs of the sender object to the value field are defined in the segment or rule, and the system reads the sender objects with value type 04. Choosing option 2 (Split Costs), the costs from the sender object are transferred to the corresponding fields assigned in the segment header into fixed and variable costs.

▶ AGGREGATED TRACING FACTOR: This indicator determines that the cycle processing proceeds on a cumulative allocation tracing factor basis and smoothing the distribution of values since period 1.

▶ CO AREA: In this option the SAP controlling area must be assigned.

▶ TF BASIS: Tracing Factor Basis. There are two types of Profitability Analysis in SAP: costing-based or account-based. In this option, select how your operating concern is configured to receive the costs.

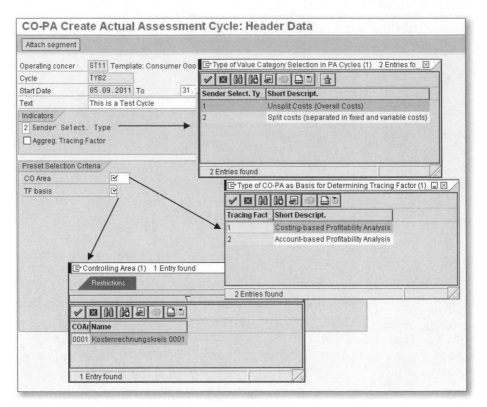

Figure 7.48 Configuring the CO-PA Assessment Cycle Header

5. Once these components have been set up to reflect the characteristics of your operating concern and how you want to transfer the cost, click on the ATTACH SEGMENT button located on top of the screen in Figure 7.48. Notice that the configuration is almost equivalent to the procedure described in the previous section for cost center. After clicking on the button in Figure 7.48, you'll be able to access the screen shown in Figure 7.49, where a CO-PA assessment cycle segment allows you to develop your own allocation rules also using an assessment cost element, PA transfer structure, allocation structure, and selecting the destination value fields in your operating concern where you want the fixed and variable costs portions of the costs to be sent. In this screen we have access to the field names that are stored in the operating concern, which would be the receiver, as well as to the same options in the cost center assessments.

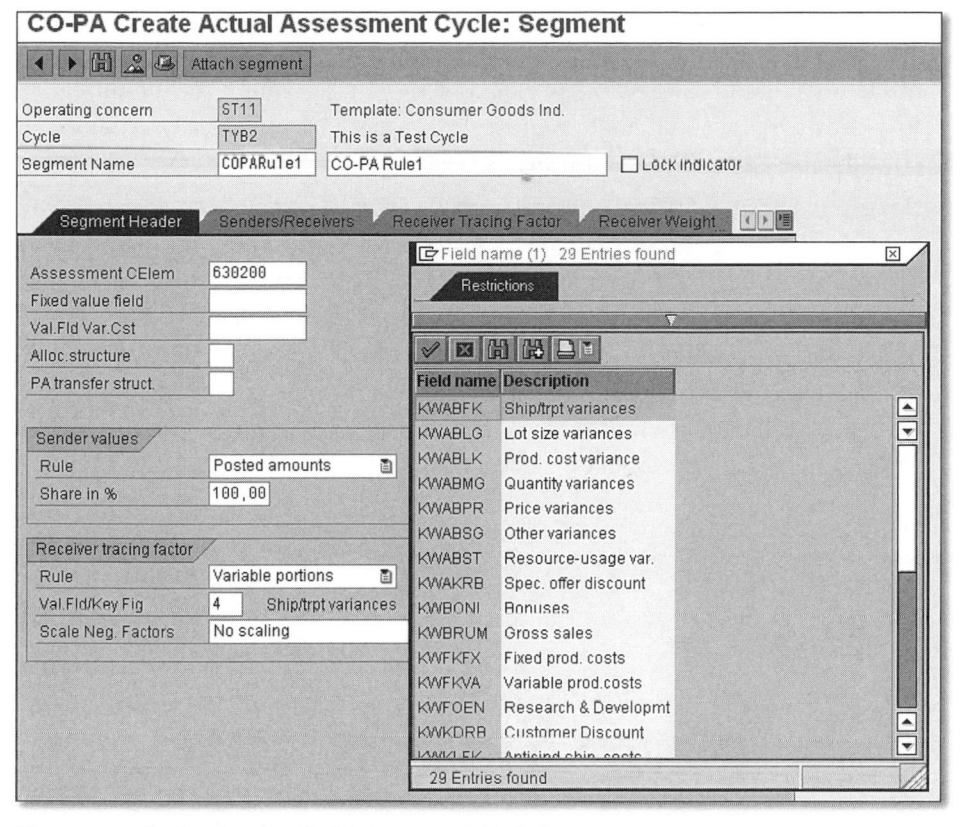

Figure 7.49 Configuring the CO-PA Assessment Cycle Segment

6. Notice the VAL. FLD/KEY FIG indicator in the RECEIVER TRACING FACTOR section in Figure 7.49. You should only use this field if you have configured the receiver to use variable portions. The system uses this selection to determine the receiver tracing factor for each allocation.

Note

You must first understand the kind of allocation procedure you want your costs to follow, and then focus on what tools are available in the assessment cycles to configure such an approach. As you can see, there are multiple options available in SAP ECC to deliver the detail required to perform your allocations. However, remember there are slight differences in the kinds of information available after allocation depending on the method selected, so make sure to understand each method (Assessment, Distribution, and Period Repostings) before making a decision.

7. You need to configure the SENDER/RECEIVERS tab, RECEIVER TRACING FACTOR tab, and others shown in Figure 7.49, depending on the rules that you want to implement. Each industry and project is different, without factoring in regulatory considerations that might require you to monitor and store the changes in your database after each allocation.

8. Notice in Figure 7.50 that the SENDERS/RECEIVERS tab has been selected, and here is where the linkage between Cost Center Accounting and SAP CO-PA operating concern is more evident. As shown in Figure 7.50, the sender is either a cost center or cost element, and the receiver is composed of the elements that are available in the operating concern as part of the CO-PA environment. In this way, it's clear that when executing the cycle costs would be moved from the cost centers or cost elements to the operating concern, and the values in the senders would be zeroed out.

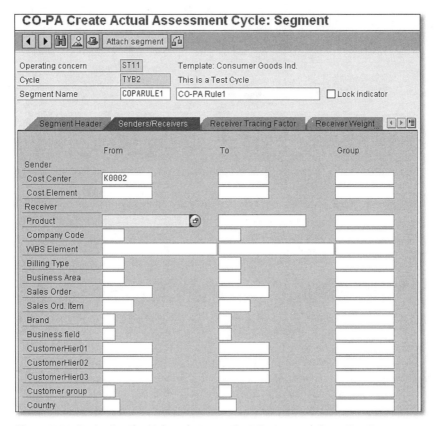

Figure 7.50 Reviewing the Linkage between Cost Centers and Operating Concern

9. Once you have completed setting the information shown in Figure 7.50 with the sender and receiver logic, simply click on the SAVE button, and your CO-PA assessment cycle will be saved to the database. Remember that after executing the assessment cycle, your cost centers or cost elements values will zero out as you continue generating reports either within SAP CO PA, SAP ECC, or SAP NetWeaver BW, so you are not looking for the information that was transferred from one cost object to another in the incorrect location. Make sure your business users understand the process.You can always go back and change the cycle details with Transaction KEU2.

10. When you're ready to transfer the costs from cost centers to CO-PA, execute Transaction KEU5 as shown in Figure 7.51. Define the PERIOD, FISCAL YEAR, identify the CO-PA cycle (TYB2), and then click on the EXECUTE button (the icon with the clock and the checkmark).

KEU5
To execute.

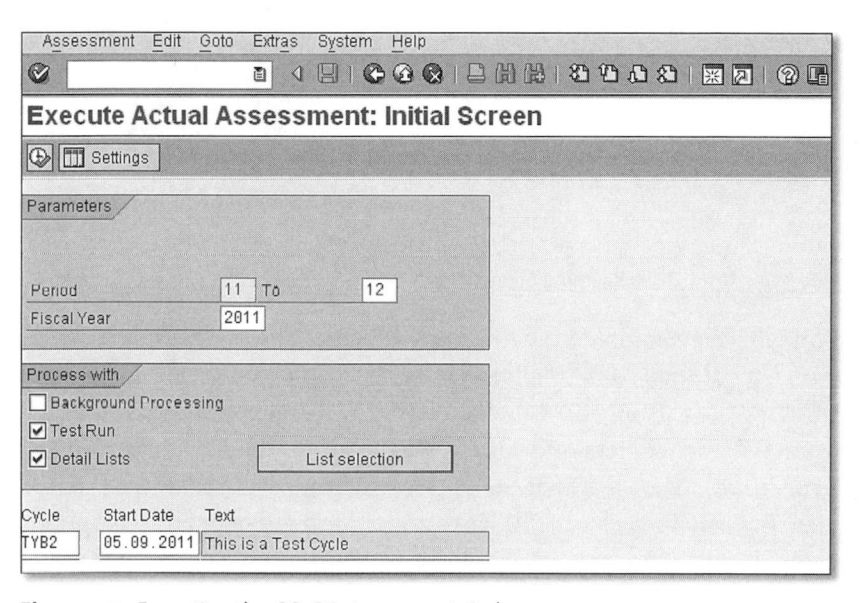

Figure 7.51 Executing the CO-PA Assessment Cycle

11. The system will initiate executing the assessment cycle and the cost will be transferred to the operating concern according to the rules defined in Transaction KEU5. Notice that there is a TEST RUN option as part of your screen where you can simulate the results. When you're satisfied with the output, uncheck that option so the values are completely transferred to the CO-PA operating concern.

12. If the assessment cycle was successful, your results will be available for viewing in your operating concern. In order to perform this verification, access the CO-PA planning framework using Transaction KEPM and the screen shown in Figure 7.52 appears.

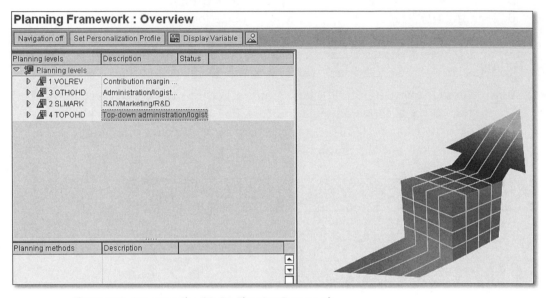

Planning Framework : Overview

| Navigation off | Set Personalization Profile | Display Variable |

Planning levels	Description	Status	
▽ 🗐 Planning levels			
▷ 📇 1 VOLREV	Contribution margin ...		
▷ 📇 3 OTHOHD	Administration/logist...		
▷ 📇 2 SLMARK	S&D/Marketing/R&D		
▷ 📇 4 TOPOHD	Top-down administration/logist		

Planning methods	Description	

Figure 7.52 Accessing the CO-PA Planning Framework

In this section we have explored how to work with cost center and CO-PA assessment cycles as part of the SAP ECC allocation types. You should now understand that when moving costs from cost centers to CO-PA, the cost centers' values are removed from the cost centers and moved to the value fields available in the operating concern. It's also clear that CO-PA assessment cycles aren't the same as the traditional assessment cycles in SAP ECC, and also the type of costing options set up in the operating concern have an impact on the data transfer as well as the assignment of the operating concern to the controlling area. For your reference, the following transaction codes are associated with the CO-PA assessment:

▶ KEU1: Creating a CO-PA Assessment Cycle for Actual Data

▶ KEU2: Changing a CO-PA Assessment Cycle for Actual Data

▶ KEU3: Displaying a CO-PA Assessment Cycle for Actual Data

▶ KEU4: Deleting a CO-PA Assessment Cycle

▶ KEU5: Executing a CO-PA Assessment Cycle for Actual Data

- KEU6: Actual CO-PA Assessment Cycle Overview
- KEU7: Create Plan Data CO-PA Assessment Cycle
- KEU8: Change Plan Data CO-PA Assessment Cycle
- KEU9: Display Plan Data CO-PA Assessment Cycle

7.4 Top-Down Distribution

Another important component when working with CO-PA is performing *top-down distribution,* which is the process of inputting data at a higher level of detail such as product group or material group, and then splitting the value to the children using reference data. This is especially helpful when you plan or receive your data at a higher level of detail, and then want to distribute the results using reference data such as data sets from actual data from previous years.

It's important to distinguish between distribution as an allocation process in SAP ECC and top-down distributions that are applicable to CO-PA. Distributions behave similarly to assessments as shown in the previous sections, and are part of the allocation procedures that are part of Cost Center Accounting. However, top-down distributions are associated to the CO-PA planning environment, and support variance analysis at different levels of detail. For example, you can plan at the product group level and then distribute the planning data to the individual products on the basis of the distribution of the sales figures from the previous year.

Top-down distributions are a pre-delivered planning method from SAP that are associated with a planning package, and can be reviewed using Transaction KEPM as shown in Figure 7.53.

Notice in Figure 7.53 that there are three tabs: Settings, Value Flds (value fields), and Description. The Settings tab provides access to a configuration environment similar to the CO-PA assessment header discussed in the previous section, where there are two methods that determine precisely which values are to be distributed:

- Only Distribute "Nonassigned"
  Using this setting, only values that are posted directly at the higher level can be distributed. For example, if your data is extracted or transferred from Cost

Center Accounting at the product group level, it cannot be assigned to the detailed level.

▶ DISTRIBUTE TOTAL VALUE

All values located at the higher level can be distributed regardless of whether they were posted directly or copied to the higher level. When working with this option, the values taken from the detailed level are overwritten by the new distributed value.

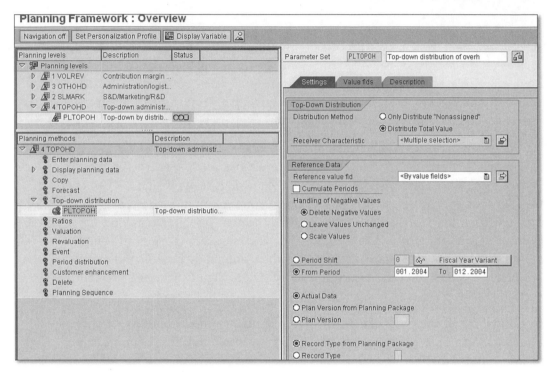

Figure 7.53 Reviewing the Top-Down Distribution Method

When performing top-down distributions, the same concepts of senders and receivers explored in the previous section are applicable. As shown in Figure 7.53 and 7.54, the equivalent of sender amounts would be set up in the REFERENCE DATA section, and the receiver would be the RECEIVER CHARACTERISTICS that will accept the information derived from the REFERENCE DATA.

As shown in Figure 7.54, we also set up sender and receiver characteristics—such as PRODUCT and MATERIAL GROUP as senders, and BUSINESS FIELD and DISTRIBUTION

CHANNEL as receivers after the distribution. Once again, the customization rules can change depending on the scenarios of your company and project.

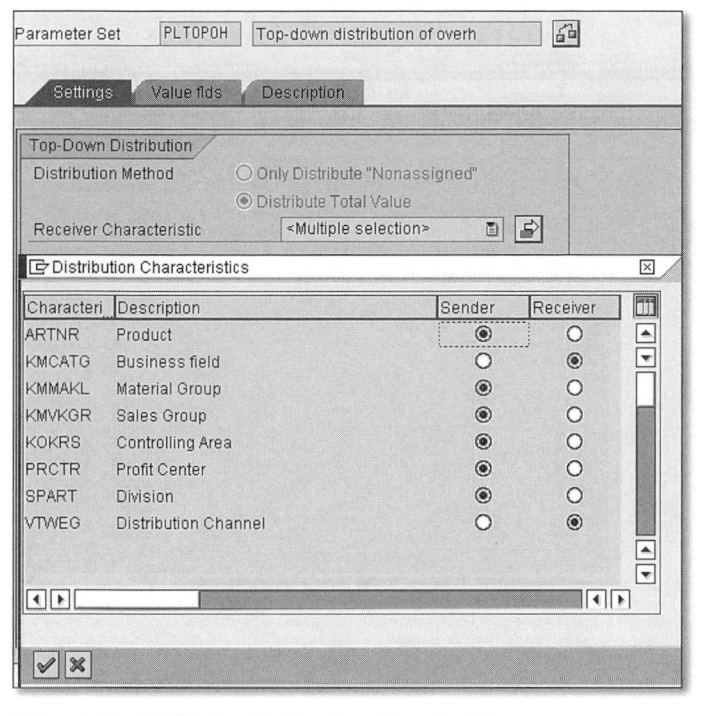

Figure 7.54 Configuring the Receiver Characteristics

As shown in Figure 7.53 in the REFERENCE DATA section, the REFERENCE value field identifies the data set to be used as reference or training in order to perform the distribution of the data entered or available at the parent level for a time period. As shown in Figure 7.55, you can enter the basis for distribution, a specific value field for reference data, or a key figure calculated from value fields. Alternatively, you can specify that the distribution occurs by value fields so that each value field is taken as the basis for its distribution.

You can configure the system to automatically determine periods that fall before (or after) the periods at the planning level or those in the planning package. In order to perform this process select under PERIOD CLOSING the number of periods that the system should count back. (If the reference data is to fall in the future, enter a number with a negative sign.) You can display the current fiscal year variant in order to enter an appropriate value.

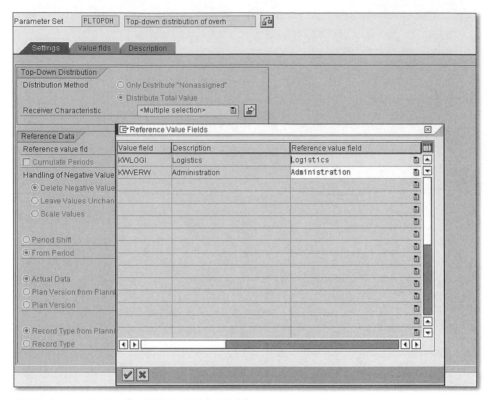

Figure 7.55 Accessing the Reference Value Fields

In addition, it's possible to enter time periods for the reference data directly under PERIOD FROM/TO in order to be more specific to only the reference data that you want to use as reference and limited using a specific time period. The interval that you enter must correspond to the period interval of the currently selected planning package, except in cases where you select the CUMULATE PERIODS indicator. It's necessary to define whether the reference data is actual data or data from the plan version for the planning package or from a different plan version that is yet to be specified.

You can specify for a sender characteristic that a different characteristic value in the reference data forms the basis for distribution. This means that you can specify that the distribution of product groups to the products in country 1 occurs on the basis of the product data in country 2. To do this, access the TRANSFORM CHARACTERISTIC VALUES function as shown in Figure 7.56.

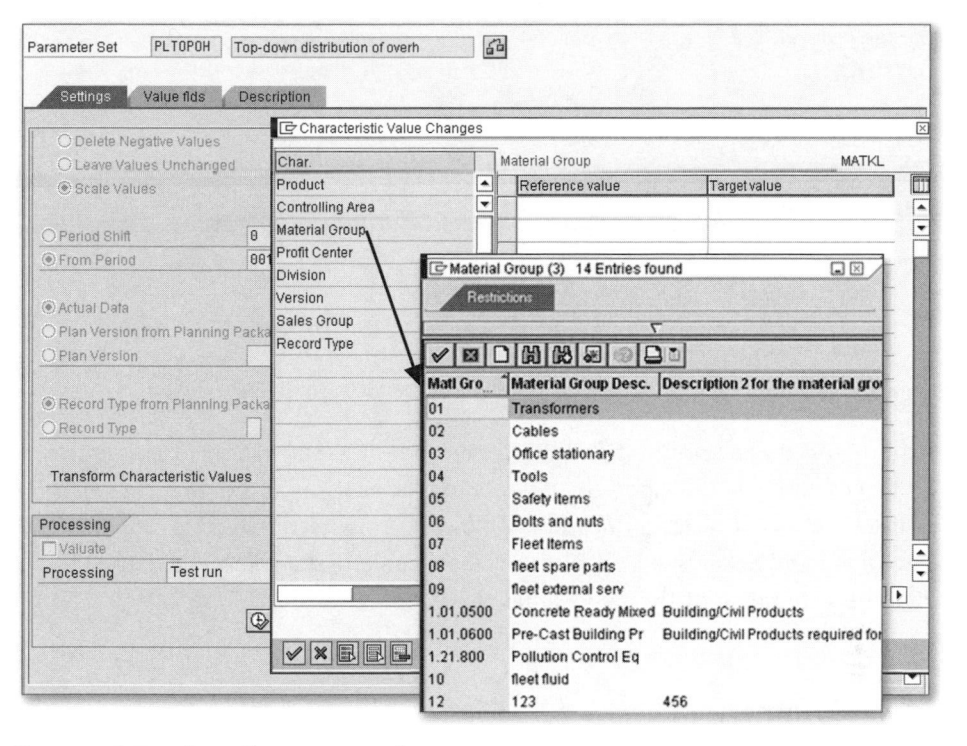

Figure 7.56 Transform Characteristic Values

You can use this functionality to determine whether the value fields are to be revaluated during top-down distribution.

Finally, when preparing to execute the top-down distribution method, make sure that you review the options available in Figure 7.57:

▶ TEST RUN: Use this option to perform a simulation of the rules defined without affecting the real data.

▶ UPDATE RUN: Executes the rules to data in the database.

▶ DECISION AT POINT OF EXECUTION: Interacts with a variable defined in the parameter set, and allows the user to make the decision to either run a TEST RUN or an UPDATE RUN when the planning method is executed online.

▶ BACKGROUND PROCESSING: Configures your method to be executed behind the scenes to improve system performance.

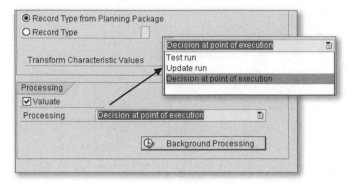

Figure 7.57 Reviewing the Processing Options for Top-Down Distribution

In summary, the top-down distribution method can greatly support budget, plan, and forecast processes, especially when variance analysis and detail is a key issue for the business. It is not a question of how exact the estimation is, but the level of accuracy and detail that you want to be available in the reference data that will drive the generation of the new values.

7.5 Summary

The CO-PA planning framework is a powerful and important tool available in CO-PA that helps you avoid increasing the complexity of your implementation, and at the same time provides interaction with data input and transformation. Planning with CO-PA allows you to create sophisticated and powerful applications without leaving the traditional OLTP environment of SAP and without the need to create complex objects that interact with SAP NetWeaver BI 7.0 or SAP NetWeaver Business Warehouse (BW) to use SEM-BPS or BW-BPS. This is because the CO-PA planning framework lets you perform operations very similar to those performed in these environments.

However, the CO-PA planning framework has limitations, depending on the data volume and based on the types of data transformation required. For example, if you need to interact heavily with the Enterprise Portal Applications (EP), you should use the capabilities available in the SAP NetWeaver BI environment. On the other hand, if you simply require data manipulation, the planning methods in CO-PA provide solutions for most requirements.

The concept of assessment and distributions are allocation procedures that are very important to quantify the real costs of the firm and for variance analysis. However, the different allocation types that occur in Cost Center Accounting don't update the SAP CO-PA operating concern, and thus a CO-PA specific assessment cycle must be created to transfer the data from Cost Center Accounting to the operating concern, as well as creating allocation rules that combine the cost center data and characteristics with the value fields that are stored in the CO-PA environment.

Using CO-PA as a tool to access information in almost real-time from different SAP components is one of its most important capabilities, making it quite similar to a SAP NetWeaver BW environment within SAP ECC. In this chapter, we'll briefly explore some of the options contained inside the Flows of Actual Values menu and how to configure some of the structures required for this functionality.

8 Flows of Actual Values: Transferring Actual Data into CO-PA

Profitability Analysis is not just about connectivity to a few tables in R/3 or SAP ERP ECC 6.0—it's also about determining whether the overall transactions from a company, business unit, controlling area, profit center, or all of these things are profitable for the corporation. For this reason, to evaluate revenues, expenses, investments, and costs in CO-PA, we need to transfer actual data from other components of the transactional system into CO-PA. We'll look at how to do this in detail in this chapter.

> **Note**
>
> This chapter will provide a brief introduction on how to connect to components such as Financials (FI), Controlling (CO), Materials Management (MM), Sales and Distribution (SD), and others, but because there are quite a few functionalities available in the transactional system of SAP, the information in this chapter cannot go into specific details. Many concepts such as how to configure controlling areas, bill of materials, and sales orders are specific components that are covered in other SAP PRESS reference sources; however, for our purposes we focus only on transfer data available in those components, and don't explain why and how this data was created. For further reference, refer to *Optimizing Value Flows with SAP ERP* (SAP PRESS, 2010).

8.1   Overview

Figure 8.1 provides a general overview of the power of CO-PA to consolidate data without leaving the transactional system of SAP, which can be uploaded into profitability segments created inside the operating concern. Processes described in this figure provide an overview of the possible data and the consolidation power of CO-PA, similarly to that of SAP Business Warehouse (BW)/SAP Net-Weaver Business Intelligence (BI) to connect to different sources of data inside the transactional system.

As shown in Figure 8.1, some of the components that you can access by using CO-PA flows of actual values include Overhead Cost Controlling, information from cost centers, cost objects from Product Cost Controlling (PC), revenues from SD, Cost Element Accounting, FI information, and more.

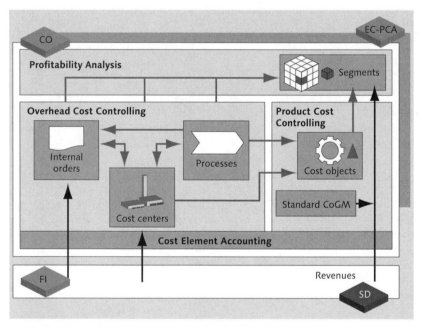

Figure 8.1 Reviewing Actual Data Flows Available in CO-PA

To enhance your understanding of the information and data available for the integration and transfer of actual data inside the CO-PA profitability segments, review Figure 8.2. It provides a more detailed breakdown of the data elements involved to generate Profit and Loss (P&L) information. For example, you can see that you can extract sales order information, such as sales quantity, rebates, and sales revenue by transferring billing documents from SD, or that you can generate direct costs values by making direct postings from FI, and so on.

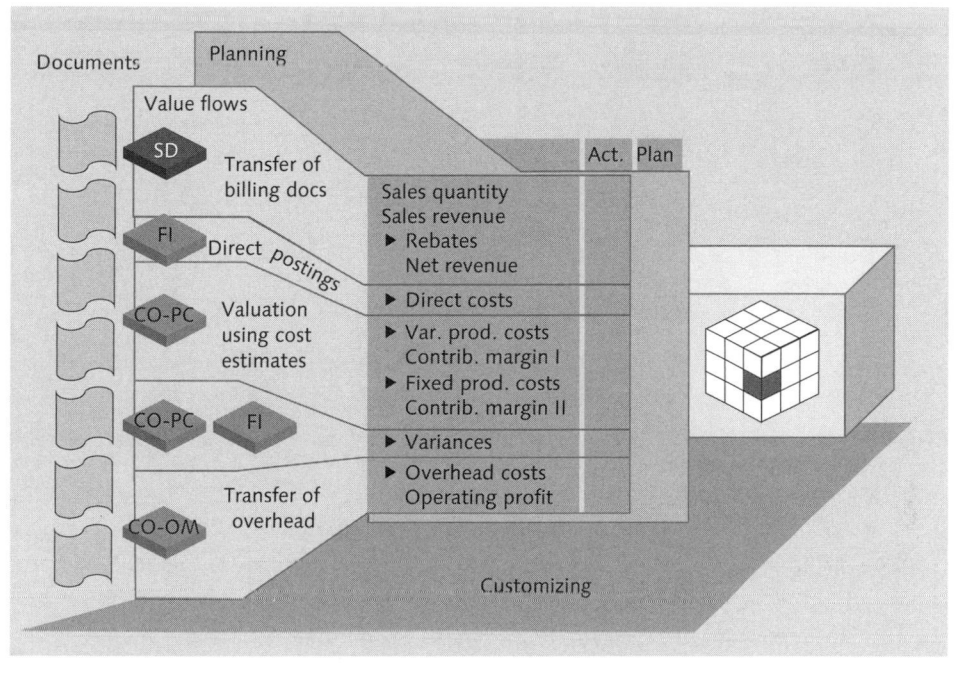

Figure 8.2 Integrated Business Model to Collect Revenue and Costs

The processes shown in the model presented in Figure 8.2 occur within the transactional system of SAP. Therefore, you combine data already consolidated inside CO-PA with other platforms such as SAP NetWeaver BW/SAP NetWeaver BI and Customer Relationship Management (CRM) environments, as shown in Figure 8.3, to perform extraction and retraction.

Note

Extraction and retraction are extensively covered in two ASAP "how-to" papers called "How-to CO-PA Extraction" and "How-to CO-PA Retraction." You can access these papers in the SAP Marketplace or at *http://sdn.sap.com*.

Figure 8.2 and Figure 8.3 identify just how much information can be connected to CO-PA using the FLOWS OF ACTUAL VALUES menu, and how this information can

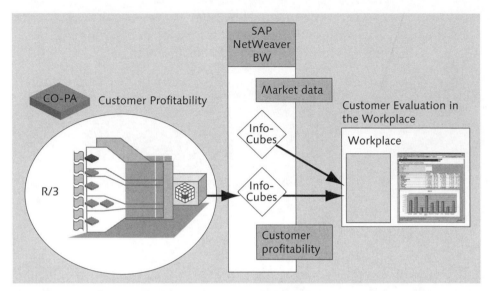

SAP
NetWeaver
BW

Market data

CO-PA Customer Profitability

Customer Evaluation in
the Workplace

Info-
Cubes

Workplace

R/3

Info-
Cubes

Customer
profitability

Figure 8.3 Data Flow into the SAP NetWeaver BW/SAP NetWeaver BI Environment Using CO-PA as a Data Source Environment

be directed into other systems, such as SAP NetWeaver BI/SAP BW. As its name implies, *flows of actual values* is what controls how actual values are accessed and included into the characteristics and value fields that define profitability segments. However, sometimes you might need to connect to other systems using SAP NetWeaver BI technologies instead.

Let's now take a general look at the CO-PA FLOWS OF ACTUAL VALUES menu.

8.2 General Review of the CO-PA Flows of Actual Values Menu

As shown in Figure 8.4, the FLOWS OF ACTUAL VALUES menu is displayed by following this path: PROFITABILITY ANALYSIS • FLOWS OF ACTUAL VALUES. As we've said before, the idea of CO-PA is that it integrates with other SAP system components to calculate a company's value every period, using transactional data to present revenues and costs as accurately as possible. In the FLOWS OF ACTUAL VALUES menu, you can see the different components, such as TRANSFER OF INCOMING SALES ORDERS, TRANSFER OF BILLING DOCUMENTS, ORDER AND PROJECT SETTLEMENT (internal orders and projects), DIRECT POSTING FROM FI/MM, SETTLEMENT OF

PRODUCTION VARIANCES, TRANSFER OF OVERHEAD, MULTIPLE VALUATION APPROACHES/ TRANSFER PRICES, PERIODIC ADJUSTMENTS, and others.

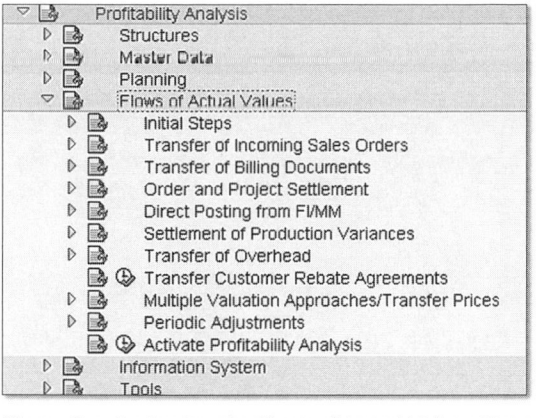

Figure 8.4 Reviewing the Flows of Actual Values Menu of CO-PA

While we won't go into detailed explanation of each of these items, let's understand how to get this information and incorporate it into your reports and planning applications to calculate revenue and costs to create cash flows for each time period within a fiscal year.

A general procedure can be described as follows, regardless of the type of component to extract:

1. Any of the actual value components shown in Figure 8.4 can be added to your operating concern. To do so, you need to associate each component with value fields or characteristics, or create user-defined objects to accept the information. Remember that value fields can be of type value or quantity to store a currency or a number.

2. Define number ranges to filter the information to transfer into CO-PA. You can define number ranges in the INITIAL STEPS submenu inside the FLOWS OF ACTUAL VALUES menu of CO-PA, as shown in Figure 8.4. When doing so, you must define value field groups, representing the possible combinations of value fields in an operating concern. These value fields groups are used to specify the following:

   ▸ Which value fields should be made available to users entering or displaying a line item

   ▸ In what order these value fields should be displayed

[handwritten margin note: need to associate each w/ value and characters]

- ▶ Whether specific value fields can be filled
- ▶ Whether specific value fields have to be filled
- ▶ Whether specific value fields may only be displayed

3. Select the fields and components you want to transfer.

Tips & Tricks

If you don't define any value field groups, then all value fields in an operating concern are unlocked for entry during line item entry.

Note

You don't have to define all of the elements in the INITIAL STEPS submenu. Most of these elements are considered to be noncritical activities that are not required to transfer actual data from the different transactional systems.

In the following sections, we'll provide you with a quick overview of the most important components for working with actual values, including transfer of incoming sales orders, transfer of billing documents, order and project settlement, direct posting from FI/MM, settlement of production variances, and transfer of overhead.

8.3 Transfer of Incoming Sales Orders

Sales orders are the source of revenue for the SAP system, coming from the SD component, which is based on the transfer of billing documents. As shown earlier in Figure 8.2, sales order information is extracted based on four components: SALES QUANTITY, SALES REVENUE, REBATES, and NET REVENUE.

All revenues, sales deductions, and other values (such as transfer prices) are defined as conditions in SD. You assign these conditions to the corresponding CO-PA value fields, with limitations, to transfer billing documents to CO-PA. Now let's review how to access and configure CO-PA to accept incoming sales order information:

- ▶ To transfer condition types for sales revenues and sales deductions to CO-PA, make sure that the condition types are linked to an account in FI that is also

conditions assigned to Value Fields

cost elements

defined as a cost element of <u>category "11" (revenue element)</u> or <u>"12" (sales deduction) in CO.</u> These condition types must be assigned to a CO-PA value field. Condition types linked to FI accounts that are defined as cost elements of another category are not transferred to CO-PA, even when the condition type has been assigned to a CO-PA value field.

condition Types in SD.

► Condition types such as "VPRS" (cost) that are defined as statistical in SD are always transferred to CO-PA if they're assigned to a value field.

► All condition types that you want to transfer to CO-PA must be active <u>in the SD pricing procedure.</u> Inactive conditions in a billing item are not transferred. If all of the conditions in a billing item are inactive, that item is not transferred to CO-PA. Conditions don't need to be active, however, to be transferred with sales order items because the transfer of incoming sales orders is always statistical.

You can also transfer conditions from MM to update billing data in pooled payment in the Information Systems (IS) retail system. These are transferred according to the same rules as SD conditions. Conditions from SD are always transferred to CO-PA with "+" signs, with the exception of credit memos and returns. The reasons for this are that the signs for revenues are handled differently in the different applications of the system. For example, revenues are positive in SD, while they are negative in FI. Consequently, CO-PA accepts all of the values as positive, and then subtracts deductions and costs from revenues in IS.

> **Note**
>
> Note that the indicator transfer +/– is not used to compare the different use of +/– signs between FI or SD and CO-PA. If you activate the indicator, shown later in this section in Figure 8.7, only the positive and negative values for the condition in question will be balanced. This guarantees that the sum of the negative and positive condition values is displayed as a correct total value in the value field assigned to that condition.

> **Tips & Tricks**
>
> In order to perform transfer conditions from the billing document, the same definitions must be established for the value fields in Profitability Analysis, and both pricing and condition types must be defined in SD.

To transfer incoming sales orders, do the following:

1. Follow the path FLOWS OF ACTUAL VALUES • TRANSFER OF INCOMING SALES ORDERS, as shown in Figure 8.5.

2. Notice that there are three elements: ASSIGN VALUE FIELDS, ASSIGN QUANTITY FIELDS, and ACTIVATE TRANSFER OF INCOMING SALES ORDERS.

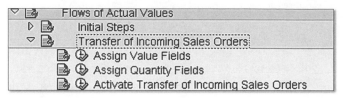

Figure 8.5 Reviewing the Transfer of Incoming Sales Orders Menu

Following SAP theory, there are two types of key figures:

▸ **Amount**
Refers to data stored in a currency format that describes monetary transactions, such as gross sales, net revenue, and operating costs.

▸ **Quantity**
Refers to basically all information that reflects nonmonetary transactions such as material levels, number of complaints, number of parts in storage, and inventory levels.

As shown in Figure 8.5, you can extract both of these key figure types using the functions ASSIGN VALUE FIELDS and ASSIGN QUANTITY FIELDS, respectively.

Assigning Value Fields

Let's review an example to assign value fields:

1. Click on the object FLOWS OF ACTUAL VALUES • TRANSFER OF INCOMING SALES ORDERS • ASSIGN VALUE FIELDS, as shown in Figure 8.5.

2. Review the screen shown in Figure 8.6 and notice that you can connect to three systems: SD, MM, and CRM.

3. Click on the line MAINTAIN ASSIGNMENT OF SD CONDITIONS TO CO-PA VALUE FIELDS to display the screen NEW ENTRIES: OVERVIEW OF ADDED ENTRIES, shown in Figure 8.7.

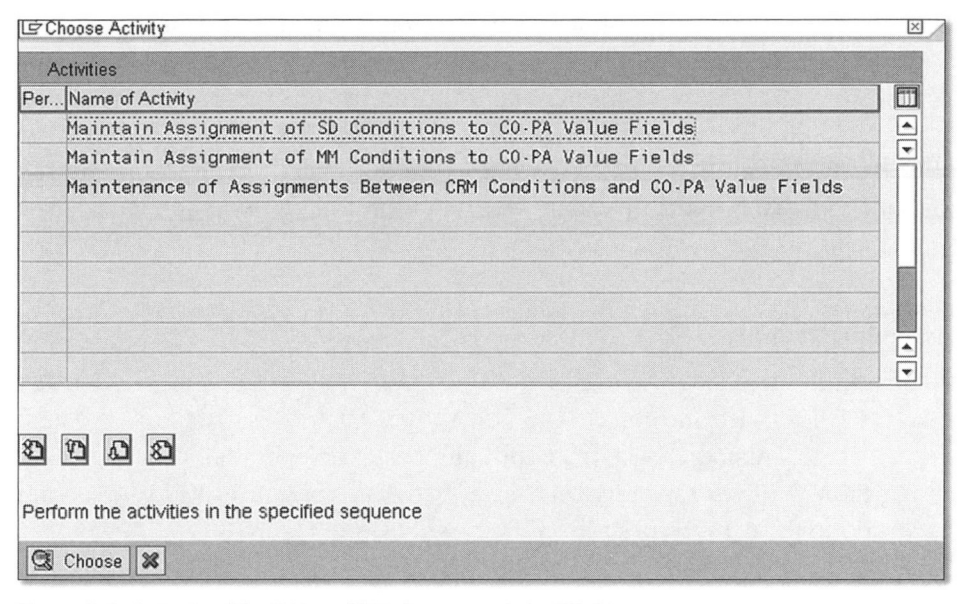

Figure 8.6 Assigning SD, MM, or CRM Components to CO-PA

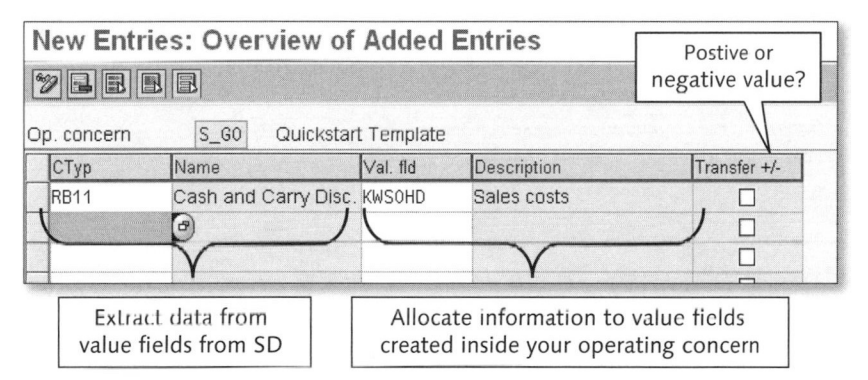

Figure 8.7 Assigning SD Fields to CO-PA Value Fields in the Operating Concern S_GO

Tips & Tricks

In the screen shown in Figure 8.7, you access the value fields defined in SD and link them with value fields defined inside your operating concern. Remember that there are default value fields inside CO-PA, but that you can create your own user-defined value fields using the path PROFITABILITY ANALYSIS • STRUCTURES • DEFINE OPERATING CONCERN • MAINTAIN VALUE FIELDS.

— majority are pre-set

327

4. In the CTYP column, enter the technical name of the SD value field you want to extract. On the right-hand side, make sure that VAL. FLD matches the value field contained inside your operating concern. In our example, the operating concern is S_GO and we're matching the SD field RB11 (Cash and Carry Disc) to the value field KWSOHD (Sales Costs) in our operating concern. You can name and assign value fields any way you want; the example in Figure 8.7 is there just to show you the assignment procedure.

Assigning Quantity Fields

Following the same logic as we just did with assigning value fields, let's assign quantity fields. Select the object FLOWS OF ACTUAL VALUES • TRANSFER OF INCOMING SALES ORDERS • ASSIGN QUANTITY FIELDS, and, using the operating concern S_GO, assign FKIMG (Billed Quantity) in the SD QTY FIELD column to KWSVME (Sales Quantity) in the CO-PA QTY FIELD column, as shown in Figure 8.8.

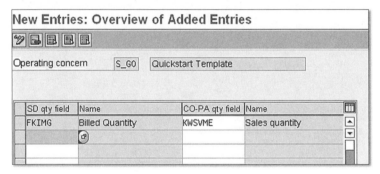

Figure 8.8 Assigning a SD Quantity Field to a CO-PA Quantity Field

8.3.1 Activating the Transfer of Incoming Sales Orders

The last object available in the TRANSFER OF INCOMING SALES ORDERS menu, shown earlier in Figure 8.5, is ACTIVATE TRANSFER OF INCOMING SALES ORDERS. Follow these steps to complete the activation of your actual data flows from SD into CO-PA:

1. Click on FLOWS OF ACTUAL VALUES • TRANSFER OF INCOMING SALES ORDERS • ACTIVATE TRANSFER OF INCOMING SALES ORDERS. This opens the ACTIVE FLAG FOR TRANSFER OF INCOMING SALES ORDERS screen shown in Figure 8.9, which contains the same table we accessed in Chapter 4 when we activated CO-PA. This

means that any changes you make in this screen will also affect any configurations we discussed in Chapter 4, so be careful!

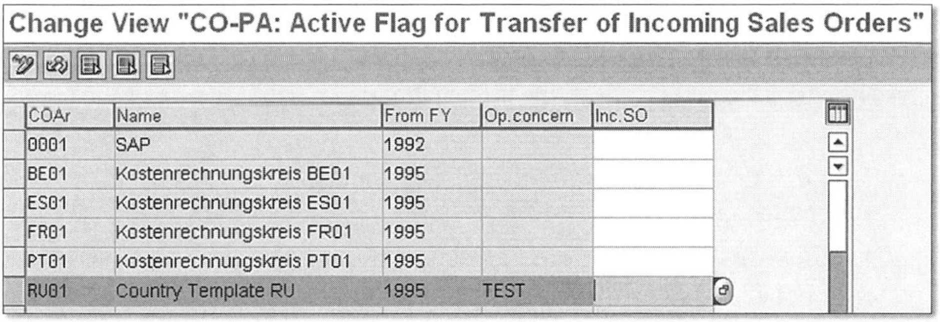

Figure 8.9 Active Flag for Transfer of Incoming Sales Orders into CO-PA

Tips & Tricks

The transfer of incoming sales order is performed based on the controlling area. Also, the INC. SO column (which stands for "Transfer of Incoming Sales Orders") next to the operating concern assigned with the controlling area describes the activation status.

---

2. To activate the incoming sales order as shown in Figure 8.10, start by selecting the line of the desired controlling area (in our example, RU01 COUNTRY TEMPLATE RU), and review the assigned operating concern (TEST).

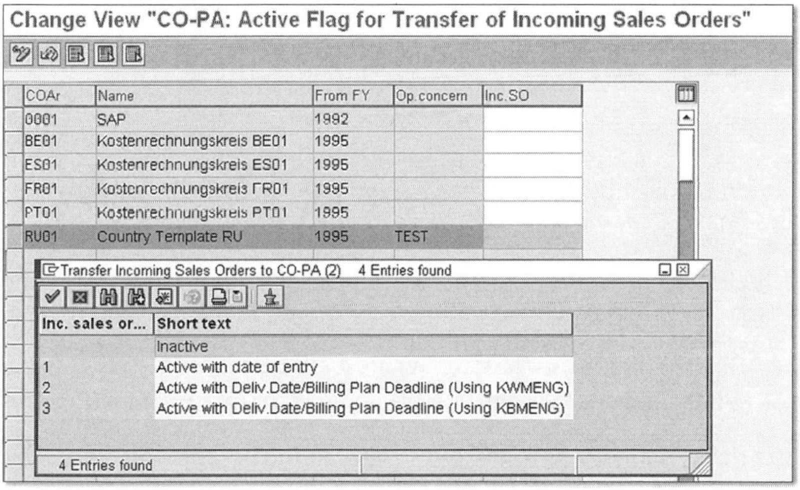

Figure 8.10 Activating Your Incoming Sales Order Actual Data Transfer

3. Click on the INC. SO field associated with the RU01 controlling area to select the type of data transfer and pick the flag value (a number between one and three), as shown in Figure 8.10. In this step, you're performing the activation of the transfer of incoming sales orders from SD component of SAP ECC into Profitability Analysis (CO-PA). This transferred sales order can be displayed in CO-PA as shown in Figure 8.10, and this information is available as part of the schedule lines as follows:

   ► ACTIVE WITH DATE OF ENTRY: This option means that the orders are updated under the same period in which they were created in the system.

   ► ACTIVE WITH DELIV. DATE/BILLING PLAN DEADLINE (USING KWMENG): This option means that the order appears in Profitability Analysis in the period of the planned delivery or the scheduled billing date. It thus comes closer to reflecting the expected billing information.

   ► ACTIVE WITH DELIV. DATE/BILLING PLAN DEADLINE (USING KBMENG): Same functionality as the second option, but a different field in Table VBAP.

You can create an example of the difference of these options as shown in Table 8.1, replicating the information associated to a particular sales order that we need to transfer to CO-PA:

Sales Order:100392	Customer	4711	Date Entered	1/9/2011
Item 10	Material 99	Quantity 40		
			Delivery date 10/8/2011	Quantity 15
			Delivery date 11/8/2011	Quantity 25

Table 8.1 Sample Sales Order to Be Transferred to CO-PA

Based on the information shown in Table 8.1 and using the options shown in Figure 8.10, the behavior of the data transferred to CO-PA would be as follows:

► If option 1 is chosen, then one line item would be created in CO-PA with the quantity of 40 PCS for September, 2011.

► If options 2 or 3 are selected, two items would be created in CO-PA with the quantities of 15 PCS delivered for period 10, and 25 PCS delivered in period 11.

Note that if any changes are made to the sales order in the SD component and its values were already transferred into CO-PA, the line items posted to CO-PA are completely canceled and new line items containing the new characteristics and values are transferred from the order.

Sales orders are transferred to CO-PA with the record type "A" and sales orders from projects receive record type "I" when transferred during the project settlement. In addition, incoming sales orders are only updated in costing-based Profitability Analysis. Only documents that are likewise represented in FI can be posted to account-based Profitability Analysis.

Please remember that you're maintaining the same table as when you activated the operating concern as described in Chapter 3. Note that if you delete any entries such as the sales order, this change will also affect the contents of your operating concern. When completed, make sure to click on the checkmark icon to save your changes.

Next we'll discuss how to transfer billing documents, which is closely related to the process we just described of how to transfer incoming sales orders to CO-PA.

> **Note**
>
> Before selecting any of the values shown in Figure 8.10, you should call your SD, FI/CO, and Sarbanes-Oxley team leads to ask for advice on when a sale is recognized in your system. A "sale" is a tricky term that can be recognized by your company when the sale order was created, when the product was delivered to the client, when it was shipped from the plant to the client, when the company received payment, and so on. Your selection in the screen shown in Figure 8.10 depends on this information.

8.3.2   Correct Errors in Sales Orders

It's easy for errors to occur when a sales order is posted to CO-PA. For example, when valuation is defined using the current standard cost estimate, but the system cannot find any value for the current standard cost estimate, a derivation rule wasn't defined completely. In these cases, no line items are posted to Profitability Analysis. The system saves the "original" records that contain errors in a separate table.

As shown in Figure 8.11, you can work with sales orders with errors by using Transactions KE2D, KE2B, and KE2C in the Profitability Analysis menu that respectively display, review subsequent postings, and delete any transfer errors associated with the incoming orders.

correcting error where co-PA posting could not be made.

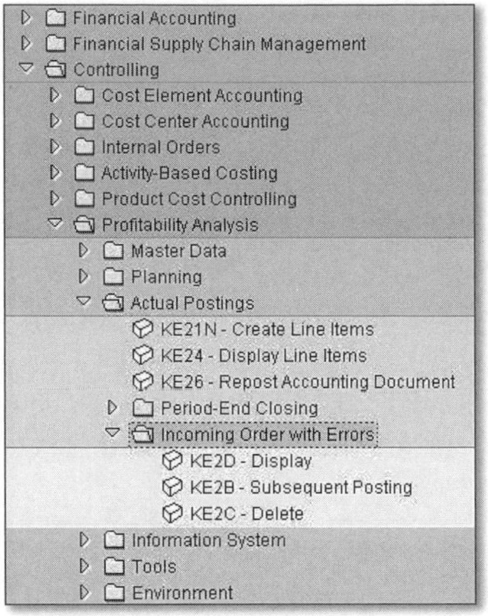

Figure 8.11 Incoming Order with Errors

To review the incoming sale orders with errors, you can navigate the menu shown in Figure 8.11: PROFITABILITY ANALYSIS • ACTUAL POSTINGS • PERIODIC ADJUST-MENTS • POST INCOMING ORDERS SUBSEQUENTLY • DISPLAY, or use Transaction KE2D as shown in Figure 8.12.

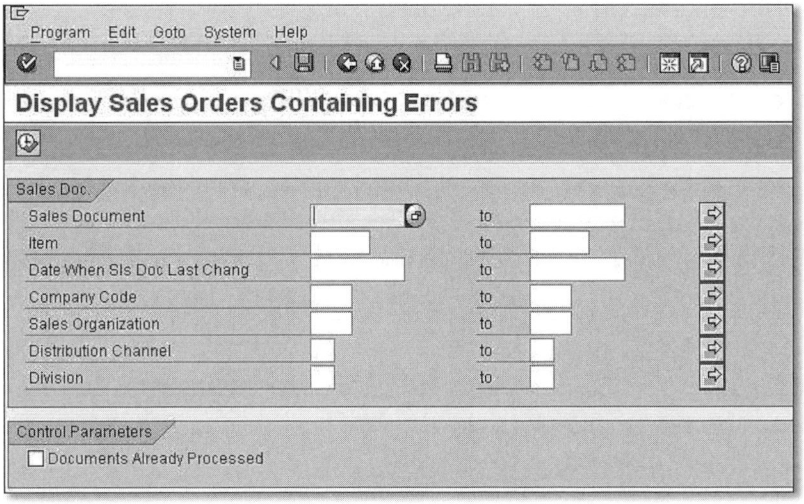

Figure 8.12 Displaying Sales Orders with Errors

Once the errors associated with the sales order have been corrected, depending on the report provided using Transaction KE2D, you can repost these records in CO-PA using the path PROFITABILITY ANALYSIS MENU • ACTUAL POSTINGS • INCOMING ORDER WITH ERRORS • SUBSEQUENT POSTING or Transaction KE2B as shown in Figure 8.13. Select the sales order that you want to analyze and click on the EXECUTE button. You can perform this function in the test run as well as in the update run.

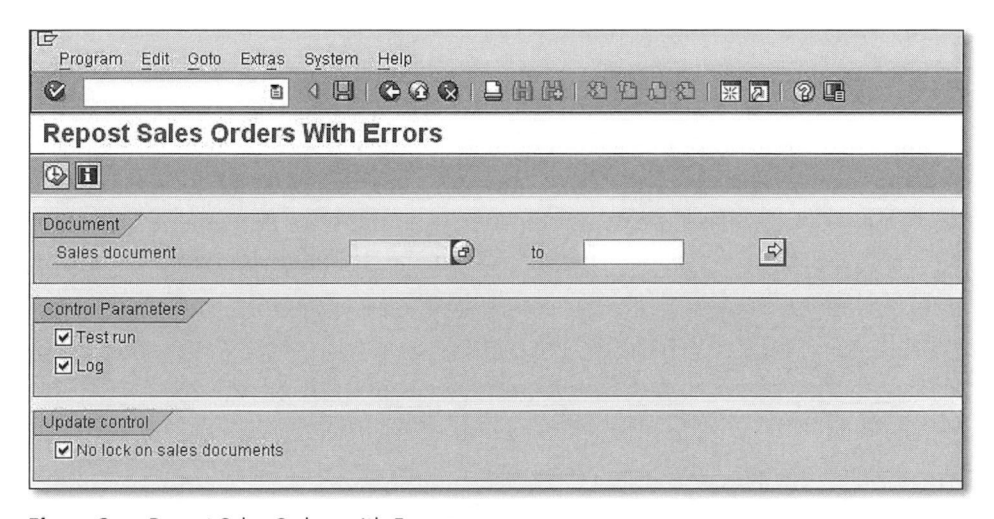

Figure 8.13 Repost Sales Orders with Errors

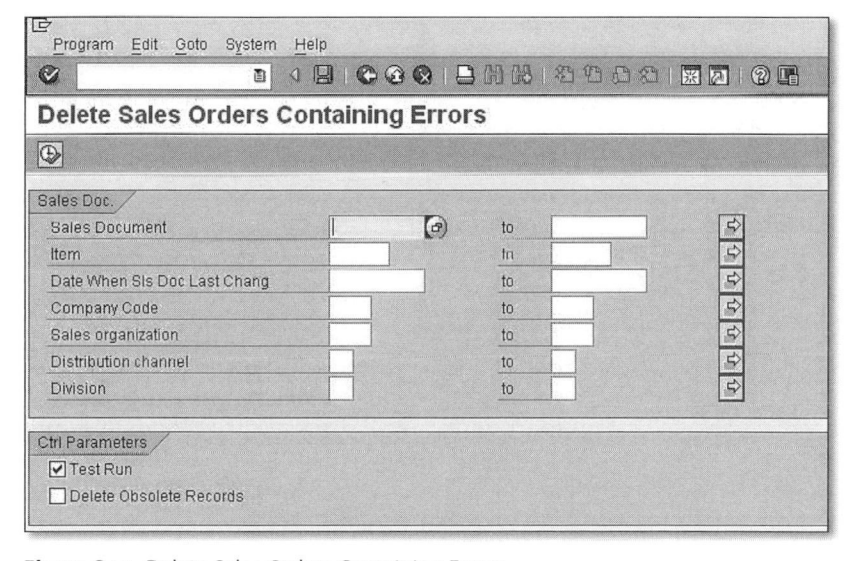

Figure 8.14 Delete Sales Orders Containing Errors

The error table then indicates which line items have been reposted. You can delete any sales order that contains errors by choosing PROFITABILITY ANALYSIS • ACTUAL POSTINGS • INCOMING ORDER WITH ERRORS • DELETE or use Transaction KE2C as shown in Figure 8.14. This screen provides you with multiple criteria available in SAP in order to find the order(s) that you want to analyze. If you don't know the exact order number, you can use different criteria such as ITEM, COMPANY CODE, SALES ORGANIZATION, DIVISION, and others as shown in Figure 8.14.

8.3.3 Post Existing Sales Orders to CO-PA

In our final discussion of sales orders, let's go over the steps you need to post existing sales orders to Profitability Analysis. This is particularly useful if you implement CO-PA after the SD component of SAP has been implemented and you wish to transfer sales orders; for example, for the current or previous periods to CO-PA.

Execute the function for posting sales orders using Transaction SPRO and following this path: CONTROLLING • PROFITABILITY ANALYSIS • TOOL • PRODUCTION STARTUP • SUBSEQUENT POSTING OF SD DOCUMENTS as shown in Figures 8.15.

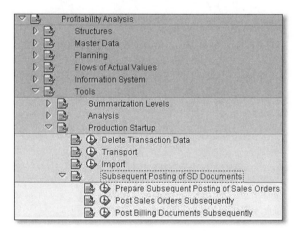

Figure 8.15 Accessing Subsequent Posting of SD Documents in the SPRO Environment

In this menu there are several options, which we'll discuss in the following subsections.

Prepare Subsequent Posting of Sales Orders

As shown in Figure 8.15, you can access the menu PREPARE SUBSEQUENT POSTINGS OF SALES ORDERS by clicking on the EXECUTE icon. Here, you can prepare to post existing sales orders to CO-PA. This function is useful if SD has been implemented before SAP CO-PA, and there's posted data from the current or past periods. Before sales orders can be subsequently posted, the system needs to determine the profitability segments to which the order items should be assigned, if this assignment doesn't exist already. This transaction allows you to perform the assignment of order items so sales orders can be posted.

As shown in Figure 8.16, a selection screen appears and requires you to set the selection criteria for the sales orders that you want to post subsequently. The system selects those sales orders that meet the criteria and have not yet been assigned to a profitability segment.

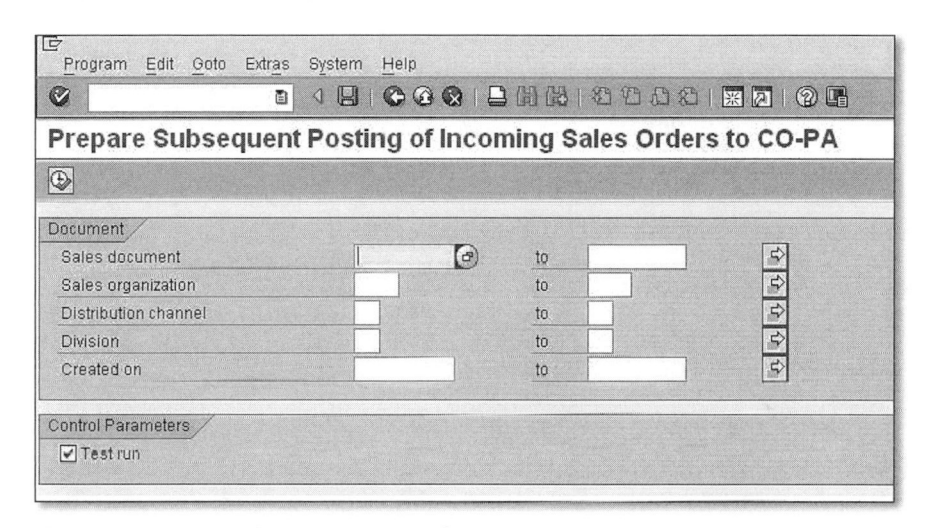

Figure 8.16 Prepare Subsequent Posting of Incoming Sales Orders to CO-PA

After defining the selection criteria as shown in Figure 8.16, click on EXECUTE to initiate the transfer of sales orders based on your criteria. If any errors occur during the execution, the system stores the corresponding messages in a log that you can access and review as shown in Figure 8.17. The errors appear as logs, and the system provides you with information that describes the number of successful documents that are ready to be transferred and number of documents with incorrect information that need to be fixed.

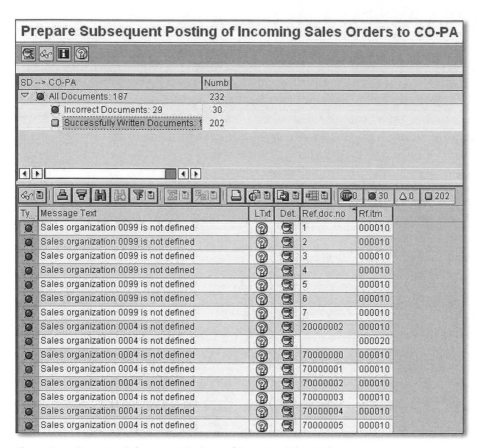

Figure 8.17 Preparing Subsequent Postings of Incoming Sales Orders

As shown in Figure 8.17 there are 202 sales orders ready to be transferred. There are 30 orders that were not correctly transferred because their definitions weren't correctly assigned to the correct value fields, the incorrect condition types were identified, and/or the sales order might not be successfully created in the system. It's also possible that there's still missing information in the sales order, such as the sales organization master data is not yet correctly defined as shown in Figure 8.17. To do this, go back to the PREPARE POSTING OF INCOMING SALES ORDERS TO CO-PA screen as shown previously in Figure 8.16, select the sales order number available in the SALES DOCUMENT field shown in Figure 8.19 that is ready to be transferred, uncheck the TEST RUN checkbox, and once again click on the EXECUTE button.

This time you're performing the preparation of the sales order selected in Figure 8.16 in real time, and it is not a test! The system will perform a confirmation as shown in Figure 8.18 that the order was successfully written from SD to CO-PA, as shown on the top part of the screen. Also notice that the number of the sales order successfully prepared must have a successful confirmation in the lower bottom of the screen as shown in Figure 8.18 for Sales Order (SO) number 11. Exit this screen, and go to the next step, POST SALES ORDERS SUBSEQUENTLY, shown back in Figure 8.15.

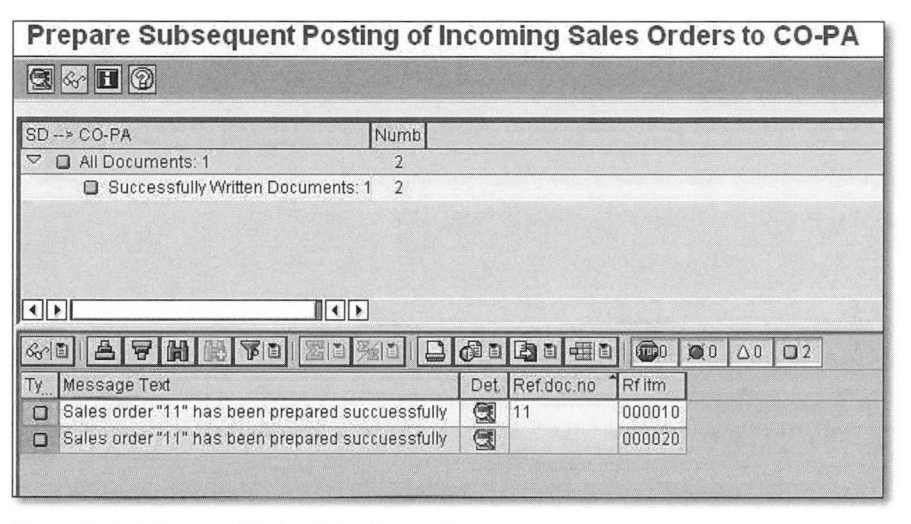

Figure 8.18 A Successful Sales Order Preparation

Post Sales Orders Subsequently

Once an order has been prepared, you can transfer it to the CO-PA environment. Before you can use this function, you must determine a profitability segment to which the data for these orders should be posted. If you have sales orders that haven't already been assigned a profitability segment, you need to prepare this step using the previous function PREPARE SUBSEQUENT POSTING OF SALES ORDERS.

Documents without profitability segments are not processed by this function. On the selection screen as shown in Figure 8.19, specify the sales orders you would like to transfer. Note that only those that have been assigned to a profitability segment will be transferred.

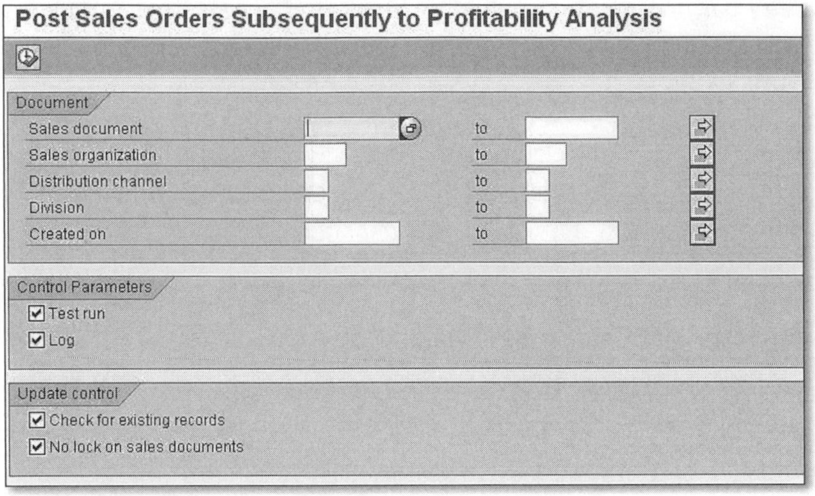

Figure 8.19 Post Sales Orders Subsequently to Profitability Analysis

Post Billing Documents Subsequently

Use this function to transfer costing-based CO-PA billing documents that already exist in FI. This is particularly useful if you go productive with CO-PA after the SD component has been implemented and transferring sales data from current or previous periods to CO-PA is required.

In the next section, we'll explore how to transfer billing documents from SD to CO-PA.

8.4 Transfer of Billing Documents

In this section, you'll learn how to define how billing document items (record type "F") for sales from stock that are transferred to Profitability Analysis. In costing-based CO-PA, you need to assign condition types and quantity fields from SD to the value and quantity fields in CO-PA. In account-based CO-PA, the system only transfers the posting lines available in FI. As shown in Figure 8.15 and described in the previous section, you can also transfer billing documents to the CO-PA environment using the POST BILLING DOCUMENTS SUBSEQUENTLY step if there are billing documents that exist in FI before Profitability Analysis has been activated.

You can transfer a billing document by choosing the billing document number, billing date, sales organization, distribution channel and/or division. When the transfer occurs, the system checks whether the billing data has already been posted to CO-PA in order to prevent documents from being posted twice (first online and then with this function to CO-PA). After posting the data to CO-PA, the program displays a transfer log and an error log. If any billing documents contained errors, you need to correct them and run the program once again.

> **Note**
>
> Almost every single component in transfer of actual values follows the PA transfer structure procedures discussed in the previous sections. For this reason, we'll briefly review the menus in the following sections without going into much detail because they all follow the same logic.

Now, to transfer the information coming from billing documents and postings from FI, you must assign condition types to the desired value fields in CO-PA as described in Chapter 4. These assignments transfer the real and statistical ("fictitious") conditions (postings in FI, such as revenues, sales deductions, and cost-of-sales accounts) and must be defined as CO-relevant accounts (cost or revenue elements).

Similar to transfer of incoming sales orders, there are two functions available when transferring billing documents from the transactional system: ASSIGN QUANTITY FIELDS and ASSIGN VALUE FIELDS. To access these functions, follow the path CONTROLLING • PROFITABILITY ANALYSIS • FLOWS OF ACTUAL VALUES • TRANSFER OF BILLING DOCUMENTS, as shown in Figure 8.20.

The screen shown in Figure 8.20 is very similar to the screen shown earlier in Figure 8.6 (for transfers of sales orders) because we're accessing the same object but with a different record type ("F" for billing documents, rather than "A" or "I" for sales orders).

In addition, you can see in Figure 8.20 that there is a function object called RESET VALUE/QUANTITY FIELDS, which is used to reset a quantity or value field, depending on the billing type. This means that the condition value set in the field is replaced by the value 0. This makes it possible to post only the revenue and quantity in Profitability Analysis (i.e., for returns) while retaining the freight costs of the original billing document. To do so, you would set "RE" as the billing type and reset the value field "freight costs."

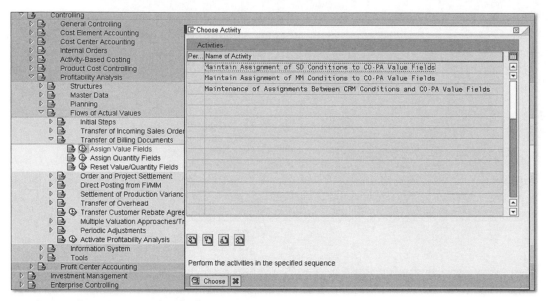

Figure 8.20 Transfer of Billing Documents

In order to be able to transfer billing documents to CO-PA there are several prerequisites:

- ▶ The level of detail of the valuation in the SD billing document must meet the requirements for value fields in Profitability Analysis (see Chapter 4).

- ▶ The pricing procedure must be defined in SD.

- ▶ The condition types must be defined in SD. It isn't necessary to activate the conditions for transferring sales order data since this transfer is solely for statistical purposes.

- ▶ The operating concern to which you want to transfer the billing data must be defined and generated.

- ▶ The fields in the billing document must be assigned to the value fields or quantity fields in the operating concern.

It's important to notice that the billing document transfer also allows the system to repost billing documents correctly if they have been transferred into CO-PA via incorrect derivation. If you activate the REVERSAL OF LINE ITEMS indicator as shown in Figure 8.21 using Transaction KE4S, the system cancels the incorrect line item and, in the same step, writes a new line item for which the current derivation rules are taken into account. You need to activate the REDETERMINE PROF. SEGMENT indicator for the latter to occur, and when ready click on the EXECUTE button.

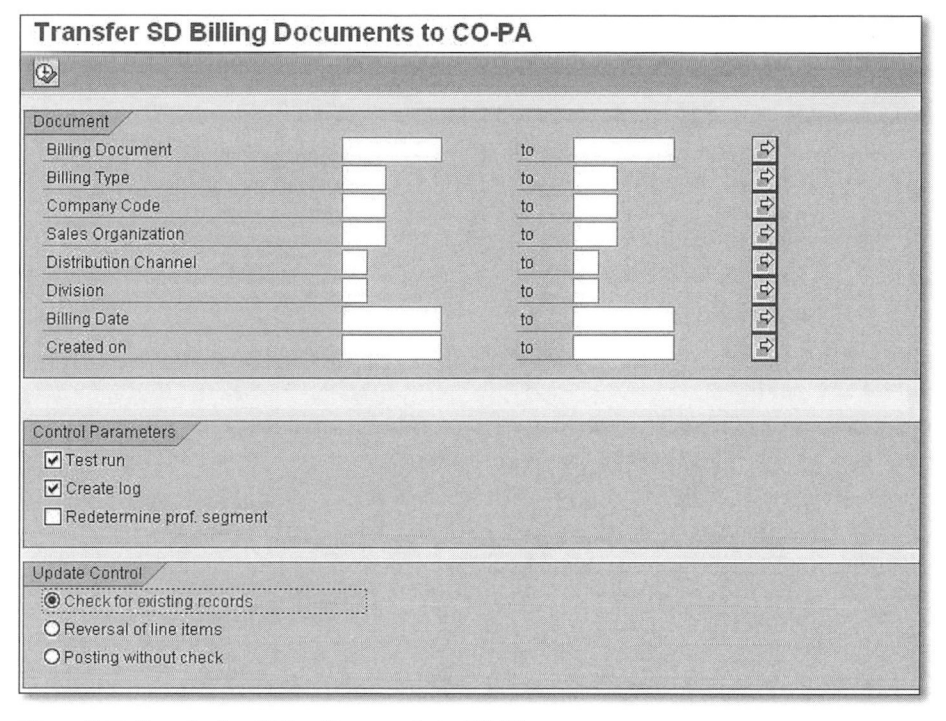

Figure 8.21 Transferring Billing Documents to CO-PA

Next, we'll look at order and project settlement.

8.5   Order and Project Settlement

In the SAP ECC system, you can settle the following to profitability segments: internal orders (component of CO), sales orders (component of SD), projects (component of PS), and production orders (component of PP). Internal orders and projects can be used to control the costs of an internal activity, such as the costs of an advertising campaign.

To transfer these costs to the profitability segments, you need to make sure that the following are done:

- The settlements to CO-PA have a settlement profile.
- Assign the objects to the master data objects you want to settle.
- Activate the controlling area or target of the settlement.
- Create a settlement rule for the settlement object with a profitability segment as the receiver.

If the settlement profile of the order allows settling the profitability segments, it's possible to enter an assignment to a profitability segment when you create the settlement rule.

You need to set up a PA transfer structure in CO-PA in order to transfer the settlement information to the profitability segments and determine how the values are settled to the value fields in the Profitability Analysis component. As shown in Figure 8.22 we have reviewed a subset of the screen shown in Figure 8.21 to focus on the Overhead/Project Settlements, there are two elements necessary when working with PA transfer structures when accessing the ORDER AND PROJECT SETTLEMENT menu. Notice that there are two functions available to transfer actual and plan data for orders and projects with Record Type "C":

- DEFINE PA TRANSFER STRUCTURE FOR SETTLEMENT
- ASSIGN PA TRANSFER STRUCTURE TO SETTLEMENT PROFILE

Figure 8.22 Reviewing the Order and Project Settlement Menu

To settle data to CO-PA, you need to define a *settlement profile*, and then assign this to the master data of the objects you want to settle. This settlement profile contains an allocation structure, which defines how the corresponding order or project is credited. It also contains a PA transfer structure, which determines how the values are settled to value fields in CO-PA. Let's look at this process in more detail.

8.5.1 Define a PA Transfer Structure for Settlement

In this activity, you define the PA transfer structures that are used to settle actual and planning data for orders and projects. To be able to transfer order and project system information, you first define a PA transfer structure to assign the original cost elements on the order or the project to lines (assignments) that are later assigned to value fields in Profitability Analysis.

To create the PA transfer structure, follow these steps:

1. Click on the Define PA Transfer Structure for Settlement object shown in Figure 8.22. The screen shown in Figure 8.23 appears.

2. Click on the New Entries button, and type an abbreviation and name for your PA transfer structures. For example, as shown in Figure 8.23, we have three structures CO, E1, and FI with their respective descriptions.

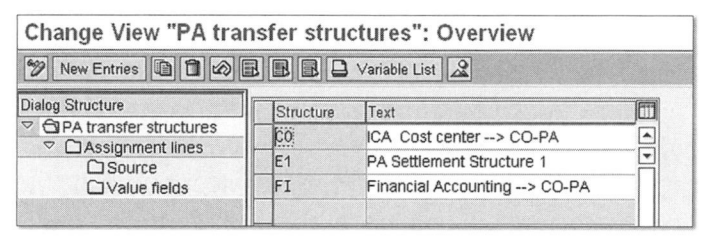

Figure 8.23 Configuring Your PA Transfer Structure

3. Next, select a structure in the Structure column; for example, CO.

4. To perform an assignment, first select the Source object on the left side of the screen and add your source fields (the SAP ERP ECC 6.0 or R/3 fields from where the data is extracted).

5. Next, select the Value fields object on the left side of the screen and specify the value fields that will receive the data in CO-PA coming from the previously defined source fields. You need to assign a CO-PA quantity field (quantity/value indicator "2") to an assignment line for the billed quantity. Now the billed amount of the settlement information is transferred from CO-PA to an assigned field.

6. Now, select the Assignment lines object on the left side of the screen. In that object, you must select the quantity billed/delivered indicator for a particular assignment line, such as CO, E1, and FI, to be transferred to CO-PA. These assignment lines are then used to transfer the cost elements to CO-PA value fields.

7. For each assignment line, enter the cost element(s) or the cost element group to be assigned into the order/project; you should usually activate the costs/revenues option as the source. The variances on production orders option is

only relevant for the settlement of production orders. In the latter case, you should define a separate operating concern. The ACCOUNTING INDICATOR FROM SERVICE MANAGEMENT (SM) ORDERS option is only relevant for the settlement of service orders.

After completing the definition of your PA transfer structure, you're ready to assign it to a settlement profile that contains all of the relevant information required for settling CO orders, sales orders, projects, and production orders. This functionality is explained in the following section.

8.5.2 Assign a PA Transfer Structure to a Settlement Profile

From the CO-PA perspective, you need to assign your PA transfer structure to a settlement profile to access the information from the different CO objects. However, this settlement profile must allow profitability segments to be set as settlement receivers. In other words, you must configure the system to accept the order and project settlement structure information into its final destination: CO-PA.

Because the settlement profile is usually entered automatically in the MASTER DATA menu of the specific objects being settled, such as internal orders, sales orders, and/or projects, a settlement profile must be specified as default. You can perform this in each of these components by object type:

▶ For internal orders, you can do this when you maintain order types.

▶ For sales orders, you do this when you maintain requirement classes.

▶ For projects, you do this when you maintain project profiles.

▶ You can assign 100% of the values to one profitability segment using Transaction KO04 as shown in Figure 8.24, or the values can be distributed among several profitability segments on a percentage basis based on your preference. This procedure can occur online or in the background. It's possible to run a simulation settlement or perform a direct update with a result log available after the process is executed.

When working with account-based CO-PA, the costs are settled to the settlement cost elements that are specified in the allocation structure of the order or project. The line item created in CO-PA can be displayed in the application menu.

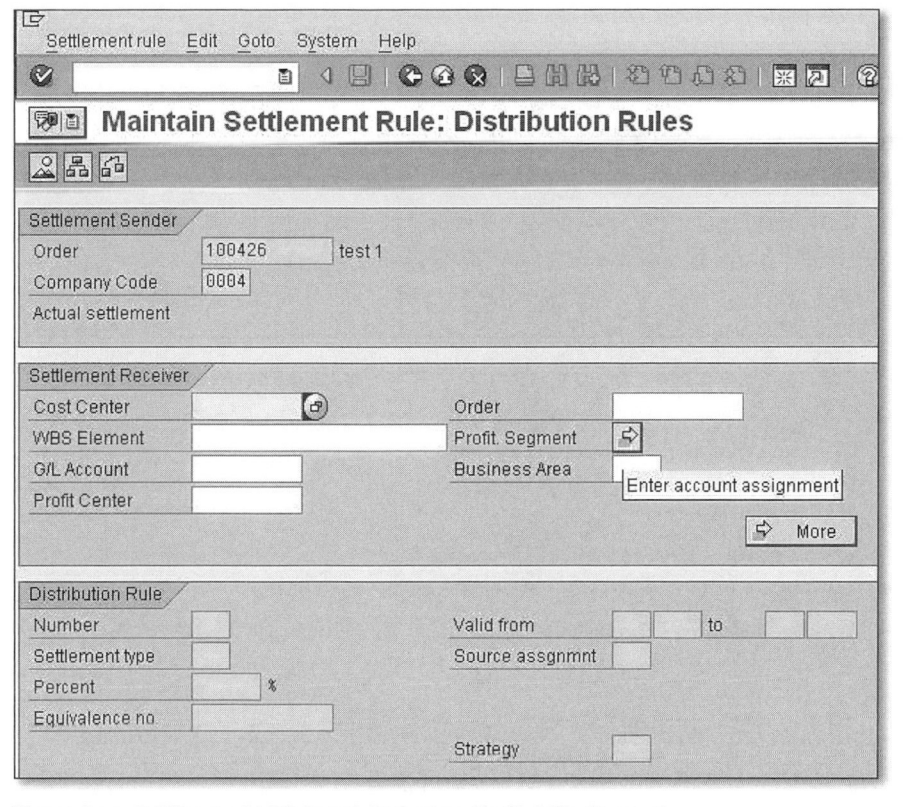

Figure 8.24 Settling an SAP Internal Order to a Profitability Segment

Before you can settle orders or projects to Profitability Analysis in real-time, the controlling area you're working in must be activated using Transaction OKKP. In addition, you also need to configure a settlement profile to allow the system to settle an order or project to a profitability segment that is set up as a receiver. As shown in Figure 8.25 and 8.26, we review the elements that must be configured to allow an order to settle to a CO-PA profitability segment. For example, as shown in Figure 8.25 we are creating a settlement profile where it's optional to settle costs to a sales order by simply selecting the drop-down menu.

Notice in Figure 8.26 that the settlement profile requires PA TRANSFER STRUCTURE, SOURCE STRUCTURE, and ALLOCATION STRUCTURE. Similarly, once the settlement profile has been created, you can assign the settlement profile to the different order types using Transaction KOAL as shown in Figure 8.27.

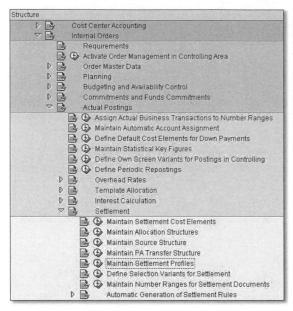

Figure 8.25 Accessing Settlement Profile Configuration in the Internal Order Menu

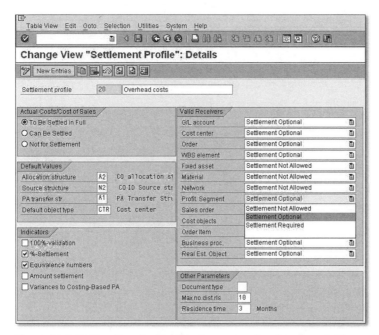

Figure 8.26 Setting Up a Profitability Segment as Receiver for a Settlement Profile for an Internal Order

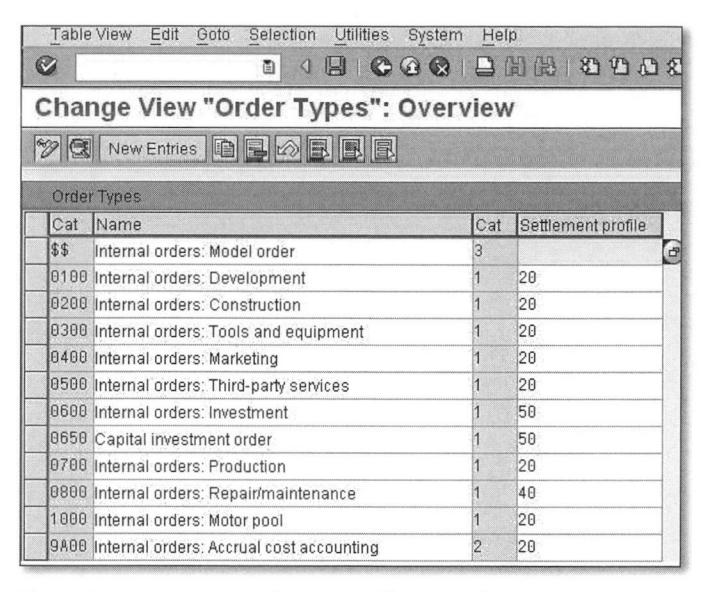

Figure 8.27 Assigning Settlement Profiles to Order Types

There are additional configuration options required that are applicable to internal orders and settlement procedures such as distribution rules, settlement parameters, settlement methods, automatic generated rules, and others, and particular to your internal order component configuration. Check with your FICO team to determine how to define all of these elements for orders and/or projects to allow data transfer to SAP CO-PA profitability segments. If the settlement profile of the order allows the ability to settle to profitability segments, you can enter an assignment to a profitability segment when you create the settlement rule.

Similarly, project settlements to profitability segments require a settlement profile, allocation structure, PA transfer structure, source structure, settlement rules, and more as shown in Figure 8.28.

As shown in Figure 8.29, once the settlement profile has been defined, you can assign it to a project definition using SPRO. Follow the path as follows: PROJECT SYSTEMS • COSTS • AUTOMATIC AND PERIODIC ALLOCATIONS • SETTLEMENTS • SPECIFY DEFAULT SETTLEMENT PROFILE FOR PROJECT PROFILE, and identify the Project Profile and open the input box next to it to review the information available in Figure 8.29.

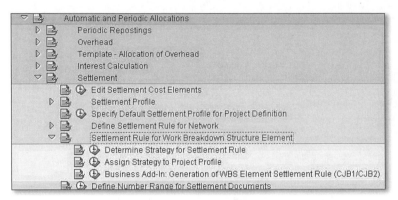

Figure 8.28 Reviewing the Settlement Configuration Menus for the Project Systems Component

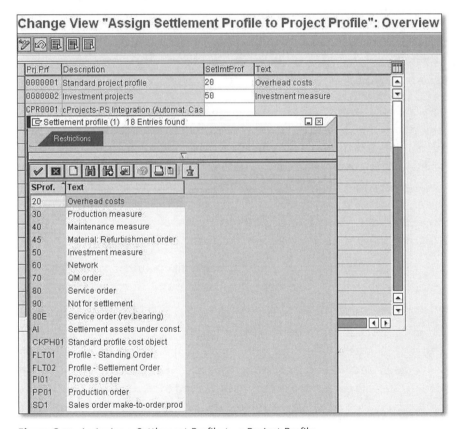

Figure 8.29 Assigning a Settlement Profile to a Project Profile

For the allocation to occur, projects use an object called a *WBS element*. This is nothing more than a cost collector that behaves like an account and stores the project values that are settled to profitability segments. In this activity, access Transaction SPRO to make the system settings for the automatic generation of settlement rules to the WBS elements as shown in Figure 8.30.

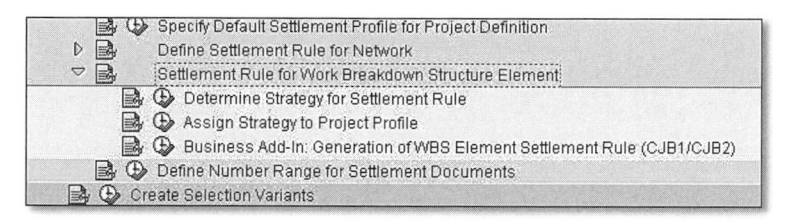

Figure 8.30 Reviewing the Automatic Generation of WBS Settlement Rules Menu

Note that the following occurs during the automatic generation:

▶ Characteristics are inherited as they are in CO-PA.

▶ Rules generated automatically stipulate period 100% settlement to one receiver.

▶ Characteristics from a sales order are only included if the sales order item or sales order header is assigned to a billing element.

▶ The organizational units controlling area, company code, and profit center are copied from the WBS element to the settlement rule. The plant is copied from the sales order item.

▶ The settlement rule from superior objects can only be inherited if no settlement rule is maintained for the WBS elements lower down in the hierarchy.

▶ Settlement rules generated automatically are recorded under commercial Transaction SRGN. You can use the user status to regulate changes to the settlement rule.

We strongly recommend that you check with your FICO team before moving forward in the configuration of the options reviewed in this chapter, due to the impact to the overall architecture of the CO structures available in your system. You use Transaction CJ8G in order to settle projects to SAP CO-PA profitability segments to post cost of sales, and we recommend that you follow these steps to execute the process in the background:

- ▶ Choose BACKGROUND PROCESSING in the PROCESSING OPTIONS, and then click on the EXECUTE button.
- ▶ In the BACKGROUND PROCESSING OPTIONS dialog box, choose START IMMEDIATELY. Note the job number.
- ▶ Choose CHECK.
- ▶ Choose CONFIRM.
- ▶ In the BACKGROUND PRINT PARAMETERS dialog box, choose the OUTPUT device, and then choose CONTINUE.
- ▶ Choose the system from the top of the screen, select it, and then select the OWN JOBS line.
- ▶ On the JOB OVERVIEW screen, choose JOBNAME.
- ▶ Choose JOBLOG to see the results.

In the next section, we'll explore how to configure and transfer direct postings from FI/MM into Profitability Analysis.

8.6 Direct Posting from FI/MM

Direct postings from FI or MM can be configured in CO-PA to identify revenues and costs for record type "B." The revenue component of MM appears when there is inventory that can appreciate, such as oil and gold. In addition, you can transfer expenses, such as gifts to customers, special promotions, or samples. Note that these are not costs because they are never billed to a client as part of a sale, but rather expenses of your operations. This is a delicate topic, however, and you should review the financial regulations in your country to understand how this type of expense is handled.

As shown in Figure 8.31, there are two components in the DIRECT POSTING FROM FI/MM menu: MAINTAIN PA TRANSFER STRUCTURE FOR DIRECT POSTINGS and AUTOMATIC ACCOUNT ASSIGNMENT. These components let you transfer direct primary postings from FI and MM to profitability segments.

Figure 8.31 Direct Postings from FI/MM

You can use these MM extraction settings under the following circumstances:

▶ When you post special direct costs from sales, such as transport insurance for a certain delivery, and would like to assign these primary costs directly to a profitability segment.

▶ When you post an invoice for promotional events and you want this invoice to appear statistically in the responsible marketing cost center, and at the same time assign it to a profitability segment in Profitability Analysis. In this case, you would assign the invoice to both a cost center and a profitability segment.

▶ When you create automatic postings in MM and you want these revenues and expenses from the revaluation of material stocks to be automatically posted to Profitability Analysis. This instance also requires that you define "Automatic assignment to a profitability segment."

Additional considerations are required in MM to perform the actual transfer of data into CO-PA. You should consult with your MM team lead or responsible consultants to assist you with this MM-specific information. Let's now look in detail at the two components available under direct posting from FI/MM.

> **Note**
>
> Other configurations are possible to allow the transfer of material ledger information into CO-PA. Unfortunately, they go beyond the scope of this book because they depend on activation of the Product Costing Component (CO-PC) and configuration of the S and V price components.

8.6.1 Maintain PA Transfer Structure for Direct Postings

As shown in Figure 8.32, when you access the MAINTAIN PA TRANSFER STRUCTURE FOR DIRECT POSTING component, you access a screen similar to the one previously shown in Figure 8.30. However, the configuration options inside of each of these objects differ, and in this case are specific for FI/MM information.

In this activity, you define the PA transfer structure FI to post costs and revenues directly to profitability segments in CO-PA. Similar to how you configured the previous transfer structures, you specify how the different cost elements and posted amounts are matched with specific components within the CO-PA operating concern in this functionality:

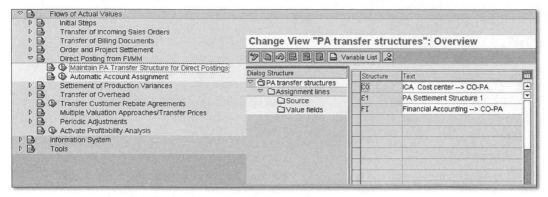

Figure 8.32 Accessing FI/MM PA Transfer Structures

1. Define the PA transfer structure to use as shown in Figure 8.33. In this case, we'll be configuring FI DIRECT ACCT ASSIGN. FR. FI/MM. The system will prompt you to select a controlling area; for this example we use the default Kostenrechnungskreis 0001 or CO Area 0001.

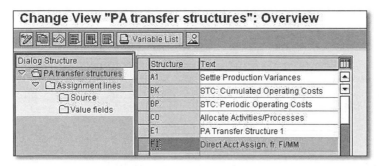

Figure 8.33 Selecting the PA Transfer Structure

2. Select the PA structure, and choose the ASSIGNMENT LINES as shown in Figure 8.34 on the left-hand side of the screen.

3. Select the ASSIGNMENT LINE ITEM 20 or RAW-/SERVICE MATERIAL CONSUMP. as shown in Figure 8.34. The screen shown in Figure 8.35 appears, where you double-click on the SOURCE icon on the left-hand side of the screen.

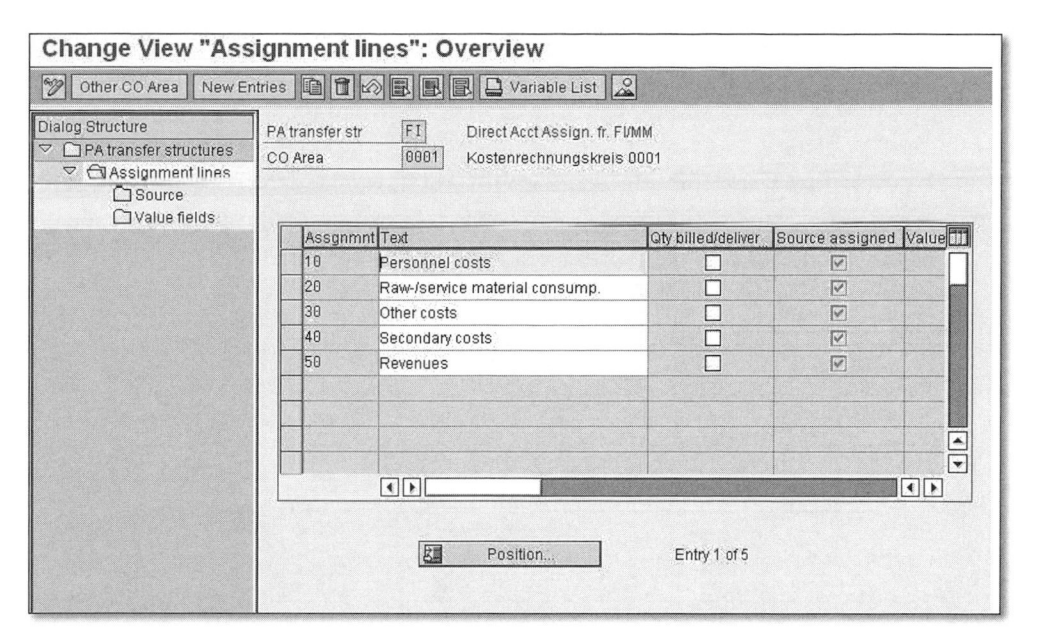

Figure 8.34 Reviewing the Assignment Lines Available in the PA Transfer Structure

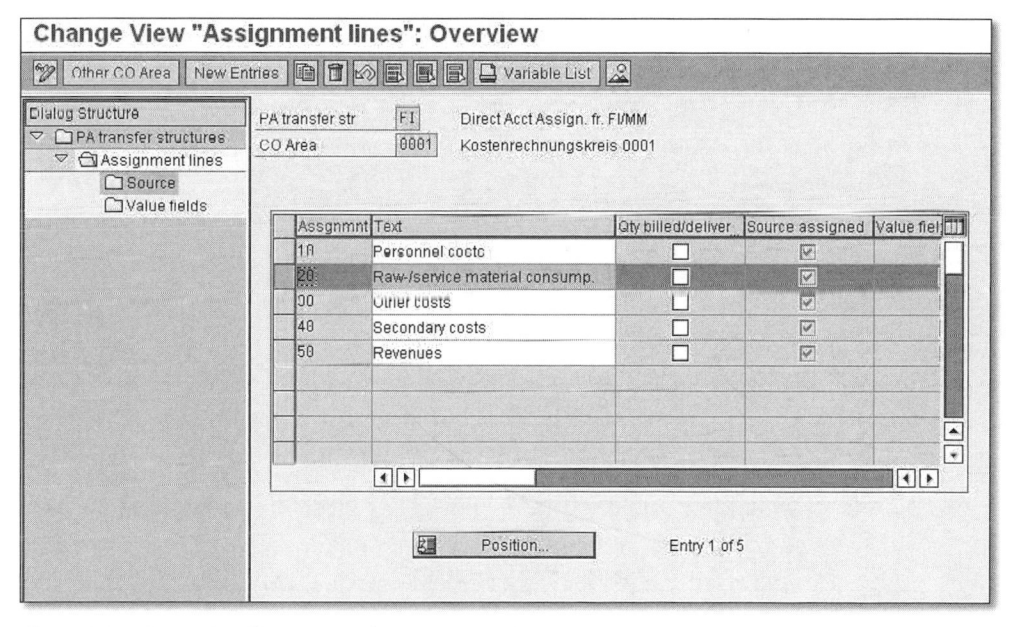

Figure 8.35 Reviewing the Source of an Assignment Line

4. Now you need to assign the source fields that will populate the RAW-/SERVICE MATERIAL CONSUMP line. Here, we'll select a cost element range or a cost element group from cost and revenue to be used to populate the required line in CO-PA as shown in Figure 8.36. Divide your cost elements according to how you want to group them in Profitability Analysis, and create assignment lines accordingly. The QUANTITY BILLED/DELIVERED indicator is not relevant for the PA transfer structure FI and therefore should not be activated.

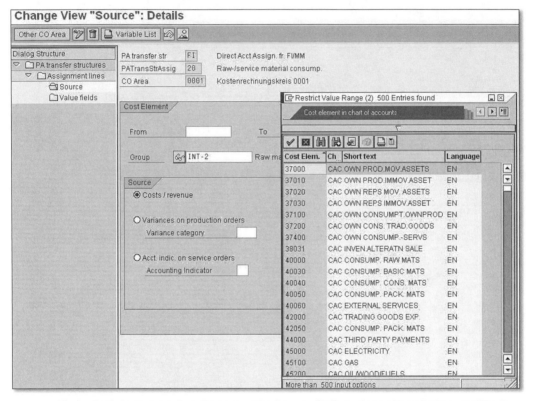

Figure 8.36 Assigning a Cost Element as the Source of Information to Your Assignment Line in CO-PA

5. Double-click on the value fields in the left dialog structure in Figure 8.36 once you have completed the assignment of cost elements ranges or cost element groups. As shown in Figure 8.37, a value field with a fixed length of three has been created, and the amount values will be stored in the CO-PA Value Field VVMAT. Once completed, click on the SAVE button located on the top of the screen.

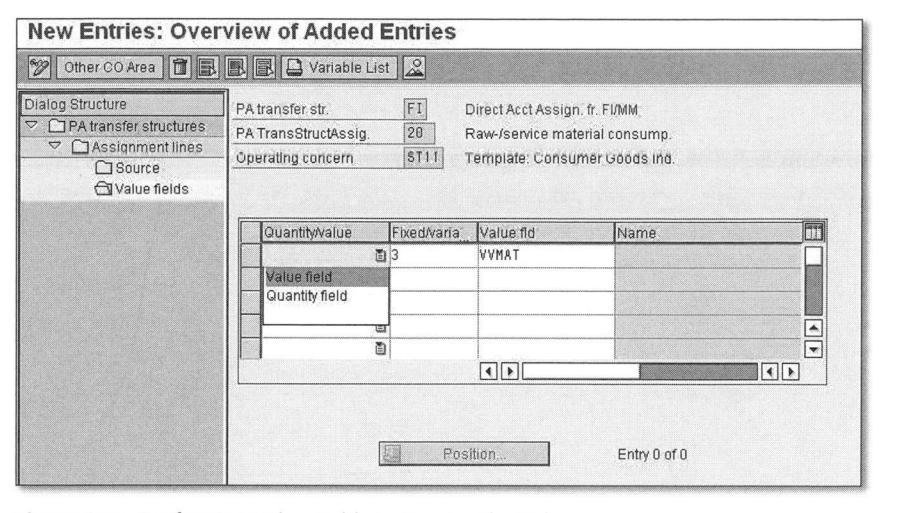

Figure 8.37 Configuring Value Fields to Receive the Values

Notice that for each assignment line you need to enter the value field (or, if the costs are split into fixed and variable portions, both value fields) into which costs/revenues are imported.

Automatic postings created in MM can be transferred to CO-PA using automatic assignment. This configuration is briefly discussed in the next subsection.

8.6.2 Automatic Account Assignment

Automatic account assignment executes an automatic procedure to identify profitability segments automatically posted, such as those generated for MM. These automatic postings can be passed on to CO-PA by means of an automatic assignment to a profitability segment, depending on the characteristics found in FI. For this reason, if the information identified in the FI documents is not very detailed, the posted values are transferred to CO-PA at an aggregated level, which can also become a drawback. This functionality might be advisable for certain accounts and business transactions only, such as the following:

▶ The transfer of price differences that are posted in purchasing due to differing order prices or differing prices in invoice receipt (as period costs).

▶ The transfer of expenses or revenues that arise due to a revaluation of material stocks (as period costs).

▶ The transfer of inventory differences (as period costs).

Now, let's review how to work with the function automatic account assignment:

1. Follow the path Profitability Analysis • Flows of Actual Values • Direct Postings FI/MM • Automatic Account Assignment.

2. As shown in Figure 8.38, in the left area of the screen, you now see the Default account assignment, Detail per business area/valuation area, and Detail per profit center hierarchy.

OKB9

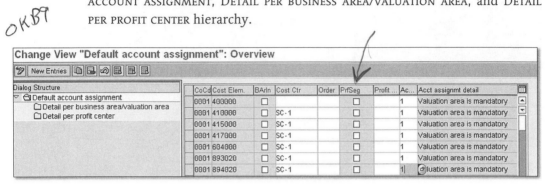

Figure 8.38 Accessing Automatic Account Assignment in FI/MM

3. As also shown in Figure 8.38, you can define the company code (CoCd), cost element (Cost Elem.), cost center (Cost Ctr), and account assignment detail (Acct assignmt detail). Notice in this case that we're using Cost Ctr SC-1 that is also dependent on the controlling area and the information stored in it. In this case, SC-1 is an SAP default MM cost center.

4. Select the profitability segment indicator (PrfSeg), shown in Figure 8.38, to transfer postings from the different cost element accounts displayed and move that information into CO-PA. Selecting this indicator means that first the profitability segment is found using substitution for automatic postings, and then the corresponding posting is transferred to CO-PA.

   Generally, a profitability segment is automatically found and updated in Profitability Analysis when the corresponding sender document is created (such as when you enter FI documents with direct assignment to Profitability Analysis, or when you create sales orders or billing documents). Therefore, it isn't desirable to have the system find a profitability segment for all of the accounts relevant to profits by assigning accounts in this customizing step.

5. Make sure that the account for automatic postings is assigned in the PA transfer structure "FI" with a cost element account, using the Source object displayed earlier in Figure 8.35.

6. Click on the line for cost element 400000 displayed in Figure 8.35, and select the DETAIL PER BUSINESS AREA/VALUATION AREA object in the hierarchy displayed on the left-hand side of the screen, as shown in Figure 8.39. Here you can configure the detail by cost center, order, profit center, and others.

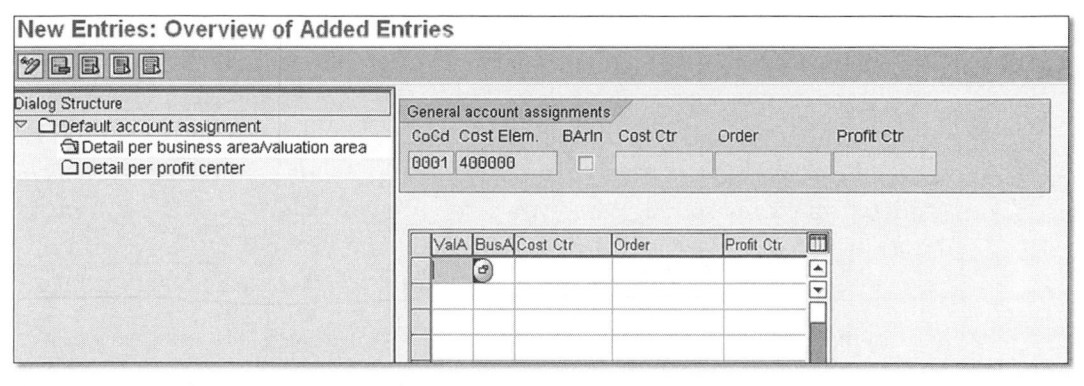

Figure 8.39 Detail Per Business Area/Valuation Area

7. Also, you can configure the detail more simplistically by profit center, as shown in Figure 8.40. In this case, you can define GENERAL ACCOUNT ASSIGN-MENTS for company code (CoCD), cost element (COST ELEM.), cost center (COST CTR), order (ORDER), and profit center (PROFIT CTR).

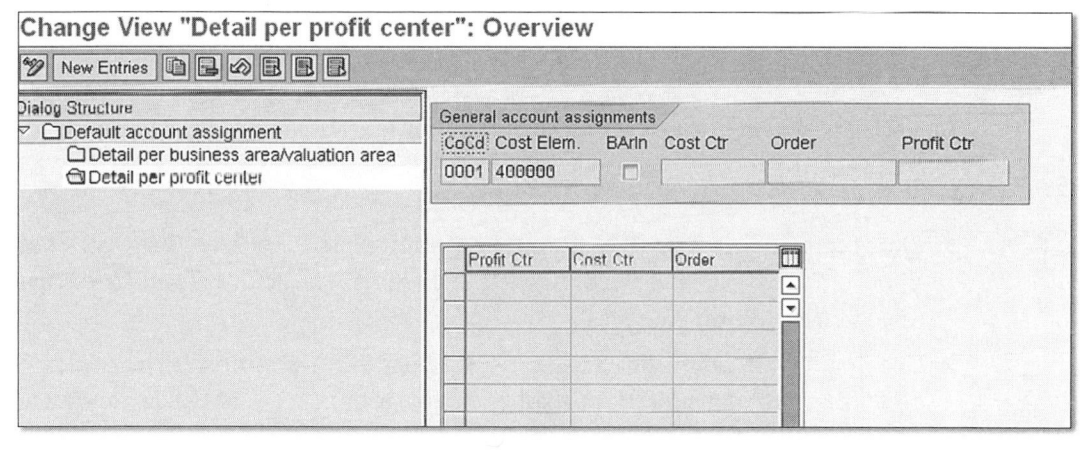

Figure 8.40 Detail Per Profit Center

Whether you'll use DETAIL PER PROFIT CENTER or DETAIL PER BUSINESS AREA/VALUA-TION AREA will depend on the type of postings you need to extract. You must analyze your data postings to decide which is more appropriate. Next, let's look at the settlement of production variances function.

8.7 Settlement of Production Variances

If you have information coming from the Production Planning (PP) component and if your company plans to produce actual products or goods, there might be differences because of scrap, shop floor delays, material defect delays, reprocessing, and others. When variances are calculated in CO-PC, production variances are determined and stored. When you settle production orders, you can transfer these variances—differentiated by cost element and variance category—to value fields in CO-PA, using the SETTLEMENT OF PRODUCTION VARIANCES functionality.

As shown in Figure 8.41, you need to configure two objects: DEFINE PA TRANSFER STRUCTURE FOR VARIANCE SETTLEMENT and ASSIGN PA TRANSFER STRUCTURE TO SETTLEMENT PROFILE.

> **Note**
>
> We highly recommend defining separate PA transfer structures for different allocation types.

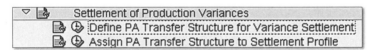

Figure 8.41 Reviewing the Settlement of Production Variances Menu

Follow these steps:

1. Click on the object DEFINE PA TRANSFER STRUCTURE FOR VARIANCE SETTLEMENT as shown in Figure 8.41. The configuration of this PA structure is similar to that reviewed in Section 8.6.

2. Decide how the variances and assignment lines in the PA transfer structure are defined, using the procedure explained in Section 8.3. The value fields are moved to CO-PA once the assignments are completed.

3. Select the indicator for the quantity billed/delivered in the assignment line that is used for transferring the quantity of the production order that has been delivered to the plant to CO-PA. As before, you must assign a CO-PA value field

under the value fields object shown previously in Figure 8.23, and in the assignment line for the delivered quantity (quantity/value indicator "2"). When the production order is settled to CO-PA, the delivered quantity is transferred to the assigned field.

4. For each assignment line, enter the cost element(s) or the cost element group from which the production variances are settled, and select a variance category as the source (such as price variances for materials input). If, instead of a variance category, you select the costs/revenues option as the source, all variances of the entered cost element are settled to the production order.

5. For each assignment line, enter the value field (or, if costs are split into fixed and variable portions, both value fields) into which the appropriate variance category is imported.

6. Save your work and return to the IMG environment, and click on ASSIGN PA TRANSFER STRUCTURE TO SETTLEMENT PROFILE. Here you need to link the previous configuration to a SETTLEMENT PROFILE object, as shown in Figure 8.42.

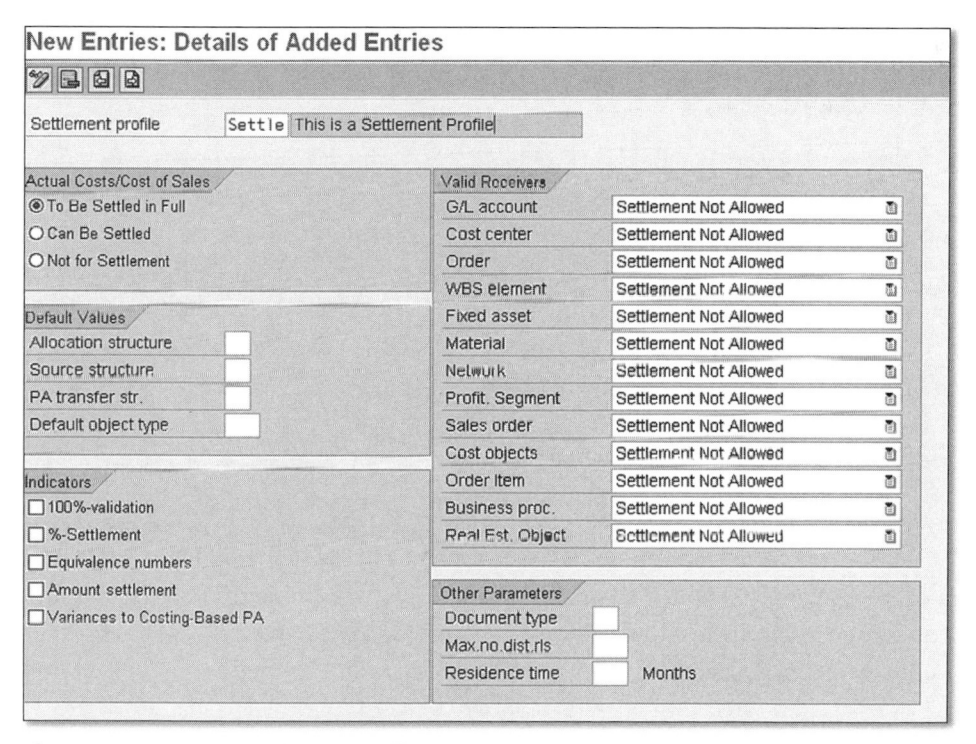

Figure 8.42 Creating a Settlement Profile

Similar to order and project management, the settlement profile contains all relevant information needed for settling CO orders, sales orders, projects, and production orders. From a CO-PA perspective, the settlement profile must allow profitability segments to be set as settlement receivers in order to settle production variances.

For this, assign the PA transfer structure (PA TRANSFER STR.) in the DEFAULT VALUES area, shown in Figure 8.42, and change the status of the profit segments in the VALID RECEIVERS area to allow settlements. Because the settlement profile is usually entered automatically in the master data of the object being settled (internal order, sales order, or project), you need to specify the desired settlement profile as a default, as follows:

▶ For internal orders, you can do this when you maintain order types.

▶ For sales orders, you do this when you maintain requirement classes.

▶ For projects, you do this when you maintain project profiles.

There are more options available, as you can see in Figure 8.42, to allow receivers from other sources, including G/L ACCOUNT, COST CENTER, ORDER, WBS ELEMENT, FIXED ASSET, NETWORK, PROFIT. SEGMENT, COST OBJECTS, BUSINESS PROC. (business processes), and others.

In the next section, we'll very briefly identify the menu options available in TRANSFER OF OVERHEAD in order for you to have a reference point to initiate the review of this topic. Unfortunately, the topic of transfer of overhead into SAP CO-PA requires further understanding of advanced topics related to Cost Center Accounting, process costs, assessments, distributions, direct and indirect activity allocations, and others that go beyond the purpose of this book.

8.8 Transfer of Overhead

As shown in Figure 8.43, the TRANSFER OF OVERHEAD function of CO-PA is a rather large submenu within the FLOWS OF ACTUAL VALUES CO-PA menu. Please note that because overhead within FI and CO can involve information and data coming from cost centers and process costs, direct and indirect allocations, project settlements, actual cycles, and many more, this topic could be a chapter or even a book on its own, and anything more than showing you the available menu options is beyond the scope of this book as it would involve activity-based costing, Cost

Center Accounting, project systems, and other concepts that are difficult to coherently relate to SAP CO-PA. If you're looking for more information on this topic, try *Product Cost Controlling with SAP* (2nd edition, SAP PRESS, 2012) for further insights regarding overhead and its configuration.

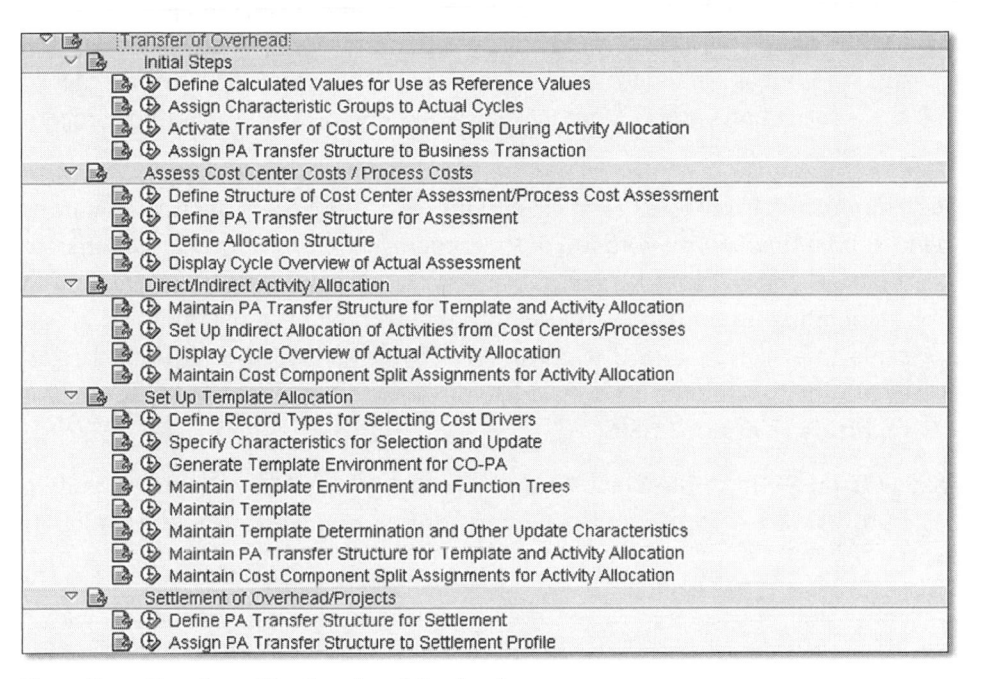

Figure 8.43 Overview of the Transfer of Overhead

If you need to use this complex functionality, interact with people in financial accounting or with the controllers in your company to review how these elements can be configured.

> **Note**
>
> Another component we were unable to discuss is the integration between CO-PA and the material ledger using CO-PC. We recommend that you review this functionality if integration between MM and CO-PA is a requirement for you when working with the COGS from the material master. In addition, you should review the presentation ML46C available in the SAP Service Marketplace for more information on integrating material ledger with CO-PA. Extensive information on this topic can be found in the book *Actual Costing with the SAP Material Ledger* (SAP PRESS, 2011).

8.9   Summary

The information in this chapter is difficult to explain without reviewing and exploring other components external to Profitability Analysis because flows of actual values is an integrator component between the data coming into CO-PA from other components, such as FI, SD, and CO. However, we can say that a PA transfer structure is a standard component that requires configuration in order to link the information coming from the source system to CO-PA operating concern components.

The aim of this chapter was to make you aware of the FLOWS OF ACTUAL VALUES menu and familiarize you with it. You're encouraged to carefully analyze when to use it because there might be alternative ways to access the same information in SAP, depending on your reporting environments. For example, you can access the same information in SAP NetWeaver BW/SAP NetWeaver BI, or you can access specific components to consolidate the data within the SAP ERP ECC 6.0 or R/3 reporting environment.

Next, Chapter 9 introduces you to the concepts of CO-PA reporting, including basic profitability reports, line item reports, forms, and working with the Report Painter.

In this chapter, we'll explore the general reporting functionalities of CO-PA, which will give you an overview of its main capabilities, as well as its role within the overall SAP environment. Typically, CO-PA fulfills most overall requirements for reporting in most implementations without the need to create objects within the SAP NetWeaver Business Intelligence (BI)/SAP Business Warehouse (BW) environment.

9   CO-PA Reporting: Basics

The ultimate goal of any SAP ERP implementation is the generation of reports to keep track of key information and to share it with different users or interested parties. However, there are several tools available within and outside the SAP system to achieve such a goal.

In this chapter, we'll explore CO-PA reporting basics to understand the concepts behind R/3 or SAP ERP ECC 6.0 reporting and how CO-PA is a useful tool for the generation and combination of data coming from different sources inside and outside the SAP environment. The analysis you can perform using CO-PA reporting is multidimensional because CO-PA provides dynamic sorting and rearranging of data within a single report.

Furthermore, in this chapter the concept of market segments or profitability segments will become clearer as a way to suppress or limit characteristics related to customers, products, time, and others for a particular level of information or user role. In addition, you'll see how market segments allow access to the information stored in your operating concern related to quantities, revenues, discounts, surcharges, product costs, margins, period costs, and other predefined value fields that are extracting data coming from different SAP tables. Let's get started by looking at some CO-PA reporting scenarios.

9.1 CO-PA Reporting Scenarios

Reporting must have a purpose, a strategy, and a general framework under which all functionalities are created. The following three types of reporting are typical scenarios involving CO-PA, the more powerful tools of SAP NetWeaver BI and SAP NetWeaver BW, as well as legacy systems and third-party tools:

▶ Reporting data within SAP R/3 or SAP ERP ECC 6.0 and sharing it with the SAP NetWeaver BI/SAP NetWeaver BW platform from a single CO-PA data source.

▶ Reporting data with CO-PA from several systems, data sources, or processes, and also sharing it with SAP NetWeaver BI/SAP NetWeaver BW.

▶ Reporting data using a combination of SAP data and data coming from legacy systems or other third-party tools.

The first scenario is shown in Figure 9.1. In this case, CO-PA is used in profitability reporting to move reporting tasks from an R/3 or SAP ERP ECC 6.0 system into an independent system using the operating concern as the data source or interface to create the link between the SAP transactional system and the OLAP reporting environment. For such a scenario, the R/3 or SAP ERP ECC 6.0 system operates as an OLTP system, which runs the operational business, while the SAP NetWeaver BI/SAP NetWeaver BW system serves as an OLAP system. By diverting the performance-intensive reporting tasks to a separate system, the following strategic advantages can be gained:

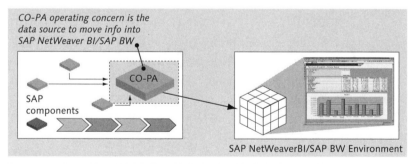

Figure 9.1 Reporting CO-PA Data Outside the OLTP Environment

▶ Reporting does not affect the response times of operational business transactions in the OLTP system.

▶ Each system can be optimized to perform its specific tasks: You can tune the R/3 or SAP ERP ECC 6.0 system to efficiently perform OLTP-typical parallel updates and single-record accesses, whereas the SAP NetWeaver BW system can be adjusted to handle complex search requests that involve summarizing large sets of hits. Competing updates are bundled via cyclic replication, thus eliminating any interference with the queries.

▶ OLTP transactions don't influence the response times of reporting.

▶ Besides the technical advantages, the efficiency of reporting is further increased by uniformly reporting across all functional areas and R/3 or SAP ERP ECC 6.0 applications.

The second scenario, illustrated in Figure 9.2, involves situations where there are multiple environments with several SAP systems that represent, for example, slightly different methods of profitability analysis for various countries or business units. For this scenario, it is essential to gain a cross-system view, such as the one shown in Figure 9.2. Here, the results from different organizational subunits are combined into a single InfoCube in SAP NetWeaver BI/SAP NetWeaver BW that contains the same reporting levels and calculations of contribution margins.

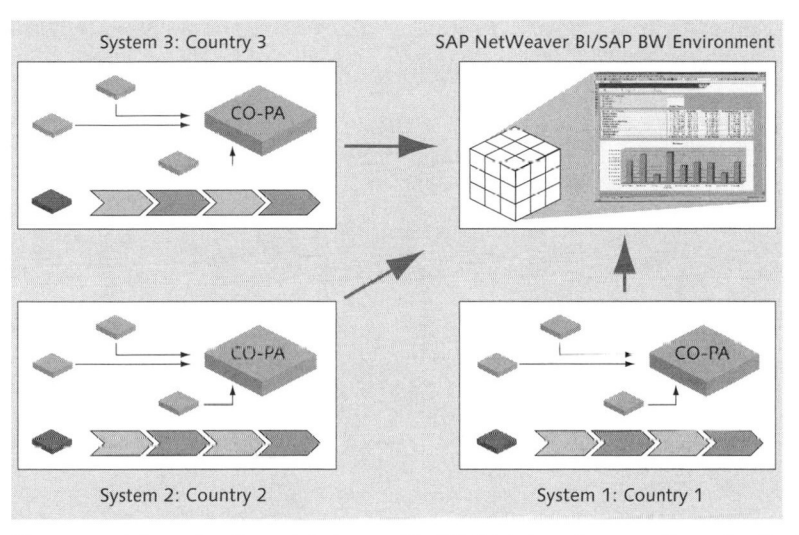

Figure 9.2 Integrating Several Systems with CO-PA into a Common Reporting Environment

CO-PA provides the necessary functions to create classification groups to analyze your business processes according to sales between affiliated companies and customers. This classification of internal and external customers enables you to report your group profit by analyzing profits from external customers as well as profits from affiliated companies.

In addition, there are several recommendations to consider when working with the scenario presented in Figure 9.2:

▶ You should valuate quantities sold with the group cost estimate in parallel with value fields in CO-PA to eliminate intercompany profits.

▶ The data prepared in CO-PA can easily be extracted into SAP NetWeaver BI/ SAP BW. The integration of CO-PA and SAP NetWeaver BI/SAP BW also allows you to harmonize heterogeneous operating concerns as previously described.

▶ If a business unit (affiliate, division, country) stores sales data in CO-PA at a more detailed level than other units, appropriate presummarization can be carried out when the data is transferred.

▶ If a division system stores a detailed cost component split for the cost of goods sold (COGS) while group-level reporting is carried out in less detail, cost of sales can be aggregated from the split during data transfer.

The third typical scenario for the implementation of CO-PA with an SAP NetWeaver BI/SAP BW installation is when affiliated companies, or portions of your company, operate systems other than R/3 or SAP ERP ECC 6.0, and their data has to be consolidated in your reporting of group profitability, as shown in Figure 9.3.

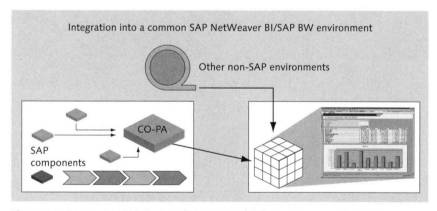

Figure 9.3 Integrating SAP Data with Legacy and Other Non-SAP Environments

The structure presented in Figure 9.3 has certain implications to consider:

▶ External data transfer into the R/3 or SAP ERP ECC 6.0 system is recommended when financial accounting and management accounting are updated simultaneously. In this case, the integrated business model of CO-PA will assure the consistency of your profitability data.

▶ If there is no need to integrate your data into R/3 or SAP ERP ECC 6.0 accounting, SAP NetWeaver BI/SAP BW can provide an excellent cross-system view when data is loaded directly into SAP NetWeaver BW. The powerful staging mechanisms within SAP NetWeaver BI/SAP NetWeaver BW provide extensive support for importing external data, data quality management, and subsequent bulk updates of the imported data.

All of this shows that CO-PA can be a logical system to integrate into high-level reporting environments, such as SAP NetWeaver BI/SAP BW; however, CO-PA has very similar and powerful capabilities that allow it to be a reporting platform by itself. This not only saves development time; the CO-PA reporting tool also operates in real time, and allows interfacing with Microsoft Excel.

In the following section we'll explore the menus and options available to access the information contained in your operating concern objects to create reports in CO-PA in detail.

9.2 Working with Reports in CO-PA

To access the reporting functions of CO-PA, you need to work with the INFORMATION SYSTEM menu, as shown in Figure 9.4. However, because there are quite a few functionalities, we'll explore only the most common. You can then explore the remaining items on your own.

CO-PA reporting will be covered in two chapters—Chapter 9 and Chapter 10. When you're done with these two chapters, you'll know how to do the following:

▶ Work with reports

▶ Work with forms, and understand the difference between reports and forms

▶ Link a form to a report

▶ Perform basic drilldown operations in CO-PA

▶ Work with line item lists, key figure schemes, characteristic groups, and hierarchies

▶ Improve the performance of your reports with frozen data and summarization levels

▶ Define headers and footers

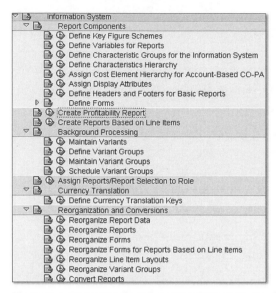

Figure 9.4 Reviewing the Information System Menu of CO-PA

In the next section, we'll look at the different report types available in CO-PA.

9.2.1 Report Types

CO-PA uses two kinds of reports:

- **Basic profitability reports**
  Delivers simple reporting requirements stored in operating concerns.

- **Reports based on line items**
  Extracts information stored in line items of different transactions, controlled by headers, such as quantities, revenues, and cost-related information.

In addition, reports can be enhanced with *forms*. Forms are predefined template-based reports that can be assigned to a particular report to maintain a desired standard format. Forms are also either basic or based on line items, and can be considered a report component rather than an independent reporting object. Forms-related options are also available in the INFORMATION SYSTEM menu.

Now let's review how to create a basic report using CO-PA data. Remember, these reports are useful to fulfill the most common report requirements without leaving the OLTP system and at the same time perform multidimensional analyses of data similar to those available in the SAP NetWeaver BI/BW platform.

9.2.2 Creating a Basic Report

To create a basic report in CO-PA, follow these steps:

1. In the INFORMATION SYSTEM menu, click on the EXECUTE icon for the CREATE PROFITABILITY REPORT object as shown in Figure 9.5.

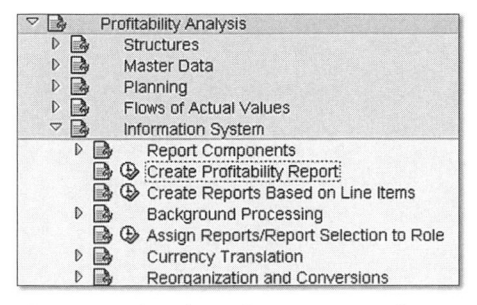

Figure 9.5 Identifying the Two Types of Report Creation Objects in the Information System Menu

2. In the CHOOSE ACTIVITY screen that displays, as shown in Figure 9.6, click on the CREATE PROFITABILITY REPORT option.

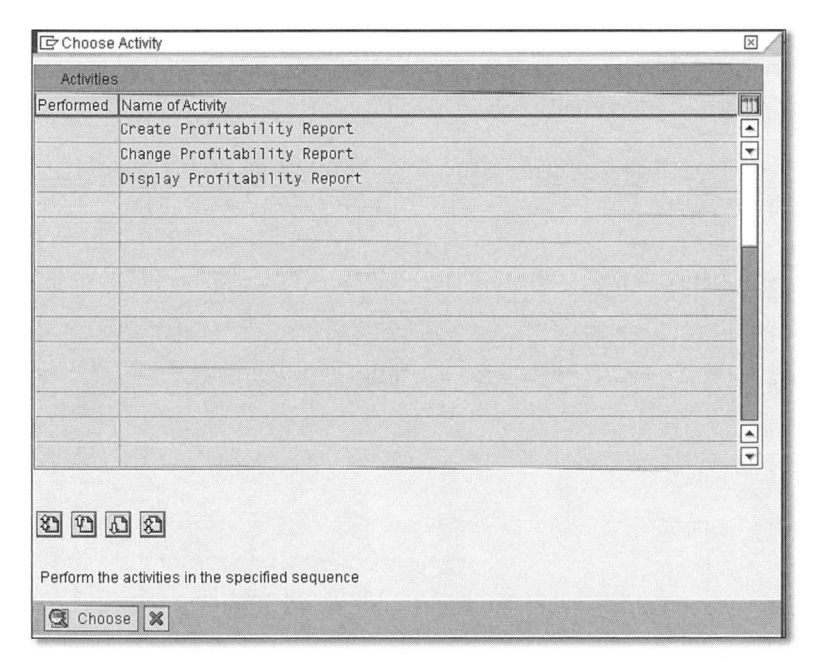

Figure 9.6 Accessing the Create Profitability Analysis Report Activity

3. The screen called CREATE PROFITABILITY REPORT: INITIAL SCREEN appears. Enter a name ("Report1") and a description ("This is a PA Report"), as shown in Figure 9.7.

4. In the REPORT TYPE area, verify that BASIC REPORT is selected. Alternatively, REPORT WITH FORM lets you build a report following a previously created form that is used like a predefined template.

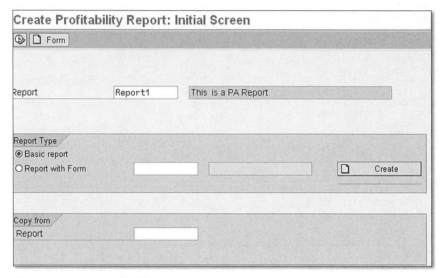

Figure 9.7 Create Profitability Report: Initial Screen

5. Click on the CREATE button to move to the screen shown in Figure 9.8.

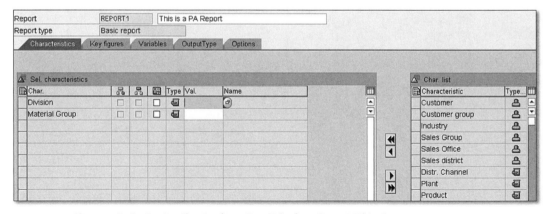

Figure 9.8 Reviewing the Configuration Tabs for a Report Object

Note

You'll be accessing the data and information contained in the operating concern that was set up as current using the object of the same name, and your report will be linked as part of that operating concern.

This screen contains the following tabs: CHARACTERISTICS, KEY FIGURES, VARIABLES, OUTPUT TYPE, and OPTIONS. These tabs let you select the elements that will be included in your report. Use the arrows to move items to be included in the report to the left (SEL. CHARACTERISTICS area) or items that you don't require to the right (CHAR. LIST area). Note that the first two columns next to the CHAR. column in the SEL. CHARACTERISTICS area identify if the characteristic is part of a node or a hierarchy.

Tips & Tricks

There are two types of characteristic values: product- or customer-specific. You can identify the type of characteristic by looking in the TYPE columns displayed in Figure 9.8. An icon that looks like a page with a key (🗝) identifies the characteristic as product-related—an example is shown in the TYPE column in the SEL. CHARACTERISTICS area of the screen. A person-like icon (👤) identifies customer-specific characteristics, as shown in the TYPE column in the CHAR. LIST area.

6. Use the corresponding tab to limit which characteristics and key figures will be included, leaving the VARIABLES, OUTPUT TYPE, and OPTIONS tabs alone for now. We'll be using gross sales, sales costs, sales quantity, material costs, bonuses, cash discounts, and customer discounts as key figures for 2009 data, and some characteristics such as division, material group, version, and record type.

7. Click on the SAVE icon and return to the CREATE PROFITABILITY REPORT: INITIAL SCREEN, which shows that your report has been created and is ready to execute.

8. To start executing and simultaneously testing your report, click on the EXECUTE icon.

9. The SELECTION: THIS IS A PA REPORT screen appears. Fill out the requested information, as shown in Figure 9.9, and click on the EXECUTE icon.

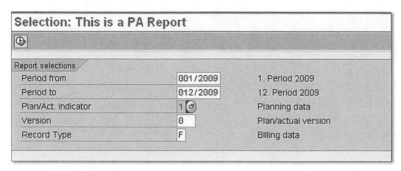

Figure 9.9 Executing Your New CO-PA Report

10. If any errors occurred during the execution of your report, the affected fields in the screen shown in Figure 9.9 are displayed in red, requesting you to review your data selections to match with the available information. If successfully executed, you should see information similar to that shown in Figure 9.10, depending on your configuration. Notice that there are four regions on this screen:

   ▶ NAVIGATION
   Allows you to perform drilldown in the report using characteristics to change the values displayed in the chart and in the upper portion of the screen.

   ▶ KEY FIGURES
   Displays the value fields' values, limited by the characteristics information, and the data graphed in the chart is based on these values. For example, in the screen shown in Figure 9.10, you see the key figure information, based on the characteristic DIVISION. To change the display to the key figures based on the characteristic MATERIAL GROUP, double-click on MATERIAL GROUP in the left area of the screen, and the displayed values and chart will be adjusted accordingly.

   ▶ DETAIL
   Shows the key figure detail, based on the defined navigation characteristics, complemented with totals information.

   ▶ GRAPHICAL AREA
   Displays charts that users can customize using the information available in the NAVIGATION and KEY FIGURES regions.

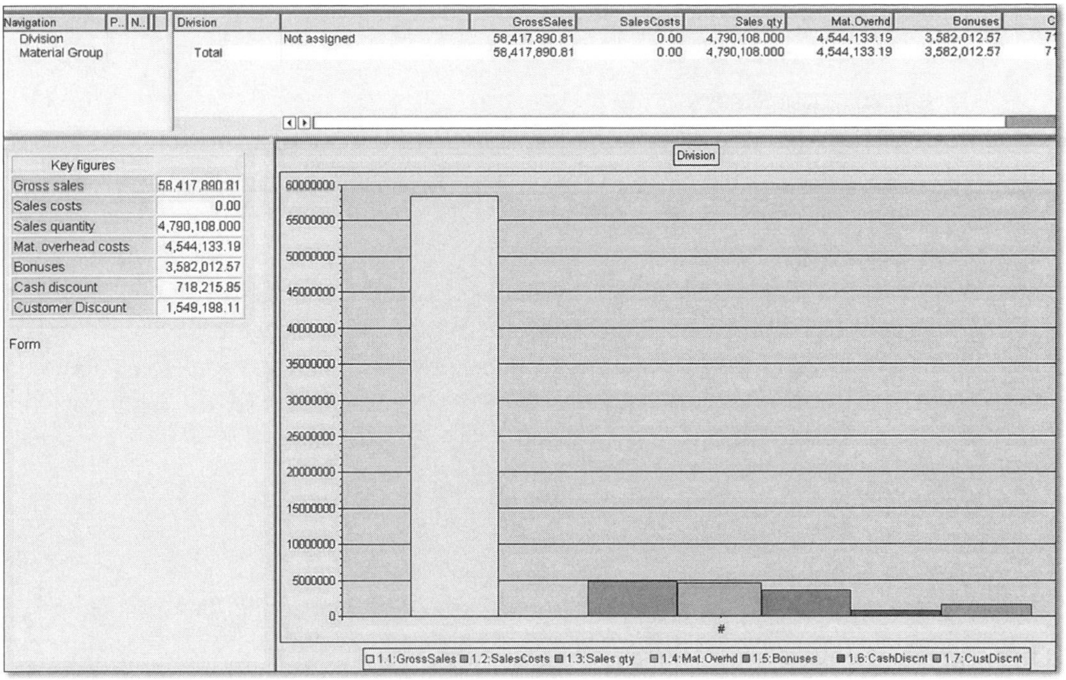

Navigation	P..	N..	Division		GrossSales	SalesCosts	Sales qty	Mat.Overhd	Bonuses	C
Division			Not assigned		58,417,890.81	0.00	4,790,108.000	4,544,133.19	3,582,012.57	7
Material Group			Total		58,417,890.81	0.00	4,790,108.000	4,544,133.19	3,582,012.57	7

Key figures	
Gross sales	58,417,890.81
Sales costs	0.00
Sales quantity	4,790,108.000
Mat. overhead costs	4,544,133.19
Bonuses	3,582,012.57
Cash discount	718,215.85
Customer Discount	1,549,198.11

Form

Division

□ 1.1:GrossSales ⊞ 1.2:SalesCosts ⊞ 1.3:Sales qty □ 1.4:Mat.Overhd ⊞ 1.5:Bonuses ■ 1.6:CashDiscnt ⊞ 1.7:CustDiscnt

Figure 9.10 Reviewing Your Newly Created CO-PA Report

Menu of Icons Available in a Report

Every report you create lets you perform additional functions using the menu of icons located at the top of the report, as shown in Figure 9.11.

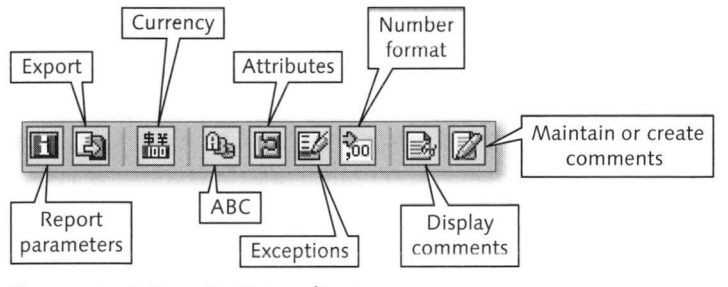

Figure 9.11 A Report's Menu of Icons

Each of these icons is described in the following list, going from left to right, based on Figure 9.11:

▶ REPORT PARAMETERS
Displays the general information of the report definitions, such as characteristic values, key figures, user that created the report, dates, and duration to generate the report, all as a way to monitor performance.

▶ EXPORT
Lets you export the report to Microsoft Excel (you'll see the letters XXL) as a table or pivot table. If successful, the system will suggest to SAVE DATA IN THE SPREAD SHEET. To keep the file, you have to save it in Microsoft Excel, and then click on the checkmark icon in the SAP system. Otherwise, the temporary file will be closed and you return to the SAP environment.

▶ CURRENCY
Performs currency translation.

▶ ABC
Creates an ABC analysis based on the 80/20 or Pareto rule for a particular key figure. To do so, you select the key figure you want to analyze, and set up your ranges for regions A, B, and C. This is a *very* important feature that improves the analysis of information, focusing on specific elements, and interacting with the SAP Business Graphics application. An example of this important functionality is presented in Figure 9.12.

▶ ATTRIBUTES
Displays any information attached to a characteristic.

▶ EXCEPTIONS
Select a value field, and select this icon in order to assign exceptions or rules, depending on the value. An example of an exception is if the value is less than x, the value will be displayed as red, rather than the standard green. Exceptions are criteria set up to the values displayed in your reports, and provide criteria to identify a particular color that meets a lower or higher threshold.

▶ NUMBER FORMAT
Lets you change your data display of the decimal and factoring places in your report, and activate or deactivate your unit of measure as shown in Figure 9.13. For example, you can display 10 instead of 10,000 or 1 instead of 1,000 to simplify your data analysis.

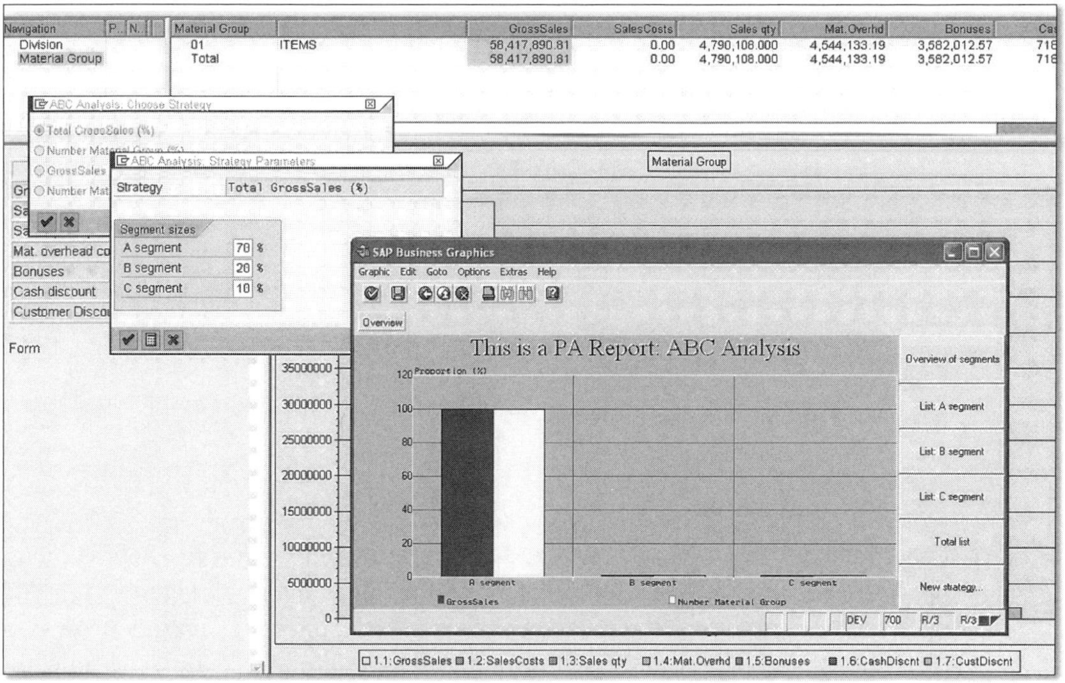

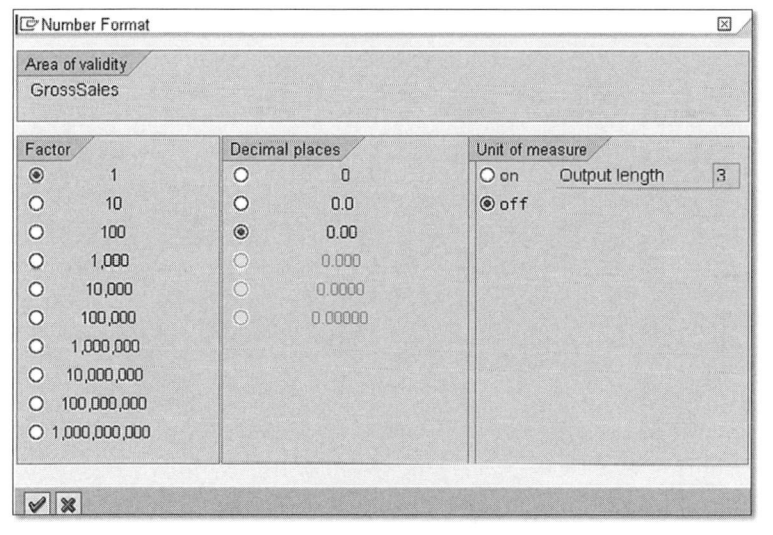

Figure 9.12 Reviewing an ABC Analysis Using the Upper Menu

Figure 9.13 Working with the Number Format Icon

▶ DISPLAY
Lets you display any comments available in the report.

▶ MAINTAIN OR CREATE COMMENTS
Lets you add headers (comments) attached to your report, depending on your needs. You can use Microsoft Word, SAP editor, binary document, and other formats, using the TYPE dropdown list shown in Figure 9.14.

Figure 9.14 Creating a Document Header

CO-PA Report Menu Options

Now let's explore the SAVE DATA and SAVE LAYOUT options on the REPORT menu available inside the CO-PA reporting environment, as shown in Figure 9.15. (The other menu options are standard for most SAP applications.) With these two functionalities, a user can create frozen data with reference to a time period without the need to execute a real-time report. The advantage is that retrieving frozen data with a predefined set of parameters is faster than real-time reporting because the latter demands a larger number of system resources.

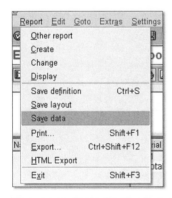

Figure 9.15 Reviewing the Report Menu Options

When you execute the SAVE DATA functionality, you see the last date and time when the layout was saved. You can then choose to retrieve the data for this timeframe or extract the CURRENT DATA (latest), as shown in Figure 9.16. The SAVE

LAYOUT option is used to maintain the same screen definition so that each time you want to access your report the same format will be maintained.

> **Tips & Tricks**
>
> When executing the SAVE DATA option, the screen shown in Figure 9.16 only appears if the selection criteria are exactly the same as those of the saved data. This means if you run your report with different selection criteria values, the screen shown in Figure 9.16 would not appear because you're executing another part of the database (for the first time). In this scenario, time delays might occur, depending on the data volume.

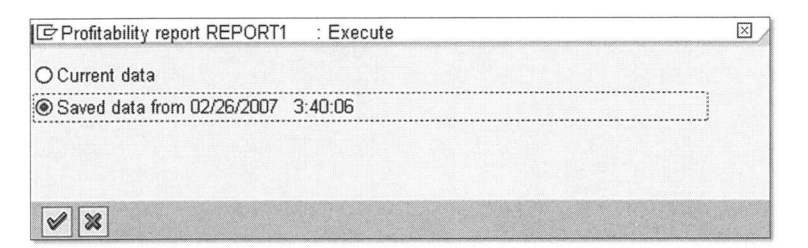

Figure 9.16 Executing Your Profitability Report with Frozen Data

CO-PA Report Edit Menu Options

We'll now explore the EDIT menu, which lets you perform functions such as CUMULATIVE CURVE, CLASSIFICATION, RANKING LIST, CONDITION, and others, to control the data display and analysis of your reports, as shown in Figure 9.17. Some of the options might be unavailable (grayed out) because they are used exclusively in reports based on line items, and also specifically to work with *hotspots*. Hotspots are dynamic links inside your report that control the data display of your report. Consider them the main delimiter of data display.

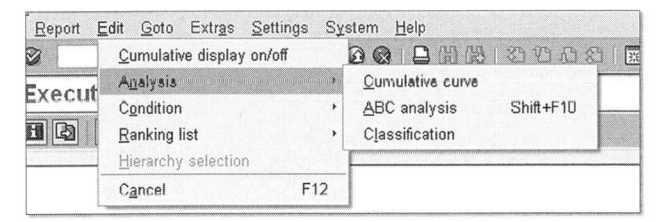

Figure 9.17 Working with the Edit Menu

In addition, you can review the information contained in the line items of the report if you need further information for specific transactions associated with your report data by clicking on GOTO • LINE ITEMS. As shown in Figure 9.18, you can also define exceptions to complement the display capabilities of your data based on a range.

So you can define, for example, that if the value for gross sales is above 1,000 USD, it will display as green, and if it is below 1,000 USD, it will display as red.

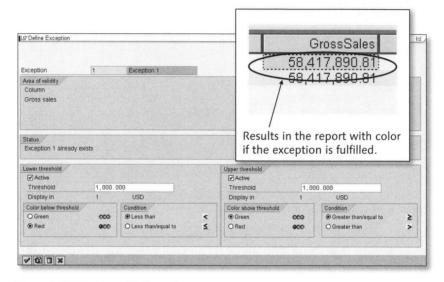

Figure 9.18 Working with Exceptions

Explore the additional options in the menus on your own, such as:

▶ SWITCH ON AND OFF THE TOTALS

▶ PERCENTAGE/ABSOLUTE

▶ ZEROS ON/OFF

▶ RESTRICT THE COLUMN DISPLAY/CHARACTERISTIC DISPLAY

▶ UNDO

CO-PA Report Options Linked to the Chart Display

Several functionalities are linked to the chart displayed in a CO-PA report, as shown in Figure 9.19. You can access them by double-clicking on the chart. Some of the functionalities available include specifying the color for a particular data series, changing patterns, determining axis, displaying error bars, formatting a specific data series, showing data values, defining value ranges for data display, displaying data labels, and others. You can also select the legend and change the chart type to meet your requirements. If something goes wrong along the way, undo your changes. You can undo them back to the last saved version of the layout.

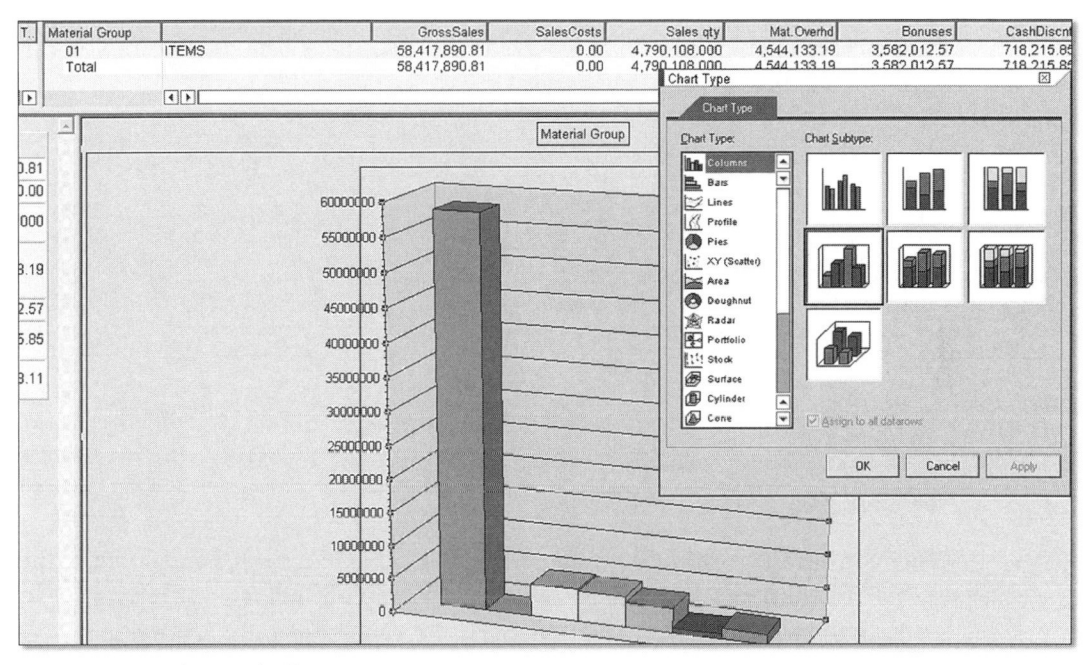

Figure 9.19 Working with Charts

> **Note**
>
> As a reminder, save the layout using the menu option REPORT • SAVE LAYOUT if you want to keep the current display for next time, and the option REPORT • SAVE DATA if you also want to save the data without making a real-time extraction.

As you can see, the capabilities for data analysis for CO-PA are quite powerful, and you don't have to leave the traditional R/3 or SAP ERP ECC 6.0 environment to design and create flexible reports.

Transporting CO-PA Reports

In Figure 9.20 you can see several reports that can be transported, including any attached subobjects, such as forms or key figure schemes, and for a specific language if desired. Now, all this information, which exists inside the objects you see in Figure 9.20, can be moved to another system by using a *transport request*. To do so, click on the truck icon located in the CHANGE REPORT: SETTINGS screen shown in Figure 9.20. Finally, your report(s) are always available to be accessed by and assigned to a user, according to his authorizations and roles, and in the change report mode (accessible by clicking on the change/modify icon), you can review and access the different reports created.

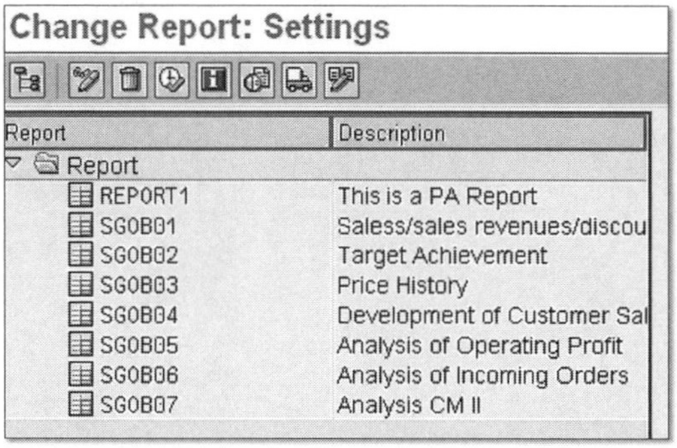

Change Report: Settings

Report	Description
▽ 🗁 Report	
REPORT1	This is a PA Report
SG0B01	Saless/sales revenues/discou
SG0B02	Target Achievement
SG0B03	Price History
SG0B04	Development of Customer Sal
SG0B05	Analysis of Operating Profit
SG0B06	Analysis of Incoming Orders
SG0B07	Analysis CM II

Figure 9.20 Reviewing the Change Report Screen

This ends our discussion on how to create a basic CO-PA report and some of the key functionalities to be aware of when working with this type of report. Next, we'll discuss the more specific line item CO-PA reports that don't provide charts, or any type of graphics, because they are focused on displaying transaction data.

9.2.3 Creating Reports Based on Line Items

In this section, we'll create reports based on line items, or change or display existing line item reports. In comparison with basic reports that display the characteristics and value fields you specify using a standard layout, line item reports are best suited to searching for trends in data classified by various characteristics.

Line item reports are also called *form reports* because they allow you to display the characteristics and key figures according to your requirements and without using a standard layout. Now, let's create a line item CO-PA report with these steps:

380

1. Access the menu path INFORMATION SYSTEM • CREATE REPORTS BASED ON LINE ITEMS as previously shown in Figure 9.5, and perform the same configuration steps done for the basic report.

2. Move the characteristics to the selected characteristics screen. When you work with line items, you can use the following characteristics:

   ▶ All of the characteristics in the segment level, plus those excluded from the segment-level characteristics.

   ▶ The creation of date of line item.

   ▶ The name of the person who created the line item.

3. Select the key figures you want to analyze. You can choose from the value fields of your operating concern and any key figures defined in a key figure scheme (which we'll review in Chapter 10).

4. If required, specify restricting values for the variables defined for the report. Select ENTER AT EXECUTION if you want users to be able to enter or replace these variables when they execute the report.

5. Select the output type that you want to use to display the report, and an HTML template:

   ▶ If you select GRAPHIC REPORT output, the report may consist of several information areas (header and navigation area, graphic area, drilldown, and details list). You can use an HTML template to include individual graphics in the report header. For this output type, you can use drag and drop for functions such as navigation and drilldown switch.

   ▶ If you select the CLASSIC DRILLDOWN output type, your reports are displayed as drilldown lists.

   ▶ The OBJECT list enables you to display reports using the ABAP list viewer. This is a particularly useful output type if you want to display several characteristics in the lead column.

   ▶ If you select the output type XXL (spreadsheet), you can display reports in Microsoft Excel.

6. Among the settings under OPTIONS, you'll find print layout settings and performance settings for executing a report. When specifying the latter, you need to decide whether current data should be read or whether the system should read the data from the last time the summarization level was built up.

Note

Not all of these steps may be possible or required because they'll depend on the report and the form. In addition, because basic reports and line item reports also allow working with variables, characteristic groups, key figure schemes, and additional elements, all of these items must be defined beforehand so you can have access to them during your report design.

Another important element when working with line item reports is hotspots, which are objects that you can click on inside the report that change the data display. Line item reports are mostly geared toward the analysis of data and review of system transactions; therefore, using hotspots is very important for drilldown. However, line item reports can also display any chart or graphic as part of the report, but you need to create these items separately using 3D and a portfolio graph option and saving the report with a *.dat* file extension.

Because you create line item reports using a similar procedure to that of creating basic reports—you execute them by clicking on the EXECUTE icon, and access the data contained in your characteristics—we'll go directly to presenting an example of a final result of a line item report, as shown in Figure 9.21.

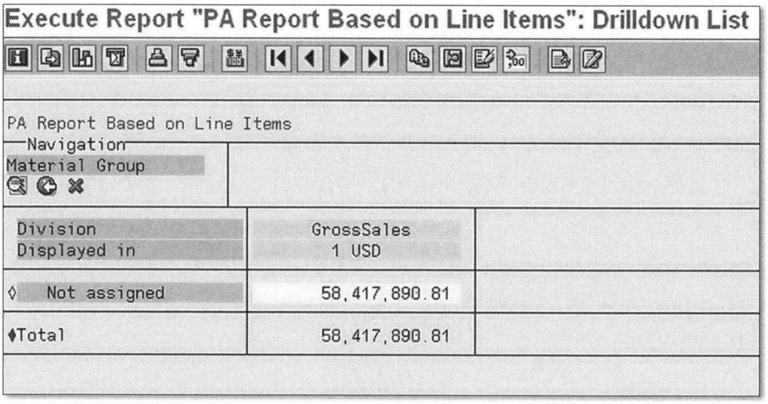

Figure 9.21 Reviewing a Line Item Report

Notice in Figure 9.21 that a line item report is essentially a more simplified version of a basic report, showing two characteristics, MATERIAL GROUP and DIVISION, to control the data display for the GROSSSALES value field. Also, notice that you can display totals for the information contained inside of the value fields displayed in columns.

The report shown in Figure 9.21 also contains one hotspot that controls the drill-down navigation display, so we'll use it to improve our analysis:

1. Click on the DIVISION characteristic (❶ in Figure 9.22).

2. Click on the MATERIAL GROUP characteristic to perform the switch of the display of the hotspot (❷).

3. See the final result of the hotspot and data display, adding the display of the ITEMS MATERIAL GROUP (❸).

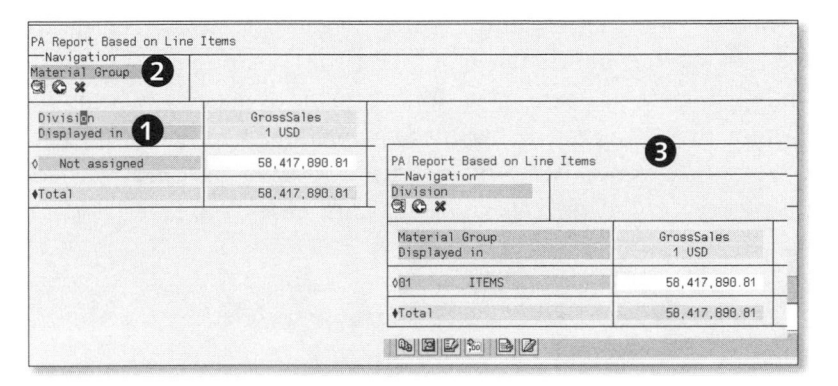

Figure 9.22 Working with Hotspots to Change the Data Display

Play around and explore other options and different alternatives to your data display by adding more characteristics and value fields. If you access the EDIT menu, as shown in Figure 9.23, you'll see that different options from those available with the basic report are now available because they are for exclusive use with line item reports.

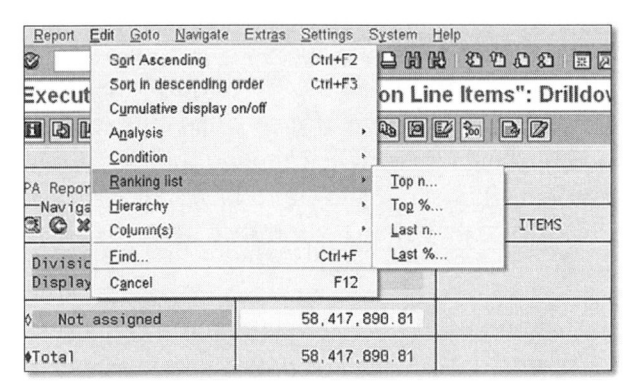

Figure 9.23 Reviewing the Line Item Report Additional Options in the Edit Menu

In the next section we'll review the concept of forms and how to interact with reports based on a common template. These types of components are useful for large implementations where different departments or businesses require maintaining a standard reporting template.

9.3 Working with Forms

You've probably already noticed that there's a FORM button in some of the screens we've worked with while creating reports; for example, the screen shown in Figure 9.7. You'll see this button when you first start creating a basic or line item report, and clicking on this button lets you create forms used by basic or line item reports. Alternatively, you can access this functionality by following the path INFORMATION SYSTEM • REPORT COMPONENTS • DEFINE FORMS • DEFINE FORMS FOR PROFITABILITY REPORTS or DEFINE FORMS FOR REPORTS BASED ON LINE ITEMS, as shown in Figure 9.24.

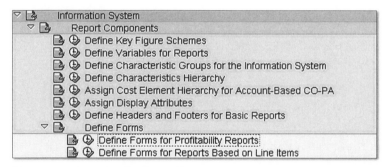

Figure 9.24 Accessing the Forms Menu

Either way, you're taken to the screen shown in Figure 9.25. The form object accesses an alternative environment of Report Painter created for forms to define a standard template based on a value field (key figure) structure that other reports may follow to maintain standard reporting values. When a report follows a form, only the CHARACTERISTICS, VARIABLES, OUTPUT TYPE, and OPTION tabs are available, but not the KEY FIGURES tab because that information is controlled by the template of the form.

Forms work with key figure structures and control the display of value fields. Three types of structures can be defined:

- Two axis (matrix)
- One axis with key figure
- One axis without key figure

These configurations let you create flexible reporting templates that can be maintained around different business areas, allowing users to modify only the characteristics needed to limit the data displays, but the information generated is exactly the same. You can also generate a form as a copy from another form and use it as a reference. When creating a report using a form, at least one characteristic must be used to limit the data extraction of the template.

For our example we'll define a matrix form for a basic report:

1. Follow the path INFORMATION SYSTEM • REPORT COMPONENTS • DEFINE FORMS • DEFINE FORMS FOR PROFITABILITY REPORTS and click on the option DEFINE FORM FOR PROFITABILITY REPORTS.

2. Provide a name of "Form1" and a description of "This is Form1" for the form. Notice that when creating forms, we're accessing a Report Painter environment, as shown in Figure 9.25.

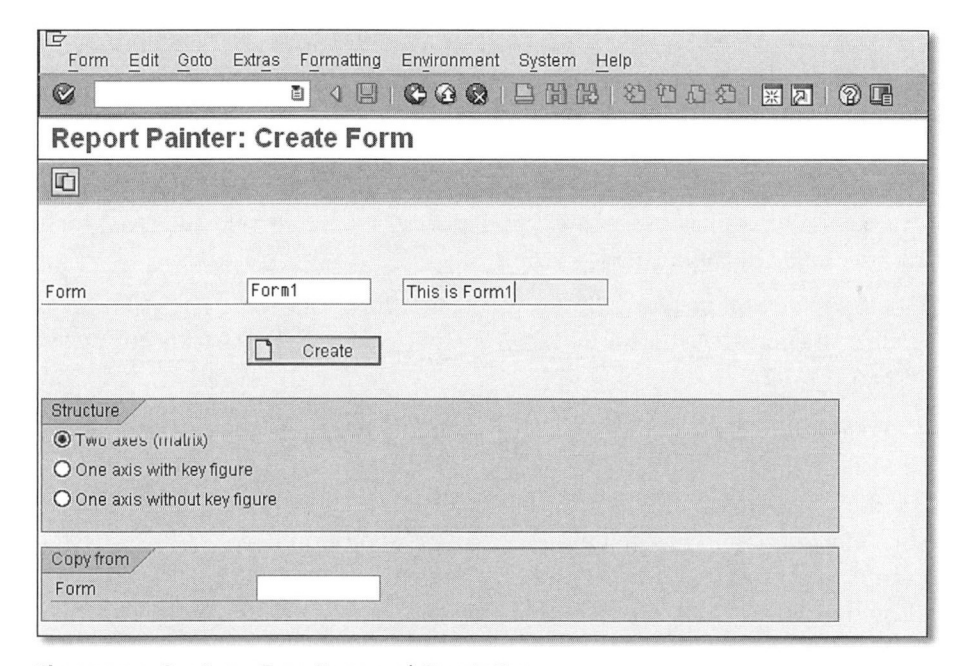

Figure 9.25 Creating a Form Name and Description

3. Select Two axes (matrix) to define the structure of your form.

4. Click on the Create button.

5. As shown in Figure 9.26, you can see a standard template with a Lead column with different rows and columns. Because this is a matrix, double-clicking on each of the columns and rows defines what data is extracted to each of those locations.

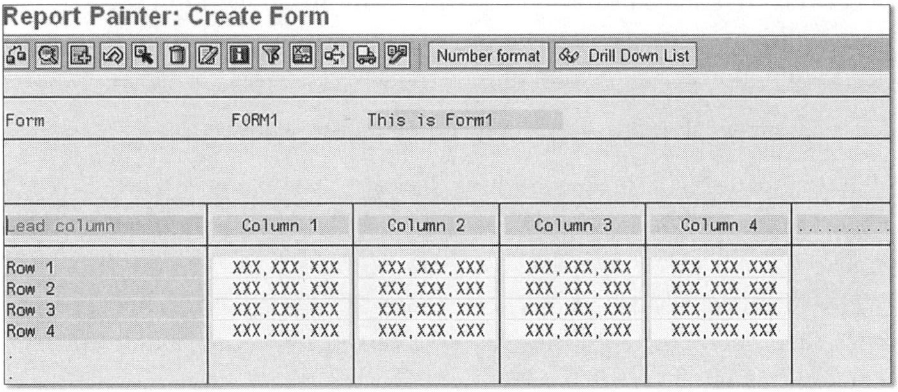

Report Painter: Create Form

| Form | FORM1 | This is Form1 |

Lead column	Column 1	Column 2	Column 3	Column 4	....
Row 1	XXX,XXX,XXX	XXX,XXX,XXX	XXX,XXX,XXX	XXX,XXX,XXX	
Row 2	XXX,XXX,XXX	XXX,XXX,XXX	XXX,XXX,XXX	XXX,XXX,XXX	
Row 3	XXX,XXX,XXX	XXX,XXX,XXX	XXX,XXX,XXX	XXX,XXX,XXX	
Row 4	XXX,XXX,XXX	XXX,XXX,XXX	XXX,XXX,XXX	XXX,XXX,XXX	

Figure 9.26 Reviewing Matrix Form1

6. Double-click on Row 1 and you'll see that you can create characteristics, value fields with characteristics, key figure scheme elements, and predefined elements as types.

7. Select from the Available characteristics section, and select and limit the characteristics values. As shown in Figure 9.27 we're selecting Material Group with a default value for ITEM.

8. Once you've completed defining the restrictions and selection criteria for your characteristic, click on the Confirm button located at the lower bottom of Figure 9.27.

9. Double-click on a column, select the Value Field with Characteristics option, and click on the checkmark icon.

10. As shown in Figure 9.28, select the Value field Gross sales, then establish the selection criteria as required. Of course, you don't want to extract the complete gross sales information of the entire database in the SAP system. As shown in Figure 9.28, the minimum selection criteria are Plan/Act. In (plan and actual data) and Version.

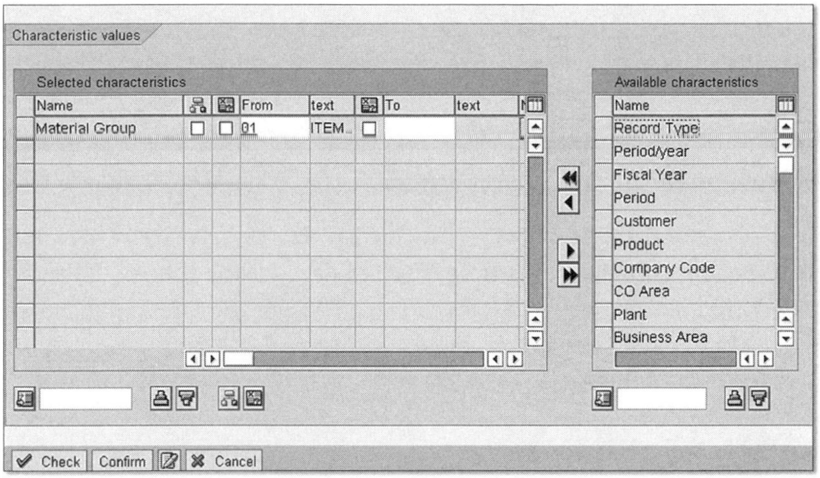

Figure 9.27 Restricting a Characteristic in a Form

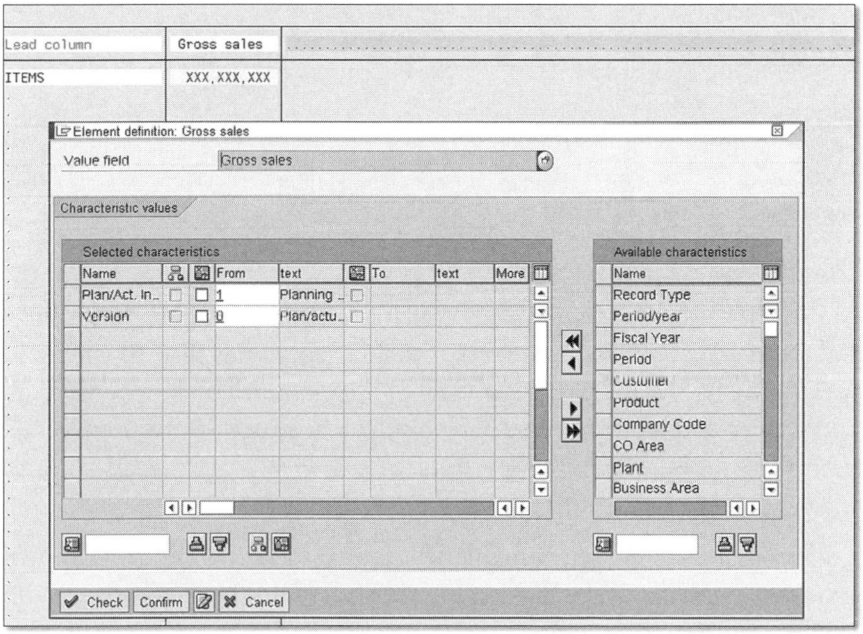

Figure 9.28 Creating a Value Field in a Form

11. Click on the CONFIRM button.

12. Save your form.

Note

You can also click on the CHECK button before clicking on the CONFIRM button to make sure that everything was created correctly.

Now you must assign the form to a basic report:

1. Return to the PROFITABILITY ANALYSIS • INFORMATION SYSTEM • CREATE PROFITABIL-ITY REPORT function. However, this time, instead of choosing the BASIC REPORT option, select the REPORT WITH FORM option, and assign the FORM1 form we just created. Also, create REPORT3 as shown in Figure 9.29, and type "Report Using Form1" as a description.

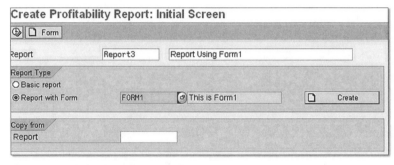

Figure 9.29 Assigning a Form to a Report

2. Click on the CREATE button.

3. Notice that there is no KEY FIGURES tab available as before, and you must select at least one characteristic on the CHARACTERISTICS tab. In this case, as shown in Figure 9.30, we'll leave the VAL. column empty to extract all of the information. You can change and modify the options displayed in Figure 9.30 at any time, but for now we'll leave them as they are.

4. Save your new report based on a form.

5. In the appropriate screen, select the newly created REPORT3 report as shown in Figure 9.31, execute it (by clicking on the clock with the checkmark icon), and click on the YES button to extract the latest information.

6. Now the report is executed and displayed, as shown in Figure 9.32. Notice at the bottom of the screen that the report confirms that this report is based on FORM1.

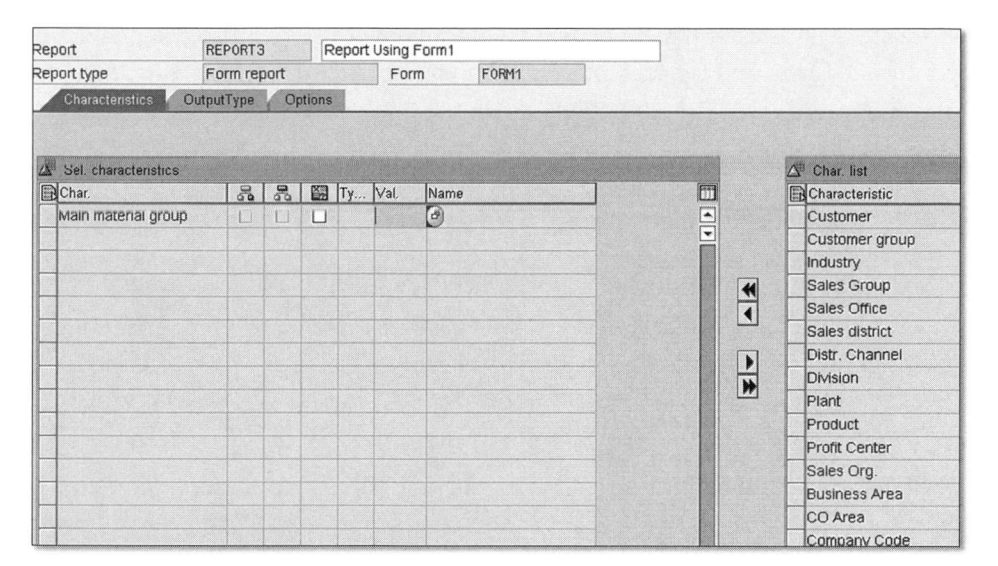

Figure 9.30 Reviewing the Configuration Tabs of a Form-based Report

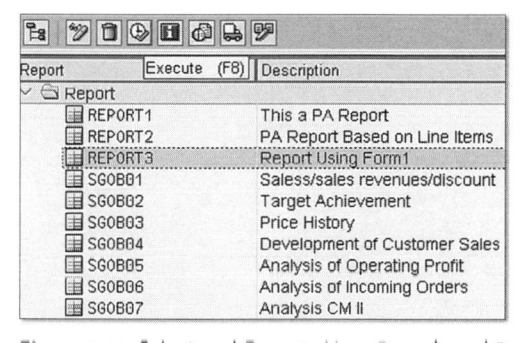

Figure 9.31 Select and Execute Your Form-based Report

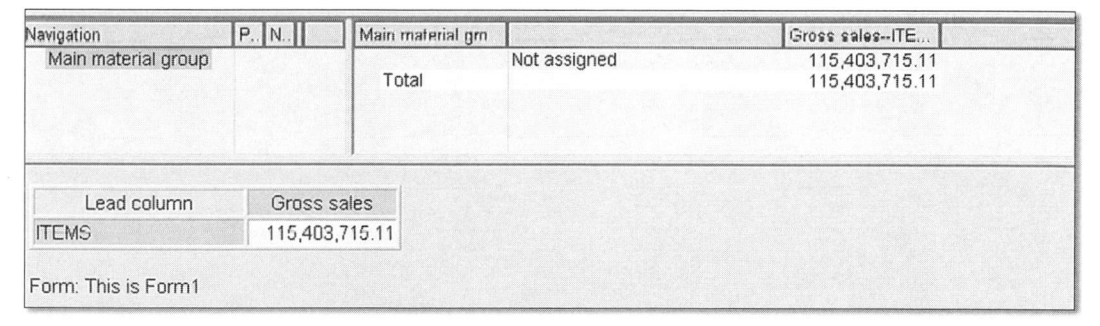

Figure 9.32 Working with a Form-based Report

This was a simple example; if you want, you can now explore more complex ways to improve forms and report generation on your own. Finally, be aware that you can create forms based on line items following the same logic.

9.4 Summary

This chapter introduced the concepts of CO-PA reporting and how similar some of these functionalities are to SAP NetWeaver BI/SAP BW. We also reviewed the Report Painter, a standard SAP ECC reporting functionality that works within the CO-PA environment. You also learned about basic reports and reports based on line items, and how to create forms and how to use them when creating reports.

We'll discuss additional functionalities in Chapter 10, such as frozen reports, variables, and formulas. All of these elements increase the sophistication and power of the reports generated within CO-PA, and it is comparable with much of the functionality available in SAP BW/SAP NetWeaver BI.

We're now moving on to advanced topics in CO-PA reporting. This chapter is not appropriate for end users, unless there is a strong interest in becoming a super or power user that allows handling and configuring objects, such as summarization levels, frozen reports, key figure schemes, formulas, and others.

10 CO-PA Reporting: Configuration

In the previous chapter we reviewed the concepts of basic and line item reports, forms, and general configuration options available in CO-PA. In this chapter, we'll explore further configuration settings available in the INFORMATION SYSTEM menu. Some of the elements we'll discuss are how to configure headers and footers if you want to provide additional information attached to your report or form, creating key figure schemes, variables, configuration of frozen reports, working with the Formula Editor, and more. Let's start our discussion by looking at how to predefine headers and footers.

> **Note**
>
> Most of the elements discussed in this chapter can be used in both forms and reports. Thus, we won't specify for which component the configuration object is applicable.

10.1 Predefining Headers and Footers

You're probably aware that a header and footer in a report allow you to include additional information, such as addresses, page numbers, descriptions, or comments that you might want to attach to the report and make this information available to the user either at the top (header) or bottom (footer) of the report, and printed on each page. We'll now review in more detail how to include these two elements as part of a report using the Report Painter environment with CO-PA.

To start creating headers and footers in CO-PA reports, follow these steps:

1. Access the header and footer definitions by following the path INFORMATION SYSTEM • REPORT COMPONENTS • DEFINE HEADERS AND FOOTERS FOR BASIC REPORTS, shown in Figure 10.1.

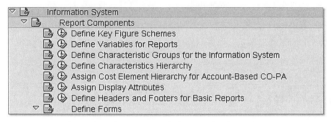

Figure 10.1 Creating Headers and Footers in the Information System Menu

2. Alternatively, when creating a basic report, as discussed in Chapter 9, access the OUTPUT TYPE tab, as shown in Figure 10.2. In the LAYOUT area, select the checkbox next to HEADERS or FOOTERS (or both of them if you need to) and click on the respective change/modify icon(s) to define the contents of each of these objects.

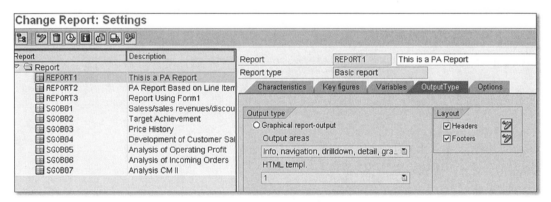

Figure 10.2 Creating Headers and Footers in the Change Report: Settings Screen

Both types of objects have a common menu, as shown in Figure 10.3. The buttons on this menu, in order from left to right, are add line, cut, paste, delete line, delete variable (VARIABLE), insert frames (FRAMES), insert general variables (GEN. VARIABLES), and insert text variable for selection parameters (SEL. PARAMETERS).

Figure 10.3 Header and Footer Menu

Now let's explore the functions of the last three buttons displayed in Figure 10.3 (FRAMES, GEN. VARIABLES, and SEL. PARAMETERS), starting with FRAMES.

10.1.1 Frames

A *frame* is a text variable with a width and height specified, as shown in Figure 10.4, that you can predefine to be maintained in all of the pages of a report. It's a line that defines the division of information or contains information details needed to comply with certain formatting requirements for a particular report. For example, to define settings similar to those shown in Figure 10.4 as part of your report, proceed as follows:

1. Double-click on a line in the report and click on the FRAMES button to add the frames object to your report.

2. Modify the formatting options by double-clicking on the frame object and configuring your settings. For our example, in the FORMATTING area, change the character length to "10" for WIDTH and "1" for HEIGHT, as shown in Figure 10.4.

3. Click on the checkmark button to save your settings.

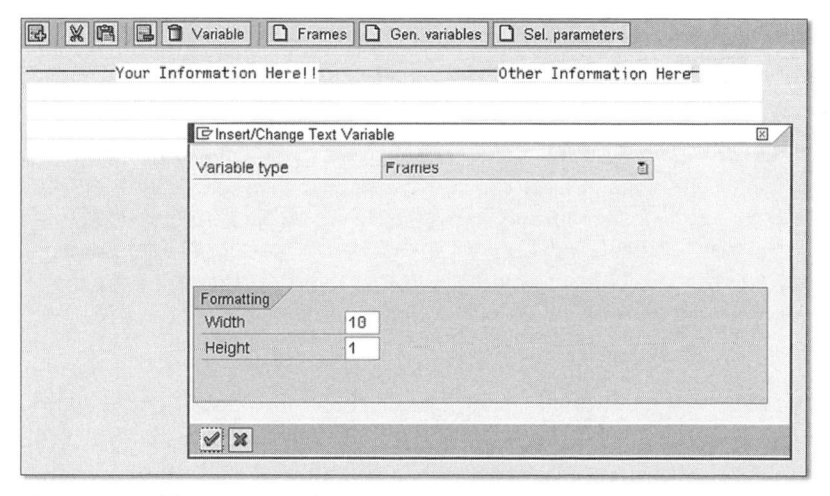

Figure 10.4 Adding a Frame Object to Your Report

4. As shown in Figure 10.4, you're creating multiple lines, some blank, some with text. For example, you can see the text YOUR INFORMATION HERE!! and OTHER INFORMATION HERE as part of the the header section, and you can add as many lines as required to your report.

5. Once you have created your lines as shown in Figure 10.4, you can type a header description, such as "This is your Header with --------Frames!!------."

6. Save your work, and go back to the CHANGE REPORT: SETTINGS screen, as shown in Figure 10.5, and, on the OUTPUT TYPE tab in the LAYOUT area, select the HEADERS checkbox option to display the newly created frame object when executing your report.

7. Save your changes.

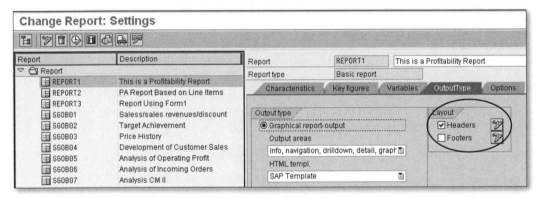

Figure 10.5 Displaying the Frame Object in the Header of REPORT1

Tips & Tricks

Remember, to modify the frame object you just created, you can either click on the OUTPUT TYPE tab shown in Figure 10.5 and access the HEADERS change/modify icon (the pencil with glasses), or you can follow the path INFORMATION SYSTEM • REPORT COMPONENTS • DEFINE HEADERS AND FOOTERS FOR BASIC REPORTS. Both paths access the same object and allow you to modify or create headers and footers.

---

8. Once you've completed configuring the frame object and making it available to your report, execute your report as discussed in Chapter 9. At the top of the report, review the information we just created; it should look similar to that shown in Figure 10.6.

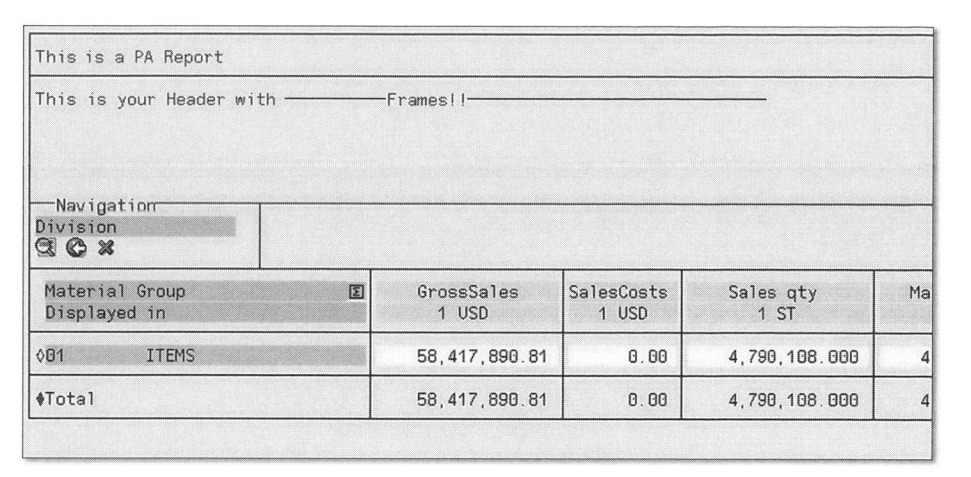

Figure 10.6 Executing Your Report and Reviewing the Frame Object

You can also increase the size of the frame, depending on how many lines you add to your report header. Just make sure that you test and print some samples of your report to verify that it fits your paper size and that all of the required information is displayed according to the required format.

You'll likely be interested in adding more information to your headers, such as a page number, page count, date, and other types of descriptive information. This is the function of the general variables (GEN. VARIABLES) button discussed in the next section.

10.1.2 General Variables

General variables are objects that store, generate, or format data depending on report settings, such as page number or additional description. To add a variable to a report, use this procedure:

1. Access the headers menu again following the path INFORMATION SYSTEM • REPORT COMPONENTS • DEFINE HEADERS AND FOOTERS FOR BASIC REPORTS, as shown earlier in Figure 10.3.

2. Add a new line and type the description "Page Number is:" as shown toward the top of the page in Figure 10.7. This description is specified before you create the general variable.

3. Click on the GEN. VARIABLES button.

4. The screen INSERT/CHANGE TEXT VARIABLE appears, as shown in Figure 10.7.

5. Select GENERAL TEXT VARIABLE from the VARIABLE TYPE dropdown list.

6. From the VARIABLE NAME dropdown list, select PAGE NUMBER.

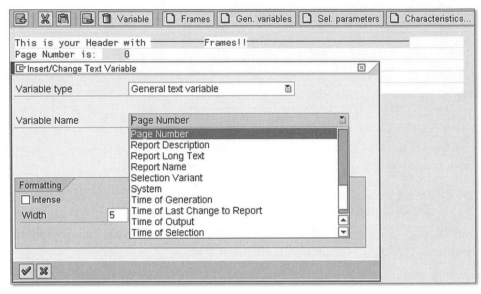

Figure 10.7 Creating a General Variable for Your Report

7. In the FORMATTING area, leave the WIDTH as 5.

8. Click on the checkmark icon to attach the PAGE NUMBER variable object to the report as part of your frame object, after the description PAGE NUMBER IS:.

9. In Figure 10.7, you see a 0 after the text PAGE NUMBER IS:. This is where the general variable will display the page number of the report.

> **Tips & Tricks**
>
> To delete any of the general variables, position the cursor on the desired object to delete, and click on the VARIABLE button (with the trashcan next to the word VARIABLE). The system prompts you to confirm your deletion. Click on the checkmark icon to remove the variable from your report.

If you wish, you can experiment with the many types of variables available, adding different ones to your report. Also, sometimes it's useful to display information related to the characteristics included or attached in your report; for example, you might like to make sure you're reporting only billing data or a specific category within a material group. This type of information might be meaningful for your users to have and adding it is done using of the selection parameters (SEL. PARAMETERS) function we discuss in the next section.

10.1.3   Selection Parameters

Before we look at selection parameters, let's quickly review what we've done so far. We have created a frame object using several lines that define a region on the header. This object allows writing or attaching information to clarify the contents of the report for your users. Next, we created a variable that provides the page number of the report (to organize reports that have more than one page). Now, we'll provide an additional functionality to display information related to data classification based on the characteristics used in the report, using selection parameters.

Let's say that we want to add a variable for selection parameters to display the value of the record type characteristic that is already stored in the report. This way, users will always know that the report is generated based on the type of data being displayed. To create a selection parameter variable, follow these steps:

1. Access the headers and footers configuration settings, using the path shown earlier in Figure 10.3.

2. Create a new line and type the description "The Record Type is:" (the result of which is shown in Figure 10.8).

3. Click on the SEL. PARAMETER button to display the INSERT/CHANGE TEXT VARIABLE screen, as shown in Figure 10.8. Notice that the VARIABLE TYPE is TEXT VARIABLE FOR SELECTION PARAMETERS.

4. From the SELECTION PARAMETERS dropdown list, choose the RECORD TYPE characteristic, as shown in Figure 10.8

5. Select the TEXT TYPE to be VALUE.

6. Remember to control the WIDTH field information, depending on the expected length of the data to be displayed. In this case, as shown in Figure 10.8, we chose a WIDTH size of 1 because the RECORD TYPE displays only one letter.

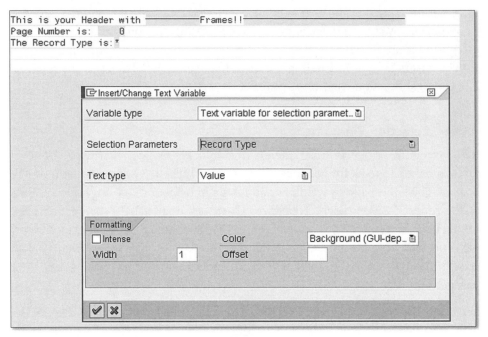

This is your Header with ————————Frames!!————————————————————
Page Number is: 0
The Record Type is:*

Insert/Change Text Variable	⊠
Variable type	Text variable for selection paramet...
Selection Parameters	Record Type
Text type	Value

Formatting
☐ Intense   Color   Background (GUI-dep...
Width   1   Offset

Figure 10.8 Creating a Selection Parameter Object in Your Report

7. Click on the checkmark icon to complete the creation of your frame, and then click on the standard SAVE icon to store your configuration.

8. As shown in Figure 10.8, you now see an asterisk after the text THE RECORD TYPE IS:. This means that a new object has been added to your report, where the record type value will be displayed.

9. Create another selection parameter in another line. As shown in Figure 10.9, add the MATERIAL GROUP characteristic and the description "We are working with" before the SEL. PARAMETER object. However, this time define the width as 15 to be able to display the complete description. As you can see, the selection parameters is just another type of variable added to your report.

10. Save your changes and see the results by executing your report, as shown in Figure 10.10. Notice the header information at the top of the screen and the information extracted using your predefined selection parameter variables PAGE NUMBER and RECORD TYPE.

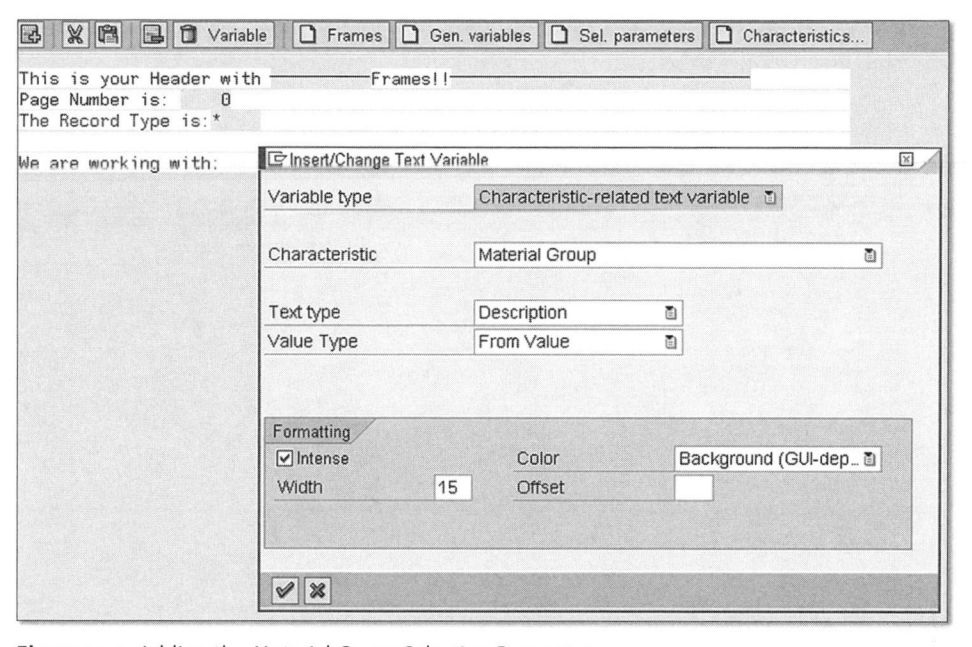

Figure 10.9 Adding the Material Group Selection Parameter

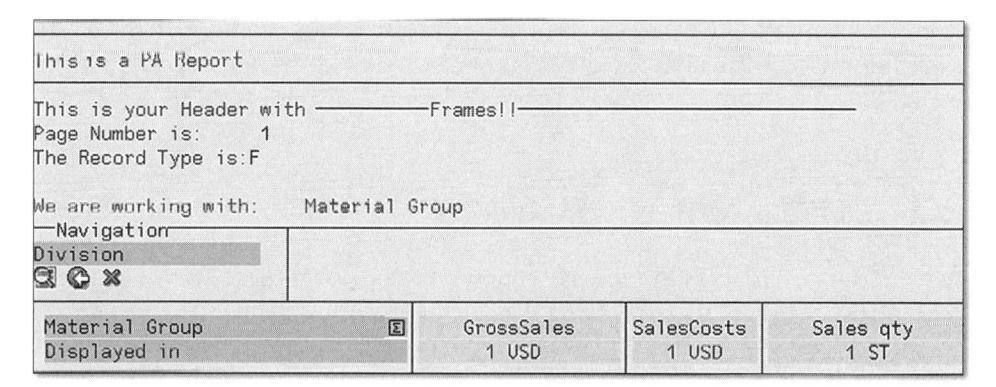

Figure 10.10 Reviewing Your Header Report with Variables and Descriptions

10.1.4 Footers

What about footers? It's simple—all of the information we just reviewed for headers applies to footers, also; the only difference is that the information displays at the bottom of the report! To access the footer information, select the FOOTERS checkbox on the OUTPUT TYPE tab, as shown in Figure 10.11, and with the change/modify icon access the MAINTAIN FOOTERS area where you can configure your footer information.

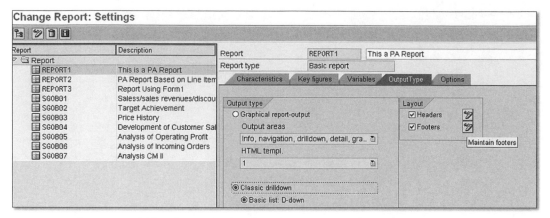

Figure 10.11 Adding Footers to Your Report

You now have a general idea of how variables work inside your CO-PA reporting environment. You can also define variables that control more than just the information displayed in your headers and footers. For example, you can define variables that control characteristic values, hierarchy nodes, texts, formulas, and other information. This is our main topic of discussion in the next section, so let's begin!

10.2   Defining Variables in Reports

You can define variables in reports using the path INFORMATION SYSTEM • REPORT COMPONENTS • DEFINE VARIABLES FOR REPORTS as shown in Figure 10.12 or access the VARIABLES tab in the CHANGE REPORT: SETTINGS screen, shown earlier in Figure 10.11.

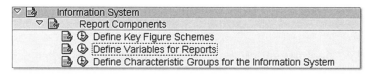

Figure 10.12 Reviewing the Variable Access Path in the Information System Menu

Generally speaking, in an SAP system there are several types of variables that are used to simplify or automate data extraction. In CO-PA the following types of variables are available:

▶ CHARACTERISTIC VALUE (variable type 1)
A unique value within a characteristic (field name).

▶ HIERARCHY NODE (variable type 2)
Identifies a particular node within a hierarchy.

▶ TEXT (variable type 3)
Instead of being fixed text, text can be defined as a variable to display text content that is not available before a report is run. A text variable can be used to make a reference to another text.

▶ FORMULA (variable type 4)
If certain constants are determined just before the formula is evaluated, you can use formula variables instead of constants when you define the formula.

▶ HIERARCHY (variable type 5)
You can assign a variable to extract a specific hierarchy variable stored in the system.

▶ HIERARCHY NODE/CHARACTERISTIC VALUE (variable type 6)
A combination of a variable node (variable type 2) and a characteristic value (variable type 1). When executing a report, you can either enter a hierarchy node or different characteristic values.

In addition to the variable types discussed above, another element called *replacement type* is required to complete the definition of the variables. Replacement type defines how a CO-PA variable will be replaced by a value, automatically or manually:

▶ AUTOMATIC REPLACEMENT PATH (replacement type 1)
For variables of types 3 and 4, you can create an automatic replacement path. You define the replacement path using the following entries: source field (field name), from/to flag, characteristic value/text flag, offset, and length.

▶ REPLACEMENT BY MANUAL ENTRY (replacement type 2)
The entry you make when carrying out the transaction determine the contents of the variable.

▶ REPLACEMENT BY USER-EXIT (replacement type 3)
A user exit defines the content of the variable. User exits can be found and are

maintained in the component pool SAPLXYEX. The function components are called EXIT_SAPLKYP1_001, EXIT_SAPLKYP1_002, and EXIT_SAPLKYP1_003. You also need to create the corresponding local objects such as ZXYEXU01, ZXYEXU02, and ZXYEXU03.

▶ REPLACEMENT BY SAP-EXIT (replacement type 4)
A path prescribed by the SAP system determines the contents of the variable. These variables begin with a number and cannot be maintained.

▶ REPLACEMENT BY A FIXED VALUE (replacement type 5)
The entry in the FIXED VALUE field determines the contents of the variable.

▶ REPLACEMENT BY USER PARAMETERS FROM THE GPA AREA (ONLY ONLINE) (replacement type 6)
Relevant for variable type 1 (characteristic value). The variable is automatically replaced by the GET parameter value of the entered field.

▶ REPLACEMENT BY A REFERENCE (replacement type 7)
Relevant with variable type 5 (hierarchy). The hierarchy display in the report list can be controlled using this variable when using a hierarchy node in the form. At the same time, the hierarchy node of the formula is used for the hierarchy display of the report list.

Prerequisite: A hierarchy node variable (variable type 2) with replacement type 2 (entry) is used for the hierarchy node in the form. The name of the node variables must agree with the name of the hierarchy variables (variable type 5, replacement type 7). This hierarchy variable is offered in the report definition with the hierarchy selection.

Example: Global hierarchy node variable &KNOTEN is used in the form (variable type 2, replacement type 2). In addition, a global variable &KNOTEN is defined with variable type 5, replacement type 7. The variable &KNOTEN can be highlighted in the report definition using the hierarchy selection. Then the report list is displayed in accordance with nodes entered when executing the report.

As you can see, not only is the variable type a configuration issue, but also how the values of the variable are handled needs to be considered. For our example, we'll limit the discussion to a standard user so we define the most basic of the variables and replacement types: a CHARACTERISTIC VALUE variable that extracts data from a characteristic during execution time with manual ENTRY as the REPLACEMENT TYPE, as shown in Figure 10.13.

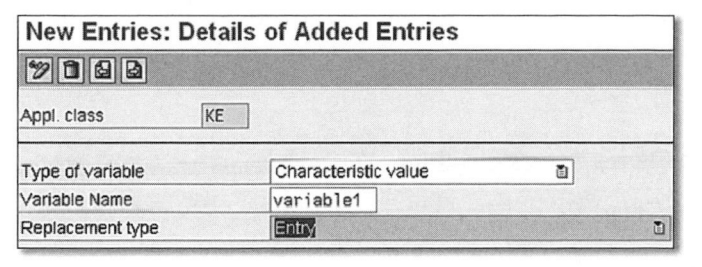

Figure 10.13 Creating a Characteristic Variable with Manual Entry Replacement Type

Follow these steps to create the sample variable, VARIABLE1:

1. Access the screen shown in Figure 10.13, using the path INFORMATION SYSTEM • REPORT COMPONENTS • DEFINE VARIABLES FOR REPORTS.

2. Notice the nonmodifiable field APPL. CLASS with the text KE. This identifies that the variable will be for Profitability Analysis use only.

3. Select the TYPE OF VARIABLE to be CHARACTERISTIC VALUE, as shown in Figure 10.13, specify a VARIABLE NAME of "variable1," and select the REPLACEMENT TYPE to be ENTRY.

4. Press ⌨Enter⌨ to move to the next configuration portion of the screen. Don't save at this point yet; otherwise the system prompts you with an error that it is waiting to use the definition of the characteristic.

5. The system changes the screen display as shown in Figure 10.14, and grays out (blocks) the fields TYPE OF VARIABLE and VARIABLE NAME.

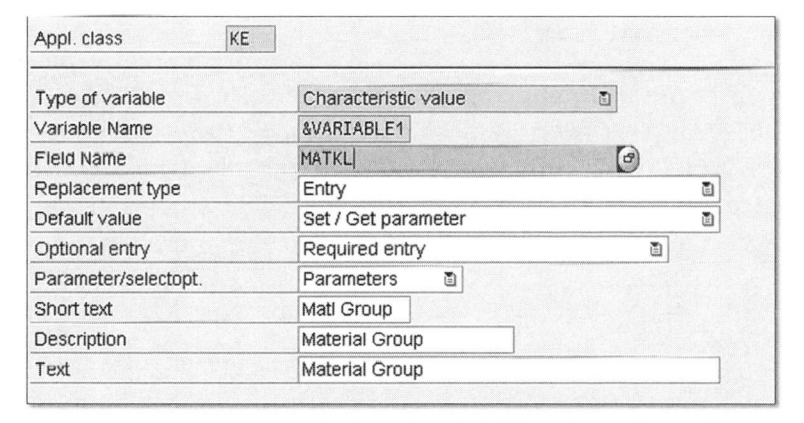

Figure 10.14 Completing the Configuration of &VARIABLE1 for Material Group

6. Type the technical name "MATKL" in the FIELD NAME to specify that you want to use the material group characteristic for the variable with the technical name &VARIABLE1.

7. Leave the rest of the options seen in Figure 10.14 as they appear in the figure, and type the description "MATERIAL GROUP." That way you'll know that you're working with that characteristic attached to VARIABLE1.

8. Save your work, and go back to the CHANGE PROFITABILITY REPORT:SPECIFY PROFIT. SEGMENT environment.

9. On the CHARACTERISTICS tab, in the SEL. CHARACTERISTICS area, notice the checkbox in the third column from the left in the line MATERIAL GROUP, as shown in Figure 10.15. This checkbox enables access to predefined CO-PA variables (such as the one created in the previous steps). Select this checkbox to access the VARIABLE1 variable we just created.

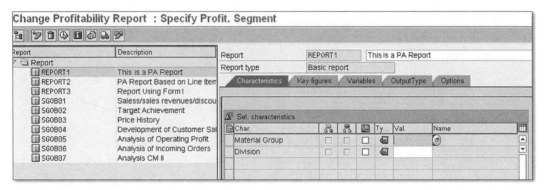

Figure 10.15 Adding &VARIABLE1 to REPORT1

10. As you can see in Figure 10.16, after selecting the checkbox in the variable column in the line MATERIAL GROUP, we're able to attach a variable to the characteristic MATERIAL GROUP. Because we only have one variable at the moment, select the line for VARIABLE1. Also, notice that in this line, you see the settings you specified in the screen shown in Figure 10.14.

11. Click on the checkmark icon to accept the selection and attach it to the MATERIAL GROUP characteristic.

12. As shown in Figure 10.16, variable VARIABLE1 has been added to the MATERIAL GROUP characteristic and it is grayed out to disallow any other information input (unless you want to change the variable, which you would do by clicking on the checkbox again).

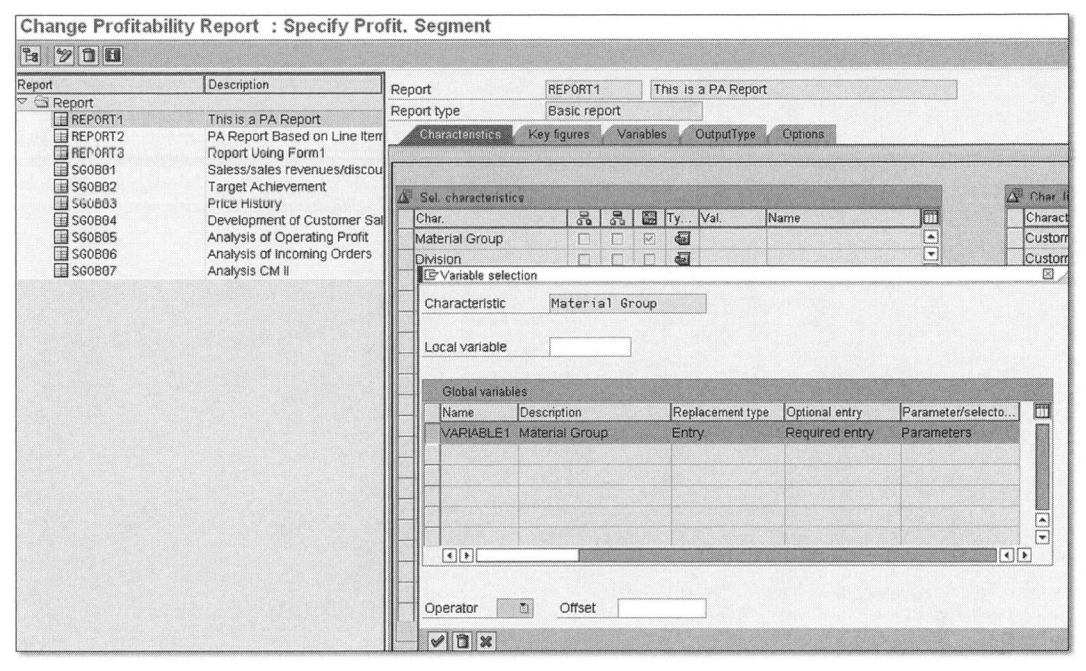

Figure 10.16 Adding VARIABLE1 to Your CO-PA Report

13. Notice that the description of the variable is visible in the column called NAME in Figure 10.17, and currently shows MATERIAL GROUP, the name we previously configured in the screen shown in Figure 10.14. You could have chosen a different name if you wanted the variable name to be different from the characteristic name.

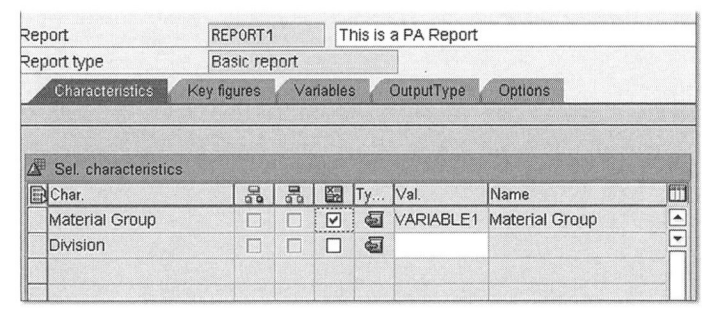

Figure 10.17 Assigning Variables to Your Report

14. Save your report to update all of the configuration settings, and execute it again.

15. Notice that in the REPORT SELECTIONS area in the SELECTION: THIS IS A PA REPORT screen, shown in Figure 10.18, the MATERIAL GROUP characteristic displays without any type of definition. We'll change this to take advantage of the VARIABLE1 variable.

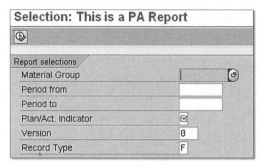

Figure 10.18 Executing Your Report

16. Go back to the CHANGE PROFITABILITY REPORT : VARIABLE ENTRY screen, as shown in Figure 10.19, and select the VARIABLES tab.

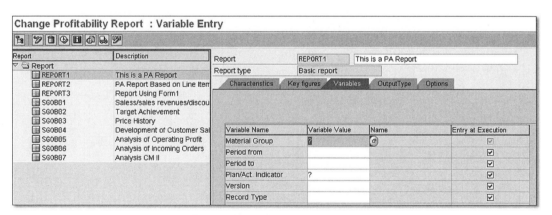

Figure 10.19 Reviewing the Variables Tab

17. Notice that all of the required data values to input before each report are also variables and that for your variable MATERIAL GROUP (VARIABLE1), the ENTRY AT EXECUTION column checkbox is checked and grayed out to inform you that a variable is attached and that it cannot be removed.

Remember, VARIABLE1 was set up to be a required entry, meaning you cannot omit inputting a value to this characteristic when executing your report. However, the other variables shown in Figure 10.19—PERIOD FROM, PERIOD TO, PLAN/ACT INDICATOR, VERSION, and RECORD TYPE—are not required during execution. Therefore, you can uncheck any of the checkmarks in the ENTRY AT EXECUTION column to remove the associated variable, but not MATERIAL GROUP.

18. Also, notice that there is a question mark (?) in the VARIABLE VALUE column. This means that the value is required, and before executing the report, this field must be either defaulted in the screen shown in Figure 10.19, or typed in at run time. Otherwise, the system won't allow the report to run and an error message appears to inform you about this situation.

19. Remove the variables VERSION and RECORD TYPE by clicking on their respective checkboxes in the ENTRY AT EXECUTION column.

20. Type a default value of "AA-001" into the VARIABLE VALUE field for the MATERIAL GROUP variable (VARIABLE1), as shown in Figure 10.20. This value will appear as the default during execution of the report.

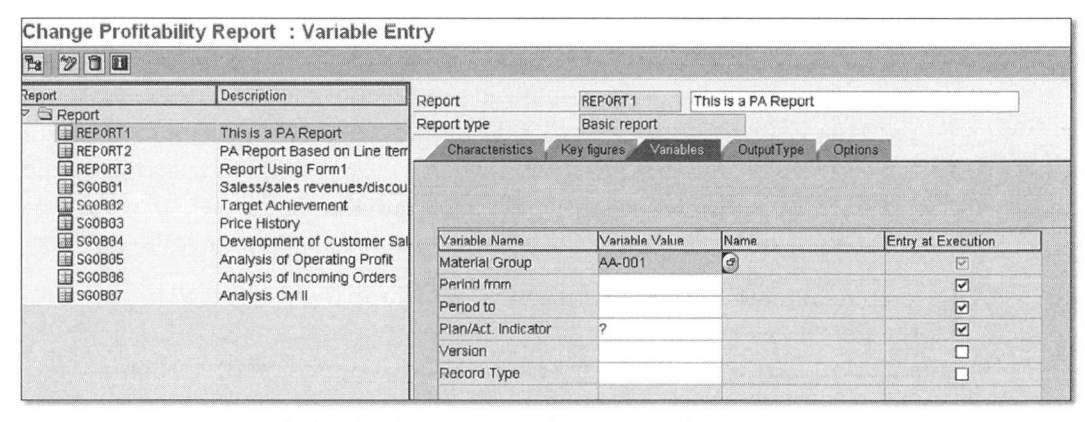

Figure 10.20 Creating a Default Value for Your Material Group Variable

21. Save your changes.

22. Execute the report again and compare the screen shown in Figure 10.21 with the one shown earlier in Figure 10.18. In the REPORT SELECTIONS area, MATERIAL GROUP now displays AA-001 as the default value that is required to

execute the report and will extract all of the information from the other three characteristics if nothing else is defined, but always specifically extracts information for MATERIAL GROUP. Also, notice that the characteristics VERSION and RECORD TYPE that we removed earlier don't display anymore.

23. Notice that VARIABLE1 now carries a default value of AA-001, as shown in Figure 10.21.

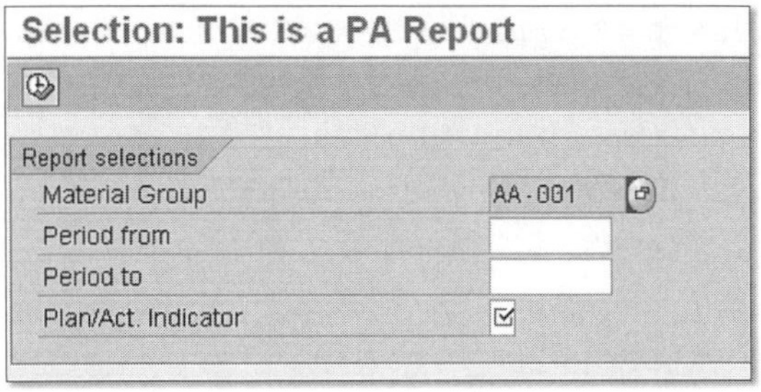

Figure 10.21 Reviewing Your Default Value for VARIABLE1

This completes our discussion of configuring variables for CO-PA reports. Beyond this, you've probably already explored the remaining tabs available in the REPORT CHANGE: SETTINGS screen that we've worked on in this chapter and in Chapter 9. Notice, however, that in the OUTPUT TYPE section of the OUTPUT TYPE tab, you can control how your report is displayed using HTML, CLASSIC DRILLDOWN, the traditional OBJECT LIST (AVL), or EXCEL (XXL) format, as shown in Figure 10.22. To switch between the different displays for your report, select the appropriate radio button. For example, in Figure 10.22, the configuration is set to GRAPHICAL REPORT-OUTPUT using the OUTPUT AREAS dropdown list for further configuration.

Overall, remember to configure the environment that will make your users feel most comfortable when working. Experiment with the various options and execute your reports several times to see the different options and capabilities.

In the next section we'll explore CO-PA reporting Best Practices, and as part of this, work with more advanced functionalities. More specifically, in Chapter 9, we worked on creating frozen reports; now we'll move to the next level and explain how to run these reports in the background to improve system performance. We'll also look at the configuration of key figure schemes and other techniques useful to improve your reporting efforts.

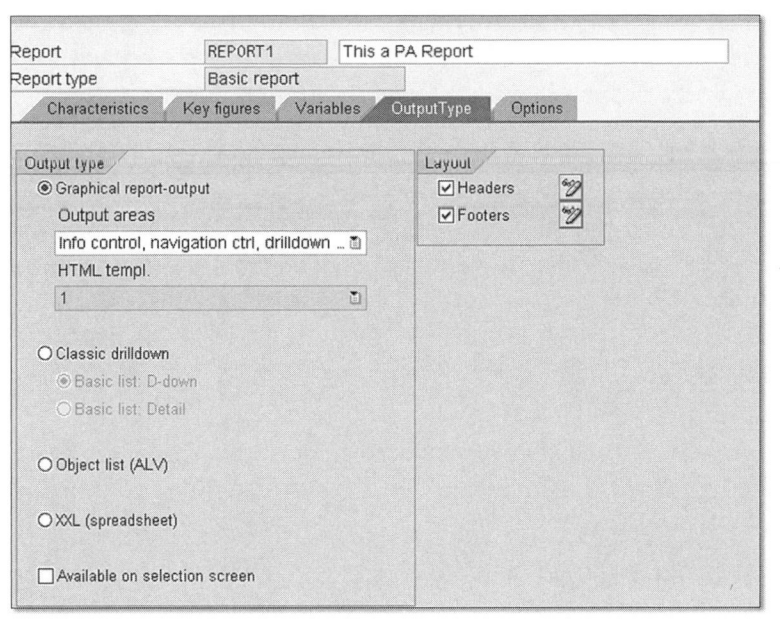

Figure 10.22 Reviewing the Output Type

10.3 CO-PA Reporting: Best Practices

We've created reports, forms, headers, footers, and variables, and modified the data selection process, so what's next? Best Practices! System performance should always be on your mind at each step of implementing any SAP component. Having a project leader who is aware of the importance of this concept and is knowledgeable about it is priceless. Unfortunately, in many projects the project leader works on multiple projects and is under pressure to deliver his projects; therefore, system performance is often not considered until the basic model is completed.

> **Note**
>
> Some terms introduced and briefly discussed here will be explained in more detail in Chapter 12.

This section addresses decisions for which a project leader should consider using Best Practices or recommended procedures in CO-PA reporting that truly improve system performance and simplify data extraction. In addition, by using Best Practices, project leaders can manage their teams more productively and avoid generating ABAP programs by using standard SAP components instead.

> **Note**
>
> Most people know that ABAP is the SAP programming language and that it can be used to create applications to perform a variety of functions. However, alternative intermediate ways to perform the same functions without requiring ABAP coding are often available. For this reason, ABAP by itself is not an SAP Best Practice, and it is not recommended unless your system requires so many fixes that it is justified. This, however, increases the risk that all of your work might be lost in future upgrades.

You don't necessarily have to apply everything written in this section, but you should keep these Best Practices in mind and see if they are useful in your implementation.

Let's start our review of the suggested Best Practices of CO-PA:

▸ Don't include too many characteristics in your reports because this practice reduces system performance and increases extraction time. A good rule of thumb is to limit your characteristics to six or less per report.

▸ Use Report-Report Interface (RRI) and Report Splitting (RS) (to be discussed in detail in Chapter 12) to link and have access to several reports, use line items for reconciliation, improve performance, remove unnecessary characteristics, and simplify reporting.

▸ Use frozen data for reports that take a long time to execute.

▸ Use mass print settings when you need hard copies.

▸ Study value fields and determine any dependencies required to be added to your report. For example, if you set up a single field called "Net Revenue" without including the components that generate this value field and the information is posted, the SAP system will not allow breaking down the data later on to identify how the number was calculated. In other words, once data has been posted to a particular value field, there is no way to identify the components that generated the value in the first place.

▸ Use key figure schemes to manage groupings of value fields across reports and ensure consistency.

▸ Improve system performance with summarization levels.

Some of these procedures are reviewed further in Chapter 12 because they are more suited for advanced users. For this chapter, we'll focus our attention on extensively explaining the concepts of frozen reports, key figure schemes, and summarization levels. Frozen reports were briefly reviewed in Chapter 9, but here we'll expand the discussion to generate pre-calculated reports running in the background with an ABAP program without any type of coding!

10.3.1 Creating Frozen Reports

We already worked with frozen reports in Chapter 9, however, in this section we'll expand on their practical usage. First, let's take a quick refresher of the concepts and procedures. Remember that extracting data directly from an OLTP SAP database might be time consuming and require a lot of memory, slowing down the generation of a report or form, especially when thousands of lines of data need to be extracted. For this reason, it's practical to have selection parameters stored and associated with previously generated data that doesn't require generation of data from scratch, but rather exists "hidden" in the memory for a particular report, with predefined selection parameters, and for a particular time and date.

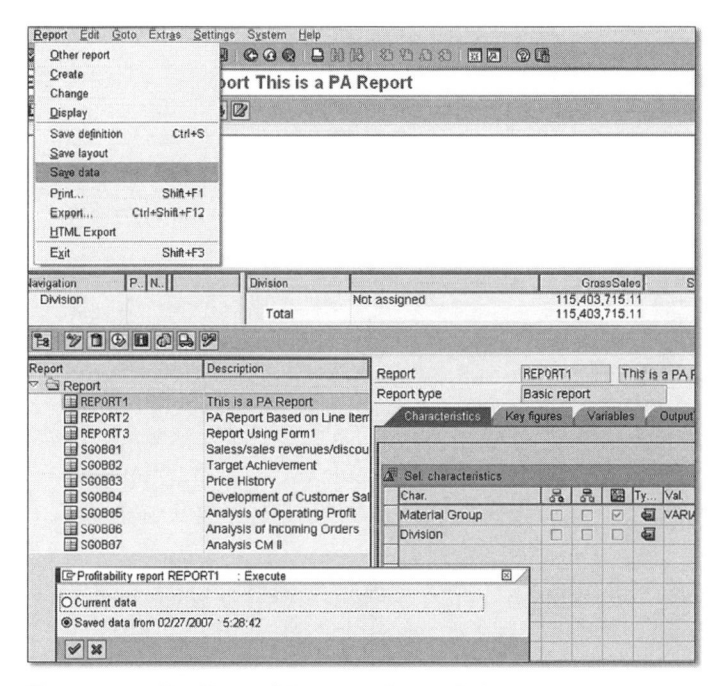

Figure 10.23 Creating and Accessing Frozen Data

This process is called *freezing data* in CO-PA and this data can be reused at any time. Users have the choice to access this frozen data or perform a new extraction to obtain the latest data with the desired selection criteria. In addition, remember that after generating a report, you can select the path REPORT • SAVE DATA, as shown in Figure 10.23, to freeze the current settings for the generation of your report without spending time and resources to run it again, especially if you have a large volume of data to extract.

Using this function, your data is saved in memory and you can retrieve it the next time your selection parameters exactly match those of the data stored and associated to your report.

To expand your understanding of this process, this time we'll update the data in the background running a variable.

To create a variable that controls the frozen data associated with a report, follow these steps:

1. Follow the path PROFITABILITY ANALYSIS • INFORMATION SYSTEM • MAINTAIN VARI-ANTS, as shown in Figure 10.24, and click on the EXECUTE icon next to MAINTAIN VARIANTS.

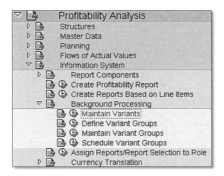

Figure 10.24 Accessing the Maintain Variants Option

2. The screen BACKGROUND PROCESSING FOR DRILLDOWN REPORTS appears, as shown in Figure 10.25. Notice that there are two field elements required, a report and a variant.

3. In the REPORT field, type the technical name of the report that has frozen data. Based on what we did in Chapter 9, and as shown in Figure 10.25, "REPORT1" is the object we're looking for.

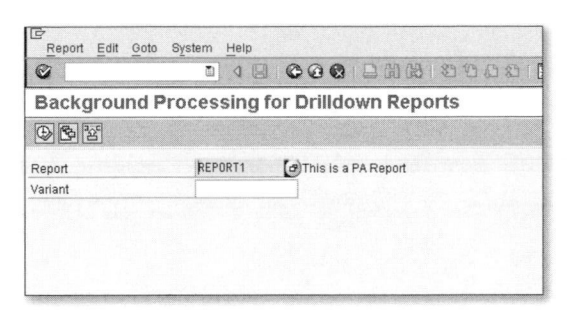

Figure 10.25 Accessing the Maintain Variants Screen

4. In the VARIANT field, shown in Figure 10.25, you need to enter the name of the variable (VARIANT) that you're associating with the frozen data stored in the REPORT1 report and that controls its execution in the background. We still need to create this variable, so follow the path EDIT • VARIANT, shown in Figure 10.26.

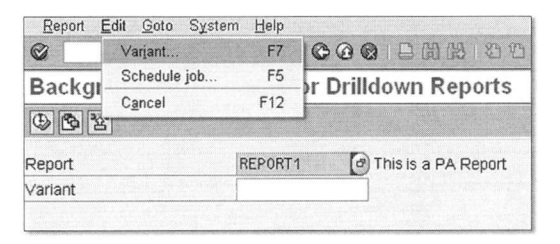

Figure 10.26 Creating a Variant Variable

5. As you can see in the screen ABAP: VARIANTS – INITIAL SCREEN shown in Figure 10.27, you're not only creating a variable, you're actually interacting with an ABAP program associated with the variant that we're creating (VARIANT1).

6. Type "Variant1" in the VARIANT field.

7. In the SUBOBJECTS area, select VALUES.

8. Click on the CREATE button.

9. The screen MAINTAIN VARIANT: REPORT displays to initiate the configuration of the VARIANT1 variant, as shown in Figure 10.28.

10. Notice that we have the REPORT SELECTIONS coming from our REPORT1, and we can even modify these selections! Remember, we have configured information for 001/2009 until 012/2009 for PLANNING DATA 1.

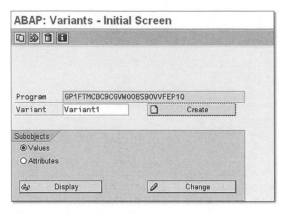

ABAP: Variants - Initial Screen

Program	GP1FTMC0C9CGVW008S9OVVFEP1Q
Variant	Variant1

[ ] Create

Subobjects
- ⦿ Values
- ○ Attributes

[ ] Display   [ ] Change

Figure 10.27 Creating a Variant

Maintain Variant: Report GP1FTMC0C9CGVWOO8S9OVVFEP1Q, Variant VARIANT1

[Attributes]

Report selections
Material Group	01	
Period from	001/2009	1. Period 2009
Period to	012/2009	12. Period 2009
Plan/Act. Indicator	1	Planning data

Status of data
Read mode	1

Print settings
☐ Print report
List type(D-down/detail/ALV)	1

Presummarized data
☑ Rebuild frozen report data

Figure 10.28 Configuring Variant1 to Use Predefined Selection Criteria and to Access Frozen Data

11. Select the checkbox REBUILD FROZEN REPORT DATA to allow the variant to access any frozen data stored in your REPORT1, and click on the ATTRIBUTES button.

12. The screen VARIANT ATTRIBUTES appears, as shown in Figure 10.29. Notice the VARIANT NAME field is grayed out, meaning that the technical name has been already created and cannot be changed. Complete your definition by typing the description "This is a Variant" into the MEANING field, as shown in Figure 10.29.

13. Click on the SAVE icon to save the values of VARIANT1.

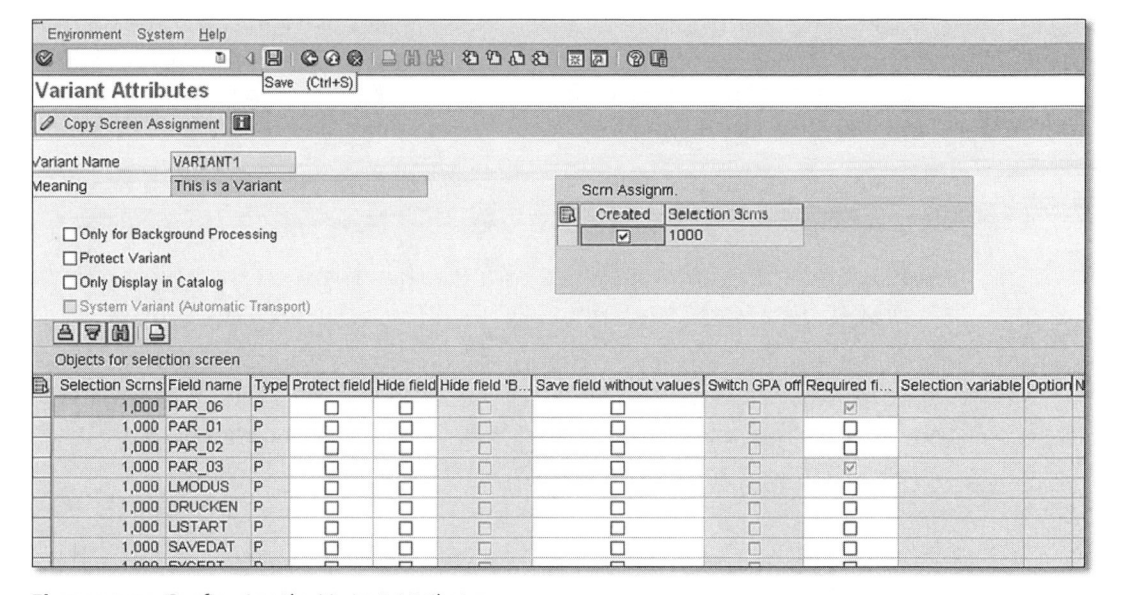

Figure 10.29 Configuring the Variant Attributes

14. Go back to the screen shown in Figure 10.30 by clicking on the BACK icon or using Transaction KE3Q.

15. Place the cursor into the VARIANT field shown in Figure 10.30 and enter "VARIANT1."

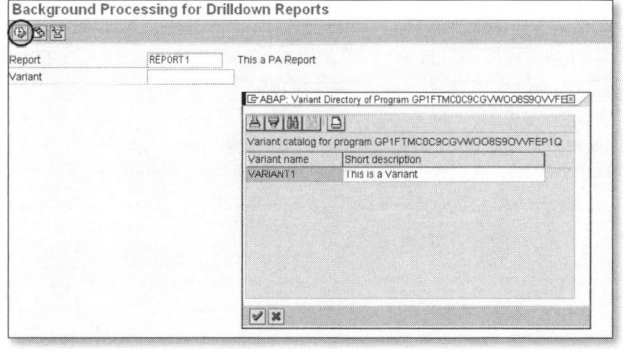

Figure 10.30 Assigning VARIANT1 to REPORT1

16. Click on the checkmark icon to accept your selection. Once you complete your assignment, you have an ABAP variant running with a predefined report without coding!

17. Click on the Execute icon, and the following message appears at the bottom of your screen: Report data for REPORT1 saved. This means that the variable VARIANT1 is now carrying frozen data that belongs to REPORT1 running with an ABAP program!

Now we need to perform some additional steps to allow the variable to execute in the background:

1. Return to the IMG and follow the path Profitability Analysis • Information System • Background Processing • Define Variant Groups.

2. Click on the New Entries button, and the screen shown in Figure 10.31 appears. Notice that the Application Class again is KE for Profitability Analysis, and that we're working with Table Name CE1S_GO, associated with the operating concern where the data exists.

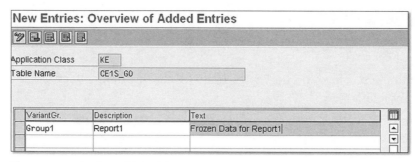

Figure 10.31 Creating a Variant Group

3. Create the variant group (VariantGr.) "Group1," with Description "Report1," and Text "Frozen Data for Report1," as shown in Figure 10.31.

However, we still need to maintain the variant groups, so perform these steps:

1. Go back to the IMG and follow the path Information System • Maintain Variant Groups to access the screen shown in Figure 10.32.

2. Select the Operating concern associated with your report information, in this case S_GO.

3. Enter the Type of Profitability Analysis to be performed inside your operating concern (in this case 1, for costing-based; otherwise you would select 2 for account-based).

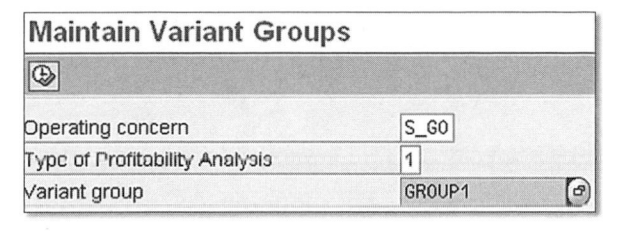

Figure 10.32 Maintaining Variant Groups

4. Select the VARIANT GROUP GROUP1.

5. Click on the EXECUTE icon.

6. Click on the NEW ENTRIES button. Notice that the information you just defined is displayed and grayed out, and that you're directly interacting with TABLE NAME CE1S_GO, as shown in Figure 10.33.

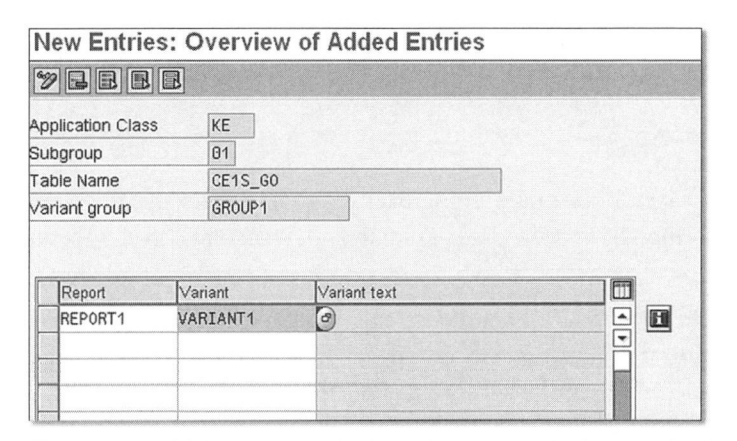

Figure 10.33 Linking REPORT1 to VARIANT1 with Variant Group GROUP1

7. With this configuration, you're saying that VARIANT1 controls the info in REPORT1, so click on the SAVE icon to complete the link.

Now you need to schedule these variants to interact with each other, executing the report extraction in the background:

1. Follow the path PROFITABILITY ANALYSIS • INFORMATION SYSTEM • BACKGROUND PROCESSING • SCHEDULE VARIANT GROUPS.

2. At this point, as shown in Figure 10.34, you're ready to execute a job by typing the following parameters:

417

- ▶ Operating concern: "S_GO"

- ▶ Type of Profitabiliy Analysis: "1" (costing-based)

- ▶ Variant group: "GROUP1"

- ▶ Report name(s): Not needed because we have it associated with the variant and a variant group

- ▶ Job name: The description used as an identification for your frozen data execution program. In this case, "We are freezing data!!!" sounds good.

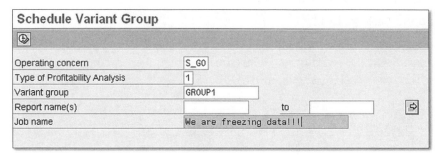

Figure 10.34 Scheduling Variant Groups

3. You're now ready to extract your data in the background without users knowing that you're updating the frozen data. To start, click on the EXECUTE icon shown in Figure 10.34.

4. The screen shown in Figure 10.35 appears and you're ready to schedule VARIANT1 for execution, using the job called WE ARE FREEZING DATA!!!. The only thing missing is configuring the frequency of the data collection, and we want to perform this in a controlled way.

5. Click on the START CONDITION button, and the START TIME window appears, shown in Figure 10.36.

6. Either click on the IMMEDIATE button, also shown in Figure 10.36, to initiate the execution right away, or select how you want to schedule the variant to collect the data periodically, using the DATE/TIME, AFTER JOB, AFTER EVENT, AT OPERATION MODE, or any other button available to control the frequency of the execution.

7. For our purposes, click on the IMMEDIATE button and then click on the SAVE icon.

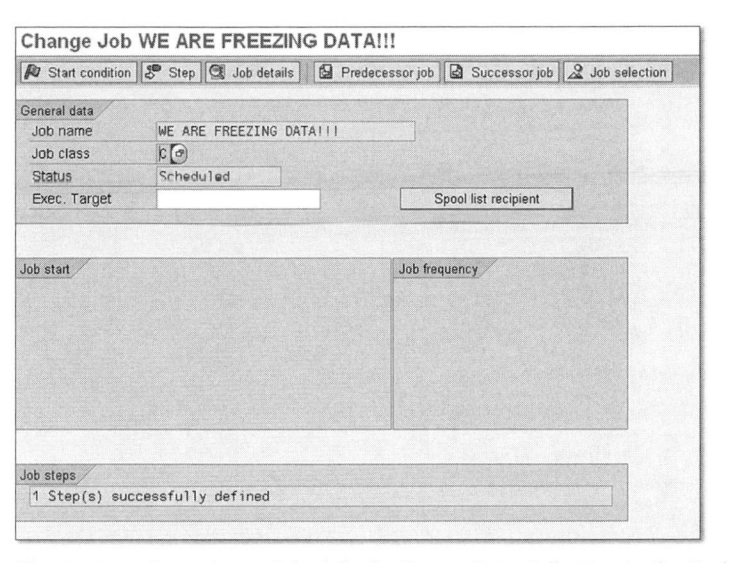

Figure 10.35 Preparing to Schedule the Frozen Data Collection in the Background

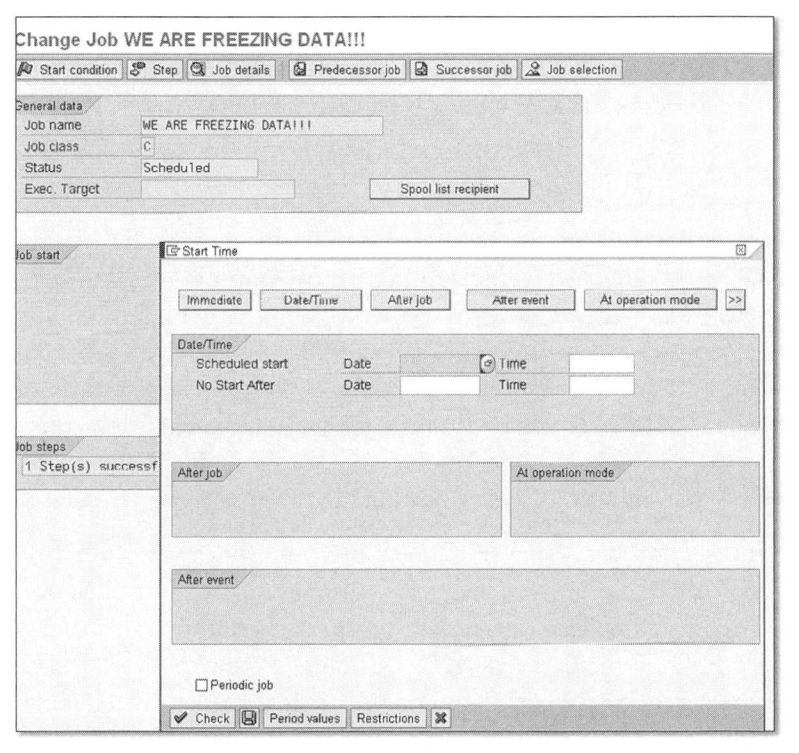

Figure 10.36 Configuring the Frequency of Execution of Frozen Data Collection with VARIANT1

8. Completely exit all screens and return to the PROFITABILITY ANALYSIS • INFORMATION SYSTEM • CREATE PROFITABILITY REPORT to access the CHANGE PROFITABILITY REPORT screen, shown in Figure 10.37.

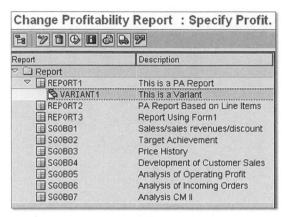

Figure 10.37 Accessing the Change/Report Environment

9. Identify REPORT1 and notice that VARIANT1 is linked to this report as a hierarchy, as shown in Figure 10.37. This means there's a scheduled process running behind the scenes associated with this particular report.

10. Execute the report and you'll see the same message on the screen the last time VARIANT1 was executed to collect frozen data.

Overall, this process allows users to access information quickly, doesn't require them to know how the data was generated, and most importantly improves system performance using a predefined ABAP program without any coding required. This is a good way to control and share information between different users in the system without overloading the system at the same time. Some of these variants can be scheduled to run late in the evening so users have new information early the next day, for example, or the data can be updated every day, depending on your scheduling configuration using the scheduler.

In summary, in this section we reviewed and explored the concept of collecting and generating frozen data with a variable. This variable can be controlled and associated with a report to collect frozen data in the background, and make it available to users of a particular report. Performing a new freeze of data overwrites the previously saved copy, thereby updating stored frozen data. Unfortunately, each report can only have one version of frozen data stored in the background unless you want to generate real-time data each time you refresh your report. Next, let's look at the concept of key figure schemes in more detail.

10.3.2 Key Figure Schemes

As explained at the beginning of this section, *key figure schemes* are groupings of value fields that are set up once and can be used several times across reports. There are two ways to access key figure schemes, either using the path PROFITABILITY ANALYSIS • REPORT COMPONENTS • DEFINE KEY FIGURE SCHEMES or using Transaction KER1.

In a key figure scheme you can define any number of interrelated key figures, referred to as *elements* of the key figure scheme, that establish the relationship. Key figure schemes work as formulas that carry out automatic operations and the results are stored in a variable that can be used as part of a report or form and behave similarly to regular value fields. Let's create a key figure scheme using the following example:

1. Follow the path PROFITABILITY ANALYSIS • REPORT COMPONENTS • DEFINE KEY FIGURE SCHEMES to start creating a new key figure scheme, as shown in Figure 10.38.

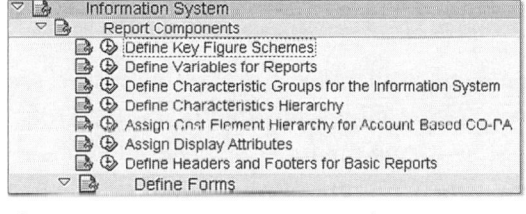

Figure 10.38 Creating a Key Figure Scheme

2. Click on NEW ENTRIES.

3. Verify that the KEY FIGURE SCHEME level is selected in the DIALOG STRUCTURE on the left of the screen, as shown in Figure 10.39.

4. Enter a number between 01 and 8999 in the KF column (we entered 01) and a suitable text, as also shown in Figure 10.39, in the MEDIUM-LENGTH TEXT column (we entered DETAILED).

5. When you're done working with the key figure scheme, in this case 01 DETAILED, you need to configure key figure scheme elements. In the DIALOG

STRUCTURE on the left side of the screen, select ELEMENTS OF THE KEY FIGURE SCHEME.

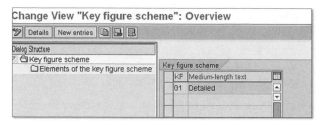

Figure 10.39 Creating a Key Figure Scheme

6. In the screen that displays, shown in Figure 10.40, there are two functions you can use to define the content of a key figure as part of a key figure scheme:

   ▶ To define an element that simply represents the addition and subtraction of different values, click on BASIC FORMULA. The system then displays a list of all of the elements available to create your formulas and select all of the value fields that you want to use in the element. This formula will then become available when you define the next element of the scheme, and will therefore appear in the list of elements under CHOOSE ENTRIES.

   ▶ If you want to define a more complex formula, click on FORMULA EDITOR. Here you can link constants and any elements of the scheme using standard mathematical operators (+, –, *, /) as well as your own ABAP functions. For a detailed description of the functions available in the formula editor, see the section "Information System" in the online documentation for Profitability Analysis at *http://help.sap.com*. Using the function "check key figure scheme" (accessible by clicking on the icon represented with two squares joined with a line), you can check all of the elements of the scheme for syntactical errors.

   In addition, clicking on the overview list icon (the mountains with the sun icon), you can obtain an overview of all of the formulas in a key figure scheme and also print the key figure scheme.

7. In the ELMNT column, add the element number and in the column MEDIUM-LENGTH TEXT and add descriptions, as shown in Figure 10.40.

8. Double-click on the element 165 CONTRIB. MARGIN I, shown in Figure 10.41, to review it as one of the components of the KEY FIGURE SCHEME DETAILED (01).

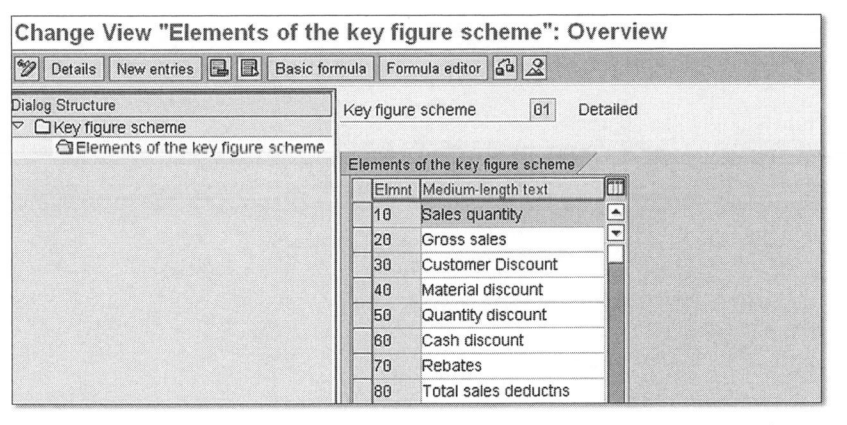

Figure 10.40 Adding Elements of the Key Figure Scheme to Your Key Figure Scheme

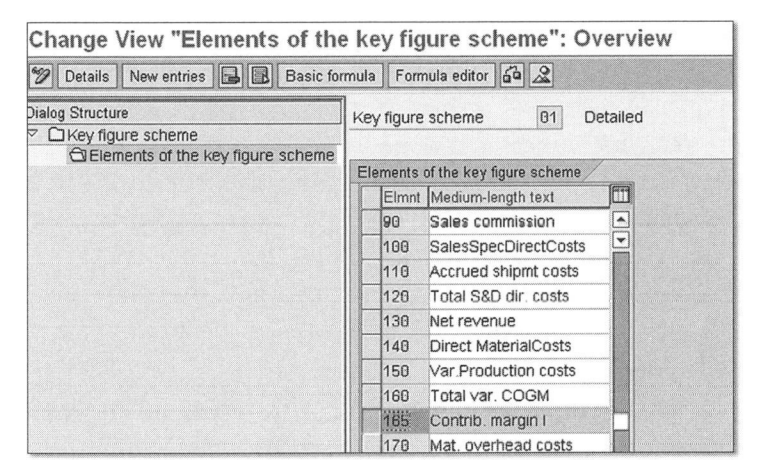

Figure 10.41 Working with Contrib. Margin I

9. The screen shown in Figure 10.42 appears. Note that the element is now in design mode.

10. Notice that the different components that form an element as part of a key figure scheme, as shown in Figure 10.42, are as follows:

    ▶ KEY FIGURE SCHEME: has a number, in this case 01.

    ▶ ELEMENT NUMBER: also has a number, in this case, 165 (the identifier for CONTRIB. MARGIN I).

    ▶ NUMBER FORMAT: includes the display factor and the number of decimal places.

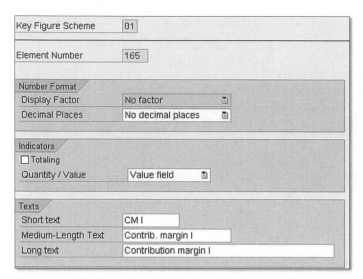

Figure 10.42 Reviewing the Configuration Settings of an Element of a Key Figure Scheme

> ► INDICATORS: the TOTALING indicator is a special function that is only used with formulas containing user-defined calculations. The QUANTITY/VALUE indicator identifies whether the format is for a quantity field or a value field; that is, whether the result of the calculation is a quantity or a value. The system will normally determine this automatically. You should set the indicator manually if you want to divide a value using a formula and then interpret it as a quantity.

> ► TEXTS: as with most SAP applications there is a short, medium, and long text to describe the element.

To clarify the concept: an element can be a stand-alone value that carries a negative or positive value extracted from a value field, and later used by another element as part of a formula. For this, CO-PA provides two environments for formula editing, which you can access using the BASIC FORMULA and FORMULA EDITOR buttons.

Basic Formula

In Figure 10.43, we're accessing the definitions of the element CONTRIB. MARGIN I using the BASIC FORMULA button. You can see that information is based on the element value of 165 that is part of the key figure scheme 01.

You can also see how simple it is to understand the equation that controls the key figure scheme element. That is, ELEMENT 165 (CONTRIB. MARGIN I) is defined as ELEMENT + 130 (NET REVENUE) – ELEMENT 160 (TOTAL VAR. COGM). Now you see why we need an element code, in this case the number 130 that identifies the data coming from NET REVENUE that can be defined as an independent value field or to reference other elements inside the key figure scheme.

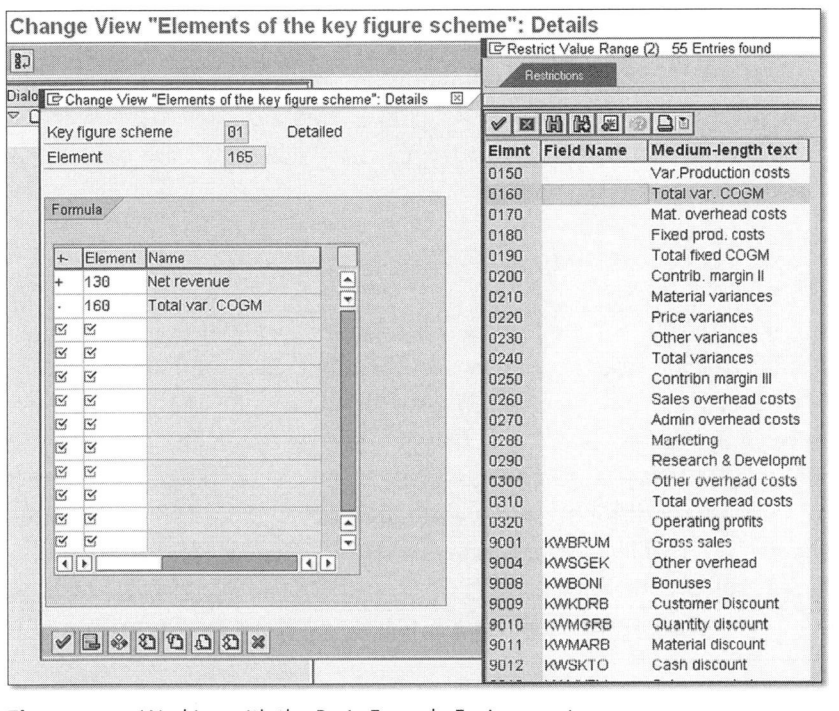

Figure 10.43 Working with the Basic Formula Environment

When working with REPORT PAINTER, we're creating formulas without overloading the system because here, values are calculated internally as if they were actual value fields with data stored.

Now, let's review the functionality accessed using the BASIC FORMULA button to better understand how the elements inside the key figure scheme work. Notice the positive (+) or negative (–) sign in the first column in Figure 10.43, then you see the ELEMENT number as part of the equation and of course the NAME.

If you click on a field in the ELEMENT column, you can either directly enter the element number, or, using the dropdown list that appears, access the RESTRICT VALUE

RANGE window that is displayed on the right side of the screen shown in Figure 10.43. There you'll see three columns: ELMNT (for the element code, using the coding system you already know), FIELD NAME (it's technical name), and MEDIUM-LENGTH TEXT (the name of the element). In this portion of the screen, you identify the element for each line to be added individually and whether the element is part of a key figure scheme following the previously displayed code numbers. To make a selection, double-click an element or select an element and click on the checkmark icon.

Notice the other element codes further down in this area of the screen, for example 9001 with a FIELD NAME of KWBRUM, and MEDIUM-LENGTH TEXT of GROSS SALES. These are the value fields from the regular SAP tables that are part of our operating concern!

Formula Editor

In addition, for more sophisticated users and complex formulas you can use the Formula Editor, which works similar to the formula creation environments of SAP NetWeaver Business Intelligence (BI), SAP NetWeaver Business Warehouse (BW), and BEx. In this environment, you first get the original value fields that you require, then create a formula assigned to an element, and then you can use this information to generate different new values and access them as regular value fields. As you can see, this lets you use value fields and create system-friendly formulas easily, without any coding in ABAP!

To access the Formula Editor:

1. Select the FORMULA EDITOR button shown earlier in Figure 10.42. As shown in Figure 10.44, the Formula Editor environment is a sophisticated environment more suited for developers and not for users new to the SAP system or advanced computer systems in general.

2. Notice that the formula and other information of element 165 (CONTRIB. MARGIN I) now appears in a different format that is more appealing to developers.

3. Also notice that there are different functionalities, as shown in full detail in Figure 10.44: the FORMULA element identifier (0165), the FORMULA LINE where the formula appears slightly differently from how it looked in the basic formula environment, the DELETE, DELETE ALL, and CHANGE VIEW buttons, as well as a variety of different operator buttons and icons.

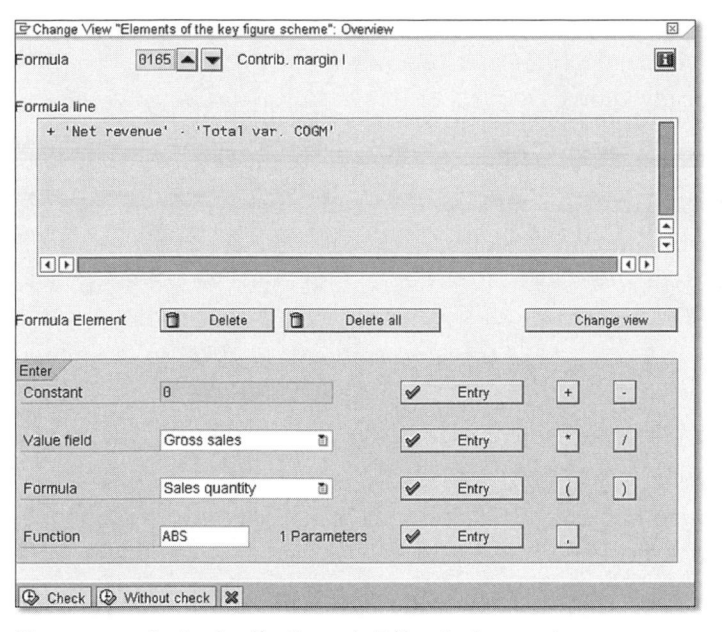

Figure 10.44 Reviewing the Formula Editor Environment

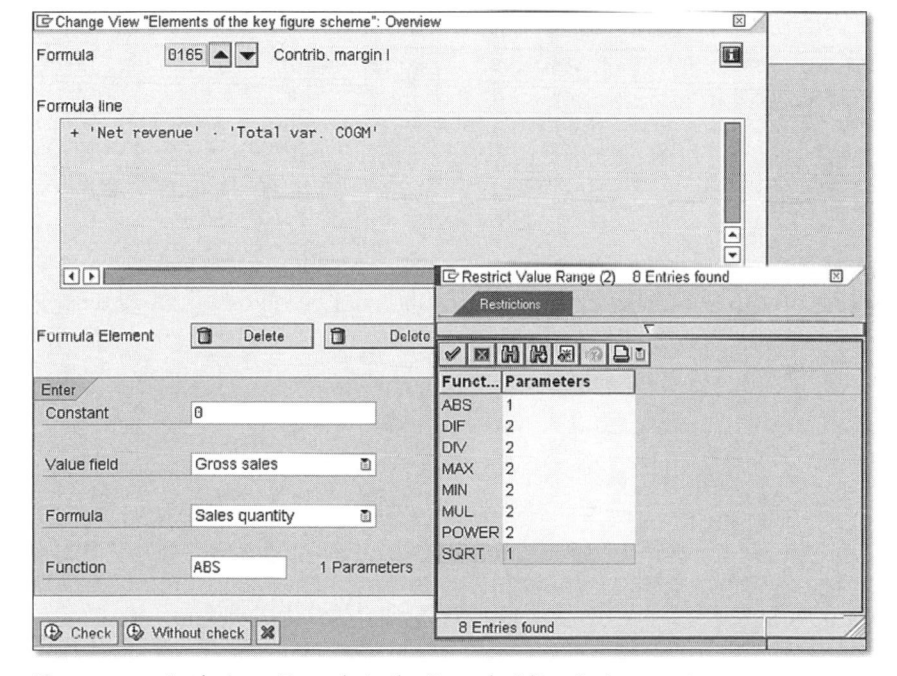

Figure 10.45 Analyzing a Formula in the Formula Editor Environment

To create a formula using the Formula Editor, follow these steps, referring to the information displayed in Figure 10.44 and 10.45:

1. First think about your formula and write it down on a piece of paper.

2. To add an operator to the formula (they are elements of the key figure scheme), in the Formula line area, type "+" (sum), "−" (subtraction), "*" (multiplication), "/" (division) , "(" and ")" (left and right parentheses), and "," (comma).

3. To add a constant, type the value (for example, "100") in the Constant field and click on the Entry button for Constant. This will add the constant to the formula, as long as an operator has already been added (an operator is required before a constant).

4. To add a new value field, select a field from the Value Field dropdown list and click on the Entry button for Value Field.

5. To add a preconfigured formula, select a formula from the Formula dropdown list and click on the Entry button for Formula.

6. As shown in Figure 10.45, there are also eight functions available that you can add, depending on the output for the calculated element and the number of parameters required in an equation. Examples include ABS for absolute value, DIF for difference, SQRT for square root, MAX for the maximum value, and so on. Explore these features on your own. They are simple mathematical terms that can be useful in more complex calculations.

   To add one of these functions to the formula, enter its name in the Function field, or select the function from the list in the Restrict Value Range window shown in Figure 10.45, and click on the Entry button for Function.

7. Finally, the Change View button (shown earlier in Figure 10.44) is useful if you'd like to change the display of the formula from being based on its technical definitions, as shown in Figure 10.46, to showing a technical name description as illustrated in Figure 10.47.

Figure 10.46 The Formula Editor Before Clicking on the Change View Button

Formula line

```
=+Z0130-Z0160;
```

Figure 10.47 The Formula Editor After Clicking on the Change View Button

8. When you're finished, click on the CHECK button.

Using Key Figure Schemes and Elements

Now the question is, how do we use this? And where? The answer is simple: use key figure schemes and elements as if they were value fields (key figures) in reports and forms. You'll be able to access this information along with your regular value field information:

1. Place the cursor into the KEY FIGURE SCHEME box and select DETAILED, as shown in step ❶ in Figure 10.48.

2. Select the desired characteristics in the list of AVAILABLE KEY FIGURES, in this case CONTRIB. MARGIN I, as shown in step ❷.

3. Move the characteristic to the left to make it a selected key figure (use the left arrow button), as shown in step ❸.

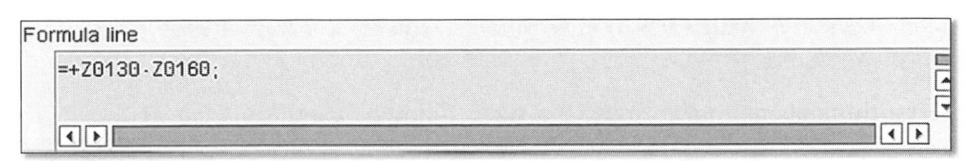

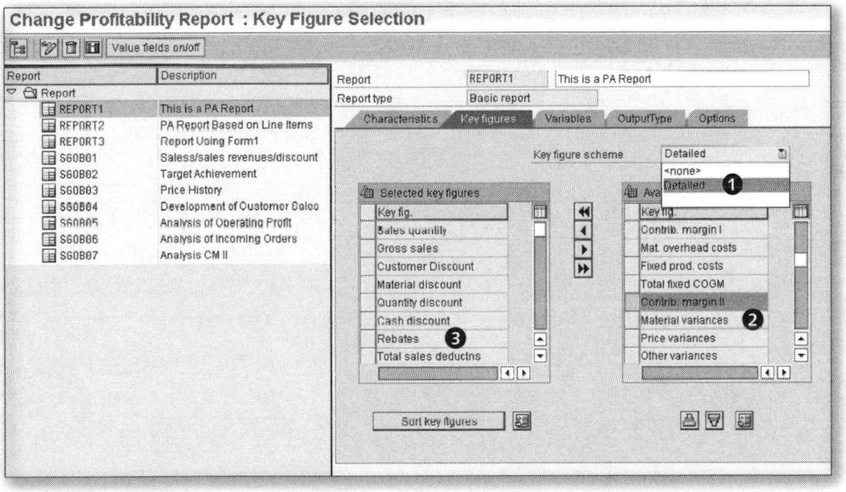

Figure 10.48 Accessing the Key Figure Scheme and Elements in the Report

Now, access the change report environment, and review FORM1 shown in Figure 10.49 and Figure 10.50:

1. Click to the right of the GROSS SALES column, as shown in step ❶ in Figure 10.49.

2. When the window SELECT ELEMENT TYPE appears, select the second option, KEY FIGURE SCHEME ELEMENT, as shown in step ❷.

3. Click on the checkmark icon, as shown in step ❸.

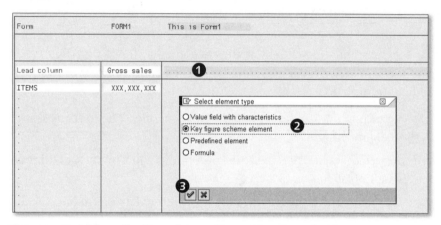

Figure 10.49 Adding a Key Figure Scheme Element to a Form, Part I

4. Select SALES QUANTITY, as shown in step ❹ in Figure 10.50.

5. Select CONTRIB. MARGIN I, as shown in step ❺.

6. Determine any selection criteria required, again as shown in step ❻.

7. Click on the CONFIRM button, as shown in step ❼.

You have now seen how a key figure scheme can be used to optimize the calculation of complex values using the basic formula or Formula Editor environments. Key figure schemes are useful when the same calculated formula needs to be used in several reports or shared with key figure schemes. They are system performance-friendly alternatives to ABAP programs, and to even the CO-PA planning framework functions. The environment is relatively friendly for formula generation, and having a clear definition of the value fields involved in the calculations is critical.

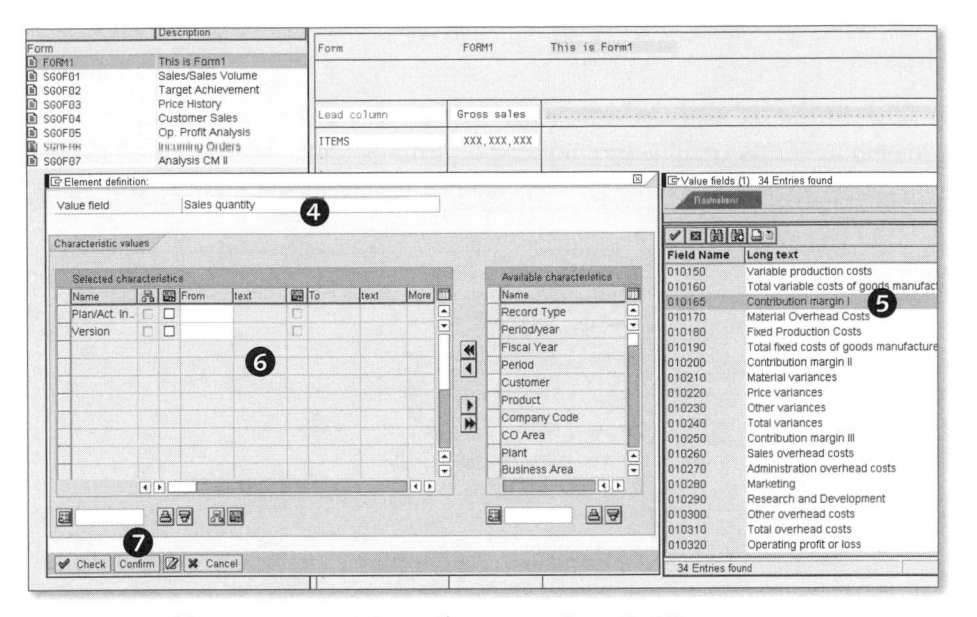

Figure 10.50 Adding a Key Figure Scheme Element to a Form, Part II

Also, you can use and reuse key figure schemes and elements in different key figure scheme elements. As long as the definitions are correct, the information will be carried over and shared across objects. We'll now finish this chapter with a brief overview of the summarization levels that control the latest posted information inside the operating concern and positively affect system performance.

10.3.3 Improving Performance in Reports and Forms Using Summarization Levels

This topic depends greatly on the concept of summarization levels discussed in detail in Chapter 12, but here's a quick definition. Summarization of data is a pre summarized set of report data stored in the database. In CO-PA reporting, it can be used to display parts of information that reside in a particular segment level. This data can be read from the database and displayed immediately when you call up a report. Summarization is a technique for improving system performance when extraction is considerably slow. Normally, summarization data is created during background processing, as we previously discussed, to avoid overloading the system with multiple users running the same reports at the same time. The data controlled by summarization levels can also be updated with the created line items, and this data is valid for one combination of characteristic values (variables) for one report at a time.

At this point we'll discuss how to work with the performance-related options available in CO-PA designed to improve report performance. You'll find these in the PERFORMANCE area on the OPTIONS tab of a report, as shown in Figure 10.51.

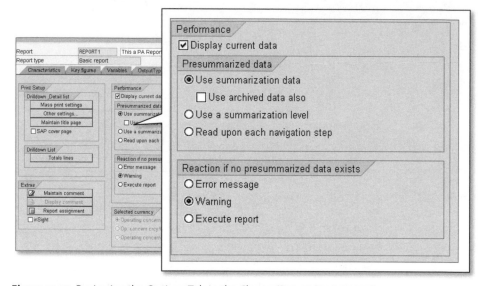

Figure 10.51 Reviewing the Options Tab in the Change/Report Environment

> **Note**
>
> PERFORMANCE is a small area of the OPTIONS tab; feel free to explore the other items on this tab if desired.

▶ DISPLAY CURRENT DATA

Because presummarized data is updated on a periodic basis, it does not always contain the latest values of postings that have been made in Profitability Analysis since the information was last updated. Therefore, if you select this setting (it's the default setting) when you execute the report, the system will read the presummarized data plus the line items posted since that data was last updated. If you don't select this option, the system displays the data as it was when it was last updated.

▶ PRESUMMARIZED DATA

There are a number of different methods for presummarizing data in CO-PA. Which method is better depends on which type of report you want to execute. The available options include:

▶ USE SUMMARIZATION DATA

All of the data required for the defined report is loaded into working memory. First, the system tries to find summarization data for the report. If this does not exist, the system creates it by reading a summarization level or the segment level.

▶ USE ARCHIVED DATA ALSO

The system reads the data that has been archived and deleted from the segment level of your operating concern as well as data from the segment level.

▶ USE A SUMMARIZATION LEVEL (default setting)

All of the data required for the defined report is loaded into working memory. The system tries to read the data from a summarization level. If it does not find a suitable summarization level, it retrieves the data from the segment level.

▶ READ UPON EACH NAVIGATION STEP

In contrast to the other options, here the system does not load all of the report data when you execute the report. Instead, it only loads the data (from a summarization level or the segment level) that is needed upon each navigation step and displays this on the screen. It does the same for each step you take when navigating through the report.

▶ REACTION IF NO PRESUMMARIZED DATA EXISTS

Here you can tell the system how it should react if no presummarized data can be found for the report:

▶ ERROR MESSAGE

The report cannot be executed. You first need to create the presummarized data in the background. You should select this option if executing the report without the presummarized data would lead to excessively long runtimes.

▶ WARNING (default setting)

When you execute the report, you receive a warning message saying that no suitable presummarized data could be found. You can then decide whether you want to cancel or to execute the report anyway.

▶ EXECUTE REPORT
In this case, the system executes the report without displaying a message. The data is read from the segment level. You should select this option only for reports that require a small amount of data.

10.4 Summary

In this chapter, we reviewed the different configuration elements related to CO-PA reporting to provide you with a view of its capabilities and functionalities from an advanced user or implementer point of view. The information presented in this chapter, along with that presented previously in Chapter 9, should provide a project leader with enough background information to consider if reporting outside R/3 or SAP ERP ECC 6.0 is required, or if certain reports can be utilized within the CO-PA Report Painter environment to make the required consolidation, and leave more complex developments for the SAP BW/SAP NetWeaver BI platforms. Remember, the SAP system is not about implementing the latest tools all of the time, but about delivering requirements with tools that provide value to your users and improve the productivity of your implementation teams.

We have now covered the most important concepts and functionalities of CO-PA with SAP. In Chapter 11, we briefly discuss how to perform the switch from costing-based to account-based CO-PA. With account-based CO-PA, it is possible to use cost elements to perform reconciliation with the FI-G/L module.

Costing-based CO-PA is not the only approach available. Account-based CO-PA allows reconciliation with Financial Accounting (FI) using cost elements by reusing the same previously configured components, but changing specific elements within the operating concern to allow account-based transactions.

11 Working with Account-Based CO-PA

So far, we've dedicated our time and resources to reviewing applications using costing-based CO-PA and studying other functionalities of the component, such as planning and reporting. Because the functionalities are relatively the same in comparison with account-based, we'll only discuss the change in approach you'll need to take if you decide to be more specific and link your general ledger (G/L) information in FI and your cost elements in Controlling (CO) using account-based CO-PA. The switch to an account-based environment can be achieved with just some minor changes in your operating concern, but it affects how the information is displayed and reported. For example, value fields are exclusively applicable to costing-based CO-PA and don't exist in account-based environments.

11.1 Differences between Costing-Based and Account-Based CO-PA

Costing-based profitability is intended for short-term Profit and Loss (P&L) statements for sales management in evaluation of planned sales volumes or the sales volume transferred from billing or incoming sales orders using costing-based values, such as sales deductions and standard cost of goods manufactured, in real time. In comparison, account-based accounting using CO-PA allows users to simultaneously access information reconciled with FI at the account level and post cost and revenue information in CO-PA and FI.

It's important to remember that account-based and costing-based CO-PA can run parallel either using the same operating concern to extract the required information to switch back and forth between the two types of Profitability Analysis, or with two operating concerns—one running account-based and another one running costing-based CO-PA. The latter is particularly useful when working with SAP NetWeaver Business Intelligence (BI) extraction because the information for each type of accounting can be sent to different data targets, depending on the reporting needs. The account-based approach can be used as a "reconciliation bridge" between FI and costing-based CO-PA, and costing-based Profitability Analysis is mostly used for short-term data analysis.

In addition, in account-based CO-PA, the cost of goods sold (COGS) is updated at the time of delivery (goods issue); revenue, discounts, and freight are not updated in the system until the billing document is created. In comparison with costing-based CO-PA, the COGS is not updated at the time of delivery when the goods are issued, but at the same time when revenue, freight, discounts, and other related information is updated. This major difference when switching between costing-based and account-based CO-PA causes differences in the information report of time of delivery (goods issue) versus time of billing.

Because of these timing differences, a change of model from costing-based CO-PA to account-based CO-PA causes these two to be out of balance. This does not mean, however, that the information is incorrect; it's simply interpreted differently.

Now let's begin our discussion of the elements and changes required to work with account-based CO-PA.

> **Note**
>
> In the next section we discuss comments related to SAP Note 69384, and complement this with information we consider meaningful to the reader. We won't provide a complete discussion of the implications behind account-based CO-PA because this requires knowledge of FI and other areas of CO. However, at a minimum, the reader should have a clear understanding of account-based CO-PA to decide which version of CO-PA to use and under which circumstances, based on the information provided in this chapter.

11.1.1 Defining Cost Elements for CO-PA

Account-based CO-PA uses cost elements, which are the CO equivalents of G/Ls in the FI system. Cost elements are not created in CO-PA, and their creation is specific to the cost element accounting component of CO, shown in Figure 11.1.

Use the path CONTROLLING • COST ELEMENT ACCOUNTING • CREATE COST ELEMENTS, also shown in Figure 11.1, to access cost element accounting. The idea behind cost elements is that each transaction in the system has an account number that transfers and monitors the flows of money, materials, resources, and other components inside the system within the CO component.

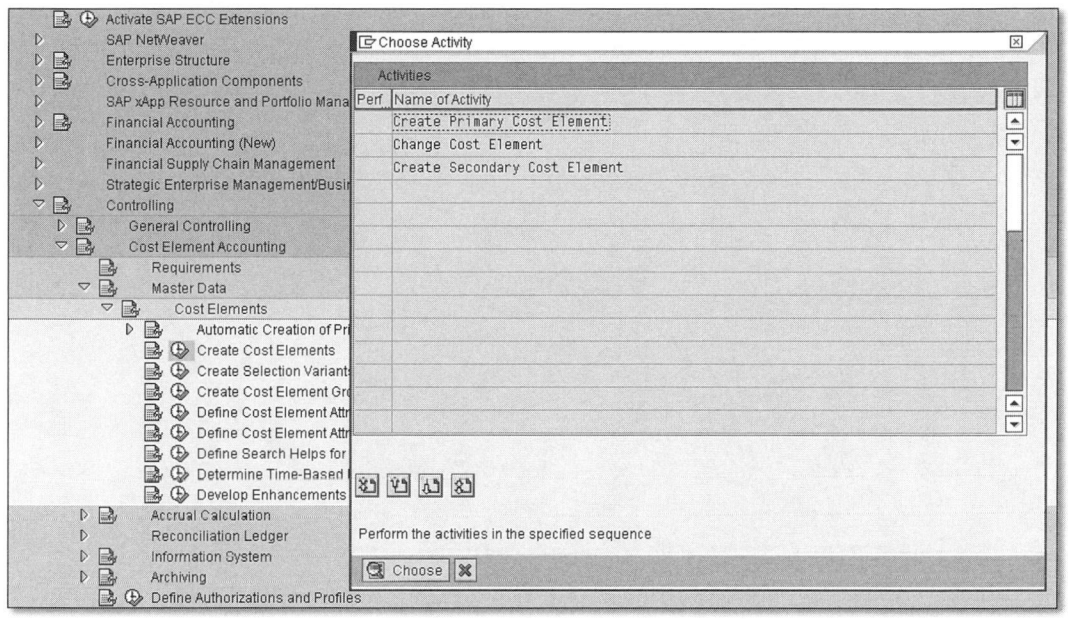

Figure 11.1 Accessing Cost Element Accounting

For example, you can monitor the materials consumed from a cost center by assigning cost element accounts that specifically control materials only inside the system and that are defined as *secondary* cost elements (read more on secondary cost elements in a moment). This lets you determine budget and actual costs based on the assignments and consumptions of this cost center. Furthermore, you can generate reports based on these characteristics. Cost elements must previously exist inside your CO system to use account-based CO-PA, and its use is limited by the configuration options set up in the G/L accounts and cost element accounting.

There are two types of cost elements: *primary* and *secondary*. Primary cost elements describe a one-to-one relationship between the G/L transactions and cost elements inside the OLTP system associated with the FI component. Secondary cost elements are created inside the CO environment, and are related to internal transactions, such as cost center, profit center, and internal order postings that move and transfer costs or revenues among them.

As shown in Figure 11.2, cost elements such as 420000 DIRECT LABOR COSTS are part of a controlling area, 0001 SAP in this case, and they have a validity period, in our example 01/01/1995 to 12/31/2400. In addition, a cost element has master data elements associated with it as also shown in Figure 11.2 such as its NAME, DESCRIPTION, CELEM CATEGORY (Cost Element Category, which describes its behavior within the system), INDICATORS, DEFAULT ACCT ASSGNMT, and others.

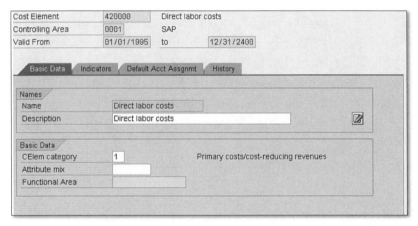

Figure 11.2 Reviewing the General Options of a Cost Element

As shown in Figure 11.2, in the cost element category (CELEM CATEGORY), we've defined cost element 420000 as a primary cost/cost-reducing revenue by specifying a value of 1. However, there are other classifications, such as the following:

▶ **3:** Accrual/deferral per surcharge

▶ **4:** Accrual/deferral per debit = actual

▶ **11:** Revenues

▶ **12:** External settlement

> **Note**
>
> Feel free to investigate the different types and classifications of cost elements and how they impact your data display. You can find help at *http://help.sap.com* or *http://sdn.sap.com*.

Next, let's review the specific configuration settings required to switch to account-based CO-PA in more detail.

11.1.2 Changing the Operating Concern from Costing-Based to Account-Based CO-PA

As we previously reviewed in Chapters 3 and 4, several processes are required to configure an operating concern, which is the main component and object to perform profitability analysis. As shown in Figure 11.3, when setting up the operating concern TEST, the option you select in the area TYPE OF PROFIT. ANALYSIS changes the behavior of your operating concern object to either costing-based or account-based. Once you make a selection, your operating concern output will be immediately affected, so if you're using structures associated with a data source in R/3 or SAP ERP ECC 6.0 generated with Transaction KEB0, this change will directly impact the information coming out of your R/3 or SAP ERP ECC 6.0 system.

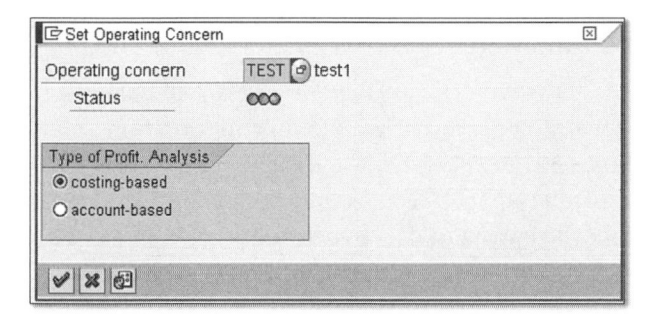

Figure 11.3 Switching from Costing-Based to Account-Based CO-PA

11.1.3 Controlling Areas and Account-Based CO-PA

As is the case in costing-based CO-PA, the controlling area is hierarchically subordinate to the operating concern in account-based CO-PA. Consequently, one or more controlling areas can be assigned to an operating concern. The operating concern determines the characteristics, and therefore the structuring, of the market segments for costing-based and account-based CO-PA. If you've configured both types of Profitability Analysis, you have the option to use one or the other, and with account-based CO-PA the data volume can be reduced considerably.

Furthermore, controlling areas can have different currencies and different charts of accounts. However, as in costing-based CO-PA, the fiscal year variant of the operating concern and the fiscal year variants of all assigned controlling areas must correspond in account-based CO-PA as well. However, unlike costing-based CO-PA, in account-based CO-PA you cannot create cross-controlling area evaluations because the charts of accounts may differ. Cross-controlling area planning is not supported either.

11.1.4 Currencies and Account-Based CO-PA

With respect to currencies, costing-based Profitability Analysis requires an operating concern currency definition to maintain a common currency for all of the transactions. For account-based Profitability Analysis, the operating concern currency is irrelevant because the data is updated simultaneously using the information contained in the company code currency, transaction currency, and controlling area currency.

11.1.5 Data Structures and Data Retention

In costing-based Profitability Analysis, you can activate the update of data in calendar weeks at the segment level (total records) while entering different actual and plan data settings. When you activate this function, the data in CO-PA is managed both in the period type of the posting periods and according to calendar weeks. In particular, you can use the update of data in calendar weeks in account-based CO-PA to support a weekly schedule in sales planning and you can only valuate data according to calendar weeks in the line item reporting.

In terms of the data structures required to create an operating concern, there are basically no differences in comparison of account-based CO-PA to what we discussed in Chapter 4 for costing-based CO-PA. However, value fields are only required in costing-based CO-PA. Therefore, if you configure your operating concern to use both types of CO-PA, value fields are only relevant when you're working with costing-based Profitability Analysis.

Tips & Tricks

If you believe that both types of Profitability Analysis are required in your implementation, make a copy of your operating concern and have it switch independently of your options and required fields. This will help you avoid confusion during data reporting and provide more visibility.

11.1.6 Characteristic Derivation and Valuation

The same characteristic derivation-related functions and procedures shown previously in Chapter 5 using costing-based examples are applicable to account-based Profitability Analysis as well.

In account-based Profitability Analysis, posted values are always transferred from the primary document (goods issue posting, billing, direct postings from FI/MM, allocations within the CO system, settlements of orders). However, valuation does not take place in account-based CO-PA.

11.1.7 Actual Data Flow and Data Transfer

Costing-based and account-based Profitability Analysis is updated when actual postings relevant to profit are made. What is updated depends on which type of Profitability Analysis is active.

The following is a general description of the main transfer components posted to CO-PA and their change when working in account-based CO-PA:

▶ **Sales order receipts**
The transfer of sales order receipts is not available when using account-based CO-PA.

▶ **Goods issued for the sales order**
When transferring billing data in account-based CO-PA when there is a stock change in FI, the goods are issued for the sales order simultaneously to CO-PA. Therefore, you must create a cost element in CO to monitor stock changes posted in FI.

▶ **Transfer of billing data**
When a billing document is released to FI, revenues, sales deductions, and imputed costs are transferred to CO-PA, whether they are FI-relevant or not. This way, the COGM is transferred to account-based profitability when the goods are issued.

▶ **Cost center assessments**
With account-based Profitability Analysis, the update is carried out using an assessment cost element under which the sending cost center is credited. When using both types of Profitability Analysis, you can specify whether the distribution base is determined for costing- or account-based data.

▶ **Order and project settlement**
When you settle orders or projects in account-based CO-PA, you also must have settlement cost elements defined by the corresponding settlement structure.

▶ **Internal activity allocation**
If you allocate internal activities of cost centers to profitability segments, you must also create allocation cost elements, which are assigned to a particular activity type.

11.1.8 Profitability Analysis Reports

When working with the CO-PA INFORMATION SYSTEM menu and the reporting components, there are a few considerations to keep in mind when working with account-based Profitability Analysis:

▶ Forms, reports, and line item layouts apply to one type of Profitability Analysis only, and cannot be combined because they are directly dependent on the operating concern set as current (active) and its type of Profitability Analysis to display information.

▶ You can use hierarchies for the cost element characteristic by entering a cost element group. There is no such structure in costing-based CO-PA because cost elements don't exist in that environment.

▶ Different currencies can be displayed in a report based on controlling area currency, company code currency, and transaction currency.

▶ For any form or basic report, a characteristic currency must be entered as a required entry for each currency needed in your report. If you want a report to be made in the company code currency, for example, the "company code" characteristic is compulsory; for a report in the transaction currency, the transaction currency (foreign currency) characteristic is required. However, in the form definition or report definition, you can use variables that are only supplied with a characteristic when they are executed. By the time you run the report at the latest, you must have specified a unique characteristic value for every cell of a report (intervals are not permitted).

▶ When working with line item reports, both account-based and costing-based CO-PA can be used. You can define separate line item layouts for the account-based Profitability Analysis; if you don't specify a layout, the system uses the standard layout.

With account-based Profitability Analysis, you can only report on active characteristics, in comparison with the costing-based CO-PA that allows displaying non-active characteristics in a line-item report. In addition, in the detail display of account-based Profitability Analysis, the system goes to the general CO document display instead of the detail screens of the costing-based line item.

11.1.9 Assessment of Cost Center Costs

For costing-based Profitability Analysis, cost center costs are updated using a value field specified during the cycle maintenance. In account-based Profitability Analysis, the update is carried out by a cost element called an *assessment cost element*. This special cost element credits the sending cost center and debits the receiving cost center. When using both types of profitability, the distribution base can be determined from the data of the costing-based Profitability Analysis or from the data of the account-based Profitability Analysis.

11.1.10 Order and Project Settlement

A *settlement* can be considered a process to assign costs from a sending object to one or more receiving objects, such as cost center, order, fixed asset, or account. When you settle orders or projects, the value fields for updating the costing-based Profitability Analysis are determined by the PA transfer structure that is assigned to the order. In account-based Profitability Analysis, the update of the settlement data is carried out under the settlement cost elements that are defined by the corresponding settlement structure. A PA transfer structure is not required for settlement in account-based Profitability Analysis.

11.1.11 Internal Activity Allocation

Allocations are useful when the breakdown of costs received to a cost object is not possible or is not very clear. Some examples of allocations can be general and administrative costs. In the case of CO-PA, when you allocate internal activities of cost centers to profitability segments, the value field for updating costing-based Profitability Analysis is defined by the "CO" PA transfer structure. The update of the values from activity allocation in account-based Profitability Analysis is carried out under the allocation cost element that is assigned to the corresponding activity type. The "CO" PA transfer structure is not used for account-based Profitability Analysis.

11.1.12 Work in Process (WIP) and Results Analysis (RA)

Work in process (WIP) is part of the working capital or current assets of a company, and is part of the balance sheet statement. We'll define WIP as partially completed goods with a currency value based on its percent of completion or other criteria to determine the book value of partially finished goods. WIP is no longer raw materials, but not yet a finished product that a customer can purchase, and thus it has already some value added within the company. From a financial point of view, WIP shows the costs in production that have not been set yet against a finished product (semi-finished or finished product), and thus is a quantification of the value of the unfinished product.

The goal of WIP calculation is the period-related assignment of revenues and costs as part of the period-end closing activities. It's only possible to perform a WIP calculation in product cost collectors, production orders, and sales-order-related production with valuated sales order stock.

There can be different accounting methodologies to calculate the value of the WIP in your company depending on your industry and if you're following IFRS, IAS, or US GAAP standards. In general, it's possible to say that WIP is calculated in SAP in the following way:

▶ By calculating the difference between the actual costs charged to an order and the actual costs credited to the order.

▶ By valuating the yield confirmed to date for each milestone or reporting point, minus the relevant scrap.

When working with SAP, the raw materials are transferred to finished goods via production orders or process orders that are generated in the product cost controlling component. During this phase, the production order is created and raw materials are issued, while any work activities performed are charged along with any overheads to the production order. It's clear that the production processes are ongoing in any firm, and at month end, it's possible to end up with open production orders.

SAP provides a feature to calculate the value of WIP, deriving the definition of line IDs in line with the cost components. The WIP will be the total debits cost in the order as reduced by the credits for goods receipt. Results analysis is meaningful in the following situations:

▶ Working with nonvaluated sales order stock or nonvaluated project stock—in this situation, results analysis is used to calculate the inventory value of the finished and unfinished products.

▶ Working with a valuated sales order stock or valuated project stock, it might be necessary to capitalize goods that have been delivered but not yet invoiced—in this case, the data calculated in results analysis is updated on the order with reference to the results analysis version. This enables you to perform results analysis on the basis of more than one Results Analysis Version.

In order to perform WIP results analysis configuration in SAP ECC, follow these steps:

1. Define a results analysis key using Transaction OKG1. A results analysis key is a six-digit ID and a name, which is used as a control parameter of cost objects that control the calculation of the WIP (periodic valuation of long-term orders and projects). This key determines if results analysis can be performed on a sales document item, WBS element, or internal orders. SAP recommends utilizing the pre-delivered standard results analysis keys as shown in Figure 11.4, or you can create your own by clicking on the New Entries button, providing a name and four letter key with its description, which is nothing more than a unique identifier of the calculation process that will be stored in the value created.

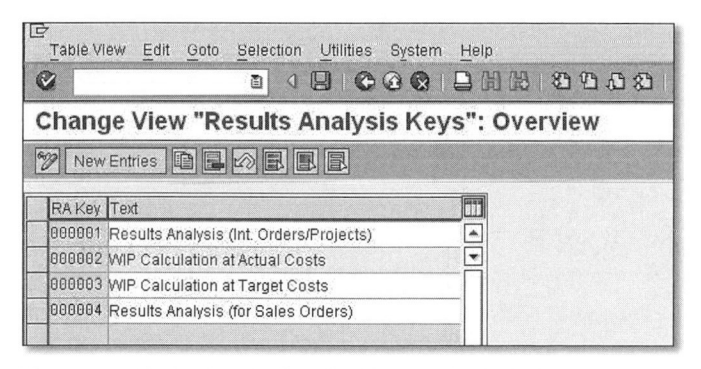

Figure 11.4 Reviewing the Standard Results Analysis Keys

2. Create cost element type 31 using Transaction KA06, as shown in Figure 11.5 by accessing the BASIC tab and CELEM category field.

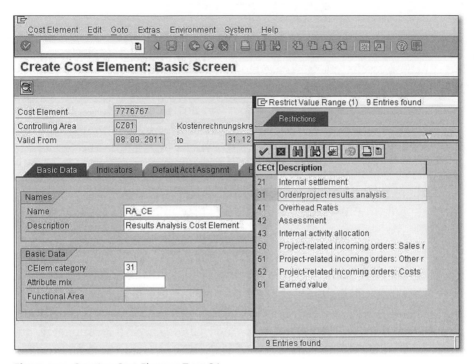

Figure 11.5 Creating Cost Element Type 31

3. Next, define results analysis versions (RA version) using Transaction OKG9 as shown in Figure 11.6. In this step, you need to define parameters that influence results analysis with sales orders, projects, and long-term orders, and then link to a controlling area. Results analysis is performed at period-end closing as part of the project systems activities and/or calculation of WIP associated to a cost object. Notice in Figure 11.6 that when double-clicking on a version (such as BE01) you access the RESULTS ANALYSIS VERSIONS DETAILS screen. Here, a version is associated with a cost element, and can transfer information to FI during settlement depending on the relationship between the company code and ledger.

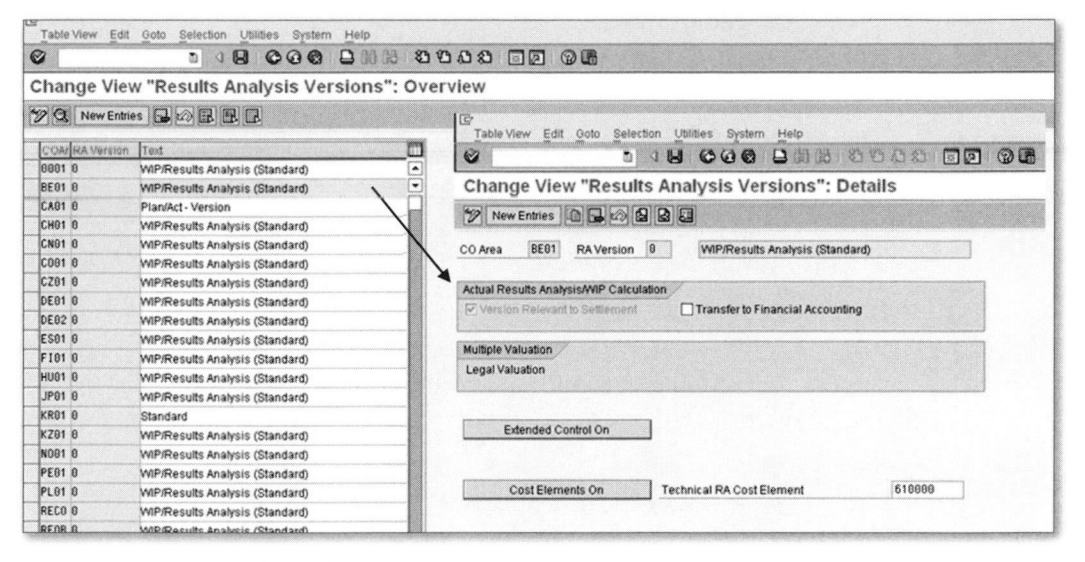

Figure 11.6 Defining Results Analysis Versions

From a CO-PA perspective, you need to define a PA transfer structure that contains at least the technical RA cost element shown in Figure 11.6. If multiple cost elements have been defined for results analysis, for example for WIP calculation, you can use Transaction OKG2 to define technical cost elements during the transfer of WIP into CO-PA. Also notice that there are two buttons—EXTENDED CONTROL ON and COST ELEMENTS ON—and when you click on these buttons, you access additional details for the configuration. In summary, these buttons allow you to do the following when you click on them:

► EXTENDED CONTROL ON button:

  ► Update/RA key: Enter the cutoff period for actual RA/WIP, the effective date before any WIP data has been generated.

  ► Separate creation and usage of the WIP or reserves.

  ► Generate a line item for each posting.

  ► Allow legacy data to be transferred.

  ► Allow deletion of the results analysis data calculated with a results analysis version.

  ► Update the results analysis data under separate results analysis cost elements depending on the results analysis key.

▶ COST ELEMENTS ON button:

   ▶ This button allows you to assign technical RA cost elements to the results analysis version for internal purposes, such as valuated actual costs, calculated costs, and capitalized profit.

   ▶ Reserves for imminent loss.

   ▶ Data for the percentage of completion method, such as calculated revenue and revenue in excess of billings.

4. Define valuation methods for results analysis using Transaction OKG3. In this step, you specify the method by which results analysis is carried out for sales document item, project, and internal orders. The valuation method is defined by the following parameters as shown in Figure 11.7 after clicking on the NEW ENTRIES button:

   ▶ Controlling area to which the object is assigned

   ▶ Results analysis key specified in the object

   ▶ Results analysis version specified in results analysis

   ▶ Results analysis method

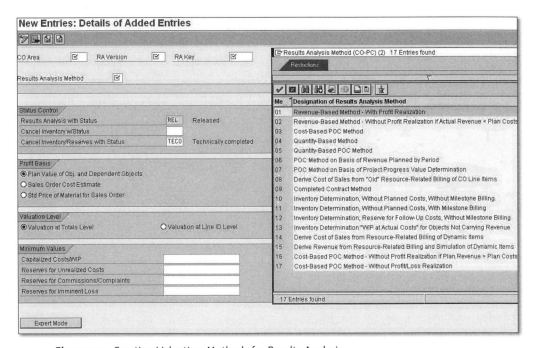

Figure 11.7 Creating Valuation Methods for Results Analysis

- ▶ Status control
- ▶ Profit basis
- ▶ Valuation level
- ▶ Minimum values (if applicable)

As shown in Figure 11.7, Transaction OKG3 provides access to the RESULTS ANALYSIS METHOD screen, and the window shown on the right-hand side appears, which shows 17 pre-delivered methods.

The results analysis method controls which formula is used to calculate the results analysis data that can be generated from SAP Product Cost Controlling (CO-PC) when working in product cost by sales order, in the project system, and for internal orders. It's possible to transfer to SAP CO-PA data generated from results analysis, specifically calculated cost of sales, calculated revenue, and reserves for imminent loss.

5. Next, define line IDs as shown in Figure 11.8 by following this path after using Transaction SPRO: CONTROLLING • PRODUCT COST CONTROLLING • COST OBJECT CONTROLLING • PRODUCT COST BY ORDER • PERIOD END CLOSING • WORK IN PROCESS • DEFINE LINE IDs. Line IDs are utilized to separate costs that need to be capitalized from the costs that cannot be capitalized for the balance sheet financial statement. With line IDs, you can assign the costs incurred for the results analysis object to specific groups such as direct materials costs, productions costs, and indirect costs. As shown in Figure 11.8, each line ID is associated with a controlling area. Its main purpose is to support the calculation of WIP separating the cost components associated with WIP such as WIP Material Reserve, WIP Labor, WIP Labor Reserve, WIP Overhead, and WIP Overhead Reserve following the requirements from FI and for RA.

The WIP, reserves for unrealized costs, reserves for the costs of complaints, and the cost of sales are calculated as a total for each order and apportioned to the line IDs. For each line ID, you can define whether the WIP for that line ID must be capitalized. In comparison, results analysis updates the WIP, reserves for unrealized costs, reserves for the costs of complaints, and the cost of sales to the sales order by line ID.

In order to calculate the WIP at actual costs, you need to create an additional line ID for the cost elements under which the goods receipts are posted. For results analysis, an additional line ID must be created for the cost element under which the revenues are posted.

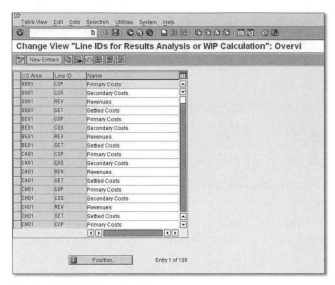

Figure 11.8 Defining Line IDs

6. Use Transaction OKG5 to assign the cost elements for WIP and results analysis to the object to be debited and credited to the line IDs. As shown in Figure 11.9, there are different relationships possible to a Controlling area where the line IDs can be assigned as a requirement to capitalize (REQTOCAP), option to capitalize (OPTTOCAP), and cannot be capitalized (CANNOTBECAP). In addition, Figure 11.9 shows that SAP provides the option to choose a percentage of the line ID to capitalize (%OPTTOCAP) and a percentage that cannot be capitalized (%CANNOTBECAP).

Change View "Assignment of Cost Elements for WIP and Results Analysis"

New Entries

CO A	RA V	RA Key	Masked Co	Ori	Masked Co	Maske	Business Proc.	D	V	Apport	Accou	Valid-Fro	ReqToCap	OptToCap	CannotBeCap	% OptToCap	% CannotBeCap
0001	0		00004+++++	++++				+	+		++	001.1997	COP				
0001	0		00006+++++	++++	++++++++++	++++++		+	+		++	001.1997	COS				
0001	0		000080++++	++++				+	+		++	001.1997	REV				
0001	0		000081++++	++++				+	+		++	001.1997	SET				
0001	0		000088++++	++++				+	+		++	001.1997	REV				
0001	0		0000895+++	++++				+	+		++	001.1997	SET				
BE01	0		00006+++++	++++				+	+		++	001.1997	COP				
BE01	0		000070++++	++++				+	+		++	001.1997	REV				
BE01	0		00008+++++	++++	++++++++++	++++++		+	+		++	001.1997	COS				
BE01	0		000081++++	++++				+	+		++	001.1997	SET				
BE01	0		0000895+++	++++				+	+		++	001.1997	SET				
CA01	0		00004+++++	++++				+	+		++	001.1997	REV				
CA01	0		000044++++	++++				+	+		++	001.1997	REV				
CA01	0		000051++++	++++				+	+		++	001.1997	COP				

Figure 11.9 Assigning Cost Elements for WIP and Results Analysis

For example, if you only want to capitalize 90% of the costs for internal activities and overhead surcharges as WIP, you need to define a line ID that contains all costs of the relevant secondary cost elements. Input 10% in the %CANNOT-BECAP column shown in Figure 11.9, and then enter the line ID in the REQTO-CAP column under which the remaining 90% of the WIP is to be written.

7. As previously mentioned, once you create a line ID, you need to perform results analysis to a cost element under which the results analysis data is updated. In order to perform this process, access Transaction OKG4 as shown in Figure 11.10.

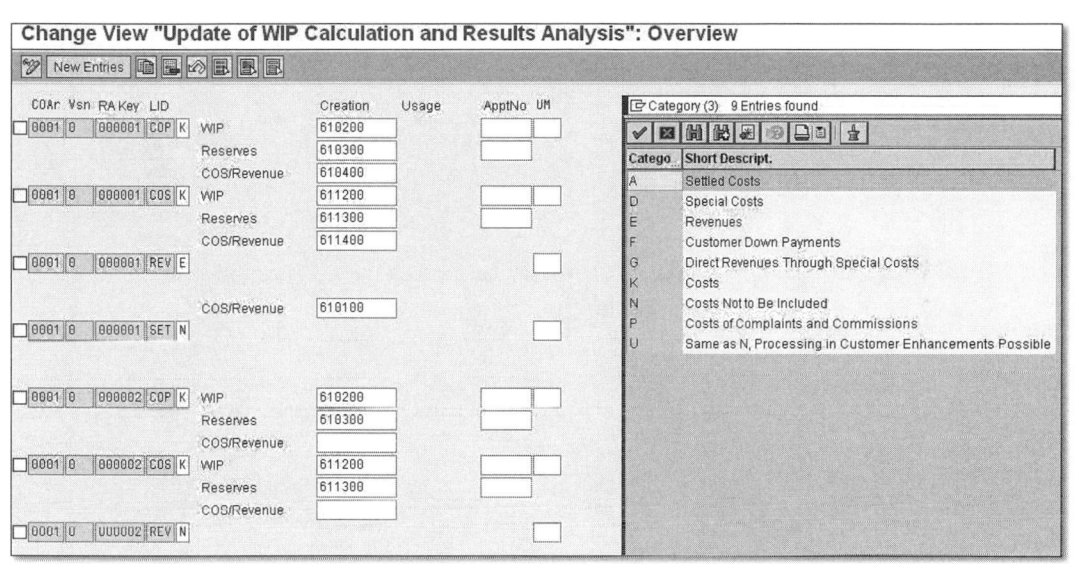

Figure 11.10 Define Update for Results Analysis

As shown in Figure 11.10, you can associate each of the line IDs to a particular cost element based on the combination of Controlling area, results analysis key (RA key) and line ID. Notice the input box next to the LID (line ID) in Figure 11.10 with different letters—if you click on it, the screen shown on the right-hand side appears, identifying the category that groups the different postings. Figure 11.10 identifies that these are the possible categories available.

In addition, the APPNO box allows you to specify the capitalized costs apportionment number that defines how the capitalized costs or revenue in excess of billings is calculated in results analysis or the WIP is calculated in WIP calculation. For example, if you enter "70" as the number for the line ID "EK" (unit costs) and "30" as the number for the line ID "GK" (overhead), then 70% of the capitalized costs created in results analysis are regarded as inventory for unit costs and 30% as inventory for overhead.

8. Using Transaction OKGC, you can define the valuation method for WIP as shown in Figure 11.11 for either actual or target costs. Here, you specify that WIP calculation mode is when the order has the status REL. The calculated WIP will be cancelled when the order status changes to DLV or TECO. You maintain this data for the CO area, RA version, and RA key combination.

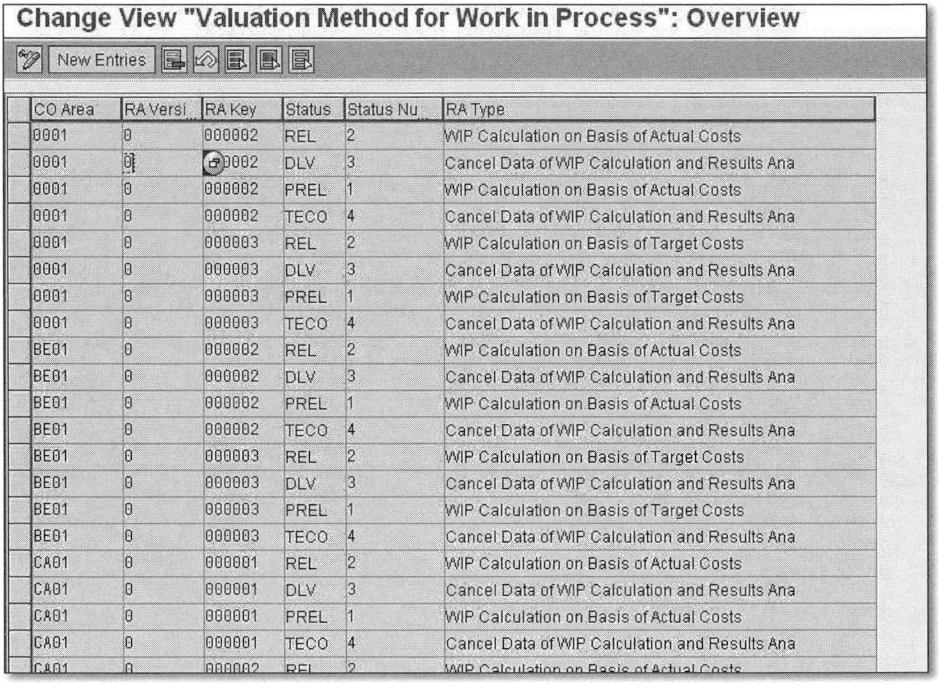

Change View "Valuation Method for Work in Process": Overview

New Entries

CO Area	RA Versi	RA Key	Status	Status Nu	RA Type
0001	0	000002	REL	2	WIP Calculation on Basis of Actual Costs
0001	0	000002	DLV	3	Cancel Data of WIP Calculation and Results Ana
0001	0	000002	PREL	1	WIP Calculation on Basis of Actual Costs
0001	0	000002	TECO	4	Cancel Data of WIP Calculation and Results Ana
0001	0	000003	REL	2	WIP Calculation on Basis of Target Costs
0001	0	000003	DLV	3	Cancel Data of WIP Calculation and Results Ana
0001	0	000003	PREL	1	WIP Calculation on Basis of Target Costs
0001	0	000003	TECO	4	Cancel Data of WIP Calculation and Results Ana
BE01	0	000002	REL	2	WIP Calculation on Basis of Actual Costs
BE01	0	000002	DLV	3	Cancel Data of WIP Calculation and Results Ana
BE01	0	000002	PREL	1	WIP Calculation on Basis of Actual Costs
BE01	0	000002	TECO	4	Cancel Data of WIP Calculation and Results Ana
BE01	0	000003	REL	2	WIP Calculation on Basis of Target Costs
BE01	0	000003	DLV	3	Cancel Data of WIP Calculation and Results Ana
BE01	0	000003	PREL	1	WIP Calculation on Basis of Target Costs
BE01	0	000003	TECO	4	Cancel Data of WIP Calculation and Results Ana
CA01	0	000001	REL	2	WIP Calculation on Basis of Actual Costs
CA01	0	000001	DLV	3	Cancel Data of WIP Calculation and Results Ana
CA01	0	000001	PREL	1	WIP Calculation on Basis of Actual Costs
CA01	0	000001	TECO	4	Cancel Data of WIP Calculation and Results Ana
CA01	0	000002	REL	2	WIP Calculation on Basis of Actual Costs

Figure 11.11 Valuation Method for Work in Process

9. Now, define posting rules for WIP calculation using Transaction OKG8 as shown in Figure 11.12. These rules are defined by Controlling area, company code, RA version, and maintaining the RA category WIPR (WIP cost, required to be capitalized) and RUCR (reserve for unrealized cost). Generally, you'll need to maintain both the P&L Acct (to reflect changes to stock) and the BalSheetAcct (WIP) columns. These G/L accounts are posted in the FI component. In addition, you can associate the posting rules that affect WIP

calculations and results analysis with the accounting standard that the rule is following such as GAAP, IAS, or IFRS.

Change View "Posting Rules in WIP Calculation and Results Analysis": O

New Entries

CO Ar	Comp	RA Ver	RA category	Bal./Cr.	Cost Elem.	Record	P&L Acct	BalSheetAcct	Accounting Principle
0001	0001	0	WIPR			0	891000	791000	
0001	RERF	0	WIPR			0	891000	791000	
BE01	BE01	0	WIPR			0	712000	320000	
CA01	CA01	0	WIPR			0	700770	132000	
CH01	CH01	0	WIPR			0	30800	12800	
CN01	0001	0	WIPR			0	891000	791000	
CN01	CN01	0	WIPR			0	91092000	14810101	
CN01	RERF	0	WIPR			0	891000	791000	
C001	C001	0	WIPR			0	14658910	14657910	
CZ01	CZ01	0	WIPR			0	611000	121000	
DE01	DE01	0	WIPR			0	891000	781000	
DE02	DE02	0	WIPR			0	521500	215000	
ES01	ES01	0	WIPR			0	710000	330000	
FI01	FI01	0	WIPR			0	494000	144000	
HU01	HU01	0	WIPR			0	582100	280100	
JP01	JP01	0	WIPR			0	891000	126000	
KR01	KR01	0	WIPR			0	51000800	12040100	
PE01	PE01	0	WIPR			0	601000	230000	

Figure 11.12 Posting Rules for WIP Calculations

10. You can restrict the number of accounts associated with the WIP calculations by using Transaction OKG6 to assign a number range for the WIP transactions as shown in Figure 11.13. Some of the types of number range groups are defined as follows:

  ► KABG AUTOMAT. WIP/RESULTS ANALYSIS

  ► KABM MANUAL WIP/RESULTS ANALYSIS

  ► KSWP PRIM. TARGET COST CALC. (WIP)

  ► KSWS SEC. TARGET COST CALC. (WIP)

  We recommend checking with your SAP ECC FICO lead to discuss further implications associated with the number ranges and postings.

11. Now you need to set up the period end WIP calculation process, which is the process of running WIP at period end. You can access this with Transaction KKAX for individual order processing or KKAO for collective order processing, as shown in Figures 11.14 and 11.15.

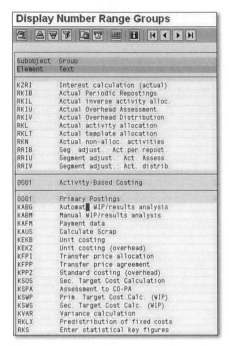

Figure 11.13 Assigning Number Ranges for the WIP Transaction Groups

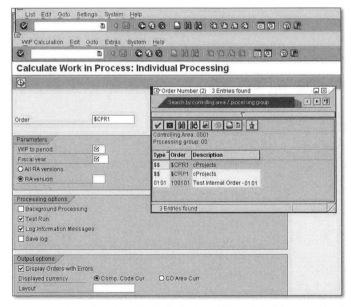

Figure 11.14 Performing WIP Calculation at Period End for an Individual Order

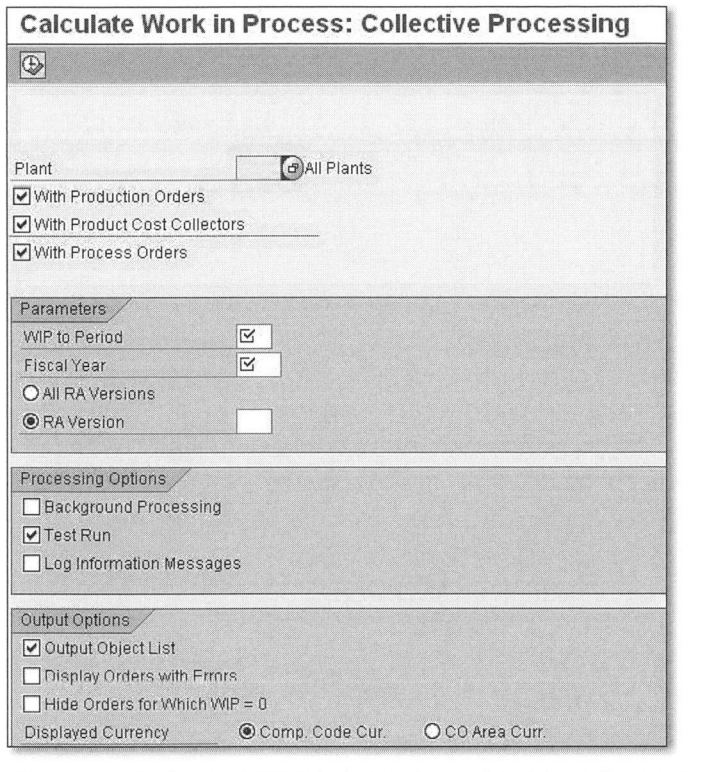

Figure 11.15 Performing WIP Calculation at Period End for Collective Orders

Using these transactions, the system debits the WIP account and credits the inventory change account automatically. The entire WIP account values are reversed and new entries are passed to the following month. When the order is fully delivered, no additional WIP entries are passed.

11.1.13   Conclusion

We've reviewed the procedure to work with results analysis in the product costing component/product cost/sales order components. It's possible to focus the information from the CO-PC component associated with results analysis information attached to the sales order items for engineer-to-order environments and internal orders that carry revenue.

Because the revenues affecting net income and the costs affecting net income are usually different from the actual revenues and actual costs posted in FI, the result shown in CO-PA is different from the profit/loss in FI. The difference between the value in CO-PA and the value in FI can be offset by means of posting reserves and inventories. Once the results analysis values are available in your product costing environment, you can settle this data to CO-PA using integrated planning ("actual and plan results analysis"). This function only applies to projects and internal orders. It is irrelevant for sales order items. The correction postings are made through the settlement of results analysis data.

11.2 Sales and Profit Planning

A main function of sales and profit planning for costing-based Profitability Analysis is the valuation of entered planning values, such as sales volume, with price lists of the Sales and Distribution (SD) system and imputed costs and sales deductions. In account-based Profitability Analysis, amounts and quantities can be entered by cost element for any market segment and user-selectable planning level. However, no valuation functions are available.

11.3 External Data Transfer

The only way you can transfer actual external or legacy data into account-based CO-PA is to post the corresponding data to FI. The long text of error message KE093 explains why this restriction applies. All FI document line items that have been assigned to a profitability segment automatically generate a line item in account-based Profitability Analysis as well.

11.4 Summary

In this chapter, we've briefly covered the general concepts and changes required to switch to the account-based model of CO-PA from the costing-based model. Costing-based CO-PA is derived from value fields. Account-based CO-PA is often used for reconciliation of data between FI-G/L accounting and CO cost element accounting. Costing-based CO-PA is more analytical but not as accurate as account-based CO-PA.

In addition, account-based CO-PA is updated during the delivery (goods issue) and the creation of billing documents. For this reason, the COGS is updated in CO-PA at the time of delivery (goods issue); revenue discounts and freight are not updated until billing documents are created. The update of COGS in account-based CO-PA might generate significant differences between revenue and billing. These differences make account-based CO-PA out of balance with costing-based CO-PA, and vice versa.

You can transfer detailed information from the CO-PC component associated with results analysis and WIP calculations to CO-PA using line IDs to provide a greater level of detail of the cost values. Valuation strategies, costing sheets, and material cost estimates all support the calculation process of costs associated with operations, and thus can be sophisticated or quite simplified processes depending on the level of complexity of the conditions set up during their configuration.

Next, Chapter 12 explores some tips and tricks relating to summarization levels, the Report-Report-Interface (RRI), and report splitting.

Tips and tricks can improve your reporting capabilities inside CO-PA. Some of the techniques we explore in this chapter are designed to make your environment as user-friendly as possible without losing powerful reporting capabilities.

12 Tips and Tricks with CO-PA

We're close to coming to the end of our discussion of CO-PA with SAP, at least with the most general and basic components we addressed in this book.

In this chapter, we'll cover some general and important tips and tricks to consider in your implementation. You don't need to apply them all; instead, select those that make sense based on your project requirements. Some of these tips come from the author's personal experience with different projects and clients, others from different literature and sources, such as *Financials Expert* magazine and others. This chapter has been written for advanced users, so keep that in mind as you follow our discussion.

12.1 Integrate Planning Layouts with Microsoft Excel

This first tip might be important for users who don't feel comfortable working within the traditional SAP environment. For this reason, CO-PA includes a configuration checkbox that allows the layout to accept information after changing into a Microsoft Excel environment. Some consultants or advanced users may already know about this, but it's a tricky change, and it's not always clear if this capability is available.

In Figure 12.1, a screenshot from the CO-PA planning framework is displayed. Notice that in the INTEGRATED EXCEL area at the bottom of the screen, the ACTIVE checkbox is selected. This changes the output of the CO-PA planning framework to display the information in a Microsoft Excel environment without leaving the SAP system.

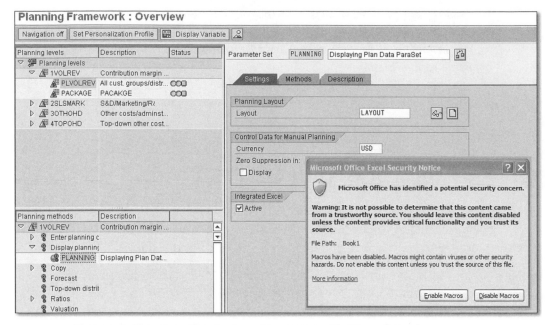

Figure 12.1 Changing a Planning Layout to Interact with Microsoft Excel

As also shown in Figure 12.1, once you execute the layout, you might receive a SECURITY WARNING message to notify you that the document you're opening contains macros. If this message appears, click on the ENABLE MACROS button and then review the change in the environment, which will now look similar to that shown in Figure 12.2.

> **Caution**
>
> If you plan to use the Microsoft Excel environment inside CO-PA, verify with your system administrator that the Microsoft Excel integration with SAP has been correctly installed.

Note that you're only able to access Microsoft Excel with restrictions in place; that is, some of its functions will be either not available or not working.

As shown on the right-hand side of the screen in Figure 12.2, the Microsoft Excel environment appears with the information controlled by the package PLVOLREV, selected on the left-hand side of the same figure. Just as with a regular layout, at the left bottom of the screen you can select any planning method; for example, ENTER PLANNING DATA or DISPLAY PLANNING DATA. As shown in Figure 12.2, we're working in the ENTER PLANNING DATA planning method; therefore, we can modify the data available to users, save, and go back to the SAP environment.

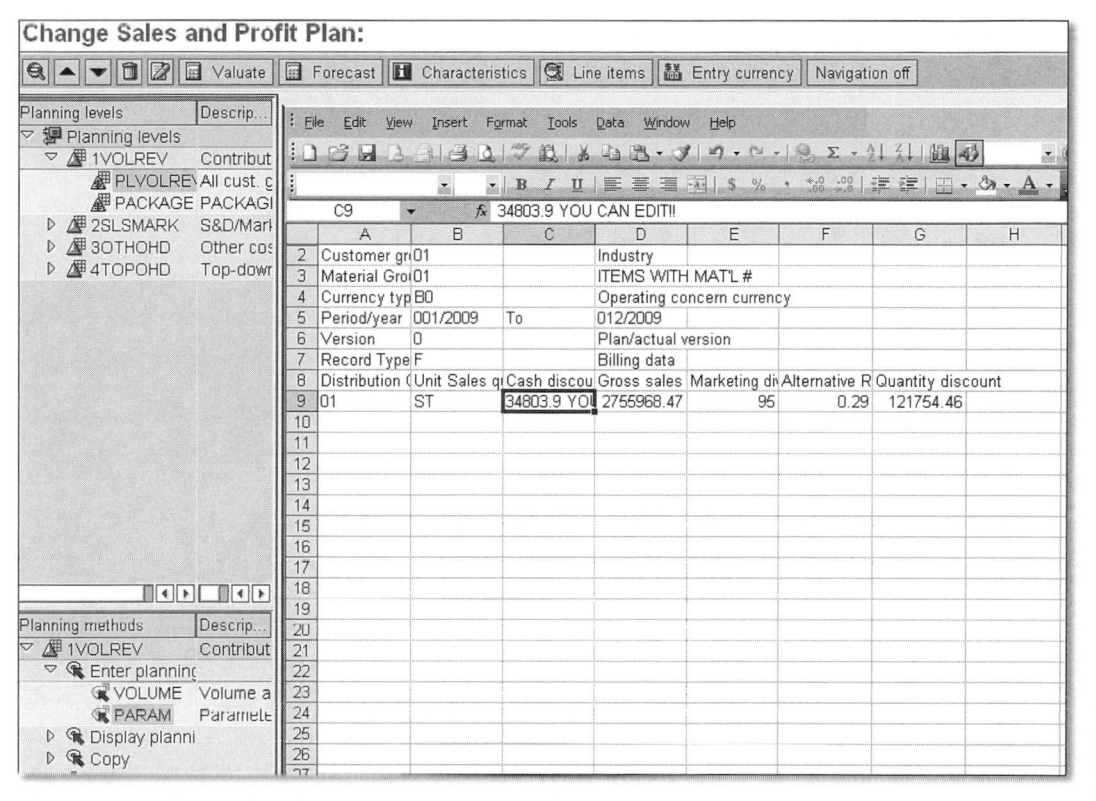

Figure 12.2 Working with a Planning Layout in Microsoft Excel

When you've made your changes, click on the BACK icon to return to the SAP GUI environment. For comparison purposes, review Figure 12.3, which shows the same layout but within the SAP GUI environment, after deselecting the ACTIVE option in the INTEGRATED EXCEL area shown earlier in Figure 12.1.

Even though it might not be the most sophisticated tip or trick, this option should be quite useful to sell your planning applications to different users, especially those in finance who actively use Microsoft Excel in their reporting.

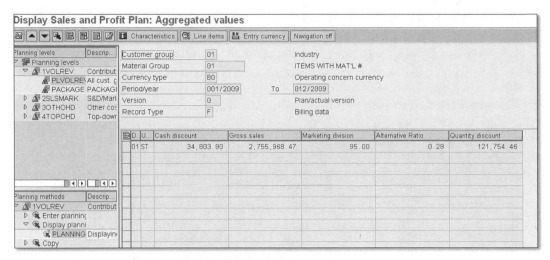

Figure 12.3 Planning Layout within the SAP Environment

Now, let's review a more important tip: working with summarization levels in CO-PA.

12.2 Working with Summarization Levels

In general, *summarization levels* can be defined as tables with an update frequency. They are presummarized data for selected characteristics that can be created to run as the first layer that the system uses for data extraction. The alternative, for the system to read the different transactional tables and extract the data every time that it is required by a report, might take considerably more time. When summarization levels are used, the SAP OLTP system generates, loads, and updates tables when extracting the data for a report, thus maximizing your overall extraction performance. In broad terms, to create and use summarization levels, follow these steps:

1. Define summarization levels using Transaction KEDV (more on how to do this in a moment).

2. Tell R/3 or SAP ERP ECC 6.0 to load the level by executing a report with Transaction KEDU.

3. To update your levels, schedule the report to run periodically by creating a variant.

4. Schedule a batch job to run the variant.

Now, let's look at defining and using summarization levels in more detail. From our brief discussion of this topic in Chapter 10, recall the summarization related options on the OPTIONS tab of a report, shown again here in Figure 12.4.

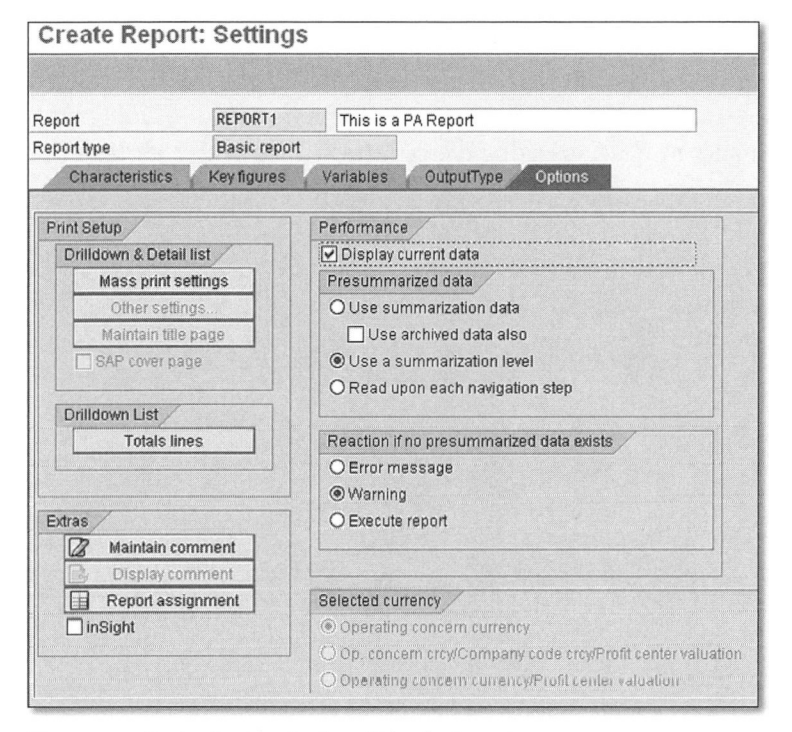

Figure 12.4 Reviewing the Options Tab of a Report

We'll use this tab to review how to create and work with summarization levels in more detail:

1. To start, click on the EXECUTE icon for DEFINE SUMMARIZATION LEVELS in the PROFITABILITY ANALYSIS • TOOLS menu shown in Figure 12.5.

2. If this is the first time that you access the summarization option, click on the PROFITABILITY ANALYSIS • TOOLS • HAVE PROPOSAL CREATED AUTOMATICALLY object as shown in Figure 12.5 for the SAP system to generate proposed summarization levels based on the use of your different reports and data in general.

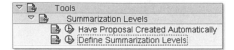

Figure 12.5 Defining Summarization Levels

3. Review the screen shown in Figure 12.6, where the SAP system suggests possible summarization levels and the characteristics used in each of them. The information shown in Figure 12.6 also includes the percentage of records you can expect to simplify extraction by using each of type of summarization level. For example, the proposal says that Summarization Level 80001 provides 42.86% of savings, and it's the first one that the system chooses, including most of the characteristics in your operating concern (identified with an asterisk [*] in the upper level of the report).

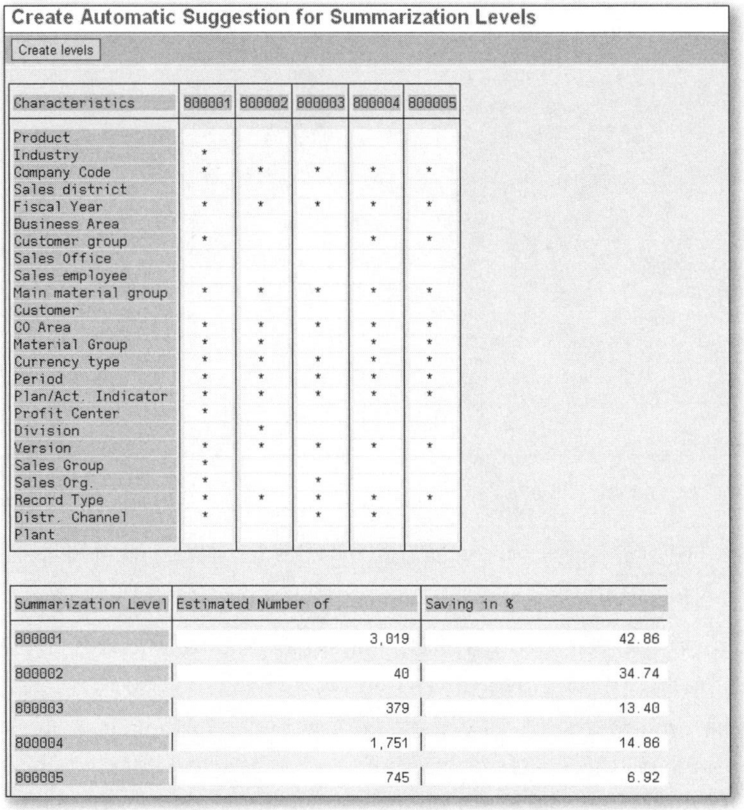

Create Automatic Suggestion for Summarization Levels

Create levels					

Characteristics	800001	800002	800003	800004	800005
Product					
Industry	*				
Company Code	*	*	*	*	*
Sales district					
Fiscal Year	*	*	*	*	*
Business Area					
Customer group	*			*	*
Sales Office					
Sales employee					
Main material group	*	*	*	*	*
Customer					
CO Area	*	*	*	*	*
Material Group	*	*		*	*
Currency type	*	*	*	*	*
Period	*	*	*	*	*
Plan/Act. Indicator	*	*	*	*	*
Profit Center	*				
Division		*			
Version	*	*	*	*	*
Sales Group	*				
Sales Org.	*		*		
Record Type	*	*	*	*	*
Distr. Channel	*		*	*	
Plant					

Summarization Level	Estimated Number of	Saving in %
800001	3,019	42.86
800002	40	34.74
800003	379	13.40
800004	1,751	14.86
800005	745	6.92

Figure 12.6 Reviewing the Automatically Calculated Summarization Levels

4. Accept the default summarization levels displayed in Figure 12.6, and identify the best choice: in this case Summarization Level 80001 provides the best savings in percentages.

5. Click on the CREATE LEVELS button shown at the top of Figure 12.6 to generate your automatic summarization levels.

The summarization levels we just created are empty tables that now need to be populated with data. To do so, we need to identify the default parameters based on the history of usage of the system, using the following steps:

1. Execute the TOOLS • SUMMARIZATION LEVELS • DEFINE SUMMARIZATION LEVELS object, and the screen shown in Figure 12.7 appears. Notice that the automatically calculated summarization levels are ACTIVE, WITHOUT DATA.

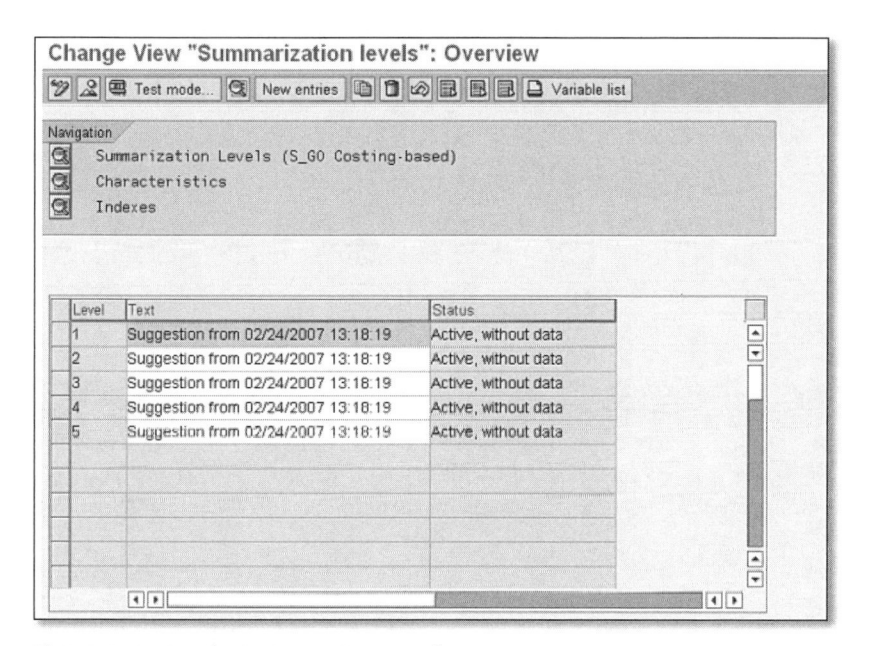

Figure 12.7 View the Summarization Levels

2. Use Transaction KEDU to display the screen where you can populate the summarization levels (tables) with data, as shown in Figure 12.8. Here you must define the OPERATING CONCERN (S_GO), TYPE OF PROFITABILITY ANALYSIS (1 = costing-based), SUMMARIZATION LEVELS (1 = 80001), and make sure that the BUILD NEW LEVELS option is checked.

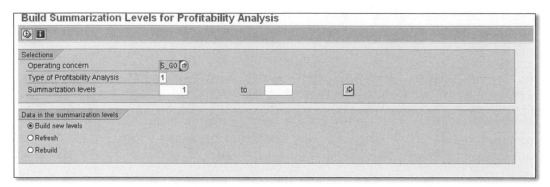

Figure 12.8 Loading Data into Your Summarization Levels

3. Click on the EXECUTE icon.

Tips & Tricks

Summarization levels can be used for specific reports (and the fields used depend on each report) for manual and automatic planning and cost center assessments, among others.

4. The screen shown in Figure 12.9 appears and notifies you that the summarization levels have been created without problems, based on the parameters established in the previous screen.

Note

To update the levels periodically and automatically, you must define a variant. Also, you can run the screen displayed in Figure 12.8 and select either the REBUILD or REFRESH option depending on the changes that might have happened in the data selection parameters of your system.

5. Return to the report, and select the OPTIONS tab previously displayed in Figure 12.4.

6. Select the USE A SUMMARIZATION LEVEL radio button. Your report performance should now be improved to make extraction faster because the system will first look in the data contained in the summarization levels to perform the extraction, which is more commonly used. If not available, the system will go directly to the different CO-PA tables to update the information.

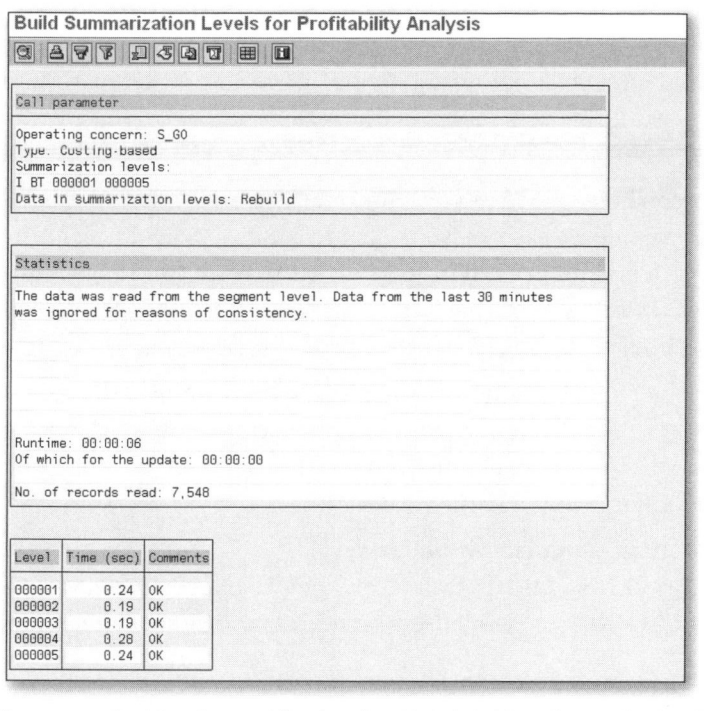

Figure 12.9 Revision Screen After Loading Data into Your Summarization Levels

We'll conclude our discussion of summarization levels with these tips:

▶ **Do not include constants**
  Summarization levels are designed for characteristics or values that change, not for characteristics or values that are always the same. For example, a customer group is more likely to change during the extraction than a company code when there is only one company code available in the system.

▶ **Avoid using redundant summarization levels**
  If summarization level A contains characteristics X1 and X2, and summarization level B contains characteristics X1, X2, and X3, it doesn't make sense to use summarization level A because it's already part of summarization level B, and the difference at the segment level in number of records isn't significant enough to use summarization level A instead of summarization level B.

▶ **Add dependent characteristics as part of your summarization levels**
  A characteristic that depends on others will affect the performance during the extraction. Therefore, if as an example you add the characteristic customer ID

to your summarization level, and the characteristics customer group, customer region, and customer category are also part of your operating concern or your CO-PA data, it's much better if you include all of them in the summarization level to avoid delays during extraction because their information is highly dependent.

▸ **Avoid fixed characteristic values in your summarization levels**
Evaluate the data volume of each of your characteristics to avoid managing small data volumes in different summarization levels that are controlled with a fixed characteristic. In other words, avoid using fixed characteristics because they will perform similarly to constants.

▸ **Do not use more than six characteristics per summarization level**
Remember, summarization levels are about being selective. You don't need to use all of the characteristics available in your transaction data, only the ones that are used most often to simplify their extraction.

▸ **Do not create too many summarization levels**
Between eight and twenty summarization levels is more than enough! Summarization levels are not "free;" they require resources that include memory and storage space.

▸ **Force all summarization levels to have the same timestamp**
In other words, build all of your summarization levels and update all of them at the same time so the data is consistent in your reports.

▸ **Delete older summarization levels**
Use Transaction KEDV and review the date-last-read status to avoid using summarization levels that are no longer used by any report or object.

▸ **Update your summarization levels daily**
Update your summarization levels each night by using a variant and a scheduled job.

▸ **Review your definitions periodically**
There are always changes during the lifetime of your implementation, and some characteristics will be used more often than others, but this might also change over time. Eventually you'll know which characteristics you must include in your summarization levels and which ones you can remove. Perform this process periodically to achieve optimum performance.

12.3   Performing Report Splitting

Report splitting (RS) means taking a report with a certain number of characteristics and generating two or more reports from it to reduce the number of characteristics used to perform the data extraction. This improves system performance. Situations in which to use RS include:

▶ When you have reports that have many characteristics, and only part of them are required for a specific level of users.

▶ When reports use a lot of characteristics and values and take a long time to generate.

▶ When multiple users require the same drilldown with the same characteristics.

Tips & Tricks

The reason for using RS and the Report-Report-Interface (RRI), discussed in detail in the next section, is to allow the breakdown of transactional data. As a general rule, R/3 or SAP ERP ECC 6.0 transactional data is indivisible once posted in the respective value fields, meaning you cannot go back to the original components that describe an account unless each component was previously specified as an independent object. For example, if gross margin (GM) is calculated as the difference between total sales and cost of goods sold (COGS), the last two fields must be specified in addition to the GM before the values are posted; otherwise, it isn't possible to go back and review the calculation performed. Using RS, you can have the GM value in one report and call the stored values of COGS and sales in a different report, if required.

To create a split report, follow these steps:

1. Using the regular SAP menu, access the following path, as shown in Figure 12.10: CONTROLLING • PROFITABILITY ANALYSIS • INFORMATION SYSTEM • KE3L – SPLIT REPORT. Alternatively, use Transaction KE3L.

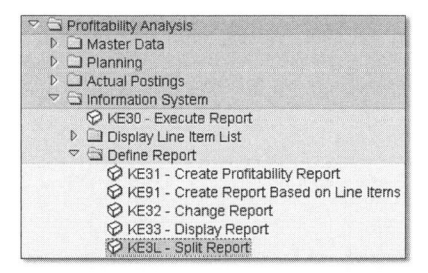

Figure 12.10 Accessing the Split Report Functionality

Note

You cannot access the split report functionality by using the IMG menu (Transaction SPRO) that we've worked with throughout the rest of the book.

2. The SPLIT REPORT screen appears and requests the following parameters: OPER-ATING CONCERN, TYPE OF PROFITABILITY ANALYSIS, and REPORT NAME. Enter "S_GO," "1," and "REPORT2" into the respective fields, as shown in Figure 12.11.

Figure 12.11 Reviewing the Split Report Screen

3. Click on the EXECUTE icon.

Tips & Tricks

It may be obvious, but still: The minimum number of characteristics required in a report to perform RS is two. (Otherwise, why would you need to use this functionality?) In addition, if you select all of the characteristics available in your current report, why are you splitting the report in the first place? RS is meant to simplify the information being displayed and to cut an original report into smaller pieces.

4. As shown in Figure 12.12, the SPLIT REPORT screen asks you to select the char-acteristics to use in the new report and provide a name for the new report. For our example in Figure 12.12, select MATERIAL GROUP as the characteristic to use and specify RECEIVER REPORT as "ReportSplit1."

5. Click on the checkmark icon.

6. You receive the information message REPORT REPORT2 WAS SPLIT. Click on the checkmark icon.

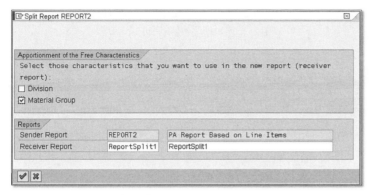

Figure 12.12 Creating the Split Report

7. Now, use Transaction KE32 to access the CHANGE PROFITABILITY REPORT object to see the list of the available reports, as shown in Figure 12.13.

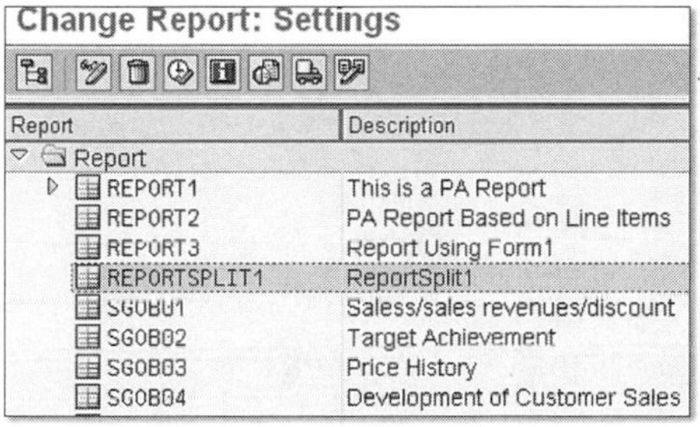

Figure 12.13 Reviewing the Creation of the ReportSplit1 Report

Here you can see that you've generated REPORTSPLIT1, a reduced version of the original REPORT2 with a selected number of characteristics. In addition, you've reduced the search time for the characteristics because you narrowed down the size of the search! However, there are cases when another type of functionality might be useful, namely when you want to attach different reports with common characteristics and generate a drilldown. This is the function of the RRI discussed in the next section.

12.4 Working with the Report-Report Interface (RRI)

What happens when you have multiple reports, and you have common characteristics between them? Can you integrate all of them to make them look like a single report without affecting performance? Can you configure a report list to manually navigate to the lower-level report using a menu path? The answer is yes to all of these questions, and the RRI has been created to address this issue.

In general, the RRI is a high-level analysis to improve interfacing with other elements besides simple reports, enabling you to connect a total of seven types of reports:

- ▶ Report portfolio
- ▶ SAP Business Warehouse (BW) query
- ▶ SAP query
- ▶ Drilldown reporting
- ▶ ABAP report program
- ▶ Report Writer
- ▶ A basic transaction

The next issue is when to use RRI:

- ▶ When you want to link different types of reports, such as ABAP programs to Report Painter reports or SAP queries to drilldown reports.
- ▶ When users don't use a single drilldown approach so RS is not a viable option.
- ▶ When splitting a report, users are limited to specific drilldowns.
- ▶ When drilldown is the best way to present your data and based on a callup chain that allows access to other SAP applications.
- ▶ When you want to combine information generated in RS.

Now, with a better idea of how and when to work with RRI, follow these steps to use the RRI process, as illustrated in Figure 12.14:

1. Access the CHANGE REPORT screen and select the report you want to configure; in this case REPORT1, as shown in step ❶ in Figure 12.14.
2. Select the OPTIONS tab as shown in step ❷.
3. Click on the REPORT ASSIGNMENT button as shown in step ❸.
4. The ASSIGN REPORT screen appears. Click on the plus sign icon, as shown in step ❹.
5. The ADD DRILLDOWN REPORT screen appears, as shown in step ❺.
6. Click on the OTHER REPORT TYPE button as shown in step ❻.

7. Now see the seven types of reports as shown in step **7**, and select the report of your choice.

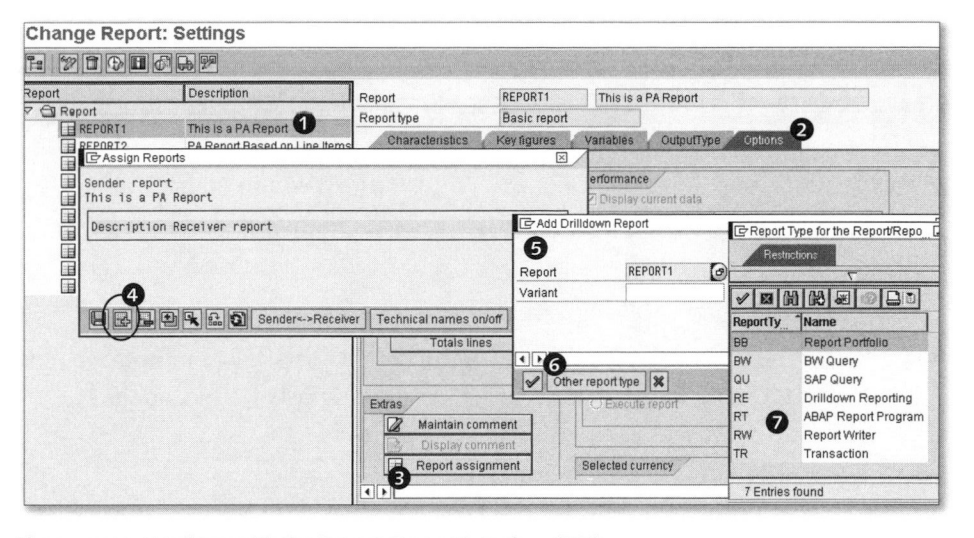

Figure 12.14 Working with the Report-Report Interface (RRI)

Now, let's say we want to perform drilldown and attach two reports to our basic report REPORT1 following the steps shown in Figure 12.14, but we want to create a drilldown structure attached to REPORT1, as shown in Figure 12.15, called PRICE HISTORY and ANALYSIS CM II.

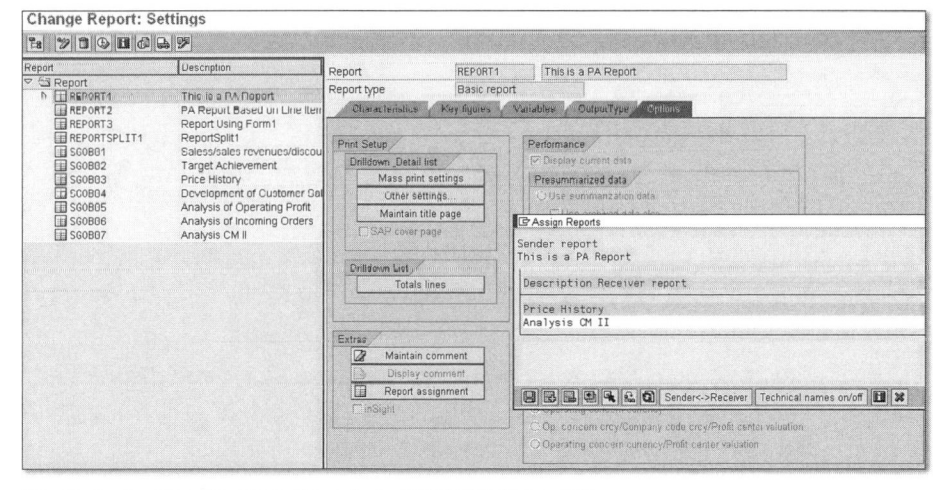

Figure 12.15 Attaching Two Reports to REPORT1 Using RRI

To create the drilldown structure based on RRI, follow these steps:

1. Using the REPORT ASSIGNMENT button, select the PRICE HISTORY and ANALYSIS CM II reports, as shown in Figure 12.15.

2. Click on the SAVE icon to attach the reports.

3. Save your changes to REPORT1 using the SAVE icon in the upper portion of the screen.

4. Execute the report REPORT1 THIS IS A PA REPORT, shown in Figure 12.15.

5. Fill out the report selection parameters like a traditional R/3 or SAP ERP ECC 6.0 report.

6. Select either CURRENT or SAVED (frozen) data, if available.

7. Review Figure 12.16. It seems like the report ran successfully, but nothing new seems to have happened, correct? Where are the reports we just added?

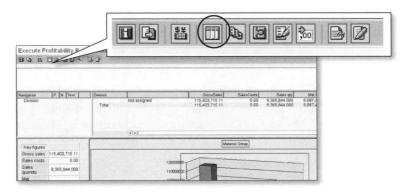

Figure 12.16 Results for REPORT1

8. Look closely at the icon menu shown in Figure 12.16. The icon that is identified by a circle is how you access the callup reports defined with the RRI functionality.

9. Click on the callup report icon, or enter the keystrokes [Ctrl] + [Shift] + [F3], or use the GOTO • CALL UP REPORT option in the menu at the top of the report during execution time.

10. The SELECT REPORT screen appears as shown in Figure 12.17, and displays any SAP executable objects available and linked to REPORT1 to perform a drilldown. Select the one you want, let's say PRICE HISTORY, and click on the checkmark icon.

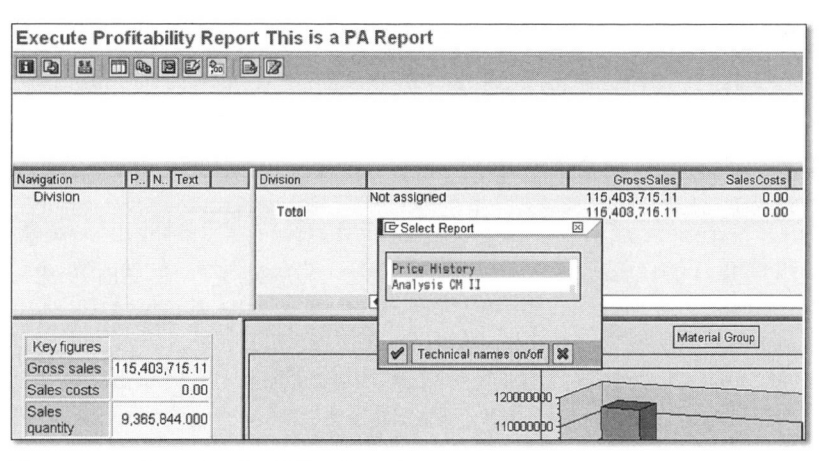

Figure 12.17 Accessing the Callup Reports

11. The PRICE HISTORY report is executed, maintaining the report selection parameters input for REPORT1 because we've built what is called a *callup chain*. This means two object reports are sharing the same parameter definition at the same time, improving system performance because the system does not need the parameters to extract the data. Instead, the system accesses data already generated. The results of this drilldown are shown in Figure 12.18.

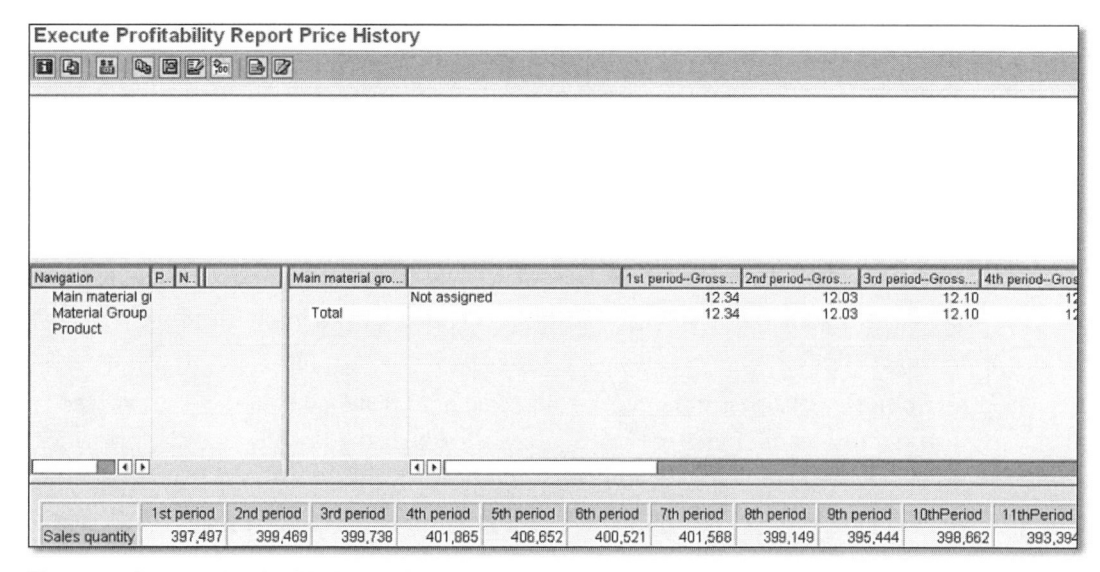

Figure 12.18 Accessing the RRI Report Price History

> **Tips & Tricks**
>
> You can break the relationship created with the RRI at any time. Based on this informa-tion, experiment with the other types of objects, such as ABAP queries, Report Writer reports, and so on, that can be linked to the callup navigation functionality.

Now, let's think of a more complex scenario using the objects shown in step ❼, displayed earlier in Figure 12.14. For example, you may have a report that depends on an ABAP program that must be generated, and once that's ready, you can access the information in another report. You can review your final SAP NetWeaver BW query that collects that information using scheduled variants that will run in the background after your ABAP program ran and update your final information reports that are accessible in your SAP NetWeaver BW query.

Therefore, the functionalities and interactions that can be performed using the reports, SAP NetWeaver BW queries, SAP queries, drilldown reporting, ABAP report program, Report Writer, and transaction objects make more sense of the power of the RRI functionality to improve navigation while improving the end-user interface. Regardless of the level of complexity you decide to use with your RRI reports, remember to maintain the best and easiest environment for your users. Try to keep things clear and simple.

12.5   Final Tips

Finally, here are a few suggestions that are important to consider when working with any type of SAP implementation, and that can also affect your CO-PA imple-mentation:

▶ Don't allow the IT department to manage your implementation and control the budget for the project. Otherwise, your project might never be implemented because your requirements and timelines don't coincide with those of the IT department.

▶ Do have a business person or project manager from a business area involved in the implementation. This helps you ensure that the business needs, priorities, and budget are correctly controlled.

▶ Make sure to have an implementation plan that identifies times and activities required for your project. You don't have to be an SAP expert, but having a clear idea of your goals written down in a document is a good idea to have for your implementation team.

▶ Have your requirements clearly defined in a formal document and communicated and reviewed with your IT department.

With these considerations in mind and a complete commitment to understanding your business processes and implementing that knowledge using the SAP functionalities of CO-PA, or any other component, you're on your way to a successful implementation.

CO-PA is a great tool to improve the consolidation, reporting, and planning capabilities of your R/3 or SAP ERP ECC 6.0 environment. However, remember to spend time reviewing your requirements and data volume to determine if CO-PA or SAP NetWeaver Business Intelligence (BI)/SAP NetWeaver BW is the best choice for your final goals and for system performance.

12.6   Summary

In this chapter, we explored important and useful functionalities to improve the performance and interface of your reports generated in CO-PA. We reviewed key elements that are useful in most implementations, such as Microsoft Excel integration, RS, RRI, and summarization levels. All of them can make the lives of your users better and improve the performance and look and feel of your application. Hopefully, these tips and tricks will be useful to you.

In Chapter 13, we'll explore how to transfer and report with SAP CO-PA as part of the SAP BusinessObjects environment, and also the kind of configuration processes required to perform reporting of CO-PA data in the SAP NetWeaver BW environment.

When CO-PA analytical and reporting capabilities are limited, there are additional support tools available in SAP to improve analysis, calculations, data display, and give you more user-friendly environments. In this chapter we'll review a few of these tools as part of SAP BusinessObjects as additional ways to support, enhance, or replace functionalities from SAP CO-PA, depending on the IT strategy and long-term goals of your organization.

13 Enhancing CO-PA with SAP Business-Objects Tools

It isn't a secret that SAP technologies are evolving and providing much better ways to analyze data, deploy applications, provide better security, and much more. This chapter has been introduced since the previous edition to provide an overview of the current developments in the SAP Business Analytics environment, and to explain how these changes can help you change, supplement, or even replace your CO-PA component in SAP. SAP Business Analytics is a new set of tools that provide further reporting functionality that runs on top of or in parallel to SAP NetWeaver Business Warehouse (BW), and that improve integration with SAP ECC and third-party systems using an Online Analytical Database (OLAP). As SAP technologies provide more flexibility, clients have the ability to choose either pre-delivered functionality or customized developments to fulfill their financial requirements.

In the last few years, SAP technologies have been evolving at an astonishing rate, supported by the multiple acquisitions of companies such as OutlookSoft, BusinessObjects, SAP BusinessObjects Dashboards (previously Xcelsius), and many more. In this chapter, we'll review a few of the software elements that can provide additional functionality for your business and that can complement or enhance SAP CO-PA reporting and data analysis. We'll also provide an overview of some of the most important trends that will radically change data analysis and decision making in the next few years.

This chapter will provide a general overview of different components of SAP Business Analytics that can be used to enhance the capabilities available in SAP CO-PA, and that can also complement its functions, such as SAP BusinessObjects Planning and Consolidation (BPC). Each of the SAP tools discussed in this chapter are a book on their own; they are mentioned to make you aware of the current changes of the SAP environment and how they might also affect CO-PA in SAP. Please note that it's not the purpose of this chapter to train you or make you an expert in each of the tools previously mentioned, but to provide an overview of their existence, their capabilities, and how they can support your SAP CO-PA implementation.

13.1　CO-PA Integration with SAP Business Analytics

Currently, SAP technologies work using basically two generic kinds of databases: Online Transactional Processing (OLTP; CO-PA) and Online Analytical Processing (OLAP; graphical and user-friendly SAP BusinessObjects tools). OLTP has been designed to generate and capture data quickly, such as the SAP ECC database. In comparison, OLAP databases have been designed for analytical purposes, reporting, slice and dice, and are oriented to support decision making. Clear examples of this environment have been SAP NetWeaver BW and the SAP BusinessObjects family of products such as Voyager, Web Intelligence, BEx, SAP BusinessObjects Dashboards, SAP Crystal Reports, Explorer, and many more that are more flexible and user-friendly than the traditional CO-PA reporting because these OLAP tools are designed for data analysis, flexible reporting, and graphics. In comparison, SAP CO-PA exists in the SAP ECC environment, and is thus part of the OLTP database, and it's not designed to process large data volumes in comparison with OLAP analytical tools.

13.1.1　Existing Technologies in the Business Analytics Suite

As shown in Figure 13.1, there are multiple technologies that exist in parallel to or on top of the SAP ERP transactional system; this supports decision making and improves data display or data capture. As shown in Figure 13.1, SAP BusinessObjects tools are the preferred way to display information generated originally from the SAP ERP or SAP ECC system and transferred into the SAP BW environment for reporting purposes and/or for sophisticated operations such as data mining.

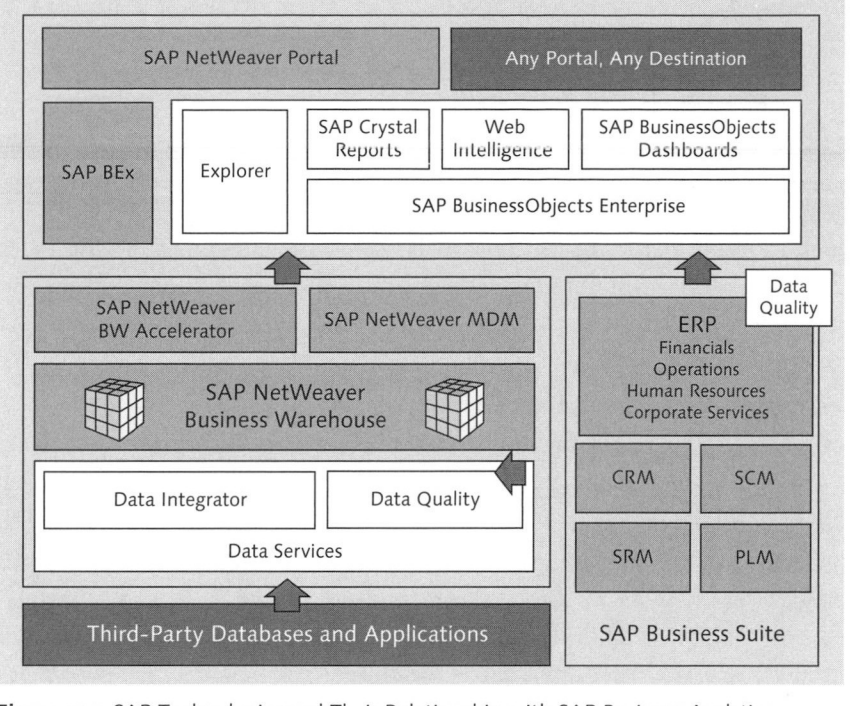

Figure 13.1 SAP Technologies and Their Relationship with SAP Business Analytics

As shown in Figure 13.1, business intelligence tools exist on top of the SAP ECC environment, and can be integrated not only with SAP ECC, but also with third-party systems. The disadvantage of these tools at this moment is that you aren't able to generate data in real time from SAP ECC because SAP BI tools literally exist in a different system. SAP CO-PA planning and reporting tools exist within SAP ECC and eliminate the need for waiting, while a batch process uploads the data and makes it available for reporting, which is the case of the tools shown in Figure 13.1. As was previously described in Chapter 3, Figures 3.1 and 3.2, having CO-PA directly integrated within the SAP ECC system with pre-delivered functionality to update the information nearly in real time is a great feature that supports why this component is so important within SAP Financials.

However, tools such as SAP Crystal Reports, SAP BusinessObjects Enterprise, Web Intelligence, and SAP BusinessObjects Dashboards have something in common—they have been designed to improve reporting, data analysis, and decision making with a user-friendly environment mostly designed using drag-and-drop, which is not the case of SAP CO-PA.

As shown in Figure 13.2, the tools supporting SAP ECC are grouped in four major areas:

1. **Enterprise performance management (EPM)**
   Includes financial tools such as SAP BPC that are designed to manage the planning, budgeting, forecasting, and consolidation functionalities.

2. **Business intelligence**
   Designed to exclusively provide data analysis and/or reporting functionalities such as SAP BusinessObjects Dashboards and SAP Crystal Reports for Dashboards and a user-friendly environment for reports with an enhanced tool for developers.

3. **Governance, risk, and compliance**
   Tools such as GRC, which provide support for internal controls and Sarbanes-Oxley (SOX).

4. **Information management**
   Tools specifically designed to manage and share large volumes of master data for different systems and using a centralized environment to perform such distribution. For example, SAP MDM provides a single version of master data for supplier, product, customer, or user-defined data objects in heterogeneous environments.

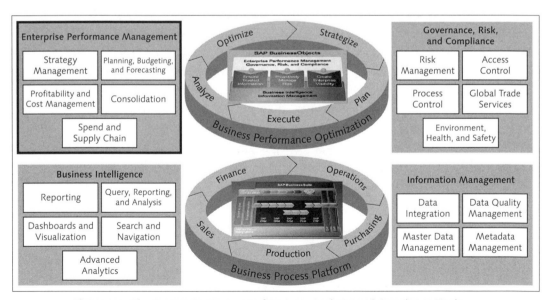

Figure 13.2 The Current Environment of Business Analytics and Compliance Tools

Based on the information discussed in previous chapters, we expect that you have a pretty good idea of the capabilities of SAP CO-PA. As shown in Figure 13.2, you may also be provided with a set of tools available as part of the Business Analytics Suite that are executed mostly using SAP NetWeaver BW as their database, and provide additional functionality that does not exist in SAP ECC and/or CO-PA. In order to make them available in your environment, we recommend checking with your SAP Basis team, SAP BI team, and if they are completely new to your company, feel free to contact your SAP representative.

As shown in Figure 13.2, the tools in which we're most interested in this chapter are identified on the left side of the figure. This collection of tools provides support for budgeting, planning, forecasting, consolidation, advanced analytics, data visualization, queries, and much more.

> **Note**
>
> Notice that tools such as SAP Strategic Planning and Simulation (SEM) and OutlookSoft are not a part of Figure 13.1 and Figure 13.2, thus making them obsolete and not part of the future roadmap of technologies that SAP will support and develop.

13.1.2 SAP BusinessObjects Tools—Activating Pre-Delivered CO-PA Functionality Available in SAP NetWeaver Business Warehouse

Currently, CO-PA information in SAP can be reported using SAP BusinessObjects tools using either data extraction into SAP NetWeaver BW and utilizing some of the tools mentioned in the previous chapter, or by directly accessing the SAP ECC tables, which is what CO-PA reporting provides. As we discussed in Chapter 3, SAP CO-PA is integrated within the SAP ECC OLTP database, and the differences between the backend (SAP tables) and the frontend (SAP screens) are easy to recognize in comparison with the SAP NetWeaver BW environment. In the case of SAP NetWeaver BW, there are two components: the backend, which is basically InfoCubes that will store the data that the users need to report and objects called extractors that are configured so the data reaches these InfoCubes, and the frontend, which is composed of tools that are designed to access the information contained in the InfoCubes and present it in a graphical way for simple reporting. In addition, from a system performance point of view, it's best that you perform extractions of large data sets into SAP BW in order to improve response times, and that you use SAP BusinessObjects reporting tools to read the different InfoCubes that store the SAP ECC or CO-PA specific data. The alternative of performing reporting on large data sets in SAP ECC or SAP CO-PA isn't recommended as a standard SAP practice, but this might change in the near future, which you'll see when we discuss SAP HANA functionalities in Section 13.4.

As shown later on in Figure 13.5, SAP NetWeaver BW has pre-delivered functionality that's ready to use—it only needs to be activated—and specific for different components. In this case, we'll be reviewing how to access SAP NetWeaver BW structures that are already available in your system to perform analysis, reporting, and data transformation. In SAP Business Intelligence, there are pre-defined templates that link SAP Business Intelligence with SAP ECC and SAP CO-PA and can be customized to meet your needs for reporting. These structures or Business Content are a combination of data sources utilized to extract the data into SAP Business Intelligence, InfoCubes, reports, queries, and more, so you can have enhanced functionalities to report data that's generated and/or stored in SAP CO-PA. To access SAP NetWeaver BW structures used to perform data extraction, transformation, and load data available in CO-PA and move it to SAP BW for reporting using any of the Business Analytics tools previously shown in Figure 13.1 and Figure 13.2, follow these steps:

1. Identify the SAP GUI icon, double-click on it, and check with your system administrator about the server numbers and other configuration required in your machine. Enter your user ID and password, and press ⌴Enter⌴ to access SAP NetWeaver BW.

2. Use Transaction RSA1, and the screen shown in Figure 13.3 appears. Select the BI CONTENT tab on the left-hand side to access the pre-delivered Business Content objects. Business Content is nothing more than SAP NetWeaver BW specific structures that allow you to extract and report information after loading data from SAP ECC, or that can be used as the reference to build your different requirements.

Tips & Tricks

SAP CO-PA, like many other components, has pre-delivered templates available in SAP NetWeaver BW that replicate the data available in the SAP ECC environment. By default there is Business Content available for the operating concerns identified in Chapter 3, such as Quickstart Template S_GO. Take note that value fields in SAP CO-PA are called *key figures*, and the interpretation of characteristics in SAP CO-PA is the same as in SAP NetWeaver BW.

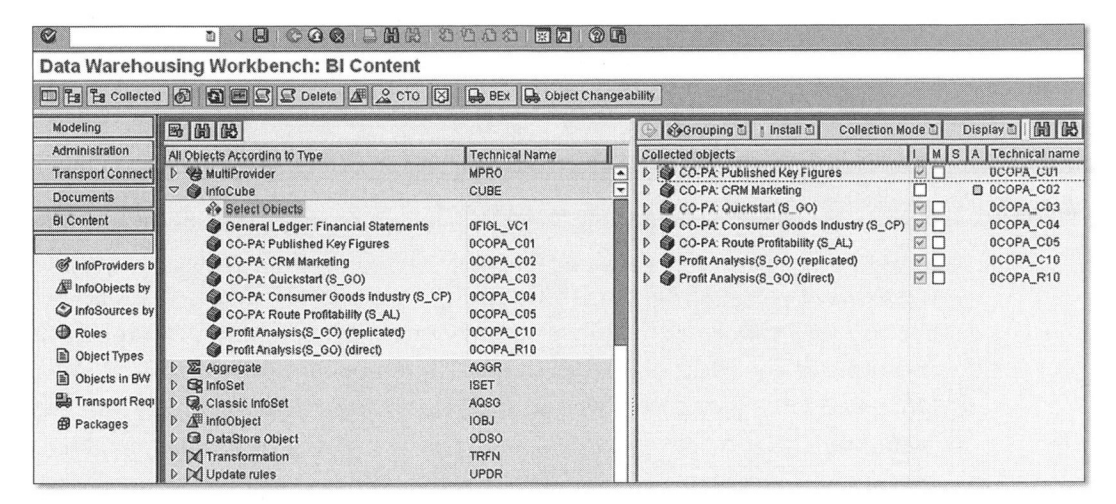

Figure 13.3 Reviewing CO-PA Specific Business Content in SAP NetWeaver BW

> **Note**
>
> Further knowledge is required to configure, design, and deploy the different technologies mentioned in this chapter, but this is a quick reference guide of the capabilities of each of them. We recommend reviewing the following books from SAP PRESS to provide more clarity on the functionalities of SAP BusinessObjects tools and components:
>
> ▶ *Reporting and Analytics with SAP BusinessObjects* by Ingo Hilgefort (2012)
>
> ▶ *SAP BusinessObjects Web Intelligence* by Jim Brogden et al. (2010)
>
> ▶ *Integrating SAP BusinessObjects XI 3.1 Tools with SAP NetWeaver* by Ingo Hilgefort (2nd edition, 2012)
>
> ▶ *SAP NetWeaver BW and SAP BusinessObjects—The Comprehensive Guide* by Loren Heilig et al. (2012)

3. In Figure 13.3, choose the Select Objects option in the InfoCube type, and perform the search for InfoCubes with the 0COPA prefix in the technical name, and then move the InfoCubes to the right-hand side of the screen by using drag-and-drop.

4. As shown, we've identified a group of InfoCubes that have pre-defined SAP CO-PA structures available, which are displayed on the right-hand side of the

screen. Notice that we see familiar names to the pre-delivered SAP CO-PA operating concerns that we identified in Chapter 3.

5. As shown in Figure 13.4, we've identified CO-PA specific objects available in SAP NetWeaver BW that mirror CO-PA operating concerns and their contents for data extraction, transformation, and loading into SAP BW. Drag the objects from left to right in order to select the structures that you would like to activate (in other words, you're copying pre-delivered objects so that you can modify them to suit your specific needs). These objects are useful for two reasons: one because they reduce development time with structures that are ready to use and transfer data from the SAP ECC-CO-PA component into SAP NetWeaver BW for reporting, and two because they can be used as reference so you can customize the pre-delivered SAP objects to your particular implementation needs.

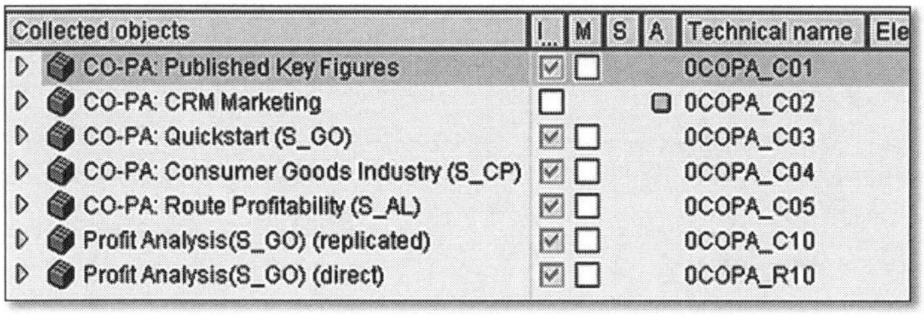

Collected objects	I	M	S	A	Technical name	Ele
▷ CO-PA: Published Key Figures	☑	☐			0COPA_C01	
▷ CO-PA: CRM Marketing	☐			◲	0COPA_C02	
▷ CO-PA: Quickstart (S_GO)	☑	☐			0COPA_C03	
▷ CO-PA: Consumer Goods Industry (S_CP)	☑	☐			0COPA_C04	
▷ CO-PA: Route Profitability (S_AL)	☑	☐			0COPA_C05	
▷ Profit Analysis(S_GO) (replicated)	☑	☐			0COPA_C10	
▷ Profit Analysis(S_GO) (direct)	☑	☐			0COPA_R10	

Figure 13.4 Reviewing the SAP CO-PA Business Content Available in SAP NetWeaver BW

6. Once you've identified the objects that you need (see our example shown in Figure 13.5), click on the GROUPING button, and select the ONLY NECESSARY OBJECTS option as shown. Here, you're simply telling SAP BW that you need the minimum number of required objects to be activated to perform the data extraction of SAP CO-PA information.

7. You can also create your own objects from scratch in SAP NetWeaver BW by accessing the MODELING tab and the INFOOBJECTS menu on the left-hand side. Based on the characteristics of the operating concern that you've defined in your SAP ECC system, you can reuse a number of InfoObjects (characteristics and key figures) already defined in SAP NetWeaver BW and populate them with data as part of the extraction process. If you require more clarity on this process, you'll need the support of your SAP NetWeaver BW consultant and/or team lead.

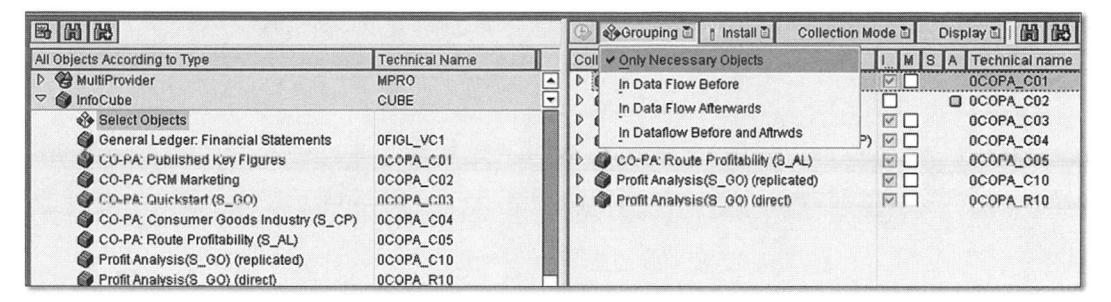

Figure 13.5 Grouping Pre-Delivered Structures with Only the Necessary Objects

8. Open the tabs associated with the SAP CO-PA objects that you've identified, and review them. Notice that there are elements called InfoObjects, which are nothing more than a different naming convention in SAP NetWeaver BW for your operating concern characteristics and value fields as shown in Figure 13.6.

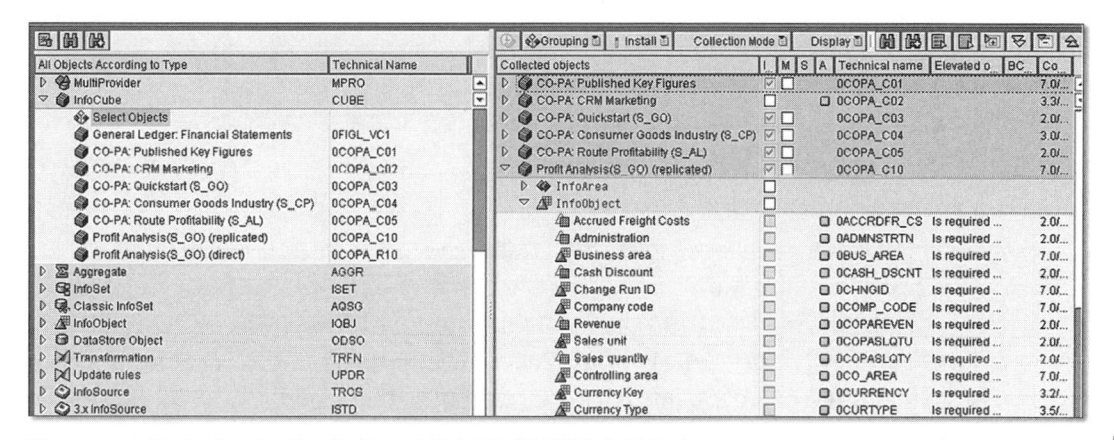

Figure 13.6 Reviewing the Pre-Delivered SAP CO-PA BW InfoObjects

9. Now, simply click on the INSTALL button as shown in Figure 13.7 and select either INSTALL or INSTALL IN BACKGROUND. This will transfer your SAP BW CO-PA Business Content to your MODELING tab shown previously in Figure 13.3. In other words, we just generated a copy of the SAP NetWeaver BW pre-delivered objects and we've installed them in the MODELING tab so they can be modified and configured. We recommend that you copy and rename these objects once they're available in the MODELING tab so that if a new transfer occurs, the system will replace the objects in the MODELING tab with the ones available in the BI CONTENT tab.

Figure 13.7 Installing the SAP NetWeaver BW Pre-Delivered Business Content

13.1.3 What Tools Should I Use?

At this point, your challenge is how to populate these cubes with your SAP ECC CO-PA data; for this you require metadata structures such as data sources, transformation, business rules, DTPs, and others. Please note that we won't explain the ins and outs of the SAP NetWeaver BW environment, but just make you aware that there are other components and structures that you should consider when working and transferring data between SAP CO-PA and SAP NetWeaver BW. If you would like to explore further the capabilities of SAP NetWeaver BW, we recommend reading *Data Modeling in SAP NetWeaver BW* (SAP PRESS, 2011).

It's possible to say that of all the SAP NetWeaver BW structures available, the data source is the most important because it is the gate to the SAP ECC environment from where the SAP CO-PA data will flow into specific SAP BW InfoCubes. Once the data has reached SAP BW InfoCubes and is available for reporting, you can use the different SAP BusinessObjects tools available as part of SAP Business Analytics such as SAP BusinessObjects Dashboards, WEBI, BEx, SAP BPC (formerly OutlookSoft), SAP Crystal Reports, Live Office, BusinessObjects Explorer, Report Designer, Universe Designer, WebApp Designer, and Pioneer.

Of the tools we just listed, SAP BPC is one of the most important, with functionalities for planning, budgeting, forecasting, and consolidation, and it can substitute and/or complement the capabilities of SAP CO-PA (such as the ones discussed in Chapter 7). SAP BPC is currently delivered with two versions: Microsoft (based on the original OutlookSoft platform using SQL Server database) and NetWeaver (which uses the SAP NetWeaver BW system as its database).

With this new set of tools, SAP has enhanced its customer base and addressed the different needs of an organization for ad hoc and flexible reporting and complemented it with a user-friendly and web-based environment. In comparison with SAP CO-PA reporting using the Report Painter functionality, SAP BusinessObjects analytical tools support a more flexible and faster platform to deliver reports of data generated in SAP CO-PA, and in high data environments, the performance of OLAP analytical databases is much better than OLTP databases.

13.2 SAP BusinessObjects Integration with CO-PA Structures

In the previous section we discussed how SAP NetWeaver BW has pre-delivered Business Content that allows you to access information contained in SAP CO-PA, and that can be used to improve your reporting environment with SAP Business-Objects tools. We also briefly illustrated the similarities and differences between the information available in SAP CO-PA and the building structures of SAP Net-Weaver BW. In this section, we'll go into further detail on the similarities and differences between the information available in SAP ECC using SAP CO-PA and that available in the SAP Business Intelligence environment, and how this information is received with SAP NetWeaver BW as the storage database. Remember, using SAP BW InfoCubes provides faster performance in comparison with SAP ECC and CO-PA reports.

As shown in Figure 13.8, the CO-PA-specific pre-delivered objects are available to use in the MODELING tab of SAP NetWeaver BW. Here, you can access the InfoObjects or building blocks that control the information available in an SAP BW Info-Cube. As reference, characteristics in CO-PA are the same as characteristics in SAP NetWeaver BW environment; however, value fields in SAP CO-PA are the equivalent of the key figures you'll see here.

Here, you can access the contents of InfoProvider 0COPA_C03, which is the SAP NetWeaver BW equivalent of the operating concern Quickstart, by selecting the specific cube you want more details on, and right-clicking on the DISPLAY or CHANGE options as shown.

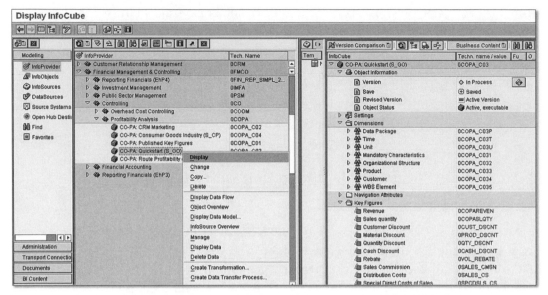

Figure 13.8 Reviewing the Characteristics and Key Figures of an SAP BW InfoCube

As shown in Figure 13.9, we're comparing the characteristics available in the SAP CO-PA Quickstart operating concern with the contents of the SAP BW InfoCube 0COPA_C03 and viewing their similarities. Notice that Figure 13.9 shows a combination of functionality from SAP NetWeaver BW and SAP CO-PA. Remember, to access the characteristics available in your SAP CO-PA operating concern as discussed in Chapter 3 you need to access the MAINTAIN CHARACTERISTICS menu available in the IMG using the menu path PROFITABILITY ANALYSIS • STRUCTURES • DEFINE OPERATING CONCERN. To access the equivalent environment in SAP NetWeaver BW, use Transaction RSA1 to access the InfoObjects contained in the pre-delivered Business Content shown previously in Figure 13.6, and also available in the MODELING tab. In this particular case, we can see in Figure 13.9 that the names and structures in each screen are literally the same, but the objects exist in two different systems.

You can reuse, copy, and modify the Business Content objects to adjust to the needs of your SAP BW InfoCubes and perform the same adjustments in SAP CO-PA with the pre-delivered templates reviewed in Chapter 3, which will receive the data from your particular operating concern. Your business users can report accordingly from that particular InfoCube to review the data generated and/or stored in SAP CO-PA.

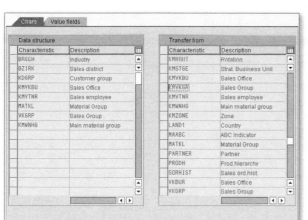

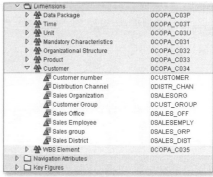

Figure 13.9 Comparison between SAP NetWeaver BW and CO-PA Characteristics

Figure 13.10 displays the similarities between the SAP CO-PA value fields and the names of the key figures available in the pre-delivered templates in SAP NetWeaver BW. For SAP CO-PA you can access value fields similarly to how you access characteristics, as reviewed in Chapter 3, and for SAP NetWeaver BW, you access key figures using Transaction RSA1 in the INFOOBJECTS and MODELING tabs.

As we already mentioned, the logic behind value fields and key figures is literally the same; both are used to either store amounts or quantities, and there can be as many multiple key figures in one cube as there can be multiple value fields in an operating concern. Once your data has a logical structure that reads, maps, and uploads the data from your SAP CO-PA operating concern into an SAP BW Info-Cube, other processes can occur besides reporting with SAP BusinessObjects tools, such as sophisticated data transformation using standard SAP NetWeaver BW DTP objects or ABAP programs, data mining operations, business rules, universes, BEx queries, SAP Crystal Reports, InfoViews, and others. Depending on your level of involvement of the implementation, you'll be more aware of these tools, and/or request to use these tools to improve your CO-PA reporting functionalities.

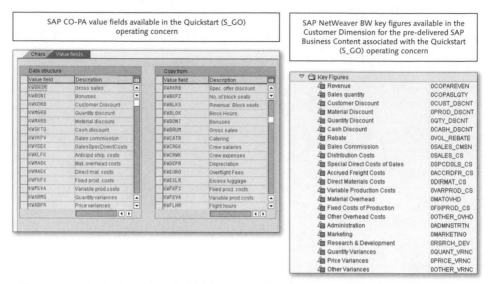

SAP CO-PA value fields available in the Quickstart (S_GO) operating concern		SAP NetWeaver BW key figures available in the Customer Dimension for the pre-delivered SAP Business Content associated with the Quickstart (S_GO) operating concern

Chars Value fields

Data structure

Value field	Description		Value field	Description
KWBRUM	Gross sales		KWAKRB	Spec. offer discount
KWBONI	Bonuses		KWBKPZ	No. of block seats
KWKDRB	Customer Discount		KWBLKS	Revenue: Block seats
KWMGRB	Quantity discount		KWBLOK	Block Hours
KWMARB	Material discount		KWBONI	Bonuses
KWSKTO	Cash discount		KWBRUM	Gross sales
KWVKPV	Sales commission		KWCATR	Catering
KWVSEK	SalesSpecDirectCosts		KWCR6K	Crew salaries
KWKLFK	Anticipd ship. costs		KWCRWK	Crew expenses
KWMAGK	Mat. overhead costs		KWDEPR	Depreciation
KWMAEK	Direct mat. costs		KWEURO	Overflight Fees
KWFKFX	Fixed prod. costs		KWEXLR	Excess luggage
KWFKVA	Variable prod.costs		KWFKFX	Fixed prod. costs
KWABMG	Quantity variances		KWFKVA	Variable prod.costs
KWABPR	Price variances		KWFLHR	Flight hours

Copy from

▽ 🗀 Key Figures

Revenue	0COPAREVEN
Sales quantity	0COPASLQTY
Customer Discount	0CUST_DSCNT
Material Discount	0PROD_DSCNT
Quantity Discount	0QTY_DSCNT
Cash Discount	0CASH_DSCNT
Rebate	0VOL_REBATE
Sales Commission	0SALES_CMSN
Distribution Costs	0SALES_CS
Special Direct Costs of Sales	0SPCDSLS_CS
Accrued Freight Costs	0ACCRDFR_CS
Direct Materials Costs	0DIRMAT_CS
Variable Production Costs	0VARPROD_CS
Material Overhead	0MATOVHD
Fixed Costs of Production	0FIXPROD_CS
Other Overhead Costs	0OTHER_OVHD
Administration	0ADMNSTRTN
Marketing	0MARKETING
Research & Development	0RSRCH_DEV
Quantity Variances	0QUANT_VRNC
Price Variances	0PRICE_VRNC
Other Variances	0OTHER_VRNC

Figure 13.10 Comparison between SAP NetWeaver BW Key Figures and CO-PA Value Fields

In summary, SAP NetWeaver BW provides pre-delivered structures to transfer data from SAP CO-PA and store it in SAP BW InfoCubes, and as shown in this section they follow the CO-PA pre-delivered templates that we discussed in Chapter 3. For CO-PA systems that don't have any relationship with the pre-delivered SAP CO-PA templates, further enhancements or configuration in SAP NetWeaver BW is required, such as naming your value fields and characteristics, making sure that these elements are available in your SAP BW InfoCube, and also the extractor to make sure that the correct information is transferred to SAP NetWeaver BW from SAP CO-PA tables.

In the next section we'll discuss briefly why SAP BW InfoCubes are meaningful for BusinessObjects tools, such as SAP BPC, in order to have a common source of data for reporting and/or manipulation.

13.3 Comparing SAP BusinessObjects Planning and Consolidation (BPC) and CO-PA

SAP BusinessObjects Planning and Consolidation is an OLAP tool available in two versions: Microsoft and NetWeaver. The Microsoft version of SAP BPC uses as the main database Microsoft SQL Server and Visual Studio components, and doesn't connect directly to SAP ECC, SAP NetWeaver BW, or any other transactional system by default, and the standard interface uses flat files. In comparison, the NetWeaver version uses SAP NetWeaver BW as the database, and thus interacts directly with SAP NetWeaver BW Business Content and SAP structures. Flat files can still be used, but it has the capability to read directly to SAP BW InfoCubes.

SAP BPC can enhance or replace the functionalities used in SAP CO-PA if we consider the reporting and planning functionalities described in Chapters 6 and 7. In addition, SAP BPC not only provides flexible reporting and additional planning tools, but can also perform consolidation, which is something that SAP CO-PA is not designed to do. However, in comparison with SAP CO-PA, SAP BPC has the drawback of not having lots of pre-designed functionality because it allows the user to create functionality from scratch using standard building blocks. It's possible to compare SAP BPC with SAP NetWeaver BW, since there is pre-delivered functionality that is generic to transform, extract, and load data, but it requires detail customization to deliver a solution. It's not similar to SAP ECC in that each component follows specific guidelines that are established and sometimes quite rigid.

The purpose of this section is to review the capabilities of SAP BPC and CO-PA and highlight that there is some overlapping in functionality. For this reason, some companies can replace SAP CO-PA with SAP BPC, or keep SAP CO-PA and SAP BPC running in parallel due to capabilities that might complement each other. For example, SAP BPC's strongest functionality is flexible reporting and pre-delivered templates that allow the user to generate a report almost instantly with a click of the mouse. In comparison, SAP CO-PA, as it was reviewed in Chapter 9, requires a set of specific procedures that require further configuration.

Another example is how SAP BPC can be integrated with multiple sources of data and SAP ECC and SAP BI, compared to SAP CO-PA, which requires a complex architecture to transfer data from other systems as described in Chapter 8. However, the complexity of integrating CO-PA with other components within SAP ECC allows CO-PA data to be updated nearly on a real-time basis. This is not the case with SAP BPC, which depends heavily on SAP BI data loads.

SAP BPC and CO-PA are quite often compared, and this section is designed to provide a closer look at SAP BPC and help you determine whether to use SAP CO-PA or to use both tools if they can provide capabilities to justify their existence at the same time.

13.3.1 Deciding if SAP BPC is Right for You

Similarly to SAP CO-PA, SAP BPC can perform planning and reporting functionalities with the capability to organize the data sources in a more ordered and simplified way than CO-PA. Also, maintenance of SAP BPC applications (the equivalent of operating concerns) is much simpler, and the adjustments in both characteristics and master data can be reflected in seconds rather than by performing sophisticated adjustments and following the different rules required by SAP CO-PA. In addition, the data transfer structure using SAP BPC is simplified using programs that pick and choose the sources of data, rather than configuring a transfer structure similar to the one discussed in Chapter 8.

However, neither SAP BPC nor SAP NetWeaver BW is real time. This is a big advantage that SAP CO-PA has over this tool. The operating concern in CO-PA can be updated each time a transaction occurs in SAP ECC that is relevant to a particular structure. In addition, CO-PA has a multitude of pre-defined structures that have to be followed to move, input, send, transform, and modify data values in a more organized way than SAP BPC, which is a blank blackboard that can be configured to deliver almost anything, but has to be built from scratch. In order to better understand the differences between SAP BPC and SAP CO-PA, let's review Figure 13.11. This figure illustrates how data reaches the SAP BPC environment for reporting, planning, consolidation, budgeting, and/or forecasting.

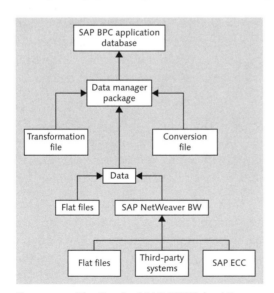

Figure 13.11 The Standard SAP BPC Upload Process

It's important to notice that Figure 13.11 shows the SAP pre-delivered process to perform uploads into the SAP BPC environment. Similar to SAP NetWeaver BW, there are building blocks that can be used, but they must be customized to your needs and are more flexible than SAP ECC components. Also, remember that the standard SAP CO-PA process was illustrated in Figure 3.2 in Chapter 3. There are basically three components:

▶ **Conversion file**
Controls data transformation rules from source to target. For example, if the account is A-12345 in the source transactional file to load and the account format used in SAP BPC for reporting is 12345 for the same account, this means that a conversion rule is required to eliminate "A-" when performing the load.

▶ **Transformation file**
Controls the mappings from source to target for each column in the SAP BPC database to each column or header of the InfoCube or flat file. For example, if the account dimension in the SAP BPC dimension is contained in the first column of the flat file or InfoCube, then *account = column(1)* assignment must occur so the system understands where to find the account information.

▶ **Data**
As shown in Figure 13.11, this represents the transactional data to load into the SAP BPC environment, and it could be flat files, connection to third-party systems, or SAP ECC, and it always uses SAP NetWeaver BW as the system that links everything together. Flat files can also be loaded directly to the SAP BPC server.

The process shown in Figure 13.11 is the standard SAP BPC process for data upload using SAP pre-delivered functionality. Custom programs can be developed, but we recommend this as the last choice. In comparison to SAP CO-PA, SAP BPC is less rigid on how to configure each of the structures required for uploading the information into the database. To provide a general idea of the navigation, display, and look and feel of SAP BPC, please review Figure 13.12, and notice the significant differences in the appearance of the application. Another benefit to note about SAP BPC is that it provides interfaces that interact with MS Office and a web environment, which allows the user to review the data in Microsoft Word, Excel, PowerPoint, or on the web. In comparison, CO-PA is limited to interacting with the MS Excel interface when working with integrated planning layouts, as described in Chapter 12.

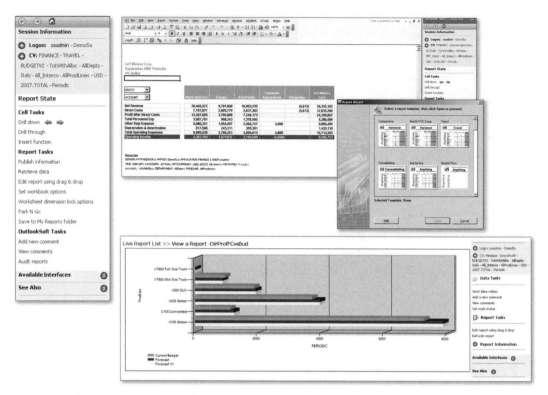

Figure 13.12 Overview of the SAP BPC Environment

SAP BPC is part of the SAP BusinessObjects family of products, thus it can integrate with other tools such as SAP BusinessObjects Dashboards and SAP BPC with an environment using either MS Excel or Web Intelligence (WebI) without the need to transfer data to another environment or system. However, even though the reporting capabilities of SAP BPC can be considered improved in comparison with SAP CO-PA, the real-time capabilities of SAP CO-PA are still a big plus from a data point of view. However, we recommend limiting CO-PA reporting to small sets of data and exploring the usage of SAP BusinessObjects Analytics Suite for larger volumes.

In addition, Figure 13.13 provides a closer look at the capabilities of SAP BPC in comparison with SAP CO-PA, and as previously mentioned, can expand the capabilities of the application since it's not only focused on Profitability Analysis, but also on planning, budgeting, strategy management, and with the support of additional functionality, on controlling and monitoring the flow of information.

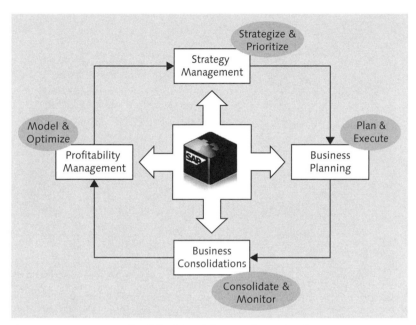

Figure 13.13 Overview of SAP BPC Capabilities and Functionality

Table 13.1 provides a general overview of the comparison between SAP BPC and SAP CO-PA, and clearly shows that the capabilities between the two systems are quite different and the functionality can be limited by either data volume or the kind of reports to be generated.

	SAP CO-PA	SAP BPC
SAP ECC Integration	Requires multiple configurations to transfer data from other components into SAP CO-PA.	Easily access the information available in the different SAP ECC components leveraging SAP NetWeaver BW pre-configured functionality.

Table 13.1 Comparison between SAP CO-PA and SAP BPC

	SAP CO-PA	SAP BPC
Pre-Configured Functionality	Extensively designed to be integrated with SAP ECC, follows SAP ECC design guidelines, and has pre-defined rules for data transformation and upload.	Greater flexibility since does not follow SAP ECC design guidelines but requires development using basic building blocks.
Reporting	Yes	Yes
Integration with MS Office	Only MS Excel	MS Excel, MS PowerPoint, MS Word, and pre-delivered portal functionality available out-of-the-box
Planning	Yes	Yes
Consolidation	None	Yes
Web Capabilities	Limited	Web portal pre-delivered as out-of-the-box functionality, plus integration with SAP NetWeaver Portal Technology
SAP HANA Integration	Yes	Yes
Usage of SAP NetWeaver BW	No, because exists in SAP ECC and it is executed in an OLTP database.	Yes, for SAP BPC NetWeaver versions only, and works with an OLAP database.
Integration with SAP BusinessObjects Analytics	Limited	Yes
Integration with SAP ECC	Real-time	Requires upload into SAP NetWeaver BW first.
Master Data Derivation	Pre-delivered content available	None, requires custom development using Script Logic or ABAP.
Transport Process	Yes	Yes, for SAP BPC NetWeaver versions only. SAP BPC Microsoft versions follow a different transport strategy to SAP.

Table 13.1 Comparison between SAP CO-PA and SAP BPC (Cont.)

	SAP CO-PA	SAP BPC
Supports Account-Based and Costing-Based Models	Yes	Yes

Table 13.1 Comparison between SAP CO-PA and SAP BPC (Cont.)

SAP CO-PA is a more stable tool that has been around for several years, in comparison to SAP BusinessObjects Analytics in general, where the integration process is still ongoing and the capabilities that are available for data display and analysis are more powerful but currently undergoing greater development by SAP as the new set of tools to drive the future of decision making. Also, as shown in Table 13.1, SAP CO-PA is an SAP ECC component that's available with extensive pre-configured functionality, in comparison with SAP BPC that is more flexible and is delivered with standard building blocks similar to those of SAP NetWeaver BW. For this reason, if being as close to SAP ECC rules and guidelines as possible is your priority, SAP CO-PA provides lots of functionality similar to those of SAP ECC components, but requires lots of work to perform the integration as described in Chapter 8. In addition, SAP BPC provides functionality that is more generic in comparison with the rules written in stone of SAP ECC, and similar to SAP NetWeaver BW, must be customized to deliver the required behavior using standard functions or programs. Because of the importance of SAP BPC in the SAP world, we've provided a greater level of detail in the following section to understand this tool in a much better way.

Let's go over a few of the highlights that the table illustrates:

▶ As shown in Table 13.1, it's possible that both SAP CO-PA and SAP BPC will be integrated with SAP HANA, the in-memory computing tool that improves reporting, performance, and calculations in large data environments (this will be reviewed later on in Section 13.4). Also, as clearly shown in Table 13.1, CO-PA doesn't require SAP NetWeaver BW, and thus its integration with SAP Business-Objects is also more limited or requires further work in comparison with SAP BPC since it's part of the family of products of SAP Business Analytics.

▶ SAP BPC not only provides planning and reporting capabilities similar or improved to those provided by SAP CO-PA, but also allows you to perform consolidation processes. SAP CO-PA unfortunately doesn't have this capability unless it's custom-made using ABAP programs that are executed within a separate data set. However, we don't recommend performing consolidation processes in SAP CO-PA as an SAP Best Practice; it was not created in SAP ECC to provide such functionality as SAP ECC-ECS, which is now considered obsolete and replaced by SAP BPC.

▶ A key element that SAP BPC lacks is the pre-configured capability of characteristic derivation associated with master data, but SAP CO-PA provides this capability out-of-the-box, as reviewed in Chapter 5. The transport strategy between the two systems is also quite different. SAP CO-PA follows the traditional object transport, and depending on the number of structures created and the integration with other components, this process can become very tedious. In comparison, SAP BPC differs between SAP BPC NetWeaver (SAP BW version) and SAP BPC Microsoft. SAP BPC NetWeaver versions follow the same SAP BW structure to move objects from one system to another, but the SAP BPC MS versions require a specific tool to move the elements created to another server, similar to the SAP transport process of moving data and/or objects across servers. The main reason for this difference in SAP BPC NetWeaver and MS is the database; SAP BW is the database for SAP BPC NetWeaver, and Microsoft SQL is the database for the SAP BPC MS version.

▶ Both systems support account-based and costing-based models. In SAP CO-PA this is more straightforward, as reviewed in Chapters 4 and 11; in SAP BPC this relationship is more sophisticated because only one value field column is allowed to store values. However, SAP BPC can provide account-based and costing-based reports; everything depends on the characteristics of the dimensions chosen and how the master data will be arranged inside each of these dimensions.

13.3.2 General Overview of the SAP BPC Extraction and Upload Process

The concept of upload and extraction was briefly covered in the previous section when Figure 13.11 was discussed. The standard extraction, upload, and transformation process within SAP BPC is controlled with an out-of-the-box functionality called the DATA MANAGER, displayed in Figure 13.13. As shown in Figure 13.14, there can be multiple functionalities available that can be customizable or predelivered. Depending on your security settings, you'll be able to see a limited number of objects, similar to the SAP ECC limitations that you might have assigned to your user ID in order to access or execute SAP CO-PA configuration settings.

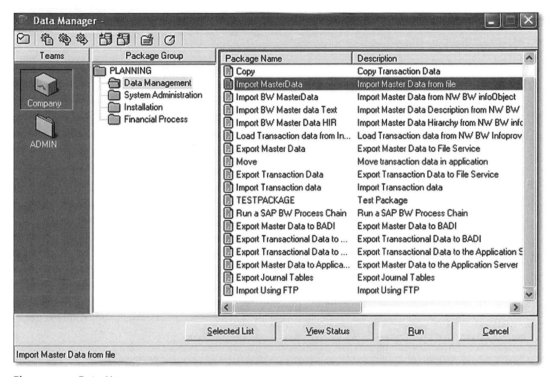

Figure 13.14 Data Manager

As shown in Figure 13.14, on the left-hand side you can see the TEAMS as folders where programs and different executables are available. Here, we've chosen to access the COMPANY folder to review the package groups and the packages available on the right-hand side. As shown, the package groups are nothing but classification folders that contain data management packages that are the programs that execute specific tasks, and as shown in Figure 13.14, we have multiple import and export options. To execute any data management package, simply select and click on the RUN button located at the bottom of the screen shown in Figure 13.14, and depending on the design of each package, there might be selection options required before initiating the program.

In order to upload data using SAP BPC, follow these steps:

1. Access the SAP BPC environment by identifying the icon or the web link available, along with your password, ID, and server information. This access is completely separate from the traditional SAP NetWeaver BW and SAP ECC because SAP BPC requires a separate design and development environment called the administration environment as shown in Figure 13.15.

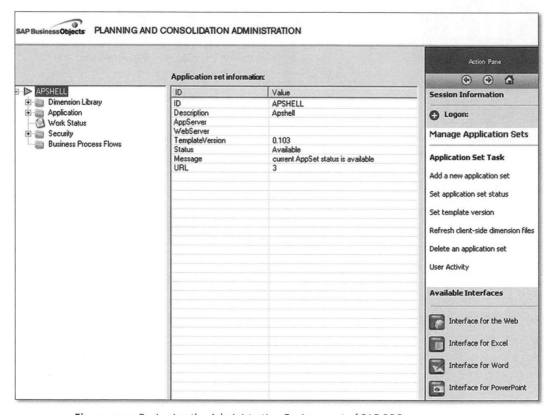

Figure 13.15 Reviewing the Administration Environment of SAP BPC

2. Access the SAP BPC INTERFACE FOR EXCEL located on the lower right corner of Figure 13.15, and the screen displayed in Figure 13.16 should appear (if it doesn't, contact your system administrator).

3. Go to the ACTION PANE menu, select the MANAGE DATA menu, and the MANAGE DATA OPTIONS menu appears as shown in Figure 13.17.

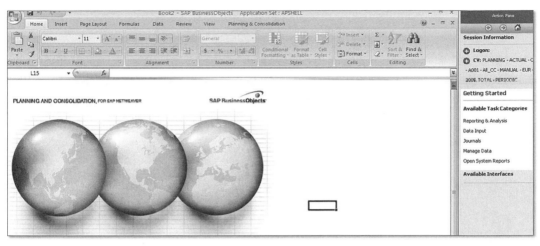

Figure 13.16 Accessing the SAP BPC MS Excel Environment

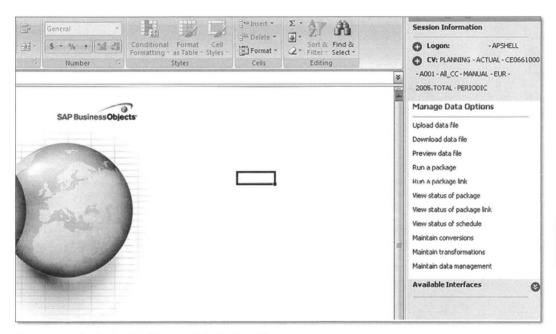

Figure 13.17 Reviewing the Manage Data Options Menu

4. Click on the RUN A PACKAGE option displayed in Figure 13.17, and select a package to execute. Let's say that we want to execute a package to load a flat file, so we select it and click on the RUN button.

5. As shown in Figure 13.18, SAP BPC requires you to define a transformation file in order to perform the data upload and a import file that contains the transactional data that you want to upload and use for reports. To assign the import file or the transformation file, either type the paths where they are located on the server or click on the first button on the right next to each of the input boxes as shown in Figure 13.18. SAP BPC can also load data directly from an SAP BI InfoCube populated with SAP CO-PA data.

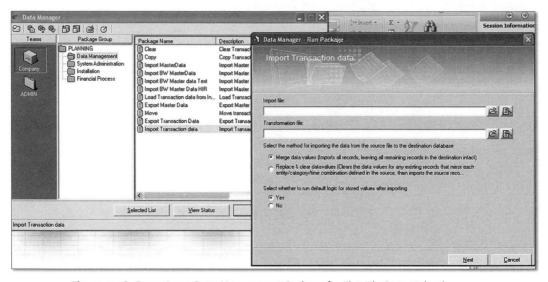

Figure 13.18 Executing a Data Management Package for Flat File Data Upload

6. As shown in Figure 13.17 in the MANAGE DATA OPTIONS menu, the system provides access to the MAINTAIN TRANSFORMATION and MAINTAIN CONVERSION functionalities that allow you to create, modify, copy, validate, and save information in these files. The conversion and the transformation files are the logic behind the data load stored in the import file shown in the first input box line in Figure 13.18. These two files control how the data will be uploaded and assigned, and establish the data transformation rules so it can be correctly stored in SAP BPC. Examples of a transformation and a conversion file required to perform the data load are shown in Figure 13.19 and Figure 13.20.

```
   *OPTIONS
   FORMAT = DELIMITED              Help on ...        ▼
   HEADER = YES
   DELIMITER = ,
   AMOUNTDECIMALPOINT = .
   SKIP = 1
   SKIPIF =
   VALIDATERECORDS=YES
   CREDITPOSITIVE=YES
   MAXREJECTCOUNT=100
   ROUNDAMOUNT=
   SELECTION=/CPMB/VJDW68R,LC;/CPMB/VJD4RC5,2005.JAN;/CPMB/VJD3EIS,France

   *MAPPING

   P_CC=/CPMB/VJD3EIS
   TIME=/CPMB/VJD4RC5
   CATEGORY=/CPMB/VJDXYWN
   P_ACTIVITY=/CPMB/VJDN9EO
   P_ACCT=/CPMB/VJDK50X
   P_DATASRC=/CPMB/VJDEY9Y
   RPTCURRENCY=/CPMB/VJDW68R
   AMOUNT=/CPMB/SDATA




   *CONVERSION
```

Figure 13.19 Setting Up Your SAP BPC NetWeaver Transformation File

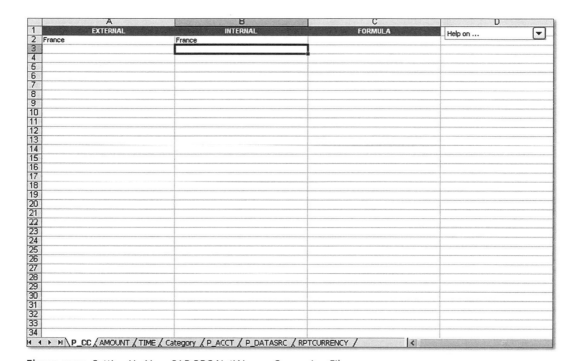

Figure 13.20 Setting Up Your SAP BPC NetWeaver Conversion File

505

7. You can also validate the configuration stored in each of your conversion and transformation files to make sure that the master data and calculations stored in these two files are correctly configured. Figure 13.21 provides an example of the validation status of a transformation file, and the results of a successful validation are displayed in Figure 13.22. To perform validation on either a conversion or a transformation file, simply open your file, and click on the eDATA menu in the MS Excel environment as shown in Figure 13.21, and select either VALIDATE & PROCESS TRANSFORMATION FILE or VALIDATE & PROCESS CONVERSION FILE. Once this process is performed, SAP BPC will execute the validation status and provide you with an output screen as shown in Figure 13.22.

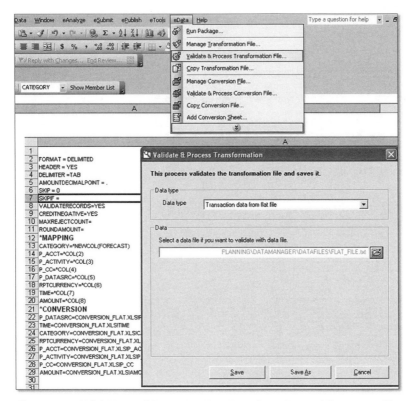

Figure 13.21 Validating and Processing Your Transformation and Conversion Files

8. Once this is completed, select the source of your data, which could be either a flat file or an SAP BW InfoCube. Choose the appropriate package or program that will perform the data upload process, and attach the appropriate conversion and transformation files as shown in Figure 13.23.

Figure 13.22 Reviewing a Successful Validation

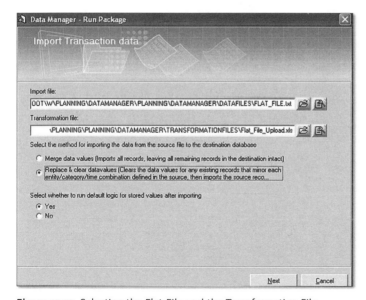

Figure 13.23 Selecting the Flat File and the Transformation File

9. You can perform a simulated upload process using pre-defined SAP BPC functionality to test your conversion and transformation files against the source flat file without updating your SAP BPC database or tables as shown in Figure 13.23. To do this, simply access the EDATA menu as shown in Figure 13.21 when peforming validation of a transformation file and select VALIDATE & PROCESS TRANSFORMATION FILE. As shown in Figure 13.21, select the file that contains the transactional data to load. This process is simply a simulation procedure that can be used to validate the logic stored in the transformation file. Click on the open folder icon located at the end of the input box of the data section in Figure 13.21 and select the SAVE button. Notice in Figure 13.24 that the results of the simulation are a record count with six records, and the accepted count is six records, meaning that six records were sent and six records were received.

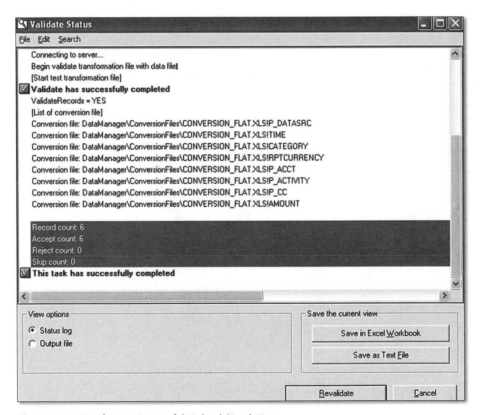

Figure 13.24 Verifying a Successful Upload Simulation

10. When you execute the package in the live system, you're able to tell if the SAP BPC package was sent and received successfully if there's a checkmark next to the program's name. As shown in Figure 13.25, the IMPORT TRANSACTION data package was completed and it was successful.

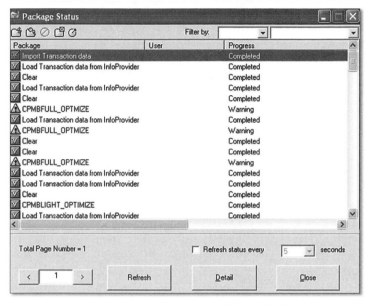

Figure 13.25 Reviewing the Package Status of a Flat File Upload

11. If you double-click on the status message shown in Figure 13.25, the DETAIL LOG screen will appear as shown in Figure 13.26, which allows you to review the following information:

   ▷ Record count: number of records available in the source

   ▷ Accept count: number of records stored in the database

   ▷ Reject count: number of records that weren't accepted and aren't saved to the database

   ▷ Skip count: number of records that didn't meet the criteria of the transformation or conversion files

12. Once you have a successful upload, you can review the contents of your database by using a report. A sample is shown in Figure 13.27 to verify that the data uploaded in this section has successfully reached your required data sets.

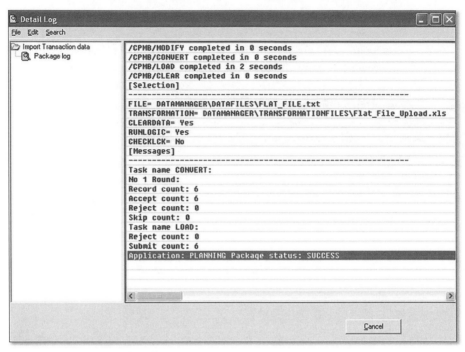

Figure 13.26 Reviewing Detail Logs

	2005.JAN	2005.FEB	2005.MAR	2005.Q1
Dynamic Report With Subtotals – Accounts				
France				
FORECAST, Periodic				
Bonus Expense	550			550
Wages and Salaries	220			220
Social Contributions	110			110
Personal Costs	**880**			**880**
Internet Expenses				
TV & Radio				
Magazines				
Advertising Costs				
Cooling (Water) Costs	440			440
Heating (Steam) Costs	330			330
Machine Repair	660			660
Electricity				
Mfg Costs	**1,430**			**1,430**
Total Costs	**2,310**			**2,310**

Report Data: France | FORECAST | Manual Planning | Local Currency | Periodic | Repairing/maintenance of manufacturing lines

Figure 13.27 Verifying That the Data Was Correctly Uploaded

In summary, we've reviewed briefly how different SAP BPC is in comparison with SAP CO-PA, and how user friendly its interface is in comparison with the SAP CO-PA reporting environment. However, the flexibility of SAP BPC is also limited by the amount of pre-delivered functionality since it's not tailored to deliver a specific need or functionality, but is instead a tool that requires development and/or configuration to fulfill specific functionality. In comparison, SAP CO-PA has the capability to have a pre-defined set of functionality and with known limitations, but lacks the flexibility to be enhanced to accommodate all planning, budgeting, and forecasting needs of a firm. The combination of SAP CO-PA with SAP BPC provides great potential to improve the functionalities at different levels (you can find more information on SAP BPC in *Implementing SAP BusinessObjects Planning and Consolidation (SAP BPC) Volume 1: Foundations* by Marco Sisfontes-Monge [Create Space, 2011]).

Now, it's not a secret that as a system evolves in time, the data volume will increase, as well as the need of more resources to manage, monitor, control, archive, and report larger data sets. However, SAP ECC, and specifically SAP CO-PA, don't work very well on their own with large data sets for reporting, analysis, and slice and dice. For that purpose, SAP created the SAP NetWeaver BW environment, which offers a number of tools to support slice and dice, decision-making analysis and reporting processes, and the additional work associated with the OLTP database. It seems that the previous scenario will be changing thanks to in-memory technology databases that remove bottlenecks typically associated with writing data to a disk, while providing significant gains in performance and reducing response times for reporting and/or calculations. In the next section, we'll provide an initial overview of SAP HANA, an in-memory computing tool currently available to provide support and improve system performance and response times for SAP ECC and SAP Business Analytics systems.

13.4 SAP High Performance Analytic Appliance (HANA) and In-Memory Computing

In June 2011, SAP AG announced the general release of its in-memory analytics appliance software and overhaul of its ERP system for small businesses. SAP HANA is the new generation of analytics and business applications using in-memory computing technology in combination with SAP BusinessObjects business intelligence. We'll define in-memory computing as a technology that allows a business to process massive quantities of real-time data in the main memory of the server, which in turn provides immediate results from analysis and transactions. This platform has been designed to help companies to better analyze large volumes of operational and transactional information in real time from virtually any data source.

13.4.1 Capabilities Overview

SAP claims that SAP HANA is able to achieve up to 3600X speed in reporting, 460 billion records analyzed in less than a second, and that it provides a business with a 21% increase in average revenue. In terms of SAP CO-PA, SAP HANA provides an in-memory application called Profitability Analysis Accelerator for ERP to accelerate reporting and allocation processes leveraging in-memory performance inside ERP. Allocations can be one of the most sophisticated and complex calculations in SAP ECC, and can drive a lot of the memory resources during period-end close. Once allocations are completed, the data volume generated by these calculations will have a direct impact on the reporting time that it takes to execute queries on line-item data in large data volumes. There are two components within SAP HANA:

▶ **SAP HANA Appliance**
 A flexible, data-source-agnostic appliance that allows customers to analyze large volumes of SAP ERP data in real-time, avoiding the need to materialize transformations. SAP HANA is a hardware and software combination that integrates a number of SAP components including the SAP In-Memory Database, Sybase Replication technology, and SAP LT (Landscape Transformation) Replicator. SAP HANA is delivered as an optimized appliance in conjunction with leading SAP hardware partners.

▶ **SAP In-Memory Database**
 The SAP In-Memory Database is a hybrid in-memory database that combines row-based, column-based, and object-based database technology. It's optimized to exploit parallel processing capabilities of modern multicore/CPU architectures.

 With this architecture, SAP applications can benefit from current hardware technologies. The SAP In-Memory Database is at the heart of SAP offerings like SAP HANA that help customers to improve their operational efficiency, agility, and flexibility.

The combination of the previous two components allows businesses to have data in real time without delays waiting for batches and/or overnight processing. SAP HANA compresses the data executed in-memory, making calculations and/or reporting much faster, and using saving points and uncompressed data backups that reside in a solid-state disk. Because the data exist not only in memory, but in a database designed to run in-memory as well, the traditional needs of application servers such as those available in SAP BW/BI for data storage, database support, and/or calculations are no longer required. Think of SAP HANA as the database or place of storage of an application, such as SAP NetWeaver BW. SAP HANA can be configured to literally be the database of SAP NetWeaver BW while removing the need of DB2, Oracle, or any other database that supports that application.

Now, in order to have a better idea on the look and feel of SAP HANA, follow along with these steps:

1. Click on START • PROGRAMS • SAP IN-MEMORY COMPUTING • STUDIO as shown in Figure 13.28.

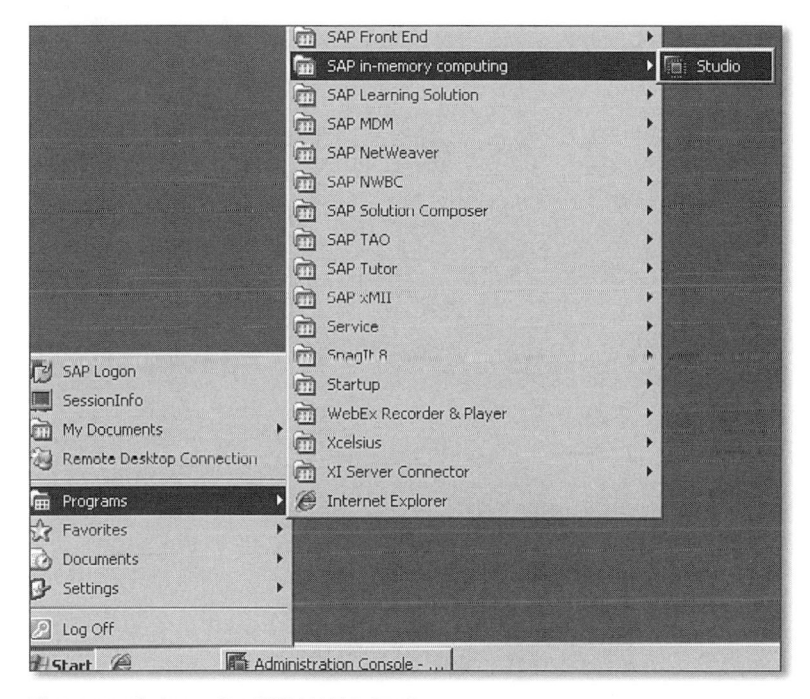

Figure 13.28 Accessing SAP HANA Studio

2. After accessing the SAP HANA Studio, you'll see a screen similar to the one shown in Figure 13.29 where the four perspectives appear:

▶ OPEN ADMINISTRATION CONSOLE: Created for system administrators to monitor the behavior of different objects and/or processes within SAP HANA.

▶ OPEN INFORMATION MODELER: Designed for developers to create tables, data sources, interaction with third-party systems, and anything required to create a real-time environment.

▶ OPEN LIFECYCLE MANAGEMENT: Provides tools that organize the development of projects and object movement between SAP BusinessObjects Enterprise systems.

▶ DOCUMENTATION OVERVIEW FOR SAP HANA APPLIANCE SOFTWARE: Accesses help and supporting information available at *www.help.sap.com*.

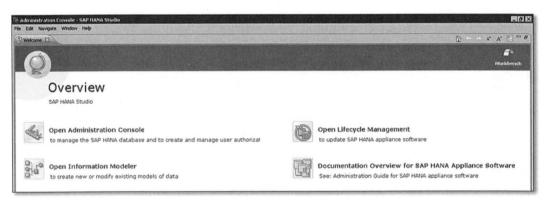

Figure 13.29 Reviewing the Initial Screen from SAP HANA Studio

3. Click on the OPEN ADMINISTRATION CONSOLE to access a screen similar to Figure 13.30. Notice that the Administration Console has a NAVIGATION view on the left-hand side that organizes the systems and projects, and a cheat sheet region on the right to assist in the development of catalogs, which are nothing more than structures that control business models that manage the data transfer to and from SAP HANA.

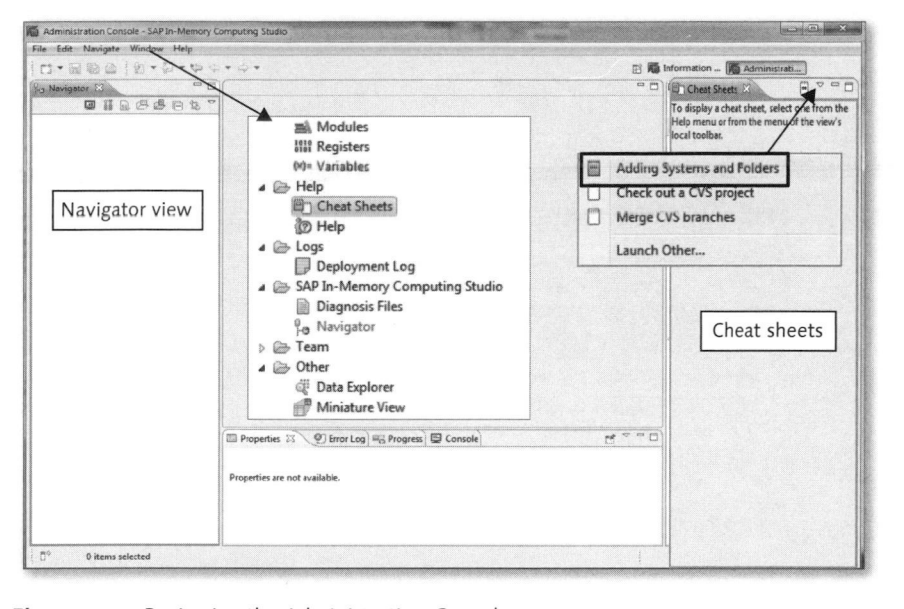

Figure 13.30 Reviewing the Administration Console

13.4.2 SAP HANA Architecture

As shown in Figure 13.31, the overall architecture of SAP HANA is displayed. Notice its similarities to SAP BW—it also has a data modeler tool, calculation engine, security, lifecycle, and data management components; extractors and data models; analyzes both historical and real-time data; and enables real-time data replication using Sybase's Replication Server. SAP HANA will interact with third-party software (non-SAP), SAP NetWeaver BW, the SAP BusinessObjects suite, and others using standard SQL, MDX, and BICS data standards. The concept of massive processing of data in a fast and reliable form was previously supported with the SAP BIA or SAP BWA technology, which is not being replaced with SAP HANA, and is part of the current SAP HANA roadmap.

Let's review Figure 13.32 to have a better idea of the SAP HANA Information Modeler, which is quite similar to the SAP BusinessObjects environment, BEx, Web Application Designer, and other SAP tools. The difference between these tools and SAP HANA is that SAP HANA relies on the fact that these models can literally be created without the need of an SAP NetWeaver BW system because it has its own development environment as shown in Figure 13.32, where SAP CO-PA reporting can also be developed.

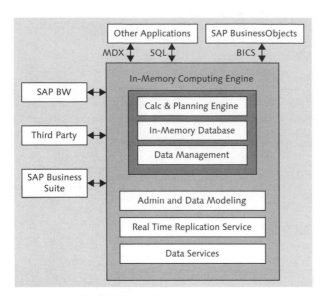

Figure 13.31 SAP HANA Architecture

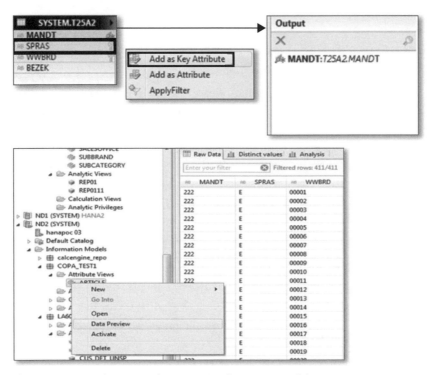

Figure 13.32 Sample Screen of SAP HANA Information Modeler

As shown in Figure 13.32 and 13.33, SAP HANA provides similar flexibility of drag-and-drop as SAP BusinessObjects, and maintains the table field names. As shown in Figure 13.33, the HANA Information Modeler operates based on views, similar to the Universe concept of SAP BusinessObjects.

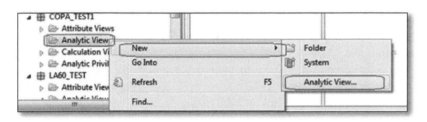

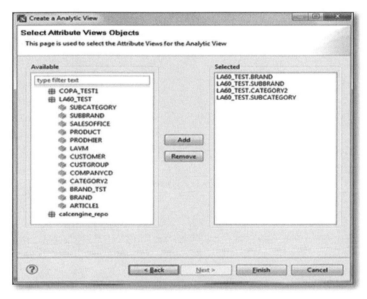

Figure 13.33 Sample of SAP HANA Information Modeler

In summary, SAP HANA is a new breakthrough and a huge leap in data analysis with its introduction in large data volume environments. The ability to wait seconds instead of hours to process massive amounts of data will revolutionize decision making in high data volume industries such as oil & gas, pharmaceutical, heavy equipment, manufacturing, utilities, and others. Also, the possibility to leverage SAP HANA for data mining, trend analysis, forecasting, and planning also supports a business in its ability to view results as they happen and not wait to get an answer. Without question, SAP HANA has captured the attention of

CIOs and business managers to have the exact answer to the lowest level of granularity possible and react faster to changing economic conditions.

13.4.3 A New Platform to Support a Variety of Tools

With the help of SAP HANA, SAP ERP (and specifically for our purposes, CO-PA) can also replicate and execute faster allocations during month-end reporting in real-time with high performance reporting on line-item levels while keeping existing SAP ECC processes intact since the memory calculations will be executed inside SAP HANA. In order to better understand the role of SAP HANA and its integration with SAP systems, different landscapes have been provided in Figure 13.34.

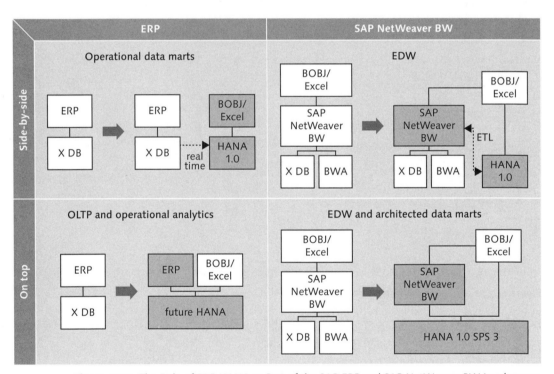

Figure 13.34 The Role of SAP HANA as Part of the SAP ERP and SAP NetWeaver BW Landscapes

Figure 13.34 provides a general description on the differences of SAP HANA SP01 and SP03, supporting both SAP ERP and SAP NetWeaver BW. The top two models, side-by-side, illustrate that SAP HANA resides next to the ERP system and the database where the data resides, such as XDB for both SAP ERP and SAP Net-Weaver BW. Notice in Figure 13.34 the SAP NetWeaver BW side-by-side landscape still maintains SAP BWA due to limitations in functionality and connectivity of the SAP HANA SP01 (service pack 01) version. In comparison, Figure 13.34 shows the on-top landscape design as part of SP03 and the future of HANA as the database that can completely replace and support the existing applications. SAP ERP, SAP NetWeaver BW, and SAP BusinessObjects literally will be on top of the SAP HANA database, and the existence of SAP BWA will no longer be required.

The improvements and differences for using HANA, opposed to a traditional landscape, have been captured as part of the integration with the CO-PA Accelerator in Table 13.2. The comparison was created by SAP AG using a sample size of data of 120 million line-items and reporting on product-related dimensions for a single company. This sample scenario was designed in order to provide a comparison between a system with and without SAP HANA as the support to improve performance in both calculations and system reporting. Based on the information provided in Table 13.2, it's possible to conclude that the usage of SAP HANA CO-PA Accelerator functionality has been reduced significantly from several hours to less than one second!

SAP HANA: SAP ERP CO-PA Accelerator Performance	Traditional SAP ECC and CO-PA Reporting
Less than one second (runtime for specific scenario, no general statement)	Up to several hours (runtime for specific scenario, no general statement)
Directly on line-item level, no precalculated data aggregation levels required	Precalculated data aggregation levels
No limit on drilldowns and details	Processing time for next navigation step depends on whether aggregate exists
Data immediately available for reporting, no waiting on data load processes to data warehouse	Parallel drilldown to multiple dimensions may not be possible anymore

Table 13.2 SAP HANA CO-PA Accelerator versus Traditional SAP ECC and CO-PA Reporting (Source: SAP AG)

In addition, SAP HANA provides applications for Sales & Operational Planning, SAP Smart Meter Analytics, SAP Dynamic Cash Management, SAP Trade Promotion Management, SAP BusinessObjects Strategic Workforce Planning, and SAP

BusinessObjects Planning and Consolidation, as well as other functionality built in SQL script (not ABAP), which is the real-time language of HANA.

13.4.4 A Quick Scenario: CO-PA and SAP HANA

So how can SAP CO-PA take advantage of SAP HANA's capabilities? Before we dive into this discussion, it's extremely important to have a clear understanding of how the process works before we start. We can simplify the process of working with SAP HANA as follows:

▶ Identify the SAP ECC tables that store the information that you need to analyze with SAP HANA using T-code SD11.

▶ Bring the metadata (structures) from these tables into SAP HANA *before* any data is loaded.

▶ Perform the initial data load in SAP HANA with data extracted from SAP CO-PA.

▶ A replication server will now take over to maintain the data in SAP HANA in synch and in real-time with SAP CO-PA using the SAP ECC replication agent as the bridge.

▶ Any changes in SAP CO-PA will be updated immediately in SAP HANA for real-time analysis, calculation, and reporting.

Note that these steps can become slightly complicated if SAP HANA requires configuration to integrate with multiple systems and processes. Even though it works with non-SAP systems, there are other technical decisions associated with the replication method chosen, and it depends on how SAP HANA will be positioned in the landscape of the business. For more information, we recommend reviewing the help section in SAP HANA Studio as previously discussed, or visit *www.help.sap.com*.

Based on the list of steps described above, let's walk through a scenario to integrate CO-PA with SAP HANA, transfer data from CO-PA, use SAP HANA to improve analysis speed, and then use report the data using SAP BusinessObjects. Please note that these steps are to provide an overview only.

1. Access the SAP HANA Information Modeler environment as shown in Figure 13.35 (refer back to Figure 13.32).

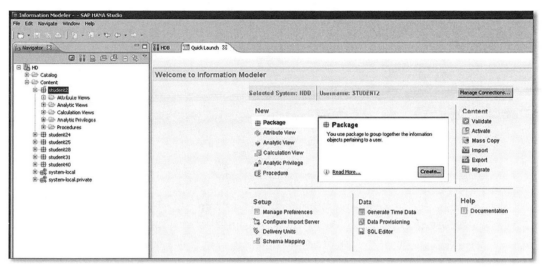

Figure 13.35 Navigating in the SAP HANA Information Modeler

2. Right-click on the CONTENT folder in the NAVIGATION VIEW as shown in Figure 13.36, and create a package by clicking NEW • PACKAGE. A package in SAP HANA is the equivalent of a logical object that stores different business models at different levels of aggregation. A package also requires an attribute called a DELIVERY UNIT that's associated with the business models stored in the package.

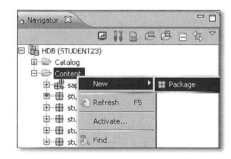

Figure 13.36 Creating a Package in SAP HANA Information Modeler

3. Once the package is created, it will display as shown in Figure 13.37, and contains five pre-delivered views: ATTRIBUTE, ANALYTIC, CALCULATION, ANALYTIC, and PROCEDURES. SAP HANA does not create redundant data for each model and does not create aggregates. Therefore, the physical tables are the only storage area for data within SAP HANA, the rest are just logical views or structures

to support the data extraction, replication, loading, and mapping such as the ones shown in Figure 13.37.

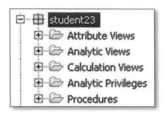

Figure 13.37 Reviewing the Contents of a SAP HANA Package

4. In order to create a mapping of tables from SAP CO-PA to destination data sources in SAP HANA, right-click on ATTRIBUTE VIEWS, provide a name and description of the attribute, and identify the tables you required. As shown in Figure 13.38, we have chosen to look for and add the SAP ECC Table T005U to the selection. Transfer it to the right-hand side of the screen by using the ADD button; once you've added all of the desired tables, click on the FINISH button.

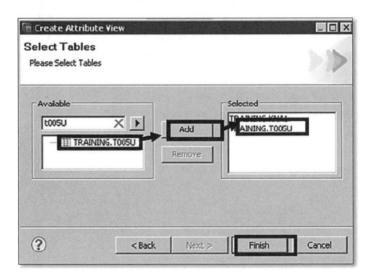

Figure 13.38 Transferring an SAP ECC Table in the Attribute View

5. After you click on the FINISH button in Figure 13.38, the ATTRIBUTE VIEW EDITOR will initiate as shown in Figure 13.39. The two tables T005U and KNA1 have been chosen to be added to the ATTRIBUTE VIEW.

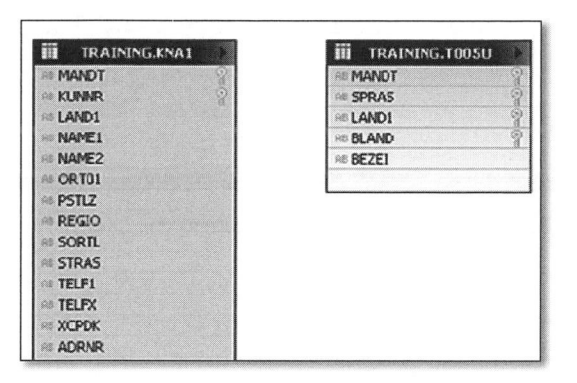

Figure 13.39 Reviewing the Attribute View Editor

6. This process of field assignment is similar to the traditional SQL database joints. You can add more tables to the relationship of fields required as shown in Figure 13.40 to have access to more information available in other tables. As shown in Figure 13.40, we have chosen to add SAP ECC Table T005T to the relationship. Once your model is completed, save your work and exit the Attribute View Editor environment.

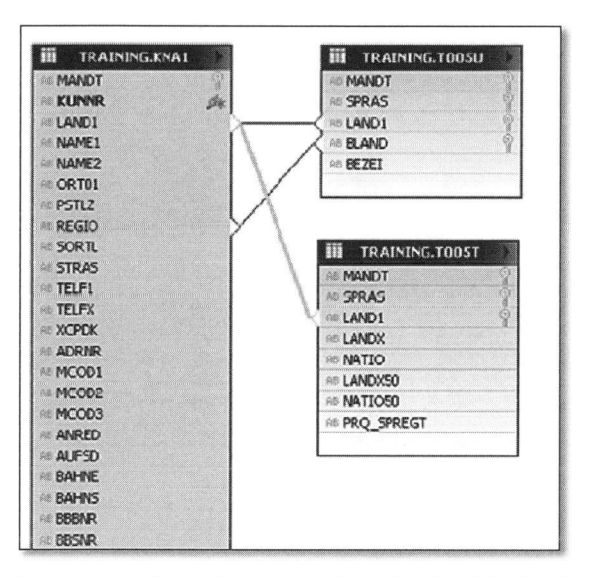

Figure 13.40 Reviewing the Database Relationships for SAP CO-PA Data in SAP HANA

7. When you exit the Attribute View Editor, you go back to the initial environment of the Information Modeler as shown in Figure 13.41. Notice that we

need to select the newly created Attribute View, in this case LOCATION_XX, right-click on it, click ACTIVATE, and then wait for a successful confirmation that the process occurred without problems.

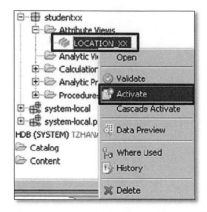

Figure 13.41 Activating your Attribute View with the SAP CO-PA Table Relationships in SAP HANA

8. To make sure that the relationships are actually reading SAP ECC-CO-PA tables as defined in the relationship, right-click in your attribute again, and select the option DATA PREVIEW as shown in Figure 13.41. When you perform this process, SAP HANA will display the contents of the SAP CO-PA operating concern tables as shown in Figure 13.42.

KUNNR	KUNNR description	REGIO	REGIO description	ORT01	LAND1	LAND1 description	MATNR	MATNR description	PERIO	VKORG	PLIKZ	GrossRevenue	SalesDeduction
0000300703	American Security Comp...	LA	Louisiana	NEW ORLEANS	US	United States	M-04	Sunny Extreme	2005011	3020	0	735.46	0
0000002000	Carbor GmbH	05	Nrth Rhine Westfalia	Duesseldorf	DE	Germany	M-02	Sunny Xa1	1996004	0001	0	25497.11	0
0000001460	C.A.S. Computer Applic...	14	Saxony	Dresden	DE	Germany	M-13	MAG DX 17F	2001011	1000	0	10767.9	265.43
0000001033	Karsson High Tech Markt	09	Bavaria	Muenchen	DE	Germany	M-01	Sunny Sunny 01	2005009	1000	0	40003.2	1392.11
0000001370	Superplus	09	Bavaria	Muenchen	DE	Germany	M-02	Sunny Xa1	1996004	0001	0	76491.31	0
0000300705	Web Design Studio	CA	California	PALO ALTO	US	United States	M-01	Sunny Sunny 01	2003004	3020	0	12586.06	0
0000002140	N.I.C. High Tech	06	Hesse	Frankfurt	DE	Germany	M-05	Flatscreen LE 50 P	2005001	1000	0	15325.4	533.32
0000002502	Miller & Son Trading Ltd.	LO	Greater London	London	GB	Great Britain	P-103	Pump PRECISION 103	2006008	2500	0	91800	2754
0000001460	C.A.S. Computer Applic...	14	Saxony	Dresden	DE	Germany	M-18	Jotachi SN4500	1997001	1000	0	2156.63	52.7
0000001172	CBD Computer Based De...	02	Hamburg	Hamburg	DE	Germany	M-20	Jotachi SN 7000	2004010	1000	0	11566.1	462.5
0000002502	Miller & Son Trading Ltd.	LO	Greater London	London	GB	Great Britain	P-103	Pump PRECISION 103	2008006	2500	0	112200	3366
0000300719	Hall Manufacturing	WA	Washington	EVERETT	US	United States	P-102	Pump PRECISION 102	2003003	3000	0	101769.19	0
0000002007	Software Systeme GmbH	05	Nrth Rhine Westfalia	Bonn	DE	Germany	M-20	Jotachi SN 7000	2002002	1000	0	12455.8	433.46
0000001321	Becker Stuttgart	08	Baden-Wuerttemberg	Stuttgart	DE	Germany	P-101	Pump PRECISION 101	2003005	1000	0	123243.2	4288.87
0000001175	Elektromarkt Bamby	16	Thuringia	Gera	DE	Germany	L-40R	Light Bulb 40 Watt red 2...	2001001	1000	0	67936	2364.17
0000001171	Hitech AG	02	Hamburg	Hamburg	DE	Germany	M-05	Flatscreen LE 50 P	1996003	0001	0	22496.84	0
0000001460	C.A.S. Computer Applic...	14	Saxony	Dresden	DE	Germany	M-17	Jotachi SN4000	2004009	1000	0	21627	501.75
0000001460	C.A.S. Computer Applic...	14	Saxony	Dresden	DE	Germany	R-1180	CD ROM Drive	2006006	1000	0	1120.5	0
0000001171	Hitech AG	02	Hamburg	Hamburg	DE	Germany	M-05	Flatscreen LE 50 P	1996007	0001	0	48143.24	0
0000002130	COMPU Tech. AG	05	Nrth Rhine Westfalia	Koeln	DE	Germany	DPC1016	SIM-Module 8M x 36, 70 ns	1997004	1000	0	2567.71	98.59
0000001175	Elektromarkt Bamby	16	Thuringia	Gera	DE	Germany	L-40C	Light Bulb 40 Watt clear ...	2000002	1000	0	216754.01	7543.04
0000001172	CBD Computer Based De...	02	Hamburg	Hamburg	DE	Germany	DPC1011	Professional keyboard - ...	2003006	1000	0	22100	769.08
0000300704	Century Software.Com	NH	New Hampshire	PORTSMOUTH	US	United States	DPC1016	SIM-Module 8M x 36, 70 ns	2002009	3020	0	112.95	0
0000003920	Thomas Clinton Inc.	IL	Illinois	MAYWOOD	US	United States	P-109	Pump cast steel IDESNO...	1996008	3000	0	5309.57	111.71
0000002402	Jashanmal International ...			Dubai	AE	Utd.Arab.Emir.	P-104	Pump PRECISION 104	2001008	2400	0	42700	1281
0000001360	Amadeus	09	Bavaria	Muenchen	DE	Germany	DPC1009	Standard Keyboard - EU...	2004007	1000	0	21182.25	493.75
0000002200	HTG Komponente GmbH	03	Lower Saxony	Hannover	DE	Germany	M-02	Sunny Xa1	2003003	1000	0	43439.36	1511.69
0000300701	Clinton Industries	DE	Delaware	WILMINGTON	US	United States	DPC1003	Harddisk 180 GB / SCSI-...	2004008	3020	0	93266.42	0
0000001321	Becker Stuttgart	08	Baden-Wuerttemberg	Stuttgart	DE	Germany	P-101	Pump PRECISION 101	2005004	1000	0	115205.6	4009.16
0000002503	Norwegian Import & Exp...	03	Oslo	Oslo	NO	Norway	P-104	Pump PRECISION 104	2006007	2500	0	79350	2380.5
0000300711	Holden & Associates	TX	Texas	SAN ANTONIO	US	United States	R-1006	Maxitec-RM 6100 Person...	2004006	3000	0	8922.1	0
0000002503	Norwegian Import & Exp...	03	Oslo	Oslo	NO	Norway	P-103	Pump PRECISION 103	2005005	2500	0	136000	4080
0000300717	JMart	MA	Massachusetts	SPRINGFIELD	US	United States	I400-310	CrossFun / 350 cm3	2002010	3000	0	27676.15	0
0000002140	N.I.C. High Tech	06	Hesse	Frankfurt	DE	Germany	M-01	Sunny Sunny 01	2005008	1000	0	34169.4	1189.1
0000001033	Karsson High Tech Markt	09	Bavaria	Muenchen	DE	Germany	M-04	Sunny Extreme	1996006	0001	0	153483.68	0
0000001033	Karsson High Tech Markt	09	Bavaria	Muenchen	DE	Germany	M-14	MAG PA/DX 175	2002009	1000	0	42515.2	1479.53

Figure 13.42 Reviewing the Contents of the CO-PA Operating Concern Tables in the SAP HANA Environment

At this stage, the Information Modeler within SAP HANA is capable of reading the contents available in your SAP ECC-CO-PA operating concern tables using SQL relationships, and creating linkages across tables.

Now we need to know how SAP CO-PA data can be reported using SAP HANA. Once the data is available in SAP HANA, you can report it using SAP Business Intelligence 4.0; MS Excel connectivity via ODBO, ODBC, and JDBC. Additionally, Analysis for Office, BusinessObjects Explorer, and SAP BPC version 10 also have capabilities that allow them to communicate directly with SAP HANA. A sample report using SAP BusinessObjects Explorer is presented in Figure 13.43 and SAP Analysis Services for MS Excel is shown in Figure 13.44.

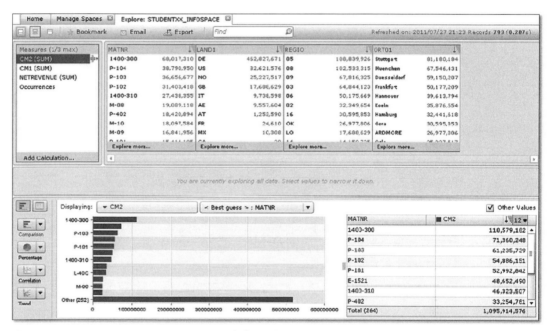

Figure 13.43 Reviewing SAP CO-PA Data Loaded into SAP HANA and Reported Using SAP Business Objects Explorer

Before making the decision to move forward with your SAP HANA implementation and integrate it as part of your system landscape, we recommend discussing this with your implementation teams to decide what service pack (SP) level will be installed, since the strategies, functionalities, and pre-delivered information will be different, and also discuss this with your SAP marketing representative to provide you with the best support possible.

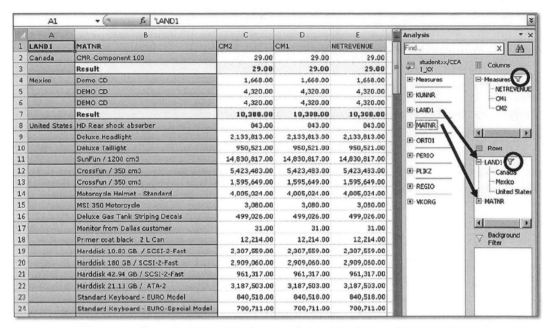

Figure 13.44 Reviewing SAP CO-PA Data Loaded in SAP HANA and Reported Using SAP BusinessObjects Analysis for MS Excel

> **Note**
>
> At the time of this publication, SAP HANA 1.0 SP03 was the latest release available in the market, and the SP03 naming convention replaced the proposed SAP HANA 1.5 version. It is very important to understand the differences between SP01 and SP03 because the functionalities and landscape requirements are quite different, as we reviewed them in Figure 13.34.

13.5 Summary

In this chapter we've explored additional tools and technologies that can complement, support, substitute, and/or enhance SAP CO-PA capabilities. The SAP BusinessObjects suite, such as SAP BPC and SAP BusinessObjects Dashboards, provides additional reporting functionalities and flexibility that aren't available in SAP CO-PA, but allows the data to be transferred into SAP NetWeaver BW and reported from there.

Additionally, we've discussed how to work with SAP BPC, one of the main technologies in the market related to planning, consolidation, budgeting, and forecasting solutions. SAP BPC may be an attractive alternative to SAP CO-PA for some businesses, since SAP CO-PA can handle only a limited amount of data before system performance and reporting times becomes an issue.

Many tools are currently available in the market that can support or enhance the capabilities of SAP CO-PA; however, its capabilities of real-time posting means that it doesn't require delays for upload and processing, such as those of SAP NetWeaver BW in large data volume environments. To supplement our discussion of large data environments, we briefly introduced SAP HANA, which has been created to support large data volumes, and can even be used as an alternative environment to SAP NetWeaver BW since it comes with its own data modeling and reporting tools. SAP HANA is a groundbreaking achievement by SAP to support and improve current technologies and perform faster calculations using in-memory technology. This new tool will be constantly adapting to the new market requirements and challenges, but it's already supported by big oil companies that already see the potential to manage their large volumes of data, and serves as an excellent solution to provide answers to key question in a short period of time.

We've provided some initial information regarding how SAP CO-PA and SAP HANA can work together, and shown you that SAP BusinessObjects tools are important elements that can provide support and/or enhance the reporting functionalities from SAP CO-PA.

Without question, SAP CO-PA is a tool that will prove itself useful in the future, and its importance is reflected in the CO-PA Accelerator component available in SAP HANA. There's no question that, in the future, SAP HANA and SAP BPC will directly affect applications and implementations as the new standards to support planning, forecasting, and other financial processes.

Stay hungry, stay foolish.
—Steve Jobs, Apple Inc. 2005, Stanford University

14   Concluding Remarks

In this book, we covered the key components and functionalities of the Controlling Profitability Analysis (CO-PA) component in SAP. Regardless of your role during an implementation, whether you're an end user, a manager, a team lead, or a consultant, we hope you've found something useful in this book to complement your current interest. In general, it's a great advantage to be able to obtain information in an environment that is similar to SAP NetWeaver Business Warehouse (BW)/SAP NetWeaver Business Intelligence (BI), Business Planning and Simulation (BPS), and Integrated Planning (IP), but without having to create complex structures to generate similar reports.

For users who are new to CO-PA, this book has been designed to be a reference guide. For advanced users, this book provides extensive configuration reviews and discussion of key functionalities to facilitate your data extraction, reporting, and planning within the SAP transactional system, in as simple a form as possible. Regardless of your knowledge level, however, using this component does require further study of the information contained in other SAP components such as Materials Management (MM), Financials (FI), Sales and Distribution (SD), Controlling (CO), and others.

The book covered the following topics:

▶ **Chapter 1** introduced the book and provided an overview of the information contained in it.

▶ **Chapter 2** reviewed basic concepts and terminology quite common in any financial-related projects. Terms such as EVA, revenues, direct and indirect costs, and how an SAP system controls and generates such information must be completely clear during your implementation. Financial transactions are a delicate issue and how Profitability Analysis information is reported to external parties is sensitive, so make sure to include the people with more financial knowledge of the organization when implementing CO-PA to make it truly successful.

▶ **Chapter 3** provided a general overview and introduction to the functionalities of CO-PA, specifically the concepts of costing- and account-based accounting within the SAP system. Costing-based CO-PA is more complex to implement than account-based. Even though some minor changes in your operating concern are required to switch from one to the other, both approaches use the same functionalities, such as reporting and planning.

▶ **Chapter 4** introduced the configuration steps toward the definition of the basic element for CO-PA: an operating concern. We've said several times throughout this book that you aren't required to implement every single component of CO-PA, but it's highly recommended to at least use an operating concern object when possible to facilitate your data extraction and reporting from SAP ERP ECC 6.0 or R/3 into SAP NetWeaver BI/SAP BW or non-SAP systems. Remember, CO-PA interacts directly with the transactional system of SAP, and doesn't require exporting the data into third-party systems or SAP BW/SAP NetWeaver BI to execute similar tasks until a certain level. However, when the data volume is high, it might be better to use an OLAP environment.

▶ **Chapter 5** explored additional functionalities in master data, such as characteristic values, valuation, derivation, and valuation strategies. Valuation, especially, is a functionality that is very difficult to replicate with alternative processes.

▶ **Chapters 6 and 7** reviewed the concepts of the CO-PA planning framework, such as layouts, planning functions, planning packages, ratio schemes, and others. Using planning applications, you can create and modify data inside your transactional system that can also be shared later on during reporting.

▶ **Chapter 8** explored flows of actual values to transfer data from other SAP components into CO-PA. This chapter also reviewed how to guarantee a successful sales order transfer to the SAP CO-PA profitability segments, internal order and project settlements, and transfer of billing documents using PA transfer structures in order to provide further clarity on the integration of SAP CO-PA with other SAP ECC components.

▶ **Chapters 9 and 10** provided an extensive analysis of the most important component for any SAP implementation: reporting. CO-PA reporting interfaces with the Report Painter functionality within R/3 or SAP ERP ECC 6.0, so it might be easy for users familiar with similar environments from other SAP applications.

▶ **Chapter 11** provided a quick glance at the differences when working with account based CO PA, and how to switch to this environment. However, we recommend reviewing SAP Note 74486 (INFO: Overview of Consulting Notes for CO-PA) for further details on using your SAP Service Marketplace account.

▶ **Chapter 12** provided an overview of advanced functionalities, such as RRI and RS, that improve system performance. The best choice is to have reports that not only have precalculated data so the system doesn't need to spend time using parameters that are accessed frequently, but that also can be reduced to only the required characteristics for each level of analysis.

▶ **Chapter 13** introduced the SAP BusinessObjects tools that can be utilized to enhance the value of information that SAP CO-PA generates using the SAP NetWeaver BW environment. In addition, we provided a detailed explanation of SAP BPC as a tool that will directly compete in functionality with SAP CO-PA with multiple benefits in end-user flexibility. We also briefly discussed the SAP HANA capabilities and environment for improving system performance, reducing reporting times by using in-memory technology, and the additional functionality available in SAP HANA to support CO-PA.

It has been a pleasure to provide this comprehensive CO-PA review. Unfortunately, some topics had to be left out of this book due to their complexity, such as the integration of the material ledger and CO-PA to access information related to material costs, prices, and movements. If you're looking for information on data extraction and retraction, which also weren't covered in this book, you can go to the "how-to" procedures available in SDN at *http://sdn.sap.com*. Even though these procedures aren't new, they can still be used as a good reference to create a data source in R/3 or SAP ERP ECC 6.0, or to save data back to the transactional system using SAP CO-PA as the link between SAP NetWeaver BW and SAP ECC.

We hope that the information discussed in this book is useful for your SAP implementation efforts, and helps you provide the best service to your clients and users.

Appendices

A   Glossary

ABAP   Advanced Business Application Programming language. Virtually the entire SAP system is written in ABAP.

Access Sequence   Determines the condition tables in which the system should search for valid condition records for a condition type.

Account-based CO-PA   Used to monitor cost elements and reconcile CO-PA data with Financial Accounting (FI) data. It is updated when goods are delivered.

BEx   SAP NetWeaver Business Intelligence (BI) tool that allows creating, setting up, and extracting specific information from SAP NetWeaver BI cubes.

Business Planning and Simulation (BPS)   SAP application that enables you to perform planning operations over data coming from SAP NetWeaver BW or R/3. It is quite similar to the SAP NetWeaver BI component Integrated Planning (IP).

Condition Types   Key used to define the attributes of a condition and identify the condition in the system.

Costing Sheets   Contain the conditions that are used to calculate expected values. They also determine the order in which the conditions are processed and how the conditions are related to one another.

Characteristic   Describes the business event and creates relationships. Can be business characteristics (customer, cost centers, and company), units (currency and quantity), time characteristics (calendar day, calendar year, and fiscal year), and technical characteristics (the number of a data-load procedure).

Characteristic Derivation   Rules used to generate new characteristic values based on inference rules.

Cost Center   Object used in Controlling (CO) to monitor internal cost assignments.

Cost Element   CO equivalent of a general ledger (G/L) that monitors both primary and secondary postings.

Costing-based CO-PA   CO-PA model that stores values and quantities in value fields. It is updated until the billing document is created.

Controlling (CO)   SAP R/3 or SAP ERP ECC component that controls and monitors internal transactions or reporting processes for non-external parties.

CO-PA Planning Framework   Environment used to generate planning applications within CO-PA. Similar to that of SAP SEM-BPS, SAP BW-BPS, and SAP NetWeaver BI-IP.

Condition Tables   Tables that store specific characteristic values and combinations to automatically control automatic procedures.

Derivation Rule   Automatic procedure used to generate or change values based on predefined criteria.

Discrete Manufacturing Production environment where the end product is the result of operations using parts or components to assemble a product. Example: automotive components.

Economic Value Added (EVA) Monetary value of an entity at the end of a time period minus the monetary value of that same entity at the beginning of that time period.

Extraction In CO-PA, setting up an operating concern using Transaction KEB0 to create a data source to transfer data from the transactional SAP system to SAP NetWeaver BI/SAP BW.

Forms CO-PA object used to create predefined templates that can be used as standard to maintain specific formats.

Financial Accounting (FI) SAP component that organizes and controls the financial accounting processes and transactions of an organization, and mostly oriented toward external parties.

In-Memory Computing Storing data in the main random access memory (RAM) of specialized servers instead of in complex relational databases that run on relatively slow disk drives.

Integrated Planning (IP) SAP NetWeaver BI planning application that uses J2EE technology using a similar environment to that of SAP BPS.

Key Figure Scheme Collection of any number of interrelated key figures, referred to as elements of the key figure scheme.

Materials Management (MM) Component of the Logistics component designed to manage and control the material flow of information inside a company, such as requisitions, bills of material, inventory management, purchasing and supplier information, and others.

Operating Concern Basic CO-PA object that contains characteristics or value fields and is used to perform reporting, planning, and data extraction.

Order Settlements Internal orders used to close any open items used to post information from a cost sender to a cost receiver.

Planning Layout CO-PA planning object that accesses the data restrictions stored in a planning package. It is the object that displays any required planning information.

Process Manufacturing Production environment that uses production batches or jobs to create the final product. Example: beer production.

Profitability Segments Grouping of characteristics used to store selected groups of data. Think of profitability segments as data sets of an SAP NetWeaver BI InfoCube.

Project System (PS) Project management component of SAP systems that controls dates, activities, costs, networks, schedule, and interfaces with different components to control how the information for a particular project is achieved.

Report-Report Interface (RRI) Reporting functionality that allows creating drilldown structures within a reporting environment to improve performance.

Report Splitting (RS)   Reporting functionality that allows dividing a larger report with many characteristics into a smaller one with fewer characteristics.

Retraction   Data transfer process from outside the OLTP into CO-PA using the operating concern as the connection.

SAP   Abbreviation for SAP AG, Systeme, Anwendungen, Produkte in der Datenverarbeitung (Systems, Applications & Products in Data Processing).

SAP BPC   SAP BusinessObjects Planning and Consolidation tool, part of the Enterprises Performance Management suite. This is the preferred tool for companies to implement planning, budgeting, forecasting, and consolidation.

SAP HANA   In-memory computing technology developed by SAP AG. It stands for High-Performance Analytic Appliance. It uses sophisticated data compression techniques to store information in RAM, which is 10,000 times faster than standard disks, enabling companies to analyze data in seconds instead of hours.

Summarization Levels   Performance optimization technique used to keep the most common extraction parameters in memory.

Valuation   Automatic calculations based on costing-based CO-PA. Can be used for both planning data and actual data.

Value Fields   R/3 or SAP ERP ECC equivalent of a key figure in SAP NetWeaver BW. They are objects that store quantity, amounts, dates, and counter-related information.

B   Bibliography

Draeger, E. *Project Management with SAP R/3*. Addison-Wesley. London, England, 2000.

Franz, M. *Project Management with SAP Project System*. SAP PRESS. Bonn, Germany, 2007.

Greenspan, A. *The Age of Turbulence: Adventures in a New World*. The Penguin Press. New York, 2007.

Jacobsen, L. *Cost Accounting*. Second Edition. McGraw Hill. New York, 1988.

Kundalia, M. "Ask the Financials Expert: Should I Report in CO-PA or BW?" *Financials Expert* magazine. Volume 4, Issue 1.

"Pick the Right Reporting Tool for the Job: CO-PA or BW." *Financials Expert* magazine. Volume 1, Issue 7.

Quentin, H., et al. *Configuring SAP R/3 FI/CO*. SYBEX. Alameda, CA, 2000.

"Quick Tip: 7 Sets of Consulting Notes for CO-PA Analyst." *Financials Expert* magazine. Volume 6, Issue 7.

Reilly, F., et al. *Investment Analysis Portfolio Management*. Thomson South-Western. USA, 2003.

Reis, V. *Actual Costing with the SAP Material Ledger*. SAP PRESS. Boston, MA, 2011.

Rogan, T. "A Quick Look at How to Use Frozen Data and Speed Up Your CO-PA Report Response Speeds in the Process." *Financials Expert* magazine. Volume 6, Issue 8.

Shizuo, S., et al. *Profitability Analysis for Managerial and Engineering Decisions*. Asian Productivity Organization (APO). Tokyo, Japan, 1980.

Sisfontes, M. *SAP CPM and Balanced Scorecard with SAP*. SAP PRESS. Bonn, Germany, 2007.

Thomas, K. *The Business of Investment Banking: A Comprehensive Overview*. Second Edition. John Wiley & Son, Inc. New York, 2006.

Williams, G. *Implementing SAP R/3 Sales & Distribution*. McGraw Hill. New York, 2000.

C   The Author

Dr. Marco Sisfontes-Monge is a managing partner of Arellius Enterprises. For more than 15 years, he has supported SAP implementers, direct clients, and other customers in Europe, North America, Latin America, Asia, and Africa in the industries of automotive, insurance, pharmaceutical and health care, logistics, software, utilities, chemical, oil and gas, exploration and natural resources, discrete and process manufacturing, retail, and financial services.

His background includes project management and performance measurement, product- and activity-based costing, design optimization, discrete and process simulation, system dynamics, and structural equations modeling. He also has finance specializations from the London Business School and Saïd Business School from Oxford University. Dr. Sisfontes-Monge is also the author of the book *CPM and Balanced Scorecard with SAP*, *Implementing SAP BusinessObjects Planning and Consolidation (SAP BPC) Volume I: Foundations* and *Volume II: Advanced Concepts*, and is an active writer for *Financials Expert* magazine. You may contact him via email at *msisfontes@arelliusenterprises.com*.

Index

D

E

F

G

H

Learn how product costing works and integrates with other modules

Master integrated planning, product cost planning, manufacturing methods, reporting, and more

Reduce long run times during month-end processing and streamline controlling processes

John Jordan

Product Cost Controlling with SAP

This comprehensive resource is for anyone with an interest in the integrated areas of product costing. You'll learn how overhead costs flow from financial postings to cost centers and then on to manufacturing orders. In addition, you'll master the material ledger, transfer pricing, reporting, and discover how to address common problem areas, including month-end processing, long run times, and message and variance analysis. This new edition includes updated content on cost object hierarchies and engineer-to-order, as well as new case studies and real-world examples.

652 pp., 2. edition, 79,95 Euro / US$ 79.95
ISBN 978-1-59229-399-5

>> www.sap-press.com

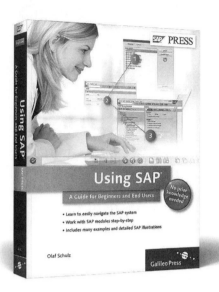

Learn to easily navigate the SAP system

Work with SAP modules step-by-step

Includes many examples and detailed SAP illustrations

Olaf Schulz

Using SAP:
A Guide for Beginners and End Users

This book helps end users and beginners get started in SAP ERP and provides readers with the basic knowledge they need for their daily work. Readers will get to know the essentials of working with the SAP system, learn about the SAP systems' structures and functions, and discover how SAP connects to critical business processes. Whether this book is used as an exercise book or as a reference book, readers will find what they need to help them become more comfortable with SAP ERP.

388 pp., 39,95 Euro / US$ 39.95
ISBN 978-1-59229-408-4

>> www.sap-press.com

Interested in reading more?

Please visit our website for all
new book releases from SAP PRESS.

www.sap-press.com